Letters from Lotusland
Ian Whitcomb

Wild Shore Press
2009

Letters from Lotusland
by Ian Whitcomb
Copyright 2009
All Rights Reserved
ISBN 978-1-4276-3164-0

This work may not be reproduced in whole or in part without the express permission of the author and Wild Shore Press.

This is a work of fancy, fiction and philosophy, and should be regarded as such. All opinions herein contained are those of the author.

Wild Shore Press is a publisher of fine literature, philosophy, poetry, science fiction, plays, and many other amazing things. You may find us on the web at:

WWW. WildShorePress.com

Books by Ian Whitcomb

AFTER THE BALL: Pop Music From Rag To Rock (1972)
20th CENTURY FUN (1973)
TIN PAN ALLEY: A Pictorial History (1975)
LOTUSLAND: A Story Of Southern California (1979)
WHOLE LOTTA SHAKIN': A Rock 'n' Roll Scrapbook (1982)
ROCK ODYSSEY: A Chronicle Of The Sixties (1983)
IRVING BERLIN & RAGTIME AMERICA (1987)
RESIDENT ALIEN (1990)
THE BECKONING FAIRGROUND:
   Notes Of A British Exile (1994)
TREASURES OF TIN PAN ALLEY (1994)
VAUDEVILLE FAVORITES (1995)
THE BEST OF VINTAGE DANCE (1996)
SONGS OF THE RAGTIME ERA (1997)
THE TITANIC SONGBOOK (1998)
TITANIC TUNES: Songs From Steerage (1998)
SONGS OF THE JAZZ AGE (1998)
UKULELE HEAVEN (1999)
UKE BALLADS (2001)
THE CAT'S MEOW (2003)
THE IAN WHITCOMB SONGBOOK (2007)

Acknowledgments:

Editor-in-Chief (moral and technical): Regina Whitcomb
Text editor: Barbara Watkins
Cover designer: Rick Whitmore
Drawing of Ian: Don Bachardy
Cover Photograph: Jane Quinn

Editor for Wild Shore Press: Don Elwell

PREFACE

A cursory glance at these preposterous pages reveal a case history of a vanishing breed — the upper class twit — at last made to disappear from the new post-post-modern Britain, an exciting new world of diversity and change. We will no doubt soon have a mosque taller than Salisbury Cathedral and hallelujah for that! Whitcomb is a curious remainder, an exiled dinosaur from a banished Britain when clipped clenched-teeth accents filled the air, when gentlemen wore bowlers and their women flower dresses and hats, when the lower classes (remember the class system?) knew their place and stayed there in the ship's boiler room as lantern-jawed officers peered through binoculars in search of U-Boats, and when the only acceptable peoples of colour were the likes of Mr. Golliberry on the Robertson's Jam jars.

Typical of so many of his type Whitcomb fled to Southern California, a repository of the weird, the outcast and the anti-social, there to amuse guileless Americans with his antiquated songs and exaggerated tales of a better place back in the Jolly Olde England of Yore.

Read at your aesthetic peril but study, as good social scientists, an enemy who may turn up another day from under some long forgotten stone.

"Smudge" X Hendon,
Chairperson,
Sir Mick Jagger Department of Pop Culture & Sociology,
Elvis Costello Section,
University of Eel Pie Island,
Middlesex,
England

INTRODUCTION

In 1996 I was approached, via old-time mail, by two baldheaded comedians, Rusty Lewis and Wayne Faust, who lived in Colorado. They asked if they could set up a website for me. I didn't know what a website was because we didn't have a computer. My wife Regina knew that I was intolerant of anything new, anything post-Elvis. "Computer" smacked of mathematics and I've always been fearful of anything to do with numbers. Numbers, being rational, are inhuman.

However, I was interested in any device that might shove my CDs and books into a wider market—they were taking up too much space in the garage—so I agreed to let the bald men include me in their umbrella website: *picklehead.com*. My wares were duly offered on-line, all major credit cards accepted. Then the webmasters suggested that a monthly newsletter from me might attract more customers since constant new goodies keep people visiting your site.

So, in April of 1996, I wrote my first Letter From Lotusland on a typewriter in the Huntington Library, San Marino, where I occupied a basement desk in a cubbyhole under a staircase. "Lotusland" is the word I had been using to describe where we live in Southern California, a place that could be ideal if only we all tried. It's also a never-never land of rocks and sand where cowboys roam and sing, where bi-planes adorned with skull & crossbones are hangered in caves, a land that haunts my dreams.

The first Letter was little more than a report on work in progress—books and articles about to be published, upcoming gigs, etc. And so the Letters continued, irregularly, as reports, as advertisements for myself. Until the 21st Century rolled in and our life started to go awry. As you will learn, neighbour problems escalated into war. We were terrorized even as other wars began elsewhere. But as Altadena life darkened so I poured more and more of my feelings in the Letters. They became a relief.

Part of the relief was brought to me by our Apple computer.

Yes, I had caved in. A friend, an ex-Apple employee, had

presented us with an old machine, a clunky great creature. At first I was wary but gradually the ease of the typing action, the satisfying tock-tock of the keyboard, and the fact that I could continue typing without having to bang a shift lever at the page margin — so that the stream of consciousness could race like a raging river — won me over to the modern age. I grew to love this mysterious machine of invisible parts and no oil. Nothing could stop the flow of words, except that steady airline voice announcing, "You've got mail!"

But was such prolific outpouring a good thing? Was I simply spewing unconsidered trivia? Was I merely another blogger bleating for recognition? I like to think that the computer is a perfect vehicle for my volatile, rushing personality. Raw stuff it is within these pages. But the rawness is everything. If I polished up then I'd just be another man of letters in tweed jacket and leather elbow patches. This medium, as is the case for millions of others, has freed me from publishing house gatekeepers. This part of the world has freed me from the strictures and judgments of my homeland. Los Angeles County is the right testing ground. Here the West is still wild and the England I yearn for lies still in country churchyards. And so, out here, I continue to struggle against current affairs, fighting a rearguard action against the present, in search of some ancient gleam of promise, some real honey of a song still to be revealed in its hiding place of perfect peace behind some sculpted rock.

Ian Whitcomb,
Altadena,
California,
July 2008.

LETTERS FROM LOTUSLAND (1996-2008)

Finding My Web Voice
Extracts from the early Letters.

The Very First Letter:

1996

APRIL

People ask me, "What exactly do you do?" and when I respond with a torrent of activities they excuse themselves. Well, I'll try again here on the magic Web, although I may be blattering into thin air.

Right now, since I don't own a computer yet, I'm typing this First Letter noisily at my desk under the stairs in the basement of The Huntington Library in San Marino, California — the world-famous repository of great and rare books. Here, in the unpopulated basement I can bang away at my typewriter and not disturb the cutting-edge scholars upstairs as they tap away on their laptops and such, raiding manuscripts quill-penned by monks and dukes and mistresses.

Why am I, a One Hit Wonder, allowed inside? Because I am a published author, having written several books here, and I also provide musical entertainment (with my Bungalow Boys band) for Huntington garden parties, and because I have donated my manuscripts, diaries, and even my laundry lists, to the Rare Manuscript Department. There they sit waiting for researchers, near Cyril Connolly's letters and a few from old James Joyce.

The Huntington is my haven of rest from the clang of the outside world. Luckily I live only a few miles away in a 1948 bungalow hard by the San Gabriel Mountains in leafy Altadena, an unincorporated town which means it can be lawless or bohemian, as it chooses.

Inside my "home," as they like to call a house over here, live my singing/cooking wife Regina, her cat Simon The Unfriendly, and our dog Inspector The Half Breed. I inherited Inspector from the late crooner Rudy Vallee, not long after the star's death. The latter, watching a TV special, had been cheering on his pal President Reagan and, rather overdoing it, had succumbed to a massive coronary. Inspector was found at his master's side, licking lovingly. He came to us with his few possessions: a megaphone, a bowl, and a packet of frankfurters.

If you want to know how I landed up in Altadena, far from my English homeland, go online and order my memoir *Resident Alien*, a real hardback book that describes my misadventures as a bachelor with a house full of miscreant boarders, before I met Regina, the Valley girl, who like a fairy godmother, waved them away with her iron wand. Actually, I miss some of them, because we all need a bit of strife in life, shadows to relieve the unthinking eternal sunshine.

And now I must return to work on the text of my next songbook for Mel Bay Publications — *Songs Of The Ragtime Era*.

TTFN!

(Editor's Note: the above letters stand for "Ta-Ta For Now!" In other words: "See you later!")

DECEMBER

The reason for such a long silence is that I've been working steadily. "Work!" says my friend Andy, a one-time executive at Warner Bros Records, now retired and living comfortably in London."You don't work! — Work is something one dislikes doing but has to do. But you — you enjoy what you do. So it's not work."

Be that as it may.

I was planning on returning to London in August to see close friends like Andy. And also my mother, who now lives in a super-style nursing home in a mansion, which includes a lake, decorated with ducks and swans that fly in especially from Canada. But I couldn't go to London: there was too much work coming up — like Johnny Legend's *All-In Wrestling & Rock'n'Roll Show* in San Francisco in which I was billed to sing my hit and join in *We're Over The Hill* with the other stars; followed by K-EARTH radio's retro-rock concert at the Greek Theatre where I shared a dressing room with Sam The Sham and was able to pick up our discussion on 18th century British philosophers. We'd left off in the summer of 1965.

1999

JANUARY

In December of each year I make a list of everything I've produced that year in order to justify my existence. I reckon I'm only here to amuse people and generally it's really hard just to get their attention. So what did I do? In 1998 I sailed on my *Titanic* CD, getting a Grammy and a nomination, promoting in France & Germany, hoping to concertize in Taiwan — but the Asian market went into meltdown. At the Oregon Festival Of American Music I sang some of the music of the Titanic Era in a special concert under maestro Dick Hyman's direction. The second half was a performance of *The Rite Of Spring*. What an odd combination! The local paper called me a "ham" — but in the very best sense of the word. *Titanic* sales are slipping so I'm now concentrating on the ukulele. A songbook, *Ukulele Heaven* is in the making.

I want to write a mystery story around my Martin ukulele, "Ukie." Had him since 1987. Had another Martin before that — bought at an L.A pawnshop in 1963. This was BEFORE Tiny Tim, mark you. Ukie talks back to me onstage. Has a high-pitched querulous voice. Hates being put back in his case when I need to play Art, the Accordion. Jealousy.

Regina and I were at the annual Scott Joplin Festival in Sedalia, Missouri last June, singing the old songs, the good ones. The Joplin Fest worked wonders as therapy for me. I'd flown in the day before from England where I'd been mourning my mother's death at a service in a crematorium in Leatherhead, Surrey. I've never cared much for Leatherhead — the name or anything about it — and I care even less now.

My mother, who had been my greatest supporter, had celebrated her 85th birthday on February 24 and, over in England on a *Titanic* promo tour, I'd sat with her in the games room of her nursing home in Esher as we'd played my *Titanic* CD and she'd encouraged sad old ladies to come out of their brown studies and sing and even dance to The *Merry Widow Waltz*. After that she whizzed off in her electric chair to *Smokie Joe's* for a ciggie with me not far behind, making sure I had my tin of Wills' *Café Creme* cigarillos with which to join her. After this it would be sherry back in her room as we watched the Little & Large show on TV with me smiling at her merriness.

She'd looked so eagle-eyed and bright on her birthday, so relieved that I was once more making money from my hobbies. I was of course dismayed to see her slump down in her electric chair after she'd waved me goodbye at the front door of the home. But then she'd always slumped dramatically after the final radiant goodbye smile.

In May though, as I was working here at The Huntington Library, my brother left word on my answering machine that our mother wasn't well, was under par. Better hurry. I caught the next plane to London but she was dead even as I arrived at Heathrow. She'd wanted to leave this world, had told my sister she'd had a happy time here, that she loved us, and that she was tired and ready to say the real last goodbye. The doctor asked my sister whether we'd like our mother to have a few months of pain or whether we'd prefer her to go peacefully in the night. British doctors are sensible in this way. She went in the night, peacefully.

Even so, what a cheat it is to experience love and life's pleasant rituals and then suddenly be robbed of them forever. My mother is gone forever — burned up into ashes — and no matter what we're told by balmy parsons about spirit and soul I want my mother back in the flesh, with her glass of gin and Dubonnet and her packet of ciggies. What age would I like her?

APRIL

The great point to remember, I tell myself, is to keep busy, to keep moving. That's the only way to sweep out depression. Black dog night will vanish howling in the blinding white light of unthinking action.

So The Salon, my Salon, is a therapeutic thing. We meet at a cheap eatery every Monday night around 8pm. It's not about the food, it's about being with people. Life is People, even when they're infuriating. Lots of people coming and going, interrupting each other, speechifying, jump-cutting from topic to topic, and heavily drinking. Usually I'm uplifted, but the other night there were too many people, the mixture was too rich and I needed an emetic.

It wasn't called a salon when we started. That title was the contribution of my fine arts friend, Paul K, who runs the West Coast branch of The Smithsonian's Archives of American Art located at The Huntington Library.

When we started it was just Jim and me. Jim is a tall, bespectacled pornographer and an expert on American roots music. We used to meet at a common-or-garden Mexican restaurant called La Fiesta Grande in Pasadena, near my mountain foothills home. Also near the radio station where, on Wednesday nights, I'd broadcast *The Ian Whitcomb Show*. Jim would bring suitcases full of obscure rhythm & blues records to flesh out the long radio hours — for I'd worn silly my George Formbys and Al Bowllys.

He'd often bring guests such as Big Jay McNeely, ebony hero of the 1940s, king of the honking sax; and Jack McVea, a black minstrel famous for his smash hit "Open The Door, Richard." On other nights, when we were featuring street corner doo-wop groups, there'd be lots of Spanish-speaking aficionados in the studio with us, finger-popping along, answering the phones. It was a jolly crowd. Sometimes too jolly and I felt I was losing control, felt this was democracy run riot. You can have too much of a good thing.

In those days I used to drink two grande margaritas (mainly tequila, a lovely and lethal cactus-based liquor) at La Fiesta before going on the air, thus continuing the freewheeling atmosphere of our dinner. And so I developed a trick of asking my legendary guests a question and nodding off during the answer, then returning to life during the sometimes-long silence that followed their speech. Like all good things this had to end: the station replaced me with a format called "Intelligent Talk & Alternative (Adult) Rock."

Not to be defeated by the radio authorities, we continued to meet at La Fiesta with selected guests from the roots music world, and to imagine we were all going on afterwards to the radio station. In fact, we'd stand in the street, when the restaurant had closed and do the show a capella.

We were always short on women. Regina occasionally put in an appearance but she didn't care much for the company and now she doesn't come at all. "Boys' night out," she says and leaves it at that. Once we snared a 1950s fashion model but she objected to the body odor of one of our doo-wop experts and has never been seen again. Mind you, we do have Gloria and she more than makes up for our sex imbalance what with her no-nonsense approach to life ("I tell it as I see it, like it is") and her severe business suit with the stiff shirt and high collar topped by the wide, fruit-laden hat stuck with ostrich feathers.

Gloria is black and of a certain age. She recently retired from an important government job ("Racked in secrecy — know what I'm sayin'?") and she must have done all right because she turns up in a long and wide late-model Cadillac with no license plates. A handicap sign is prominent on the dashboard. She walks so straight and true I had to ask her, at our first meeting, what exactly was her handicap. Quick as a vaudeville star she replied: "Being an African-American female in the United States Of America!" Then she gently rubbed my knee and that really won me to her. Little touchie things like that mean a lot over here.

She and Jim were born in the same town in West Virginia, years apart and from different sides of the railroad tracks. While Jim is full of facts about old black music and culture, Gloria shuns all that: "For a person of color such as I, the past is pain and there's no use regurgitatin'!" Jim brings the earthy folk to our salon — rockabillies, security guards, doo-woppers. His new book, which he waved at us the other night, is called *Who Cut The Cheese?* a history of farting. You can't catch him on that subject: *The Miller's Tale* is old hat to him. He can tell you how, in ancient times, a Roman soldier in Jerusalem lifted his tunic and broke wind on a devout group of early Christians thus raising a riot that left thousands dead. Jim's down there with the demotics.

Whereas all I can produce are high art people, via my friend Paul K. I met him at The Huntington. He works for The Smithsonian, as I mentioned earlier. He brings conceptualists, performance artists, Chicano cartoonists, de-constructionists, to the meetings. He told us that a salon used to refer to "a large and lofty reception room in a palace or other great house" but that we qualify as a fin-de-siecle neo-salon. "You mean a cheap burrito joint," said Jim.

La Fiesta Grande is in a currently unfashionable part of Pasadena, nestling second-hand bookshops and a live theatre. We're over a mile from trendy "Old Town" with its shells of historic buildings now occupied by up-market chain stores and chic bistros, and its street corners guarded by knots of surly Latino gang-bangers in black baggy uniforms. Next to them sit their low-slung black vans shuddering as they blast out the thudding hip-hop beat, putting the fear of God into the yuppies waiting in line for the restaurant table of their choice.

There's no wait at La Fiesta. Our long and curvy booth is always free for us. Some nights there's only me and Jim, other nights there's more than a dozen — and that's too many, as we shall see. But no matter — it's my salon, and my saviour. The waiters are fair, treating us with the same indifference they treat any gringo, keeping the chip and salsa bowls full to the brim, lively with the bill, and always following briskly — since we're the last customers — with the raucous advance of the cleaning machinery and disinfectant blasters.

Then it's out onto the pavement for the long goodnights, the vows to meet again next week, the understanding that the art business — both high and low — is controlled by cliques and conspiracies.

And off I roar home to shoot some final salvoes against the world at my wife as she lies in bed trying to watch a late-night reality cop show.

But the other night—the night in question — was a terrible discordance: too many of us (plus a few strangers) cramped together in the booth, so that I could feel and smell them and I don't care for that; and what I usually care for—the conversation — now seemingly oppressive, what with Ray, a retired king of rockabilly, banging on about UFOs and how Clinton has a 13 year-old black love child — he heard this on his radio — and Gloria, dressed-down in a white T-shirt and baseball cap on backwards, telling us there should be mandatory reparations for the descendants of slaves, and me — worst of all — butting in to inform Michael McMillan, the world-famous installationist that, yes, I visited the room he created at the L.A. County Museum of Art and, yes, I admired his "virtual 1930s old man's garage" complete with oil pools, period radio playing period music, and stacks of period paper ephemera. In fact, I was so impressed, so excited, that I contributed to the work by dropping a crushed Kleenex full of a recent sneeze. McMillan smiled but some strangers didn't. One hissed: "Philistine!" I knew I'd done wrong, but it's my party and I'll do what I like.

Next Zorthian arrived and everybody was all over him and I was off the hook. Good old Zorthian, that Armenian runt with the satyr smile and the bedraggled but loyal wife in tow; he who has lived in the mountains above us for fifty years, building a ranch of unfinished houses, studded with broken glass and female breasts fashioned from hub caps and dustbin lids, and encouraging people to come tip their garbage into the surrounding canyons so as to eventually create a plateau of pure garbology, and welcoming one and all into the gloom of his adobe hacienda to take a chance perhaps on a dirt-encrusted bottle of 1949 California champagne, part of a consignment given to him by Charlie Parker, the legendary jazz sax man, in return for the time Zorthian rescued him from a boring party on the plain below, took him to the ranch and persuaded the gangster-suited jazz-artist to join his host in a mad horse ride, in the nude, up and down the canyons that were still free of garbage.

Afterwards, as a red dawn broke, they sat in the studio and admired the Armenian's gynecologically-accurate oil paintings of voluptuous female nudes. "Man!" exclaimed Parker, "This is T & A and it's legit!"

We all hush for Zorthian. A chair is pulled out for him. At once there's ample room at the table — and, mysteriously, a glass of fine wine is set in front of him. Paul K, the Smithsonian man, produces a sheet of paper and a Pentel Rolling Riter and spreads the work tools in front of the artist. Zorthian takes a sip of wine, rolls it around in his mouth, spits it into a glass provided by his wife, and gets down to work. His Pentel line goes for a fast, snaky walk, leaving a trail depicting a young woman with ripe melon breasts and our attention drawn to her dark triangular forest. "Hola!" he shouts and everyone applauds.

For some unknown reason, I seize the pen and impose upon the erotic forest a snub-nosed rocket of a penis. Nobody finds this clever and the party breaks up.

Outside, in a doorway, our party — the pop people — try to calm me down. Jim takes the lead. He's clever that way, he understands life.

He explains: "You were pissed off with those artsy-fartsy types."

Right.

"And so you made a statement."

Right again.

"It seems to me," I say — getting into the spirit of bile — "It seems to me that these creatures, unlike us working stiffs, contribute nothing to the joy of mankind."

"Right on," says Jim, "Why, an epileptic having a fit is a real performance artist."

"Exactly — these people sow not, neither do they reap."

"Well, they sure couldn't fill a night club or sell a magazine."

"Where did they vanish to, that motley bunch of conceptualists, constructionists, post-modernists, and installationists?"

"Round the corner to the back bar for absinthe margaritas. They're talking of creating a happening or rave."

After our people — the rockabillies, doo-woppers, bluesmen, and off-duty security guards — have sauntered off (with many a "goodnight!"), Jim sits me on the hood of my Honda and says: "What you need is a good clean break. You know I'm a pornographer by trade .... well, I get lots of invites to attend hard-core movie shoots. There's one coming up next week that I think will be just what the doctor ordered."

He hands me a pamphlet printed on creamy art paper, blazing with colour: "Be our guest at *THINGS CHANGE* (The More They Change, The More They Get Fucked Up) – A Michael Zen Production for Cal Vista, starring Misty Rain & Nikki Sinn. Got wood? Got a camera? Be there!"

With only a week to go before the big day, I got genned up a little about the movie by studying the pamphlet: this production will be shot on proper film, not video, and will boast multi-partner matings, a 5-way all-girl orgy, "and, of course, plenty of anal sex... Our customers have told us over and over: "Keep the Mona Lisa's smile — just let me see her butt."

The director, Michael Zen, is a UCLA teacher specializing in the work of Eisenstein, Pudovkin, and Welles. He has "learned to love the human element, exploring the motivations, desires and hypocrisies of the human psyche." Has the business changed this essentially contemplative artist?

Says Zen: "Well, now I don't recognize people with their clothes on."

Next, I turned to facts about the hard-core porno business, a burgeoning one, to be sure: over 800 million videos rented and sold in 1998 and that's just the USA. Of course, in Britain the business is all under the counter, which is probably one of the reasons I live over here. Sex has always been a siren for me — fancy free and anonymous, out on the West Coast where the best-built pneumatic girls and boys are. No more Macintoshes, no more cottaging, no more sitting on the old school bench!

Now, in my late 50s, I live safely, cozily, respectfully up in Altadena in a cottage with my wife. So how can I live out the dream at my age, in my state? Through Michael Zen's magic perhaps! The thrill factories are all, we're told, down in the San Fernando Valley, not far from home, in and around Chatsworth where once rode singing cowboys like Rex Allen and Jimmy Wakeley and now pump Titman and Buttman. I was getting into the spirit. Fantasies were leaping about like sparks from a Boy Scout bonfire. What if Mr. Zen asked me to take a small role? After all, I recently did a cameo in *Contact*.

Jim and I had a decent breakfast before setting out for the location. I must admit I was nervous. Had we been properly cleared? Weren't gangsters involved in this business? As we approached the address, an old shack of a club called Martini Lounge off Hollywood Boulevard, he reassured me: "Times have changed. It's all legal so there's no shady guys. Nobody cares what you do, so long as kiddies aren't involved. I remember, in the old days, when an anonymous caller would tell me to be at a certain phone booth at a certain hour and when I got there the phone rang and another voice told me to look south-west for a fluttering handkerchief from a half-opened window in a warehouse."

Jim was right. Times have changed. The front door to the club was wide open and the sunlight streaming inside revealed women in high leather boots chatting and smoking while men, mostly tattooed, rushed around with lighting stands, reflectors, walkie-talkies — the sort of workaday equipment one associates with the mundanity of movie-making. I did catch a twinkle, activated by the sun, from off the ringed nipple of one of the women, reminding me that sex was the business being conducted today on these premises and that it was now an important part of the economy of California. Pedestrians, bent on other matters, passed by the open door without turning their heads for a peep. In such conditions I began to feel schoolboy-smutty. For, unlike the times, I haven't changed.

"Look!" said Jim as we parked in a side street "There's one of the male studs, adjusting his dress in preparation for work." He pointed to a nondescript young man making his way towards the building's back door, an awkward progress for, as Jim pointed out, he seemed to be having trouble with his crotch, constantly twitching one or other of his legs and then, finally and with exasperation, pushing the recalcitrant equipment of his trade firmly against the left thigh. "I wouldn't lose too much sleep over him," said Jim. "The studs are the lowest on the totem pole—mere functionaries, no more than hired guns." Still, I was very interested in their place on the scene.

Suddenly, like Alice's rabbit, he'd disappeared, gobbled up by an intense blackness tasting acrid and slightly foul (and, therefore, promising sexual excitement for me). Eventually, a little light came to our eyes revealing that we had started to make our way down a narrow corridor lined with bubbling hot snacks (constant food on hand is a staple of popular entertainment). Now we were bumping against a man of our own age, immaculately turned-out in blazer and striped tie and bearing a big clipboard.

"Ha, ha!" he greeted us. "The gentlemen of the press! I'm Cal Vista's publicist and my name is Peter Pecker."

As he said this he raised a pen above his clipboard in a dramatic pose.

Jim stepped in: "I'm from *Slut* as you know. And this is Ian of *The London Observer*." I interrupted Pecker's furious scribbling with a correction: "Actually, I write for *The London Magazine*."

Pecker lowered his pen, stared at me with piercing blue eyes. Coming close, so that I got whiffs of his honey breath, he said: "Even better — a magazine. Meaning glossy pages and pictures. I can provide you with any amount of pussy-close colour transparencies."

I let the matter rest and, thankfully, Jim stepped in to congratulate Pecker on the style of the Cal Vista pamphlet for "Things Change." Pecker bowed and revealed that he'd written every word and — brightened perhaps by the compliment — he led us in a brisk march to the very heart of the set: the dance floor and stage of the club and its snug little back bar.

We were introduced to the screenwriter, Delysia Ravenscroft, a tiny woman in late middle age, armed with a large deaf-aid, and very personable (she immediately gave me her card). Pecker shouted: "I hope the next scene is sex action, Delysia. I love your lines and I'd like to let our guests see the core of our business." She assured us that in a few minutes there'd be enacted "full sex scene number 6" and that it would be "run to the pop." Run to the pop!

This was another world, another language, except for the outward gear of filmmaking — the camera on the crane, the arc lights, the recording desk — and I was burning with questions.

Wait, for God's sake! Here we are at the eye of the coming storm, standing at the little back bar, about to meet the director, Michael Zen himself. A past master of high quality porn (and on proper film, not cheap video), as Jim told me earlier. And, as Pecker quickly advised, he refers to his work as "erotic fantasy" not hard-core porn. Careful now . . .

"Hey Mike — You mother-fucking son-of-a-bitch!"

Michael Zen, seated with his back to us at the bar, swung slowly round in answer to Pecker's call. Dressed completely in black, from turtleneck to dress pants and patent leather shoes, his smiling saturnine face, framed by a monkish fringe, reminded me of someone.

"Isn't he like Nero?" said Delysia and Pecker laughed automatically like it was an old and trusty joke. Zen pulled a smile, but his concentration was on my face as if dredging up some ancient memory. Then Pecker introduced me. Zen slapped his hand to his brow: "Of course! The radio show! How many times have I been saved by your civilized tones from going mad as I edited vibration, masturbation and penetration sequences . . . This is indeed well met my friends!"

Jim seemed a little left out so I quickly agreed when he suggested a visit to some of the female stars in their dressing rooms as they prepared for the coming action.

"You must sit at my side!" shouted Zen as Pecker led us out of the dim bar and up some rickety stairs. In the make-up room Jim was in heaven because there he met an Asian girl in nothing but a G-string. He adores Asian girls; they're like delicate dolls. "She'll be in the lesbian orgy scene later this afternoon," said Pecker consulting his clipboard. "Now Ian, I want you to say hello to Misty Rain — who'll be visiting your country this Christmas, won't you dear?"

Miss Rain, sitting in her make-up chair, to my relief seemed quite ordinary, almost spindly. "Petite," perhaps, is the word for her. She smiled at me with wide sunflower eyes and gushed girlishly about her upcoming European trip: "A few days in Amsterdam — on business, of course-and then we hit London. I'll bet you know all the great clubs there?" I recommended a visit to The Tower of London where my brother-in-law, having once been Governor, has connections.

She thanked me with a little touch on my left side. But I felt no thrill. Next we were introduced to Misty's opposite number, Nikki Sinn, a big broad-shouldered (but beautifully proportioned) girl-woman wearing nothing but black leather boots.

Nikki advanced on me, her thick and sturdy thighs slotted into her hips and calf muscles — as if assembled from a heavenly construction kit. I almost didn't spot her huge twin breast turrets with their rivet nipples pointing.

"Pleased to meet you, really," she rasped at me and I had to lean back athletically in order to shake her hand. She was offering me herbal tea and a dunking biscuit when the bell rang for action. Jim and I strolled back as casually as we could to the little bar while Pecker and Miss Ravenscroft gave us a quick résumé of the plot:

"Diane and Ken are married . . . All he desires is a good orgasm, a bowl of ice cream, and Diane beside him as he watches Monday night football on a 50 inch screen with surround-sound . . . But she wants some spice and so off she goes to experiment with lipstick lesbians and even full bull-dykes . . . Strap-on dildos, toys, lap-dancing, the whole shebang . . . But that's for later this afternoon . . . Right now we're gonna shoot a straight sex scene taking place on top of the bar between Diane and a fantasy man . ."

The bar, so stygian before, was now lit by a concentrated battery of lights. Men and machinery were encamped in a circle around the bar-top. I was reminded of an illuminated Nativity tableau. Michael Zen sat back in the shadows, looking into a TV monitor, notes on his lap. He nodded his head to indicate that Jim and I should press forward for a good view when the action began.

"My friends, all I ask of you is that you stay clear of JD and his very mobile camera. Mark my words, he and his crew will be on the move constantly . ."

He grows serious, even somber.

"Action!"

Just as in a regular film a clapper boy steps out to mark the scene. I stand on tiptoes to get a full view: Misty Rain, now completely nude and shaved in all the right places, is lying on the bar with one leg arched. From out of the shadows appears a young man. He has clipped black hair and the classic bland face of a model. He is nude and is in tip-top shape — firm chest, firm legs, firm buttocks. The way American males used to look in the 40s and 50s — these days they're mostly butterballs.

He vaults onto the bar, with not a wobble from his body (but with a graceful swinging from between his legs) and joins Misty. He begins by licking up and down her legs. The camera, manned by a paunchy fellow in jungle fatigues, hovers above on a zigzagging crane operated by a young woman in baggy clothes, chewing gum. Misty starts to moan as the stud (he must be the man with the trouser trouble whom we saw on the street) noses into her mid-region. I notice that her breasts, perfectly shaped balloons, have gleaming metal rings hanging from the nipples. There is silence from the watchers. Are any of them feeling trouser-strain? It's the last thing on my mind. I hear traffic going by in the street and that's a good thing.

Suddenly our silence is broken by orders from Michael Zen. "Move in close, JD, so we can see the desire." I didn't know that directors can talk through the action, I thought that went out with the coming of sound.

"Bring in the pussy light!" A grey-bearded old man who had been crouching under the camera emerges with a tiny hand light and thrusts it towards where the stud's tongue was flicking before it disappeared inside Misty. "Let's have a close-up of the tongue as it goes in and out, in and out, in and out of pussy! . . . Long tongue, long tongue!" Zen is the DW Griffith of erotic fantasy films. I must tell him later. "We're on you, dear...Let me see that head go back, that's a good sport...Now look into the bar as if Ken is there...Pull on his hair . . . Good...Now Billy, get some saliva down there — I want to see strings of saliva . . . JD! Pick up on the pubic hair . . . Watch out you don't hit his balls . . . Long licks . . . Don't lose your energy, children . . . More sound, please . . . Something different than ummms and yeahs, Misty . . . I like your positions, Billy . . . Misty, keep your legs arched — we're still filming for cable audiences . . . Tell me when you need a break — We have all kinds of beverages for you — and, of course, BABY WIPES."

Zen's directions are interrupted by a crash. The elaborate crane system, enabling the camera to snake around and peep into any nook or cranny or orifice of the couple, has collapsed. Dumbbells, vital to the crane balance, roll around the floor and have to be retrieved by the chewing gum woman. Billy and Misty fall about laughing. "Baby wipes, anybody?" asks Zen. "Ian, come sit at my side." He proceeds to talk to me about *Citizen Kane* and the film course he teaches, while the crew re-balances the dumbbells on the crane, and the camera is reloaded. Jim is looking at another Asian girl who has appeared, readying for this afternoon's lesbian orgy scene. The clapper boy is reading the *Los Angeles Times*. Miss Ravenscroft is munching a bagel. I am supposed to be listening to Zen but I'm not: I'm transfixed by Billy, the stud.

He's standing by the bar, sideways, bottom clenched tight, hips stuck forward, and he's manipulating his penis in a workmanlike manner. Penis — too Latin, too dry dictionary. Dong — too comic. Cock — a little better, but not much. No word can describe what I now see: a splendid, thick, ripe, banana-bent but reddish-brown shaft with a pulsing wide vein running up the side, leading to a beautiful mushroom head that is nodding, nodding like flowers do in romantic poems. Meanwhile, beneath the shaft are two delicious ripe plums gently swaying as if to say, "Easy now — we are all part of God's works and will perform our ancient magic in good time."

I realize that Billy is only doing his job, as a stoker on a ship might grease some rods or shovel coal into a boiler, but Billy's quivering rampant prick (to use a coarse word) is greater than a work tool. It is Life, it is Art—it is the Be-all and The End-all. If only one could own Billy's entire tackle and keep it safe and primed forever! I wouldn't want Billy, or any Billys or Jasons or Bruces or Zanes, because you can be sure they'd talk of Rock or New Age or macrobiotic diets or the latest trends. All I want is the cock itself, to treasure forever. There'd be none of the complications that the other body parts bring.

"Right, children!" snaps Zen, waking me from my reverie. "Let's go for some internal probing — and then, with any luck, for the pop shot." Billy is now fully primed and rampant-ready, a magnificent picture of soldierly sturdiness — the cock quivers and shines. So clean and well maintained. As is Misty Rain. No obnoxious smells from them when they're working, only the reassuring smell of nursery unguents. What if Billy has a sudden attack of the squitters? Does he have a last name? "He's of little importance," says Zen. "In a straight show like this the men are merely servicers, functionaries. Billy does a workmanlike job and can pop to order — that's why he's always working. I use him in my gay movies too, because he performs without emotion — are we ready, children? — and doesn't seek romance like my gay actors do. My dear, it's a positive soap opera with some of those divas! I like your lighting, JD — reminds me of a forties film noir. Perhaps a little smoke, too . ."

We are reaching the solid meat of the movie: on the word "action" Billy shoves his engine inside Misty's crotch and starts thrusting in a fast but regular motion. She gets into a series of gymnastic positions as if working out at a health club. Every now and then Billy retracts for some sucking from Misty. "Strands of saliva!" orders Zen. "Get in close, JD, for some hard-core!" He whispers to me: "No time for second takes when they get hard and horny. You must grab your shot fast . ."

Billy is back inside, thrusting for all he's worth. Oops! He stops and snaps his fingers: "Condom!" I never realized he'd been wearing a rubber johnny all this time. Now, in the excitement of the action, it has torn. A youth in a baseball cap appears, carrying a long box which he opens and presents to Billy. As if selecting a cigar or a tea bag, Billy gets his new rubber. Then it's back into the fray, with Misty spread-eagled on the bar and Billy crouch-balanced over her in the military push-up position. "Work out! But if your knees hurt tell me!" shouts Zen. "Now assume the doggy position." This back-passage stuff I don't care for. Just as when childbirth is described to me, I feel I'm the victim. The pain is awful and can lead to fainting. "I think our man is coming to the pop!" calls out the chewing gum woman from the crane. "Then extract, extract!" orders Zen to Billy. Why it's necessary in straight porno to show the cock shooting is a mystery to me. I must question Zen about this important matter, later. It's all rather contradictory. Or does it prove what my gay friends claim — that all heteros are closet queens or, at least, interested in the homoerotic?

Anyway, out comes the magnificent, now glistening and shuddering instrument, and off comes the rubber johnny. At this moment Delysia Ravenscroft approaches me with a tray of little chocolate madeleines. "Baked 'em myself — just look at the fluting," she instructs. "Dunk it in that coffee." Not wishing to upset my hosts I do so, but all the while I'm watching the cock. It appears to have grown bigger and brighter since I first saw it — positively radiant and exuding an ancient godlike aura — and Billy is pumping away professionally with a red face full of grim determination.

Zen leans over to me: "Let us hope, my friend, that the goods can be produced swiftly so that we can proceed to the more enjoyable business of lunch." As Billy slaves, Zen decides on an artistic touch. Addressing the cameraman who has been whizzing about on his special cranes, he screams: "JD, let's utilize the photogenic possibilities of Misty's buttocks. Let's think John Ford — close in on Misty's buttocks and remain there till the first load falls . . . Yes, yes . . . Oh, that's so beautiful . . . like craters of the moon or the velvet hills of Oklahoma . . . alabastine . . . Misty! Undulate, dearie, undulate! This is a motion picture . ." Misty slowly waggles her bottom as Billy wanks away. "Anyone for baby wipes or bottled water?"

Finally, after perhaps only a minute and with just the tiniest beads of sweat on his brow, Billy gives birth to the required pop. Zen heaves a sigh of relief. "Excellent work! Now rub your dick on her buttocks . . . Very good . . . Gentlemen, you may come in for still shots." Several cameramen surround the exhausted couple and coax them into poses re-creating their recent acts. "This is where the spin-off money is generated. Ancillary photo rights garner us revenue worldwide." Noticing my surprise at his having dropped the aesthetic mode he'd been using up till now, Zen quickly follows with: "Let us feast — I can recommend the pasta pesto."

We ate lunch off a packing crate, Zen and me and a man called Zak (who had materialized from the darkness into which everyone else, including Jim, had disappeared). Zak looked older than me or Zen; he seemed to have been around the block several times and had the grids of facial lines to prove it. First off he produced a salt and pepper shaker set in the shape of elegant penises complete with golf ball-sized balls. Then, when we were well tucked into our lunch, he started, without any cue from me, a stream of information which he reeled off at such speed and with such precision that I more than suspected he'd dealt with people like me countless times before:

"Michael has many types of arrow in his quiver, you know. He has made lots of documentaries on all kinds of subjects. For example, his film on tattooing is considered a classic of its kind — he showed one man with Dante-like flames shooting from his ass. Another had butterflies round his balls. He is as much at home in the straight as in the gay scene. A dick is a dick is a dick, to paraphrase the poet. But as to the question of why there's so much erect dick in a hetero movie the answer is simple: the customers want to know that what we're shooting is for real. Now this afternoon we'll be concentrating on a bull-dyke orgy with plenty of toys involved and much lap dancing. Michael will, of course, put an artistic spin on proceedings, because it's necessary to be several notches above the 75 other adult movie outfits in the San Fernando Valley. Michael, you know, can talk Fellini or De Sica . ."

"Oh do shut up, Zak!" cut in Zen. "You're taking all the joy, all the fun, out of this business. Go and fetch me some more pesta and tell Billy he's finished for the day — I can see him still working desperately with his unit, poor devil."

The disgraced Zak was replaced by Delysia who wanted to remind Zen that this afternoon's scene would be in the club's show room and that although there'd be little dialogue beyond the usual "oohs" and "aaahs" she'd procured some really archetypal lesbians to act as audience. "Straight from Fantasy Casting—berets and heavy tweed, riding britches, you name it. One of the dykes smokes a meerschaum pipe!"

"You know," said Zen, tapping me on the knee, "At moments like this I feel like Judas on Resurrection morning—eternally grateful. Thank you, thank you, Delysia darling!"

I was enjoying a blueberry Danish pastry when Delysia started on about her philosophy of life: "All of us are only on loan from God and eventually we're returned to His storeroom. The restitution of all things . ." Thank God that Zen suddenly got up, clapped his hands and shouted, "Come now, kiddies-let's get down to some solid sucking and fucking!"

And now into my head there sprung a magnificent epiphany: a headless well-built naked body offering me any cake, sausage, fried onion, beer or wine I desired; and any kind of sexual permutation, too. This perfect body having no head there was, therefore, no brain and thus no ideas, no theories, no rules of government to get in the way. The day with Zen and his porno people had brought about this wonderful image of Truth and the promise of Life.

This was the meaning of that great American motto: "The Pursuit Of Happiness." Washington had started it; Clinton was presently paying for it.

The rest of the afternoon at Martini Lounge was a daze of activity, of the slapping of titties and bottoms, of tongues flicking up orifices, of bull-dykes in berets egging on the Asian girls (directed by Zen with such questions as, "Wouldn't you just love to go Dutch and put your finger up a dyke?"), of Nikki Sinn resplendent in black boots over muscular thighs and with her whip at the ready and a giant dildo strapped to her waist ("Do you approve of this one, Michael?" "I've no opinion — all dildos terrify me"), of JD rushing around on his fluid camera crane, pushed by the chewing-gum woman (who was able to eat sandwiches at the same time), followed by the older man with the pussy light ("Get closer to the hole, JD!" "Any closer and I'll be right inside!" "Exactly, JD, exactly!"), of Zen nudging me to offer his headphones ("Listen to the slurping of saliva in hi-fi"), and then, as a six-way lesbian tangle was reaching its climax, of the sound of a sneeze followed by a fart. Everybody broke out into their own peculiar laughter. Except for me. "Experience the joy of our business," said Zen gently to me. Then he ordered a break.

"You see?" he said to me at tea, "You must realize that while we may enjoy a little laugh every now and then, our customers in the world at large take our work extremely seriously, sitting alone in their homes as we work up their fantasies. We bring solace to the physically challenged. Why, my own doctor prescribes my films to help couples with marital problems. We are doing good work." And he pressed my hand gently. What I really wanted was a bit part in one of his films, but I said nothing.

At five o'clock Zak came up to tell Zen that Misty was "ready and lubed and prepped for DP." What was DP, I asked. "My dear boy," said Zen, "your ingenuousness is most attractive. Or is it disingenuousness?" Zak gave me a horrid look. "We are talking double penetration," he said, giving each syllable a different note. The announcement, DP, had the effect of producing people I'd thought were forever lost in the darkness: Pecker re-appeared, so did Jim. "This is what our lonely customers really enjoy," said Zen. "This is the icing on the cake."

But I took one look at the men involved — two British louts, built like bulls and equipped with genitals that hung too low and reminded me of things Neanderthal, slimy and scarred, of the earth, of the mud-and I begged to leave, saying I had a pressing appointment. Was it because I was squeamish about what they were embarked upon? Or was it because they were British, and therefore anti-romantic and down-to-earth. I feared that, if we were introduced, they would be quickly onto my game. "But they're your fellow countrymen," protested Pecker. Jim said he'd see me next week at the salon. Zen added that he'd like to come, too. "Perhaps I'll bring some of my actors — and their families." Their families? "Yes, you see we have husbands and wives and children. Don't look surprised—we are an American business like any other business, and when we play I assure you we leave our work behind us . .''

    I returned the next day but it wasn't the same. The thrill had gone.

DECEMBER

    Astonishingly, I am writing this on a computer! It is very slow going — much slower than the electric typewriter — but this is the way the world is moving and I shall have to move along with it or die. Friends who are in the computer business gave us this machine but it's very old (three years!) and marked with a cracked half-eaten apple and it huffs and puffs and groans. Funnily enough, I don't mind the tock-tock sound, even preferring it to the clack of the Smith-Corona and the long-ago clang of the Remington.

    At the moment I'm relieved to have enough projects in which I am the boss. Creating one's own universe. Where I have trouble is in the mainstream of show-biz (or "The Industry" as they arrogantly call it out here). Sometimes the Industry call by way of my agent, Sheila: an audition for a movie, TV series or, more likely, a commercial. Invariably it's for a part as a butler.

    I'm fed up with being sent out for butler parts — because I never get them. I like to believe this is because I haven't the necessary superciliousness (mixed with lower-class origins) you need to play butlers. Every time I report to these "cattle calls" the place is overflowing with butler types. They pour out of buses in full regalia— boiled shirt, frock coat, wing collar and serving napkin. They all know each other too, comparing notes, discussing casting directors, making golf and soccer dates. The humiliation is excruciating. You wait around on hard benches for hours in an impersonal holding room as the bastards blather and joke and name-drop until finally you're called. And then the director calls you "Jim" and tells you the role for this high-fiber cereal commercial is "many-layered" and is still "in a state of flux." Two lines, that's all there is. But I was so annoyed at being called Jim that I fluffed the two lines. Why do I go up for such demeaning work? A pathetic desire to be a star again, to be recognized in crowded street and bar.

    Some Friday nights I go out as a Volunteer On Patrol for the Altadena Sheriff's Dept. I have a uniform — what a sexy one! Sheriff badges on shirt and jacket. My partner (a cartoon scriptwriter) and I are allowed to commandeer a big white marked car with a searchlight and those waltzing colored lights on the roof. My partner drives and I grasp the radio. We prowl around the neighbourhood using only our eyes and ears — and the searchlight

— to seek out crime. But everyone's at home from 8pm onwards, it seems. What are they all doing? Frustrated at having no bad guys, we call in on the radio to report a young man who has been talking far too long on the public phone by the park; and then there's that Black man snoozing in his car nearby.

Trouble is, I was tuned to the wrong waveband and my call was channeled down to police HQ in central Los Angeles. The authorities expressed mystification over an alarm call from an Englishman overexcited about African-Americans in and around a public park. From now on I'll try to spend more time at home, sitting still, or practicing the piano or reading Proust.

Of course, I'm at home now as I work the blessed computer. But now I must stop in order to relieve Regina in her duties of disciplining our new puppy Rollo, making sure he doesn't pee on the carpet, chew up my socks, tear up her ball gowns, eat the newspaper. When he's bad he's Rollo H. Danks. His mother married beneath her so we don't know his family background. But we guess he's part Greyhound and part Rhodesian Ridgeback.

He's rapidly taking the place of Inspector — who died under mysterious circumstances: just disappeared one day, then turned up at dusk, rolled over in the driveway, did a few pants and expired. Regina is sure our next-door neighbour, a glum-faced brooding Iranian woman, let him out the front gate. I say no, I can't believe it. But Regina has never liked the woman and the woman does make a lot of strange trips to Germany. Once she asked Regina whether she was expecting a baby because she was putting on weight in a place where it just shouldn't be.

Christ! I must have leaned on a wrong key — there's a series of nnnnnnnnnns racing up and destroying everything in its path. I'll have to "Force Quit."

Tunefully Yours & A Very Happy Xmas!

2000

JANUARY

How therapeutic it is to type out the new year, the new century — with all those clean zeroes standing for a New Beginning! Another chance, another go-round on the carousel.

Do you worry about where the next money is coming from? I've been self-employed for years and have no skill that the world needs. I can't even competently flip a burger.

Right now I'm putting together another songbook for the Mel Bay Company but it's just an excuse to avoid settling down to write a proper book — I mean a book that relies solely on words and isn't supported by music and pictures. Music and Art are nothing but sauce without meat.

Time was when I used to write real books, published by conglomerates with branches in Delhi and Auckland. Since those days — over a decade ago — I've been avoiding proper authorship by messing around making records or writing liner notes and articles or playing tiny parts in movies. The Real Thing is pure writing. The novel, the autobiography, the memoir.

Proust was the master of writing about one's life and making it magical by elevating life above the quotidian. A hellishly hard read but ultimately rewarding. He made me laugh just describing a snob's bow to a minor landed lady. There followed, he writes, a "rapid straightening-up which caused a sort of tense muscular wave to ripple over M. Legrandin's rump, which I had not supposed to be so fleshy; I cannot say why, but this undulation of pure matter, this wholly carnal fluency devoid of spiritual significance, this wave lashed into a tempest by an obsequious alacrity of the basest sort, awoke my mind suddenly to the possibility of a Legrandin altogether different from the one we knew."

Superb minutiae! Exquisite Camp! But do I have the time for such close study in the rush of everyday life?

No — I must be brace and settle down to write a book-book on spec. But what shall the subject be? Maybe the adventures of Smiling Jack, the character I invented for *Stanley's Gig*, the ukulele movie I also wrote songs for last summer. The one with Faye Dunaway.

Maybe Jack can roam the Far West with Ukie and a talking dog and a small orphan boy in search of a mysterious ranch where all is melody and light. But on the journey there are trials and tests...

The test for me lies in dreaming up the details. We shall see whether I can ever knuckle down to the job, to dare to face the unknown.

Sadly,

TTFN

PS From Regina: For God's sake! Please write back to Ian and tell him how great he is because he IS great and wonderful and sweet. I don't know why he's in such a dark mood. I'm going to prepare him a favorite supper of macaroni cheese with fried tomatoes and bacon on top and hope that it helps. Then we'll watch 'Old Mother Riley' on video.

APRIL

Oh, to be in England now that April's here! — as the poet sang. I get pangs of Proust-like memories too often: crisp, cutting mornings rushing about the Sussex Downs as a Boy Scout, followed by the loving rubbing onto the thighs of the salve by TDM, chief scoutmaster with his reassurance that this would do the trick; lushly-bordered racing-deep rivers on a Dorset afternoon as you swim with your best friend in the nude (a school rule). The clean virgin English countryside, the good manners of the 1950s, the tranquility of hedges, fields and copses, relieved by Odeon visits where American violence, swollen and beefy, lowered in ten gallon hat or fedora bringing tingly fear from the snug of a seat.

There are plenty of Englishmen over here but not the kind I care to remember from the 1950s. I encounter them constantly at auditions. A motley crew. Sometimes I throw them off by getting through to a near-final stage of selection. I achieved this recently via the commercial for a brokerage company where I got to "call back" status three times. Unfortunately each time it was for a smaller role.

Anyway, the scene was an awards ceremony in 2010 for Doctors Of The World. A speaker announces that AIDS has been conquered and everything else as well, including spinal injuries. And to prove it, on marches Christopher Reeve, completely cured and grinning like Mr. Tambo. (This would be achieved by something new called CGI, they said, and never you mind how it's done).

By the final callback I'd fallen from the prime role of Awards Speaker to a wordless doctor in the audience, flanked by a Pakistani male and a Korean female. We were ordered into a shabby casting office in a shaky packing crate of a building on Third Street. There we were introduced to the director, a smooth-talking Englishman in khaki supported by a row of sour-faced and deadly serious associates in T shirts and black jackets, sitting rigid behind him.

"Right," drawled the Englishman in an accent I couldn't place, "I need to see your reactions when Christopher miraculously walks in." The ethnics were called on to perform first; I felt they were over the top — keening and prostrating themselves and so forth.

The director was most grateful, thanking them for traveling so far and dismissing them with a wave. Now he pointed to me with his chin. "Now let's see your reaction to the miracle of Christopher."

I put on my best smile, giving the imaginary Reeve a pleasing up-and down look while indicating that I wasn't to be confused with the role I was playing.

"Tell me, do tell me," said the director, "what was running through your head?" He leaned forward to study my reply.

"Well, I was really glad that Mr. Reeve had been cured but I didn't want to appear to seem proud of having helped cure him." A silence all round. I felt pretty good.

"OK — get outta here!"

And that settled that, as the mother said when she laid an egg in the teapot. Later I caught the commercial on network TV on Super Bowl Sunday. It had cost several million to make and several more to be shown on prime time TV. But I couldn't see any British doctor faces in the crowd so I was relieved. In fact I've not seen any of the audition bastards who've been chosen over me. I simply avoid going to the movies when I recognize the titles as ones I auditioned for. That way I can feel better.

2001

MARCH

Rain is pelting down as I type. And I'm safe inside the burrow of our house, almost a home, and I'm enjoying the rain, getting a thrill out of hiding away. Maybe a memory of World War Two days when, while there was brutal racket outside, there was Rupert The Bear and Buck Jones comics for inside, under the eiderdown.

Right now there's unnatural snow sitting on the mountains that stand straight up behind us in Altadena. Snow! Last weekend, when I was waiting in Lone Pine — up the map in the middle of California — for Regina to join me there after her nannying trip in Mammoth, ski-land resort of the rich, I got lost in a snow storm.

Between Lone Pine and the mountains lie the Alabama Hills. There, for decades, rode singing cowboys like Roy Rogers and Gene Autry in a dreamscape of rocks and sand, a land I wanted to live in after watching these western heroes on a tiny TV screen at home in soggy London in the early 1950s. I wanted these men to be my father, my uncle, my buddy, my friend.

I wrote a song about the Hills; made a little video, starring Regina and Inspector The Dog, shot on the same roads where Gene, Roy and even Hoppy had ridden; produced a short called *On Location in Lone Pine* for the BBC; had an article published in *London Magazine* called *Lone Pine Blues*; obsessed about a New Zealand boy actor and his name, Ra Hould, who'd been Gene Autry's saddle pal in *Boots And Saddles*; wished I'd been Ra Hould instead of a British Invader; sought him out in his 70s and found him dying at home in an L.A suburb.

And here I was once again in the Alabama Hills, alone except for Rollo The Dog (now almost as big as a pony), tramping off confidently along a track leading to a *Boots And Saddles* location not far from where a *Gunga Din* charge had been staged, not much further from Whitney Portal Road where Humphrey Bogart had fled in a car with cops in hot pursuit at the end of *High Sierra*. I had parked the Honda close to a set of tall but friendly rocks; I sang "Slow Poke" as I tramped.

Out here alone, in a past summer, I'd torn myself away from the BBC crew to stand in the still blackness and stare up at the too bright and too many stars in a firmament informing me that we're of no consequence in the enormity of things that go on forever and ever without benefit of a sense of humor or understanding of the pleasures in a dry martini.

Now the snow fell silently around us and a mist swirled up so that the scene seemed very different from that of sunnier days when I'd strolled here, different even from the nothingness of night, different to the land of Roy and Hoppy. I should have known better than to be out in such inclement weather.

I strolled and I strolled, up hill and down gully; I admired a cactus or two. Rollo, off-leash, did some fruitless sniffing and cocked his head to sounds foreign to me.

After an hour I decided we'd better turn back since I was to rendezvous at noon with Regina, back from her Mammoth trip, at a Lone Pine Coffee Shop, a spot where motherly waitresses make sure your coffee cup is bottomless. I anticipated a squashy tuna melt and a heap of onion rings.

But I couldn't find the Honda. The rocks I thought I knew were no longer my friends. Changed, all changed utterly. Strange and hostile, with no western melodies bouncing off them. Snow was pounding, no longer silent, coming down in blankets; wind lashing. I was lost.

I trudged and sang and swore. "When You Travel Down The Road That Leads To Nowhere" — a number sung by Ozie Waters accompanied by His Colorado Rangers in a 1940s western starring Charles Starrett. Information of no use to me now. Rollo was unfazed, lucky dog.

Unprepared for survival: no cell phone, no emergency rations, no compass, no nothing. Hands getting redder and redder. By all means, don't panic. Find main road, the one called Movie Road, where the camera cars used to rattle-race in the old B western years, traveling alongside a runaway stagecoach containing the girl.

Ah, Movie Road! Relying on the sense of direction I'm proud of, we set off to the right as the storm grew angrier and my hands grew purple. I knew that soon we'd arrive at the road's entrance, off Whitney Portal Road. Then I'd backtrack and locate the place where I'd left the car. On and on we walked. "Tumbling Tumbleweeds" was now the song of the moment. More and hideously grotesque rocks and hills and even snaggle-toothed snarling mountains. They were never here before.

No cars, no hikers, nobody — except....I could have sworn I heard an excited conversation high in the jagged cliffs to my left. But no sign of life. Rollo heard it too and his ears went into red alert. The chatter became a screech, a hideous inhuman noise. Another hour had gone by. Almost noon and she'd be waiting for me, like a Rose of Picardy, at the rendezvous. What a fool I'd feel, even if dead, when at last the emergency services find me and they see the jacket with the Sheriff's badges and the small "Volunteer" underneath. What kind of a man is this?

Time passed and snow fell mercilessly and I'd run out of Kleenex. Songs were of no use anymore. Had they ever been? No — they were merely stupid habit. Now I was really considering an ignominious death: Middle-aged One Hit Wonder Dies In Snowstorm In Police Jacket With Faithful Dog At Side. Would I even get an obituary? At least I had the consolation of having been a clue in the *Los Angeles Times* crossword puzzle.

Just as I was abandoning all hope I heard the beautiful sound of a motorcar and then, up behind us, there emerged chugging through the gloom — an SUV. Never was I so glad to see such a monster. I flagged it down.

The driver, a photographer for a Calendar publisher, told me I'd been heading in the wrong direction — North into a wilderness that goes on for miles until it ends at the site of the Japanese Relocation Camp of World War Two. I promised to visit it that afternoon as penance. I was only a few minutes late for Regina.

So now I'm back home and not going away. I'm looking forward to providing period music for Peter Bogdanovich's new movie, *The Cat's Meow*; to more gigs with Janet Klein's Parlour Boys; to the release of my new CD *Sentimentally Yours*; to a Florida ragtime concert with Dick Hyman; to correcting proofs for *Uke Ballads*, the upcoming Mel Bay songbook; to Vintage Dance Week in Oxford, Missouri.

In short, I'm plunging once more into the hurly burly of Life, leaving no time to ponder rude thoughts about Death. But he's there alright, waiting to welcome me with a silly smile and no tune that I'd recognize on his thin, pale, deathless lips.

Tunefully — more than ever.

SEPTEMBER

September 11 was a bad day for us for a different reason: we learned that Regina's father, Morris, had died (peacefully) the night before in his current hometown of Thousand Palms out in the low desert. So we've been preoccupied with certain arrangements. I wish

I'd quizzed him more about the time his parents ran a speakeasy in New Jersey in the 1920s, upstairs in a low-ceilinged room while down below on the streets slow-moving limousines roamed the street gunning down rivals every so often. Odd that a Jewish family ran a speakeasy. Doesn't the Torah forbid alcohol?

Morris wrote a few songs on the side. Mostly he sold household appliances for Sears Roebuck — and very well too. In his honor Regina and I sang songs that he didn't write: "Till We Meet Again" and, brightening up, "Everywhere You Go" with the fine line, "Children love you, they seem to know/You bring roses out of the snow." What would we do without the balm of these songs? I must admit they can be more potent and pithy than anything by Proust or Joyce. The latter used to unblushingly steal lines from old songs and plop them in his books without any credit to the writers.

While the funeral arrangements were being made I was, surreptitiously, writing songs for a TV movie to be shot next month — about Scott Fitzgerald's last year when he was living here and trying to finish *The Last Tycoon*. The director, Henry Bromell, is a novelist as well as a director. We get along fine, so far. He wears tweed jackets with leather elbow patches. A good sign. But he's a Tom Waits fan. A bad sign.

DECEMBER

Bromell kindly arranged for Showtime, the cable company funding the movie (*Against The Current*) to fly me up to Toronto so that I could supervise the dance band in the night club scene. There is nobody flying anywhere, it seems — a result of this Twin Towers business, no doubt. I described myself as "movie composer" when questioned by immigration. A new position! Joining the ranks of Max Steiner and all those European exiles with unpronouncable names.

Toronto is vilely modern but the movie crew had found a few Art Deco streets and there they were busy shooting. So, once again, I was able to hide from the present day. On the night of the recreation of the Trocadero night club in Hollywood there were no less than 200 actors and extras. The band mimed to my song "Goodnight." Jeremy Irons danced to it with Neve Campbell. I was in a transport of delight, standing there as composer in my speckled black and white vintage 1940s suit, bought for $25 at a Salvation Army thrift store.

To cap it all, Irons approached and in his sauvest voice asked: "Who is your tailor?" Always wear a suit and you can't go wrong. I asked him where he'd gone to school but he wouldn't tell me. Maybe he's not a Public School man. "Oh, and one more thing,

Ian," he said as he turned on his heel to return to the dance. "Do you have any other tunes? I'm becoming frightfully tired of the one they keep playing."

Saddened to read of George Harrison's death, in Los Angeles of all places. Never actually met any of the Beatles but George and Paul, I'm reliably informed, knew of my uke playing and taste for old songs. Not long ago I was descending the stairs from the Green Room at McCabe's Guitar Shop in Santa Monica — following a performance at a uke show — when a woman came up and told me she was George's sister-in-law and that George likes my uke records. Well you could have knocked me down with a feather! A connection with the Happening World!

"Just a minute," I said — and pulled out of my briefcase a bunch of my CDs (at least a half dozen), plopping them into her hands. She was taken aback. "He likes you," she said as she staggered. "But not that much!"

Dr Kevin Starr, the State Librarian Of California — who really is a fan — has appointed me as a sort of State Minstrel. Starting next year I'll be roaming around rural libraries giving talk-concerts. Funded by the federal government. Regina is included in the contract to travel. So is Rollo. A wandering troubadour, as of yore!

2002

JANUARY

A new year starts before I've even got to grips with the last bloody year! They say that as you get older so time passes faster and faster until you've not even time to recognize that you're dead. Anyway, happy new year. Last year wasn't bad for us here in Altadena: I provided over an hour of music for Peter Bogdanovich's new picture, *The Cat's Meow*, and I wrote the songs for a new Showtime picture starring Jeremy Irons as Scott Fitzgerald. That was the big show-biz stuff. On a smaller scale I played Harry Potter's headmaster Mr. Dumbledore in a skit for *Mad TV*— dressed in Richard Harris wig and having the time of my life overacting but <u>not</u> overacting as much as the precocious kid playing Harry, a real English boy who couldn't stop snarling that it should have been him in the movie and not the wretched Radcliffe child because he, this kid on the Hollywood TV set who was actually here on holiday and happened to be picked for this *Mad TV* sketch, was next in line to play Harry.

The Scott Fitzgerald film (set in Southern California but filmed, as is typical today, in Canada) is supposed to be ready for the Cannes film festival in March and may be on Showtime around the same month.

But, *what's new* in this first month of 2002?

On Tuesday, January 15, accompanied by Regina and the dog Rollo, I will be embarking on the first of my official California State Library tours. This is a program to bring fun and frolics to the rural libraries. I will be doing my usual act: ostensibly delivering a lecture but actually performing a rambling entertainment about my obsession with pop songs and I'll be illustrating these songs with the ukulele and recorded music from our little boom box. Regina will sing a few numbers. What Rollo will do is, at the moment, unclear. We start in at Kern Valley canyon and then, next day, we journey to

Rosamond, a little town in the desert, and on Thursday we end up the first tour in the big city of Bakersfield. Our next tour will be in March and we'll continue every other month giving these little entertainments at rural libraries throughout the State for two years. We'll be like a traveling minstrel show, or troubadours of old, coming to spread the good news gospel of song.

The other night I dreamed that I was back at my alma mater, Trinity College Dublin, and found myself in a finely-panelled dining room with several aged dons whom I remembered as my lecturers. There was Miss Otway-Ruthven, a cranky old bat in black gown who used to read a lecture to us on British constitutional history in a drone, and put more animation into the roll call when she made every name seem racy.

Old Otway was, in my dream, talking shop with some aged gowned profs as they sat around in huge wing-backed chairs sipping sherry. She told of a student of hers who, in an essay answer, "parsed rather well." She enunciated the word "parse" as if it was some some perverted sex act. Anyway, all the Academics ignored me and so I asked a stooping servant (in full livery) if he'd kindly show me the way out because I had to be going to my hotel. The room was high as a cathedral and the other rooms he led me through were equally large and daunting and gloomy too. Then down long dark corridors lined with fusty shields and crossed swords. Finally he let me out at a gold-encrusted side door. "Where are you abiding, sir?" I told him my hostelry was near Bryanston, my old school (which in fact is in Dorset, England, across a sea). "There is Bryanston, sir," he said, pointing me to a huge brick castle right next door, swimming in a romantic fog. Then I discovered that my hotel was my mother's old flat on Putney Heath in London, only now it was next door to Bryanston, one along from TCD. And when I couldn't find my mother's place I went back into our present house in Altadena which was, conveniently, round the corner.

So I woke up in my own bed. And then it dawned on me why I'd dreamed about TCD. Just after Christmas I'd received an e-mail from Mick Molloy, lead guitarist in Bluesville, the band I'd helped found in Dublin back in 1962. He'd played on my chart records, "This Sporting Life" and "You Turn Me On." He was a real Dubliner, a good quiet steady fellow, a little like George Harrison. His "sad news" was that the co-founder of Bluesville (Ireland's first band to ever make the American hit charts) had died "peacefully" on Christmas Day: Barry Richardson — my old pal Barry whom I hadn't seen since the 1960s, had died. But what of? Mick mentioned "chemo" so I suppose it must have been cancer. He was living in Belgium. Why Belgium? I'd lost touch with Barry and that was such a pity because in the early 1960s at Trinity I'd spent so much time with him, grand and glorious times they were, playing American blues and boogie records, listening intensely and occasionally whooping with joy, enthusing about the music and what we were going to do about it. Barry played any instrument he could get his hands on: bass, clarinet, mouth organ (he played the latter on my very first record release, "Soho" on Seattle's Jerden label). Barry, it must be admitted — and admitted it was by many of his friends and associates — could be prickly at times but he was always full of enthusiasm and ardor and he fired me up. He was an Englishman too but he was a practical down-to-earth, salt-of-the-earth one. He came from the North of England where life was supposedly much harder and he looked on me as a softie from the South, a wet who'd been to boarding schools and had been mollycoddled. We were yin and yang but we got along because of our mutual fire concerning American roots music. Look, I must have liked Barry because I had a nickname for him: Barold Pilchardson. I keep repeating it these days, to the distraction of my wife. So Bluesville was formed and became the toast of Dublin and the desire of a hundred local biddies. We were a hell of a good band. They still talk about us in Dublin. There's a photo of us affixed to a wall at an exhibit in Dublin called *The Irish Music Hall of Fame.* Truly, I was at my best as a raw rocker. And Barry had egged me on, had inspired it all. I have no letters from him but there are pix of him on some of our record sleeves, standing near me as I fling myself about the stage — Barry, like a sort of gray eminence, a sort of Svengali of rock and roll. I wish I'd seen more of him in his later years. How was I to know they were going to be his later years? In rootsy music we were ever young with no thought of tomorrow. That's the trouble with that music — it never pauses to reflect. But I'd have never been the rocker I was if it hadn't been for Barry Richardson. You can read more about him and Bluesville in my book, *Rock Odyssey*. Meanwhile, good-bye Barry and thanks for all the great gigging and the jars of stout that we consumed!

Tunefully, and a little thoughtfully,
Ian

FEBRUARY

Up until now, as I have dashed off these letters from the top of my head, I haven't given much thought as to who'll be reading them, apart from a handful of friends and supporters (who become friends). But since the publication of last week's edition of *The L.A. Weekly*, in which there is a full-page article about me, I shall have to watch my words: the writer has been regularly perusing my on-line stuff and has quoted liberally — my cheeky remarks about a film director, and my really rather nasty description of a veteran film actress. All "out of context," as people say when their rash off-the-cuff words become sound or print "bites." But there we are — I really did write such vitriol.

Of course, the point of these letters is to write raw and not to polish for posterity or my place in literature, so I'll probably go on stating the first feeling that comes into my head and let it translate itself onto the computer screen via my left forefinger............

The article in question is called "Ukie and Me Against the World." I come across as a curmudgeon and I look like an old fool in the photo. All true, I suppose. Our house is described as a "cultural bomb shelter where he tries to pretend the real world doesn't exist." But I'm very aware of this real world whenever I step outside. And recently I've been out and about in communities I don't normally have a chance to visit.

In the middle of January the state sent me on the first leg of my lecture tour of rural libraries. An actual employee of the Federal Government. A real job! I am described as a "scholar and performer" reviving the old-time "chautauqua" so that deprived rural areas can have "fun in learning." Well, we certainly had fun and we also learnt: "we" meaning me, Regina, and our dog Rollo. We set off in our rented Windstar van (packed with boom box, songbooks, CDs, and Ukie) on a Tuesday and were soon over the Tejon Pass and into the great Central Valley with its vast level fields of agribiz and little else except Denny's and the like. Our base for the first three lecture/concerts was Bakersfield and we put up at a Best Western because they take dogs. This one, conveniently opposite the grand terra cotta Beale Memorial Library, is called The Hill House, although I couldn't find the hill. In fact, there were no hills in Bakersfield, as it turned out. Like so many motels it was run by a fellow from India whose name was, as usual, Patel. I sniffed around for the normal (and agreeable) aroma of curry. All You Can Eat crab legs were being offered on Wednesday night, so said the big marquee outside. A Live Band was promised for the near future. Rock, no doubt. Our room was in a large white building with pillars over the entrance in *Gone With The Wind* style. Rollo was very excited about his new quarters, but then he's excited about everything.

After we'd finally achieved plastic key cards that actually worked, I left Regina and Rollo sampling the cable TV channels (we don't subscribe to cable so it's exciting when we stay at motels) while I strolled across the street to the Beale Library to introduce myself. In fact, I didn't stroll — I limped. Back at our athletic club, you see, the day before our departure, I'd stubbed a bunch of toes on a bench in the locker room. I think I may have broken a few, but the resulting limp has its good side: it makes me literally take life a step at a time, so I can stop and smell the roses (so to speak), and I can take measured steps and be humble and even pathetic. This is quite a change for me, and a welcome one. Certain people are relieved.

On entering the Beale I was greeted by a chap at Information.

"Geoff "(pronounced "Joff "), he told me with a wrinkle of his nose. "Apologies are in Order! But, you understand, I was born that way." Then: "Just been reading about you! Fascinating character!" The book, it turned out, is *Playing For Time*, a memoir of Trinity College Dublin student life written by my old roommate Jeremy Lewis, now a Big Man in the Literary London scene. In this memoir, which I've read several times, he'd revealed that I'd been so constipated one term at TCD that I'd had to seek out an enema. And as I'd been too shy to ask for the machinery at the chemist shop, Jeremy had stepped up to the counter and dealt with the matter. Of course, I've also made fun of friends in my books. I quickly unloaded some of my own books onto Geoff so that I could really trump Jeremy. Then the librarian showed me via a mere click of his computer that the library already had tons of my work. I was going to enjoy this tour.

Next he led me upstairs to meet the lady librarian in charge of the Kern County system. Most of these libraries are run by ladies, I was warned. On our way we passed walls of delicious oil paintings of plein air California — golden days of the 1920s, so romantic, so distant! — and past rows of heads concentrating on computer screens like medieval monks on illuminated manuscripts. Were they filling themselves with information? Or checking where they could locate a rare edition of *The Waste Land*? No: they were all playing video games. One of them was deep into blackjack. Another deep into pictures of semi-naked youths with knotted muscles and big bulges, wrestling each other. As we passed this last computer student, Geoff slapped the old man's wrist: "Now, now! We know that's not Ancient Greece but modern Chatsworth!" My time as an observer of the porn movie industry enabled me to understand the Chatsworth reference. But I wondered how Geoff knew.

After a stimulating meeting with the lady librarian — all the library folk I met were ebullient and enthusiastic about my impending tour — we set off in the Windstar. The vast ranges of the Tejon ranch — a ranch that seems to encompass all of the Kern Valley — impressed me what with the sheep and cattle munching contentedly and the promise of adventure just over the far hills; then the narrow mountain pass with the rushing river; then suddenly a great low stretch of land and there we were at Lake Isabella. It was hard to find the lake itself and when we did it seemed rather desolate, with no sailing boats and a lot of fish carcasses littering the shore.

But Rollo had a good time as he always does. Sniffing fresh smells. The Lake is full of activity in the summer, we were told. We learned this in Shady's Saloon, a dark but cheerful spot decorated with beer ads showing busty young women, where we joined the locals celebrating something or other. Toasts were made and songs were sung. The locals had the look of pioneers about them — grizzled and versed in the hard knocks of life. A sturdy race, unlike what you see in Los Angeles. There was a woman called Donna and a burly man wearing a leather jacket with a patch reading "Proud To Be An American."

We dined on fresh trout at The Fisherman's Grill across the street. The waitress told us the trout wasn't local because the FDA wants too much time-consuming testing done. I wonder where the fish actually comes from? Still, it was tasty, especially with the tartar sauce.

Down the road to the smart and well-appointed Kern River Valley Library and a small but extremely appreciative audience. It was too cold and too late (7pm) for the local seniors who'd expressed interest in attending. There are a lot of retirees in this area, happy to be out of the L.A. rat race.

I set up the little Target-bought boom box and I laid out my wares. The lady librarian gave a short introduction. Earlier she'd confided that a friend of hers, an elderly woman, used to wait outside hotels in the hope of catching me — back in 1965 when I was a British Invader. Regina and I sang "Shine On Harvest Moon" (to accompaniment by Ukie) and the audience joined in. What a relief that such people know a song from 1909! I fear that in the near future we'll being singing alone to a silent moon.

I talked a bit of cultural history. Rollo ate a paper plate and had to be removed. We were back in our Best Western room by 11pm and ready for old movies on cable. Rollo carried on a conversation with the dog on the floor below. A man howled nearby. Upon inquiry Mr. Patel assured me that the man, Jebb by name, was a harmless lunatic who, like so many unfortunates in these parlous times, was a regular guest at the motel with his bill being footed by the state of California. Thus I took his howls into consideration and Regina turned the TV louder. However, the problem became moot when Rollo, stimulated no doubt, began howling louder than the lunatic and soon succeeded in shutting him down.

The dog's successful tactic reminded me of my Dublin days when "eejits," the local equivalent of Jebb, used to waylay us students as we reeled back to our digs after a night on the town. In those days the city was riddled with eejits due to their being no mental asylums, only the Catholic Church. One eejit, a particularly nasty old bag armed with independently-moving teeth and breath that could lance you at twenty-five yards, had a habit of springing out at us from a certain religious niche in Grafton Street, raising her arms like a Macbeth witch and screeching to high heaven. On advice from one of our history professors we employed a preemptive strike: spotting her as she emerged from her pre-Christian gloom to launch her attack, we uttered, as one man, an Early Irish "Wailing Lament For The Dead" (taught to us by our professor) so effectively that the wretched woman was struck dumb even before she could go into her act. She was last seen racing professionally towards the bushes of St. Stephen's Green. We had, for the moment at least, cured her of her particular illness.

Back to the Library Tour.

Next day we headed away from the mountains and into the Mojave Desert, to the little town of Rosamond. More rolling hills and meadows with contented sheep and cows. The families who run the agribiz contributed more than a million dollars to help build the Wanda Kirk Library. We had a railway line to the right of us, a picturesque sight, winding along and every now and then disappearing into a tunnel. I'd love to take trains all over California but unfortunately a lot of Amtrak travel seems to take place on a bus.

At the end of a lovely afternoon, as the sun was painting the distant mountains a dusty gold, we approached our destination — and almost drove right past it. Rosamond has but a tiny sign off the freeway, upstaged by the cacti, and the rows and rows of remaindered jumbo jets parked in a nearby airstrip. But, like Bakersfield, the Wanda Kirk Library was an imposing structure, the largest building in the town. And, as before, we were greeted expansively by the lady librarian. Lots of school children deep into computers.

The librarian, a comely woman in rhinestone glasses and with a tendency to wink, recommended the fish at a gringo Mexican restaurant a few blocks away at the airport. After that and a margarita we were fully primed to perform. Again, a small but attentive audience. Many of the Rosamundites, I was told, commute to L.A. and so when my chautauqua began they were probably getting ready for bed. Again, Rollo grew over-excited and had to be removed.

As we left the library a man resembling a grizzled prospector approached us and doffed his ten-gallon hat. After telling us how much he'd been entertained by our show and regretting that we hadn't sung any Hendrix or Dylan he said: "Don't be fooled by the apple-blossom atmosphere of Rosamund and the Mojave Desert." He waved his arm slowly from left to right, embracing the evening panorama. As he did so he added a flickering of his fingers. It was a rather beautiful sight, almost balletic. "Don't be fooled, pals. That there desert's a dumping ground for dead bodies, a sprawl of meths labs, and a centre for train robbers. Jest thought I'd tell you as you seem good, if gullible, folks. The dog knows what I'm taking about." Indeed, Rollo at present was involved in some heavy sniffing.

Thursday was the climax of the first leg of our tour: a show in the auditorium of the Beale, back in Bakersfield. As we were on base there was time to explore Bakersfield, a place I hadn't visited since 1972 when I'd been the guest of a Warner Bros. Records executive and we'd come up for the first West Coast Country Convention, an answer to Nashville's domination. My executive friend, Andy Wickham, and I had stayed at the famous Bakersfield Inn, a rambling neo-Spanish resort with ponds and fountains and an impressive great arch of a sign stretching across the street proclaiming, "WELCOME TO BAKERSFIELD." In those heady days it was hoped that Bakersfield would become a centre of country music, led by its local heroes Buck Owens and Merle Haggard, voice-coached by legendary disc jockey, Bill Woods Of Bakersfield. The latter had been sung about on a record of the same name.

But the Bakersfield Inn has long been felled and the dream of West Coast country evaporated. We did visit the county museum where, surrounded by roaring mechanical dinosaurs, there's a glass case containing a Buck Owens guitar and bits of his clothing, plus a vintage picture of Bill Woods squinting from behind a radio station microphone. Afterwards we had an awfully hard time finding a decent cup of coffee. Where was Starbucks when we needed it? In the search for custom coffee we ran across rather too many "antique" shops (full of Elvis collectibles and the like) and used furniture stores (bar stools and dinettes) occupying what were once proud and bustling Woolworth or Kreske palaces. Rollo found a lot of interesting lampposts. I realized that the state libraries are like Dark Ages monasteries where culture is kept protected from the barbarians roaming abroad, those who want to develop, to wire us into a world of always-available cartoons, video games, cell phones, hip-hop chants. I thought of the Mojave Desert and its dark secrets.

The Beale Auditorium is extremely well-equipped: a large stage, a Yamaha grand piano, projection TV onto a big screen, excellent sound system, stadium seating. Quite a decent audience, eager, expectant, as videos of my past performances flashed across the screen. Rollo had finished running up and down the aisles greeting people and I was getting into my stride with a uke song when a couple started to walk out. "Why," I asked. "What have I done?" They explained that they had been expecting a talk on cruising in Alaska. "But you'll still have a good time — both entertaining and instructional!" I pleaded.

To no avail. Off they went. Still, I wasn't thrown. And I was pleased to see that there were even young people present: a little boy sat in the front row cradling his baby brother, listening intently, ready with a question. Thus I put more than the usual instructional information into my presentation. After all, I was now a state employee. In the system. I got applause for the piano solo in the middle of "Kiss Me Big," a Tennessee Ernie Ford specialty. Afterwards a woman said that seeing me felt like being with family, as she used to listen to me night after night when I had my radio show back in Los Angeles on KPCC.

It was a very rewarding night in all senses. Pity Rollo couldn't have restrained himself. Maybe on the next leg he'll become more of a seasoned trouper. In March our base will be Madera. I must look it up on the map. The minstrels on the move again! The new chautauquans! I learn as much, if not more, than my audiences. It's good to get out of the hothouse of L.A. and experience America proper.

We were home in Altadena by noon the next day. By 6pm I was down at McCabe's in Santa Monica ready once more to take my place as a Parlour Boy in Janet Klein's band. I must say I've had a hard job explaining to friends what I did on the tour and why I was hired. But I think the audiences understood. And I long to trek out once more into the hinterland.

MARCH

I'm late and I'm sorry. Too much going on, too little time. That's the excuse of all older people, especially retirees. Oh, they've never been so busy in their lives! This and that — but when they tell you what they've actually been doing it turns out mostly to be trivia. Just killing time and the fact of approaching death. And what I've been up to hasn't been that important either.........

Let's look to the immediate future: on Friday, March 15 our traveling chautauqua is off again, courtesy of the State Library. Regina, Rollo, and me — in our rented van, packed with CDs, books, and musical instruments. The accordion is with us because our first stop is the Ahwahnee Hotel in Yosemite, and this first gig is not a Library one, but it has the Library's blessing.

The famous old Ahwahnee is celebrating its 75th year and we've been hired to provide entertainment and education revolving around 1927, the year the hotel opened. I will be doing two lecture/concerts on the pop music of the 1920s as well as providing music for dancing with my Bungalow Boys. I'll also be appearing as one of Janet Klein's Parlour Boys. They're doing two cabaret shows. And the Crazy Rhythm Hot Society Orchestra will be playing for dancing, too. Regina will be giving dance instruction just before each dance. And what will Rollo be doing? Being a good dog, I hope. Our contract provides for accommodation and companionship for him: a fenced yard and another dog, plus plenty of coyotes howling away nearby.

A few weeks ago I went into the studio to record the songs I'd written especially for *Last Call*, a Showtime movie about Scott Fitzgerald, and starring Jeremy Irons and Sissy Spacek. You may remember I went to the shooting in Toronto last November when the movie was still called *Against The Current*. The recording was successful, everyone loves the songs, and I feel the music is some of my best. But the road since November has been a rocky one......................

I had been led to believe that I was in charge of the music — not just the songs (which are what's called "source," meaning music heard from a radio, a juke box, in a nightclub, etc.), but also the "underscore," that moody background stuff. But then, early in the new year, I learned that, no, the director had hired some composer he'd worked with before. And only four of my songs were to be licensed. My world fell apart. Anyway — typical of the constantly fluctuating world of movies — a few weeks later, and much pain, too — the director, a charming, civilized man — rang to say that he'd like a dozen of my songs and he'd pay well, and not to worry, and please come in and work with him and the editor in going through the movie to see where we need to place songs. So I had a creative time suggesting new songs to replace vintage recordings — Billie Holiday, Benny Goodman, etc. — that were too expensive to license.

I brought up with me my ukulele and accordion and as the film played through the video machine I sang my new songs, my soundalikes, as if I was a Tin Pan Alley song plugger. I could feel the ghosts of Harry Warren and Irving Berlin hovering over me, egging me on. And the movie people liked what I sang! So I went away and hired the band and booked the studio and paid for the arrangements. And no film executives came to the recording sessions to interfere.

But there was another hurdle to get rid of. Showtime has a policy of owning any songs and recordings created for its productions. Which would mean I'd lose all those lovely royalties and I wouldn't be able to reuse the recordings or make my own CD soundtrack. But I knew I had the trump card because I owned the recordings of the new material — I'd produced and paid for them. I physically had the tape.

When I went once again to Showtime's post-production office to deliver the music I made sure I had my new Bose Wave CD player with me (well, it's not exactly mine — it was bought for me by the State Library for lecture demonstrations).

I set it up in the main room and then I played the new songs to the director and editor. They were soon smiling and making notes. I think it was the Bose that really won their ears. What a sound! Yes, yes, they wanted that music right away. In fact, a messenger was waiting to take the tape to be dubbed. Hold it!

Then I did an amazing thing — I stood up for my rights. I refused to hand over the tape, clutching it close to my heart. I told them that this was my property until a deal was done allowing me to retain all the rights to the master and the publishing.

In other words, Showtime — and its mighty master Viacom, lurking in the shadows — would have to license this music from ITW Industries and Ian Whitcomb Songs — companies that were founded years before such upstarts as Showtime and Viacom! Take that, Sumner Redstone!

And you know what? There was a lull. Executive doors slammed shut, the messenger slunk off. I went home with my McGuffin, my tape. Next day my representative called to say that the attorneys had agreed to simply license the songs. I could retain all the rights, and to hell with it. David had beaten Goliath! At least — in my fevered mind.

Ta Ta for now.

APRIL

Last month I was anticipating our trip to Yosemite and the Ahwahnee hotel, to be followed by three days of lecturing at rural libraries in Madera County (Please see a California map — nobody seems to know where this is). The trip went off smoothly — too smoothly because in my life I never expect anything to go well for long. We drove up from Altadena in a rented Chevrolet Astro, towering above everything except trucks, above those wretched SUVs driven by hatchet-faced soccer moms on cell phones; we ate at Denny's-style coffee shops, we saw bikers and truckers and waitresses who call you sweetheart — all the hard-core Americans we never see in Los Angeles. And the number of American flags has decreased. I don't need to be told I'm in America. We arrived in the Yosemite Valley in the early evening as snow was starting to swirl and mists were gliding around the steep cliffs. We were welcomed like stars to the 1927 hotel. Rollo was escorted to his digs nearby where he was given attention and company. In the Great Hall, which resembles Hogwarts, we dined for free on filet mignon, sitting a few inches from where Queen Elizabeth II dined when she visited in 1983. She, we were told, was a little on the dour side whereas the Duke was all smiles and jokes ("Do the redskins still war dance?").

Next day we woke to a blanket of snow. Quite delightful, especially if you're inside and there's a great fire crackling and spitting in the main lounge. Every room was tall and natural — boulders and wood — mirroring the steep cliffs surrounding us. In the lounge I gave my lectures. In the afternoon Regina gave vintage dance demonstrations. In the bar Janet Klein & Her Parlour Boys performed in the early evening — and I was one of the Boys. Me, a boy at age 61! The Park superintendent was there and thoroughly enjoyed himself. So we were able to prove that our old-style entertainment fits naturally with Yosemite and isn't an urban incursion. In fact, in my lectures I drew a parallel between the Park rangers as the custodians of nature and us as the custodians and curators of the endangered species called classic popular song and dance.

Between the music I was able to take Rollo for walks through the snow where he was flabbergasted by deer and so entranced by virgin snow that he ran around in mad circles.

On the last night my Bungalow Boys (actually Janet's band under a different name) played in the dining room and people danced. We were a great success and I wish I had something to complain about but I haven't. All was sweetness and light and snow. We did hear rather a lot about John Muir, the Scotsman who championed this area and liked to get right into nature by climbing to the top of a tree in a storm and swaying with it. Luckily there weren't too many Britishers around while we were in Yosemite.

On Tuesday we headed down to the plains for Madera, a city in the flatlands of the agribiz. Not much architecturally but full of friendly folks. I gave my three lectures at nearby libraries and in our free time we walked by a lake or two. We also discovered a most hospitable cocktail bar in our motel, tended by a tough-looking but intelligent woman called Malcolm, who could tell us anything we needed to know about the world and its problems. She is against the death penalty, to the consternation of the barstool regulars, most of whom are bikers and off-road vehicle enthusiasts. We met the local public defender in the bar and also a squirrelly-looking man who turned out to be a big contractor and owner of hundreds of acres on which he grows almonds, "for fun." The only time he'd visited Yosemite was when he was in a team of Harley Davidson cyclists. "Boy, did we raise a ruckus! We destroyed everything in sight!" When we got back to Los Angeles we were at once struck by the rush and the rudeness, the honking of horns and the boom of the rap.

Have I told you that I host a Salon every Monday night at Mijares restaurant in Pasadena? I've done this for almost a decade. We started at Fiesta Grande but they were unkind to gringos so we left. Anyway, a group of us meets and drinks and yarns from 7.15

till they start vacuuming the joint. When we started the Salon we met at 8pm. But we're not as young as we used to be.

One of our regulars, Ray Campi (The King of Rockabilly), so enjoys "Mijares" that he goes there every evening, usually when Happy Hour is in play and he can scoff refried beans, etc. Well, the other night, when I was away in the desert, who should come in but Paul McCartney! Ray spotted him at once — nobody else did — and went over to slap him on the back. They talked for 20 minutes about rockabilly and Buddy Holly. Ray says that Paul took my name "in vain." When I protested Ray said, "There you are, you see! The English have no sense of humor." What could he mean? Next week Ray says he may get an audience with one of The Doors. And Ray doesn't even like that stuff, cursing hippies constantly! Well, I must close now because I'm off for another voice-over audition. Don't know what it's for, but I rarely get the job. They are calling for a posh-voiced Englishmen but the common ones always get picked. Last week I was at Warner Bros. studios making bird and beast noises into a mike for an upcoming movie called *Signs,* directed by that Indian-named fellow who made *The Sixth Sense.* I cackled and groaned and whistled. I went into a primal scream which wrecked my voice for a day. But all to no avail. There's been not a word since from my agent. Why do I subject myself to such humiliation? And who was the bastard who got hired?

See you next month.
Tunefully,
Ian

MAY

It's May 11 and at last I've got around to writing this letter. It's not as if I've been busy doing anything important. It's procrastination, the thief of time. Rather than tell you about the recent past — about the premiere of *The Cat's Meow*, about the struggle to pull together all the material for my next Mel Bay ukulele songbook (also called *The Cat's Meow*), about trying to get my first name spelled right in "Noah's Bagels" when ordering the lox and bagel I always have on a Friday morning (Ian is spelled with an I not an E), about how my dream of once again taking my place in the pantheon of show biz has been shattered by word from Lion's Gate that "Meow" is fast fading at the box office and that the CD has only sold a meager 1000 copies (while *Spider Man*, with our same costar Kirsten Dunst is raking in the dollars), about my letters to Little, Brown, the established New York publishers, informing them how their author Nick Tosches has plagiarized a part of one of my books and how the head man at this esteemed publisher has told me, in polite East Coast language, to piss off because I'm small fry and they're big boys, about how the child next door, raised by dogs, screams and screams all day so that Regina has to resort to pointing a boom box at the child's house and playing "Sentimental Journey" as loud as possible in order to drown out the dervish howling — rather than tell you all this I'll just talk briefly about what's coming up..................

First of all, thank you all for the positive response letters about Meow. I'm sorry it won't be long on the big screen before it's consigned to video limbo. Catch it while you can. Meanwhile, watch for *Last Call*, the feature movie about Scott Fitzgerald and starring Jeremy Irons and Sissy Spacek, for which I wrote thirteen songs. They've all been used in the final print and I think you'll find them a little more advanced than most of my music: in other words, I've advanced into the 1940s.

Ongoing is my sideman job with Tom Marion's Italian Novelty Band at Cantalini's Salerno Beach Restaurant at 193 Culver Blvd. Playa Del Rey, California on Sundays from 6.30 to 9.30. Here I play accordion and sometimes sing a song or two with the help of Flukie, the other ukulele.

So that's it for now. But keep writing to me. I always, in the end, reply.......

Tunefully,
Wistfully,
Ian

JUNE

I'm happy to announce that a fat conglomerate, AOL Time Warner, and in particular, an odious little editor-in-chief of Little, Brown, a once-fine publishing company, have been humbled, if not humiliated: via one of their servile lawyers they have admitted that their "author" Nick Tosches, commandeered a chunk of one of my books and stuck it in one of his "books" without acknowledgment. The "book," by the way, is called *Where Dead Voices Meet*. At first, as you know, this editor, whose name I cannot pronounce because it is so very off-the-boat East European, wrote me an insulting letter to the effect that I was a wannabe upstart writer and had no right to accuse a great author like Mr. Tosches — a man who had spent 25 years of "primary research" — of stealing. I had made the mistake of writing humbly, in person, in pen. It was only when I got my good friend from the Pasadena Athletic Club, a fellow swimmer and a former judge, to write a legal letter that I got a reply. A swift one. Now, after admitting that Mr. Tosches was mistaken and meant me no harm, and is aware of my work, we will get due compensation. And the chunk of my writing will be removed from any new editions of the books (if there are any).

This is the second victory I have scored against these disgusting leviathan conglomerates who sprawl the world, smothering creativity: I also beat Viacom recently when they tried to claim all the songs I'd written for their Showtime movie, *Last Call,* as "work for hire."

Let's all get together and battle these brutes. Not with bombs and planes and twin towers, but with words and a bold breast.

Now to June and what's happening............

Regina and I were at the premiere of *Last Call* at the Academy of Motion Picture Arts & Sciences and it was a thrill to see it up on the giant silver screen and to hear the songs pumped through on massive speakers. And to stand up and take a bow together with Jeremy Irons and Neve Campbell, etc. Yes, yes — I know — once I'm accepted and applauded by the showbiz establishment I'm purring like a pussycat. But most of the time I'm battling indifference and that's a good thing because being on the outside keeps the creative juices on the boil.

Last Saturday I had a reunion with Gordon Waller of Peter & Gordon. We met up again at Riverside, a 1950s town surrounded by slag-heap mountains, on the way to Palm Springs. We were both attending the annual Vox Fest, a celebration of vintage Vox amplifiers, held at the local Elks Lodge. We were both there as celebrities, old GB invaders. Gordon seemed to spend most of his time consuming cheeseburgers from an outdoor barbecue pit manned by two tattooed old gentlemen. I think he'd been trying to escape a fan-pest who'd been telling him that his favorite album was *Cabbages And Kings.* That was Chad & Jeremy, I told the oaf so many times. To no avail. Gordon had taken the matter philosophically, quietly puffing at his Camel. Why does rock attract cretins?

Gordon and I had first met in the summer of 1965 when we were acts on a Dick Clark Caravan Of Stars — which meant traveling for months on a Greyhound bus mostly around an unreconstructed Dixie, stopping only at night in some tank town to clamber onto a hay cart and sing our hits. It was on this bus that I became friends with Gordon and also his partner Peter. We needed each other. We were all exiled temporarily from a privileged class in England and now here we were down among the savages. Gordon was quite happy on the bus because he was snuggled in the arms of Jackie De Shannon. I was struggling to read (and understand) my history text books so that I could get my degree that autumn at Trinity College Dublin. Peter helped me understand the books. He was in Mensa.

Both Peter and Gordon seemed adept at picking up the groupie girls who hovered around our bus when we'd arrive in a new Dixie town. I was never adept and so I spent many nights alone in my Holiday Inn room — reading Karl Marx. Or admiring myself in the mirror.

Gordon reminded me, at the Vox Fest, that the Caravan of Stars was sponsored by Dr Pepper and that we were encouraged to swill it on stage. It tasted of prune to me. Filthy. It was certainly a bowel liquefier. Anyway, Gordon got fed up with the stuff and so he made his road manager nightly replace the Dr Pepper with something stronger — Old Sour Mash or some such moonshine. One night, thirsty, I went on stage to pant "You Turn Me On" for the umpteenth time, and Gordon lent me his personal bottle of Pepper. I swigged and swigged and the result was an extraordinarily animated show in which I bounced from hay bale to hay bale, ending up in the arms of the audience. I vowed never again to be drunk on stage.

Gordon currently lives near us in Glendale, a few miles from us, and he seems to spend his time playing with model trains, the British variety. In fact, he's a recognized expert on British steam trains. That's where his happiness lies, lucky man. Of course, he'd rather be back in England, specifically in the fishing village of Foy where he used to have a boat and a gang of fellow drinkers in the local pub. But that England has all gone. For him and for me. So we make do in Lotusland with our memories.

We were on a Local Access TV show a few days after the Vox Fest and I asked Gordon to fill in some details I'd forgotten from that halcyon summer of 1965 when we were so young, beautiful and irresponsible. "I can't remember anything, old chap. It's all gone with the wind." I told him he was quoting from Ernest Dowson. "You always were like that," he replied with a smile.

Perhaps I should give up trying to recreate the past, to clamber back inside.

SEPTEMBER & OCTOBER

I can't believe it and I do apologize: I have neglected writing this newsletter since June! Why? I just don't know. Maybe I've been doing too much. But let's catch up.........

June 23: Regina and I, plus Rollo, the Dog, drove down to San Diego where we took part in their first Vintage Dance Week. If you remember we used to attend these Dance affairs in Ohio for ten years or so. But the Flying Cloud Academy there decided to call it a day and so a San Diegan couple took up the cause and put on a very good show. We were based at the attractive San Diego University, a Catholic College, and daily Regina would instruct on ragtime and 1920s dance steps while I accompanied her on piano. At lunch time I gave my usual lecture/concert infomercials. I also did a little Music Hall show one evening and Regina sang "Under The Bamboo Tree" which I fouled up in my piano accompaniment. She scolded me and told me to do some practicing. I have been seeing a piano pedagogue for several years now but all his lessons evaporate in the heat of the concert moment. While in San Diego I was able to have dinner with my good old pal Joseph Wambaugh who's lived down at Point Loma for several years. He was busy promoting his new book, *Fire Lover*, about a fireman who was also a murdering arsonist.

I was back at Cantalini's Salerno Beach Italian Restaurant that Sunday, playing in Tom Marion's novelty band. How I love that pie-wedge place with its cheerful decor of Chianti bottles hanging from the ceiling and the rush of waiters with plates of hot rich pasta and the free wine! Cantalini's is near the beach at Playa Del Rey, where the planes roar overhead from LAX, and the beach bimbos saunter by and sometimes come in and ogle-eye us. Each member of the band thinks that the girls are eyeing us individually. I love to sit there with my accordion, as Tom Marion picks out a violent tarantella, and watch the customers behave in their separate worlds. And when they leave and their table is empty I feel empty too because a life, a drama, that was so lively for a while has gone forever.

I see that I scribbled an appointment in my Executive Desk Diary — from where I'm getting all this information — that I actually went with Regina to see one Al Stewart performing at McCabe's Guitar Shop in Santa Monica. This was quite a sacrifice on my part — I've never been a member of that audience (nor would I be one — unless Ukulele Ike decided to make a trip down from Heaven) and Mr. Stewart's music is not to my taste. But for some reason Regina has a soft spot for him. It was a pleasant experience: I sat back, closed my eyes and wandered in a land induced by recent margaritas-on-the-rocks. In between the songs Mr. Stewart would tell us a good deal of world history since his songs seem all to have been inspired by his wide reading. We heard, for instance, about the King of Sweden invading Russia. And I think Nostradamus put in an appearance as he usually does at Al Stewart concerts. Altogether this singer/lecturer is a very personable fellow and must be raking in the money since he lives comfortably in the Napa Valley. Yet when you bring his name up most people say, "Year Of The Cat" and can't dredge up any other work. Rather like those who believe all I ever achieved was "You Turn Me On."

On Sunday, July 14 we set off in our rented Pontiac van for another State Library Tour — and, I'm glad to say, NOT our last one. I'd been informed from Sacramento that due to a budget cut there would be no more indulgences — no more real authors going out to talk to real readers in neglected rural libraries. But bold Dr. Kevin Starr, the State Librarian, said dammit we're going to continue these minstrel chautauquas even if they're on a limited run. So this tour wasn't to be the last.

We will start going forth again in the winter months, possibly up in the snowy Sierras, or possibly around Sacramento. But for now we were conditioned against vile hot weather inside our large (but not SUV aggressive) Pontiac. Our first stop was in the middle of that grand flat plain known as the Salad Bowl of America, scarred by the freeway known as #5: the Harris Ranch, an oasis amidst the dust. We swam in the Olympic pool, we ate tri-tip beef in the restaurant, we saw the big sky at night and the nothingness that was around and above us. I took Rollo for a walk into the flat nothingness and thank God his forceful tugging prevented me from feeling I was a speck in oblivion.

Next day we drove across to the little town of Sanger where I gave one of my typical lecture/concerts: the history of popular music, some uke songs, some laughter, some learning. Although I actually learn more from the locals who speak up at question time. Our accommodations were not the best: the motel, bang next to an active railroad track, seemed to be the headquarters of drug and illicit sex lovers. Next day we moved to Shaver Lake near Aubery, which was to be our library of the evening. At Shaver Lake we rented a log cabin and then we went to the lake itself and took a dip. To our amazement Rollo, who hitherto had abhorred immersion, suddenly decided to jump in and swam out to us. He proved to be a most energetic swimmer. Where did he learn? Instinct, I suppose.

From Aubery we motored to Fresno and the Gillis Library where we had a decent turnout and I was videoed for the local Access TV station. On Thursday we were in Modesto, staying next to a Victorian mansion, the home of one of Modesto's founding fathers, a self-made grim-faced Victorian of high principles and lots of dead babies. That evening we drove down sunkissed country roads to a delightful little town called Patterson built around a circle. The time for the talk was 6pm but nobody appeared. Then in peeped a Latino family — a mother, two preteen daughters and a toddling son. Should I pack it in and call it a day? No, I stayed and gave them their own private show. The daughters sang along to the ukulele songs from my songbook. They were keen to show how well they read, how fast. They said they love reading, a very rewarding evening. Worth all the traveling.

A week later I was setting off for Eugene, Oregon to take part in the annual Oregon Festival of American Music. This is a big affair involving hundreds of young people, and symphony orchestra and jazz bands, and music camps. Eugene has more opera houses, live theatres, book shops than any where else in the country — so the locals enjoyed telling me. Many are refugees from nasty places like Glendale and Orange County.

Dick Hyman, the renowned jazz pianist, has been the jazz advisor at the festival for many years. He'd had me up there a short while back when I helped present an evening of music from the Titanic era. This year the accent was on George and Ira Gershwin. What was a vaudevillian like me doing in the exalted realm of Broadway and concert-stage George Gershwin? Well, Dick Hyman had hired me to sing neglected gems by the brothers, accompanied by a Flukie. George Gershwin and the uke? Whatever next? Actually, the brothers had originally written "Fascinating Rhythm" for Ukulele Ike to perform in 1924's *Lady Be Good*. So I ended up not only accompanying a great jazz songstress on this number but also playing the part created by Ukulele Ike in the Broadway production of *Lady Be Good*. Dick also had me reciting some Ira G lyrics to his polished piano — music by Kurt Weill. Boy, was I up with the masters! I'd told Dick earlier that I wasn't sure I'd be able to remember all these clever lyrics. Yes, you can, he admonished. It's good therapy for you to learn something new and difficult. You can't spend your life relying on the same old sure shtick. I feel like a new man now — though I'm not putting "Fascinating Rhythm" into my songbag for future shows. It's a little too tricky for me. Not exactly a flowing, natural song.

Eugene is an extraordinary place — or maybe it's typical of the America outside of a metropolis like L.A. What I mean is — it's almost totally white. I only saw one black man when I was there — and that was BB King, who was in town for The BB King Show. All these strapping whites are so neat and clean, striding off to climb local hills witth calf muscles rolling and glistening, chewing at carrots, with knapsacks on their backs. Happy to be away from the corrupt city I come from.

I returned from Eugene for exactly one day back in Altadena. Then it was off to Milwaukee, Wisconsin. Regina had met me at the airport — but she was laboring under crutches: while I'd been swanning around in Eugene she'd tripped in our street and sprained her ankle, badly. She'd lain at the side of the road for some time with cars whizzing by and no one coming to her aid. Eventually our next door neighbours, the little man with the Iranian wife, heard her scream at Rollo to behave and they kindly came out to carry her in. After that bit of good Samaritan work I suppose I'd better tolerate the incessant screaming of their wild child who, at age three, can still only gurgle and keen and scream — and eat dog food.

So here was I shooting off to Wisconsin and leaving her hobbling about. Still, she had the comfort of a brand new DVD player — and copies of both *Man Of The Century* and *The Cat's Meow*. These, of course, are movies containing my songs. What must it be like to live with an egomaniac, even if he is self-deprecating at times?

I had been invited to Milwaukee to appear as The Father Of Irish Rock. Every year they hold the world's biggest Irish Festival and they'd felt that a history of Irish Rock would be appropriate. Since I had made "You Turn Me On" in Dublin and it had reached the American Top Ten in 1965 I qualified as the father of their music. Milwaukee is a handsome city — full of sturdy solid nineteenth century buildings proclaiming the endurance of insurance and banking. Milwaukeeans seem to have adopted an Irish brogue even though they may be of German extraction. It was odd and I felt I was back in Dublin. Meanwhile planeloads of real Irishmen were landing in the city and soon I was enjoying pints of stout and listening to tall tales of Irish life.

Every morning for three days I gave my rambling talk in a classroom at the university. How could I fill the time with a history of Irish Rock? What did I know or care about Van Morrison or Bono or Sir Bob Geldorf? Luckily I was able to settle into being an Irish storyteller and revel in the blarney. I made my audiences laugh with my tales of tussling with Dublin biddies. Soon my students put away their note pads, settled back and enjoyed themselves. President Bush flew in for the umpteenth time but nobody paid him any attention. It was all Guinness and tall tales.

I returned just a day before our annual dance band concert at the Workman & Temple Homestead in the City of Industry. What a superb band! And we had a record crowd — sitting with their picnics on the grass with the lake and ducks nearby on a summer's evening. But how could I explain such bliss to those in other parts of the country who can't picture Los Angeles County as a place of beauty and history and traditions and happy families? A few days later I played in a fake Hawaiian band at a Mormon Church in Hollywood. How's that for a varied life? And a week later I was with Ukie performing George Formby's "When I'm Cleaning Windows" song at a film folk banquet near the Chinese Theatre in Hollywood to an audience that included Mickey Rooney and Tippi Hedren. She has a very nice muscular back, by the way.

Those of you who like to come to our salons — those democratic no-invitation dinners we've been having for a decade — must be told that we have yet again changed our venue. We had been meeting at Mijares, a Mexican restaurant, in Pasadena, for several years. Occupying a long table and some nights giving the management the benefit of a ton of money due to our party growing to sometimes over 20 people.

But two weeks ago the manager told me that our favorite waiter — dear Jesse who used to prepare our table in advance and be there immediately we arrived with a tray of large margaritas at a special price, dear Jesse who comforted Regina one night when she was down in the dumps — had been fired that very evening. He'd been skimming money or something. Who cares? He was always so nice to us.

In a hostile tone, the manager informed me that right now the police were in the parking lot clapping Jesse into handcuffs. "And so," added this manager — a surly fellow with a fishy wandering eye (I never did care for him) — "You people won't be getting any more of the sort of attention that Jesse gave you. Oh no ... You'll have to have separate checks from now on!" Change and decay in all around I see, runs the old hymn. And things certainly have changed in a hurry!.........

Next week when the four of us who'd founded the salon went to try out the new regime we sat for ages without any service at all while those around us were greeted with smiles and drinks and salsa and chips. I believe that the management saw us as accomplices to Jesse's unfortunate acts. To cap it all, as I left, the manager shouted at my back : "Sir Paul was in the other night! Elton's next!"

We have decided to go elsewhere. In future we will be at Bona Corso's Italian restaurant on Lake at Walnut — still in Pasadena. As Jim Dawson, one of the founders of our salon reminded me: it was at Bona Corso's that we first met to dine and yarn back in the days when I hosted my nightly radio show on KPCC. We would dine and wine well and then roll into the station showing no pain at all. In such good spirits we made some pretty ripe shows.

So until next time then I will leave you with the cry of Pancho, sidekick to the Cisco Kid. At the end of each episode of their TV series he would shout from his rearing horse: "See you soon, ha! HA!"

NOVEMBER & DECEMBER

Sorry — I missed a month. Too much drama happening. Will fill you in as we move along.........

On Friday, September 13, The Bungalow Boys, with me and Regina took part in the annual vaudeville show at The Alex Theatre in Glendale. Last year had been an emotional experience since it was only days after the explosions of September 11. I had found myself vociferously singing, "God Bless America" without knowing that I don't really know the number. But it was one of those inexplicable moving experiences that you're grateful for afterwards: I became a regular human. Is it called "The Human Condition"?

At this year's vaudeville show I felt I was with family: even the mention of George Formby, and, more oddly, King Zany, drew applause. So the performance was a breeze — we could do no harm.

The following Sunday found us at yet another Uketopia concert at McCabe's Guitar Shop in Santa Monica. How many years has Jim Beloff, the prime mover of this ukulele renaissance, been organizing these gatherings? This year's theme was Songs of Spirituality.

I was amazed to find myself getting into the spirit of "In The Sweet Bye And Bye" and even "Amazing Grace." Fred Sokolow, a normally down-to-earth Bungalow Boy, confessed that so potent were the hymns that he was considering giving up being an atheist in order to become an agnostic. It's amazing where a good tune can to lead you. Lots of Asians were moving around backstage with video cameras and boom mikes. Uke documentaries are in the works, it would appear.

The next day marked the second salon at our new venue: Bona Corso's Italian Restaurant on Lake Avenue and Walnut. We get a warm welcome from management. Very different from Mijares. Ray Campi, the rockabilly king, still hangs out at Mijares bar, and he tells us that they don't miss us one bit. That's a little disconcerting — I mean, we brought a lot of business their way and I thought we were making a point by leaving. Still, I have to face the fact that we meant nothing. I hope that's not the case when I kick the bucket. Just last week I returned home to find several calls on my message center from Fred Sokolow, each one getting more frantic: where was I? Call him at once, etc. Turns out that somebody had told him they'd recently read an obituary of me. Well, I never! Still, I was happy to even receive an obituary. And I wonder which paper it was in? My life is spent trying to build walls against oblivion.

At this second new salon only Ray Campi turned up. We had a pleasant time chatting together in a comfortable booth. I shared his jug of rose wine, not my favorite color but any wine's OK with me. Usually we have to shout to be heard so large is our group, and then there are cross-talks I want to eavesdrop on, and people interrupt each other and thoughts can't get completed. Towards the end of the evening Gloria, our black member, turned up, dressed, as usual, in a fascinating ensemble. She treated us to an interesting sidelight on African-American life: recently she was having her false teeth serviced at a dentistry and was shocked to be handed back a set of teeth that weren't hers. How could she tell? Because the gums were of a darker hue than her own set. You see, she's light-skinned and these were deep black. I had no idea.

We moved to the bar for nightcaps and further discussion of aspects of her life. In fact, what happened was that we stood close together and sang a close harmony version of "We'll Meet Again," the World War Two British anthem which turns out to be one of Gloria's favorite songs. In this way disparate cultures become as one.

On Sunday, October 6 The Bungalow Boys were stars at a big

street block event honoring Glendale Memorial Hospital: A Night of Wine And Roses. Local restaurants provide the food and wine; at two large stages, facing each other, entertainment continues all evening. Unfortunately the subtle, acoustic Bungalow Boys had been scheduled to face a stage opposite occupied by a reincarnation of Three Dog Night, a loud 1960s rock group that, like every other 60s group has grown louder with the years even as the players have died or become AARP members. My songs were drowned out by the electronic blasts and shouts of "Put your hands together and rock out!" I have to admit I grew so frustrated that I looked up to the sky and called upon Bin Laden and his men to drop something on this wretched example of western decadence screaming at us from across the way. Luckily those who heard me dismissed my prayers as characteristic of me.

Monday, October 14 was rather special.
During the night I'd dreamed I was leading my Dance Band (a ten piece outfit, bigger than The Bungalow Boys) at a concert and that when I ordered them, in the middle of a number, to stop and start again because the tempo was wrong, they simply held the note they'd been playing. On and on. Was it a rebellion or a joke? Life never gives reasons and so you can't expect dreams to be any more understanding. I told the audience—playing the populist card and thus counting on sympathy—that I'd fine the band a dollar for every second they continued to hold that blasted note. But they persisted, sounding like a stuck CD. So I delivered a tongue-lashing for all to witness. And I knew that by so doing they'd vow never to work for me again. A self-destructive, over-the-top outburst on my part. Something building up inside.

Later, over an egg'n'sausage breakfast I read an article in the *Los Angeles Times* health news section about narcissism. I was horrified to see I have many of the traits of this "personality disorder." A partial list: "a grandiose sense of self-importance," "a desperate need for admiration," "an almost absolute blindness to the needs and feelings of others," and "a fury at being treated normally whether at a dry cleaner or library checkout counter."

For moment I was stunned and lay down my fork. Even the Dijon mustard-smeared pork sausage had lost its allure. But after a little reflection I resumed eating: why worry?— these traits fit almost everyone I know—except Regina and the dog Rollo.

The rest of the day I spent mucking about in the Music Room—the wooden shack we've had erected in the back garden. I avoided practicing the classical keyboard exercises by playing around with an old country song called "The Utah Trail," killing time before leaving for the salon at Bono Corso's.

It was a crowded one. After some wine I got a bit argumentative.

It was like this: Libby, one of our richer members, had been telling how she can't return to Bali, her "paradise," because terrorists have just killed hundreds of tourists discoing way in an Oirish-named night club.

Well, I must have incensed one rather sensitive male member, an artist, by suggesting that the young Australians who go to such places as Paddy's Bar in Bali in order to be rowdy and "pull birds" might not be of the best breed, might not appreciate exotic cultures. "How dare you!" he screamed, "I adore Disco and I'm tired of your silly opinions!"

I was astonished because usually it's his wife, a stiff-backed English woman with views, who does the talking while he stays silent and grins. Don't you hate people who say nothing at parties while you're trying to be a genial host by filling up silences with small talk and then later these people attack you as silly, stupid, fatuous? Anyway, I apologized profusely, as I always do under such circumstances, and later, at nightcaps in the bar, he rubbed shoulders with me. I made a mental note to make mundane remarks at the salon or to keep silent. After a diplomatic space of time I bid them all goodnight and made for the Honda. Up Lake Avenue I roared, feeling fine again, playing a CD track of a 1920s radio duo harmonizing on "The Utah Trail."

I found Regina sitting upright on the bed, hugging Rollo. We'd been burglarized, she said. This wasn't the moment to tell her that "burgled" is a shorter and friendlier expression. Yes, even as she had been watching TV in the bedroom somebody had dared to steal our CD/cassette Sharp boom box from the kitchen table via the open window. Plastic pieces were scattered about. The police had arrived within minutes, two nice young sheriff's deputies, and their guess was that this was a random theft by some passing kid. The boom box wasn't worth replacing, but the fact of one's private lair being violated is quite scary and then infuriating. In fact, it felt like rape. What a pity—because earlier, just before I'd left for the salon Regina had been playing vintage dance band music on the boom box and dancing energetically with herself in the kitchen with the windows wide open.

I have my own theories as to who did the deed. At first, I'd assumed it was black kids. But then I remembered how Kaleem, our neighbour's Iranian wife, has been invading our space of late, coming over to reclaim stuff. You see, their kid, who I call Mowgli because he was raised by their dogs, has a habit of tossing objects over the fence— the one I paid for and had put up years before they arrived. Our kitchen window is only a few feet from their side door; they seem to spend most of their lives going in and out of that side door, sometimes holding forth at the entrance. We hear all about them and don't really want to know. That's the trouble when you live so damned close but aren't family, aren't friends, aren't really neighbours in the folksy sense of the word—as in the 1950s British hit "Friends And Neighbours" by Billy Cotton: "Just take your little troubles and share 'em with the folks next door/ Makes it twice as easy to bear 'em—that's what friends are for!"

Anyway, Regina has made a list of, and has numbered, the objects landing on our property: mainly audiocassettes of, say, Chopin, Bach and—I was sorry to see—a tape of my instrumentals called "Tango Dreams." I probably donated it to them in an attempt to be friendly—or to have them admire my music and, thus, myself.

That night, while Regina slept with Rollo and Simon, the cat, between us, I flipped through a copy of one of my journals in order to refresh myself on these neighbours and in particular the rather strange and unfriendly wife, Kaleem. Here's what I found in an entry for June 5, 1990:

"Not a good day. Didn't receive a single phone call. Regina came home in the early afternoon, bright and breezy, and floated the great idea of inviting our new neighbours to dinner. Harold Hodge accepted but said that his wife was 'too tired'. So far we've never seen hide or hair of her. Very odd. We took him to Ernie's Jnr, the Mexican restaurant in Pasadena where, a few years ago, after a second margarita, I'd proposed to Regina and she'd accepted. Tonight we ordered a jug of margarita and soon Mr. Hodge, a stubby and balding man, was answering my questions. We learned that he'd been married once before, but that this time he was determined to get it right and have a child one way or the other. He has a nervous laugh, rather disconcerting. His little eyes dart around like tiny silver daggers. He said he'd met his present wife at a match club called A Fine Romance and that she had been in an arranged, or 'forced', marriage back in Iran. This 'marriage' produced a son, now aged 24. She left the same time as the Shah, and now works for the city of Los Angeles, inspecting restaurants. We said we hope to see and get to know here someday."

I'm not going to pursue my suspicions because an ex-judge friend, a fellow member of the Pasadena Athletic Club where I exercise, has said that you should always keep a truce with your neighbours. But fingerprints have been taken. I greet every neighbour with a wave and a hello, like the song says: "What a wonderful word—Hello!"

So the burglary took place on the Monday night. I took a sleeping pill to calm me down and I was deep in the arms of Morpheus when the phone rang at around 8am. It was my agent: "You're wanted on the set as soon as possible!" Whaat? Yes, an "experimental" movie called *Open House*, shooting conveniently down the road in San Marino. Then I remembered: the previous Friday I'd auditioned for this film but put it aside since the director had told me shooting was to begin on Tuesday. This was Tuesday. "How did I get the part?" The selected actor, a "very elderly man"— a few years older than me, in fact — had woken up this morning to discover he had a medical problem: swollen testicles. So I had landed the large part of "Dr. Santee" by default? "Oh no, you were their second choice." Anyway I was down at the house location within the hour and tucking into a "craft services" bagel with cream cheese. I got to glance at a script just before we shot my first scene. This was with an actor I recognized: Anthony Rapp who'd played a major role in that excellent little cult musical *Man Of The Century* (to which I'd contributed the end credits song vocal).

It was odd to be in *Open House* because I soon discovered it's a musical — and I didn't have a song. This was fortunate since the songs I heard weren't from within my rarefied world: they were sort of Lloyd-Webber/Elton John and I don't know what. You needed to be able to hold long and theatrical notes. But I settled into being an actor for a few days. I learned my lines and was also allowed to improvise. They all thought I was quite funny what with my silly ass upper-class British accent (With this voice there's no chance of my stuttering, you see). And so the week rolled by and I was happy to be part of a team: reaching my mark, finding my cue, and oblivious to the two digital video cameras darting around and about us. One afternoon we had Sally Kellerman with us and we had a couple of lines together. Another of the actors had been a regular on "Babylon Five." If I'd had a cell phone I'd have truly been a part of the team.

A week whizzed by.

On Sunday there was much anticipation excitement: my older sister and younger brother were arriving at LAX to stay with us for a week. My sister, Suzanne, hadn't been at our house since our wedding in 1990; my brother Robin was last in America in 1965 when he was playing drums for Sonny & Cher (and me) at The Hollywood Bowl.

Regina had been feverishly preparing for months for this event. The house was spotless, having been virtually rebuilt by armies of workmen, craftsmen, cleaners, gardeners. My sister, who works for the Queen Of England and used to run the Queen's House at the Tower Of London when her husband was Governor, has an eagle eye for the spic and the span.

But all was well — she loved our house and especially Rollo. My brother bonded with him better than anybody else he met. On the Monday night they were able to see me in action at a gig. With a black beret pulled over my head at a rakish angle and my musette accordion strapped on, I was appearing as one of the Hot Club of France in Johnny Crawford's regular re-creation at the Argyle Club on Sunset Strip. I introduced Johnny to my sister because he wanted to inform her that his ancestor Lord Lovett had been executed at the

Tower of London. My sister gently corrected him: Lovett had actually had a public execution on Tower Hill. Only the true nobs were given the honor of having their heads chopped off within the Tower itself.

Next day the grand tour began. Regina and I dutifully, and with great pleasure, took Suzanne and Robin to Beverly Hills, to Malibu — and of course to Hollywood so that they could see the famous footprints in the cement. And what d'you know? As we emerged from the underground parking lot in the new plaza at Highland and Hollywood Boulevards who should we see sprawled on the pavement near Mann's Chinese but Harrison Ford in the flesh. Blood was pouring out of the side of his mouth.

It was perfect. We were bang in the middle of one of those typical Ford movie chase scenes. Bullhorns blared. The star suddenly got to his feet and raced off down the boulevard waving his gun at a clown. My brother snapped some great photos before the gaggle of assistant directors pounced on him. I felt so relieved: they'd seen a real movie star in action. And they had pictures to prove it. We also took in the Huntington Library and the Norton Simon Museum, but nothing compared to Ford sprawled on the pavement.

On the Saturday night I had a Bungalow Boys gig at a very upmarket wedding in the Atheneum Club at Cal Tech. The bride let my brother and sister take part as bona fide guests. And persuaded my brother Robin to join us on the drums. What a great job he did! It was as if we were back in my British Invasion days. The next day we dropped them at LAX and said sad farewells. Not too sad for me since I'll be over with him this Christmas in England.

We're almost up to speed. What else has happened? Oh, I suppose I should mention that we attended a Rolling Stones concert last Thursday at the Staples Center in Los Angeles. I only went because my best friend from school invited me and Regina was determined to go and we were taken in a limousine and had VIP passes. Even with all this we didn't get backstage — which was just as well because I published a rude passage about Jagger in the last issue of *American Heritage* — I wrote that he was no more than an engorged crotch enhanced by bunched hankies.

Our seats were on the side in this huge stadium. We studied the band through binoculars — and I must admit that Jagger looks extremely fit, has all his hair and not a fleck of gray. Supposedly this is their farewell tour. Sinatra was fond of giving farewell tours most of his life. In retrospect I'd have liked to have been in the receiving line to meet Sir Mick: we were on the same bill at least three times in 1965 and Jagger once engaged me in a long quizzing conversation backstage before a Seattle show. After this I concluded we'd become good buddies but when I strolled up to resume our intimate relationship at our next gig (The Olympia Theatre in Paris) he cut me stone dead. Funny sort of chap.

Next evening I was the star — with my show at Boulevard Music in Culver City, a much smaller venue, but at least you could hear every word and see me up close without any need for binoculars. Afterwards we trooped across the street to a most eccentric restaurant called Dear John – a sort of Culver City equivalent of Faulty Towers. They seem reluctant to serve you. I asked for two olives in my martini. The bartender fixed me with a glare: "You'll be lucky to get one." Somebody asked me to sing a song. Reluctantly I agreed. But the piano was being guarded by a man even older than me. He clamped his hands on the piano lid. "Oh, no you don't," he growled. They have great onion rings, though.

In conclusion I must pay my respects to two performers who had a great influence on my musical life: Lonnie Donegan, the king of skiffle, who died a few days ago. It was his hectic, kinetic vocals and hard-driving strumming that inspired us future British Invaders to take up guitars and form our own groups. I once appeared on a British TV show with Donegan and he impressed me as a squirrelly strong performer. Much later, in Hollywood, we had dinner at a cafeteria where, surrounded by wife and children, he asked me for tips about getting into movies. This was odd since I wasn't yet in movies myself. I think he was living in Lake Tahoe at the time. I notice the obituary in today's *Los Angeles Times* reports that he died near Cambridge, England, while on tour.

Ragtime Bob Darch, who died a few weeks ago in Missouri, was a good friend of mine and a mighty mentor. Even as I was studying skiffle, blues, rock 'n' roll and country & western from the dinginess of late 1950s England, I was also getting hooked on Tin Pan Alley and ragtime music. Then I encountered Bob Darch's playing and persona and I knew I had struck the true gold.

Here is my memoir of this great artist......

BOB DARCH – MY ADVENTURES WITH THE GREAT MAN

I first came across Bob in 1960 when I was working as an assistant film editor in London. I was helping to cut a documentary about the joys of Canada. The chief editor took a break and told me to have a go at assembling a Toronto sequence featuring an ebullient gentleman in straw hat, red vest, and sleeve garters, pounding away at an enormous upright piano and thoroughly enjoying himself. There was a sign on the side of this piano: "Ragtime" Bob Darch. I worked for hours on the sequence because I never tired of it. In fact, I became bewitched by the music: Bob was playing his energetic, stress-free version of "Maple Leaf Rag." I ran the sequence over and over, emerging a fanatic for (a) Maple Leaf Rag and (b) Ragtime Bob. I was hooked. I was a born-again Christian who'd never been properly born.

I mean, during the Fifties, I'd heard plenty of tinny piano honkytonk and raggy songs but I'd never heard them sound so pure, so bright, so jolly, so solid. I had become a Ragtimer — from the Branch Darch.

In 1964 I was in Seattle, having established myself as an entertainer in a local coffee house and having parlayed my way into a recording contract as a future rock star with a local label. My recording manager and I were sitting in a swell hotel talking turkey over Jack Daniel's when my attention was deflected from royalty points and how I was to become bigger than Jagger by that certain sound of "Maple Leaf Rag" — the documentary soundtrack.

I rushed into the room from whence came the glorious music and there he was! Straw hat and everything, pounding out the good news. To the consternation of my manager I spent the next few days in the company of Ragtime Bob. Songs, stories, jokes came pouring out of this avuncular genius as I followed him around like Boswell followed Dr. Johnson in 18th century London. I hung on every gravelly word, I vowed to remember the lyric of every song gem that kept falling from him as we walked and talked and drank and drank. One afternoon I found myself sitting in the home of Joe Jordan, the great black rag composer, as Bob interviewed him about his days in vaudeville and how he wrote "That Teasin' Rag." One evening we, together with my local girl friend, were having dinner in the home of a wealthy local couple when in came their young son to say goodnight. Later Bob trapped me in the wet bar to inform me that the boy was really his son. Even later my girl friend emerged from the powder room to tell me that Bob had proposed to her. I put the whole matter aside because I so admired the man's art.

We went our separate ways — Bob to peregrinate the country as the last of the great itinerant ragtime entertainers; me as a member of The British Invasion. But though I was supposed to be a teen idol I still yearned for the solid music of Bob and when I got the chance I'd drop off a rock tour to catch Bob in his act: the most notable was in Colorado at The Cherry Creek Inn.

Luckily I had a tape recorder with me and managed to capture one night of Bob at his very best, in the environment that suited him: an upright piano in a saloon full of merry folk. He presided like the king he was — "The tender bartenders will satisfy your every need, won't you dears?" — and I got a record of the variety of entertainment provided by this great man: songs like "They're Wearing 'Em Higher In Hawaii" and "A Lemon In The Garden Of Love"; classic rags played with vigor and fire (unlike the effete, careful "classicism" that was to be the hallmark of certain players in the unfortunate 1970s revival); and a constant commentary on the writers of the music and the attributes of certain females who happened to be in the bar. The evening ended at 2 am, with a bang. After 13 martinis Bob toppled off the piano stool and hit the floor but suffered no injuries.

Next day he was right as rain and off we went to *The Denver Post* where they interviewed us as "Ragtimer Meets Rocker" and pictured us together at a piano. Later Bob set fire to the piano as a stunt in order to get more coverage. The subsequent headline read: "Man Plays Hot Piano." After that Bob took me for a tour of the old gold mining towns — we didn't see much mining but we saw an awful lot of saloons and we played every kind of piano, in-tune, out-of-tune, no keys. Until finally Bob just stood in the middle of the floor and sang a capella, snapping his fingers and sometimes clapping. Everywhere we went we collected disciples, converts, evangelical ragtimers. Old-fashioned Americans who smoked cigars and chewed steaks. And all the while I was getting a priceless education as an entertainer.

Back in my Hollywood digs I played the Cherry Creek tapes over and over, learning every song. And when I got a booking at the prestigious Troubadour club in West Hollywood I virtually reproduced Bob's act, but as a young British whelp. Stars came and gaped. The rockers and the hippies were amazed and entranced. They would come in and drop LSD as I sang such Darch memorables as "Silver Sardines In Your Hair." Wow, was I hip! And this was <u>before</u> Tiny Tim. I got everything from Darch.

Over the years we kept in touch. I mean, I'd get postcards in that familiar block letter printing: "Dear Friend..." He was in Alaska one moment and Russia the next, the whole world was being exposed to his enlightening virus. And then we met up again at the Scott Joplin Festival in Sedalia. He looked the same but now he tended to wear Jungle Jim outfits. Some of the newer, more serious ragtime people, were puzzled by Bob. He didn't act like a scholar, he was having too much fun, he didn't go to bed at 9 o'clock.

Actually, he was truly living the ragtime life. He was the Real Thing In Color. And, after they turned their back on him so that they could look at the backs of po-faced pianists plodding sedately through yet another classic rag as if they were about to be executed, Bob decided he'd regain the attention of these "scholars" by stating that he had the score of the lost Scott Joplin opera and that it lay safe and sound somewhere in the Midwest. Where exactly he never divulged. But I guessed it was probably over the rainbow with Dorothy. Bob was the real entertainer right till the last.

I heard from him a few months before his death. Another of those postcards: he and I and Regina and a whole slew of like-minded performers were going to put on a grand minstrel show in the White House and George Bush would be so dancing mad he'd forget about declaring any wars. Bin Laden would be there too, possibly on tambourine.

My most enduring image of Ragtime Bob is of him in a Sedalia motel room at dawn. Dressed in his bush outfit, complete with broad jungle hat, his legs are placed squarely apart, his arms are akimbo, his head is looking straight up towards the ceiling, and he's singing — without any accompaniment — "Goodnight Little Girl Goodnight." As he finishes the last line "And if I couldn't win ya with all the booze I put in ya — Goodnight, little girl, goodnight!" — I realize that his gaze, his reach, his power, goes beyond the motel ceiling and up into the sky to radiate forever for all us poor souls who need a little spice, a little exaggeration for elevation, to see us through this gray earthly trek.

Bob Darch is my inspiration. I will continue trying to travel in the footsteps he made for me.

2003

JANUARY

A very belated Happy New Year. I've just returned from England and I'm still in a bewildered and bemused state, nevertheless Regina ordered me to the machine and told me to get reporting.

First of all I'll catch up on the immediate past: during last summer I kept moaning about the incessant sun here in L.A. and so Regina suggested I take a trip home to England to stock up some soft refreshing rain. I'd been having glorious nostalgic visions of sparkling Devon bays backed by white cliffs topped with velvet grass and a storm in the offing. My brother had sent me postcards re-enforcing this dream. And then an old Trinity College Dublin friend wrote to me from his Devonshire seaside cottage: "I'll have to break off now because the evening is drawing in and so the tide will be out, revealing a rather tempting wreck that I want to explore." The picture was exquisite. I wished I could be there and not sitting in the oppressive heat, finding fault with everything, especially the fish in my pond who never made an appearance, even when I threw food pellets for their enjoyment.

In late December I left LAX on a Virgin flight for London. What a miserable airline is Virgin! The seats are cramped, and are not for today's wide-bottomed Americans; the stewards are stingy with the drink, frowning if you ask for wine or spirits. There are no longer those rosily-written menus. And have you noticed that at the baggage terminal there are always strange bags traveling round and round the carousel when you arrive — and that nobody claims them? What mysterious flight and country are they from? I got a panic attack after half an hour's wait. Then, like waking from a bad dream, they arrived.

All I did on this trip was to see and stay with family and friends. I perambulated around between my sister's house in Berkshire and my brother's house in Wimbledon. I also stayed alone in a central London house belonging to a woman friend who writes an agony aunt column for a leading daily paper. No hanky panky — we are just good friends. She was happy for me to house-sit while she motored around the West Country visiting stately homes. She lives in an area full of many cultures — women in the veil, Serbo-Croatians, you name it. She says she loves the racial diversity — but I had to deal with her elaborate security system whenever I entered or left her house.

One of the joys of Britain is the wide range of daily newspapers — and most of them shout and scream and are full of great tittle tattle and frightful crime. The following appeared in the *Daily Mail*, a tabloid: "Thugs ambush 84-year-old spinster for her purse ..... containing thirteen pounds ... Catherine Wrenn was a midwife for 50 years and delivered 5,000 babies. Just thirteen days from Christmas, she was brutally mugged and left to die in the area she had served so well." Covered in blood from the street attack, she staggered into her flat and asked for a cup of tea. "I've got a terrible headache." Those were her last words.

On January 3 there was relief in a light-hearted story about an irate farmer who was refused a drink at the pub he owns as a hobby. The management had informed him it was too late and they were closing. So the farmer stamped out only to return a few minutes later astride a JCB tractor and proceeded to demolish his pub, sending women and children fleeing. Turns out the pub is a listed Grade A 16th century landmark called The North Star, a favorite of the Real Ale crowd. Now it will probably have to be demolished.

A few days later the papers were screaming the story of the two innocent black girls at a hair salon party slaughtered by gang members armed with machine guns. This was a battle by rival members of two street gangs, The Burger Bar Boys and the Johnson Crew. Their turf feud dates back to the early 1990s and the cause is a dispute about who was the winner in a violent computer game. Sweet England is following America's example.

Speaking of America, I've never run across so much anti-Americanism in England before. Of course it's all because of the man they call "Dubya" and his threatened war. But while you hear and read about the Evil One in the White House you look around and see that there's a Starbucks on every corner and huge posters for *Gangs of New York* and every other American film. Burger Kings, of course, have abounded for years.

But then, Britain has been a dumping ground for American culture ever since the coming of Ragtime in the days before World

War One.

I tried to avoid stepping out into the seething gray masses of the London streets. I raced between the safe houses of my friends and family. Once I was negotiating my way from a friend's flat in Earl's Court to the Underground and I suffered another panic attack. Nobody was threatening me with a mugging but I just had a feeling of fright, of foreboding — here I was born and bred in England but feeling a stranger in a strange land: brutish whites with shorn heads, hulking blacks, Arabs in traditional garb, and a million alien tongues. I longed for the safety, the sleepiness of Southern California. Yes, I know — all this is purely subjective and silly. But that's how I felt.

How anybody, short of the Lloyd Webbers or Elton Johns, can afford to live in London is beyond me. It's extremely expensive. Here's an example: I had dined out in a very safe house — an elegant gentleman's club in exclusive St. James' Square in the heart of London's West End: The Public Schools Club. I was a guest of Andy Wickham, late of Warner Bros. Records. Andy likes to see me humiliated so he had introduced me to the president of this club, a Mr. Mickey Steele-Bodger, and got me to strike up a conversation by way of an opening gambit. Bear in mind that in Britain the term "Public School" means private school and they're pretty pricey too. I asked Mr. Steele-Bodger: "Sir, I attended Bryanston. Would you consider that a major or a minor Public School?" Mr. Bodger glared from a beet-red face: "Sir, I wouldn't even consider it a Public School! I went to Rugby. You know we do have standards!" Shaking with laughter Andy saw me to my taxi.

Now I was staying at my brother's house — called The Molehouse, in Wimbledon — a mere 15 miles away. Well, the bill came to forty pounds. Forty pounds! You can take a plane trip from Heathrow to Venice, Italy, for forty pounds! And a few days later when I offered to pay my friend Charles' petrol station fill-up bill and gave him a 20 pound note he just chuckled. The fill-up came to over 50 pounds.

But enough of this bad stuff. Regina keeps telling me to think positive. Yes, and many of the songs I sing tell me to keep smiling. So ... I went with my brother to The Tate Gallery to take in the Gainsborough exhibition. "The Blue Boy," his most famous work, wasn't there, because, of course, it hangs permanently in our very own Huntington Gallery right here in San Marino, not far from my desk.

The best times were with the people I know — long late night dinners at their homes or in raffish restaurants — talking, reminiscing, yarning, laughing. Why can't my friends live over here? Every day grew grayer and grayer, and then there were great floods — the Thames burst its banks — finally there was ice and freezing temperatures. I took to wearing my overcoat indoors. I started to yearn for the very California heartless sun that I'd come to England to escape.

My sister and brother-in-law invited me to join them for a New Years' Eve party in the heart of the countryside at the home of the most beautiful woman (of a certain age) in the county of Royal Berkshire. She lives among fields and hedges in a low-ceilinged 16th century (listed) cottage. We arrived — in full evening dress — to a room full of like-minded upper middle-class people braying in a very secure manner. Including my brother-in-law there were two Generals in the room so I felt safe. We played party games. There was one where we were shown a tray of objects and then had to write down as many as we could remember. One of the objects, I was informed later, was a tampon. This rather rattled me. Then a karaoke machine appeared and the next thing I was presented with was the sight of Captains of Industry and Generals uttering "Rock Around The Clock" and "That'll Be The Day" with much energy but little accuracy. The Moet & Chandon champagne didn't help matters.

When it was my turn I tried to set a good example by singing the lyrics accurately but it was hard because my partner, a hard and buxom woman (who has made a packet in real estate and would eagerly inform anyone that her son is at Eton and the fees are 20,000 pounds a year), kept thrusting her thighs into me. This was a case of our betters behaving badly. But on the whole a good time was had by all and my friend Charles (an art dealer and author of the classic swimming book, *Haunts Of The Black Masseur*), finally managed, with the aid of his cigarette lighter, to launch the firework rocket into space. "Christ!" said one of the Generals, "I hope the bloody war in Iraq moves faster than that!"

And so, eventually, and several jolly dinners later, back to L.A. to the warm welcome of Regina, followed by the wriggles of Rollo, the Dog, and the indifference of Simon, The Cat. Everything in the garden's lovely, except for the never-ending problem of the leaking pond. No matter how many pond liners I put down on our converted hot tub of a pond the thing invariably leaks. There's also the usual New Year worry about whether I'll ever get another paying job.

Fortunately, since I returned four days ago I've already performed at Sunset Strip's House of Blues — at the annual Elvis's Birthday Bash. I took part of my Bungalow Boys band — all acoustic and with a terrific new member, Russ Blake on slide guitar — and we were received well, probably because of our not being typical electric loud rock & roll. I performed "Are You Lonesome Tonight?" from the original 1927 sheet music. The L.A. Times reported that "music historian Ian Whitcomb strummed a ukulele and sang in the style of a '20s balladeer." On Friday night I shared a bill with Noel Harrison at Boulevard Music in Culver City. A full crowd and much singing along. There was a busload of seniors,

"The Happy Travelers," all the way in from Santa Clarita, home of the ancient tree that the developers are trying to destroy in order to make room for more ticky-tacky "homes." A man has been sitting in this tree protesting for 70 days (how does he go to the bathroom?) but the cops took him down today.

All quiet on the neighbour front. Of course, I'm now pretty certain they were responsible for the burglary. But for now my tactic is to shine it all on. Am I acting like Neville Chamberlain?

FEBRUARY

It's the afternoon of February the 5th as I write this letter, so I'm late again. I'm active every moment it seems and yet achieving little that will last. But Regina is fine, and so are Rollo The Dog and Simon The Cat. The house is standing and the sun is shining. So I shouldn't moan while the world beyond my cocoon is trembling on the brink.

Phil Spector is out on bail, but I don't believe he's armed or dangerous. The woman he allegedly shot, the poor B picture actress with the little house in Venice she'd painted herself, was our hostess, it turns out, at The House of Blues on Jan 8 when The Bungalow Boys performed "Are You Lonesome Tonight?" at the Elvis's Birthday Bash. Did our guitarist try to get her number that night? He likes older women — says he can "polish them up" as he would an old Victrola.

Since my return I've been scuffling about trying to line up work. Every year at this time I get into a panic that I'll never get another job and will be reduced to working at Jack In The Box. Actually, I don't think I'd even have the skill for that. I did try a day at a friend's offices in Pasadena—he runs a legal services company that gets settlement money for motor cyclists who've been injured. Most of them do get injured. The business is done on the phone. You talk to insurance companies, you make a deal. So much for an arm, a leg, or an eye. Talk of liens and depositions, pain and suffering, emotional distress. A $70,000 settlement was agreed upon. I pretended to be a reporter taking notes. At the very end of the day my friend allowed me to try one call to a client, as he laughed softly in the background: "This is Ian Whitcomb of Eagle Legal Services. We're sending you the release from our client Harold Haig, notarized. Please send your draft for $70,000 straight away. I am diapering this file with a tickler for follow-up." I was pleased to have mastered the business argot. My friend told me next day that the money had already been wired. Perhaps they were fans of mine. No, no, I'm living in another world, like Don Quixote.

In that other world, the safe one of old songs: in January I played accordion with Johnny Crawford's band at the Argyle Club on Sunset Strip, not far from The House of Blues. I begged a couple of Jack Daniels from a pair who represent the Constitutional Rights Foundation and talked to a teacher about my becoming one too. $100 a day, but you spend most of your time disciplining and trying to teach "immersion."

I'm playing regularly now at Cantalini's in Playa Del Rey. In addition to cash we are also offered dinner and wine. The hard stuff is obtainable at the Harbor Bar which is attached to the galleon-shaped street corner restaurant. It's the smallest bar in L.A. They serve a very nice vodka martini with two olives but you have to battle with Sports TV and thick tobacco smoke.

Last Sunday, in our Cantalini corner, we were blissfully in our world of old songs when a horrific car accident happened in front of our eyes. We could see it through the open front door: a car whirling around at a vicious speed and then smashing into the building opposite, coming to rest as a pancaked car ready for the scrap heap. A pay phone had been demolished in the process and our bass player told me he saw a passerby busily collect spilled coins as the squashed car hissed and smoked. Somewhere inside was a driver. Diners left their tables to take a look. But, despite a base desire to view the mashed dead, I decided the band must play on, no ghoulishness. However, "Home In Pasadena" seemed awfully artificial under the circumstances. My songs are no solace, no remedies.

Last year — ah, last year! — there was heaps of work: movie soundtracks, library tours for California, the Oregon Festival of Music, Vintage Dance Week in San Diego, and more. This year my appointment book is pretty white. The book I bought is called a Time Master and every day's blank page is headed "Objectives." To the right of that are two boxes: "Priority" and "Results." I ignore them.

Now is the opportunity to do what I've been telling myself to do for years. To go to my Huntington desk, the one under the stairs in the basement, and start writing that novel. I've even bought a book called *On Writing* by Stephen King. He says — go for it! But then he has a rock sensibility that alienates me. Besides I've never been able to get beyond the first page of one of his books. He makes references to The Ramones. It's all very well to go for it and start writing regularly every day. But what do I write about? No ideas come popping into my head.

At the end of this month I will be up in Seattle—where my show biz career began — as the vaudeville act in the Silent Movie Tour. Maybe in the audience there will be seniors who were juniors in the summer of 1963 and who might remember me from when I was entertaining and preparing pizzas at a student coffee house in Pioneer Square. This job eventually led to a record contract and the release of my first record singles. "You Turn Me On" and notoriety followed. I got the job at the 92 Yesler coffee house through my cousin Anna who was then a student at Seattle University. She had led me down to the place that summer evening, almost immediately after I'd got off the Greyhound bus. I always remember that she got me started.

When we were in our teens and on summer holidays back in the England of the 1950s, she bought a rather expensive pair of yellow shoes and her father asked why and what exactly were they for. "Well," she said, "I bought them for walking and watching, and for listening to Ian playing the piano." A few days ago she died after a long struggle with cancer. I'd spoken to her on the phone — she lived in Canada — from her father's house in England about three weeks ago. We knew it was goodbye. We talked about the days back in Suffolk at the coast when I played "Love Letters In The Sand" on the country club piano and Anna danced in her bright new shoes. There would be a dance that evening and Anna was much in demand. At the end of the call — how do you end such a call? — we said we'd see each other sometime, somewhere, soon.

Her parents, my aunt and uncle, are still alive. That must be quite a blow — to have your child die before you. I'm going to think about Anna — she always encouraged my songs — and be content in this life to be getting by on the wings of music. "Music of a sort" as my housemaster used to say sniffily at school. Yes, but music just the same. The same as ever.

Tunefully,
Ian

MARCH

My apologies for reporting so late into the month. My excuse is that I have actually been working for money—and out-of-state, too. I started in Seattle as the vaudeville section of a "touring" attraction called "The Silent Picture Show," organized by Charlie Lustman who runs the venerable Silent Movie Theater here in Los Angeles. The idea is to take the show on the road augmented with a live act (me) and an organist who was accompanying movies back in the 1920s (Bob Mitchell).

Bob is in his early 90s and is full of beans. We couldn't stop him on the plane journey, regaling us with stories, singing songs, and telling us about the ancient church modes. He does an amusing impression of a very prim Carrie Jacobs-Bond intoning her famous

"The End of A Perfect Day." Bob had witnessed her. Bob is famous for having started the Mitchell Boy Choir in the 1930s and lending them to such movies as *The Jolson Story* and *Going My Way*. I've seen the Jolson picture many times and I've always been intrigued by the credit "Mitchell Boy Choir" because I'd assumed that this referred to the boy who played the part of the kid Jolson and that he was probably a full-blown Red Indian. Bob disabused me of this theory pretty fast. And so we talked on, even as we entered Seattle.

This was where I'd gotten my first record contract, where my first hit was polished and released, where I'd experienced my first lay. Yet, to my dismay, nobody at first remembered me, the city was unrecognizable, and Paul Allen's multimillion dollar monstrosity called "The Music Experience Project" failed to mention me in its Northwest Rock History section. I felt like James Stewart when he returns to his hometown and it's as if he'd never been born. If only I'd kept a journal in 1963-65. Then I could remember the name of the girl who deflowered me on my birthday, and I'd know what I'd done day by day in those halcyon years. I do remember returning in glory to Seattle in 1965, as a teen idol, and performing at the Coliseum on a bill with The Rolling Stones, and how Jagger had been obsessed with me, grilling me for ages about who exactly I was and where I came from and how I'd come to pant on record. Later, in Paris, he cut me dead.

Our shows at the Uptown cineplex in the "Bohemian" Queen Anne section of Seattle went OK. I mean we didn't exactly overwhelm the theater, but then Tony Bennett was in town. I had time off to take a boat trip on Puget Sound so that I could learn from our garrulous guide that Seattle is full of millionaires and that Los Angeles is hell on wheels and off wheels.

No sooner had I returned to Los Angeles when I was off again: to New Orleans, The Big Easy (in other words, nothing gets done efficiently but there's lots of soul and good vibes). This time I wasn't singing. I was part of an entertainment service hired by a corporation called Countrywide who lend money for "sub-prime" mortgages, whatever they are. They have a branch that deals with those who don't have a good credit rating (but will still get "finance" as long as they accept an "adjustable loan rate") and we were providing a show for one of their sales persons meetings: a "Masters Summit." By God, these were quite tough cookies, experts at phone warfare, no doubt. A little like gangsters. The boss, a swarthy brute, gave me a handshake that crunched my bones audibly and clearly the man disliked my English accent. I must have appeared very pink and summer puddingish, as Noel Coward would have said.

My job was to pretend to be a BBC host of a business show, and, with a real camera crew, interview the sales people as they arrived at the hotel. They'd think it was the real deal. Later we'd edit the film and when shown at the Friday culminating banquet the employees would laugh almost as loud as the boss. For example, one of the questions I asked in the interview was: "What would you say to Saddam Hussein, given the chance?" To a man they hurled invective. "Shit" was one word they preferred. Then, later and clandestinely, I'd be filmed in a reversal shot asking, "What do you think of your boss?" Get the joke? Well, it's a living.

I did manage to get away down in The French Quarter, avoiding the tourists for a while. (Mardi Gras was, thankfully, over and done with — of course, the garbage was there and lingered a while, but, you see, this is "The Big Easy") The buildings are still quaint and all that, but the music is dire: copycat Satchmos all grunting, "Hello Dolly" or, worse, "New York, New York." The bright spot is at the end of Decatur Street where my old friend and patron George Buck resides and works. George owns a beautiful 19th century building and inside he operates the only large jazz record conglomerate in the world. He is keeping the true old jazz alive (I mean pre-bebop), with his collection of old record labels he's bought and with new releases of today's revivalist bands on his own labels. He has released 5 CDs of me and my Bungalow Boys on his Audiophile label — I share the same stable as Ukulele Ike and Little Jack Little: good company. George also runs a restaurant downstairs called "The Palm Court Cafe" where nightly jazz bands play on the stage. The night I was there we had a guest appearance from the last surviving Ink Spot.

Now I'm safely back at home and trying to drive carefully — as my Honda was crumpled up on the Ventura Freeway a few days ago as I cruised along in a reverie listening to Isham Jones on a CD. Yesterday I gave a lecture on pop music in the 1920s for the Constitutional Rights Foundation. I'd met two of their lawyers when I was playing the Argyle Club and they'd bought me Jack Daniels and so one thing led to another: work!

The gig was at my old hunting grounds, The Huntington Library, and I was billed as a Fellow. Which is true. They've very kindly made me one for a while. I think I will study radical movements in California in the 1930s. I don't know why but I've always been interested in communists, Wobblies, radicals, etc., in America. The United States and Radicalism seem so very alien to each other. Of course, I may be under a romantic spell because I've just finished John Steinbeck's gripping novel *In Dubious Battle* about Reds organizing a strike in the California fruit fields in the 1930s .

Now I must get back to my current work: putting together a list of 125 of the best love ballads for a projected CD collection called "The Great American Song Box." This is a difficult task because, as you know, my tastes lean more towards "The War In Snider's Grocery Store" and "Masculine Women, Feminine Men."

What lies in store?

I'm concerned as we all are. There seems as much good reason behind this promised war as there was behind World War One. But, like *The Pianist*, I simply try to carry on, trying to bring joy through my performances. Is this escape? Is this shirking the issue? I shall have to watch and wait till the clouds roll by. Only then can I, as a historian, examine in tranquility.

APRIL

I've been following the Iraq follies with all the guilt of somebody who is hooked on soap operas. I'm well aware that anything I see on TV has more in common with video games than reality. Mostly I get my fix from print: where we live it's the stodgy *Los Angeles Times*. Today they apologized profusely for having front-paged a photo from the war front which had been altered by computer trickery by their photographer. They published the two originals side by side together with this faked collage. Personally, I think the faked one made a much better point than the actuality: a nice British soldier helping an Iraqi and his cradled child get to safety.

In the right hands, poetry is more truthful than actuality.

Anyway, the photographer has been fired. Meanwhile, I've been gleaning some choice bits from the newsprint: there's characters like Chemical Al, a Hussein associate who loves to gas by the thousand. Of course, with their broom mustaches they all look like their master Saddam. There's also the bold British troops who've been sneaking into Basra by night in order to steal an Iraqi or two just to demoralize the natives (We didn't run an Empire and learn nothing). Said Major Nanson, who led the raid: "By extracting someone in their midst, it unsettles them, you see. I expect they didn't get much shuteye the next night — after all, the last thing you want when you wake up is to find 25 Geordies in your bedroom!"

Geordies, by the way, are residents of Newcastle, England —and I can tell you from experience that they are crude bastards. I've been in their country — just south of Scotland. They even have their own impenetrable language.

I spend much too much time looking up mentions of me on Google. Going in too deep can lead to a sharp comeuppance. Eg: last night I'd got as far as the 75th entry when suddenly I was aghast: here was a fellow in a guitar chat room discussing ukuleles and he had the nerve to say that he's tired of me and I'm an old fart who publishes songs nobody young has ever heard of.

When I wrote last month I talked about how I'd been preparing a 125-track CD box set on The Great American Song. My work is now complete — and I think I got every deserving standard in plus a few that people have forgotten about. For example, "You Call Everybody Darling."

It was a big late 1940s smash for Al Trace & His Orchestra. Stayed ages in the top ten. And Al had two versions of this song (his own) in the chart. Two versions — both by him! Who else has ever achieved that? And who the hell was this Al Trace? So you see, this is how I spend my time.

No sooner had I completed my hit list when I got a call from the Oregon Festival of American Music. My dream had come true: they've invited me back to Eugene for a second year in a row! Last year had been bliss: singing Gershwin in concerts directed by the greatest pianist in the world, Dick Hyman. And now it would all be happening again. Oh, how I loved those leisurely hotel breakfasts of fruits and nuts, etc., as I perused a newspaper full of world horrors far removed from this tree-choked, mountain-guarded state.

This time there will be a wider field: The Great American Song. Oh boy! Am I primed for this—my territory exactly. No more kowtowing to the rarefied Gershwin! No more feeling the knowing Michael Feinstein over my shoulder grimacing

Just a few minutes ago Dick Hyman, the Headmaster, called to invite me to perform a couple of Chuck Berry songs at the African-American songwriter concert, as well as give my own lectures and shows on my fave Tin Pan Alley writers.

Regina has been busy making money. She is now the working Hollywood person in our family: she won an audition yesterday to dance a Victorian waltz in a big ballroom scene in the Disney movie, *The Haunted Mansion*, based on the Disneyland ride. She's perfectly qualified for such a job, having attended Victorian Balls, and Vintage Dance Weeks, for donkey's years and me shunning them. And — I'm not even jealous!

On the home front, things are quiet right now. I mean the neighbours we've been having trouble with for years. The ones with the Mowgli child who screams and, poor devil, is left to be raised by the dogs while his bulbous-nosed Iranian foster mother lazes around inside. Eating Turkish Delight? No, that can't be right. It's like a microcosm of this war. Recently matters have escalated: she threatened to have us shot by her wimpy Wasp hubby — all because a note she'd posted for the gardener had blown from her gate to our driveway. Rightly, Regina had assumed it was trash and had consigned it to our dustbin.

We will keep you posted about Western Front news......

MAY

Yes, like any oldster, I have had an active month. Monday has become our regular salon night. It's well over ten years since Jim Dawson and I started these restaurant gatherings of like-minded (and sometimes rather tetchy-touchy) people. These days we're down to a stubborn core: Jim D (the pornographer, rock historian, and author of the best-selling fart book), Libby (a race horse owner and world traveler), and Ray Campi, (the famous king of rockabilly) and me.

The moment I treasure is when I enter the bar and the barman (a would-be actor) immediately starts to prepare my vodka martini with two olives). Next I repair to our corner booth and I order the antipasto. Always the same routine, always delightful. Why can't life run along these predictable lines? By the way, I have given up reading the international news. I'm so fed up with Shiites and Sunnis. What I enjoy are the local American stories — about the Redondo Beach insurance salesman who left the beach in his tiny sailboat in January in order to sail round to Cape Town and hasn't been heard of since. He had a Jack Daniels bottle among his meager provisions. Good for him. I have sworn off Jack because he makes me snore.

Last Thursday Regina and I were the guests of Dr. Kevin Starr, our state librarian and a terrific historian of California, at his annual dinner for USC professors. This was our second time. We cocktailed on the third floor terrace of the famous old California Club in downtown L.A. with its great view of all the capitalist skyscrapers glistening with power. With the professors I talked DNA and such, because these boffins know Crick and Watson, the men who discovered DNA. Regina quickly corrected me when I spoke about DNA's "inventors."

I said I was so relieved that these discoverer-scientists have still not found the soul, the spirit, the secret of personality, of individuality. At that moment a Catholic priest, complete with dog collar stepped forward to shake my hand and congratulate me on my statement.

Then a Chinese gentleman banged a gong and we trooped inside for a dinner. There was a long line of glasses at every table setting: a different wine with each course. And a sommelier to explain where the wines came from. Michael York, the actor, sat beaming at the other end of the table. I never got to speak to him. I'm sure he's charming but it rather queered my pitch to have a rival Englishman present, if you see what I mean. I'm still not quite sure why he was there. But he beamed mightily.

When the sommelier spoke of the King Rufus wine and asked whether we knew who Rufus was I put up my hand and said he was an early Norman King of England who got shot through the head with an arrow. Very good, said the wine man. And the professors were impressed. Top marks for me — until I added that Rufus is notorious as England's first known bugger-boy monarch.

Me and the Bungalow Boys had been hired to provide an afterglow of entertainment — which we did, but terribly late because we were preceded by a busty novice mezzo-soprano who shrieked out standards and a bit of Wagner for so long that by the time we came on the professors were weary and well-wined. Still, a good time was had by those who remained. And Dr. Starr led the final chorus of Jerome Kern's "They Didn't Believe Me."

Tonight, Saturday, I'm dining at a house in the Hollywood Hills where back in the 1960s I used to stay during my rock star years. Jean Clyde Quinn will be hosting the gathering. She and her late husband, the banjo star Spencer Quinn, introduced me to the real American Song when I met them in 1965. And I met them through another of tonight's guests, Barbara Pohlman. She and her husband Ray had befriended me when we were all in Hawaii that autumn of 1965 making an episode of *Shindig*, the ABC television show. Ray was the musical director of that splendid pioneering rock and roll show.

Ray, a bass player, had been one of the original Wrecking Crew, those great studio musicians who played on almost all the hits made in Hollywood, most notably Phil Spector's. I wonder where he is right now? I mean, Spector. Poor Ray died many years ago.

Of course at this moment I'm trying to learn the many Great American Songs I've been set to perform at the upcoming Oregon Festival Of American Music. After spending my post-rock years rolling around in Tin Pan Alley I'm finding the tricksy lyrics of Hart and Porter very hard to memorize. Mostly because much of the rhyming is rhyming for its own sake and makes little sense. I mean, have you ever examined "The Girl Friend," an early Rodgers & Hart hit?

Here's the chorus: "Isn't she cute? Isn't she sweet? She's gentle and mentally almost complete. She's knockout, she's regal, her beauty's illegal — she's the Girl Friend!" Now I don't relate being gentle with being knockout and regal. Also — what about being "mentally almost complete?" Does that suggest she may have a screw or two loose? I don't think so. I think it's just Lorenz Hart striving too hard for a clever rhyme. That's probably why I'm more at home with the predictable world of, say, "Just A Little Street Where Old Friends Meet" (by dear Harry Woods who wrote "Try A Little Tenderness" and was fond of starting fights in bars). Anyway these Hart songs are damned hard to remember but I'll do it, I will.

On the home front — I mean the next-door neighbour problem — there's been all-quiet. They failed to turn up at the Dispute Resolution meeting. Another mark against them. Next day I saw a policeman strolling out of their house arm and arm with them, all parties wreathed in smiles (which annoyed me). Still, I've decided I'm going to ignore them from now on. This'll be hard because I can't stand not being liked.

Mowgli and the dogs continue to greet us with grunts and barks. Nevertheless, I remain stoic, staring straight ahead. I don't want to be shot-gunned just yet.

JUNE

This month and this year mark the 40th anniversary of the time I first set foot on U.S. soil: June 1963. So I think I'll reminisce for the rest of this letter because I want to see if I can remember much of that memorable summer......................

The very end of June 1963: I had booked on a charter flight to America organized by the Union of Students Of Ireland. I was then in my second year as an undergraduate in modern history and political science at Trinity College Dublin. Since the late 1940s I'd dreamed of coming to America, the land of my fantasies, the land of westerns, and blue jeans, and then rock 'n' roll. The land of glamour and great physical beauty — or so it seemed from my reading of movies, comic books, and magazines.

Two of my pals, roommates of mine at TCD had booked on the flight: Jeremy Lewis and David Shaw, both in my history class, both English — as, it seemed, were most students at TCD. Jeremy has since published a very amusing memoir of our times in Dublin (*Playing For Time*). David Shaw disappeared from my life decades ago. Jeremy has a theory that David is now Yasser Arafat.

Anyway, they were bent on visiting high culture America — Yosemite and San Francisco, etc. — whereas I was determined to visit Nashville and New Orleans in a search for hillbillies and hot black jazzers. In preparation for the trip I got myself a crew cut from a Dublin barber and I happened to have a private glimpse of President Kennedy. This was happenstance: the night before our departure I was ambling down a Dublin street when suddenly round the corner came a motorcade and there, in an open car, were President Kennedy and Jackie. Off to some local do, no doubt. I stopped and cheered. They smiled and waved. This was a good omen for my trip.

When we set down at Idyllwild airport an official came aboard and marched down the aisle spraying two disinfectant cans with great skill and self-assuredness. I was most impressed. And then when we were in the airport proper I noticed that all employees wore smart uniforms, as if they were officers in some fairytale country. Even the colored man who pushed our luggage wore epaulettes and had gold braid all round his cap. Everybody seemed on casual military alert.

My pals set off almost immediately on their culture trip — by Greyhound bus. We had all bought 99day/99dollar Greyhound tickets in advance. I stayed a sweltering night in the New York apartment of the grandmother of my best friend from childhood, an American boy called "Speedy" McKeachie. His father was a big advertising executive with McCann-Ericson and had been posted back to America, but when he'd worked in London the family had lived at Wildcroft Manor, Putney Heath and that was how I'd gotten friendly with their son, Speedy. What a great name! There's a picture of Speedy (with my brother and me) in *Rock Odyssey*, the book I wrote about the 1960s. In the Fifties we'd played Cowboys and Indians games on Putney Heath, and also one called North & South Armies, a civil war affair. I'd always insisted on being a Confederate soldier. Speedy was more than content to represent the North. In the Western games my younger brother Robin was forced to be the Indian. We used real bows and arrows as well as pellet-shooting Daisy repeater air guns. Sometimes we got pellets in our bodies and arrows up the rear end.

The first pop song I heard in America I heard on that sweltering night in that un-air-conditioned apartment with its fusty smell of the forties and long-dead swell parties on Park Avenue reeking of Cole Porter sophistication. The song, on the radio, was "Tie Me Kangaroo Down, Sport" by the Australian Rolf Harris. I had come all this way to hear a song that had bugged me back in England!

The next day Speedy, who'd met me at the airport, took me by train to his parents' house in Bucks County, Pennsylvania. Everything was so new and exciting that I didn't dare talk much. I was overawed. And the few times I did speak to people they didn't understand my accent. At Speedy's I saw my first American television show: it was a film called *Kentucky Kernels*, starring Wheeler and Woolsey. A very old film. Kentucky! That was where I longed to be!

We went to a few local affairs but I can't remember anything about them. It did seem rather formal and even faux European in Bucks County. Where was The West? Sometime during my stay I managed to get to Atlantic City. My cousin Rebecca, who'd emigrated to America the year before, was working as a waitress in a casino there. We had a day on the beach. I have a picture of that: I'm wearing swim togs and a T-shirt emblazoned with *Eh? What? No!* the title of a cheeky TD revue for which I'd written the songs (Next year's revue produced my recording of a bluesy instrumental that eventually got me my first record contract — in Seattle and for a label called Jerden. It was released in the summer of 1964 as "Soho").

After quite enough time in Bucks County, Speedy had me dropped off in Washington, DC. Upper-crust friends of his family were willing to entertain me. In their house I found a guitar and I dared to strum a few chords and sing an American song. This moment I'll never forget because I considered myself to be very brave by singing an American song in the land of origin, and me an Englishman. For some long-forgotten reason and connection, I was lunched in Georgetown by a rather grand lady, something to do with government, and I was so tongue-tied I stammered and stuttered an awful lot. That was July 10, my birthday. I was all of 22. Did I feel young? I can't remember. I do know that I was still a virgin. And still blissfully happy, on the whole, and all things considered.

Next I moved to Falls Church, Virginia where I stayed with friends of Jeremy's. The father worked for Time magazine. The children were called Kerry and Kelly — I'd never heard last names used as first names before.

From D.C. I journeyed by Greyhound to Nashville, Tennessee, in search of country music. I'd never been on a bus with a lavatory before. In fact, for many hours I didn't know there was a lavatory because the driver kept referring to it by an even deeper euphemism: "You folks are encouraged to avail yourself of the clean rest room." But I could rest in my seat, thank you very much. This was one of the many jolts I received during my first American visit. In my fantasies I had imagined the country to be full of wild, vulgar people who talked in tough slang, in a blunt manner. But America of 1963 turned out to be a Sargasso of bourgeoisie.

I was reading British classics on this trip: *Roderick Random* by Tobias Smollett and H.G. Wells' *Tono Bungay*. Why was this? I should have been immersed in Zane Grey or John O'Hara. Perhaps nostalgia for the England I'd left behind — worlds away, cultures away. An embarrassment of youth, that I now recall, is the sudden rush of unwanted blood to the groin: as we were pulling in to Nashville and I needed to rise and be ready I realized that I had an erection (for no reason). My mind was unable to order it to cease and desist. As it happened, nobody noticed me. Nobody paid any attention to me on this trip, until I opened my mouth. That awkward accent.

In the centre of country music I had my first taste of a YMCA. Back in Dublin we had been advised that YMCAs would be our best and cheapest places of rest. So far, though, I had avoided them. I was scared by talk I had heard. Danger was said to lurk there. Doors were said to be left ajar and one might be invited in and then who knows? Plucking up courage I checked in to a YMCA that overlooked the main city square of Nashville — and nothing happened. I could have been invisible for all they cared. The inverts were out, it appeared.

In my lonely room I looked out at the square. I saw buses chugging along. Buses! That might be a problem! I must remember that this was the South and if I traveled by bus I'd need to sit in the front and never, never sit in the back. Negroes sat in the back and at all costs I must obey the laws of Dixie. I was so terrified of making a bus mistake that I never took a bus. Instead I walked from the YMCA to downtown where I found a radio station called WLAC. I went in and announced myself as a British visitor. They immediately put me on the air as a curiosity. As a news item I was quizzed about the Profumo sex scandal then raging in England and in particular about the luscious call-girl Christine Keeler. Americans were fascinated to learn that sex existed in Britain, land of tea and crumpets and tally-ho. I was soon tired of the tally-ho stuff.

WLAC was a country station so I was much pleased. I made a hit with the station owner's son and he showed me around and let me sit in on a down-home cracker show hosted by an avuncular jock who would start his six-hour shift, I was told, by ringing a cowbell. While I was there he talked, as he chewed, about being a kid and lyin' there at night listenin' to the drummin' o' the rain on the ole tin shed. Then he spun a remarkable record, a current hit: Dave Dudley's "Six Days On The Road." The most masculine song I'd ever heard, a trucker/cowboy telling in a rich, lusty voice about his "rig" with its ten-four gears and a Georgia overdrive and how he could have had a lot of women but he wasn't like other guys. At the end of the song he tells us that his home town's acomin' in sight and if you think he's happy you're right: "Six days on the road and I'm a gonna get me home tonight!" At this point the disc jockey inserted a tape of screeching brakes followed by a terrible smashing and crashing sound. It was a very creative piece of radio.

The station boss's son had taken to me and invited me to stay at his place. Which I did. He knew every important person in town. So I was able to see a performance of *The Grand Ole Opry* at the Ryman Auditorium, famous as hell. The old wooden church pews were very sticky that hot night but I was privileged to be present at what would now be considered a classic show: the WSM radio host, Ralph Emery, brought on the acts and they all quickly knocked off their current hit and ran. It was a whirlwind and I really admired the backing musicians who calmly accompanied and knew every song and style. My hero Hank Snow, calm and debonair but still folksy, ambled on and sang a railroad song. Afterwards I forced my way backstage and pressed his hand. He was a tiny fellow, very spangled. On another night I slipped away to see *Lawrence Of Arabia*. And towards the end of my stay my host took me to a record session at the RCA studio. Jerry Wallace was the artist. He sang from a stool, sipping constantly from a Dr. Pepper bottle. The session was all-live with no overdubbing. There was a whole heap of session men, calm and collected, as was Jerry, as was everybody. As were all Americans I had met so far. The Anita Kerr singers provided a lush harmony backing. A short, fat and comfy man was wandering around, very casual in a Hawaiian shirt. Occasionally he'd make some musical point. This man turned out to be the arranger, Bill Justis. Of course, I knew him as a rock hero of mine because of his 1950s hit, "Raunchy," a smashing instrumental. After a few takes they'd captured their A side and now they went on to the B side, an easy-going bluesy country song. The A side, however, wasn't at all country: it had a Latin-American beat and was written by a man called Alfredo Thomson. I rather liked the harmonies, quite old-fashioned Alley.

The title was "Bamboula" and when it was released on the Challenge label, later that summer, I bought a copy. It was never a hit but I still give it a spin now and then and whenever I do that glorious first Nashville trip floods back. Such is the power of old music.

I was to meet Bill Justis again — and in Nashville: during the early 1970s I worked as a songwriter and producer with Andy Wickham, an A&R vice president at Warner Bros. Records. He and I recorded a number of eccentric singles there — "Hands" and "There Goes That Song Again," both by Debbie Dawn — and our arranger (and friend) was that same Bill Justis.

From Nashville I bussed on to Tulsa, Oklahoma to stay with another cousin, Rebecca's brother Tim. He'd been out there for a year or so working for DX-Sunray, an oil company whose boast was "The Fastest Moving Company in the West." Oil was at the bottom of any wealth in our family: our grandfather ran a venerable oil company in England, established in the 1860s. DX was my grandfather's American supplier.

The erection problem came on again as the bus pulled in to Tulsa. But I put on a long jacket and all was well when my cousin met me. He introduced me to his fellow workers at the DX Company and I learned about "cat crackers" and the like. I think Tim was working in the lube plant at the time (He now works in the cell phone biz and has done successfully for years — and to prove it he has built a mansion for his family in Atlanta, Georgia).

During my trip I was lunched at the powerful Petroleum Club by DX's president, a Mr. MacDowell, who yarned about the 1930s when Tim's father, my uncle, had also worked for the company. "Boy, was he one for the ladies! I do believe he pipped that Cherokee gal and just got out of town in time! Yessir, I do believe!"

Tim was staying with a wealthy local family called the R. B. Hurlbutts of 2003 S. Norfolk Ave, a suburb of that once rip-roaring city of Tulsa. Back in the 1930s there'd been gunfights and fisticuffs but in 1963, like so much of the America I was witnessing, Tulsa was trying its hardest to be middle-class respectable. The Hurlbutts house was bungaloid — that is ranch-style, long and low. It was bang up-to-date complete with noisy and billowing air-conditioning system. I'd never experienced such a system before. The house was certainly chilled by the commotion from the big tinny machines but I caught a cold due to the constant coming and going from outdoor humidity and into an icy indoors.

Mr. Hurlbutt was a busy businessman and I hardly saw him. At 6pm he'd return in his seersucker suit (I took to seersucker and bought myself a suit which I proudly wore, on my return to England, at a cocktail party hosted by my grandfather — but I was mistaken for a waiter and spent my time serving drinks or else answering questions concerning this strange costume) and be immediately handed a bourbon filled with loud clinking ice. Then he'd disappear to his "den," a place of mystery.

Mrs. H busied herself with local affairs and one evening made me accompany her to an "orientation of foreign visitors" meeting in a local church hall. There we foreigners were made to rise and talk about how we felt about America, about how pleased we were to be there. I remember a German boy, Manfred, made a couple of criticisms but he was swiftly dealt with: Mrs. H had a withering glance.

The Hurlbutts had two teenage sons, rather spotty, who liked to go on beer busts and holler at sports games. They liked rowdy rock & roll but they were surprised by my serious interest in down home black blues. Jimmy Reed was OK for a beer bust or necking party but he was not to be taken seriously or socially. And Mrs. H went further — she considered Negro music to be an embarrassment and a reminder of a past that was over and done with. She talked of Oklahoma's symphony orchestras and grand opera. I had heard such talk before and it depressed me.

Thanks to help from my cousin I was able to prove my love of rootsy pop music: Tim fixed me up with a guest appearance on a local TV station, a lunchtime magazine show called *Welcome Inn*, hosted by one Pat Robinson. There was even a write-up in the morning paper: "He has composed a sea chantey in a North Country dialect." I was quoted as claiming that "It's all about a woman who could be Christine Keeler." A photo showed me looking rather raffish — "like a cocky gangster," I told reporter Jim Newton.

On *Welcome Inn* I talked, without stuttering, about the blues and how Britain had its own sort of blues and country music. To prove this I played the old Liverpool bawdy ballad, "Maggie May," accompanying myself on the piano. I don't remember any comment from the Hurlbutt family. Maybe Mrs. H was offended by the

Christine Keeler reference and the nature of the song.

She was fond of inviting me to take a swim in their kidney-shaped pool. "Dress comfortable." We paddled around near each other. She seemed to be far older than my mother and more formidable. Her swimsuit was heavily boned to show off her bust. She introduced me to another American novelty, after air-conditioning. (This was to be a summer of novel sensations for I was later to experience the thrilling taste of pecan pie, of onion rings and patty melt).

The novelty was a floating drink holder. Her bourbon floated beside her as we paddled around the pool. I think I had a beer. Whenever we floated too close I made an excuse and dived. This may have been a mistake:

The day before I left — in order to take my trip to New Orleans, land of jazz — I sought out Mrs. H in the washing machine room (another novelty: there were no such machines in the England I knew). I was thanking her effusively as she folded clothes. Suddenly, with that withering look, she turned on me: "You are not a good representative of your country. I am speaking of housework. You have not helped around the home — with dishes and clothes, — and you have not been a good team player. You have been content to run with the ball rather than be part of our team. I am not pleased with you." I was staggered. I was speechless. All the way on the bus to New Orleans, I reflected on her severe dressing down. I can't bear not to be liked and I have always been terrified of women with authority. So stunned was I that I forgot to look out at magnolias and old southern mansions and shacks full of blues legends........

-----------To be continued next month----------

JULY

Some of you have written to say how much you're enjoying the memoir of my first trip to America in the summer of 1963, exactly 40 years ago. I sent a hard copy overseas to my friend Charles Sprawson, the art dealer and swimmer who was at Trinity College Dublin at that time and writes to me regularly from his flat in London. Almost immediately I got a handwritten reply inquiring whether the Greyhound bus erections ever came in useful or "did you remain a virgin?" You shall learn as you read on............

THE SUMMER OF '63

Still shaken by the dressing-down I got from my Oklahoma hostess, — the gimlet eyed Mrs. H whom I had spurned in the swimming pool — I arrived in New Orleans aboard a Greyhound bus on a typically humid day in late July, 1963. After a wash-up in the bus terminal I felt I had ridden myself of that awful experience. Now I was ready to explore the cradle of jazz. The jazz I sought was the real stuff, the traditional jazz of rough and ready ensemble players rendering hot and earthy versions of pop songs with hill-and-dale melodies on a bed of wrenching romantic Victorian harmonies. I certainly wasn't seeking the sterility of "modern" jazz. No altered nerve-jangling chords and nasty, jagged, dangerous melodies.

I wish I could remember where I stayed. Why is it we have certain lacunae? Why can't I recall from somewhere in my brain every moment seen and felt? Proust tried to do it but he made up a lot I'm pretty sure. Well, let's say he disguised what really happened to him. I mean the chauffeurs, delivery lads and such. So: I think I stayed at a motel near the French Quarter — because that was where the old jazz had originated and some of its echoes might still be there I hoped. I do recall that I made friends with a boy of my age, a touring Scandinavian student, and we walked together around the town but he didn't show any interest in trailing jazz.

My first experience in the French Quarter was courtesy of a business associate of my Uncle John, the man who'd met Hitler and then fought his airmen and finally settled into being an executive in the family's oil company in London. The Arthur Brown Co. had many American contacts and Uncle John had supplied the phone number of an oilman here in New Orleans: "He'll be good for a decent lunch I can assure you." I certainly got the lunch — at a 19th century restaurant with a French name and lots of polished wood that looked liquescent; and stooping waiters with napkins draped over their arms and steaming bowls of fish recently torn from the water and boilingly annoyed with their predicament.

The executive must have been in his 30s but he looked senior and serious to me. Very self-confident in a casual manner I'd never encountered back home. This was American savvy, know-how, relaxayvoo — it was the executive equivalent of the way American soldiers marched in World War Two newsreels: with a swagger-slouch but with confidence, to the tune of a swinging brass band playing "St. Louis Blues." It was as if all true Americans were Negroes, only a lot of them were disguised with whiteface.

The executive hung up his jacket on a rack and lunched in a crackling crisp white shirt. His tie had wide stripes in primary colours. A musky, not unpleasant, smell exuded from him. He wore big horn-rimmed glasses and for a moment the name "Clark Kent" flashed into my mind. To cover my tracks I started gabbling about the true jazz. He listened politely. Then, at an intermission, when the waiter had presented us with a bowl of writhing crabs and lobsters, the executive leaned towards me and asked in a deep radio voice: "To hell with your tourist jazz — d'you wanna get laid?"

I was in confusion. "Get laid" — I'd never heard the word used like this: laying the table for supper – yes — laying down your life for your country as the stained glass windows depicted in my prep school church — laying down your life, in the church window, looked a lot like dropping off to sleep with Christ stroking your head. But getting laid?

"Yes," he continued, flipping open a box of cigarettes and propelling one into his mouth. "What's the expression in jolly old England? Do you guys even do it? Oh, yes — Christine Keeler! Well.....Hey! Don't look so shocked. I just wanted to be friendly and steer you to a cat house — you know, the true jazz package, historically accurate, don't you know."

I thanked him and declined. But it's a jolly good lunch, I added. By now I was stammering. "You gotta try the cheesecake — a substitute for the sex."

I did try it, I relished every mouthful. A totally new experience. I'd never associated cheese with cake and the combination being so sweet and ecstatic. He paid the bill, wished his best to Uncle John, and gave me directions to Preservation Hall. "You'll get what you want there."

Was he joking? I had a wonderful afternoon in the Hall, surrounded by old red bricks and respectable tourists. White women in flowered hats. Their menfolk in seersucker. Soon I would have one of these natty suits. On a rickety old stage sat a row of very old and unthreatening black men playing a halting but touching music that may have been jazz but to me conjured up romantic sultry nights on Bourbon or Rampart streets or any of those colorful places, and a Jelly Roll or a One-Leg or a No-Leg or a Slow-Drag ladling out a tart syrup of solace music. Maybe some of it was hot and hurried and even out-of-tune, but to me it was all flowing from an old place long ago and far away and safe as a goodnight tumbler of warm milk.

After about an hour of this soothing entertainment the old men shuffled off the stage for a break. And then: another side of me took command: I found myself rising from my sticky seat and heading for the piano. Next I was sitting at it and starting to play a kind of blues. My blues — with a tip of the hat to Jimmy Yancey. The tourists were astonished but stayed put. The musicians slowly moved back to the stage and one by one and, as in a movie musical, joined me. In the last chorus we achieved a climax, a grand blast of triumphant music.

I had become part of the jazz scene and all through the international telegram off just twelve bars. What a clever invention is the twelve bar blues! What an easy way to a fix between different cultures! We finished to great applause. The band made me take a bow and I hastened off into the gloaming of the French Quarter full of joy and sassy of walk. Surely this experience had been more satisfying than a lay? Of course, I'd never had a lay (or "charver," as it was known as in Dublin) so how could I compare? But music affords me instant satisfaction and for the moment that was enough. However, given the right circumstances an American lay would have been a nice topping to my trip. The sensation of full sex had been described to me by a friend as being like a bird taking flight, soaring higher and higher. "A trip to the moon on gossamer wings," said a Cole Porter song. It certainly sounded worth doing but my problem was that, as in everything else in life, I'd have to be carefully taught. And then I might never learn but end up doing it my way. The mechanics of sex had not come naturally to me. I was not a true animal. In fact, I hated my body and wished to be just a spirit or a flying sprite, as in dreams. Back at boarding school, when I was fifteen, I'd had to enlist the help of Carlisle, also known as the school tart, a youth with hair like a Brillo pad, to explain in simple language how masturbation worked. He was a nasty little sod with yellow skin but his directions proved effective.

Aboard the Greyhound and reading H.G. Wells, head buried in book. Crossing the heart of Texas, bound for the Mexican border. Heart pumping with excitement. Soon I'd be seeing Jeremy and David again: we'd agreed to meet at the Greyhound station in El Paso when we were parting back in New York. We'd simply looked at a map and decided with a pin. What adventures had they had? I couldn't wait to tell them of my triumphs (and disasters). All I knew was that they had planned to venture across the border into Central America even. For myself, American culture was sufficient — always had been, always will be. Plus a little P.G. Wodehouse and H.G. Wells and Graham Greene for relief.

I checked into a motel near the bus station. I knew I was early — we'd given ourselves a window of just under a week — so I plucked up my courage and walked across the border into Juarez, the border town abutting El Paso. Of course I was terrified, as I always am in spots where English is not the language. Without language I'm lost, I'm flaying, I'm certain I'm going to be gypped.

Juarez was hot and dusty. Dirty too. Not a bit romantic. Women approached me. They had refreshments. I was thirsty and by handing out change I got a drink. It was banana juice — not very refreshing. Luckily I'd changed some traveler's cheques so I had enough dollars to buy a pair of cowboy boots. I hadn't the nerve to haggle, I just handed over the $10 and the shiny black leather boots with the pointed toes and high heels and indented decorations were mine to show off in England. I tried them on and found that I had to hobble but I think it made me look like a cowboy. The locals cheered me. I might have lingered south of the border — I remembered a song that made it seem exciting — but I had to get back to the motel in order to be ready for my pals.

Days and days went by. I finished *Tono Bungay* and started *The Napoleon Of Notting Hill Gate* by G.K. Chesterton. I went for my meals in the cafe or "Coffee Shop" of the Greyhound station. There I had another sensation, as good as the cheesecake, as good as sex was supposed to be: I ate a pecan pie. You have no idea what this rush did for me. I was elevated. I was in ecstasy. Then I came down with a bump and a bloated stomach. But I kept going back for more pecan pies. How could a mere nut taste so delicious? "Try it a la mode, sweetie" said the old waitress. No, that would be going too far, too soon. She shrugged and blew smoke at me. I went back to my room and read some more.

It strikes me now that during my entire U.S. trip I never gave a thought about my home on Putney Heath, London, England. About my mother, for instance, who had been suddenly widowed in December of 1962, only a few months before.

In January, when we reassembled at our digs for the Easter term I must have seemed pretty low: Jeremy was keeping a diary at the time and I sneaked a peek: "Ian in another of his gloomy moods..." A little later, perhaps after discovering that everyone was reading his diary, he tore it up into little pieces. But I pieced it together.

Why didn't I give a thought to my mother, my brother, sister, and home? Maybe the excitement of America, my land of dreams. Maybe a trait I've had since childhood: if I'm abandoned or fate deals me a blow, I'm able to settle into any new situation — find some friends or acquaintances or anyone who'll listen and let me pursue my mission of trying to make people laugh, listen, pay attention. Maybe it was the jungle of boarding school, of being packed off there at age 8 and having to fight or fail, that taught me emotional toughness. Never give any of yourself away.

And then, just as I'd given up hope, Jeremy and David turned up in El Paso, bright as bees and spotless but trussed up with wretched rucksacks. Both had the beginning of beards and looked alarmingly like Latin American revolutionaries. I may have been eating a pecan pie at the time. I know I tried to interest them in the delicacy, but they were full of stories of their adventures. It seems they'd traveled right through Mexico and out the other side and into Guatemala where, boomed Jeremy, they'd been worshipped as Gods. As Gods, indeed! David, ever the stooge, chortled. No wonder I'd always been uneasy with us as a trio. I really didn't want to hear about Aztecs and the like. I've never had any interest in past times outside of America and Britain between roughly 1890 and 1965.

Still, I was happy to be with them again. To tell them my stories. And we resumed our old routine of them talking among themselves and me telling them jokes whenever there was an intermission. They especially liked the jokes while we were on the Greyhound trundling across dull deserts sporting promising names — "The Painted Desert," for example.

I was planning to stay with them till Los Angeles. "Ugh!" muttered David. "Horrible blemish. Won't stick around long there." No, the two culture vultures were bound for San Francisco so that they could admire the beauty of the hills and the little cable cars and the museums and the painters dashing off masterpieces and the poets spouting verses 24 hours a day. Not for me. I would stick around Los Angeles. Hollywood was there, world centre of romance and thrills.

My jokes were cut off at the Grand Canyon which they insisted on seeing. One look over the top was enough for me. Just a bigger version of a Welsh slag pit. We stayed in cabins and laughed at the tourists going up and down the canyon on donkeys. I really didn't care for Bermuda shorts. Wasn't America supposed to be sexy and full of human cheesecake and beefcake? These donkey tourists seemed a flatulent bunch. Breakfast — eggs, bacon, hash browns (another new one), toast and coffee — cost one dollar and I thought that was a lot.

On we rode to Los Angeles. I had imagined that on arrival we'd be greeted by vistas of palms and great stretches of golden sands and breaking waves and splendid physiques. But the bus pulled into the city of Los Angeles, the downtown. What a disappointment! The tall buildings looked exactly like New York only grimier and sad to be sitting under sun. There didn't seem to be as much life as in New York. No taxicab men in dazzling uniforms. "Ha! Ha!" cackled David. "Chuff! Chuff!" They simply changed buses and set off for San Francisco. "See you back in New York on the plane!"

So, alone, I stood there in the baking fetid heat and haze and felt pretty low. Must take action! I found a contact number I'd been given by Uncle John. More oil biz connections — an Englishman who'd emigrated here but who once worked in my grandfather's oil company: Steve Heller, The Golden Bear Oil Company. I rang and spoke to Mr. Heller.

He was very welcoming but had an odd British accent — a touch of guttural mid-Europe, words a little too precisely pronounced. He told me I'd be welcome to stay with him and his family. At present, though, he was busy in the office, a few blocks from the bus terminal. It was now 1pm and he wouldn't be free till 6pm (They worked long hours in America). Why didn't I kill some time by exploring downtown Los Angeles and then meet him at 6pm up at the Golden Bear Company HQ?

Off I went and pretty soon I was in a wide street dotted with ornate old theatres, encrusted with everything. They'd obviously seen better days but now their marquees were advertising non-stop features for 50 cents. You could watch them for 24 hours. Mostly science fiction and horror. Films offering creatures, zombies, things from outer space and black lagoons. I saw two and a half before I realized I'd better be on my way to Mr. Heller's. I left when a group of American scientists, up in the frozen wastes, were being mysteriously murdered by some abominable snowman type who bumbled off howling when a hero hacked at him. In retrospect I suppose I ought to have been admiring the beautiful beaux-arts buildings of downtown Los Angeles. Jeremy and David used to jeer at me for always preferring the darkness of a cinema to the delights of old architecture, trees, statues, and so on.

Steve Heller was a small dumpy man in glasses with what I supposed was a London-Jewish accent. He never mentioned his Jewishness but I couldn't believe he'd been born in Britain. However, he was very loyal to the old country and wouldn't have a word said against her. We drove out of L.A. in his enormous car and soon we were on my first freeway, clogged with cars, as if in a race, lines of them in competition, all heading west to the ocean and their respective blue heavens. Steve told me about his wife Bridget, who'd been to an exclusive English girl's school, and about his two daughters who'd been born here. He told me what a great country America is compared with Britain. "Problems they have, many. Not comfortable, I was not!" and he hammered the wheel to make his point.

At San Pedro we abruptly turned right, climbed a hill and were suddenly in a different world. I saw big blue skies, with none of the downtown haze (which had hurt my eyes); I was presented with a grand vista of the Pacific breaking gracefully, silently, and rows of stately palm trees; at last I began to feel that beauty, American cleancut beauty, was not far away. Eventually, after cruising along the cliff top we turned right in and through a stone entrance, designed like an old Spanish mission: "Portuguese Bend — Residents Only" announced a sign painted in monkish script.

"Welcome to our happy home!" said Steve. Their house was in a community surrounded by fences and gates so as to protect them from the ruder elements of life. Possibly these were the rude and All-American elements I was so eager to meet. However for now I was delighted to be the guest of the Hellers in their reproduction English cottage with its neat flower beds and Mrs. Heller greeting me warmly in a plummy home-counties accent as she showed me with my own room and folded towels and tissue box. I was told the rules of the house and the busy schedule that awaited the family this coming weekend. For the two daughters, sprightly pre-teens, whose breasts were just beginning to sprout, now entered the house (or "home" as they call any house over here) hot and sweaty and clad in riding breeches. They were avid horse riders and I, they said, could help out tomorrow when they went about their horse business. Meanwhile, I should feel at home — take a shower. Yes, surely I'd like to take a shower. Followed by cocktails and nuts and then a pot roast. "Oh, you will notice quite the Californians we are. Standing on ceremony we do not do," said Steve. Bridget, who'd attended a very posh English boarding school, winked and smiled at me. The daughters rushed about in their jodhpurs, telling private jokes, giggling, ignoring me. I had a feeling this was not my America. But they were awfully nice and kind people in their way...........

To Be Continued

AUGUST

For the last few months I've been trying to learn a lot of sophisticated Broadway numbers by Rodgers & Hart and Cole Porter (not down my usual alley) as well as some rootsier pieces by Fats Waller and Eubie Blake, and even some early rock & roll by Chuck Berry. All for my appearance at the Oregon Festival Of American music. I hope I will satisfy my taskmaster, the maestro Dick Hyman. I'll be performing those songs on a concert stage without benefit of a music stand.

This has been good exercise and has pushed me into a revision of my piano playing — even scales and arpeggios, etc. In fact, I have enrolled at the local music conservatory so that I can get a grounding in the classical way of approaching the keyboard — something I rejected strenuously all through childhood and adolescence. The result was some rocking & rolling but now, in my senior years, I want to study the keyboard and play fewer notes and with more intelligence.

One of the reasons why I've sent myself back to school is because I've had a lot of involuntary time on my hands recently: the TV movie I was all set to work on for Peter Bogdanovich has fallen through. Quite a blow — at first.

As is generally the case in Hollywood matters, my agent doesn't know the real reason. After months of work on this three hour movie about Natalie Wood — sessions of music "spotting," conference calls, and my writing several songs — we came down in price and, at their request, "messengered" to them several old recordings of mine that we thought could replace recordings that they couldn't afford —

Glenn Miller and such.

To my agent's astonishment a call came last week from their post-production chief that none of my records worked in the film and that my services would not be required anymore. The official background music "composer," together with his pet arranger, would be writing all the replacement songs thank you very much. Well, this should be quite a hard job since the music that earlier I had been asked to replace included five classic Frank Sinatra hits of the 1950s complete with Nelson Riddle string arrangements for 40 piece orchestra, some 1970s Rolling Stones plus a couple of Cheap Trick tracks.

In a way this is all a relief because I'm not a musical chameleon. Let someone else make copies, pastiches, sound-alikes. However, I could have done with the money. And not a word from Mr. Bogdanovich, my onetime champion. It was he who'd recommended me originally and at our one meeting he'd praised me to the heavens, telling the bemused producers, "He can play any instrument!" Typical of Hollywood types, they had no idea who I was or what I'd done. Even when I left them CDs of my work they were none the wiser. That's because they never play music. They "crunch numbers" instead.

I should have seen the writing on the wall during my one meeting with Peter B: when I brightly suggested that I could write and record songs that could replace unaffordable Glenn Miller tracks there was an explosion from Mr. B: "Will you stop pushing your songs! I don't want your songs! I want you to make me swing version of public domain songs, that's what I want!" We turned to consideration of the only stuff available to us: 19th century ballads like "When You And I Were Young Maggie." I felt like a cheap hack hired to make copycat music. Music created by my betters—like Cheap Trick and The Rolling Stones. When I'd suggested they substitute my 1965 Top Ten hit for a Gary Lewis record of the same period the Hollywood types looked blank. They'd never heard of my hit. What was the name of the group? And so it went as I sank deeper and deeper into my chair. I wasn't even offered coffee. But Peter demanded and received a big plate of delicatessen delights. He also had a chauffeured car bring him to the film company office — suitably located — for a TV movie — on Ventura Boulevard in the heart of the Valley.

Now I'm getting bitter. Very different to earlier, when I was part of the production team and watching the VHS of the epic and telling everybody who'd listen: "Oh, it may be just a TV biopic but it's really well made — that's because it's directed by Peter Bogdanovich." But as soon as I learnt I was no longer needed the film became a worthless piece of crap.

Since being dropped from the film I've left messages at Peter's number but never a word back. I suppose he considers that I've let him down.......... So now I'm studying classical keyboard privately and preparing for the Oregon concerts. Spending a lot of time with the dog Rollo. Hollywood has once more eluded me. "Rejection" would be an inappropriate word—psychologically.

And now for the conclusion to my memoirs of the summer of 1963 and my first trip to the USA. When I started writing this I had no idea it would stretch to a three parter. But it's taken my mind off the problem next door.

THE SUMMER OF '63
Part Three.

I minded my Ps & Qs while staying at the Hellers — he ran a tight ship, a rather Germanic one. Mrs. H was always bright and kept us all neat and well-fed. She'd attended, in her day, a posh English school, Cheltenham Ladies College. I didn't ask when. It seems to me she wore tweeds. She had a deep, husky and hearty laugh.

The weekend at Portuguese Bend, in that rarefied gated community, was full of activity, mostly around horses. The daughters took their riding very seriously and I was content to watch and wait for orders. Mr. H gave a lot of them. We were in a dusty riding ring dotted with shedding eucalyptus trees, high on a hill. I knew that just the other side was the ever-blue Pacific, rolling and crashing and waiting for me to plunge into the arms of adventure.

But we never got there. Instead it was horses and steak & kidney pudding and neighbours who were curious about the visitor. "Tell me about yourself — *I'm interested!*" said a pert, well-upholstered woman, pushing her sunglasses up to her frozen bush of hair and lowering her bifocals. What could I say at this stage? I had achieved nothing. I was a mere apprentice in the West. I was in awe of all things American — except maybe my present surroundings. There was something un-American about them. A little too much refinement, class, good manners. Obviously what I'd dreamed of encountering was rough America, wild America, an outdoors paradise, teeming with fast-moving gods and nymphs wearing next to nothing.

What else did we do? I was introduced to a lot more neighbours. We may have visited Marineland and admired the dolphin show. But we never went swimming in the deep blue sea. A pool perhaps, but not the sea.

One evening Mr. Heller, rubbing his hands vigorously, said he had a surprise for me: we three, without the children, would pay a visit to a jazz club. He knew that I liked such music. We motored down the hill and along the coast road to, I think, Manhattan Beach. I remember that these coastal communities back then were just rows of ramshackle huts and summer houses interspersed with bars and cafes.

Our jazz took place at The Rumble Seat, a narrow bar with a small stage. On it sat some very earnest white men with crew cuts in a uniform of striped shirt tucked into white trousers belted way above the belly button. This made their stomachs stick out but it was de rigueur at the time. What was I wearing? I can't remember. And who had been doing my washing since I'd left the Hurlbutts? Perhaps Mrs. Heller had obliged — and here am I poking fun at all these practical, sensible American women!

The jazz was strictly traditional, what is termed "Dixieland" in America. Trumpet, trombone, clarinet, banjo, drums and piano — all working hard at their own business but somehow starting and finishing together. Solos, rigidly ordered, were as rigidly applauded. I was experiencing an American ritual of a certain caste.

At intermission, repeating my New Orleans effrontery, I asked if I could play a little piano. Fine, fine. But when I started hacking out a slow blues in the Jimmy Yancey style one of the jazzmen, flushed and perspiring, clambered onto the stage and whispered loudly in my ear: "Boogie-woogie is off limits at The Rumble Seat." Oh, of course — I'm awfully sorry. But I was furious, puzzled and perplexed. This was the same earthy boogie-blues I'd performed to great acclaim recently in New Orleans. I was learning every day about the complexities of America.

Back in my room, amid all the neatness and sweet smells, I made a decision to skip the national parks that tourists raved about — Yellowstone, Yosemite. I could get more than enough trees and mountains and nature back in the British Isles. Instead I planned to take the bus up the coast to Seattle. Why Seattle? Another cousin of mine, another of Uncle John's children, had recently moved there: Anna Burningham. These cousins were more than relatives, they were pals of mine and we'd spent idyllic summers together on the Suffolk coast during the late 1950s. Anna had recently converted to Catholicism and had enrolled as a student at Seattle University where she could both learn and study her religion of choice among priests and nuns.

My Seattle trip would be a short one, I told the Hellers. I'd be back to spend more time with them and possibly get to the pleasures of the beach. (I must say, in retrospect, they were very hospitable people. I seemed to come and go as I please, without as much as a by-your-leave. But maybe I've forgotten some of the details of that 40-year-old summer. Maybe the storyteller is taking over).

On my chosen day Mr. Heller dropped me off on his way to work, and so here I was again in the dirty downtown of Los Angeles. The Greyhound for Seattle wasn't scheduled for hours so I set off for a wander. On my way to catch another triple bill at one of those shabby movie palaces on Broadway I spotted a pawnshop. More than that: I saw a good-looking ukulele in the window. It was brown and burnished and it needed me. I paid $45 dollars in traveler's cheques for this Martin, complete with cardboard case. I didn't know then that I'd bought the finest brand.

I was no stranger to the uke. Thanks to my Burningham cousins I had discovered the instant joys of the ukulele when, while staying at their home in North London, I'd found a discarded one, a mere toy but I soon got a sound out of it and by studying the diagrams in sheet music of the 1920s I learned a clutch of chord shapes. I played upside down because I'm left-handed and I strummed with the middle finger because that was how I'd strummed guitar at school. I soon found that the uke was a handy accompaniment to my singing of old songs, when there wasn't a piano about. Better still, you could roam around with the uke, you weren't stuck behind a keyboard set in hefty furniture, like a businessman at a desk. I was on the move and ready to win hearts, if not minds. This was my perfect entertainment vehicle. Already Jeremy and David, on motor trips into the Irish countryside, had enjoyed my renditions of comedy songs on a cheap uke picked up somewhere. But now I had a real one and it rang superbly.

The bus trip to Seattle took two and a half days. As usual I slept on the bus. I'll never forget Portland, Oregon because there, at the depot, I found a cafe that sold miniature pre-wrapped pecan pies and I stocked up on the delicious dainties. El Paso, Texas, you'll recall, had been the site of my initiation into the thrill of pecan pie.

Cousin Anna met me at the Greyhound station. She was as excited as I was to be here in the Great Northwest. We repaired to her digs, a big old house which she was sharing with other students. I remember that they all sang me some inspirational folk songs such as "This Little Light Of Mine" and we all joined in on the line, "I'm gonna let it shine!" Even me. There was an eager rectitude in the air and this was good because it kept me off thoughts of pecan pies and sex. I can't remember what Anna showed me in Seattle. I must have slept in her big student house. What I do know is that on the night before I was to return to Los Angeles my cousin told me she was going to take me to a place she knew I'd like.

We visited Pioneer Square, a once-disreputable part of the city (a section of Skid Row, I believe) but which had recently been taken over by students with their coffee houses and jazz and folk clubs. We descended into the basement of a heavy stone Victorian building to a club called "92 Yesler" where Anna introduced me to the managers, fellow Seattle University students Mick McHugh and Kip Toner. I also met the Angevine brothers, more Catholics, who had been entertaining on piano and bass. They wore sleeve garters and red vests. This was the uniform of Dixieland or honky tonk performers. It was just about closing time but, in my usual way, I soon found myself sitting at the piano and showing off some British music hall songs. The boys were impressed. "Say, would you like a job here?" demanded Mick McHugh, bright-eyed and bushy-tailed. Would I? Only a month or so in my land of dreams, in the country of show business and here I was being offered a job?

The upshot was that I traveled the two and a half days back to L.A., stayed with the Hellers a short time and then returned to take up my new position. Why didn't I simply remain in Seattle? Memory fails to hold the door. But for the last few weeks of my trip I entertained at "92 Yesler"as a curiosity, regaling audiences with ragtime songs at the piano and George Formby songs at the ukulele. I also told jokes. When the Angevine boys were doing their set of Scott Joplin rags, I worked in the kitchen heating up miniature pizzas. The Angevines lent me a multicolored vest so that I looked like a honky tonker but I also sang a few rock & roll numbers which the girls liked but the folkies disapproved of as commercial junk. At the time there was a folk movement afoot, a revival of roots music without dirt or suffering, songs about hard traveling sung by flaxen-haired student girls with their eyes shut, accompanying themselves on daintily strummed guitars. But the folkies weren't a big threat to me. Generally they were gentle souls. The wrath of Dylan & Co. was yet to come.

I was paid nothing but I got to stay for free on a couch in the basement of Mick McHugh's mansion on a hill where he lived with his parents. I became the McHugh's "boy" and as such was paraded around the district, playing for priest parties and drinking a lot of whiskey. Yes, I had the time of my life and never regretted spending my final weeks in basements rather than seeing Yosemite and Yellowstone. At the appointed time I met up with the members of our charter group in New York — I took the Greyhound across the country, stopping off in Idaho where I bought a letterman jacket embroidered with a big "I" (in my case standing for "Ian" and not "Idaho). In my luggage was a Seattle University sweatshirt and other items of American clothing such as plaid shirts. I'd always found American clothes to be very sexy, very masculine, like the men's magazines you'd see on every newsstand.

Jeremy and David must have returned on an earlier plane. There was no sign of them. The students on the plane had no interest in hearing about my great success at the coffee house. They were full of national parks and the beauty of San Francisco.

It was the same back in England. Of course, my mother was enthusiastic, as she always was. There had been a revolution in popular music while I was away. The whole country was in the grips of Beatlemania. I first encountered the phenomenon while riding a bus in London: the conductor looked at my Seattle University sweatshirt and said, "Wot's that then? *Seetle* University? You must mean Beatle!" I'd never heard of the group. Nor did I want to hear about them. I was full of America, of its country music and jazz and ragtime — even its folk music as sung by flaxen-haired girls. But everything was Beatle in Britain. I was glad to get back to Dublin for the winter term and a new digs with Jeremy and David: we had our own flat in Fitzswilliam Square, we were no longer lodgers. And there were exams to get prepared for and articles to write for the college magazine. My trip to America had fired up an ambition to return to America as an entertainer, to make my mark there. To this end I started a rhythm & blues band called "Bluesville" and eventually we were playing up a storm in Dublin. Next year I would return to Seattle at the request of Mick McHugh and Kip Toner: I would coast in on the fame of the Beatles and the other British Invaders; I would be encouraged to sing rock & roll as long as I kept up my accent. In 1964, in Seattle, I would get my first record contract and first 45 rpm release — recordings I had made in Dublin with Bluesville, in a basement. My life was based on basements it seems. In 1965 I would become a rock and roll star, a teenage idol — but that's another story and well-documented in at least two of my books.

Let us, finally, return to the winter of 1965: one November night I was walking up a Dublin street on my way to a gig in an Italian restaurant called Quo Vadis. The gig involved me on piano plus a drummer and a bass player. Just before I reached the venue I met up with the bass player, lugging his instrument up the hill. This was Chris Hart, fellow student. "Have you heard?" he asked breathlessly, "President Kennedy has been assassinated!"

My American summer had come full circle. When I returned next year to Seattle it was to a different society. My life since 1963 has been devoted to preserving and adding to the American culture that had drawn me there in the first place. From 1964 onwards the America I loved was under assault and I suppose I have become a fighting preservationist. I hope I haven't become a reactionary. I truly believe in the idea — my idea — of America.

SEPTEMBER

"Lotusland" has recently become a misnomer for where we live — but I'll leave the details till later.

Last month I concluded my memoir of the summer of 1963, when I first set foot in America. Forty years ago I'd started my showbiz career here, and never looked back. Almost every year from then on, until 1979 when I bought a house in Altadena and finally decided to settle in America, I visited, as a performer.

In 1966 I changed course from being a simple British Rock Invader to becoming an archivist and performer of Tin Pan Alley songs of heart and humor.

The transition point was in the summer of that year when I appeared at Doug Weston's Troubadour in West Hollywood: celebrated as a folk music bastion I was the first rocker to be invited to perform there. There was some fuss about this. But I had informed Mr. Weston that I would be dividing my act into two: part one would be my rock hits, part two would be Tin Pan Alley and Ragtime. "Where Did Robinson Crusoe Go With Friday On Saturday Night?" featuring my ukulele and raggy piano, had already been released and was in the local Top Twenty. I was on the path back into the past, forsaking rock and also the big money.

Just before starting the Troubadour gig I met a man who convinced me that this path was righteously correct: I met Ragtime Professor Dick Zimmerman at his birthday party at a ranch in the San Fernando Valley. To be precise, I heard Ragtime Dick. No one in the vicinity could escape hearing him: he was thundering out a piano rag called "Bric A Brac" by Maurice Porcelain and it was an experience. The whole house shook. At one stage Dickie rapped with his knuckles on the top of the poor piano. Afterwards I introduced myself and within seconds I was breathlessly informed about the rag, the composer and the instructions for knuckle-rapping. Dick was a proselytizer and what an impressive one! Next day I visited him in his one room apartment and as I consumed the sandwiches left over from the party he entertained me with more rags. His every other word concerned ragtime. I was hooked. Already I'd started collecting Tin Pan Alley sheet music of the ragtime years, already I'd started knocking out my own rags. Now I knew I was not alone. Now I was inspired.

So at The Troubadour I sailed into my sermon right after the rock hits. The teenage electric guitar band that was backing me melted away and there I sat at an upright piano ready to win over audiences to these grand old songs. David Hockney came. So did Christopher Isherwood. Hippies began attending, blown away by these strange songs, getting high to "Sadie Salome, Go Home!" and "A Lemon In The Garden Of Love." But the visitor I treasured the most was Ragtime Dick — who had come to check out my ragtime. His verdict was that I was on the right track but might need some help.

The help turned out to be an act — Whitcomb & Zimmerman, or was it Zimmerman & Whitcomb? Dick accompanied me on the rag songs and there was always a portion of the show when he pounded out some rags. From a high school gym we graduated over the years to clubs like The Ice House in Pasadena, to the Scott Joplin Festival in Sedalia, Missouri, to the Montreux Jazz Festival in Switzerland where we opened for Art Blakey & His Jazz Messengers (Dick put the Bosendorfer grand out of tune so that the Blakey band sounded distinctly honky-tonky). We made LPs and CDs, we made videos. Recently Dick moved from California to Illinois and I don't see so much of him. But — and here I come to the point — on Wednesday, September 13 Dick and I will be reunited at The Old Town Music Hall in El Segundo. There we will be taking a trip down Tin Pan Alley and reminiscing about our careers. Regina will be there to lend some class to the concert by singing sweetly.

Two days after the Music Hall show I will be appearing with my Bungalow Boys & Regina at the annual Vaudeville Extravaganza at The Alex Theatre in Glendale. We will be the headliners in a show that also stars a magician, a balloon man, a human calculator, and a visual comedian. The climax of our bit will be a sudden entrance by members of The King's Royal Rifles led by their commander, General Redvers-Buller. In full military uniforms they will march across the stage to-and-fro, flaunting their banners, and leading the audience in a chorus of their signature tune, "Hello! Hello! Hello!" I taught them this number because I am a member of their group, dining out as The London Club, where I attend in my character as Sir Ray Day, a vulgar Australian gold millionaire. Don't miss this event!

And now to the recent past: the days that I spent at The Oregon Festival Of American Music.

The days sped by — because every hour I was involved in some activity. And I loved it. I stayed at the same hotel as Dick Hyman, the Jazz Advisor to the festivals. Dick, of course, is one of the greatest living pianists and is also noted for his music to many of Woody Allen's films. I have worked with Dick several times over the years. We are an odd couple — yet we admire each other terrifically. This year he had me singing songs I've resisted in the past — too classy, too sophisticated, too Broadway. I mean Rodgers & Hart, Cole Porter.

But, like a good professional, I learned every word and every note and I'm proud that I did a disciplined job at the concerts. I also lectured to Elder Hostel folk on the history of Tin Pan Alley, and I took part in kiddie camps where I taught the little ones such British songs as "We All Went Up The Mountain," which involves them crouching and then stretching as they reach the mountain top. Then they all go down, down, down, down again.

And I took part in a teenage song and dance camp in which I became the kids' sergeant in a rousing version of "There Is Nothing Like A Dame." One teenage girl asked if I'd marry her. "Because of your neat accent!" Others clung onto my arm and my every word. I was in raptures. But I was also aware of being 62 years old and could be a grandfather if I'd so wished in days gone by.

They sang "Anything Goes." Can this jaundiced Cole Porter campery be the correct medicine for teenagers? Still, it's more literate than rap. Of course, you don't encounter much rap or hip-hop in Eugene, Oregon. This is a healthy city, surrounded and protected by clean green mountains and a rushing river. Everyone is keen and clean and shakes their head sadly when I tell them I live in Los Angeles. It's a Nirvana up there in Oregon, safe from alarm......

On my last day I climaxed a concert salute to African-American songwriters with a couple of Chuck Berry songs. How thrilling it was to have Dick Hyman and his Class A jazz musicians pounding and honking to rock & roll! The teenage girls from the Song & Dance Camp screamed kindly from the balcony. I shimmied and shook. I felt like a rock star again.

As an encore I leapt off the stage and ran into the audience and then out a side door to a waiting car which whisked me to the airport so that I could catch my late afternoon plane back to Los Angeles, dread city.

The last time I made such an exit was in 1965 at the Cow Palace in San Francisco at the end of a show I did with The Beach Boys. In that case the limousine actually drove up to the stage. We all piled in and raced off, pursued by teenagers.

And so, with some trepidation, I arrived back at LAX and was soon in the car with Regina and Rollo, the Dog. Trepidation — because I had heard from Regina by phone, while I was in Eugene, that all hell had broken loose around our house (I would love to say "home"). Almost immediately after I'd left they went on the rampage. Regina hadn't informed me at once because, kind soul, she didn't want to spoil my work at the Festival.

You've heard in previous Letters about our neighbours From Hell. I hope none of you ever has to suffer this endless agony. You're so helpless because the authorities can't act until an actual crime has been committed — like, say, murder.

The troubles started in earnest last year and they have gone on every so often since then. We do nothing to cause the trouble. All we do in our lives is try to spread a little happiness with music and dance. I have never encountered evil before but here it is, unyielding and unreasoning, right next door to us. We are accused of doings we haven't done. Why? Because there is a crazed Iranian woman next door to us who has it in for Regina.

Objects are tossed over our fence while Regina is quietly tending to her flowers. One hot Sunday afternoon early in the year a miniature whiskey bottle flew over and landed near Regina. Acting on the advice of the neighbour husband (in friendlier days) she tossed it back. Immediately his bilious face appeared over the fence and from it came a hoarse scream: "IANNNNN !" I rushed from my desk in the far side of the house so stentorian and crazed was his voice. "That woman just threw a bottle at us!

From behind him a foreign accent screamed even louder: "She try to murder me!"

Sheriffs were summoned. Unfortunately, the neighbours intercepted them first. And so it was that a sheriff came to our house and told us that if the bottle had struck the Iranian and blood had been spilled then Regina would have been hauled off to jail. But he did admit later that the woman appeared deranged. He advised security cameras, Restraining Orders. It sounded like the usual list they reel off to warring neighbours. It sounded like they deal with this kind of trifle every day. "Now we have to go deal with real crimes like burglary and gangs," said the cop in parting.

Here's another incident: a few months ago, the Iranian woman came rushing up to our door accusing Regina of stealing a note to the gardeners. So loosely was it attached to their grim iron gates that it easily blew off and into our driveway where Regina, thinking it to be litter, tossed it into our garbage can. Then Regina drove off to join her brother and his family on their vacation in Mammoth — leaving me to guard the fort. I tried to reason with her the woman but she just spewed out uncontrollably. How would Lawrence of Arabia have dealt with such people? An irrational culture, one steeped in revenge and blood feuds and tribalism......

Her parting words were a threat: "You need to control your wife, like they do where I come from! If you do not—-we have many guns and we will revenge ourselves, like they do where we come from!" When the Anglo husband came home from work I managed to have a word with him. He's a stooping harried-looking man, but can be a reasoning soul; he once used to accept our offers to dine out; he once used to enjoy videos of my films and recordings of my songs. He let me enter the house — a sort of twin barracks from the outside but clean and neat inside. Why there was even a piano. A copy of *Ukulele Heaven*, one of my Mel Bay songbooks lay on the floor nearby. And they do have two sweet dogs.

He assured me, with his eyes firmly closed, that there'd be no shooting. We shook hands. I tried to win their hearts by singing "The Woody Woodpecker Song" to their three-year-old adored son (also known as "Mowgli" because of his blood-curdling screams and also the tosser of the objects that sail over our fence). I hoped that the matter was settled. But no......In fact, the Anglo husband soon joined the Revenge Team........

On the Sunday before I left for Oregon I was in the bedroom, packing, when Regina came in crying. She had been in our backyard tending to her plants when she heard loud voices, intended for her hearing, from over the fence. Our neighbours: "Lubricate the shotguns and the automatics!"said the husband.

"We can put a gun turret on the garage roof so then I will have a good view of them" said the Iranian.

I went out back to see if I would witness this madness. Yes, within minutes I got a whiff of the hate speak: "Lubricate! Lubricate! All the guns! And we got a lot!" Still hoping for the best, looking at the bright side through rose-colored glasses, I told myself that maybe this was their idea of noir humor, a bad joke. Maybe the police had told them that we'd heard talk of an arsenal.

Regina, though, spoke to the Sheriffs station. There's nothing we can do, they said. You see, anybody can say anything they like in the confines of their backyard. Amendment rights, Constitution, Free Speech and so forth. They can have guns galore and say whatever they like. A Free Country. Democracy............

Next day, my wife drove me to L. A. airport so that I could get to the Festival. And while I was having the time of my life in Eugene there was poor Regina at home under constant attack. They had been waiting for me to leave. Months ago, when they actually communicated with me, they had told me that they had nothing against me. Oh no. It's Regina they're fixated on.

Because it's Regina who won't take their bullying. I had been trying to play the Gandhi, the non-confrontational one. It wasn't working. It never works with bullies. I should have been Kevin Costner in *Open Range*. But I am a uke player, and an avoider of action. A coward?

Anyway, to return to when I was swanning about in Oregon: Regina had taken the precaution of inviting her sister and nephew to stay while I was away. But that didn't stop the Iranian.

While the sister was out for a few hours the Iranian took action. Lurking in her black sedan behind a street corner, she waited till Regina was driving her nephew up the main street. Then she struck: suddenly the Iranian's Volvo came hurtling down the street straight towards my wife and the boy. Just in time Regina swerved and thus narrowly avoided a nasty "accident."

Again: a police report: "Attempted murder." No witnesses proper. No evidence. So no action.

Another time: the Anglo husband returned home from work — their driveway is slap bang right next to ours — got out of his car and started hurling obscenities at Regina, who was working on the roses. Next he was throwing rocks at the side of our house. Clearly, the Iranian had phoned to tell some lies to him about misdeeds by my wife and thus he was in a fury. Again the cops were helpless. You have to have witnesses, evidence. Get tape recorders, security cameras, Restraining Orders. Get them. So long.

Restraining orders yet again. What worries me about having one of these documents served by a marshal is that such an act could send our neighbours off the deep end and into our house with guns blazing. Or am I wrong? Please tell me if I'm wrong. Please.

However, I'm not a complete action-shunning wimp. I've promised my wife we will install video cameras that will sweep our fences and driveway night and day, day and night, like a prison or a filthy rich person's gated estate.

The pity of it all! When I've lived in sweet Altadena for almost thirty years without wars. And now neighbours seek to destroy our life. Yes, we've asked our realtor to look for another house. You see, the Iranian won't give up — she calls the cops regularly on fantasy complaints. They are obliged to respond and make a report. And so these lies pile up at the sheriff's station and we look bad. Soon perhaps some judge will believe them and grant a Restraining Order against us.

Is there no justice in this country except the vigilante kind? Of course, I will be stoic and obey the law. Funnily enough — if there is any humour in this — when I tell friends about our troubles they cap me with worse tales concerning their own neighbours from Hell. For example, we've recently become friendly with a great couple who've moved into a house on the corner.

They lived in England for over a decade and there, in my supposedly peaceful homeland, it was necessary for them to have surveillance cameras due to the constant burglary attempts. The husband was even mugged and stabbed near his London house. Actually, I'm not surprised: most of my British friends have been robbed and mugged at some time. Then there's our D.A friend who told us a horror story about Saudi Arabian thugs with too much money who took over a house in his Beverly Hills neighbourhood and terrorized families for two years. Again, no help from cops.

You have to catch them at it. You have to be the cops. Because the real cops are engaged in sexier crimes like murder. In this case, eventually the I.N.S., tipped off by my D.A friend, deported most of the thugs. The rest flew off in their Ferraris for greener fields of terror.

Well, I'm now getting too hot under the collar. I'd better stop.

But what can be done? Any ideas. Have any of you experienced the use of Restraining Orders? Are they effective? Or do they only provoke and lead to worse things? I'd like to hear from you....

Exasperatedly,
Sadly,
Ian

POSTSCRIPT: Regina had a good idea — try writing a cool, calm, and conciliatory letter to the husband. In days past he used to be so civil. On July The Fourth I wished him a "Happy Fourth of July" and he wished me back.

So I composed the following letter and mailed it a few days ago. No response. On Labor Day we noticed that they'd installed their own video surveillance camera — pointing, it seems, at our driveway. We wave and do a little dance as we alight from our car. The day after Labor Day — today — I caught the husband slinking off to work. He saw me and before I could say, "Hello!" he smiled and said, "Hi, Ian!" Amazing. "Did you get my letter?" I asked. "Yes — very nice." "Shall we have that drink soon?" "Yes." This is a breakthrough, I feel. I'm always the optimist. But we're still in the market for a new house.

Tunefully, perhaps,
Ian

And now, the letter...

August 27, 2003.

Dear Harold,

You have been our neighbour — and I like to believe our friend — for several years. When you first moved in we invited you to a restaurant dinner and you came and we had a good time. Subsequently, you attended one of my Monday night gatherings at Mijares restaurant and, again, we had a very pleasant evening.

You had a sweet dog, Jimmi, and we had that poor old Inspector. Sometimes they barked too much and we notified each other in a friendly way. We both wanted to be good neighbours. When Inspector got hit by a car and was wandering around the driveway, your wife very kindly notified us. When Regina's father died suddenly — we heard the news the very morning of 9/11 — you sent us a touching condolence card.

I lent you videos of some of my movies and you enjoyed them. I gave you CDs of my music in the hope that you and your family would get a kick out of them. I knew you had a piano and that you were fond of music. We'd sometimes commiserate with each other about the loud rap or hip-hop booming from across the street.

When Jimmi died I gave you a CD song I'd written about Inspector's death hoping that it might give you some consolation. I once even played "The Woody Woodpecker Song" on your piano — and Jason seemed quite taken by it!

We have watched Jason grow, becoming a fun and lively little boy. He and Regina have shared many songs ("I'm A Little Teapot," etc.) through the fence. He's even started calling out "Rollo!" and he's always shouted a warm "Hi!" to us.

There have been differences, I'll admit, but I believe each one was dealt with on a one-to-one basis.

In short, I hoped that we were becoming good neighbours and even friends.

But over the last few months relations have deteriorated. At times, the sheriffs have been called. This is a pity because it would have been better if cooler heads had prevailed and we'd simply told each other face-to-face what was bothering us. In an attempt to get to the bottom of any problems you might have with us we arranged a session with the Pasadena branch for Dispute Resolution. We were so disappointed when the meeting couldn't materialize.

Harold, we really would like to make a fresh start as neighbours.

If there are issues you have with us then we'd like to know about them and work them out and solve them. Let's try to work out a way of living next door to each other in an amicable manner.

I realize that there's very little space between our houses — and that living almost on top of each other may lead to irritations and annoyances. We'd like to find a way of living so that both our privacies are not disturbed. I'm sure we can do it. We want to be at peace with you and your family.

So, at your convenience, let's talk. Maybe you'd like to come and have a drink with me — or even a meal — at a local restaurant, like we did in the old days. Please let me know.

All we want is to be good neighbours and we're sure you do too.

Sincerely,
Ian and Regina Whitcomb

****

On reflection, perhaps I should have used the American spelling of "neighbour" as in "neighbour." I hate to do this but I must. I live in America and will therefore do as the natives do and talk American from now on, to the best of my ability.

OCTOBER

Editor's Note:

There was no entry for October — when Ian would have been looking back, as was his way, on the month before — because the neighbour turmoil was taking up too much time and also taking a heavy toll on his equipoise, which has never been in the best of balance even at the best of times.

However, rather than leave the reader in a cliff-hanging situation (wondering, for instance, whether neighbour Hodge ever did take up Ian's offer of a drink and a meal) we have decided to fill in the gap by giving you selected samples from his journal for that awful September. These journals, dashed off in barely legible longhand in the heat of the moment, are kept deep in the bowels of the Huntington Library, strictly off-limits; they are not normally exposed to the world in all their brute nakedness. But, after considerable rumination on our part, and with Ian's permission, here we go...

Wednesday September 3
The Hodge security camera, recently installed, is bothering Regina. She calls it a spy camera and says it's trained on our driveway. So what? We've nothing to hide. And if Kaleem dreams up any more of our 'crimes' she'll have to prove them in court with actual tapes.

Regina packed for a visit to her sister and husband in San Diego. "This business is exhausting me," she said as she left. "I'd like you to start looking for another house." I said I would and at once.

Total earnings for August were $8,830. Not bad.

Friday September 5
Helicopters hovering over the house woke me at 6am. Usual villains, I supposed. Later I went out to take a look. I heard a rattling at the front gate: a deputy sheriff trying to serve some papers. He was most apologetic. What was it? "A Restraining Order, sir," he said with a wan smile and left hastily. They're titled "A Request To Appear At A Court Process" and are addressed to Regina Whitcomb. Not to me. The work of the Hodges no doubt. But the Order can't take effect till it's actually served on Regina.

Dutifully, I called San Diego. Regina wasn't around. Her sister said, "Good—this means Regina can have her day in court!" But the Hodges have aced us again: first the camera and now court papers. I always felt neither would do any good—only exacerbate the situation.

Happened later to catch Hodge at his front gate. What has my wife done exactly? "She's been calling us at all hours." But your number is blocked. "She calls from Sacramento." She hasn't been there. "The calls have stopped since the process began." But the process only began this morning. (I was following him like a dog, as he moved from spot to spot). "The sheriffs told us to do this" (Yes, they told us to do this too—but I took no action). And the camera—what is it trained on? "You and your movements." He's so shifty—won't look you straight in the eye. How on earth could

Charles Sprawson, my TCD friend who used to visit me here in the good old days, describe this miserable shrimp as resembling James Dean?

These realtors are fast workers. Two tidy young men arrived at noon and started inspecting pronto. The spokesman, highly scented, pronounced the house "charming" while his associate bounced on the leather sofa. "This'll go for as high as five and a quarter." He wants an immediate Open House. In return he'll find us the "Dream House Of Our Choice."

Called Regina in the afternoon and she told me to leave off selling the house for the time being. She also said she's not stepping inside our house again till we get a Restraining Order against the Hodges. And a security camera. Promised to do all this.

Saturday September 6

This has been one of the worst days of my life. When at last I managed to speak to Regina—she's been evading my calls—she informed me that as a result of my not standing up to the Hodges, of letting them trample all over us, march across our fences while I behave like Neville Chamberlain, we may well split up. That's why she's told me to put a hold on any house hunt or sale. Later she e-mailed me to say that she'll be staying in hotels till the day of our court hearing. No process server will get her till after we serve them first. Thus she won't be appearing at the Vaudeville show because I stupidly included an announcement of our appearance in the soft-soap, beseeching letter I sent Hodge last month.

She's disgusted by my cringing. She's probably right. I can't bear conflict, except when watching it on the screen. I can't bear not to be liked. And if I go to war with the Hodges then I'll be their enemy as well.

After consultation with a female psychologist friend, who surmised that Regina is feeling victimized and unsafe and therefore needs protection, and needs to have her fears allayed, I e-mailed her to that effect. Then I took a Valium, washed down with Jack Daniels, and stroked the ever-faithful Rollo for ages. And so to bed.

Sunday September 7

On the ride to the Cantalini's gig Dave, the bassist, said he thought I'd have been good as a telephone salesman. A compliment, I suppose, as he used to be one himself. Arriving early we both took separate walks by the ocean. The waves made me feel better. In our corner of the restaurant we played sweetly, my accordion fingering accurate and crisp. Every table paid attention and applauded. Tip bowl was crammed.

At home there was an e-mail from Regina: "Hit the Hodges with everything you've got!" She added: "Hugs & Kisses!"

Thursday September 11
With help from a retired judge friend I've written up a Restraining Order request that is pretty hot stuff — with such headings as "VANDALISM" and "ASSAULT WITH A DEADLY WEAPON." In the Ethnicity section I described Kaleem as "Arabic." As is my right I'd been allowed to read in advance the Hodges petition for their Order — so I have a bead on them. Their complaints are ludicrous: we are racists because we stuck a British flag in a bottle in our driveway (this was in fact a way to. identify our house to guests coming to a party); we have a dangerous dog who threatens their baby (the boy adores Rollo); we don't pay taxes, and we are providing shelter to a runaway terrorist called Simon (the name of our cat). How could the judge grant the Hodges an Order based on this nonsense? What is American justice coming to?

At Pasadena Courthouse, after sitting in silence to commemorate the dead of 9/11, the female judge granted me a Temporary Restraining Order. This means Kaleem can't come within a few feet of us without being arrested. I was very pleased. The court hearing is set for October 1. The Hodges process servers haven't yet managed to trap Regina. This Order cost me $260. This was offset by a cheque for $4000 for use of my songs in a documentary about burlesque.

Friday September 12
At 6.45 am Rollo's barks woke me. I saw a sheriff at our gate. I hid. The phone rang twice. I ignored it. Next I spied Kareem, in nightclothes, accepting something from a sheriff. She opened it. She read. "What the fuck is this!" Then she turned and screamed: "Harooooold!" God I felt good.

Sunday September 14
The price I have to pay for telling my troubles to people is that they counter with neighbour stories worse than mine. One woman told me about a neighbour who objected to her new puppy's barking and crying. Next thing the woman came home from work to find the headless corpse of the puppy on her front door mat. She moved to a different State.

Those who have never had such trouble advise, "Hire a hit man!" and laugh. I could kill them. Speaking of killing, I met a man at our local coffee house who offered his gang of vigilantes, all fully accredited ex-cops or FBI agents. What could they do? "You name it, buddy!" I paid for his bagel and left.

Wednesday September 17

My old friend and ragtime colleague Dick Zimmerman is here from Illinois to appear with me at the Old Town Music Hall in El Segundo, by the sea, near Cantalini's.

Amazingly the present turmoil—I can't eat much and my stomach grumbles—played no part in the show. Or maybe the situation acted as a palliative. At any rate, I did one of my best performances. Songs like "Settle Down In A One Horse Town" held new meaning for me—escape from the city's strife. And "In The Land Of Beginning Again," a 1918 Tin Pan Alley number, had me forgiving and forgetting even the Hodges. On my own song, "Dreams" I almost broke down. Is this sentimentality at work? Or just plain sentiment? I was thrilled to see Noel Harrison (Rex's son) with Van Dyke Parks in the audience. Had a drink with them later. Made $1000 in cash.

Thursday September 18
Saw Regina again! We met at her hotel in Pasadena. She was having a swim in the pool when I arrived. At first it was a little sticky but later we found common ground in her showing me how to use the new cell phone I've bought—on her advice, for more security. I also bought a video camera and tape recorder in order to capture evidence. She gave me notes on the clothes and shoes she wants me to bring her from home. To my distress I realize I've never touched her clothes or shoes before. They're in another part of the house.

Monday September 22
Kaleem, immaculate in black business suit, ignored me while I was in our driveway watering the roses. She strode up her driveway head in air. She didn't look crazy, she looked professional. Rather frightening.

First night of the Salon at a new location. Bona Corso's food too stodgy and getting more expensive. The noise from the indoor fountain drives me to distraction. The new place, Conrad's Family Restaurant and Cocktail Lounge, is across the street. Cheap—it's basically a coffee shop with a liquor license. We had a good showing tonight and, thankfully, the Right Wing salonists stayed away. So everyone, except me, could indulge in some Bush-bashing. Personally, I'm apolitical.

Wednesday September 24
Regina has moved to a motel called The Glendale Lodge. We arranged to meet there in the evening to watch a TV political debate in her room. Rollo I kept in the back of the Honda for her to pet on our way to dinner. I brought wine and cashews with me.

The motel is not exactly prepossessing. In a row of similar

nondescript motels this one distinguishes itself with a Swiss hunting lodge motif. Lots of curly wood and what look like gargoyles. The desk clerk is Asian. Little English at his command. Next to the elevator there's an Alma Tadema print. I felt like striking up a conversation about Tadema with the clerk but thought better of it. Regina on the third floor.

 She sat red-eyed at a small round table. Her only books are a Buddhist history and "Real Estate For Dummies." I spotted several packets of those dry noodle meals you heat up in seconds in a microwave. She has one. And a tiny fridge and tiny TV. During the TV debate she fell asleep. Eventually we got to the nearby Ernie's Taco House. She perked up while telling me how my uncle's songs, "Let's All Sing Like The Birdies Sing," is played every day in the Tiki Room at Disneyland. She's always loved Disneyland. And she told how, while at The Lodge, she's watched all of a 5 hour PBS documentary and was surprised to learn that Britain had its own holocaust when Edward II launched an attack on the country's Jews. I had no idea. A pleasant evening on the whole. A ray of light perhaps.

Friday September 26

Regina continues to stay at her Lodge. Went to Ralph's supermarket and bought the Nippon food and Odwalla Wellness juices that she's requested. Also: People magazine because it has a feature on her favourite TV show, Friends.

 It always feels strange going up to her motel room, passing that smirking desk clerk. Regina insists on referring to the upcoming Restraining Order hearing as a "Trial." When will this all end and we can return to normalcy?

 Coming home I played a tape of Tom Leamore singing his late 19th Century song, "Percy From Pimlico," a shabby-genteel number, and decided it's a masterpiece. Something rather sinister about it. Wonder what his home life was like.

Monday September 29

Audition in The Valley at Zydeco Studios—for a Swiss pastille company. Actors paired off as Lords or Butlers. As usual one Brit came dressed in complete butler outfit. I was picked as a Lord. Did my scene with a Brit whose last name is Brigadier. His real name. The commercial shoots in Switzerland. Fingers crossed.

 Met Regina at her Lodge. Always feel like a John visiting a Tart when I pass that awful desk clerk. His smirk grows worse day by day. Regina has been perusing her Buddhist literature. She asked what the word "Enlightenment" means to me. I improvised— I said I get my spirituality through my music. Felt a bit glib. She came with me to the Salon at Conrad's and was chatty. Very pleased with such *progress.*

Tuesday September 30

Regina in a blue mood when I visited her tonight—the night before "The Trial." She kept saying that Kaleem had invaded and violated her space, all the while with that empty dull look, staring past me at some distant mysterious other place.

She didn't feel like eating but I had brought take-out spaghetti and a bottle of red wine. We pretended to dine, sitting at her little round table near the growing pile of Buddhist books. Watched Larry King interviewing Royal watchers of the two princes. All the calls were from women. At 7pm she said she needed to be alone. Didn't even want to visit with Rollo who was in the back seat of the Honda.

In the parking lot there was no sign of the car. Gone. Exploring, in a panic and yet feeling my fate justified, I finally found the Honda in a street behind the Lodge—jacked up on a tow truck. Rollo was nearby, tied to a railing, tail wagging, lucky dog. Suddenly a van appeared with a sign reading "Animal Control." What was happening?

The officials, big men in T-shirts, explained that the desk clerk had reported my car as not belonging to any registered guest and therefore had called for its removal.

I had arrived in the nick of time—the Honda would have been impounded and Rollo taken to a shelter and possibly destroyed. I sweet-talked the officials into going away. Then I marched into the Lodge and up to the front desk. I gave that wretch a piece of my mind. Hadn't he got to know me over the week that Regina had been staying there and I had been visiting her? Hadn't he smirked many times at me? I called him a piece of Eastern filth, an uncivilized shit from a dark and unenlightened part of the world. Then I exploded so I don't know what else I added. He said, "No comprenez" and smiled. I felt bad.

I drove carefully home as I considered my good fortune. Just in time to watch a terrific documentary on PBS about Blues in Memphis. Wads of great gospel music. Early to bed—for to-morrow's trial. Took a Valium.

Before falling asleep I wondered how I'd taken this strange trail from Bryanston School and the lush Dorset countryside of Thomas Hardy, through Olde Worlde Dublin and studies in general Medieval History and monks in particular, to end up on a street in Alien Glendale begging for dog and car. Had I taken a wrong turning at some stage of the game? Or was I rightly clinging to the cliff top, determined to stay a part of the main, of the continent of mankind?

Involved ....

Wednesday October 1

CASE: WHITCOMB Versus HODGE

My friend The Ex-Judge accompanied us to the Pasadena Courthouse. He and I flanked Regina, walking in lock step, carrying heavy briefcases. We were prepared.

At 8.30 am the doors opened and we, together with the shabby crew (except for the shiny, chatty lawyers), filed in to be searched and patted. Regina finally accepted being served the Temporary Restraining Order papers ordered up by Hodge. Didn't matter. We were prepared. We'd win. Their case would be all moot soon. Maybe the Hodges wouldn't show. But they did—at the last minute. A small courtroom; we were uncomfortably close to them. He was reading a copy of "Nature" magazine. Can he be all that bad? She was in black.

Woman judge—actually she's really just a commissioner—was friendly, sympathetic, and dumpy. We sat there till noon and she didn't get to our case. Instead we witnessed sad divorces, child custody cases, bankruptcy. There were silent tears from a tiny Asian woman. I felt sorry for everyone. The commissioner listened intently, never in a rush. Regina was buoyant— humming, sketching cartoons, passing me notes about how we'd celebrate later.

Lunch break was announced. The commissioner asked whether, for convenience sake, we'd combine with the Hodge Versus Whitcomb case, scheduled to be heard on October 16. Yes, that would be convenient, I thought. A chapter could be closed. But Regina was adamant: no. Perhaps, continued the kindly co-missioner, both cases can be heard this afternoon. Regina: No. In that case, we will re-convene at 1.45pm. Kaleem Hodge protested she couldn't make that time. Then you'll be in default, she was told.

We walked in a sprightly manner to lunch at Marston's, a lawyer hangout. Our ex-judge friend knew a lot of the customers. Regina struck up a conversation with the next table. I picked up the bill.

Back at the courthouse Regina was very merry, even executing little vaudeville time steps.

But there they were again—the bloody Hodges. I was called up to the desk where I adjusted the microphone in a professional manner. I like mikes and they like me. I might even enjoy this—in the spirit of a gig, a concert. A show. I read out my complaints. Then Kaleem was called. "I am not an Arab," she screamed. I had written "Arabic" in the ethnicity box of the papers. "Get your geography right!" she spat at me. "But you certainly have an Arabic complexion," said the kindly commissioner.

From then on Kaleem, under oath, lied and lied: she'd never threatened me with being shot; they keep no guns; she'd never aimed her car at my wife; she'd never done anything bad, it is us who are the racists. And when she has her time in court she will bring policemen and "confidential files" that will tell of our misdeeds, you wait and see.

Decision: The commissioner ruled that the Whitcombs have no evidence and therefore she must refuse us a Restraining Order.

As the Hodges left Kaleem came close to Regina and hissed: "Ha!" And sashayed out.

Regina was silent. Then she pronounced herself to be "devastated." She was silent in the car. Silent when we got home. At least she was home. I persuaded her to dine at our favourite Mexican restaurant, the one where we had got engaged. She agreed.

After Regina had gone to bed I watched another in the PBS Blues series—Willie Dixon singing "N-Nervous," the song I "borrowed" from him and made into a Top 50 hit in 1965.

NOVEMBER

There has been an ominous gap in the letters: October was missing. You know what was happening prior to October: Regina and I were having the worst time of our lives, dealing with the neighbour problem. Thanks to all of you who sent sympathy letters — and told me stories of your troubles that made ours seem pale in comparison. I won't recount all the horrible details — suffice it to say that, after two court battles, there is no Restraining Order hovering over poor Regina's head. She is home and no longer has to hide in motels. Eventually I had realized that we needed to hire a professional — a lawyer. In our second court appearance we were represented by a lady attorney who was tough and to the point: the temporary Restraining Order was lifted and we got a "continuance" so that we could make our neighbours come to dispute resolution sessions or else. The judge also agreed to consider our requests for all costs at this next and last court session in February, 2004. This had our neighbours rattled: they don't like to be confronted by a clear daylight matter. They are dark as night people, scurrying from the light of truth. They love to lie. Thus far they have refused to attend any hearing about the dispute. So in February we're hoping the judge will throw out their request for a Restraining Order and give us our costs. These costs have been considerable. Our house now resembles a prison camp: security camera and monitor, floodlights; we carry cameras and a tape recorder. But the main point is that

Regina is home and getting back to her old self. Of course, we'll never be really safe until these people move — or we move.

Meanwhile, through all this turmoil, I have been trying to bring home the bacon: oddly enough, my work hasn't been held up at all. I've done concerts and shows, I've completed an article on the 40th anniversary of The British Invasion that will be published early next year in *Hemispheres*, the magazine of United Airlines. I've acted in a radio play based on a Ray Bradbury short story; film and TV companies continue to license my music. The dog Rollo — named in our wicked neighbour's complaint as a "vicious dog" — thrives and is the love of our street. Actually, one of the good things that has come out of our troubles is that we have become friends with almost all our neighbours — so the baddies are surrounded. Why even their adopted son loves Rollo and likes to say his name, to the consternation of his father and mother. What feeds hatred?

DECEMBER

I shall be glad to see the back of this year. Due to hostilities on the neighbour front, which have changed our lives forever, Stalag 17 blazes nightly. We carry a tape recorder, as well as still and video cameras whenever we leave the house.

Does life for you seem to get worse and worse as you get older? I am daily full of dread that something awful is going to happen. When I was younger that foreboding never came to me. In fact, I remember a wonderful moment when I was a student at Trinity College, Dublin and I had what I think is called an "epiphany" in the middle of some dull constitutional history class: I looked around and in a flash realized I knew THE TRUTH about everything. And the truth felt good. But what the truth actually was I never learnt. Anyhow, the only time I feel safe is when I'm at our athletic club and sitting in the Jacuzzi, or wrapped up in bed with a glass of wine at my side and a biography of Bill Haley, or — as I will be tonight — sipping my vodka martini at Conrad's family restaurant in Pasadena, waiting for the fun of our weekly Monday night salon to begin.

This year has had no big work. No movies, no new book writing. And yet I've made money — off shows and concerts it seems. However, next year I intend to shut myself away at my Huntington basement desk and write that book. About what? That's the problem.

Well, I suppose that's it for this month. I must get back to work finishing off the script for the audio channel on the 40th Anniversary of the British Invasion which will be narrated by me and available as in-flight entertainment on United Airlines starting in February.

Ta ta for now and see you next year. And thanks for all your attention and feedback.

PS: We have decided to motor up to the Dickens Fair in San Francisco. This is not normally an event I should care to be involved with — I fear that, like the Renaissance Faire, I will be assaulted by Americans attempting Ye Olde English accents and superannuated hippies in tights and bodices — but Regina wants to go and take part in the dancing and, besides, our dear friends from The London Club have taken a booth or site or something. Renditions of British Music Hall songs are promised and I dread that — and rather resent it as I haven't been invited to sing any. Anyway, my point is that on the way up to the Bay area we will be stopping in at Santa Cruz so that I can be the guest of the Ukulele Club of Santa Cruz. I shall sing and strum and plug my songbooks.

Hello ... Regina here. I would also like to add a few words to this month's letter.

You've all been so kind and supportive through the neighbour ordeal and I appreciate it so much. I can only hope that the woman next door is getting the help she needs and she doesn't erupt again. We still look at houses but it's not proving easy.

We're all in good health. Rollo and Simon (dog and cat) are so much fun. Three days ago Ian got his fingers twisted into Rollo's collar. There was a lot of noise — Ian was shouting because he couldn't break loose. Simon dashed across the house, jumped up on the table and started slapping Rollo. This made Rollo behave immediately and Ian could regain his composure.

Lastly, Ian and I went to see The Haunted Mansion last night. I think he mentioned that I had danced in the film last April. Well! Although the dance scene appears in the commercial and previews — it's not in the film! I love this town. Where else can you be under contract with a major studio, work with hundreds of talented people, get paid (and fed) handsomely and have it end up on the editing floor? Maybe we'll see it in the DVD release of 'extra material' ...

Happy Holidays. Celebrate yours. Good health to you!
CHEERS!

125

2004

JANUARY

2004 — it looks right and I'm determined it'll be a better year for us than last year. I mean, we had, as you know, our own war right next door. And it hasn't been resolved — like Israel, we never know when the next terror attack is coming. In a microcosm we have the Middle East a few feet from us.

At present, all is quiet: the security camera records night and day life on our front drive: a black & white image that has a spookiness: nothing seems to happen but every day Regina reviews the tape in the VCR which sits in our kitchen. At night floodlights snap on and our perimeters are lit up like a prison camp.

A few weeks ago our 74-year-old carpenter erected a very high fence in our backyard, so high we'll now never be able to see the folks who live next door again — unless we get on the roof, which I do from time to time — only to clean out leaves from the rain gutter, you understand. Of course, we do sometimes have to pass within a few feet of them because our driveway parallels theirs and there's only their tall and vulgar wrought iron fence between us and them. That's when — providing I'm not there — they scowl at Regina and sometimes give her the finger and say, "Fuck you!" They never do it to me. Oh no, when they see me they scurry like rats.

We still hear those bloodcurdling sounds — the pathetic screams and crying of the adopted child, Mowgli. He still — even at age 5 — can't speak in sentences. He mutters and shrieks and the rest. But he's essentially a good kid and loves our dog Rollo (described as a "vicious animal" by the Iranian woman in her court complaint against Regina), calling out plaintively, "Oller! Oller!" which is better than "Allah! Allah!" I suppose. The cries when the boy is left outside on cold nights are really chilling, and we've recorded great sad stretches of them. But will we call the child abuse services? I don't think so somehow.

Our third, and I hope our final, day in court is on February 24, my late mother's birthday. This is the day the Iranian chose after postponing month after month with no good reason. On the 24th the woman's baseless demand for a Restraining Order against my wife will be finally thrown out. Last time we were in court our lawyer got the judge to agree that this matter should be resolved at a Dispute Resolution meeting — something we'd tried to set up early last year and at which the neighbours, having agreed to attend, failed to show up. The judge has now ordered that they attend but — what do you know? — the husband told the Dispute Resolution people that his wife — the one who accuses Regina of phoning her every 15 minutes for four years — has suddenly developed "cancer" and is too ill to attend. Too ill? We see her striding down the driveway, dressed up to the nines, pulling open the big wrought iron gates, closing them, and sailing off at speed in her black sedan, the same car that she drove at Regina last August in her attempt to kill my wife. Is there no end to this lying and cheating? Every time I read in the newspaper about middle easterners and their anti-westerner propaganda — their refusal to face the truth — I'm reminded of our situation next door.

Enough of this! I get carried away and start sliding into a hate state where I condemn all of those beyond the pale of my own western culture, of my gentle English upbringing. In court, when I was trying to stop the Iranian's campaign against my wife, the woman had the nerve to accuse us of racism — because we had put two small flags — one was the Union Jack and the other was The Stars And Stripes — in a bottle and placed the object at the end of our driveway because we wanted to tell some out-of-town friends the location of our house. This is a family custom originating with my late mother who used to place a milk bottle, with a Union Jack stuck in it, outside the back door of our flat in London to welcome me home from America. Since the first time I brought Regina to meet my mother she'd always included an American flag as well. One of the few things I brought over here after my mother's death were those flags. Regina has continued the family tradition. And this, pronounced the Iranian in court to the judge, is racism!

I must attend to the New Year. 2004 — it looks good, as I say. Of course, as in past years, I face January with absolutely no work in sight. Will I ever get another job? No movie music, no club dates, no book commissions. And yet, this time around I'm feeling calm and collected. I can always go to my Huntington Library desk and start writing that great novel I keep promising. Maybe I should make a book on the lines of Proust. A thinly disguised memoir, fat slices of my life. After all, that's all I know and even that I find hard to understand.

There are a few regular ports in the story sea of my life. Every Monday I look forward to the Salon at Conrad's restaurant in Pasadena. We've had these salons for over a decade now but the location has changed. Conrad's is the most congenial of all. The staff treat us well and our waiter remembers exactly my order. Always the same — salad with beets and croutons and ranch dressing, followed by the Spanish-style ground sirloin with side dishes of mixed vegetables and sautéed onions, and a plate of garlic toast. The same dishes every week.

When I enter the restaurant at around 6:30 I have a vodka martini with two olives, at the bar. Always the same — until last night when the barman, including a five-dollar bill in the change, remarked: "I know, senor, that you dislike singles." What could he mean? And then I realized: I usually tip him a quarter on the $4.75 drink. Personally I think that's enough but my colleagues tip in dollar bills. So as it was near New Year I got him to change the five-dollar bills into singles and I gave him one. "Gracias, gracias, senor!" Well, I so love the steadiness of this place that it was worth the over-tipping.

Some of the Salon regulars are turning up tomorrow, January 2, at the Santa Anita racecourse to watch the horse of one of our regulars take part in a race. I have no interest in racing but I do enjoy the fraternity of our group. When me and the Bungalow Boys performed last year at a Hollywood nightclub several salonites turned up and even had more than one drink (at $10 a go). I must remember to tell them about the annual Elvis Birthday Bash on January 8: once more I'll be part of the show, singing my version of Elvis' second million seller, the hot ballad, "I Want You, I Need You, I Love You." Every year you have to be fast in calling the organizer to tell him your choice selection. Most of the well-known Elvis numbers are usually snapped up early. But, it seems, nobody revives this 1956 ballad, written by two Tin Pan Alley men. I suppose it's not exactly a hot rocker but it was the very first Elvis record I ever heard.

I remember exactly where I was: my father was driving me back to Bryanston, my boarding school in Dorset, England. He was always kind enough to let me listen to whatever I liked on the car radio. I managed to tune in Radio Luxembourg, the "Station Of The Stars." Located in a European duchy the station broadcast all the latest rock & roll, unlike the BBC, which disdained the new music. Through the static I was thrilled to hear Elvis singing — breaking up the words deliciously, making them rhythmic: "H-ho-hold me close....." And "Hi-hi-hi-hi want you, hi need you, hi love you.." and "With all my hah-hah-hah-hah-hah-heart!" Terribly exciting stuff, exoticism from a far country, received in the old world musty leather of my father's old Bentley as we muttered through the nature-clogged and historic Dorset countryside and all else that oppressed me at the time. (And right now, here in exile, what I long for).

So this record has a place in my heart. But I shall perform it in my own way, because I'm not and never will be an Elvis impersonator. The Bash takes place in what was once The Hollywood Palace, opposite the Capitol Records tower — the theatre where Dean Martin made disparaging remarks about The Rolling Stones when they guested on his show in 1964.

Another meeting place for me — and Regina — is the Coffee Gallery, our local coffee house on Lake Avenue. I so enjoy this oasis that I sometimes drop in twice a day. But early morning is the best time, when, at the big round table near the front door, there gather the local sages and oral editorial writers. With the daily papers spread out they pontificate on current affairs. To a man they are all anti-Bush. And some of the women too — the few who sit at the round table. The sages will give you an answer to all of life's problems, but they prefer to deal with faraway trouble spots rather than local affairs and gossip, which is what I prefer. I mean local stuff and gossip.

I have no interest in politics at all. I'm afraid I like the human-interest stories in the news. I always ask Steve, the leader of the Altadena sages, how his court case is going. A few years ago he naively posted an e-mail concerning an L.A. city councilor, whom he thought was long dead, in which he accused him... But I'd better stop there since I don't want to get embroiled in the lawsuit too.

Suffice it to say that the wretched councilor was still alive, if retired. But not so happily retired that he didn't have the strength to sue poor Steve for libel. The case has cost Steve a fortune. He has to see a shrink regularly. Some days I see him staring into the far distance with a look full of the sorrow of centuries on his face. Local restaurants have benefit nights for him when we all go and enjoy barbecued ribs in the knowledge that a portion of our bills is going to the Steve Defense Fund.

I believe that to be an ethical form of charity. I mean, it's not like what my one-time friend Frederick used to engage in: he'd go to fundraising dinners at fashionable Hollywood restaurants — the kind of places where they don't even put up a sign to identify the place but you know it's the spot because valet parkers are hovering about — and there he'd stuff himself with truffles and filet mignon knowing that he was helping the starving in Ethiopia.

What's wrong with that, you ask. Well, Frederick used to get into these fund-raisers for free. Some sort of movie industry connection. And he would crow about the good he was doing, even as he belched out an aroma of glazed or drizzled duck.

We can only go to pricey restaurants when we're with well-to-do friends. Like Buck Henry, the famous screenwriter, who I've known for years and who always grabs for the leather-bound bill when it arrives. His excuse, he explains, is that he has too much money and needs to "spread the wealth around."

On the night before Christmas Regina and I joined Buck at an exclusive Italian restaurant in West Hollywood. One of those places I mentioned above where the name is so small, so discreet that you drive by. Which is what we did that night — we passed by several times, so that Regina had to call the restaurant on her cell phone. When we eventually found the place we were shown an entry through a dim alley which led to a front door small enough for a private residence. Which it looked like when we entered: a large living room with a fire crackling in a friendly manner. But it wasn't a residence because we knew none of the other people crowding the place — except Buck who waved to us. Now, since my writer had chosen the dining out spot I knew it was OK to let him pay. We had a merry time — so long as I stuck to stories centering on my humiliation. If I dared to direct the talk to his movie career — what projects he was currently working on, etc. — I was at once rebuffed, as if I have no part in current mainline showbiz. At a moment when I was trying to think of a safe subject — I'd just said something rude about Van Morrison only to find out that people around us had overheard me and some rabid fans of this ex-member of that frightful tuneless Belfast group, Them, who I remember as the only rivals to my band Bluesville of Dublin and I considered "Gloria" to be about as bad as "Louie, Louie" and wasn't my record, "This Sporting Life," better than anything Them had done? A woman with a man's haircut and a hawkish nose nudged sharply me in the ribs—we were that close in this exclusive restaurant—and informed me that "Sporting Life" was nothing compared with what Van Morrison has done subsequently. I was impressed that she remembered "This Sporting Life" and was about to congratulate her when Regina, bless her, spied an elderly gentleman with a rubicund face negotiating his way past our table while at the same time greeting and being greeted as if he were Santa Claus. "It's Ronald Neame," Regina told me.

Now you must all know that I hold Ronald Neame very close to my heart. He directed *Tunes Of Glory* when I was his 5th assistant director (in other words, I made the tea). And before that classic movie he'd been George Formby's cameraman and had produced *Brief Encounter* and *Great Expectations*, working with David Lean. Mr. Neame at over 90 is one of the last surviving artists from the golden age of British cinema — the days when directors wore a suit and tie to work. I worshipped Mr. Neame.

I rose to my feet and stood in his path, stopping Santa Claus for a moment. And he remembered me! "You're the boy who spilled the tea!" We got along famously — until I breathlessly told him that the article I've written about my experiences with him on *Tunes Of Glory* is to be published this February in a most esteemed British magazine. "And what, pray, is the name of this magazine," asked the avuncular Mr. Neame. His young wife and protector seemed too interested. "It's called *The Oldie*," I replied. "But it's very well esteemed." Mr. Neame was taken aback and his youthful wife fairly bristled. "*The Oldie!*" they pronounced almost together.

Eager to change the subject I next introduced Mr. Neame to Buck Henry because I saw a historic moment: Ronald Neame meets the man who wrote *The Graduate*. They shook hands and there was politeness, but neither of them, I felt, was impressed as much as I was. After the Neames left Buck talked about British cinema but it became clear to me that his taste is for the kitchen sink, gritty reality pictures of the early 1960s — stuff like *Saturday Night And Sunday Morning* — working class rebels, not men in ties. The England of yobs and thugs and those who come up the hard way and want to bash the genteel. The people who destroyed the gentle England, controlled by the middle and upper classes, that existed up until the early 1960s. How I miss that sweet flowering England! How I rebelled against it at the time. How I regret even being a part of the British Invasion. Maybe that longing to get out of an England I found repressive is crystallized in that long ago evening's ride with my father as the enticing erotic voice of Elvis crackled from Radio Luxembourg beckoning me to the vulgar fairground full of cowboys in tight jeans, lusty men with twangs and guitars promising a world of raucous and racy thrills...

I must go to bed and watch a harmless DVD — Gloria Warren, the teen with the operatic voice, groomed by Warners to be a second Deanna Durbin, but who only made the one film, *Always In My Heart* — what a lovely tune, by the great Cuban composer Ernesto Lecuona — how sympathetic is Walter Huston, who plays the father, an ex-jail bird who can't let on that Gloria's his daughter — a sealed world supposedly near Monterey, in the fishing district but really shot on the back lot of Warner's because I can see the hills of Griffith Park looming in the background of the great musical set piece when Borrah Minnevitch leads his Harmonica Rascals and an army of lads down the street set. It never fails to warm my heart....... I must get off this machine and retire to the bedroom to continue the film. I dreamed of Gloria Warren the other night. I was at a cocktail reception and there she was, a little blue-rinsed and wearing, thank God, a name tag stating: Gloria Warren. She was so pleased that I recognized her. Like the dream in which I was about to meet Hitler at a garden party only I didn't because he'd had to leave since it was almost 6pm and he had to be put to bed as he wasn't as young as he once was and, besides, he had a lot of remembrances that bothered him in the daytime.........

FEBRUARY

I wish I could make this month's letter as exciting, as racy, as tragic, as the ones I've been writing previously. But I can't because all is quiet. Lull before the Storm? On the morning of February 24 we will once more be in the Pasadena civil courts doing battle. This should be the end of the matter.

It's funny how almost everything they do mirrors in a micro manner what's happening in the Middle East. For example: we're now told that there were no weapons of mass destruction (or weapons of mass distraction, as they're termed in the British press); that Saddam was all hot air, all bluster and lies.

Well, that's what the Iranian woman neighbour deals in too: last year she claimed they had an arsenal of guns next door and that they were placing a gun turret on their garage roof so as to get a good aim at us. Turns out that they have no weapons, to speak off, according to the police. All bluster, all lies. Now, on the court day, we'll see if the woman appears: she's claimed she couldn't attend Dispute Resolution — as ordered by the judge — because she has suddenly developed cancer. No doctor's letter, of course. No nothing.

At the annual NAMM convention — where the world's music merchants make a mighty noise for money-making in the enormous Anaheim Convention Center — I had a crisp little meeting with Bill Bay, chief of Mel Bay Publications, my songbook publisher. "Take a seat," he said. I've never had such treatment before. I was almost speechless, a rare state.

I obeyed and descended onto a tiny stool at a tiny round table amid the din of NAMM. I didn't tell Bill I was suffering from severe back pain and was under the care of a chiropractor, not just any chiro, but one who has indoctrination classes and gives lectures on the religion of adjustment and how you can't trust doctors. I descended, as I say, with care, gritting my teeth because I didn't want Mr. Bay to know my pain. I couldn't believe he was "taking a meeting" with me.

I was stuttering around, trying to win him to the idea of another uke book maybe with a Tin Pan Alley title or else a... when he cut in: "Why don't we call it *The Ian Whitcomb Songbook*?"

Terrific! That means I can include not only my raggy songs but my rockers as well. Even "You Turn Me On." How would that sit as a uke arrangement? Possibly I'll write some new songs, too. Freedom! I was, as they say in England, gob-smacked.

Apart from writing and assembling this next uke songbook — my 4th — I'm also researching a chapter on Bill Haley & The Comets in England in 1957. This will appear in Jim Dawson's next book, *Rock Around The Clock*. Jim, of course, is the author of the best-selling history of farting, and currently he has a book out on the history of the 45-rpm record. He's one of the founders of our Monday night salon.

As you know, we're now to be found in Conrad's, a family restaurant at the corner of Lake and Walnut in Pasadena. Lately there's been a very decent turnout. Do come — the bread pudding is excellent and tastes nothing like bread or pudding, thank God.

There are so many conversations taking place simultaneously that it's like radio used to be when reception was bad — a chaos of Charles Ives-like competing sounds, stations falling on top of each other, interfering — and I promiscuously flit from chat to chat.

Sometimes, in order to get attention, I announce something outrageous: did they know, for instance, that our old friend, the fading film director Curlew Worthington, had a dead body in his garage last week for 48 hours before he knew it was there? This is a better topic than the usual Bush-bashing.

I've managed to return to my desk in the basement under the stairs at The Huntington Library — all thanks to the Haley chapter. I've been soaking myself in 1950s England and feeling nostalgic. I was 14 when "Rock Around The Clock" hit us and I immediately bought the 78-rpm record and then the LP. My chapter will focus on the tour that Bill Haley & The Comets made in early 1957.

They disembarked at Southampton and boarded The Rock & Roll Express for Waterloo. Bill was immediately surrounded by fans from hell, hungry for action. They jived on top of his hired car and he didn't like it all. "There's a time and a place for rock & roll — and it's not here and now," he said. His wife Cuppy was terrified. This was a taste of the terror to come. Riots and bad behavior, British style.

Bill was basically a family man and he wasn't ready for the whirlwind he'd reaped. Nor were the British teddy boys and girls ready to accept this avuncular roly-poly man. He was not the Messiah they were expecting — to whisk them out of austerity England and away to Freedom, USA. Haley was no Elvis.

By the end of the tour Bill was no longer hot. From having filled the charts with hits all though 1956 he evaporated. He never recovered — and later he went crazy in a trailer home in Texas, alone and forgotten. It's a tragedy and I hope I can do justice to the story.

Every Saturday I get a brief respite from the hurly-burly when I report to a room at The Pasadena Conservatory of Music for my piano lesson. No jazz, no blues, no faking. Under the watchful eye of a teacher who's young enough to be my daughter, I read sonatinas by the likes of Handel. My posture must be just so, the bench the right distance from the keyboards, and I must observe the articulations, dynamics, rests and trills. Oh, this is very good for me; this is discipline in a precise and ordered world of music. I come out refreshed and may even be playing the piano with a little more sensitivity than hitherto. Classical music is like math and is a corrective to my daily mess of blues.

I would have told you that we are preparing to take an early summer trip to Italy, to gaze up at great historic buildings, all encrusted, to be truly awed, and, possibly to be taken for a ride, to be robbed by the natives.

But we've decided — to my relief — that we'd rather stay here in the Golden State and enjoy and explore what's near and should be dear to us. As it is, we've instigated a once-a-week jaunt. On Tuesdays, we take the day off and, with Rollo, drive up the coast. This week it was Santa Barbara where we have Barbarian friends; last week it was Ventura. Both lovely seaside towns with fresh air and good walks along the beach for the dog and us. Next week we may simply spend a day exploring the new Metro railway system: on a whim we'll catch a train to wherever — possibly to Sierra Madre — what sonorous names the towns have round here! — or Union station — and ride for the sake of the ride, watching the world at work as we do, feeling smug, thumbing our noses at strife and murder and road rage, enjoying our environs, safe from the Patriot Act and Bin Laden and Iraq and everything but what we know or thought we knew.

MARCH

I was determined that 2004 would be a good year, for a change. I said so right in this letter. January it was. But the last few weeks have been pretty awful. However, it's March so I ought to cheer up. I mean, the weather is bright and clear and as crisp as in a Christopher Robin poem.

I'd just got rid of my back pain — by swimming and stretching at our athletic club, working hard to get better because I couldn't bear returning to the chiropractor because he resembles a Serbo-Croat tough, his huge hands punishing me so harshly I felt like a Mel Gibson hero — when I fell down a flight of stairs. That was the night we had five inches of rain and I was playing the gentleman by going up these same stairs in order to help a woman we know get down them.

A few days before, in another of these grotesque downpours, she'd fallen down the stairs all alone and had to call an ambulance, which means the full treatment: fire engine and paramedics and cops. "Hold on tight," I told her as we started down the wretched stairs this second time, with her in a back brace and me as fit as a fiddle and ready to play a million gigs.

As she's young and attractive and curvy she didn't hold on tightly which was lucky for her because on the second step I started my slide and was soon sprawled at the bottom feeling ridiculous and cursing to high heaven.

So I've sprained my left wrist — and I'm left-handed. Can't grip anything and my strumming on the uke makes the hand swell up in retaliation. But I've completed all my gigs successfully. Got to make money.

On February 24, my mother's birthday — she would have been 91 — we had our third, and I hope our last, bout in the Pasadena court. Regina and I thought it would be a walkover — what they call a "doddle" in England. Our lawyer was going to ask, and get, costs and the judge would find the Iranian woman (who started all this business) in contempt of court for not attending Dispute Resolution as ordered.

But life never works out the way you intended it to. The woman never came to court. Her pathetic little husband, a Timothy McVeigh type, handed the female judge a paper claiming that his wife has cancer and was at this very moment undergoing chemotherapy. The judge looked ashenly sympathetic. She was so sorry. Case dismissed. "Off calendar" as they like to say. Our lawyer stepped up to the plate. What about our court costs? Her clients have been subjected to false accusations for months all because of a baseless Restraining Order and have spent thousands of dollars defending themselves. "Off calendar!" said the judge in the same manner that the Queen in Alice In Wonderland says, "Off with her head!" And that was that. All over in five minutes, with the husband sloping off — smirking, no doubt. There'll be champagne popping at their house, said Regina. Yes, we've seen the strapping Iranian heaving open her huge wrought-iron gates in a trice. We've got her on camera swerving so that she can bash dents in our garbage cans as she returns from wherever it is she goes in that big black Volvo.

Right now there's peace and quiet. But the security cameras stare at each other, and our videotaper rolls night and day. "It's like Jerusalem," explains Regina. " There's a lull and then suddenly the violence starts all over."

****

STOP PRESS!

Regina comes in to the office to tell me that in future our dog Rollo must not be let out in the backyard without an escort. Why? She just picked up several chicken bones from the backyard, fresh bones and found very close to our neighbours' yard. Obviously they were thrown over a short time ago and equally obviously it was the work of a certain woman. We have therefore to be vigilant.

On another sad note: a few days after our court appearance, on the Friday, Regina's mother Shirley died. She was 81 and had lived for the last few years in an assisted living establishment, with the unlikely name of Eldorado, in Calabasas, not far from here. Shirley was a sassy proud Virginian and had been a super school sports teacher. She was very bright and Regina must have inherited her own smarts from her. In the good days when we first met I used to call for her stories of Old Virginny and also the one about the college dance when Tommy Dorsey, just one of many bands hired for the evening, brought a skinny singer with him called Frank. The college girls weren't that impressed but Shirley found him "dreamy." Happy dreams to Shirley. Regina is holding up well, considering.

* *

I have been trying to get stuck into the writing habit again. To this end I have been visiting my desk at the Huntington Library, under the staircase in the basement where the American literature books are kept. This is usually a perfect setting in which to think and write and think. No windows, no phones, no people. I'm supposed to be writing a chapter for a book about "Rock Around The Clock," a tale of Bill Haley's ill-fated tour of Britain in 1957 and I have a good title, *The Hell-Bound Express To Waterloo*. But I've sidetracked myself: following the success of my piece about veteran film director Ronald Neame in the British magazine "The Oldie" I was commissioned to write about my songwriter uncle, the man who wrote that immortal song "Lady Of Spain" and many others.

My uncle Stanley Damerell's real name was Jack Stevens and in fact he only contributed to the lyrics, together with Harry Tilsley and Robert Hargreaves. How did they portion out who was to write what? Did they all sit down and have a brain storm? These and other questions need to be answered — and what I thought would be an easy article to write is turning out to be an epic full of mystery. My natural inclination in the past has been: when in doubt make it up.

But in this case reality has taken over from imagination. I've spent time poring over my uncle's collected and bound songs and also reading very carefully a small pile of magazines from the middle 1930s entitled *The Trap*, being a record of the meetings of The Grand Order Of Water Rats, a charity fraternity of performers who liked to get together and yarn and drink and generally talk about doing good works. All male, of course.

But I remember my mother telling him how at their public banquets the ladies were allowed to attend and how she had been invited to come along with her father — whose sister had run away with Uncle Jack in the first place, a shame on the family. After all, our family had been working hard to be respectable, to be upper middle class. My mother had told me about the fraternal greeting of the Water Rat members — a synchronized dropping of the dentures resulting in an unholy clattering noise. Next was the ritual of passing from lap to lap, from table to table, the midget wonder comedian "Wee" Georgie Wood, a gentleman of uncertain years with a face like a devilish baby.

I found his face in a copy of *The Trap* from 1937. It was taken at a banquet at a big London Hotel and my uncle was on the throne as King Rat. He, my uncle, has a very cadaverous face and he's giving away his humble origins, and his desire to be accepted as a gent, by accepting a proffered cigarette with his little finger crooked in a dainty manner. This was a very common gesture — the lower classes pretending to be upper class by crooking their fingers and the like.

The cigarette is one of several housed in a silver cigarette case held by Sir Malcolm Campbell, the debonair ace racing driver. Standing between them with his hands on their respective shoulders is the mighty midget "Wee" Georgie Wood looking very pleased with himself because, for the moment at least, he is towering above the seated gentleman (Sir Malcolm) and the gent (Stanley Damerell). A picture to be treasured and studied. Maybe I should post it on this site.

I was writing away, fully inspired, when all of a sudden my dear old 1976 electric Smith Corona typewriter started wheezing and coughing and spluttering. Finally it had a seizure and couldn't be shifted. So I carried the poor thing to the only typewriter place in town, established 1912. They repaired it — three times.

Each time I started up again in my little hideaway under the stairs in the basement the Smith Corona would try to be normal; but then the noise grew louder and more varied, eventually turning into screams. Finally — the big seizure. I took it back to the typewriter people and said that the poor old thing had given up the ghost. They sadly agreed. Even the old owner, recently retired but still pottering about, came out to have a look and to offer a prayer.

He turned out to have some of my CDs which he and his wife enjoy playing while racing around the country in their motor home as old folk do. With his fandom on my side, he agreed to give me a break on a new typewriter. Wouldn't I prefer an electric? No longer built in the USA of course, made in Mexico or China. Nothing's made in the USA anymore, is it? Well, that's progress for you. Wouldn't you prefer an electric?

No, I replied nicely, I'd like a manual machine because they don't make that motor racket and they're mechanical so you can see things when they go wrong. With modern technology you can't see anything anymore. State of the art electronics are like magic — the parts are invisible. You have to trust the digits to add up to sound and picture. You have to have faith. No one can mend modern technology except God. And I'm a little tired of him at present — mainly because of the trouble wrought by his son and his followers.

So I now have a brand new manual typewriter going by the name of Olympia but only a shadow of the good old sturdy Olympias made in the USA. This one comes from Mexico or even lower down the continent. But I'm happy because it's light and it's a machine and when you tap the keys they attack the paper with a satisfying metallic banging. You feel you're really working hard, you're chiseling out the words. It's all too easy on this computer keyboard. The computer will be the death of careful writing .

TTFN!

PS: I may be a little late with next month's Letter because I am taking a holiday in England to see friends and family. I especially want to visit old Uncle John, my late mother's brother. He knew Stanley Damerell and said he wasn't funny like his songs ("Let's All Sing Like The Birdies Sing,"etc) and was inclined to be a bit of a bore — so much so that, after Christmas dinner, my grandfather would set off for a ritual walk side by side with Damerell but invariably they'd return many yards apart. A certain frisson had been added to, no doubt, an already cold English day. Uncle John never had much truck with bores. If he met them he could always get some fun out of them. Everywhere he went he made things happen. Like when he was visiting Germany as a young man in 1936 and he was at the opera — Wagner, naturally – and he marched up to greet Hitler during intermission. Nazi brutes tried to intervene but Hitler stopped them: "Let the boy speak!"

Uncle John was a good speaker and never one to be shy. "My name is John Burningham and I'm an Englishman holidaying in your lovely clean country. Well done!"

Hitler replied: "I know your country, too. I have spent time in Liverpool — but that was long ago and much has happened since." They shook hands—and a few years later Uncle John was dutifully dropping bombs on German submarines that had dared to trespass into our English Channel. These days my uncle lives in Kent on a cliffside overlooking the frigid gray North Sea with a distant prospect of World War 2 gun emplacements. I shall enjoy sitting in his glass sunroom, sipping a sherry as friendly rain pelts down on us.

APRIL

This will be a short Letter as I'm off for England tomorrow — to see my brother and sister as well as my few remaining (but very good) friends over there. Not forgetting Uncle John about whom I wrote in the last Letter. Regina, sadly, isn't able to make the trip because she is flying to Virginia to bury her mother and meet up with her relatives there. She hasn't seen them for years.

I finished my article about my great-uncle, Stanley J. Damerell, and I've sent copies off to London in the hopes that papers and magazines there might be interested. The piece is very English — riddled with class distinctions. When I return from England I'll get back to my basement desk at the Huntington Library and start writing the chapter on Bill Haley's 1950s tour there when he boarded "The Hell-Bound Express To Waterloo" — the article that I should have completed months ago. I'm happy to now have the new portable manual typewriter and I can resume my writing methods: notes in longhand, rough drafts on the manual, final version on this here Apple computer. The computer is like the printing press — I make sure every word, sentence, is just so. Even so, my handwritten journals resemble paintings, sort of.

Recently we welcomed to our Monday night salon at Conrad's coffee shop my friend Robert N, who was here doing work at the Richard M. Nixon Library. Exactly what, I couldn't quite make out. But Robert is an erudite man who knows more about my work than I do. And the Nixon Library is a peaceful place. I have visited several times and found it to be airy, cool, calming, and empty. Scott Joplin's mellower rags waft through the halls. And in the Nixon family homestead next door lies an accordion — it was that detail that finally won me to the man. If a man plays accordion he can't be all bad. As I write I am wearing a beach boy striped T-shirt emblazoned with the Library & Birthplace's spread eagle that I bought at the Library gift shop so many years ago.

Robert N. brought with him two delightful people: a lovely lady in a cowboy hat who does burlesque dancing and was featured in the movie *The Velvet Hammer*. Our dance lady's friend is called Julien and he writes for TV. He's also helping to write a memoir with another fascinating woman: Cynthia Plaster Caster.

Do you remember that sterling bunch of super groupies from the late 1960s who immortalized their fave rockers by wrapping these stars erect members in plaster and then casting a mold? This was achieved with the help of fluffers or platers (as they say in England). Stars who submitted included Jimi Hendrix, Eric Burdon, and Mark Lindsay (of Paul Revere & The Raiders). Mark would certainly have made a good subject since I remember attending an after-hours gathering back in my rock tour days where he displayed his wares to certain female fans. Quite frightening. Anyway, my new friend Julien had told Cynthia in advance that he would be dining with me and she was ecstatic. She wished she'd gotten a mold of me back in the 60s.

But she was based in Chicago and I guess I never played there. I was so flattered that immediately I got home I went on-line to look at the Plaster Caster website. Very professional — and there's a warning to those who might want to be cast that Cynthia chooses you, you don't choose her. I e-mailed her to introduce myself. She was quick to reply: could this be the real Ian Whitcomb? The one who made a million girls' hearts flutter back in 1965. Oh, how she wishes she'd molded me back then! But it's not too late, she added. "It *is* too late," riposted Regina. Still, I'm very flattered. Wouldn't you be? If you were me?

Last weekend I took another of the traditional desert trips with Andy Wickham. An Englishman with a similar background to me, Andy and I go back to 1965 when he met me on the *Shindig* TV set. At the time he was working for Lou Adler, the record label maven. A little later he joined Warner Bros. Records and was their house hippie, gaining the company access to the burgeoning rock scene. He was instrumental in getting Joni Mitchell signed; he produced many of Van Dyke Parks' albums; he and I produced some odd country records in Nashville — singles like "Hands" by Debbie Dawn, a story of a massage Parlour girlie who accepts Master Charge (as it was then called) for her massage (good rhyme). The reference to the credit card company got us into trouble with the FCC and, I'm told, prevented the record from becoming a smash.

Andy is now retired and living in the better part of London. As we tooled along the freeway in his cool rented car he filled me in on what to expect in England when I arrive there this weekend: he says it's getting coarser and more brutish every minute; that soccer is the religion; that Blair is trying to be like an American President; that even in old-world market towns in the countryside it's not safe after dark. Mugging abounds.

So I am prepared for the worst — but I will confine myself to reaching safe havens: my sister's cottage in Royal Berkshire where she lives with the General; my brother's maisonette in Wimbledon, near the Common; my Trinity College friends — Jeremy Lewis, who's a big literary man in London and commissioning editor of *The Oldie* magazine, and Charles Sprawson, the art dealer. It's on the journeys to the safe havens that one is likely to encounter trouble — violent school kids and falling down drunks. There's graffiti decorating every underground train. Not a pleasant prospect, especially with Muslim bombers preparing their gifts in suburban houses near airports. Of course, this is an England never seen by American anglophiles who take the protected route of Cotswolds, Bath, and Shakespeare country.

Andy is the kind of Englishman who loves the desert, a worthy tradition. So we always start our trip in the Morongo Valley and eat Mexican everywhere. He's particularly fond of strong salsa.

Morongo is in the high desert and populated by a sturdy and endangered white blue-collar class who have escaped Los Angeles and tell one and all about the bliss of desert life. They all look mighty healthy in face but down below is the telltale gut and often the nervous tapping of the feet. After a night in an Indian-run motel — East Indian, I mean — and all managed by the family Patel, who seemed to have monopolized every motel in America — we set off through Joshua Tree National Monument where Andy insists we stop to admire the cholla cacti and the ocotillo. In the company of back packers and hikers in shorts Andy cuts an exotic figure in his expensive Savile Row dark jacket, trousers and white shirt. His favourite stopping off place is Mecca, close by the benighted Salton Sea — a place of dead fish and foul waters and boarded up motels — a place of broken promise — where we always stop for a Tecate at Elfie's bar. She, a Mexican-American from El Paso, sits behind the bar regarding us quizzically, curiously. Andy won her by telling of how, years ago, he went to a big Mexican boxing match at the Olympic Auditorium and how the movie star Cantinflas got more applause than any of the boxers. I asked her opinion of Mexican wrestling — the only subject I reckoned I might have in common with her— but got no response.

Onward to the border town of Calexico where Andy always impishly tries to lure me across the border knowing how fearful I am over there. I'm terrified that someone will crash into my Honda in a jalopy and I'll be sued and jailed and only get out via bribery. He knows that, because I'm a verbal person, I'm stymied in any place where I can't be understood. Luckily we only skirted the border and looked at the poor devils trying to get across into the land of plenty. Saturday evening we chose, as usual, a popcorn movie, something mindless but engrossing: *Mystic River,* a detective mystery thriller that was gripping at the time but afterwards gave me that Chinese meal feeling: unsatisfied.

Next day we motored nonstop back to Pasadena. Andy whiled away the hours by delivering an engrossing history of the Palestine Mandate under the British. We British seem to have affected the course of history everywhere. Still, I think it might be a more civilized world if British gentlemen still administered.

In Pasadena — home — Andy visited Vroman's bookshop and bought a Henry James novel for his trip back to London. We rendezvoused with Regina at the Paseo multiplex and caught an excellent old-fashioned adventure picture called *Hidalgo,* spoiled only by the usual gangs of uncontrolled children running all over the place screaming.

I will see Andy next week in London. I'll be his guest at The East India Club for dinner. Such is the parlous state of London clubs that this esteemed one has had to join forces with The Public Schools

Club. Andy always insists on teasing me that Bryanston, my school, doesn't qualify as a real Public School because it was founded as late as 1927. We often dine under the oil painting of Warren Hastings, one of the scoundrels who helped found the British Empire.

MAY

Oh to be in England now that April's here, sang the poet. And I was in England in April and it was all oh, oh, oh. Good ohs, friendly ohs — ohs to be in England permanently if only the work were there.

But now, as I write this on the first day of May, I have to tell you that we are moving. We have had enough. We cannot live under siege, in a place that is starting to look like a prison — floodlights at night, security cameras, portable video cameras, pocket tape recorders. Our cottage of honeysuckle and ivy and persimmon and lemon trees, of the vegetable garden that produces delicious radishes, of the hummingbirds hovering on the fountain outside the bathroom window, of the riot of flowers and bushes that Regina has lovingly nurtured. Our cottage of a thousand memories going back to 1979 when I moved in as a bachelor and went on to entertain a mixed bag of boarders, and many members of my family including the Governor of the Tower of London, and BBC television crews, and the sax honker Big Jay McNeely, and Gordon Waller of Peter & Gordon, not forgetting the full membership of The London Club in all their British Empire uniforms and of course the many visits from my best friend, the great swimming writer Charles Sprawson, and so many others just as important — this dream house has now to be abandoned because of a barrage of pure hate coming from next door. A hate that has been gaining momentum since last year.

The very day we returned from the heaven of the Santa Cruz uke festival and the pleasures of Monterey Bay, the onslaught had already started. They had trespassed onto our property at 9pm on the previous Friday (that's the time the security camera went dead) even as I was master of ceremonies at the festival's grand seven-hour concert in the Cocoanut Grove on the Boardwalk, even as I was strumming out happiness songs on the uke, they were breaking into our yard. Over the fence they came, smashing Regina's flowerpots, in order to trip switches and turn off our electricity. On our return we were greeted by the "fuck you" that had been the farewell from them when we left. Now it's every time I dare to even walk out into our driveway: the crazy-like-a-fox woman shouts: "You piece of shit! Your wife has boy friends and you have no balls!" Under advice I say not a word. Then the husband returns and joins in: "We're gonna nail your ass!" he shouts to Regina — and this in front of the cops we just called. The last outburst was late on Thursday night when we dared to bring friends back to see our home and our Front Line. "Come outside and fight!" challenged the little shrimp. But the cops arrived just in time. Again, I said not a word. Standing still, Ghandi-like, thinking of Martin Luther King and Christ. Did the cops help us, protect and serve? No. The cops are automatons. To them we're typical civilians having a dispute. Seen it every day. Get cameras, get lawyers, we gotta go fight real crime. Yes, but you've known about our situation for years, you know that I'm a sheriff's volunteer. No dice. It's like talking to a slot machine, hoping it'll pay out. Goodnight, sir. Added one tough looking cop who was young enough to be my grandson: "You know what, sir? You're screwed."

On April Fool's Day, with Regina in Virginia for her mother's funeral, I set off for London to see my family and friends. It has been over a year since I last saw them and I really miss them. The flight was made easy because *The Third Man* was playing constantly on one of the channels. After much wine and spirits I watched this classic in a state of inebriated trance, dozing off as Harry Lime is chased through the sewers and then waking to see the beautiful Valli walk from the graveyard after Harry's final funeral and walk and walk until she passes poor Joseph Cotten as he waits in the side of the frame, hoping she'll give him the time of day. And all the while Anton Karas' plaintive zither plucks out that haunting melody. A decent way to reach England.

I achieved everything I intended over there and the weather was my delight: raining, sunny, raining, sunny. I stayed at my sister's cottage (where she lives with the General, who is much better, thank you) in Royal Berkshire where we laughed and laughed even as it rained. My sister, Suzanne, cooks only English fare, which is alright with me. Then I stayed at my brother Robin's house in Wimbledon. He's a sports master at Dulwich College and he once played tambourine for Sonny and Cher on "I Got You Babe." I was amazed and proud that, like almost everybody else I know who didn't used to be a writer, he has become one. He has a contract to put together a book about English Village Cricket.

So the next day we set off on a research drive through the heart of English cricket — the lovely county of Sussex. Stopped off at village greens where this game has been played for centuries. I'm not going to explain the rules: so many of my American friends complain that the secrets of the game are impenetrable. To me it's all perfectly simple. I played it as a boy, as we all were forced to do, just as we all were forced to learn Shakespeare and I can still spout reams of the man (without even understanding a word but it rolls well); just as we all sang the Victorian hymns and can sing them still. If we wished to. But it's all meaningless to me, even though an indelible part of my past.

Sussex is lovely so long as you are inland. Once you reach the coast it's mostly desolation: dreary storm-lashed seaside towns with rusty trailers attached like barnacles; weather-beaten, life-beaten seniors in flat hats biffing their way along the forlorn sea front beside a beach of pebbles, or else sitting in their cars facing the gray sea and reading the tabloids, which, at the time I was in England, were obsessed with this glam soccer star David Beckham and his just-exposed extra-marital affair with a woman from the isle of Lesbos. The other news consisted of pictures of barbecued portions of American contractors hung up on Iraq bridges for the delight of the natives. The London *Times* is now a tabloid, by the way.

I took the train to Herne Bay, on the Kent Coast, to pay a visit to my old Uncle John, the last remaining relative from the World War Two generation. Indomitable, he drove in a meandering and rather dangerous way to the Dickensian town of Broadstairs where we took one look at the blustery sea and quickly retired to a pub. My uncle starts dramas wherever he is — and within minutes he was engaging an old sea salt, who was rolling his own ciggie and nursing an amber liquid in a dirty glass. I had ordered a Guinness and my uncle announced that Nigeria has the biggest brewery in the world. The grizzled old salt came to life. "Ho no it doesn't, mate!" He went on to tell us that he had spent many years in darkest Africa, building cities and getting to know all the powers. "I bin through seven coups and three dictators — count 'em — and I can tell you there ain't no brewery of Guinness in Nigeria."

"I can assure you there is," said my uncle. It was fun to hear the clash of accents: my uncle's upper class plummy tines and this drawling cockney remaindered by the seaside.

"No, mate. They brings in the liquor from Dublin in constituents and then they, they..."

"Distribute," I suggested.

"Thank you, squire. Yes, they distribute it round the tribes.."

My uncle insisted on making a bet on the subject and an ugly moment was averted due to his offering to stand everyone a round of drinks. When we got back to his house my uncle called the London office of Guinness to find out the facts but they'd all left for the day since it was Good Friday.

That evening my uncle and aunt (who was once my uncle's secretary) dined me at Le Beau Rivage, near Herne Bay — as you can tell, a place of French pretension and actually excellent food, but set in a tiny room complete with even tinier bar and a seven foot barman. Everybody knew my uncle as "John." Everybody spoke in those ubiquitous cockney accents. Many had just returned from cruises in faraway exotic places.

Next morning, before entraining back to London, I accompanied my uncle on another potential adventure. Dropping in to a new Bed & Breakfast on the Herne Bay seafront; he has booked his son, the Reverend Burningham, and family into this place for a summer holiday. The B&B also contains The Cafe Mozart and Viennese opera was wafting out of the little basement cafe, set for "Real Coffee & Real Cream Cakes." A burly man appeared and asked if he could help. Turned out to be the new owner, a Macedonian and an ex-ballet dancer.

"You've certainly gained a few pounds," said my uncle in his typical direct manner, backed by a smile. The Macedonian admitted it and then went on to bemoan British society: why, even this very morning he had to chase away a youth who was "urinating on my wall." He told him to go and urinate on his own wall.

And as for local workers — they never show up so the Macedonian called in his relatives from away in that country and over they came to complete the work on the B&B and the Cafe Mozart. Is Britain that bad? "Well, most nights, rain hot or cold, you can look out of the window and watch the teenagers copulating on the seafront grass, by the bandstand. You can see their white bottoms go up-down, up-down."

That morning the sea front appeared charming, a relic of Edwardian summers. I found it hard to imagine the copulation in such a lovely old-world setting. And I wondered about my cousin and his visit: would the Reverend and his children open their sea view bedroom windows to be greeted by the up-down couples? I'm sure the Reverend would keep the curtains closed because he daily experiences the coarseness of modern Britain down at his parish in Southampton. He tells me that not a day goes by without incidents in and around his rectory. He walks from the rectory through the churchyard and the local youth shout out "fuck you!" and the like. The other day he dodged just in time to miss a flying brick aimed at him. Nearby there are blocks of low-income housing and prospects for the youths growing up there are not good. The Reverend's back garden is often used for the homeless to "doss down" in. The Rev. draws the line when he finds perfectly able-bodied male teenagers having fun on his grass. A particular youth refused to leave so the Rev tackled him rugby-style and soon had him in a Half-Nelson. Police were called but they were reluctant to help.

So please remember that Britain is not confined to Stratford, Bath, The British Museum, the West End theaters, and the Cotswolds. It's a jungle out there — unless you stay within the pale of the tourist circuit.

Back in London I spent the rest of my trip talking, walking, dining, drinking, talking, talking, talking with Charles Sprawson.

We visited his lady friend Margaret Vyner, a great beauty of the 1950s who seems to have known everybody who is/was anybody and shares it with one and all. She's still a rare beauty and has a delightful laugh and a special way with a Bloody Mary. She lives in one of London's most exclusive Squares with its own inner park. And yet, even here among money and Mercedes, there's crime. The very morning Charles and I were visiting Margaret, a neighbour, by chance looking out her window, saw a car pull up in the square and a swarthy man alight. Another swarthy sat at the wheel with the engine running. In a trice the first man had jimmied open the door of a spanking new Mercedes parked outside the owners' flat. In a second trice he'd driven off in it with the first car following calmly. This, I'm told happens all the time. Last week robbers removed the front two wheels of a Rolls and two days later returned for the other two.

But, all in all, and taking everything into consideration, I had a lovely time in England — because of the people I know and can chat with. I was hoarse by the end of my stay. On the plane back I watched *House Of Sand And Fog*, mesmerized by its closeness to our situation. You can guess whose side I was on.

A week later we had heaven in Santa Cruz, courtesy of the Ukulele Club of that city of true angels. The club quartered us at a hotel originally called The Dream Inn. Erected in 1963, a curious dog's mess-colored multi-tiered egg box plumb on the corner of the beach staring out at the historic Wharf and with a view of the equally historic Boardwalk and its Giant Dipper and Cocoanut Grove. Once we were inside the Dream (now prosaically called Coast Santa Cruz) and in our suite, provided by the club, we were really in that heaven, due to the magnificent view of the bay, etc., and the sight and sound of relentlessly crashing waves. We arrived on Monday night and the festival didn't start till Friday so we had a mini vacation, even going so far as actually swimming without wetsuits in the invigoratingly cold sea. Curiously, hardly anybody else seems to actually swim in the sea. At all times of day you can see clusters of seal-like wetsuiters waiting for that wave, rather like fishermen waiting for that special fish. Maybe part of the joy is simply waiting and contemplating life. We explored the rebuilt old town and found it delightful and quite up-market, marred only by the aggressive panhandlers, mostly young folk. "Gimme a hundred dollars!" and that sort of demand. Many were extremely attractive, I have to admit. There appears to be no law against beggars but there are lots of laws against dogs so Rollo had to make himself scarce.

There's a terrific dog-friendly beach near the lighthouse and surf museum so Rollo could prance there every day and make friends with all sorts. He likes to rush up to a dog without so much as an invitation. There's a flotsam log in the centre of the beach which the dogs use to leave their calling cards.

One afternoon, while I was plugging the uke festival on the local NPR station Regina was taking in the world-famous Mystery Spot, "as featured in *Life* magazine." No-one, not even the all-knowing Regina, can explain what it is. But it's set among beautiful redwoods and seems to have been discovered, hut and all, suddenly in 1939. The brochure explains that "the laws of physics do not apply" and there's "excessive carbon dioxide exuding from the rocks." A certain Dr. Oscar found the "highest dielectric biocosmic radiation known anywhere in the world." I am none the wiser but better informed. At any rate, Regina and our friend Christopher, he of the Wisteria, took the tour and even, while waiting their turn to be led to the Spot and its Hut, sang and danced with the one-man band trombonist who runs the gift shoppe at the Mystery Spot. I envied them their adventure.

By Friday morning our hotel was overflowing with ukesters from all over the world. Well, Cyril had come from Paris, bringing with him the odor of Gauloises. There were workshops during the day and I conducted one although I don't see what people can learn from my strange left-handed uke strumming, but the class was very kind and applauded loudly. Anyone who carries a uke has got to be OK. In fact, I posited the theory that if we ukesters shoulder-armed our instruments and marched into the world's trouble spots those spots would lay down their arms and surrender to joy and laughter.

In the evening we celebrated the seven-hour show inside the Cocoanut Grove. Over 500 ukesters and almost as many performers, it seemed. I hosted most of the show and I must admit there wasn't a moment of monotony — every ukester had his/her own style, ranging from the authentic Hawaiian to "The Flight Of The Bumble Bee." I led the room in a chorus of my militant anthem, "The Uke Is On The March." I got so excited I fell over but gamely carried on. Let the world know: I was not drunk, just merry, intoxicated by the sound of so many ukes.

By Sunday noon the hotel was empty of our people and the regular folk, the dullards, took over. Cool jazz sax, Kenny G style, once again poured out of the Muzak system. Baseball was the topic and also the freeway traffic and the current price of real estate.

Regina and I decided to experience the Boardwalk. We were entranced by the old merry-go-round — the children rising rhythmically, gracefully, up and down and trying to grab the brass ring. I'd heard about grabbing the brass ring — as a metaphor for seizing your opportunity — but had never seen its origins at work, and I felt I was back in the ragtime era, especially as the mechanical organ was playing "Ragtime Cowboy Joe."

We rode on the Giant Dipper and I screamed with pleasure like I haven't screamed since the 1950s. I also lost my expensive sunglasses as we left the rails to race down the Big Dip. No matter.

What innocent childlike fun we had that last day! How grateful we are to the Ukulele Club of Santa Cruz! How we'd love to relocate there! How I dreaded turning that corner in Altadena onto our street! Yes, our worst fears were proven well-founded. The neighbours had broken in, had turned off our power, the war continues. And so now we beat the retreat to a safe haven for a while, a rented house, a quiet place, a hideaway. The police have failed to protect and serve, the community has failed us. Watch this space for what happens next in our opera without scented soap. Our impossible melodrama.

As always,
Tunefully,
Hopefully,
Ian

P.S. from Regina:
Ian has told you about Santa Cruz. We loved it. The people, the time together, Rollo's romps. It was heaven. Like a honeymoon. I felt restored and ready to be so productive once home again.

As for my trip to Virginia I wanted to tell you how unexpectedly nice it was. Some of the relatives I hadn't seen in 36 years and it was as if no time had passed at all. My family is wonderful.

I cried a lot at the funeral. I spoke. And, I was afraid that we'd become strangers to each other but my Aunts, Uncles, and cousins were warm and put me at ease. It was a measure of how I'd grown-up I guess.

I became aware that this was the first time my sister, brother, their spouses, their children, and I had traveled together. Not a single problem. I hadn't anticipated that it would all go so smoothly. Our mom and dad must be smiling from heaven to see how harmonious we are. I'm so lucky.

The plan for the days between my return and Ian's was for my sister to come here. We both felt the need to spend a little time alone to grieve.

We did that as much as we could. You see, I discovered I'd have to carefully inspect our (completely fenced in) backyard for rusty nails and chicken bones, EVERYDAY, several times a day.

I should add that these neighbours knew about my mom and why I was away. Nice welcome-home, huh?

So, perhaps I was naive to hope that a change had occurred just because we felt good again.

I got to Rollo just in time on April 29 to dislodge a chicken joint from his throat. That was the same day I saw (on the surveillance camera) the neighbour do 'something' in my front garden. Upon inspection I found tiny shards of glass on the soil. Not pieces as if a bottle had broken. Tiny bits that would hurt me next time I worked there. I garden <u>all</u> <u>the</u> <u>time</u>. I know what's there and what wasn't

until he waved his hand over it.
We're defeated. We're leaving.
Thanks for reading.
Love,
Regina

AUGUST

There has been an awful long silence from me. But not a silence of lambs: we have taken action and now we live in Monrovia. Not the African country (I get too much unsolicited mail from recently deposed African prime politicians and presidents and the like, begging for lots of money), but a tasteful city a few miles from our old home in Altadena. We are renting the upper floor of a house built in 1906. It is like being in a garret because the rooms are shaped by the slope of the roof. You could say it's the same setting as a late nineteenth century bohemian in Paris. You could say that but it's not true. Our old life is mostly in boxes stored in the attached garage.

Our old home in Altadena is now let to four renters — all respectable graduates, studying biochemistry and the like at nearby Cal Tech — clean and polite lads who, no doubt, will be inventing gadgets to save our lives, or shoot us to Venus, or destroy the Middle East. Even on the day the movers came Kareem wouldn't allow the van to park outside their house. A bitch up till the end. How will she treat the new tenants? If she starts on them she can be arrested for "interfering with commerce" since we are now landlords doing business — and business in America is sacred and not to be interfered with. Ordinary citizens are not so important. Amazingly I offered my hand to Hodge as we left with the movers. He took it— limply but he took it just the same.

Kaleem is dragging us to court yet again, in October, in another attempt to get a Restraining Order on Regina. More made-up complaints — claiming that my wife deposited dog poop on her garden table, that we play "obnoxious music" (i.e., it's not Persian wailing). I hope and trust the case will be thrown out of court but you never know with the super-liberal female judge that we are always landed with. If you're tinted she loves you. If you're regular white like us — watch out! However, we now have (for our fourth time in court at a cost in thousands and mounting) a stack of statements from neighbours testifying to the awfulness of our oppressors; and two cops are coming to talk on our behalf. After October I hope there'll be an end to this dreadful business. Regina still has nightmares in which this hideous gargoyle of a woman leers at her.

We plan to stay in Monrovia for at least a year. It's a pleasant and peaceful spot, very family oriented. A main street festival every Friday, with a farmer's market and "entertainment" (bad blues bands and bland harpists). The wide western-style main street is full of gift shops — stuff you don't need such as faux hand-painted wooden signs reading "My Garden" and "God's In His Heaven." But at least it seems safe out here. Nevertheless I find myself driving in everyday to my old haunts in Altadena — the dusty trail in the foothills where I let Rollo run, the coffee house where the talk is contrary and contentious. Monrovia is too family, too much into soccer and vintage cars (1955 is old).

It's such a long time since I last wrote. Is it three months? Had I told you about the Santa Cruz ukulele festival? What an idyllic time that was! A hotel on the sands so we could run right into the sea. And then the news that our neighbours had turned off our power while we were away, clambering over the back fence to do it, and leaving overturned flower pots in their wake. Back to the continuing harassment — the husband threatening Regina he'd "kick" her "ass" in court, and then he challenges me to a fight right there in the street. The reason? Search me. Unlike mystery movies there's no solution. So that evening was when I decided we had to move. It took us a month, thanks to friends who lent their vans, pickup trucks, cars. The Huntington Library even sent their head man and several assistants to load up my books and drive them to the Library where they are now shelved, in safety, next to the Christopher Isherwood and Kingsley Amis collections.

On the last night at the old home I took Rollo on our nightly walk. On ritual trees and telephone posts he lifted his leg; nocturnal animals scurried about their business, sternly regarded by Rollo. After all, this was *his* street and he pulled me along as rearguard, intent in a world of sniffing.

My attention was drawn to the barriers on our street: fences, walls, iron gates, iron railings with spear tips — all culminating in the prison camp of our bungalow compound, our front line facing their barracks, a battleground where so much inventive had been hurled, so many policemen had wearily but dutifully trod. Tonight, as every night since the crisis, floodlights lit up out driveway, ready for sudden assault.

Barriers! Fences make good neighbours some silly poet once wrote. So wrong! These barriers have prevented good neighbourliness. It was not always so — but it was I who had started this alienation back in 1979 when I moved in. In those carefree days I was a refugee from West Hollywood. So one wet day, enticed by a lady cellist who'd joined a suspect commune in an Altadena mansion, I bought the very first house-for-sale we ran across. "It's you!" she decided.

And the first thing I did was to erect a high wooden fence all around the property. What a kerfuffle! This was not the American way. Americans let their green swards roll down to the street. Democracy in action. But I was English and demanded a castle.

Inside this castle I built a little England complete with hunting scenes on the lampshade and old school group photos; after my mother's death I imported the family piano from London. Keeping at bay anything new and changing, using Altadena as a dormitory, playing no part in the community.

Meanwhile, as I occupied this cocoon, so the street imitated me, erecting their own fences —not just of wood but also of iron, concrete and brick. And the most daunting barrier of all grew around our neighbours, the Hodges. Their dark brown spear railings seemed razor sharp and ready to impale.

Now the house, my home for 25 years, is empty — as of yesterday — and being painted, scrubbed, and shampooed, in readiness for the squeaky-clean science boys.

Other stuff: I've had my article about my songwriter uncle accepted by *The Oldie*, the British magazine for oldsters, a prestigious monthly.

Tonight I'm off to play with Janet Klein & Her Parlour Boys at the coffee house in Altadena. Then I leave for Eugene, Oregon, to take part in concerts at The Oregon Festival Of American Music. This will be a thrill: the theme this year is "The Fabulous Fifties" so I will be in my element singing "Green Door," "Rock Around The Clock"— and, on opening night, a version of "Hound Dog" accompanied by a 32 member male chorus and big band. Dick Hyman is the musical director.

Also on the bill are Dave Brubeck and Mort Sahl. I have been persuaded to sing "You Turn Me On," even though it wasn't part of the Fifties. "Doesn't matter" said Mr. Hyman: "It's a good Silly Song." That's the title of that particular concert.

I'm thrilled to have been allowed to provide the clink-clink piano when we do the Connie Francis version of "Who's Sorry Now?" Mr. Hyman has threatened to replace me if I play one wrong clink-clink. He will replace me since it was he who played the clink-clink piano on the original 1957 hit recording by Miss Francis. This should be fun, this must be fun. It was during last year's festival that I heard from Regina that the neighbours' assault on her had begun. This year she'll be safe in Monrovia, among soccer moms and computer experts.

Now I must rest. Will I sleep? It's too darn quiet in these parts. Maybe we need someone to oppress us?

SEPTEMBER

"Too soon came cool September, with songs that I remember, a soft refrain that said good-bye, we must part — Autumn Concerto breaks my heart!"

A fragment of a song I know mistily; from the 1950s when I was at boarding school and homesick or in trouble and I'd find a song in my mind that somehow took me through the crisis.

Recently I've been singing "Autumn Concerto" because the walls of our world have been crashing in, even though we moved away from the evil one on Alameda St. in Altadena, even though we moved ten miles away to the neat and trim towne of Monrovia with its shoppes and civic pride and Mark Twain in bronze sitting in the Library Park reading *Tom Sawyer*.

I returned like a Victor Ludorum, a wreath round my head, from The Oregon Festival Of American Music. Two weeks of bliss, of doing what I love doing, and being paid for it. Regina picked me up at Burbank Airport (now named Bob Hope Airport and draped with a sheet printed with his trademark ski-jump nose) and all seemed merry and bright. We drove into Laurel Canyon and up Lookout Mountain Avenue, on our way to a sort of party.

In the summer of 1968, that heady and dreadful time when we were young and beautiful and careless, I had lived in a house there — the summer that my rock career drew to a close and Robert Kennedy was murdered one evening as I sat alone in this house, pondering my future and what the hell direction it was going to take. All I was concerned with was my life while all round was assassination and violence. What a year was 1968!

Well, I got out of California and returned to my London home, to the safety of my mother and family. It was while sequestered there that I had the idea to propose a book to Penguin. The result — three years later — was *After The Ball*.

But back to Lookout Mountain Ave. Also living on that street at that time were Steve Martin, Frank Zappa and the Nitty Gritty Dirt Band. I ran into some of them. I reminisced to Regina as we drove up the Avenue, with Rollo in the back high-sniffing. Regina's very tolerant — she's heard all my reminiscences before, knows every place I ever lived in Hollywood and puts up with it.

The "party" we were heading for was actually described in the email invite as a "memorial service" but it turned out to be a pleasant affair. David Raksin, an old friend, had died the previous week at the decent age of 92. David is best known for composing "Laura" but he also scored some now classic films including *The Bad And The Beautiful*. He had phoned me one morning at the

Laurel Canyon house — when young flaxen-haired girls had been coming to the canyon, trailing dreams — that very summer of 1968. I had written an article about the growing pretentiousness of rock and the delighted L.A. Times had published it on the front page of their arts section.

David was delighted too and called me up. We became fast friends and I used to visit him at his Valley home and entertain his children with ukulele songs. He played me "Run Rabbit Run" by Flanagan & Allen, a British recording by a British institution I'd revered for many years and now was so pleased that this great All-American film composer enjoyed it too.

Later David agreed to conduct the orchestra for my studio recording of my musical *Lotusland*.

The memorial party was jolly because I was able to talk about the present with his son, Alex, whom I've known since he was a child when I taught him the Monster Man game in their swimming pool, involving the sign of the cross. These days Alex is an editorial writer on the *Los Angeles Times*. After a while Alex asked whether we'd like to stroll across to his neighbour's home, there up in the hills, because his neighbour "remembers you fondly."

Danny Hutton — gosh, I hadn't seen Danny Hutton since 1965 when we were on a rock & roll stage show together in Denver, I think it was, and Danny was riding high with "Roses And Rainbows." We'd also known the same girl friend, a busty go-go dancer on the TV rock show, *Hollywood A Go-Go*. He'd impressed me by ambling on stage in sandals, an early hippie gesture. I was into stage costumes. Of course, he went on to be a part of that super group Three Dog Night and we lost contact with each other, so I was touched that he remembered me "fondly."

Off we strolled and soon were high up in a rambling 1920s house, all lit up and full of happy people, young and old, thronging all over the house, swimming in the pool. Danny Hutton was true to his word and I too felt like it was yesterday when last I saw him. Almost immediately he turned, saying, "Come and say hello to Brian — Brian Wilson."

Now, I really did know Brian Wilson, just as I had known Danny Hutton — briefly in that starry two years of 1964-66. I had been on *Shindig* with Brian and the Beach Boys, had done concerts with them, including the Hollywood Bowl and the Cow Palace, had become friendly with Dennis and had lunched with Brian and his then wife, Marilyn. This was when we were sharing the same publicist Derek Taylor, a memorable Englishman, and Derek had arranged a lunch: what I most remember was that Brian's wife had warned him against eating too much cheesecake. As I recall she was fairly hefty herself. I also recall that Brian established a friendship with my brother Robin, who was over here temporarily between school and college. Dimly, somebody from that time is telling me that Brian had said Robin was very talented. More than his older brother? Dimly, as I say.

But I didn't bring any of this up with Brian. I talked and talked at him and he seemed to brighten and swell, as if I was a power source. He's tall and is trimmed down. He responded to me like the best of an unspoiled child. I wasn't there in the years in between our first encounters but on this Sunday evening he was direct, exuberant, happy. Danny stood by and seemed amazed.

What did we talk about? I told him how I loved the way he and his Boys pronounced "Girls" as "Girrrrls" on their records — so very Californian; what had he contributed to "Surf City," the Jan & Dean hit? He wrote the immortal line: "Two girls for every boy!" and he sang it right there and then. He also sang a snatch of one of four songs he's written in the last month. "I was thinking I'd run out of songs. You see, all I am is a backup singer." How did I write my songs? Did I spend a lot of time producing them? No, I replied, I like to write and immediately go and record live in the studio. "You do?" Astonishment. "You mean you don't produce and produce?"

I went on to rake up the past — the glorious past — and he loved it, smiling all the while, enthusing. I passed on a compliment from Frank Capp, the drummer, who only the day before had opined that working with Brian was easier than with Phil Spector because Brian came prepared with arrangements and Spector never knew what the hell he was doing and could spend up to a week recording one song, with poor Frank stuck banging a skull block and shaking a maraca. Brian beamed.

I also apologized for being part of the British Invasion that had ruined the beach party that was American Pop in the early 1960s. Yes, he agreed vigorously. The Beatles weren't always a good thing. But now, I said brightly, I play the ukulele. No threat. "The ukulele," he exploded. "I love the ukulele! I had one when I was a child!" I promised I'd locate a uke for him, possibly for free, one he might endorse. Sure! "Then we can write songs together." For my next Mel Bay book? "Yes, yes." Emboldened, I sang him a song I've been obsessed with: "When You Travel Down The Road That Leads To Nowhere," a cowboy number from a 1946 Durango Kid western called "Terror Trail ", performed by Ozie Waters & His Colorado Rangers. I got it off the Starz Western cable channel. Brian was entranced. Then I told him that the song is in E flat and that the second chord is C7. "C7!" — he almost fell over. And I reacted too: was C7 really such an amazing chord in that context? He seemed to be excited — overexcited, perhaps — with everything I was saying. Would we really write songs together?

Whatever the truth was, Brian Wilson was clearly enjoying himself as we stood facing each other in Hutton's kitchen with children and dogs, including our Rollo, swirling around us. Brian was now staring hard at me, swaying slightly. "I really like you and I trust you, Ian Whitcomb. Why, our names are almost the same! B-R-I-A-N and I-A-N!" It was a revelation.

When we took our diplomatically timed leave Danny escorted us down the drive "You really made Brian happy," he said. "He hasn't been like this in years. This would be newspaper headlines in England."

Next day, Regina went to our Altadena home where now live four bright young Cal Tech students — only to discover that the wretched Iranian woman, far from laying-off now that we have beaten a retreat to Monrovia, has launched an attack on our property — hacking down our ivy hedge, the ivy planted by my aunt Grace back in 1982 when she and my uncle visited me, in those dear dead days beyond recall. It was like a stab in the back. It certainly was illegal destruction of property, something to add to our legal papers, something to add to that feeling of nausea. And so the attacks continue and, as I wrote above, our world crashed once more. The Beach Boy episode was only a respite....

A few days later I read in the paper that Brian Wilson had just returned from a sold-out concert appearance at London's Albert Hall where he had performed his resurrected opus, "Smile." The next week The *Los Angeles Times* contained a big ad for an upcoming Disney Hall concert of the same work, the musical saga of American history that I remember he'd been working on with Van Dyke Parks back in 1966 when I was current. And I also knew the reality: that Brian was Big Time Legend and that I was a footnote. That our encounter up in the Hollywood Hills was freestanding, a one-off. I knew there would be no song collaborations and that I should simply savor the time I'd lucked into. That I must face being back on the sidelines of pop culture. That, as I write, I must ready myself for my Sunday gig at the little Italian restaurant in Playa Del Rey, where we play in a corner for tips and pasta and a glass (or two) of wine. That I must, must, remember to close the lid of the lavatory bowl in our new digs — the sloping, creaking, rickety flat on the top floor of the old house in squeaky-clean Monrovia — because if I leave it open Rollo might come in and drink from the bowl, as was his wont in our old home in Altadena. We allowed him to drink out of the clean bowl in the old home, but in the exile digs he mustn't be allowed to drink because Regina has added a toxic cleanser to that bowl and I must, must, remember that. There are warning signs everywhere, but I just this minute failed to close that lid once more. We have now, at my insistence, resorted to $20 fines.

So that is the reality of my life. The land of the sloping floor................

But now I'm determined to organize my days into work, work,

work — and closing the lavatory lid. I will focus my energies onto my next Mel Bay songbook. No songs from Mr. Wilson, much as I'd like that dream to come true. Instead a bunch of new ones by me and all about Regina, who will sing them for the CD. The book is called *The Ian Whitcomb Songbook*. I will pour my all into this vessel. I will, I will.....

OCTOBER

We have, I hope, made our final move for the time being: from the top floor apartment of the 1908 house in Monrovia to the more spacious and elegant ground floor — from a Bohemian garret flat, not befitting my age, to a high ceilinged suite of rooms that are not unlike an Eighteenth Century drawing room in London. Of course, there's not enough space and so much of our old life remains in boxes stored in many places; it's not the signature home that Regina had made at our house in Altadena. But — things could be worse. Meanwhile, four young boffins — mathematicians, biochemists, and the like — live in our old home and love it. I can't stay away from Altadena: every day I drive in with Rollo to walk in the hills, take coffee in the Coffee Gallery where I listen to the sages at the round table solve the problems of the world today, go to the P. O. Box hoping for contact from the real world, and pretend that we still live in Altadena.

Sometimes I enter the old place, to get some CDs (for website sales) from the garage, to see if the fish and the turtle still thrive in the pond. And as I pass the windows and glimpse the new arrangements I get sad-sweet memories — this was the guest bedroom where my sister slept on her visit, this was my office where I talked to Peter Bogdanovich and ended up getting hired for his movie ("Yes, yes — you've convinced me! I need no more proof!"), this was where we had jolly parties and, when the London Club met, decked out in full military uniforms, there were champagne toasts that could last for hours ("And what is the nature of your toast, Your Highness?"). Laughter and tears, drama and comedy. Almost a quarter of a century in this house. Now, in Outer Monrovia among the Kinkaids, we talk and talk about where we will make our next home.

I have an urge to move back to Hollywood, where I first lived when I was a rock star in 1965-68. Being in Hollywood, or better still, in Burbank would mean sleeping next to the factories that produce the dream world where I really am happiest inhabiting. More and more I want to retreat into that misty, fragrant dream, only emerging when I have some packaged dreams to propagate around the world: CDs, movies, songbooks.

It's forty years this month since I proudly displayed my first record release in Front Square at Trinity College Dublin to my fellow Bluesville founding musician, Barry Richardson, as he sat on his bicycle. A 45 rpm disc on the Jerden label of Seattle: "Soho" on one side and "Bony Moronie" on the other. We'd recorded the tracks in a Dublin basement in the same Square where Oscar Wilde had been born. Barry regarded the blue label, nodded and cycled off. Nobody was that impressed and rightly so. That was the nature of the society in which I grew up. There was to be no showing-off. Barry died recently, and Bluesville is history. Some academics in England have included our band in their upcoming survey of Irish Rock. Both Barry and I were from England.

From England! How far away that now seems! When I see the marquee advertising the latest Kirsten Dunst movie, *Wimbledon,* I'm jolted back. Wimbledon was next to where we lived for decades, a walk or bicycle ride across the Common to Wimbledon. The very letters spell a magic that is vanished. It has nothing to do with tennis, but a lot to do with theatres where real live comedians commanded the stage in tons of paint and made us sing "On Windmill Hill" as we waved our handkerchiefs and my mother remarked on how unhygienic this all was; where "We'll Meet Again" was introduced unexpectedly during a harmless comedy thriller causing my mother, stuck next to me and my aunt, to look for an exit. She couldn't bear to hear "We'll Meet Again" and I never asked her why. Was it memories of my father, of the War? I expect so but I never asked. At the Wimbledon Theatre that night she was trapped and in anguish and tears.

Wimbledon was toy shops, too, and a dirty hole in the wall where I could hire 9.5mm films to show on my projector back at our family flat on Putney Heath, charging a few pennies to my friends for the pleasure of silent Renfrew Of The Mounties. What a pleasure it was to make money out of fun! A boy showman. Soon I would have sound. Wimbledon! And the Common — where we would run to play on straight after we'd thrilled to a BBC children's hour TV showing of a Hopalong Cassidy, inevitably ending with a shoot-out among those giant rocks, set in a desert backed by snowy mountains and a big sky. The western would be reenacted out on the Common, in and out of the bracken and gorse and into the woods and among the shrubs. Shrubs! There's a nasty word! Among the shrubs there lurked men in macintoshes armed with bags of sweets.........When George VI died the BBC, in respect, canceled the Hopalong Cassidy that week and I was rattled. My father, always attentive to my equilibrium, wrote to the BBC, complaining in no uncertain terms. He was a good man, my father, and I wish I'd known him better.

Why did parents, who loved their children and could prove it, send them away to boarding schools? I've been shot back to prep school days recently thanks to the arrival of the latest Newlands School Magazine. Between the winters of 1949 and 1954 I attended Newlands. But the school I knew was worlds away from present day Newlands. The school I knew was boys ruled by men, with a matron or two and a music mistress thrown in. We ate toothpaste to stave off hunger. As punishment for sitting on a bun at tea I was caned. The headmaster, a World War One veteran, was terrifying but reasonable. "This is hurting me as much as it's hurting you," he said as his cane swished down. Afterwards he shook my hand and assured me I would still be allowed to play his gramophone records of 1920s popular songs. All he was doing was what his duty told him to do. All my parents were doing was what their parents had done. If you came from my class and you had the money then, naturally, you sent your children away. A sacrifice but a necessary one. Suffering was our duty.

At 8 years old I was escorted by my loving parents to a train at Victoria Station, London, and handed over to a bluff ex-sea captain, busily corralling a herd of same-aged boys in grey uniforms, some brave and some blubbing. Prior to being handed over, I'd been taken to the railway station News Theatre for a tonic of Tom & Jerry and the Atom Bomb latest; I'd been lifted into the engine driver's cab and seen the blazing furnace and drunk in the smell of locomotion, down-to-earth, manly, grown-up. But now there was no more distraction, no more putting off the inevitable. The time had come to say good-bye, and I was determined not to cry, because it embarrassed my father. After a few weeks at Newlands School, in salty Seaford on the south coast of England, far, so far, from Putney Heath, I had abandoned all hope of ever seeing my parents again. "Your faces had faded," I told them when, miraculously, they reappeared at half-term in the vestibule of Newlands.

That was the winter of 1949. Now I hold the glossy, multicolored, magazine-sized Newlands School Magazine for 2004, printed on thick art paper. The cover is credited to a pupil called Noriko Sasamoto and described as a "construction using wire and wax." Inside is an editorial by a Caroline who writes of the "excellence" and "diversity" of the Newlands "experience." There is opera, ballet, musicals — performed by the school. There is excitement about the imminent anniversary of the school, founded in 1854, chiefly for sons of aristocrats. There will be a laser display and arts and sports events involving Sri Lanka. The headmaster calls himself "Buster" Price and I'm sure is an up-to-date teacher, kind and tolerant and understanding.

When I was at the school I once dared to ask the headmaster why we needed to have an Empire. "Because we do, Whitcomb — because we do!" And now the descendants of our one-time subjects excel in ballet, maths and cricket at Newlands in the same old red Dutch colonial house that faces the rolling Sussex Downs, and from which I stared and longed for a time when I could fly beyond the Downs and the grey sea to a place I'd seen on a map in the big schoolroom — a city at the end of the map, falling off the edge, with only flat blue in front of it: *Los Angeles*. We all pronounced it together, led by our master, and were awed.

Today's Newlands is "very much on the up," writes Buster Price. "The fastest developing school in the County. The quality of pupils, staff, resources, results and expectations is improving by the day!"

The fearful place that was once the only world I thought I'd ever know is now modern, multicultural, multi-sexual, not in the least intimidating. No need to be afraid, no need to kick against the traces. No need to be angry and write and paint and make up songs.

In my time the school magazine was very small and unadorned — mere black & white, set up by inky printers in metal type a letter at a time. After I'd settled in and accepted the tough community within the house I established myself as a writer. Soon there appeared, in that type you could feel if you ran your hand across the page (and I did) a poem of mine in the magazine:

> *The silent cottage stands so still,*
> *Its windows bleak and black*
> *No flowers adorn the window sill*
> *No garden at the back.*
> *The hinges on this haunted house*
> *Are creaking to and fro,*
> *And e'en the solitary mouse*
> *Has rightly crept below.*

I was thrilled. My teachers noted the alliteration and the interesting use of "rightly." There was hope I might enter the kingdom of culture. But at the same time I was drawing pictures inspired by American tough guy comics. (Read clandestinely because comics were prohibited at Newlands) There was one of my drawings, which I still have, depicting a New York cop firing his revolver as he hugs a fedora-ed gangster in front of him as a shield. The boys loved my comic book drawings. I formed a comb & paper band to sing "Answer Me" and other hits of the time. I can't say these were good or bad days — they were simply my days and I know no other. "He'll either go on the Halls or he'll go to jail," said the master, the old sea captain, I liked the best.

Normally he preferred pretty boys but he made an exception in my case because I liked Sophie Tucker songs and acted in his annual play productions.

For a time after I left prep school, I kept up with the Old Boy reunions. I remember an address to us by the Headmaster's son (whose father had caned me with great regret and pain): "You'll notice, as you tour your old school, a change from your time. A change of hue, a touch of the tarbrush....Let's not beat about the bush: the truth is that we need to pay our bills so we're letting in a lot of wogs." Hence the present glories of Newlands, the only Seaford prep school to survive. There were 22 of them when I arrived in 1949. George Orwell had attended a grim one nearby. In adversity and despondency I learned whatever it is that now keeps me afloat and furious in and around show business.

NOVEMBER

I'm happy to report that we're happier than before. Although happiness doesn't exactly make for interesting writing. But anyway, and, however.......

A chapter in the horrible neighbour war has closed: the Kaleem and her lackey husband were supposed to be taking us to court once again, for the umpteenth time, on October 29 at 10.30, in Dept. L of the Pasadena Superior Court.

The charges: depositing dog messes on their garden table and hosing water into their mail box — all false charges, of course. Regina had been preparing for months — the case kept being postponed — and this time she was armed with supporting letters from our friendly neighbours (the ones surrounding the enemy), and with videos culled from our security camera, and also, in person, a subpoenaed cop, glad to come along to attest that these people who drag us to court continuously are, in his words "nuts."

A day before we were to appear in court — to be once more in the Alice-In-Wonderland "Liberal" court of a Judge who tends to be overly sympathetic to those whose skin is tinted— our lady lawyer called to say that our accusers had decided to drop the case.

She had received a fax from the enemy lawyer stating that as we have left Altadena and as there has, therefore, been no more harassing of his clients, they have decided not to pursue the matter of obtaining a Restraining Order against Mrs. Whitcomb.

But — if the Whitcombs should dare to move back to Altadena and start harassing again then his clients would not hesitate to take legal action once more. All pure fantasy — a microcosm of America today, of a virtual world of lies and disinformation and the abuse of democracy.

We have retreated for now. But we will return.

Despite past misgivings about Monrovia as a trifle twee and frou-frou we are quite enjoying life here. It's startling to be greeted by smiling faces instead of black scowls and four-letter words; to hear the sounds of our new neighbours and not be offended or frightened or disgusted.

Above us in the old house are a young mother and her little daughter, Dixie Lee; in the little house out back is an even younger family — a Starbucks manager with a brand new baby and a two-year old. Regina and I are like the Lord and Lady of the Manor because we rent the largest floor — and that's as it should be since we are the elders. So this is our new community of cheerfulness and greetings and mutual aid: when it rained last week Dixie Lee's mother pulled my freshly delivered newspaper from the front lawn and placed it by the front door in the dryness of the porch.

This old-fashioned porch is perfect for ukulele songs like "When You Travel Down The Road That Leads To Nowhere" ... No — perhaps that's not quite apt, but you know the sort of number I mean. Traveling down roads to nowhere is how I feel in a black dog mood. I mean, where is my life heading when associates that I used to call friends have overtaken me and are jetting here and there, breathless with projects and productions — Taylor Hackford's assistant tells me her master is in New York at present and will be in London next week but messages will be picked up; Michael Feinstein is currently in London, too, preparing to open his one-man show at the Haymarket Theatre and messages can be left at his Los Angeles home, and how is your name spelled? I knew these men when they were lads and I was the one with the name.

Getting back to the Nowhere Road song: it certainly excited Brian Wilson when I sang it to him in Danny Hutton's kitchen last summer, during one of our rare encounters with real mainline entertainment industry people. I suppose that, like me, the genius Beach Boy wasn't thinking through the lyrics, was under the spell of the charming melody and harmony. Perhaps Brian and I are victims of today's virtual world of wishful thinking under a blanket of fantasy?

Monrovia takes Halloween very seriously. In Britain it's hardly observed. There we're more interested in burning Guy Fawkes in effigy on bonfire night, November 5. Our street, Myrtle, is famous for its ghoulishly decorated homes on Halloween. Tombstones started appearing weeks before the night, and there are bloody bodies popping out of front lawns where gardeners usually tread. Instead of leaf blower noises there have been howls. Instead of old folk discussing the latest friend who has "passed" or been "lost" there are streams of blood flowing from bay windows and disembodied heads with tongues lolling out are to be seen leaning against a Bush/Cheney sign. The celebration scares our dog Rollo no end.

In my new office, which takes up what should really be the family drawing room, my keyboard is in easy reach of my desk. From the desk I can see the bookshelves crammed with my music reference books, the collected sheet music, the books on British Music Hall acts such as Max Miller and Old Mother Riley.

Also from my desk, where I sit in an old wooden chair that once sat in my mother's flat on Putney Heath, I can see Regina in the front room, her office, working at this computer at her desk (which she won on a game show just prior to my asking her to marry me). All round us are windows from which we can see the good, law-abiding people of Monrovia passing by — with baby carriages, and cuddly dogs, and contentment on their faces. This may not be diversity but it's all right with me. And English is spoken. Of course, this is not the stuff that art is made of. But it means a good night's rest for the wife and me.

Recently I've been writing songs for my next Mel Bay publication, to be titled *The Ian Whitcomb Songbook*. This was Bill Bay's idea and he's the boss. The top lines and chords will be suitable for ukulele players and pianists — and everybody else. When all is said and done music, if it's any good, can be reduced to melody, harmony and rhythm, plus words, of course. Unless you're providing a service for dancers or mood music for movies, you have to have words. Otherwise music is abstract. And who wants that? Abstract art, like twelve tone scales and atonality, was part of the aberration movement of the 20th century, driven by "artists" who couldn't connect with the wishes of the people. Artists are artisans, servants of the people, providing a little glimpse of God for their edification and enjoyment. A little bit of the forbidden fruitcake.

So, amidst the recent turmoil of our life, I have been turning out songs at my electronic keyboard. It's better than a real piano because it has a marimba effect with an echo and that makes each note and chord ring out true and pure and terribly rich. I don't need any frills — any ornaments or arpeggios or flash chords — to fool people with. This is pure words and music. My songs are dance numbers you can also listen to as part of continuous saga: there's a song about losing our house, and one about Regina's new imaginary garden; one about her need to dance, about her hope that her lover will prove true and really change, even as she continues to launder his clothes, his theses and his thoses.

There's a rumba, "Restless," concerning a woman sitting at home alone with her knitting but who's itchy to get out and dive into a dance hall. This she does and in the swirl of the crowds she meets a lounge lizard who sweeps her into a sexy rumba from which she has to wriggle her escape — perhaps even slap her way out of. The song shows the dangers inherent in reckless no-holds-barred dancing.

I take a pride and a satisfaction in setting down the notes and the rests and the rhythms onto music manuscript paper. I like the lead in the pencil and the magic of the eraser. I like inking in the final sheet and making a shiny copy on the fax machine. I like the look of my scrawl—like a painting. Then into a folder goes the song, ready to be removed for performance at Cantalini's restaurant in Playa Del Rey on Sunday. This is the test of the song. Will the diners be distracted from their pasta by my song? Will they applaud? Will they stuff money into our tip mug? My music is taken straight into the front line and battle-proved. I am no ivory tower artist.

Eventually, in the first week in December, we will record the best, the most proved, songs in the collection. I have reserved Rick Cunha's Rainbow Garage studio in the San Fernando Valley.

This is where we recorded the music for *Stanley's Gig, The Cat's Meow*, and *Last Call*. Regina will be there to make sure the songs are in her key.

The rest of the songs in the Mel Bay songbook will be selected from stuff I've written going back to my first efforts in the days when I was a student at Trinity College, Dublin and playing in Bluesville, Ireland's first successful rock and roll group. From those days came my first recordings, "This Sporting Life" and "You Turn Me On." But will these rock songs work in a songbook? Will they stand up on the printed page and be transferable to ukulele and piano? Or will they remain electric slices peculiar to their period. I mean, would you want to play "Wooly Bully" on the uke or piano without benefit of guitars, sax and the distinctive chant of Sam The Sham? I am ruthlessly selecting my old rock songs to see if they work.

I must temporarily halt this letter: Regina and I need to start motoring along the old Route 66, or Foothill Blvd., to Pasadena and Conrad's Family Restaurant for the Monday night Salon, a venerable institution.

What is a Family Restaurant? Conrad's has a cocktail bar — is that correct for families? Do we qualify as a family? We have no children, but we consider our pets as sacred. Anyway, we always get a warm welcome in the cocktail bar at Conrad's: the waiter immediately brings us vodka martinis with two olives in each glass. A charming fellow, he's often disappearing into Mexico where his family lives. The waiters here work 12-hour days, saving up their money for spending back home across the border. Am I that attached to England? I still have my accent and my passport and, like our waiters, I can't vote — but the mileage that divides me from my motherland is only one reason why I don't keep popping across, geographically, spiritually, or politically. The thing is I like America and that's why I live here.

I do wish our waiters were a little more loyal to the local culture. I can't discuss the films of Tim McCoy with them, nor Charles Starrett ("The Road That Leads To Nowhere" was featured in a Starrett western called *Terror Trail*). Still, we get along famously, me and Juan and Jesus and Xavier — smiling and tipping and I always get the delicious signature bread pudding, specially reserved by tacit understanding. The best things in life are ritual, are tradition.

I've been eating at Conrad's since I first moved to this area, in 1979. I used to breakfast my guests after my morning shift on KROQ (6 am to 10am). Then, when I moved to KPCC and was broadcasting from 10pm till midnight I'd bring guests to Conrad's for a late night cocktail or bread pudding.

One night I grew irritated because the waitress seemed to be taking an awful long time fetching me my onion rings. I walked to the front desk to register my complaint, but there was a crowd at the desk and I couldn't get through. An odd crowd, standing motionless, like statues in a wax museum, among them the manager and my waitress. In the middle, and seemingly touching them, was a disheveled man in a raincoat and slouch hat. "What's holding up my rings?" I said as I walked on by, heading for the restroom. No reply. And no word or even a look as I returned and strode past them, head in air.

When, after an eternity, the waitress appeared with a plate of heaped and deep-tanned onion rings, I admonished her for the delay.

"Delay?" she said, fixing me with a very hard and un-service industry stare. "We were the ones who were delayed! No – we were being held captive!"

What was she talking about?

"I'm talking about the hold-up that was taking place — the raincoat guy had a gun pointed into the manager's ribs and the crook had his boot on my foot, too! The getaway car was right outside and, boy, did they getaway fast and straight onto the 210!"

Well, I never! "Yeah, and you were bitching about onion rings while we were in danger of losing our lives!"

That was a long time ago and maybe I'm wiser. These days I tiptoe about and let them bring my rings and martinis without me ordering. I always have the same dinner: salad with plenty of beets and croutons, covered in ranch dressing; followed by a lump of meat smothered in a Spanish sauce with a raw onion on top (my touch, the raw onion). All this leads up to the grand climax of the bread pudding, a delight that has nothing in common with its English namesake, a glutinous mess of porridge-like awfulness, a reminder of post-war prep school fare. No, this is the American pudding so it's bright and cold, tasty and sweet and fattening.

I usually enter Conrad's, with or without Regina, at 6.30, and, of course, the martini is immediately mixed and served. Then there's the wait to see who will enter the stage. And it is like a stage: the salonists come in through a side door that lets them appear as if by cue in a play. Of course, we are truly democratic in that anybody, of whatever stripe, can join our group — geniuses, bores, even our neighbours are welcome (Indeed, a few years ago the husband of the Iranian turned up, dashing to the table like a schoolboy eager to please and pouring out his life to us without prompting).

Later:
I made notes at tonight's Salon.
Usually I return in a blur and can only remember that I had a good time from the moment the martini arrived. I'd like to leave you with a flavor of a typical Salon night. I counted ten of us, but I'm not going to account for everybody. Here goes: young Joseph, a recent high school graduate, was already seated in the booth when we arrived. He is having a U. S. Cavalry uniform especially tailored for him in India. Vainly he tried to explain to me the difference between a republic and a democracy. Ancient Greece entered the explanation and I disposed of it at once. I never got a pithy answer. And what is the Electoral College and can I become an undergraduate? Why can't you have one man/one vote and be done with it? The election was tomorrow. Everyone was a-twitter. I simply observed.

Co-founder Jim Dawson entered the stage next. He's always ready with a pun. Tonight's first one concerned the salmon I was considering ordering (as a change from the smothered steak). "You are an a-fish-ionado," he punned. Very clever. Certainly a welcome diversion from politics. Edgar, the children's librarian arrived and ordered his first Foster's and then returned to Jim a DVD of a B picture he'd borrowed: called *Carnival Of Souls*. We discussed scary films, Regina stating that the films that scare her have to do with being "wrongfully accused." Was she thinking of our neighbours? Libby came on stage with her trademark glasses pushed up into her hair. She announced that one of her racehorses, "Hot Sea," is to be escorted up to Stockton for a breeding session. Have the animals been introduced to each other? Will they be attracted? Libby assured us that the horses simply get stuck in without standing on ceremony... No mucking about. Gloria, our old black lady, rolled up in her trademark leather cap back to front. She gallivants about the country attending college reunions and the like. She and Jim hail from West Virginia, a very impoverished state, so they say. Gloria has played many roles in her long life. Right now she's an inspector of polls. Steve, a vociferous hater of President Bush, and who can be found most mornings holding court and solving the world's problems at the round table at The Coffee Gallery in Altadena, was ordering Conrad's celebrated fried chicken when Ray came in.

Now Ray, a rockabilly star in faraway countries like Finland and Slovenia, is a rabid Republican and considers many of our Salonists to be unreconstructed hippies. He usually comes in to us from his perch at the Mexican restaurant we used to frequent and he's fresh with news of what Paul McCartney has just told him over a margarita. Then, after the Salon, he returns to his bachelor flat to get information from Art Bell, the AM radio host who broadcasts from a hut in the desert. Mr. Bell has the latest sightings of UFOs and news of traitors and other threats to the American way of life. But such is the spell of our Salon that Ray and Steve and the rest all get along fine.

Is this a republic or a democracy, I ask, as Regina tugs at me to leave, for our agreed departure time has arrived. And, as we are heading through the cocktail bar door, I follow up with: "And does the Electoral College have a decent canteen?"

Next week, with any luck, I will be in Japan and starting a tour with Janet Klein & Her Parlour Boys. I hope I return a fan of that country. I know that we British and Japanese share a sense of reserve and good manners.

DECEMBER

This is my last epistle of the year. My father, long dead, used to use "epistle," writing to me when I was away at boarding school. He used the grand, biblical word because — my guess — he was uneasy writing to people, especially to those he loved. He was shy, finding it hard to express emotions of love. Hence long words, euphemisms and circumlocutions. In short, he was the opposite of myself — who lets it all hang out, never tucking anything in. Verbal diarrhea, as my mother would say.

So, Merry Christmas! — as it says on the plastic bag that held the toy I bought in Kiddy Land, Tokyo, Japan. They were merrily celebrating Christmas half way through November. Boy, do they love Christmas! It should be spelled "Xmas" because poor old Jesus Christ doesn't seem to put in an appearance in Japan. Come to think of it, I didn't see much of Buddha there either. Japan is a very modern country, in the best sense of the word. Of course, I'm gearing up to tell you about the November tour of Japan as one of Janet Klein's Parlour Boys. No, you're much more than that, interjects Regina. You're a star, you're more than that. Yes, but no-one was requesting me to come over to the Orient and tour as me myself. I grant you I'm far from being a Boy, but I really enjoy being a part of Miss Klein's outfit; I like accompanying; I like being a craftsman.

We played ten days and they were amongst the most unforgettable days of my life. My journal is crowded with the details. I love Japan; I'm homesick back over here; it was a glimpse of paradise. If only America had such consistently public good manners, cleanliness, consideration for others, the nimbleness not to bump into others in the street. In short, civilization.

I saw only one fatty the entire time I was there. And I had left America reluctantly, saying I had no interest in Japan or its culture. I foolishly joked that I was frightened I might step on somebody there. Sensibly, nobody laughed at this...

A company called Seven Gods (or Tom's Cabin) brought us over. They've been in the business since the 1970s and back then they brought in the likes of Tom Waits, Elvis Costello, Leon Redbone. Lately they toured The Ukulele Orchestra Of Great Britain, friends of mine. The uke is popular in Japan. Jolly, clean and sprightly, like the Japanese. None of that dark, brooding Delta blues guitar and guttural moaning. The sun's always rising and radiating over there. Everything with a smile.

Mind you, the pocket history of Japan that I read from cover to cover on the United Airlines flight wasn't all smiles — from Commodore Perry's arrival in 1853 until MacArthur took over in 1945 there was lots of bloodletting: prime ministers were routinely assassinated, usually by disgruntled young officers; there was a good deal of self-disembowelment by shamed officials - keeping face, I suppose — and generally swords flashed and in trice a head was neatly chopped off to roll ritually away. It all seemed a bit removed from my experience, so I was relieved to read that the young Emperor Hirohito — the Divine One in charge during World War Two — had a smashing time on his trip to the West in 1922. He adored British upper-class manners, a sort of casual formality, and came home with a taste for fried eggs and bacon, a dish he ate regularly even as Japan was being pulverized by American bombs.

The first thing I saw from the plane as we landed in Tokyo was a Holiday Inn. Nearby was FedEx. There were no Customs but lots of greetings. Every uniform was immaculate. Big TV screens blazed the latest news about Bush — and in English, too. Another screen told you, by way of an animated red line, exactly where the latest traffic congestion was on the freeway.

Janet Klein specializes in "naughty and obscure songs" of the 1920s and 1930s. I've played ukulele and accordion in her band for several years. Occasionally, she lets me sing a novelty song. No rock & roll is allowed. Pity — I was told the Japanese would eat up my Elvis songs. But Janet has an image and it's very effective. She has

CDs released in Japan and the Tokyo Tower Records store has the latest one, *Living In Sin*, displayed prominently. Janet takes great pains with her stage wear — always flowers in the hair — and she does look a trifle oriental, like a dainty doll. Of course, you can tell from her name that she's not a local. But they love formality and good manners and grace — and Janet has all these. I, in turn, dusted off my English gentleman background and was on my best behaviour. I witnessed my first bow at the airport: a female official — possibly a parking lot attendant — seeing off a fully laden taxi. Deep bows. I took note. I could use this bow on stage. Lucky I'd brought my best suits and ties, especially the Trinity College Dublin (Old Boys) tie.

Our tour band was a stripped-down version of the American Parlour Boys. In fact, only half the band are American: Dave (bass), and Tom (guitar). Our violin player, Benny, is German. We really got to know each other since we had to double up in most of the hotels at which we stayed. These places are where your average Japanese businessmen stay and so the cramp of our quarters was offset by the privilege of living native.

Tiny, dear little rooms, furnished with thoughtful objects such as a flashlight, a tea pot, with bags of green tea, that you heat on a Sony hot plate set in your bedside table, and a kimono. Ah, a kimono! Regina had asked me to bring her back a kimono — and here was one for the asking, or taking. But no! I resisted — and later, guided by Janet and her brand new husband Robert, I was led to a quaint shop in a narrow alley where there were rows of vintage classy kimonos. And relatively inexpensive (I mean a few thousand-thousand yen), but don't tell Regina.

Our first night stay was in Yokohama, to which we'd traveled over a ribbon of concrete. Well kept and very clean concrete, but concrete just the same. Above us along the route were tasteful towers of business and industry and, perhaps, plain living. Down in the streets were electric signs running downwards because that's how Japanese script is — so that the advertising signs looked like decorative lanterns. Everything appeared to be new, or at least not old, not antique, maybe collectible. My historical reading told me that nothing much dated from before 1945. All the big cities had been reduced to rubble in the war. The war against the Americans, I mean, as opposed to the war that the Japanese began in 1931 against Manchuria and then China.

At this stage, let me note that our road managers, as well as everybody else we met, were young — entranced by us as much as we were entranced by them. So enthusiastic, so eager to communicate with us in English, so keen on American music, American everything. Therefore I soon realized that it was pointless and tasteless to bring up the past. Early on I asked one of our drivers, a lad in his early twenties, what was the name of the current emperor. He didn't know for sure. He was apologetic. He said he'd find out. And none of the wonderful crew who accompanied us were religious in any way. They laughed politely at our fresh-off-the-plane comments as we adjusted to a strange new country. Well, not strange to Tom, our guitarist: he's been to Japan several times and once he won a steak-eating contest in Kobe. He's always hungry and was constantly looking for food bargains. The nearest steak house in Yokohama offered steaks starting at $75. But never mind: Tom had spotted a Denny's, next to a McDonald's, where he hoped to purchase a Grand Slam. "You come 5000 miles for that!" spluttered Benny, the violinist.

Benny, from Munich, had armed himself with a guide book and a dictionary. He was my first roommate and the next day he led me on a walking tour of Yokohama, speaking Japanese with dictionary in hand, smiling and bowing as we ventured onto the subway, making sure I took my shoes off in the restaurant before stepping onto the parquet floor, expressing horror when I stuck my chop sticks into the rice and left them there ("No! No! That's a funereal gesture — it means bones!").

We stood with shoppers, obediently in columns, outside Japan's biggest department store — 20,000 employees, all contented — waiting till the clock struck ten and the manager signaled for us to enter. When the hour arrived figures in native costume from all over the world popped out of each hour as the clock played "It's A Small World After All." I must tell Dick Sherman, the composer, when next I see him at a show biz party. On second thought, I'm sure he already knows. Dick's Disney songs are everywhere.

Our first appearance was that evening, Saturday, at a venue called Thumbs Up, decorated like a Deep South shack along the lines of House Of Blues: stained wood bar, Dixie road signs, Jack Daniels and leathery hamburgers. An odd contrast to the streamlined, sterile building it's housed in (on the umpteenth floor). Some of our venues had names exotic to Japan but downright homey to America: Banana Hall, Blue Jay Way. Our opening acts (all excellent, if a little derivative) had names seemingly Anglo-Normal but yet, on closer look, odd: Fresh Lemmon, Izumi & Doggies, Milky Banana, The Rats Orchestra.

When Janet danced trippingly on in all her finery, with her cries of "Yippee" and "Whoopee," the audience was squealingly delighted. When we performed they immediately clapped along. This was to be a national trait on our tour. They answered my "Hello" community song with appropriate "Hellos" and they were consistently well behaved and polite in their enthusiasm. I bowed deeper and deeper, till Benny whispered to me that maybe I was rather overdoing it and could be misunderstood.

Janet and I featured a duet called "How Could Red Riding Hood Have Been So Very Good And Still Keep The Wolf From The Door?" From the first night onwards Janet and I had no luck trying to explain the meaning of this slightly off-color comedy song. We couldn't even explain who "Red Riding Hood" was. Polite silence. Movements, gestures, smiles, were all effective. But not sentences.

We soon realized that the Japanese, in general, do not understand English. Quite right, too. I'm glad they prefer just the veneer of Western culture — the joyful noise, the splashy movies, an old pair of Levi's — and not the substance. They have nothing to learn from us. We have old-fashioned good manners to re-learn from them. For myself, I was knocked back to my 1950s childhood when I was taught to be quiet, to shake hands gently, to be deferential. Here in Japan I saw a dainty and charming version of that teaching enacted all the time.

We Parlour boys, not stage centre like Janet (and how the audience gazed at her, enraptured!), had the opportunity to observe what lay before us. And from opening night till our last venue, at Blue Jay Way in Tokyo we watched and watched, like voyeurs. I, for one, was struck by the extraordinary beauty of the Japanese: girls and boys with slim figures, gorgeous dark sleek hair, clear skin. Actually, the boys look rather pretty — just a passing fashion so I'm told. My fellow Parlour Boys were admiring of this delicate figurine beauty but disappointed that the island women lacked big bottoms and chests.

After a few days I felt as if all of Japan belonged to one family. But where were the parents, let alone the grandparents? Another history book told me that the vast majority of Japanese were born after 1945.

We were able to look at the old — the old culture, I mean — when we arrived in the ancient city of Kyoto on the first leg of our tour. A day's sight-seeing had been thoughtfully arranged by the tour promoters. So in this city, the old seat of the Emperor, we traipsed happily around, admiring centuries-old buildings, guidebook stuff from before the embarrassments of the 20th century and the incursion of machine guns and jazz: shrines, an over-golden temple (fully rebuilt in 1955 after being burned down by a disturbed monk), and a shogun castle complete with creaking floorboards (to warn the warlord of any intruding would-be head-choppers).

It was raining and there were lots of fellow sightseers (mainly native) but nobody disturbed the peace and nobody collided with us. The school children, herding close together and always happy, were particularly well behaved. They wore neat uniforms — the girls in disturbingly short pleated skirts.

Tom, who as I mentioned before, has toured Japan before and

seen this/done that, stayed near our tour vans, only straying away to go on music shop sorties in order to offer for sale to startled store owners — startled but polite, of course — a guitar or mandolin. I wonder why, after all his local experience, he hasn't learned that the Japanese don't haggle. Still, despite no sales he came back contented — he'd found that local delicacy: the pastry bun filled with hot pork. I never did fancy the pork puffs but the lightness of most of the food we ate was a delight. Of course, a wash-down with a Starbucks latte later crowned off the meal. Yin and yang, East meets West.

I noticed that our vans were parked near two enormous tourist buses emblazoned with two different slogans: "Heartful Sightseeing" and "Relaxable Sightseeing." I found this touching rather than amusing.

Into the night we journeyed, two vans charging down mountainous country — Japan seemed to be all mountains relieved by ultra-modern cities — and frequently roaring through endless, but well-lit and friendly, tunnels. Hajime, 29, head road manager and our paymaster-general, drove the Parlour Boys and was politely happy to be taught American slang; I sat in the second, smaller van (the one reserved for Janet and Robert), next to Taku, our 23 year old driver who plays rock guitar and who was breathtaken when I told him that Jimmy Page had played on one of my early records. I felt I was sitting pretty with the VIPs. And why not? I'm the senior member, at 63.

Here's what my daily journal says: "We were on our way to Hiroshima. Hiroshima! The very name evokes atom bombs and thousands killed instantly. As we spiraled down into the twinkling city set in a plain surrounded by mountains I had an eerie feeling — as if we were entering the Valley Of Death, where shadow figures from that horrid fission flash were fixed forever on the spot where they were on that fatal morning in August 1945. When I was four and snug in England, searching, with Thomas The Tank Engine's help, for Nutwood, home of Rupert, The Bear."

So there was a different tone to our sightseeing in Hiroshima. Taku led Robert, Janet, and me to the Peace Memorial Museum, bang at the epicentre of where the bomb exploded. We thought we'd be a short time there — we stayed for hours. We were almost ineffably moved. I emerged into the sunshine as a newly-minted pacifist. Wall information inside had informed me that the Bomb had been preceded by a flurry of parachutes carrying scientific equipment for measuring the effects. That the exercise was really a demonstration to the real enemy (the new bad guys — our recent Soviet pals) to warn them about what they'd be in for should they choose to anger America and her allies. A callous exercise, an experiment. That's what the wall information said.

However, it was the human details that really got to me. Burned into my eyes was the encrusted tricycle the three year old boy had been riding when the great flash came. This trike had been buried with the child until the family grave was ready. Now the trike is on view in the museum. Around that time, in 1945, I was riding my own trike down green and pleasant English country lanes in search of Nutwood.

Back at our hotel I was jolted back into the present: Hajime asked if I would be so kind as to accompany him to a record store around the corner. The owner would be honoured to meet me — he has some records of mine. He has? I am known in Hiroshima? At the shop, several flights up a staircase in a tall and narrow building, were displayed several of my LPs, some dating back to my rock splendour in the 1960s. Even as we entered they were spinning a track from *Yellow Underground*, a rather off-beat LP on my first label, Tower, and one that certainly blazed a trail to my rock demise: the track consists of 20 minutes of spoken word, being the memoirs of a crusty old British Empire Colonel.

There was much shaking of hands in the shop. I was touched and amazed and thrilled. My message had penetrated Japan, even as far as Hiroshima. That night, as we performed and as the audience clapped along and cried and danced, I felt good that we, the latest foreign invaders, were bringing not mass destruction but music of delight, music that doesn't hurt, to a place that had once been decimated but was now, in the true sense of the word, born again.

More cities, more mutual acclaim, more delicious unusual cuisine. I can't remember what the dishes were, they came flinging at me like plates in a high-speed juggling act. I do know I was relieved to have missed one dining experience: Janet and Robert joined Hajime for a late night snack at his favourite eating place, a hole-in-the-wall cafe no bigger than an outhouse. Commanded by a chef with one eye and a cigarette dangling from his lips, together with dribbling spit caused by culinary excitement, the cafe's fare consisted of near-dead sea creatures. The chef, talking and dragging and dribbling as he worked, would reach below his counter, as cockroaches fox-trotted across the wall behind him, to pull up some struggling sea creature. After a cursory examination the poor thing was dropped into the boiling pot — but only for a few seconds. Then — Plop! — and the wriggling object was now on a plate, mattressed with seaweed and such. Hajime ate with relish. Janet and Robert observed as would have Dr. Livingstone. I'm glad I was in bed with Jack Daniels.

Our ten day tour climaxed in Tokyo. There I could Starbuck and Subway to my heart's content. Oddly familiar. Ideal chains. Dreamlike. Was I in a virtual movie? At Tower Records, the best-run I've ever been in, I was pleased to find my five Japanese CDs well-displayed in both the Country and Folk sections. We sold-out for the two shows at Blue Jay Way, a futuristic club owned and operated by Sony. There I met a gentleman, whose card told me he was something big at Warner Music Japan, who used to listen religiously to my radio show back in those dear old days when Los Angeles had free-spirited radio shows, when I ran a nightly two hour farrago on KPCC. He told me he has precisely 30 of those shows secure on DAT. He fondly remembered me refereeing Jim & John on rock & roll night, Wednesdays at 10pm. I was staggered.

Tokyo is a city within itself like New York or London. I don't mean it's cosmopolitan like those other great cities; I mean that Tokyo isn't like the rest of Japan. So the audiences, sartorially elegant and physically smashing though they were, were super cool about audience participation: in fact, they were as hushed as the tomb. But they loved us, keeping the demonstration of that love till after the show. Our encore song, "Ballin' The Jack," was thus received reverently despite my singing braggingly of jazzing 98 girls against a wall and only finishing off the other two — to make a round 100 — after my John Thomas had been re-invigorated by a plate of oyster stew. A decent dose of Vintage American popular culture.

Tom's Cabin, our promoter, hosted us to a late night supper at a very refined Chinese restaurant. Toasts were made, presents given, a few tears quietly shed. We expressed enduring love. I hope to see them all again, to return to Japan and sing some old-fashioned rock & roll. But I doubt that I will. As Andy Wickham likes to remind me: you only go round once so enjoy it for the moment's sake.

As we took off for Los Angeles I tried to prepare myself for the shock of returning to a relative barbarism. The in-flight movies — *Harry Potter, King Arthur*, and *The Terminal* — were watched without sound: they looked as plainly stupid as they probably are. The breakfast omelettete tasted like cardboard. Gently, gently, back to reality.

And then, to really tell me I'm back home in the U.S.A, a shriveled crone in Vegas-loud clothes shoved me hard as we waited in the aisle to disembark upon landing at LAX. In order to make way for her I would have had to topple several hundred passengers in the aisle line in front of me. But she would have none of this, continuing to shove and butt. Finally, succumbing to modern western life styles, I back-elbowed her into her seat. From there she cell-phoned her friend across the aisle. In a hideous New York cackle she informed her: "I can't move because of the orchestra!" I've never heard "orchestra" sound so vile and damning.

However, I'm settled in, back near the trenches of show biz, content to be here typing in peaceful Monrovia, watching the Christmas decorations start to blaze and twinkle, listening to a CD presented to me by Tom's Cabin: Petty Booka, two Japanese ladies with tingle-making little girl voices singing, "I Saw Mommy Kissing Santa Claus." I'm sure they learned this phonetically and that they understood not a word. And that's how our western culture should be received in Japan, the land of apparent paradise.

Happy Xmas!

An afterword & greeting from Regina...

Hello all,
I wanted to take this opportunity to wish you a very happy end of year — however you observe it. May you stay warm, loved and stress-free. Protect your health and increase your joy.
Thank you to all of you who have bolstered me up during this very strange year. It does help to know that others have been through similar trials. I truly believe that everything happens for the highest good and we'll emerge from this grateful for the journey.

Dance every chance you get.
Affectionately,
Regina

175

2005

JANUARY

These letters are not about the present or future but about the past — in this case, December of last year. You see, the past is a safe country because I can control it, and even change and distort it as I write. Sometimes I can even understand it, get a little proportion.

In the early 1960s, while working as a brewer's drayman during a Trinity College Dublin vacation, a cockney worker — someone who really did work up a sweat as a member of the working classes, as opposed to me, a mere student drone — commented on the history honors degree I was then working towards: "'Istry?" he scorned. "Wot you wanna study 'istry for? It's all 'appened and there's not a fuckin' thing you can do abart it, know wot I mean?" But, as I say, the very act of writing down the past fashions capricious happenstance into a sort of art, or a tissue of lies.

Yesterday, December 28, 2004, we were forced to flee from Lone Pine — but more about the reason later....

Lone Pine is my demi-paradise up the map to the right of the High Sierras; that town of one lone traffic light, where skiers bound for the mountain resort of Mammoth — impatient SUV commanders, phones clamped to ears — often have to skid to a halt due to an intersection with Whitney Portal Road. The commanders, with lean-boned supermodel wives at their side, and kids, buried in video screens, scattered out of sight behind in the vast recesses of the luxury truck, are, no doubt, irked to have to stop in this hick town of Lone Pine at this obscure road.

But for me Whitney Portal Road is the way to a sort of heaven. Here Humphrey Bogart, pursued by cops, raced his car to the High Sierras and poured down defiance before getting snipered to death. The road he flew up travels through the Alabama Hills, a strange land of twisted boulders and rocks set in sand marked with winding trails that lead to nowhere, but with a stunning and inspirational backdrop of mountains capped with white. Up and down and all over, sometimes crisscrossing each other, sometimes colliding, once rode the heroes of the B Western accompanied by their camera cars and bull-horned directors. Here were countless other action men, even including Gunga Din and a lot of Bengal Lancers. Now all is silent, a fine spot for meditation.

Regina and I first discovered this neverland in the 1980s — on our way back from Mammoth — and have been coming ever since: to the Lone Pine Film Festival in 1992 when Douglas Fairbanks, Jr., Clayton Moore, The Lone Ranger, were guests of honor, and we filmed the proceedings for a BBC documentary; sometimes we'd attempt to gain entry to the mysterious ranch hotel run by one Irene Cuffe (pronounced "Coofay"in the French manner), and who advertised herself in stills posted around town as "The Actress of a Thousand Faces" and who always demanded and was granted an appearance in the Grand Parade at the Lone Pine Film Festival, sitting in Gay 90s costume in a vintage car, waving in a British royalty manner and displaying a sample of her thousand faces, especially a special grimace if she felt the press weren't paying their proper respect.

Later I would travel here alone, except for the dog Inspector, and sit among the rocks in the darkness, and realizing as I looked at the stars how pathetic I was, how nothing we earthlings did or said was of any importance to the universe, and how that universe was without plan, scruples, conscience or consciousness. But after I pulled out my ukulele and sang "Lone Pine Blues" I felt a lot better and Nature seemed to approve too.

The trip we made on Monday was a mercy one: to take Regina's 10-year-old nephew as far as Lone Pine where he'd be picked up by her brother, another uncle, and thence to Mammoth where he could ski or play in the snow or play video games to his heart's content. Originally it had been planned for the boy to drive up with his father but, as Nature will have its capricious way, his father was diagnosed with numerous cancers only a few days before the holiday season. This is a truly good man who has patented and is developing a medical appliance that will be of benefit to the world. But that's the way Nature goes — randomly, unfeelingly.

Since we were already in Lone Pine on our mission and staying at the Dow Villa, the hotel where all the western stars stayed — and where we were entertained one unforgettable afternoon in 1992 by the great western director William Whitney who, between bourbons (which he kept in a wardrobe closet, a fully-stocked bar/closet) confessed to us that he always had a far richer relationship with Trigger, the horse, than with his master Roy Rogers — since we were there and with Rollo and a video camera, we decided that ITW

Productions should spring into action once more and start shooting a sequel to that monumental singing western melodrama, *Inspector To The Rescue*. This epic — four minutes in length and thus never boring — had inspired my film director friend Mike Dibb to convince the BBC to commission a salute to Hoppy and his Pals of The Saddle. I was employed as producer and Regina as continuity girl/production assistant. Naturally, this being the BBC, we never were properly paid, nor were we credited.

The form of the follow-up film is to be a James Joycean ramble by the dog Rollo along the highways and byways of California. One moment he'll be in Monrovia, the next in Altadena, and then we'll find him among the rocks and sand of the Alabama Hills. All the time he rambles he's soliloquizing in voice-over about his master and mistress and their lives.

On the evening of our Monday arrival we took Rollo up to the hills so that he could reacquaint himself with the landscape where he and I had been lost. Of course, I don't believe Rollo had felt lost at all. And he certainly didn't act worried like his master had. He simply ambled along sniffing the ground, the air, and generally searching for edibles. I've never seen him scared, except in the darkness. He doesn't care for the darkness, whereas I embrace the darkness like an old friend, one with whom I'll soon be spending eternity or oblivion or whatever.

We had a grand game of hide and seek that late afternoon with Rollo. He always found us. I felt the ghosts of Gene and Roy and Hoppy hovering around the boulders. I heard the harmony of the Sons of The Pioneers. I also heard the din of motorbikes much too nearby roaring and spluttering where hoof beats and wagonwheel clatter should have been.

Later, we ate tough steak in the Mount Whitney cafe surrounded by stills of John Wayne (in his portly eye-patched latter days rather than his sexy-slim youth of *Stagecoach*) and several stills of Robert Blake when he was Bobby, the Injun boy. God, he looked cute — as opposed to the gargoyle he's become. Does evil always show up in the evil one's face? Audrey Hepburn was on the wall too, but I don't recall her being in a western. Still, it was nice to be in a Wayne temple — makes you feel safe.

Our cocky fast-moving waiter kid, when asked whether he cared for cowboys replied, "That's all before my time." Regina riposted with the fact that Beethoven is before his time too but that doesn't mean he's not to be considered. The cocky boy hopped off.

We retired to our room at the Dow, across the main street, a room just a few feet from where John Wayne had stayed on his last trip to Lone Pine in the middle 1970s: he'd sat, all gussied up, on a horse out on Movie Road in the Hills being filmed as a still for Wells Fargo Bank. This was to be his last screen appearance.

Next morning I stepped outside with Rollo to be enveloped in softly but determinedly falling thick snow. Lone Pine had all but disappeared. We were advised not to attempt to go into the Alabama Hills. In fact, the wise old local varmints told us, we'd be darned lucky if we got back to where we came from. All snowed up. You gotta have chains. But I made a command decision. ITW Industries would have to abandon its first day of principal photography on *Rollo's Ramble.* Production would start back in Monrovia and environs — possibly with a close-up of Rollo looking out the window of our apartment determining whether the weather was going to be clement or inclement. Dogs are clairvoyant, you know.

I stood at the roadside and surveyed the traffic. Since I could see plenty of cars and trucks and SUVs churning peacefully by me — indeed splashing Rollo and me with slush as they passed — and I could see that none of these vehicles sported chains, and I knew that the road south must go downhill, as in the map, and that therefore there'd be decreasing snow especially as we neared Mojave — because that's a desert, isn't it? — I made another command decision: we'd leave immediately. Regina congratulated me on my firmness.

We caravaned back to the sunny Southland with Regina at the wheel and me in charge of feeding the CD player with rollicking themes from Laurel & Hardy films. At the start we were led by a blinking snow plow; later the snow departed and we were in sunshine, but as we reached the tip of the San Fernando Valley the sky darkened and we were enveloped in heavy rain, but we were at least back in the land of home, of culture, of what's happening — even if it is a newspaper filled with movie ads blazing names of people I used to know years ago and have now climbed way ahead of me and never return phone calls, the kind that are received by an assistant who demands, "And what is the nature of your call?" and "Please spell out your name" — and yet, and yet, all this humiliation is better than being holed up in a small town full of the ghosts of long-dead western stars and a live waitress who says, "We don't got no fruit juice."

The holidays are almost over and I'm sad. I wish life was one long party. The decorations will soon be down. We've only two more parties to attend. I'd like to have Christmas every day because it's a way to be with like-minded people, to not be alone. Christmas gets more and more to be a bind as you grow older. The Xmases I remember fondly were the ones I had as a child in the England of the early 1950s; the lumpy nylon stocking I felt reassuringly on top of the bed blankets on Christmas morning, proving to be crammed with oranges and Cadbury's Fruit & Nuts and *Film Fun* or *Radio Fun* annual; the wrapping violently stripped to reveal a toy that if I'd bought for myself in a store wouldn't have seemed special but when wrapped and given to you by someone else becomes special as if made just for you and you alone in a faraway toy factory. There's no joy in buying yourself a present.

Then there were the winter shows we went to: the pantomimes where men dressed as women and vice versa, where a young Peter Sellers rushed on stage as an impersonator of current local stars, his vocal gymnastics amazing, culminating in an uncanny impression of Al Jolson wailing "Waiting For The Robert E Lee," and then the traditional singalong at the end of the pantomime — *Cinderella* or *Babes In The Woods* when the comedian, dressed as a dame, led us in a song chorus with the words printed on a huge sheet that was rolled down behind him: "I Love Cinderella — Don't You Love Her Too?" and we'd all be required to answer "Yes, I Do, I Do, Yes, I Do, I Do!"

And not forgetting the home entertainment: family get-togethers round the piano where we'd take turns to contribute a limerick to that old chestnut "Rhymes," the verses getting progressively dirtier as the adults chimed in: "A plumber who hailed from Swansea/ Was plumbing a girl by the sea/ Said his girl, 'Stop your plumbing there's somebody coming'/ Said our plumber, *still plumbing*, 'It's me!'" — and my aunt chiding my uncle for having dared sing such a verse ("The very idea!") in front of the children and us children not having the foggiest what the rhyme was about. Xmases past! At today's' parties it's chit chat with one's peers, about who's doing too well in the Industry, and who's just passed on, and cancer and Alzheimer's.

I think I'd better stop and be positive by letting Regina take over with one of her cheerful messages.

FROM REGINA:
I'd simply like to wish you all a very good year. Not just wish you one happy day but that everyday should be happy. And if it's a blue day I hope it's a building block for future happiness.
Learn a song this year then come and sing along with us.

Tunefully,
Regina & Ian

FEBRUARY

This will be more like a letter rather than a literary effort. I'm happy that some readers have been so enthralled by our unfolding saga that they have bought bound hard copies as if my writing should be preserved like a real book rather than being thrown away into the ether like blogs are.

News: we are leading a peaceful life here in the ground floor apartment of the 1906 house on Myrtle Avenue in Monrovia. What a civilized place! neighbours and strangers greet you on the street. Of course, it helps to have the beautiful Rollo with you, tugging at the leash, eager to meet new friends at Starbucks. The emergency services work like greased lightning over here: when Regina called them after I'd acted strangely — babbling of a room full of sailors and tottering about — suddenly there they were, peering at me as I cowered from under the bedclothes. "What is your name? How old are you?" I passed the tests and they were gone in a flash. Comforting to know they're ever-ready. A policewoman waved to me the other morning. She hailed Rollo by name. You'd never get that treatment back in Altadena. There we had surly sheriffs, and scavengers pushing loaded shopping baskets, as well as Jehovah's Witnesses. A cultural thing, you know. I have to be careful at this point....

We still pop in to see the old home, which is now rented out to some very clean-cut egghead Caltech students, in order to tend to the garden or see if the fish are still living. But we'll never live there again: the Iranian witch is still spleening from her lair: Regina was quietly gardening the other afternoon when suddenly came a shout from the other side of that wretched Berlin Wall fence: "Why don't you come over and fuck me?" cried the witch.

Everyone had assured us that these neighbours would implode fairly soon — that was over a year ago. But they seem healthier and sassier than ever. So we live peacefully in Outer Monrovia in the land of scented candles, New Age books and Thomas Kinkade. And continue to shop around for a dream house costing less than a million.

This time in this year my mind's been ranging back to 1965, forty years ago. For forty years I've been a professional in show biz—I mean, I've been paid to do what I enjoy doing and unhappy otherwise. In February, 1965, what became my first hit record was in release and clambering up lots of local charts: "This Sporting Life," an adjusted folk song, eventually got me to #100 in the "Billboard" chart. Don't laugh—it was quite an achievement for a young fellow who was supposed to be studying Modern History & Political Thought at Trinity College Dublin. A few months later "You Turn Me On" was released and shot me into the Top Ten and teen idol stardom. However, I had the sense to realize that the pop world was transitory — or, at least, not my vocation — and so at the height of my fame I quit a Dick Clark "Caravan Of Stars" tour in order to return to Dublin and take my Finals. And, showing Irish understanding, the powers at TCD gave me a Second Class degree. I kept my mind and my health. I eventually became a published author.

I decided to dig into the archives — my old journals — because of the recent death of Johnny Carson. I guested on his "Tonight" show about a half dozen times and so I can claim to be part of a bygone era. I determined to look up my reactions to being at that pinnacle — sitting on a couch next to Mr. Carson's off limits desk, in the strange position of pretending to be the guest, the focus of attention, being quizzed by the interviewer, when the truth was that Carson's the star and I'm a nonentity. So there he was asking me questions and feigning interest. Still, he must have approved because I was invited back several times.

Once, while I was rehearsing a 1920s sentimental song called "Baby Your Mother," using an authentic period arrangement, Doc Severinsen, the band leader, lectured his men about playing the music straight and not hokeying it up, camping. "This music has its own special integrity," he said. I really appreciated him for that. Of course, the show having 10 million viewers, I assumed that my appearances would bestow stardom on me. But I was to be disillusioned: I hardly encountered a soul who saw me—then or now. But, being an assiduous collector of all my work, I have those Carson slots safe on video and even DVD.

But now to the archives — to find the date I first made the Carson Show—as people called it then — not *The Tonight Show*.

We will get to that date in a moment but bear with me while I skim through the pages of my 1974 journal. For just as in a real library — as opposed to the get-straight-to-the point Internet — the search can lead you into alcoves where you stop and find treasures you never sought. So here goes...............

The year is 1974:

January 7: London:
To dinner with Tim Rice and wife, Jane. Tim's hair oily and he wears a blue wide-lapelled corduroy jacket, very old, I should think. I like his careless dress. And he liked my new Debbie Dawn release ('There Goes That Song Again'). Said his greatest joy would have been to be a pop star like me: a One Hit Wonder. But I had three in the charts, I felt like protesting but stayed quiet because Tim is a man on the way up. Says he's going to try a musical about the life of Eva Peron. Has given up on the Jeeves project.

A few weeks later I was over in L.A. again — on a hard-to-get H1 work permit — putting together a PBS special about Tin Pan Alley with Taylor Hackford (these days best-known as the director of *Ray*, a film whose ads you can't avoid if you try to read a newspaper). He was then on staff at KCET.

I was also doing my act at the Mayfair Music Hall in Santa Monica, and I got a spot on the Merv Griffin show where I had to compete with the buxom but asinine wife of Xavier Cugat. His band leading days were over and he was running a restaurant in West Hollywood. One night there he learned I was English—and expressed horror. "Not a good country!" he said. "Why they wouldn't let my dog in — but they did let my wife in!"

March 1: Health food lunch with Taylor Hackford and Mexican producers from KCET. Had to be careful to differentiate between 'Chicanos', 'Latinos', and 'Mexicans'. When topic came up we speak very quietly and reverentially. I had to drink a disgusting herbal tea because the health place won't serve coffee. It contained, claimed Taylor, an aphrodisiac additive, but the effect it had on me was as if I'd consumed an atomic bomb laxative. So much for my current love life — which doesn't add up to much anyway.

March 24: Tea with Chris Isherwood and Don Bachardy. Both distressed by changes made to their Frankenstein movie which they'd taken 2 years to write and had been assured was 'sacred'. Isherwood reminded us of Somerset Maugham's comment on a film made of one his books: 'I liked the bits I wrote'. Herr Issyvoo is currently writing about his life in Germany—being honest about himself but diplomatically sketchy about those he knew. Said Hitler entranced him because he couldn't believe that such a puppet-like creature could actually have existed.

April 24: Was admitted to The Huntington Library today as a Reader In Rare Books (!) by a dotty lady with a strident schoolmarm voice. Got accepted because I told them I'm going to write a novel about Southern California. An atmosphere like being back at school. But with an added quiet of learning—where truth may at last be found. Men in baggy trousers and women in knitted wear. Far from the telephone and show biz and rejection. No call back yet, by the way, about the McDonald's Commercial I was up for the other day. I settled in rare book dept., with 'Sunshine And Grief In Southern California', a pamphlet by 'An Old Promoter'. Typewriters clacked away in a civilized manner. I'm grateful to Taylor for having got me in here via my KCET connection. But the 'Visiting Scholars' notice board doesn't show much lively research subjects: 'Synchronicity & The Frontier', 'Black Africa In Medieval Times'.

April 25: Was introduced at lunch at the Huntington today to the head of 'Americana Ephemera': an old fellow crippled by arthritis, with a peeling face. Looks sideways at you and speaks in machine gun bursts. Like many dons and profs. Said he's an antiquarian and wrote a pamphlet on the use of the word 'shit' by American soldiers. Gave me book tips for my research on my novel.

Then, in return, asked me whether I knew much about the 'de-bagging' of boys at English prep schools and/or genital painting rituals in place of birth. And I wasn't taken aback because the questions were posed in a hallowed academic setting where the seeking of knowledge knows no restrictions. Saw Randy F for dinner. Took me to a queer joint in the Valley. When I asked for dessert the waiter took a step backwards in horror. There are no desserts, he explained, because summer is near and customers are readying their bodies for the beach.

In late 1973 I'd been booked for the *The Tonight Show* but hadn't got on camera due to other guests talking too long. Another chance now came:

May 23: Conference at noon with Paul Block, talent coordinator for the Carson Show. He was very merry. Unhappily married—says it interferes with his career. He read through to me the question cards from last year's attempt to be a guest on this the most watched show in America, if not the whole world. Asked me to repeat the 'cute' Mae West tales. 'Keep funny—period', said Block. 'This is an entertainment show for people to relax to after the grind of real life — and wives!' I started to sing my composition, 'Wurzel Fudge, The Village Idiot', which was always sure-fire at the Mayfair Music Hall. Block made a sudden throat cutting gesture. 'Nix that one. Got a shorter cuter number?' We agreed on 'Hungry Women' in the end. Block dictated some no-no's: Don't ever pause, but keep talking. Don't show your stutter because he can't take cripples. Don't make cracks about Johnny. We had a fashion designer on and Johnny asked the man his opinion of his bright plaid jacket and the fashion queen says 'It's perfectly acceptable for Halloween'. So the guy was never invited back.' Rehearsal at 3:15 PM at KNBC in Burbank, with cameras. Severinsen's combo accompanied me as I sang and strummed my uke. They're really jazzmen but they were sympathetic. Block said, 'You gotta take it faster. You can't bore people'. Then we retired to his office to go through, one last time, the Carson question cards and what my responses should be. Soon it was 5pm and time to shoot. All rather impersonal. Never got to meet Carson or McMahon in advance. Glimpsed them in corridors, looking grim faced. All business. But then, I must remember that I'm in a business and not merely having fun. Then Carson turns up on set in plaid jacket and wreathed in smiles. Bad night for his monolog: 'Charlton Heston, my guest tonight, came into my dressing room and you know what happened? My sandwich opened up.' A titter or two. Carson presses on: 'Hey, my martini was so dry the janitor found dust in the urinals.' Racing: 'I see Dr. Kissinger is back from a round of peacemaking. Now he faces his biggest task: getting Sonny and Cher together again'. Hearty laughter. He's won. He does a golf swing, smirks and shrugs his shoulders. I sat watching all this in the 'Green Room', swilling free scotches. Heston was first guest. Rather than talk about the earthquake disaster movie he's currently shooting he wants to discuss suicide. In the Green Room the next guest, a comic called David Brenner, groans, 'That's a helluva topic to follow'. But he does well with a string of ethnic jokes. Norman Mailer was one of the guests — I keep encountering him on my book promotion talk show rounds and he always bangs on and always gets me bumped off the show. Tonight he talked endlessly about the art of graffiti and whether Marilyn Monroe committed suicide or not. Paul Block by this time had me standing in the wings, clutching Ukie, waiting to go on. He gave me the thumbs down. 'Keep a stiff upper lip — we'll have to bump you'. This is the second time it's happened. I could kill that garrulous Mailer. However, he did apologize.

Two weeks later I was called back. At last I managed to appear on the show.

May 30: This time I was in luck. Carson warmed up audience well: 'Let me tell you how to make an impeachment cocktail — first, break into a refrigerator.' Johnny Mathis was dull and Cloris Leachman talked too much and interrupted Carson — a no-no. So suddenly it was me. The curtains opened and I dashed on as if shot out of a cannon. Blue velvet jacket with red piping, platform heeled shoes. I said, 'Here's an old song from 1929 — I think it's rather good' and straight into 'Hungry Women' I went. Carson liked me. I got laughs. But, my God, you have to keep it jolly and lively! I made some crack that was over the heads of the audience and Johnny immediately seized the moment to look into the camera as if to say, 'This guy's a kook. I'm with you, folks.' However, we chatted amiably in the commercial break. And he generously held up my book, 'After The Ball' — the real point of the entire exercise. At the end he said, 'Let's continue this some other time'. In my dressing room Fred De Cordova, the producer, praised me. Wants me back again soon. Block said he was so relieved. A lot of his colleagues had had doubts about me. They didn't see me as weird as Tiny Tim. Watched the show later back at the apartment. Was pleased. Seemed natural. Had a dream that Carson was my Boy Scout leader and I was his willing cohort in the patrol.

June 11: Pan Am flight home to London. Mummy made me a mushroom, sausage, and bacon dinner, served at the Bridge table in the lounge. Very comforting and safe. Watched documentary on the Rosenberg trial as we ate. Tried calling all my friends but most are away or too busy. Suzanne [my sister] has to host the Queen next week at a garden party for the regiment.

June 15: Went on the Thames with friends. Picnic on launch- a trip from Richmond to Hampton Court. Asked questions like, 'Do we need passports?' What fun we had. Simple fun. On board was an old Colonel, dreaming, no doubt, of Afric's shores and the 1914 Congo. Had dinner with Evelyn Waugh's daughter, Hattie. England seems so tranquil and cozy, like a long running Ealing comedy. Or maybe I'm becoming more American in my sensibility. Maybe I'm a fake or fading Englishman.......

MARCH

What did you do when the Oscars were on? I worked — well, I played music in our corner of Cantalini's Italian restaurant in Playa Del Rey. I had been hoping to get away from all the Oscar fuss, all the preening over mediocrities, all the fol-de-rol of a competitive sport, the idea that there's such a thing as a best movie.

So I try to put the Oscars away and concentrate on the here and now of our particular reality. We had, for example, a successful evening the night before, on the Saturday, when we were employed as Greeters at a fundraising event for the L.A. Chamber Music Ensemble. Walter was our leader and he was waiting for us outside the Dorothy Chandler Pavilion as we pulled up on the dot of 5pm. He was already in costume — a natty 1940s brown pin-stripe gangster suit — and he directed us to the vast subterranean parking lot, assuring us that our names would be on a list. Amazingly, they were. And we could rest assured that we'd be properly fed later. We were: a white paper box containing a veggie wrap, an oatmeal cookie and an orange. With the other greeters we changed into our costumes — anything vaguely between-the-20th century-wars, as instructed. Walter said it was OK to wear my British Royal marines uniform (Colonel) even though the label inside the jacket reads 1958. The evening was to be an odd mixture of Vivaldi and 1920s-1930s fashions and music. Since I can't play anything sophisticated like Gershwin or Kern I had nixed on providing a dance band for the dinner later.

All I had to do was to stand at the foot of the grand spiral staircase and direct the guests thus: "Champagne reception is upstairs and to the left. Restrooms are also located there." My uniform was, as usual, most effective, generating a respect I never had before. "Thank you, sir" said the guests — proceeding up to the right rather than the left as I had instructed them. Maybe they were overawed by my splendor. At any rate, at the top they were politely reversed by Regina and her sisters in costume.

Several people we know in civilian life greeted me with surprise, glad to know that I had the money to support chamber music. I quickly disabused them, but with hauteur and a slightly overdone British accent. Actually, Regina's brother does have the wherewithal — he and his wife's names are up on the Founder's "Thank You Very Much" wall. But we're the relations and we need the money.

I got a little windy on spotting another marine officer patrolling around at the top of the staircase. Would I be had up for impersonating an officer? Regina informed me later that the marine in question, a slip of a boy, was windy too. From a distance I'd looked like the real thing in full colour, and a Colonel to boot. When we met he forgave me for being an impersonator. But he wondered whether the British accent was also fake. Good God, no! My parents spent a small fortune on getting me that accent.

We watched the Vivaldi from high up in the balcony as we ate our box dinners. Next we directed the guests to the silent auction. Finally we set an example by dancing on the postage stamp floors near the dinner tables. The band, a bunch of men even older than me, were clearly not attuned to Paul Whiteman or even Guy Lombardo: they started off with "Hello Dolly" and stayed there as we, poor devils, foxtrotted for what seemed like an eternity as the diners filed in and sat down to starters. Some got the idea and eventually joined us on the dance floor. I can tell you I was ready for the glue factory by the time Walter told us that our duties were over and he could be found writing checks upstairs in our dressing room. We were up in a jiffy.

That was the night before the Oscars.

As I was saying earlier, I was looking forward to a retreat from the success of others by playing quietly at Cantalini's. Alas, there were televisions hung high and blaring out the show. I had to suffer the sight of a tuxedoed streetwise black comic pacing about the stage and shouting, as they do. This is the Age of the Shout, isn't it? What will be in store for the next Age? A scream, no doubt. Still, we had a decent crowd considering the competition and I made a point of congratulating every table for ignoring the Oscars. I sang "I Am A Mole And I Live In A Hole" to an appreciative long table of black children and their parents. Waves crashed a few yards away, mists swirled, concealing Avalon, and planes continued to form a line in the sky as they came in to land at LAX. A British Airways jumbo, taking off in the other direction, dropped an engine with a pyrotechnical display of sparks and great flashes, but proceeded onwards to its destination of London. Not to worry, said the pilot. This was the real world — getting on with proper business, far from red carpets and self-congratulation.

Weekends are usually when we work. The other days are easily whiled away. Every morning I take Rollo out for the early walk. People stop their cars, approach me at Starbucks, collar me everywhere — "What kind of a dog is that?" "He's beautiful," etc. Rollo loves everybody and they love him. The only exception is old ladies. He barks and lunges at them. I have to believe there must be some concealed nastiness in little old ladies.

Recently Regina and I have been inspecting used houses for sale. So often they're called "Homes" in the ads. But they're not homes till you make them that. Sometimes, on dark days, I talk about England as being my real home. Regina shoots back that it'll be an English home minus her. The house hunting can be depressing because our dream is outside of our price range. What is affordable is what has to be fixed up, or utterly transformed. I'm amazed at the bad taste in the houses we see in which the sellers still dwell. Most sport enormous TV screens and few books. I'd rather see a litter of books, magazines, papers, records, — than the sterility of these neat and tidy rooms with the washer, dryer, air conditioning, completely remodeled kitchen, etc. — as the realtor tells us. Everything you could want to make life easy — and dreary. At one large house, built in the twenties, but completely re-modeled so that every bit of the 1920s had been erased, everything old gone, every tree removed, I was dwarfed by the obligatory big screen TV. Sitting nearby still wrapped was a sole DVD, *Ray*. The sofa was wrapped too, in plastic. Only the Bill Cosby books were naked.

The only dreamy house we were shown, described as English Cottage with built-in charm, was too small and too expensive. Like a chocolate box. And anyway there had already been six offers and tonight the sellers would be deciding which offer to accept. At just under a million dollars — who has this kind of money? The seller, a retired schoolmarm, was retreating to Arizona to live among rocks and sparkling new buildings. The realtor told us we'd better buy ASAP because inventory is depleting, there'll be soon be no more building space left, and in a few years time there'll be several million more people here. Altadena used to be a remote and blighted foothills community, overloaded with bargain houses, huge estates, and mysterious mansions. White flight, due to the Watts Riots in 1965 and bussing in the early 1970s, was responsible for the state of affairs. Today the tables are turned and the well-to-do blacks, who settled in during the blight age, are selling and moving away. Where, I wonder? To sparkling new communities, no doubt, out in the Inland Empire, or maybe Arizona. Fresh air, no crime, no libraries, and Blockbuster.

There was such a good response to last month's extracts from my old journals that I thought I'd give you a few more choice bits.

Let's go back thirty years this month and see what I was up to. Things happen differently but my reactions are always just the same. Have been since lord knows when............

MARCH 1975

The Situation: I am in Los Angeles on another work permit, but in the process of applying for a Resident Alien card. I am staying at the Studio City apartment of George Sherlock who used to be the West Coast Promotion Man in charge of my records. It was George who forced Capitol Records, my label, to release 'You Turn Me On.' It's very obliging of George to let me stay at his place — after all, he got married only recently, to a luscious girl and you'd have thought they'd like some privacy. I mean, I came barging in one night and found them billing and cooing and they stood up and apologized. I know America's full of kindly people but this is too much. Workwise, I'm hustling about every which-way, involved in far too many projects, spreading myself thin, and having an even thinner skin in my reaction to people.

March 1: George & I had our respective cars cleaned at Oxnard & Laurel. Nobody spoke a word of English so we talked among ourselves. We got into a blarney about Bill, the tuba player in Crystal Palace, the local ragtime orchestra I'm involved with as a singer. I'd asked Bill to be a roommate in an apartment that's come free in George's building. Bill wonders if there's enough room for his cats. George warned me about spoiling my career by rooming with a known homosexual. Pop-eyed with apoplexy, I lectured poor old Geo. About how he ought to change his attitude because there's a lot of homos in show-biz. And he'd better stop calling them 'fags' — why, that's as bad as talking about 'Jew Boys.' Geo. studied his shining golf shoes, the ones with the tassels. As I drove off, even as Mexicans were still polishing the car, waves of guilt washed over my body. What a bloody hypocrite I am! I was really lecturing myself!

To Vik Greenfield for dinner. He used to be Bette Davis' butler and must have been very good because mum's the word with our Vik. You'll get no spice from him. Funny spelling — 'Vik' — but there it is. A special person. At present he's general factotum to a Mrs. Doris Hall, widow of Mr. Mutual of Omaha, the insurance tycoon. The house is a solid brick Scotch Baronial in Hancock Park. He took me on a tour of the endless rooms. In one, high up, we discovered Mrs. H in the midst of a backgammon game with her miniature dogs. She was in a bathrobe and without make-up. On being introduced she covered her face with her hands and moaned. We left her and went shopping for dinner. Vik cooked an expert filet mignon and spinach. Talked about his life: how he'd been stationed in the early 1950s with the RAF in Egypt during the time we ran the *country. Talked of how officers would drive him out into the desert where, under moonlight, they'd tell him that their wives didn't understand them. Vik had a delicate face in those days. Nowadays, he says, his only worries are health and hair. Never use soap, he warned. Very bad for the skin. Never sleep on a bed. Bad for the back. He's found an electrolysis, whatever that means, treatment that keeps his hair stuck on. Turns out that Vik is a quarter Jewish. So I said I was, too.*

March 4: Spent morning with dear old Harry Warren. He's written so many standards — as many as Cole Porter and all those precious theatre types — yet he gets little recognition. Looked same as when I interviewed him for my Tin Pan Alley book, only now he's brushing his hair straight down to the front so he looks like a Caesar. Very interested in the Crystal Palace orchestra. Particularly in Jackie, the cellist. She's got a pair, he said. But why, he demanded, do we play all this Scott Joplin music? No-one in the Alley ever heard of Joplin back in the old days. Never had a hit. If you want some rags, he offered, he'd write them. And I'm sure he could, too. I quizzed him about Walter Donaldson, who wrote as many hits as Harry. 'He was a married man who traveled with a nurse,' he said with a wink. An 'ear-man' — couldn't read a note. I had more Donaldson questions but Harry stopped me: why didn't I ask him about his own songs? We sat down at the piano and sang some British Music Hall songs. He signed my copy of 'Home In Pasadena' with: 'To my historian and Friend.'

March 10: Horrors! I've been doing too much and have left days un-written up! Now I've lost the details. It's all in the details. Well, I was summoned to a meeting at the Continental Hyatt (Riot) House on the Strip with the dreaded Tony Palmer this afternoon. He's over here filming his vast series on the history of pop for British TV, and there's a book tie-in. I've contributed with an essay on Tin Pan Alley. Tony was all biz, and brusque. Watched him eat a plain steak with milk and fruit. Probably has an ulcer. He commands me like a schoolmaster. Ripped into my essay as he ate. Took it apart. Dislikes in particular a sentence at the beginning: 'Somewhere in the blue ridge mountains of Virginia there roamed one Cecil Sharp.' He really hates that one. Says I don't have enough anecdotes. That I could learn from Derek Taylor's essay in which, using just three stories, he sums up the essence of the 1960s. Why didn't I make a TV series on the heels of my 'After The Ball' book? One I could steer myself instead of taking orders from others. Must get pushier.

March 11: Meeting in the Polo Lounge in Beverly Hills with Jon Brewer, my record producer from England. Has tons of money, from mysterious sources. Always laughing so you can't help liking him. Gave me a $5000 advance to sign with him. Says he has a deal for a release with Ray Davies of The Kinks. When I last saw Ray he was belligerently demanding cups of tea and payment in cash at a big show we were doing at the Cow Palace in 1965. Since then he's gone respectable and become a custodian of old British culture. He has a record label called Konk. He said I could record all the ancient songs I like, so long as I included 'My Girl's Pussy.' Jon was with his gorgeous wife, plus a hanger-on black girl who seemed very street, or even back alley. Still, she said I was beautiful and then Jon's wife told me I have lovely hands, so I felt relaxed. But it's enough to make one solipsistic. I was trying to get the laughing Jon to agree to a definite recording date and budget when all hell broke loose in the Polo Lounge, a nest of agents and wheeler-dealers. Actually it was a very hushed hell. Nobody spoke a word. They were all frozen, especially the agents. What had happened was that Keith Moon, of The Who, had suddenly made an entrance dressed up as a Nazi officer in full regalia. He strutted around the Lounge to an audience of catatonics. Then a squad of security men, in full uniform themselves, dashed up and bundled him out. Jon roared with laughter. 'What a character!' he said. 'Now, you fancy yourself as a character but you can't compete with old Moony!'

March 12: All day filming my song for KCET, the local Public TV station... Still waiting to get a go-ahead from Taylor Hackford for our Tin Pan Alley special, but in the meantime I'm doing a few song-movie shorts for the station. This one's called 'Swinging Singles.' Bit of a hoo-hah about some of my lyrics. Found out it's Taylor's lady friend who objects — and I thought she liked me! They won't let me sing about 'Well-stacked girls.' They say it's 'sexist.' That's a new term for me. First set-up was in a Mexican restaurant posing as a singles bar. It's almost like a real movie; only 16mm rather than 35mm. Maybe one day I'll be trapped on 35mm. Three sexy girls fondled me in the scene, and even after the scene. Our final setting was the Oddfellows graveyard where we swung in time to the playback of the song. After dinner we shot the last scene — outside Gazzari's on the Strip. God, it was a decade ago when I went into Gazzari's as a teen idol and there were all the pneumatic girl go-go dancers from the Hollywood A Go-Go TV show and how we ogled each other. Hot bods. Bliss was it to be young! Now all I do is worry about my thinning hair. Perhaps Vik has the answer. Meanwhile I've grown a beard. Before we filmed tonight the girls had a meeting: then they came up and told me they considered my tight white trousers, while certainly revealing my prospects of marriage in front, were OK — but were too tight behind: the thin transparent polyester was showing everyone the brand name. I got no phone numbers.

March 13: Drawing session with Don Bachardy at the Santa

Monica house. Calming view of cliffs as I stared out trying to be still and he eagle-eyed me and drew. I always feel relaxed there, actually. Herr Issyvoo was absent. We discussed the difficulties of novel writing and of my 'Ramona Schmidt' in particular. How some friends had picked to bits my first chapter. Don advised me never to show a work in progress. He did three drawings, making me look wild-eyed. Said he likes the beard. We listened to an LP of L. Bernstein discussing the dangers of ambiguity in music. Don said B sounded full of 'self-regard.' Always has the 'mot juste', has Don. He sounds exactly like Issyvoo if you close your eyes.

March 14: Appointment downtown with my immigration lawyer, Sidney Kaplan, at 12 noon. The office was locked. Furious, I stamped over to the Federal Building to make some calls and rearrange my day. While there, on an impulse, I decided to drop in on Mrs. Hansen, the INS headmistress I've had to see before in order to stay here legally. She terrifies me like so many women in authority do. And yet at the same time I'd like to have sex with her. She's old enough to be my mother. Last time I saw her was when Taylor Hackford accompanied me. We needed an extension so I could continue my KCET work and she'd held court interminably before getting to the point. We had to hear about all the stars whom she'd 'processed.' How she loved that word! 'I've processed Peter O'Toole and Richard Harris and Sean Connery. You name 'em — I've processed them!' There they were up on the wall, framed and signed, like a game hunter's trophies. Would she like one of me? I slid an 8 by 10 glossy across her great desk, despite Taylor's sharp kick to my leg. She'd automatically put it in a drawer as she continued her interrupted monolog. Taylor handled her well — such a politician — and we got the OK for me to stay in the country a little longer. Out in the corridor Taylor laughed and said he'd never seen me so nervous, never seen me stutter so much. Today, when I waltzed into her office, she was in an expansive mood. Gave her a copy of my new book, 'Tin Pan Alley,' which she actually glanced at before consigning it to the drawer. Didn't care for my beard. Said it would have to go. I thanked her and beat a retreat.

Kaplan was back from lunch when I returned. Very apologetic. As usual his office was snowed under with Mexicans clamouring for help. He saw me right away, though, handing me a white H1 work permit approval, signed by Mrs. Hansen. All I have to do, he said, is take that to the U.S consul in London and get my passport stamped. Must be a reason, though, for the trip to England. I told him I'd say that my mother is gravely ill. Fine, fine, he said and turned to address the clamouring Mexicans. Once outside the office I felt dreadful about using my mother in this way.

March 17: I successfully starred with Crystal Palace in a show at the Mayfair Music Hall in Santa Monica. We set the show in segments: 'On The Bandstand,' 'At The Cabaret,' and then, 'In The Ten Cent Dance Hall.' The theatre was full and a lot of important show folk turned up, including Tony Bill, producer of 'The Sting.' Curtis Harrington, the horror film director came, as well as Vik Greenfield and Sidney Kaplan. But even better — Jon Brewer brought with him Jerry Leiber & Mike Stoller, those songwriters who wrote hits for Elvis, The Drifters, and The Coasters. Also David Puttnam, a British film producer, another friend of Jon's. He knows everybody. The evening spoiled somewhat even before curtain went up: the clarinet player in the band, stating he was representing the others, told me backstage that I was using the band to further my career. I was stunned. Surely it's the other way around? Well, this little bit of frostiness had the effect of making me really give my all on stage in the manner of Al Jolson. And afterwards Jon hosted a big dinner party at an expensive local joint called 'Valentino's.' I sat with Leiber & Stoller who told me how much they'd liked 'Lazy,' an early Irving Berlin number I'd performed. Jerry L was tickled by the line, "With a great big valise full of books to read where it's peaceful." He laughed his head off. Funnily enough, when I tried to tell them how much I loved 'Yackety-Yak' and all those Elvis songs they'd written the pair took offense — they didn't want to know. In fact Leiber went off on a rant about how great some obscure South American novelist was and how I should do myself a favour by reading this man with his unpronounceable name. I was aghast. David Puttnam saved the day by leaning over and, sotto voce, asking my permission to take out my current girl friend Kathy, a waitress at the Mayfair who'd snuck her way into the dinner. Of course you may, I said. I'll keep you in mind, said Puttnam, for my next picture, 'Bugsy Malone,' he said. Yippee!

March 19: The Los Angeles Times report on our concert is out. I was described as 'Not much of a singer or dancer but......' and then went on to praise my verve and enthusiasm. Is this good or bad?

March 20: TWA flight to London. Read 'Double Indemnity' by James M. Cain. Worrying about whether U.S Embassy will stamp my passport when I arrive. The anticipation is awful. Felt like the insurance man who's the murderer in 'Double Indemnity' — making up lies about my mother having to go to hospital, etc. How could I do such a thing? Maybe by my inventing the lie this emergency might actually happen. But Mummy was there at the airport. Looking a little wan admittedly. But she was there. Pouches under her eyes as well. A drizzly day in London. Pre-occupied with whether I'll ever get back to America, the land of excitement, danger, flesh and fun. Was I going to be stuck in England forever? So stultifying, drab and grey. A place where I can't pull the wool *over anyone's eyes. Come off it, mate, they'd say. Pull the other one — it's got bells on.*

APRIL

As I write there are only a few days left before I return to England, the place I still call home in my heart. Just before departure I will be making the annual desert trip with Andy Wickham. He has written a minute-by-minute plan of where we'll be and what we'll do: exactly the same as before, of course:

Late breakfast at Conrad's, which will include a Heineken for Andy followed by a strict order to the waiter for his eggs and bacon to be served without — and he means it — any California garnish of lettuce, tomato and/or parsley. We will hope that the black-robed, gold-medallioned priests from the Greek Orthodox church across the way will process in, swinging their chains to a pleasing clank, to discover their regular booth prepared and gleaming.

Andy will kick me under the table if he sees an obese person eyeing the hamburger they hold up as if readying for a holy ritual before opening their jaw till cracking point in order to take the big bite that will hopefully be so efficient that no ketchup or other matter will spill. "Look!" Andy will say," There's a man who swallowed a football!" I've always enjoyed the joke, as I enjoy everything he says. The fellow is brilliant and I am merely his Boswell. Evening will find us in the high desert in a windowless local Mexican joint with endless chips and salsa and the company of our longtime teacher Dr Randy who will talk of Wagner in exchange for Andy's red hot information on the current political scene in London, including a list of Tony Blair's new boy friends. Here are the rest of Andy's instructions mailed from Chelsea:

"The following morning we will have our traditional debate about which coffee-shop serves the best coffee. We will then progress to the border, catching a film of the undisputed quality of *Sideways*, for example, and dining again at Camacho's Place in the bean fields of El Centro, stopping at a suitable bar on the way back for the margarita that you require but that this fabulous discovery of a restaurant fails to provide. We would then return to Pasadena for bookshops and CDs before meeting up with Regina for another flick plus Nippon snackeroo. It would seem that all of the above might be do-able — if so, count me in (Come in Gary & The Playboys)."

This is vintage Wickham and I hope he doesn't mind me printing his words without the feel and smell of the beautiful writing paper he uses. Naturally, he writes in fountain pen and the address at the top of the first page is embossed in green, but page two is plain.

This is real taste — matching the perfect gentleman outfit he will wear in the desert: dark trousers well-creased, a crisp white shirt and a not-too-blue blazer. Nothing ostentatious, nothing that displays too much flesh. The reverse of his traveling companion.

Not only do I have no taste, except my own, but also I have difficulty with any form of culture higher than "The Teddy Bears' Picnic." It could be said of me, as it was of Andy's former record label boss: "It is easier for a camel to pass through the eye of a needle than for Ian Whitcomb to enter the Kingdom Of Culture."

Let me give you an example. I'm always trying to self-improve: how-to-write hit song books, how-to-speed-read music books, how-poetry-works books, etc. Recently I read *The Writer's Voice* by A. Alvarez, the noted poet and literary critic — a rather daunting figure, but attempting a wry smile in the photo on the flyleaf of the dust jacket. The blurb quote says: "For a writer, voice is a problem that never lets you go and I have thought about it as long as I can remember — if for no other reason than that a writer doesn't properly begin until he has a voice of his own."

Well, of course I felt pretty certain that I have a voice and a very recognizable one. I mean, no one could mistake my writing voice. I write like I talk — only better, and without the stutters. But if I thought Alvarez was going to comfort me with examples from P.G. Wodehouse or Julian McLaren-Ross I had another thing coming. Nothing of the sort: the voice in question is the *poet's* voice.

I've always found modern poetry difficult to understand. Even stuff from the last hundred years onwards — except the really popular and accessible poets like A.A. Milne and John Betjeman, those wonderful rumpety-tumpety-tump bards who no doubt would be beneath contempt to Alvarez.

He writes of the "concept of the work of art as something perfect, a supreme fiction that can be ruined by a single word out of place." And then he prints as an example of perfection a six line, 33-word poem by W.B. Yeats, the Irish bard. I don't understand the last part: what Alvarez describes as "the sudden shift of key in that extraordinary final image":

MEMORY
One had a lovely face,
And two or three had charm,
But charm and face were in vain
Because the mountain grass
Cannot but keep the form
Where the mountain hare has lain.

Oh, it looks and sounds lovely and it has charm, like the ladies in the first part of the poem. But why is a mountain hare's impression in the grass claimed as "perfection"?

I sent "Memory" to my literary friend, one of my oldest and dearest friends, Jeremy Lewis of *The Oldie*, at his publishing desk in London. He replied that he completely agreed with Alvarez but didn't have the time to explain to me right there and then because he was off to a literary luncheon at Simpson's-On-The Strand, lucky devil. I'd take their roast beef — carved from the trolley and according to your directions, right at your table — anytime over a poem by the old Irish bard.

I also sent the poem to our dear friend, Buck Henry, the great screenwriter. His reply was terser but more to the point: "As I recall, the Yeats poem is a warning to young ladies not to have sex with rabbits. But I could be wrong."

Incidentally I was once in Yeats country, during my Trinity College Dublin days, and standing near the Lake Isle of Innisfree, trying to hear the famous lake water lapping in low sounds and also trying to transcendentally escape the bloody cold. I became aware of an odor oppressing me from over my shoulder. I turned and was greeted by an ancient coot in a fishing hat stuck with hooks, and wearing dirty tweeds, source of the smell.

"I knew the man," he told me in that sing-song boom so beloved of tourists.

"You did?"

" I did indeed, yer honor."

"And so......?"

"He was a queer fellow."

"In what way, may I enquire?"

A pause. A sniff, and an adjusting of dress by the old coot. I got his point and fished out a few coins. After biting them and touching his hat he carried on.

"What was I talking about now? My head is peopled by so many grand and glorious things..."

"So's your pocket."

He got my point.

"Yeats was queer in this manner: ye'd be with him in the bar of an evening and he was yer best friend, hugging yer and pinching yer cheeks."

"That's not worth what I just tipped you."

"Wait....And he'd be tearing it up like it was a hooley or a wake."

"Can you be more specific? I've a few more of the readies, you know."

"Ah. Well, he'd stand on the table and sing lewd songs. British music hall songs, you understand."

"Like?"

The coot climbed onto a handy tree stump and sang like a trouper:

Like this, like this—bobbing up and down like this!
There was Gus and Gertie in their bathing socks
All mixed up like chocolates in a box.
I cried: "What ho!"
Such fun I would not miss—
When I saw my Mrs. and the Man Next Door
Bobbing up and down like this!

Very impressed, I gave the coot every penny I had, including folding.

"That was terrific! With the detail of the bathing socks and then the cry of 'What ho!'. Incomparable! Why couldn't old Yeats write poems as good as that?"

"You took the words right out of my mouth, squire. And I'll tell you something else — for free."

"Yes?"

"The next day you'd see him in the street and he'd cut you dead like he never met you in his life."

"I'm amazed!"

"Whatever you say, your lordship. And mind how you go!"

Getting back to Alvarez, I'm definitely on his wavelength when he writes of Freud being acclaimed "the discoverer of the unconscious" and then the man himself protesting that "poets and philosophers before me" had already done the discovering— how Coleridge used a dream for his best-known poem and how "dreams, in their dotty way, seem creative." I love the world of my dreams and, indeed, have kept a Dream Book since March 1972 — about the time I started my daily journal. These days I don't seem to have such vivid ones as I used to, or maybe I'm simply not remembering them.

But there's a recurring setting, a dreamscape that I love returning to: a vast sprawling black city of brick and stone and no trees, connected by railways everywhere, overground, underground, almost in the air. Using the trains I rush across this inky city in search of...? Always something different: my dead mother, or Rollo, who lives in reality nowhere near my dream city, because my city must be London, I realize, the London of the late 1940s, of bomb sites and grime and mysterious passageways and furtive men involved in the black market—spivs, nylons, salt beef sandwiches, but no candy floss. Some nights I'm lifted aboard the seaside express, a train pulled by an enormous black and hissing iron monster, manned by a burly driver who waves to me. At the seaside there's candy floss and Al Jolson captive in a slot machine at the end of the tottering pier singing "Swanee" at the drop of a penny.

In the very first entry of my Dream Book I'm back at the coast again, having lost a horse that belonged to somebody else. Next I'm involved in a gunfight in a strange house, a house full of malevolent rooms. I am unarmed, but I enter these evil rooms and shout imprecations. Masked men are creeping up on me and it looks like curtains — until I bring a stop to the dream, by shouting an order: "No more!"

Impending death plays a big part in these early dreams: black gangs, spouting R&B lyrics, attack my brother at home; I'm marching in a front line battle, executing silly steps to amuse the other soldiers, passing by men writhing about in messes of blood, awful slices of bodies, a head in a sheet; I look the other way. My best friend and his wife are skulking way at the back, behind the lines. I argue with my one other best friend, punching him several times in the head...I'm in countless crashes from the sky.........

At other times I'm with celebrities: Lennon & McCartney are in the studio playing an old tape and I walk on by, oblivious. They are insulted. Later, in a theatre, I try to explain a Weber & Fields routine to Lennon, but Weber comes downstage to tell me to quit gabbing. Sitting at a table with Dick Clark: I ask for a spot on *American Bandstand*, like I used to have in the old days. He shakes his head: "I'll give it to you straight — you're passed it as far as the field of rock is concerned." I reply that I'll prove how wrong he is (1974).

On March 19, 1998, I meet Hitler at a garden party, what we English call a "fete." He turns out to be a ukulele enthusiast and I'm so excited I tell him I'll go and fetch my uke. I leave him in the tent with his ice cream and his nurse. When I return with Ukie I'm terribly disappointed: his nurse tells me it's long past his bedtime and he'd not as young as he once was. "You must have so much to remember!" I tell Hitler as he's wheeled off. Before vanishing he says, "Yes indeed — and an awful lot to forget!"

But luckily that same night, in another dream, I'm at a cocktail party and I'm told that my idol, the early crooner "Whispering" Jack Smith is present. Where? There — over in the corner all alone. Trembling with excitement I approach. "Can I call you 'Whispering'?" "Of course, my child." I have so many questions to ask him—so little is known of him. "Ask me anything you like, dear boy." "Well — where were you born?" "Ah, now that's a real tough one!" I wake up in a sweat!

Many of my dreams are of plane crashes and how I witness the crash but am too chicken to rush up and help survivors. I seek out a phone box in order to call for help—999.

But are any of these dreams "creative"? Can they provide

material for writing, help plots, create characters? I've never used any. Real life is far more useful, and molding a story from what happens to me usually turns out best. Here's an actual event which is really an adventure and could never come to me in a dream (dreams are too weird, dreams are for art film directors and wacko poets) and could certainly have never been made up (the so-called "imagination" which we are told to rely on if we claim to be fiction writers and which I believe is poppycock: made-up characters and actions are cardboard fakes).

Here it is: one day in the early 1960s, when I was living at my mother's flat in London, on vacation from undergraduate studies at Trinity College Dublin, I was invited to take a spin in the air by my "Flying Uncle." He wasn't a relative, he was my real uncle's best friend from school: Dick Blackburn. My real uncle had teased Dick mercilessly at school, failing to rescue him, for instance, when he was buried by bullies under a mountain of school furniture at the end of one school term. In an important exam he sat for two hours without being able to write down one word. Well, he did manage to put his name at the top of the paper—but even that was mis-spelled. Dick was a simple soul and quite unlike his canny, savvy father, Robert Blackburn, a pioneer of aviation who'd been flying his own crates on the Yorkshire sands at almost the same time as the Wright Brothers.

In World War One his factories had built bombers and in the following war they built the biggest air freighter anywhere. Never mind that these were very dangerous planes. My uncle, the real one, wooed Dick's sister, the daughter of the aeroplane mogul, and they were married the day the war was declared. He went on to have a terrific war — commanding flying boats and occasionally dropping them into the sea off England where they are now marked on maps as historic wrecks. He never engaged the enemy, to my knowledge, but he did a lot of flying and had a lot of fun. Dick, on the other hand, didn't take to flying in a natural way. The first time my uncle met his school chum in the war he had to tell him to buck up and stop crying. I think he gave him a hankie.

Back in Civvy Street Dick became a barrister, which in England means the lawyer who takes the case in court, as opposed to the solicitor who prepares all the paperwork. Dick fancied himself as a bit of a thespian and liked to recite Shakespeare in an overly dramatic manner at the drop of a hat. But he proved to be not so hot when in court and without the Bard of Avon's way with words. Representing a client up on a charge that should have resulted in a five shilling fine Dick got so mixed up, addled, befuddled—he would tend to argue with himself—that his client was sentenced to five years. Dick was stricken with remorse and went to visit the poor man every week, taking him bon-bons and novels and flowers.

So I should have guessed there'd be an abnormal train of events when I volunteered to go up in the air with "Uncle" Dick. He was flying a Cessna at the time, a small light plane, fine for short joyriding trips. We'd take an hour's spin, said Dick. And be back at the club in plenty of time for cocktails and a slap-up lunch.

We encountered some fog near the south coast. Next thing we were over another coast and it looked like France. Yes, it was France, said the voice from an airport tower control below. "Allez! Allez!" We followed railway lines—"An old war trick," said Dick—until we reached Belgium and then we were over Germany and at this point Dick got a little rattled. He radioed down to another airport and managed to get the controllers to phone my brother-in-law, the General, at his HQ in the British-occupied section of Germany. Could the General arrange for us to stay the night at their place? Yes, yes, but hurry, said my relative, it's getting dark and we have tickets to a nightclub.

But Dick's calculations went awry and the airstrip we landed on was not the British HQ but a top-secret position for spying on the Reds in East Germany. Our landing was fairly smooth but our reception was brisk and bumpy. As we taxied to a halt several jeeps roared up and surrounded us. Military policemen made us raise our hands and we were taken in for interrogation. Luckily they were British Intelligence. Their commander looked at Dick in his old school tie and dark blue suit and barked: "You sir will be accommodated at the officer's club." Then swiveling smartly he fixed me with a fierce eye. I realized he was scrutinizing my outfit—which was All-American: jazzy college stuff I'd brought back from my first trip to the USA: a bright red and blue letterman jacket, a lumberjack plaid shirt, cowboy boots and a hat to match. "*You!* You will report to the sergeant's mess! For special duties." I can't remember what the duties were to be. But a quick call to the General cleared matters up and we were soon in a military motorcade on our way to the safety of my family—and in time to join them for a night on the town. The club turned out to be a strip club and Dick, no doubt feeling dizzy after our extended hour's trip, had to be held back by his suspenders when he got carried away by the contortions of one of the strip girls as she did her act— wrestling an engorged python.

An adventure like that you couldn't dream up.

I've told you next to nothing about what's in store for April. Or what happened in March. What happened was that we, The Parlour Boys, were up in Yosemite with Janet Klein, performing a 1920s show in the famous Ahwanee—the gig I was bitching about last month. It all turned out well and I was pleasantly surprised to be greeted by the splendidly-hatted head lady of the San Francisco Art Deco Society with a "Why, helloooo, Ian!" Now it's my duty to match-make the two Art Deco branches into a working pair. After the performance we retired to the bar where our guitarist Tom seemed a little the worse for drink. But always a gentleman. I gave him the key to his cabin in the Curry campground and bid him goodnight.

Next morning I peeped into his cabin, the one next to mine. The bed had not been slept in. We Parlour Boys breakfasted and were soon on our way back to Los Angeles. However, we became concerned about Tom. So I left a message on his cell phone. He returned it as we were driving up the Grapevine. This is his story: he was searching for his cabin that night when he suddenly became aware of a rather too large bear lumbering towards him in dire need of something or other. So Tom took to his legs, reached his car, and high-tailed it back to Los Angeles. Pursued, presumably, by the bear. This is one creature he can't try selling a vintage guitar to.

There'll be no extracts from my old journals for the time being. I have to vet them carefully—an old friend whom I haven't seen in years put his name into a search engine and Bingo! Up he came in my Letter. He seemed embarrassed to be exposed to the world and yet I was quite nice about him. "I shall NEVER lunch with you again!" he screamed in his e-mail. Serves him right for being so vain as to look himself up on the Internet. Whenever I look myself up there's eventual trouble: the further I dig into references to my name the more I find insults. I end up feeling very small and I switch off the computer a humbler person. And so, on this Uriah Heep-ish note I will conclude this Letter and pack my bags for the flight to London. I only hope my friends will be able to find time in their busy schedules to see me. All they seem to do in London is go to dinner parties and luncheons and book launches....

MAY

Last time I wrote it was close to departure time for an England trip, a fix I need at least once a year. Poor Regina has to put up with my threats to return to my country of origin. But of course the place I want to return to vanished decades ago: the England of the 1940s and 50s when my parents were alive and thriving. And the England of today has no work for me, unless I want to serve in a Starbucks — you'll find two in every London street with a Wendy's in support.

As before I was met at a drizzly gray (and thus delightful) Heathrow by my sister, Suzanne and her husband, the General, and off we went into the Berkshire countryside, to their Victorian cottage which has all mod cons. I'd forgotten the General doesn't drink anymore so I had the Chivas Regal bottle to myself. I'd bought it duty-free as a present for them. Still, the duty-free macadamia nuts coated in chocolate went down a treat. My sister remembered to prepare the macaroni cheese I so adore and that our mother used to make (with the trademark bacon on top). And we ate our supper in their glass conservatory with the view of the lawn and then fields beyond promising lush English countryside further south climaxing with Devonshire bays and coves where shipwrecks lie waiting to be examined. During supper we watched the local version of *The Apprentice* commanded by a pockmarked cockney millionaire called Sir Alan Sugar, nothing like as tough and nasty as Mr. Trump.

Next day, while the General played golf in the drizzle, my sister drove me down into Dorset to visit the old school, Bryanston, setting of so many of my best dreams and unrequited loves. As she bustled about the great neo-Georgian pile asking questions of the service staff, keen to learn what's current and what's happening, I of course was trying to dive back into the past and finding the going rough. There are now more girls than boys at Bryanston. The new Head is a woman.

In my day it was all males, grey open-neck shirts and grey shorts. Many confirmed bachelor masters, much romancing and fantasizing. At Bryanston I rebelled against the fustiness of the Fifties, forming a skiffle group and then a rock & roll band, bringing vulgar modernity into the quiet and pastoral. Today the tide I rode in on has overwhelmed me and I'm now an old fogy. Rockers are knights or lords. Pop art is no longer outlaw.

Nude paintings by the boys and girls adorn the school walls. There are electric signs winking you to the "Toilets." The old school group photographs have disappeared.

There's no record of my having attended the school, no record of the paintings, stories, bands, passions I had there. I did manage to locate my old dormitory, the one with the view of the headmaster's house — but the house has been replaced. So I couldn't show my sister the window we used to leer down into after lights-out back in 1957 or thereabouts — where we could nightly watch the headmaster's religious sister, the Baroness de Ward, disrobe in silhouette until she was starkers and ravishingly exciting. All feelings of inversion were banished, for the moment, by this vision of loveliness, made piquant by the knowledge that the Baroness served Jesus as her lord and lover.

After I left school and she was reduced to a tiny flat in a dreary suburb rightly called Surbiton, near my family's London home, I used to visit her for tête-à-tête bible study. "You don't know it," she liked to tell me soothingly, "But you're really rather religious at heart." Since then I've always felt there's something illicitly sexy about religion.

The trips I make home — to England, I mean — are mainly for

talk marathons with family and friends who go back a long way. We've so much catching up to do and in a way you can't achieve in emails. As you chat, in car, kitchen, street, bus and underground, subjects come up in the flow that wouldn't so easily in an email exchange. For example, on the drive back to Berkshire after the school visit, my sister filled me in on the chronology of our housing in the World War Two years.

My father had volunteered with the RAF immediately war was declared in 1939 and was posted to the seaside town of Torquay where, as a Squadron Leader with Initial Training Wing, he was in charge of new recruits — not, alas, in the air, but on the training ground, marching them up and down the town in their new serge uniforms.

One day, according to family legend, my father set off at the head of his men across a busy intersection. Proudly he walked, as pedestrians gawped in silence, past the church, the post office, the cinema. When the gawping turned to laughter he grew puzzled, stopped and turned around. Not a recruit in sight. Where the hell were the little buggers? When they eventually caught up with their commanding officer the explanation given was that at the time my father stepped into the street at the traffic crossing the lights were green — but about to change to red. Which is what they did and thus the men waited obediently until the green came round again. "Don't you know there's a war on?" offered my father as a mild reprimand. True, but what would you have done?

Later my father was posted to Scarborough, another seaside town, this one in northern England in the county of Yorkshire. By this time, late 1941, I was alive and kicking. My mother used to patronize a grocer's called "Land's," a tiled place with a long marble counter. Butter was in short supply but my mother used to get extra by holding hands under the counter with the proprietress, a spiritual denizen of the isle of Lesbos.

My sister kept me entertained with such war stories until we were safely back at the Berkshire cottage. Now it was cocktail time for me and TV time for my sister and the General. Tonight another Reality program, this one a British effort: contestants trying for a position as a chef on a cookery show. One woman, really cheery and well spoken, was disqualified for having a "posh accent." Such is the England of today.

The next day my brother Robin, accompanied by his number one son, Patrick, came to pick me up/ have lunch/ hit a few golf balls about. Yes, I found myself at a golf range and enjoying it. Patrick is a splendid fellow at 21 and about to start studying electric bass at a recognized college for such bass. They never had pop music education centres when I was his age. We had to teach ourselves. Robin, who is in his last year of teaching sport at Dulwich College prep school, has enterprisingly written and photographed a coffee table book on village cricket grounds—and it's being published by a real publisher next month. I'm proud to have given him the title: *Wielding The Willow* — you see, it's about cricket in Sussex, in the Wield, which is where the game began. The title has a reminiscent ring: *Wind In The Willows*. On the dust jacket blurb it tells how among his accomplishments he played percussion on "I Got You Babe" by Sonny & Cher.

At the weekend I was back in Robin's spare room, in the squashy bed I so enjoy. A quick trip to the Indian-run corner store brought me a container of taramasalata and greetings from the Indians. They are not Pakistanis, by the way. They also sell Retsina, the strong resinated Greek wine that tastes like diesel oil, and I bought my customary bottle and polished it off that night. The papers were full of the Pope's death. I had no idea that Britain was so Catholic-conscious. I thought we got rid of the Catholics in Henry VIII's time. Maybe the coverage was because the Pope was a personality, a celebrity like Elton John. "Gone To Heaven," said the tabloid *Daily Mirror*.

I got a lift the next day to Putney: Robin was taking Patrick to an important soccer match there, just over the bridge. I got swept up in the waves of fans heading there, louche youths with brutally short hair, or else totally shaven, marching with beer bottles and cans. Everyone seemed younger than me in London.

Leaving my family to their soccer I caught the underground to Earl's Court to hook up with my old and close friend, dating back to Trinity College Dublin days, Chas Sprawson. He's the hero of my memoir, *Resident Alien*, which, of course, you've all read. If you haven't, there's still a chance — our garage holds dozens of unsold copies.

Chas lives in one magnificent room in the busy Earl's Court Road, handy for shops that sell cigarettes and such. He showed me a fan letter from an Anglo-Asian novelist, a very well reviewed fellow, who wrote that Chas' swimming book had changed his life. He asked Chas for the honor of a swim and Chas, taking the first name of the novelist to be feminine, accepted sight unseen. The fan turned out to be an exquisitely built male, not unlike Sabu The Elephant Boy, and they swam side by side in a Chelsea pool.

Just as in the past, we talked and talked and talked. We somehow found ourselves at Lord Leighton's house, now a museum and art gallery. Lots of Arabic-themed rooms but I didn't mind. We looked at an exhibition of Millais illustrations. Our family once owned a Millais oil. My grandfather had bought it from J.P Morgan. We sold it at auction and Andrew Lloyd Webber now owns it. I never cared for it that much.

Near the exit was a visitor's book, open for comment. The last entry read: "We are Simon & David. We are lovers of art. We are also LOVERS!" My entry went: "I am Harold — and why don't we make a threesome and go cottaging at the urinal of your choice?" As I finished writing the superintendent approached to thank us for coming. I dragged Chas out in the nick of time.

Chas saw me to a bus at Olympia — my next stop was a supper with my other best friend from Trinity College, Jeremy Lewis, the well-known man of letters and I don't mean he's a postman. You've all read his memoirs, I'm sure, in which my 1962 search of Dublin for an enema is well described. I had to change buses in Putney, a source of annoyance. Public transport in London is not what it's cracked up to be: traveling a few miles takes an hour at the least. Cars are impossible. There's an ever-present smell of fuel. But while I was waiting for the next bus I assessed the houses, wondering whether I could live here again. The average price for a place round here seems to be at least a million pounds sterling. As a child I used to see these stern Victorian brick houses set in rows as fit only for the common people.

The Sunday evening was soft and cool. I envied a slender woman walking home with her shopping bags. From the rear she swayed in a most enticing way. I imagined her happy in her flat, cooking and eating alone, curling up later with a book and a cat, or else watching an intelligent reality show — maybe "Literature Ho!" — on a cable channel.

Jeremy has been married to another Trinity graduate, Petra, for countless contented years. They live in cozy East Sheen, a short walk from Richmond Park. Their house sits in a lovely row and is overflowing with books. You can't get more civilized than that. Petra always makes me a junket to round off the supper.

I used to live with them when my mother was in the nursing home. We have always been a jolly trio. Back in the 1960s I was Jeremy's Best Man and afterwards drove the happy couple from their wedding reception to their first love nest, a tiny flat in Barnes. Not far, but far enough, from the river Thames. I used to sit on the side of their marriage bed and read the women's magazine stories I wrote at the time. Jeremy would make us laugh with his stentorian farts. I dubbed him "Farting Jack Stewart." These days he has sometimes been caught short while out on the street — a fart has "followed through" thus necessitating a change of clothing when he returns home. Petra is very obliging, always has been.

On Monday I killed the time before meeting Andy Wickham by trudging the West End streets. At HMV, the vast record shop in Oxford Street, I failed to find any of my records. We used to stock them, explained the assistant, but they never sold. So sorry. I bought a Max Bygraves retrospective and two more Proust readings. At Fortnum & Mason's I picked up the required rose chocolates for

Regina, but balked at fulfilling her request for Havana cigars. It was 6:30 pm and the quality shops were closing, about the only un-American activity you'll find these days in the West End. Starbucks & Co. is encroaching by the hour. The evening newspaper poster ads informed us that Prince Charles had postponed his wedding due to a clash with the Pope's funeral. All the heads of Britain were planning on attending.

This news really got Andy's goat. What have things got to when we kow-tow to the Pope? Andy had been waiting for me in the hall of The East India Club in St James' Square. Times are tough for gentlemen's clubs and so the East India now shares space with the Public School's Club. It's worse than that, though: from the accents and demeanor of the current young members you can tell they didn't go to the right schools. Andy always points this out to me as we enjoy a cocktail in the bar which, as he also points out to me, bars entry to women. We had our usual delicious dinner served by his usual jovial Irish waiter (who told me proudly that Ireland is now the "buzzingest" country in Europe, that Ireland rocks, due to its having thrown away or destroyed all that leaden old history). Andy, wearing a Huntsman bespoke suit that he said had cost him 3 thousand pounds sterling, was irritated that our table had been commandeered by coarse youths from the wrong schools led by a rotund and red-faced priest who looked like he might be a cottager. Andy was also irritated by my not having come up with one decent story concerning my being humiliated by somebody — such as the one I told him on our desert trip, the one in which, during a St Patrick's Day gig where I was employed as accordionist with a Celtic jig and reel ensemble, I had groveled on the floor of the Irish-American bar in order to retrieve a $100 bill tossed to me by a millionaire who hadn't the time nor the inclination to stop and hear my music. Yes, I retrieved the note — but then I'd had to share it with the band.

Next morning I traveled with Robin up to the Tower Of London on a reccy for his next book project: about people who live in odd places. Courtesy of the General there was a Yeoman Warder — vulgarly known as a "Beefeater" — waiting for us at his hole-in-the-outer-wall dwelling at the Tower. The General met us and in his wake we sailed into the old prison where so many heads have rolled. He was a very popular Governor because lots of Warders came out to salute him in greeting. Robin snapped pix of the Warder standing in front of his dwelling regaling us with facts about the Tower. It's now the #1 tourist attraction in Britain and pays for the upkeep of the rest of the palaces, he said. The General topped this with his story of a previous Governor who blotted his copybook by taking ads in American magazines offering a private dinner at the Tower with himself, plus a tour of the Crown Jewels, climaxing with the famous Ceremony Of The Keys at 10 pm sharp. A Warder got wind of the ad and the rest is untold history — until now. Our current Warder chimed in with a fact about the tin-roofed garaging just behind me, against the Tower wall. "That, sir, is where we used to shoot spies. A few in World War One, lots more in the second one. We shot them as they sat in a chair not a yard from where you are standing. Blindfolded, naturally."

The day after this I had lunch with Chas at his club, the raffish Chelsea Arts. You have to be in the arts to be a member but a lot of the regulars look like businessmen to me. I suppose art is a business, though. Chas certainly can make money from painting when needs be — a quick trip over to the Channel Islands with gold-framed oldie oils for viewing by wealthy tax exiles. We joined two elderly brothers called Michie in the bar. Chas was immediately called upon to provide the second line of a certain poem by Horace. In Latin. Chas provided something passable.

Turns out that one of the brothers, Donald, was a key member at Bletchley Park in World War Two, one of the "Enigma" team who broke the Nazi code. His partner was Alan Turing and the two of them went on to invent the computer. To invent what I'm writing on now! But being a well-bred Englishman he didn't bring any of this up in our bar conversation. Instead he offered that he'd taught Artificial Intelligence at Stanford and loved California. And that he loves American films even more. He'd just been watching *River Of No Return* on TV and it had him weeping. Since you're a popular music expert, he said, perhaps you'll know that lovely number that Marilyn Monroe sings in the film. Really lovely. But no, I didn't know the number. Chas pulled me away before I could start in on choruses of my own songs such as "Wurzel Fudge, The Village Idiot." However, I did manage to tell the brothers the main story of the song and how my music publishers are at present threatening to cut the number from my new songbook. The brothers agreed that it should stay in the book.

After lunch I left Chas in order to rendezvous with our TCD pal Jeremy at one of his work places. This one is in Soho, down a narrow, dark and sooty Dickensian street. Actually it's earlier, from Dr. Johnson's era. Jeremy informed me of this as I gazed admiringly out of his poky but quaint office window at the story-book street below. I had climbed rickety and creaking wooden stairs to reach his workplace — a monthly magazine called *The Literary Review*.

Here I met two fresh young university graduates, backbones of the mag. One of them, Tom, greeted me enthusiastically after he heard my name: "I've read about you in Jeremy's book! You're the fellow who searched Dublin for an enema!" Jeremy helped matters by indicating a mountain of books on the floor and inviting me to choose one for reviewing. I took *Hatless Jack*, about the decline and fall of men's headgear. To further soften the enema business he took me for a drink in his club. This club is next door, up more rickety stairs, and consists of one room, rather like Chas's or a large bedroom, with a tiny corner bar and some literary chaps in deep discussion on a ratty sofa. There was the old-fashioned and comforting smell of tobacco. We had cocktails, even though it was 3pm.

Next stop, a few streets away, was Jeremy's other workplace, the great magazine, *The Oldie*, where he is commissioning editor and I'm an occasional contributor. My latest article is about the uncle who wrote "Lady of Spain." They make their money from incontinence underpants advertisements. Again, the skeletal staff inhabited one room and were all frighteningly young. But they laughed at my jokes and the youngest and most powerful really liked my idea for a piece about Cynthia Plaster Caster, the 1960s groupie who is famous for her casts of rock stars' erect dongs, most noticeably the prehistoric tree trunk one she made of priapic giant Jimi Hendrix. So my holiday was turning into a basket of writing commissions. I returned to Robin's Wimbledon house a happy man.

But Hollywood's temptations caught up with me, even here in the living land of my past. Robin had left me a note saying that a film executive at Elstree Studios had called about some music matter. Next day I returned the call and grew excited about a film he said was about to be made on a subject I love musically. A script was sent immediately by motorcycle messenger. Before I'd finished reading it I had whipped up a few songs. When I met with the executives and creators my dam burst and I couldn't stop singing, to the accompaniment of a ukulele borrowed off my brother. I fairly doused them with enthusiasm. The film simply had to include me............

A happy time was had on my last night in England. I hosted my sister and the General to a dinner at the restaurant of their choice. As they live in the countryside I imagined we'd go to some unpretentious hostelry that serves steak & kidney pudding or shepherd's pie, washed down with foaming tankards of ale. They chose The Cricketers, a local pub. Just as I'd imagined.

However, I'd forgotten that England is now a gastronomical centre, no longer the laughing stock of Europe. No more plain pub grub like sodden fish'n'chips and rocklike scotch eggs. At The Cricketers the talk overheard at the next tables was about recent trips to China and the Kingdom of Dubai. Then the waiter called out the dishes of the day: rhino, zebra, or lion, steaks complete with nouveau squiggles on the plate. And to follow perhaps a mountain eagle pie au gratin. "Have you emptied the local zoo?" I asked. The waiter didn't care for that one. Back at their cottage, while my sister and the General dozed to *The Apprentice*, I helped myself to treacle tart in order to get rid of the exotic animals screaming politically inside of me.

Tunefully,
Ian

P. S. from Regina –
  I looked after home & pets.

JUNE

It isn't even June yet as I write this Letter and already there's a blasted heat wave here in Los Angeles. And to make matters worse we live in the hottest part of the San Gabriel Valley — Monrovia. Sounds like Africa, feels like Africa. I'd rather be back in England within a minute of Wimbledon Common or Richmond Park. I long for the vagaries of an English day: a spot of rain, a spot of sun, more rain, then the sun peeps through.

In the England of the 1950s, when I was at prep school, I used to say "hooray" when the rain came because then it meant no sports in the afternoon and so I could stay indoors and peruse my Buffalo Bill Wild West Annuals or Kid Colt Action Westerns.

These days, with sun most of the year, I instinctively feel I should be outside and active — digging a hole or striding down trails or surfing. But of course I can't because I have this nagging voice saying work, work, work. Is this work — what I'm doing now? Or is it time-wasting blogging? Be that as it may, I will try to account for May, sketch what's coming up in June, and try to remember the summer of 1965 when I was in the throes of being a teen idol — forty years ago.

At the end of the last Letter I hinted at a skirmish with Hollywood and a possible chance to be back in the mainstream of showbiz, rather than the usual scuffling about on the bank, on the margin. As it now seems unlikely that I will be involved in the movie I can now spill the beans: a World War One aviation picture called *Flyboys*, directed by my old pal Tony Bill (I considered him my old pal, he *did* attend our wedding — late but present in the end), and just the ticket for me since I'm bursting with songs of that period. One of Tin Pan Alley's most fecund times. I also have a taste for those early talkie flying ace pictures with dog fights and scenes back at base where they live it up round the piano and try to forget that their best friends have just copped it.

Well, while I was in London in April and staying at my brother's home, The Molehouse, I was sent a script for *Flyboys* and asked to discuss possible music for certain bar scenes. Tony Bill had employed me a few years ago on *Last Call* for which I'd contributed over a dozen songs. Tony had always had faith in me and tried to involve me wherever possible. Now he was in England, at Elstree Studios to be exact, and embarking on this war genre pic, based on the story of the Lafayette Escadrille, those brave American boys who volunteered to fight in the sky for the French in 1916-17.

I was terribly excited — too excited — and immediately gutted the script, in an easy chair, at The Molehouse, not only finding songs for the bar sequences but also making up ballads and squadron songs and even dreaming up a squadron band to be led by one Major Rollo Pryors, whom maybe I could play, or failing that an old French peasant with a musette squeezebox inhabiting a corner of the bar, a kind of Greek chorus commenting sadly, wistfully, on the fate of the Yankee flyers. Clearly I was jumping the gun, overdoing it, getting carried away.

The day before I left England I traveled to Elstree to take a meeting with Tony Bill and the producer. It was a long journey, by foot, by bus, by Tube, by train, eventually alighting at Borehamwood railway station. What magic the name had, together with Elstree! For it was here at the dawn of sound that British cinema established a super studio, wired for talkies. Here was where *Elstree Calling* was made, with sequences directed by Alfred Hitchcock and songs that included my uncle's, "Fairy On The Clock," as performed by butterball xylophonist Teddy Brown.

Furthermore, I would be exorcising the spirit of film failure in my country of birth, a ghost that had haunted me into exiling myself far away on the edge of the West Coast. I'd once, as a boy, been a humble fifth assistant director (or tea boy) at British film studios, helped in the door by a family friend, John Bryan — an Oscar-winning art director, an associate of David Lean's — and it was hoped I'd eventually work my way up to being a film editor and finally a director. But I huffed and puffed and argued and grew red in the face and eventually spilled tea all over VIPs having an important meeting and was generally a hopeless case.

Mind you, I'd ended up, decades later, near Hollywood where the movie factories sat. But still, I'd always wanted to make it in English cinema if only to prove to relatives that I had what it takes.

In a rather large and austere room, at a nondescript table I conferred with Tony Bill and his producer Dean Devlin — about whom I knew nothing. Immediately I went into my act, singing to ukulele accompaniment ("Never go anywhere without your uke" has been my motto), making them laugh one minute and sit with heads in hands the next (when I performed a sentimental ballad). They were bemused, and sometimes amused. I'll be leaving tomorrow, I told them, and immediately I get back to Hollywood I'll record these songs. Yes, yes, they said, and Mr. Devlin excused himself. An important meeting to attend, no doubt

Tony let me stick around, and even order a tuna sandwich. I was being invited to lunch at Elstree studios! He stared into his computer and occasionally answered my questions. Is it a TV movie? No, it's theatrical. Is it on 35mm? No, it's on digital, a new kind of digital, state of the art. I interrupted Tony's assistant from a fish and chips desk lunch to get him to play some of my CDs that I'd brought along. As they spun Tony nodded and seemed pleased. He had an idea: maybe we should have songs instead of big strings in some of the fighting parts. Yes, yes, I said. And I'll write them.

On my way out, I told the executive producer, a no-nonsense Englishman with a dubious accent, that Tony Bill is excited about my songs. Why, he might even feature them in the dogfight sequences rather than have the traditional heavy orchestral music. The executive frowned. "Wait a minute! Hold on, Sunny Jim! We already have a composer on board" Yes, yes, of course. "Well, and what, pray, is his function going to be if you have songs in the flying bits? Eh?"

I didn't stop to ponder; I just bid him a good afternoon and strode out proud in my London Fog raincoat and Fedora at a jaunty angle.

Moving from my brother's to my sister's couldn't stop the inspiration: more songs poured out, one about a French farm girl watching lonely at the farmhouse door as her love flies by, never to return; a touching number called "My Pal," leaving the listener in no uncertain state about the fate of the pal — God had called him. Oh, the juices were flowing. I was still scribbling as I waited at Heathrow for the return flight to Los Angeles.

Scarcely had I kissed Regina hello when I was in the recording studio laying down demos for *Flyboys*. Nine songs in two days, mixing and all. Then to FedEx and presto! Off went the CDs to Elstree. How pleased they'd be! A call would come from Tony: "We all love your songs! We can't stop singing them on the set!" Yes, and I'd pop across and actually sit on the set with a live trio providing atmosphere music for laughter and tears, just like in the days of silent pictures!

I'd already informed my agent, Julie, about the movie and my involvement. She, being sensible and knowing the wily ways of the industry, was skeptical. We'll see, she said.

Soon we saw: An email from the canny executive, the Englishman: "After careful consideration ... we do not require the level of talent and input that Ian is used to providing. We already have a composer on board and he will be responsible for any songs we require. I am sure you understand. Best regards, etc."

When I read this email a bottomless pit immediately installed itself in my stomach. Some of you will know this feeling. At the time

— cocktail hour actually — Regina and I and our best friend couple were assembled on the front porch holding champagne flutes and celebrating being alive. I had been called to the computer by a warning message from Julie, the agent. When I reappeared on the porch everybody noticed the drained look. Shall we abandon our dinner plans? No, no. So we ate Mexican but the guacamole almost choked me.

I tried to put the movie debacle behind me and concentrate on other work, small potatoes compared with the brass ring of a movie, but work all the same. However, every time the phone rang I hoped it was my agent telling the good news: they love your songs, the deal is on. But, like the French farm girl in my song, I waited and waited for the good news that never came. And now, as I write, the phone sits silent in its cradle. If it rings the caller will probably be a friend and so I have to check my initial disappointment and quickly reckon that I'm lucky to have friends, to have Regina, and Rollo The Dog, and Simon The Cat. And a (rented) roof over our heads.

Speaking of roofs: we seem to have spent the last month, and even the past year and more, looking at houses. Open Houses. Our weekends are spent inspecting other people's ex-homes. I have seen everything from plastic-covered sofas in antiseptic spanking-new "homes" to cluttered and quirky old houses with dark wood-paneled rooms and comfy armchairs with a side table containing a pipe recently smoked and a view of a delightful overgrown lawn surrounded by eccentric trees.

On the few occasions when we've gone so far as to put in a bid we have been gazumped within the hour. Or else the orders from the sharkish realtors, their eyes glittering with big money, are that you must have your sealed bids in by four pm. An auction, and we've lost to folks who have no hesitation in upping their offer a cool half million in a matter of minutes. Who are these bastards? Where does their money come from? Are they all extended families from South Korea and Taiwan, as the local newspaper insists — hard workers whose riches are the result of American out-sourcing? Or are they pornographers, or film producers? Are they working on *Flyboys*?

PS: my agent recently informed me that the movie isn't a little indie for TV but a bloated multi-million dollar epic and that producer Don Devlin has a string of blockbuster popcorn hits to his name, including *Independence Day* and *Godzilla*. Perhaps I should have shown him more respect and not whipped out the ukulele so fast.

Thus we have given up trying to find our dream house for the time being. The housing market gets more bullish by the day. Everyone says the bubble must burst soon. No one will be able to afford the prices. A million dollars buys little these days. Yet, the realtor friends tell us, this is what everyone was saying two or three years ago: the bubble must burst. But the soaring has never ceased.

So what do we see for the future? A Los Angeles inhabited by only the very rich and serviced by the very poor, who will live outside the pearly gates in ghettos exuding loatheing and resentment. Like the Dark Ages when castles studded a Europe carpeted with serfs.

My gloominess about the state of California, and Los Angeles in particular, may be due in part to my having recently read and reviewed Dr. Kevin Starr's Dream book, *Coast of Dreams*, the latest in a series he began in the 1960s when he was brimming with optimism about his Golden State. The latest offering grapples with contemporary history and it is not a pleasant sight — mainly the statistics of violent death and overcrowding. The middle class is being forced out into what was once farmland or citrus groves, inhabiting neo-Spanish developments of samey-sameness, with nonstop sun bouncing off the terra cotta and nay a bookstore in sight. Even where we live in Monrovia the signs of sterility and non-culture are appearing: last week our Penny Lane video store, an oasis of oddball movies and eccentric CDs, manned by assistants who loved to talk film, closed down. It seems that Monrovians are only interested in basketball hoops hanging from their garages and Thomas Kinkade on the drawing room wall.

The review was sent off to London and well received by my commissioners, *The Literary Review*. They also approved of my article on *Hatless Jack*, a history of the decline and fall of men's hats. A short walk away, in Soho, is *The Oldie* and there they have been rocking with laughter at my article on Cynthia Plaster Caster and how she assured me that even though she failed to get a mold of my engorged Hampton Wick in the 1960s she can still have a go today. "A Hampton never ages!" she told me. "It's not too late."

I informed Regina and she issued the following fiat: "It is too late!"

The article, titled "What Is/Was A Plaster Caster?" will be in the July issue of "The Oldie" graced with a photo of me as a desirable toy boy of the Sixties. "Much mirth around the office at your pix," wrote my old pal and commissioning editor, Jeremy Lewis.

My next job will be to write an article about Cole Porter without mentioning his homosexuality. That's a hard one. I have been asked to contribute this to the programme for this summer's annual Oregon Festival Of American Music at which I will be teaching and performing. The organizer, a very nice fellow, has asked me to hold down my normal exuberance and fun-loving ways: we need to take Cole Porter seriously, he tells me. He means it — and I will.

I can't feel too neglected: last Sunday's *Los Angeles Times* crossword gave me a tremendous fillip. There I was: a clue! 109 Across read: "Whitcomb, Holm, & McKellen." And what do we all

have in common? I'm a household name and that cheers me up no end. However, a curious thing happens when I tell some people about my being a crossword clue. These are people I hardly know, even complete strangers, such as a waitress showing us our seats in a new restaurant. I tell them I'm a clue and they say yes and carry on. No puzzlement, no enquiry as to why I should be in the crossword, and who am I. My theory is that they ignore my bombshell because, like so many people these days, they're not listening. They're waiting to make their next statement. Of course, this never happens at the Monday night Salon at Conrad's — there we all speak at the same time and so there's no question about one's bombshells going off. There we all celebrate our society by yelling at the tops of our voices and having a rattling good time, even forgetting that some of us are Bush haters and some Bush lovers. As for me, the guy doesn't bother me.
TTFN.

JULY & AUGUST

I note, from my journal, that recently I woke myself up with a start from a nightmare in which a very good friend of mine, a fellow ukulele player, Will Ryan, had become a huge star — with managers, flunkies, and limousines. And in his new TV show he intended to use Janet Klein & Her Parlour Boys as his house band — all of the Boys except me. My friend, the new star, would take my place, singing my songs and strumming his uke. As everybody was so fond of me they couldn't bear to tell me the news. So they pussyfooted around, offering beverages and snacks of my choice, and switching on sad smiles of sympathy.

But I knew what was going on, especially when, in a big room, I attempted to exchange pleasantries with my old pal. For suddenly up trotting came managers and flunkies with stop watches and clipboards and pleas to my pal to hurry to the limo since everyone had to be on the set ASAP. They gave me cold looks. I was holding up the schedule. Who is this guy? they asked with their eyes. Soon I was left behind in an empty room with a canapé in hand. I was in a sweat when I woke. I called my nightmare friend, Will, and he laugh-ed and assured me he isn't yet a star and that he'd never usurp my position such as it is.

Still secure, in real life, as a member of Janet Klein's band, I flew to Bloomington, Indiana, a few days later, to take part in a concert at a restored 1920s vaudeville theatre. Indiana, like the Midwest that I already know, seems to be nothing but dense woods from the freeway, and a cute Old Towne when you arrive, having driven past the usual Big Box businesses and convenient malls and fast fooderies. Our eager booster guides told us that in the 1920s Indiana could boast more vaudeville theatres than anywhere in the U.S.A; that Cole Porter's home town of Peru was where the circuses rested for the winter; that Hoagy Carmichael dreamed up "Stardust" while strolling down the very street our venue is in — he had to dash into a nearby café in order to nail the tune on their piano. Today Indiana is the pharmaceutical manufacturing centre of the U.S.A, in the legal sense of the word.

What can I say about the show? Except that we got a standing ovation, but then everybody gets one these days, don't they? On the flight back to Los Angeles we changed planes in Memphis where back in 1965 I'd performed at a rock concert and talked of Elvis — but that's for later. Janet Klein treated us Boys to a spare rib lunch at a Dixie-style shack in the airport. Ample black waitresses mothered us. When they enquired as to what kind of music we played I obliged by pulling out my ukulele and performing "When You're Smiling." Two of the Boys produced guitars and soon we had the whole place reeling and rocking. To be more exact, the waitresses were executing authentic Charleston steps. The only party poopers were at a table on the side: three white men deep in a business conference concerning semi-conductors.

On the last leg of the journey I found myself seated next to what looked like a superannuated heavy metal rocker: tank top, jeans, long stringy jet black hair, and a husky voice talking into a cell phone with words that clipped the Gs off of the end. I thought: oh dear, oh dear. But then he turned to me and asked whether I was *the* Ian Whitcomb. After confirmation he raved about what a hepcat I was once and how he dug what I did back in the 60s. It turned out that he's the harp player in a Blues Brothers band that tours the world with Jim Belushi and Dan Ackroyd. The band was spread over the plane and they were heading home for a brief respite before taking off again — this time for Europe and points east. Jimmie Wood (the neo-hipster's name) told me that in the row in front was Air Supply. The name rang a distant bell. I was introduced to one of their members. He had that creased and in-need-of-dry-cleaning look that you see in musicians of a certain age who are constantly on the road. Like Jimmie, he had earrings. He also had what sounded like either a working class British accent or an Australian one (of any class). Where was he heading for? Wearily and in a monotone he replied: "Indonesia, mate, but don't ask me the name of the bloody city."

At the United Airlines carousel, awaiting our luggage, Jimmie and I, accompanied by Ukie, sang a version of "But I Do," the hit record by Clarence "Frogman" Henry. As we were in Los Angeles no one responded.

The next morning, with Regina away in the Simi Valley on child-care business, I locked myself out of our apartment again. A locksmith arrived within 20 minutes and within 30 seconds had the door open. Rather frightening. This cost $50, as much as I make for a full night's playing at Cantalini's restaurant. I put off writing the article on Cole Porter as a writer of sweet love songs — a rather contumacious approach to the darling bard of the Smart Set — by driving out to a part of L.A. I'd never heard of before, Arleta, to rescue hundreds of cassettes of my old radio shows from the 1980s and 90s.

An elderly woman had written to say that she was getting on in years and thus clearing out her life and would I like these recordings. She had religiously taped every show I'd hosted on KCRW and KPCC. I deposited the boxes at The Huntington Library archives where they were received gratefully. Thus they now have everything, including my laundry bills. My legacy is secure. But will anyone ever peruse this stuff? Ah, there's the rub. A researcher friend of mine from England was over here at the Huntington a few years ago and he found odd pages of some archive contributor's legacy scattered over a dusty floor in a deep basement of the library. There were ketchup stains on some of the pages and wedged into a box of the donor's memoirs was a lady's high-heeled shoe, circa 1940.

But I continue to try to leave my mark or stain, bearing in mind Alec Guinness's credo, made at the end of his life: "I believe time ceases for the individual at death, so that there can be no after-life (as there is no before-life) but that probably the personality lives in God's keeping."

The rest of June was spent writing the article on Cole Porter for the Oregon Festival of American Music's program. I will be working there for the first two weeks of August. I always look forward to performing Dick Hyman's superb piano accompaniment. This year I have to be on my best behaviour — no more "Hound Dog" or "Green Door" — because the boss has ordered that Mr. Porter is to be taken with the utmost seriousness, and there is to be not a word about his taste for male prostitutes.

I have been able to practice some of the more melodious and less brittle Porter songs, like "Rosalie" and "True Love" at the private parties that me and the Bungalow Boys get hired for. We play in lovely big gardens at lovely big houses and are allowed to eat the delicious catered food. On July 4th, for instance, we will be once more in Brentwood at the home of an affable shrink where the cuisine will have a patriotic flavor: hot dogs and buns, and an enticing potato salad studded with bacon bits. The doctor's friends are all fellow shrinks but none of them are getting any younger and so every year the party gets smaller and the dancing is reduced. But there will be much to-and-fro-ing by means of walkers or Zimmer Frames, no doubt.

Sadly, Bobby Bruce, one of my original Bungalow Boys, will not be with us. He's in hospital, in the intensive care section. But Bobby is determined to pull through and make our next event. He's toughed his way through many decades: a boy fiddler in a 1930s vaudeville act, a marine at Iwo Jima, associate fiddler with Bob Wills & The Texas Playboys, and part of the Henry Mancini string section. I first became aware of Bobby via a movie soundtrack: "Pennies From Heaven," for which he contributed a jazzy obbligato to the title number. Wondering where he was and whether he was available for a gig, I used my KCRW radio show, in 1988, to ask on the air if any listener knew his whereabouts. A trumpet player called in with Bobby Bruce's phone number and Bobby joined the band for that first gig. He has the will to recover if Nature, a beast without conscience or caring, will allow him to.

SEPTEMBER

As those of you who have followed these Letters will know, we now camp on the bottom floor of an early 20th century house in Monrovia. We camp because we still don't have a proper home with room for us to hang our paintings, to place the great dark ottoman and the sideboard that keeps the silver and gold cutlery and all the other furniture that Regina had so lovingly and painstakingly collected and then carefully placed in our old home in Altadena.

All those objects that went to make our house into a home, a statement, are scattered — in garages and in the Huntington Library basement; every time I go into the garage that comes with our Monrovia apartment in order to gather a few CDs to sell at my gigs I struggle past boxes marked "ice bucket," "wedding gifts," "paintings" and I feel pangs for the times when we had our own world in our own home and there were parties with dancing and singsongs and couples danced in the corner dark of the dining room, sparking and maybe making plans for the future.

There used to be two 1920s plein air oil paintings of Palm Springs desert mountains that hung forever in the hallway and now are god knows where. I miss them very much. They're just material objects I know, but they were the solids that made up the set on our Altadena stage where laughed, sang, roared and ranted our actors: those who came to see us. As I get older I believe that having friends and being with them in one's own created setting is the essence, the answer, the riddle solved.

The Monrovia house has a long front porch, typical of the early 1900s, and when we first moved, a year ago, when life was rotten because we'd been driven from our home by the witch next door, I sat and sang "The Trail That Has No End" to my plangent ukulele accompaniment. These days I like to sit there at 6pm (cocktail time) and rock and read and watch the people walk by, as they do out here, thus refuting the common belief that Southern Californians never walk anywhere. The parade that passes has plenty of young mothers pushing their children in prams, young men running with their dogs, and a bearded man who resembles an Indian holy man and who seems to pass from left to right and right to left every few minutes and always laden with brown paper bags, and always smiling. There's also an older man in grubby overalls whose face and accent betray a Middle East origin, in fact a prime subject for pursuit by British policemen with orders to shoot to kill. But this man, this terrorist profile, is so sweet and tender. He doesn't speak a word of English but he likes to stop and stroke Rollo the Dog and Rollo in turn gets extremely agitated with affection whenever the man approaches—wriggling and sneezing and finally crying with joy.

Yesterday evening, while Regina was inside preparing dinner, I sat on the porch with a Newcastle Brown Ale and scanned my *Weekly Telegraph*, a combination tabloid of two moderately conservative—in other words, sensible—English newspapers. I don't like the fact that the tabloid has a banner at the top stating "North American Edition" and giving the email address as www.expat.telegraph.co.uk. I'd like to have the real thing straight as it reaches London's newsagents where tobacco is dispensed by the second together with Kleenex mini packets and Mars bars. I don't like being labeled an "ex-pat" because that evokes sunburnt Brits hiding in Spain to avoid taxes, demanding better fish and chips from the natives, following hometown soccer teams. Or else, over here, those wretches who run Olde English Pubbes in strip malls and audition for butler parts, arriving at the casting office in full costume. I know because I'm often sent out for those same butler parts, but I've told my agent to cease and desist.

The real British patriots, a vanished breed, never talked about their daring deeds. They were modest gentlemen like my friend Chas' father, a World War Two bomber pilot whose plane was hit in a raid over France. He and his crew parachuted out but his co-pilot, a friend, never made it. For the rest of his life Chas' father took care of his friend's family. He felt bad about what had happened. Yet he never talked about the war. I learned the story through others. The man I knew was a quiet prep school headmaster who always greeted me from the huge Tudor fireplace with an offer of a beer which he produced by unscrewing a stopper from a bottle and carefully pouring out the liquid so that there was no excess foam. Following that ritual the headmaster would offer me an untipped cigarette from his silver case. No emotional self-serving gush from this man. One of that noble caste of taciturn well-bred Englishmen soon to be all gone to dust, leaving Britain as the land of the yob, the would-be yob, and loose tribes of angry young Muslims who may follow soccer and even cricket but who have no intentions of following British values and customs.

But what are those cherished values and customs? In response to the recent London bombings the *Daily Telegraph* and other papers have been worrying about what exactly it means to be British. Statutory patriotism being foreign to Britain the journalists have tried to number our treasures—not only real ale and cricket and double-decker buses but also fair play, politeness and tolerance for other people. Rudyard Kipling put it neatly when he wrote: "The Saxon never means anything seriously till he talks about justice and right."

But the trouble with the England that I see whenever I return is that the country, as represented by its media, is a country of heathens, of materialists, of searchers for flat TVs and video cell phones. What kind of a culture is it that votes, as recent poll shows, for the "Cultural Moments That Changed The World" and votes Bob Dylan's "Like A Rolling Stone" at Number One? What happened to "We'll Meet Again" or "Mad Dogs And Englishmen"?

All this reading about what constitutes Britishness has made me look inward and consider. Internalizing and generalizing has never been my forte but I had a go the other night on that old front porch...

The Britain that lives in me is that of the England of my childhood—the seaside summer holidays, buckets and spades and end-of-pier shows with singalongs led by my uncle, a whole long-dead world that is still lurking ready to perform like an old-time concert party. The Britain that is alive—in flesh—today consists of my friends and family, nothing more, nothing less. And there are two friends of mine who regularly send me palpable evidence of their friendship and, as a consequence, of their personification of the real British culture: handwritten letters, derogatorily called "snail mail" by the computer crowd.

My two pen pals are Andy Wickham and Charles (Chas) Sprawson, friends who go back to the 1960s. *They* are friends of *mine*, not necessarily of each other. In fact they have a kind of guarded relationship. I've known Charles since my undergraduate days at Trinity College Dublin, while Andy Wickham I met later when I was a rock star in Hollywood. Both are Englishmen of impeccable background, certainly a better class than me, and both went to older and more established Public Schools than me . Charles became a dealer in Fine Art, mostly Victorian painters, and maybe the slight frisson between him and Andy started over the sale of an oil painting of a Victorian cricket team.

I was there when Charles, at his gallery, showed Andy this neo-

Victorian work, copied from a vintage photo of geezers in flannels and beards. Chas, encouraged by me, persuaded Andy that the colour scheme of this otherwise not very distinguished piece of work by a man called Gerry would go perfectly in his Chelsea flat.

So Andy was persuaded and soon the large oil adorned a wall of his small but finely appointed place. All was well until one day when a visiting American, who fancied himself a connoisseur, pointed out that while there was the correct amount of cricketers in the team there was an extra foot in an extra boot. The original photo had distorted the foot placement, or so Gerry The Painter explained after Andy complained. But Andy persisted until finally the exasperated artist, a rather common little man, let his guard down and exploded: "Well, git yerself a paint box and brush and just paint out the bloody foot yerself!"

Since then my two best friends only meet when I talk about them. Or until recently when, according to Andy's latest letter, written in immaculate handwriting with a proper fountain pen, they ran into each other: "In Jermyn Street the other day I came across Chuck Sprawson who looked burnished and healthy and fixed me with a piercing stare while suggesting we get together, a suggestion with which I concurred though we both parted knowing neither of us would make the first move."

Chas' letters usually arrive around the same time as Andy's. His are written with fountain pen too but while Andy's are on correct small creamy notepaper with embossed address on the upper left hand corner, Chas prefers Royal Mail Airletters, the kind you have to slit open carefully for fear you'll lose the bottom flap which usually contains the juicy stuff about local love affairs between married couples, etc. And with Chas' letters you know that he'd been enjoying a Marmite sandwich at time of writing because aromatic and colorful clues are staining the paper.

Chas is world-famous now because of his one-off book, a literary history of swimming called *Haunts Of The Black Masseur*. Much of it he wrote while staying at our old house—the one we've abandoned—in Altadena. He used to work on the patio, smoking hard, and writing his book in longhand. I accompanied him to some of the interviews with famous swimmers, supplying a tape cassette recorder for asking Olympic swimmers about whether they shaved all their hair off prior to a race.

I got to swim in a lane next to former Olympic champion Murray Rose, with Chas on the other side of me. Chas didn't seem to care for this arrangement. And when the book was published and the famous swim described I was no longer present. I became the opposite of Zelig. And I was reminded of a Graham Greene book concerning his daring African adventures where he was all alone, threatened by dangerous natives. In reality he had a female relative with him, but admitting to her presence would have spoiled the atmospheric narrative.

Anyway, because of Chas' fame he's always getting letters from readers dying to have a swim with him. A beautiful girl turned up at his front door recently demanding a swim a deux and at once. In his latest letter to me he writes: "A professor from Ottawa has just written to say that his dream is to meet me and have a swim —he ends, 'Please Charles, let me know if we can get wet together sometime'."

Every time I get a letter from my two good friends I'm honor bound to reply. Of course, I've written myself to death in these Letters and I could just direct them to the Website. But neither Andy nor Chas has a computer. In fact, they despise computers. Both write with pen and ink. They don't even own typewriters. Having their letters is to own a part of them—palpable expression of their personalities and essence.

For the record: I had another successful two weeks participating in the annual Oregon Festival of American Music in Eugene. The theme this year was Cole Porter. I was obedient and stuck to Porter's work and hardly changed a lyric. I taught at the two children's camps — we danced the Lambeth walk to "Let's Be Buddies"— and I sang, as a butler, "Miss Otis Regrets" at one of the afternoon concerts. Next year the theme is Irving Berlin so I'm hoping to take a big part in that since, according to my biography of the great man, he visits me in dreams and tells me all.

OCTOBER

I've been reading a fascinating article in *The New Yorker* about the disappearance of intrepid explorer Colonel Fawcett, an Englishman with an aristocratic background, in the Amazonian jungle in 1925. Together with his son Jack and Jack's best friend Raleigh, the Colonel was in search of the Lost City of Z. In one of their last reports they describe a concert they gave in a hut, out in the wilds, to a band of naked Indians. The Colonel strummed his ukulele and sang a few songs while his son backed up on a piccolo. I wonder what the program was, and how pacified the natives were. "I'll See You In My Dreams" was a hit that year, as was "If You Knew Susie." I'd love to have seen the native reaction, but I'll be bound they were delighted. I've never met a soul who's not been moved by the pleasing plangency of the uke. An army of ukesters marching through any world trouble spot would immediately result in a cessation of hostilities and a good time all round.

We were uking—Sunday, September 25—at the annual UKEtopia concert at McCabe's guitar shop in Santa Monica. Jim Beloff, tireless promoter of all that is uke, has subtitled these concerts, "Ukulele Heaven On Earth." The theme this year was Country & Western, since Jim's latest songbook is devoted to that field. Everyone was in western garb and it was interesting to see who can wear a ten-gallon hat and who looks perfectly dreadful. I did not wear a hat.

I sang "A White Sport Coat And A Pink Carnation" as well as "Chattanoogie Shoe Shine Boy," two of the numbers that always go down a storm at Cantalini's restaurant. They went well at McCabe's, but what I can't figure out is why the fine response I always get there from the assembled ukesters is never matched by sales. I sold just one DVD, nothing else. Is it that my audiences are entertained, laughing and such, but feel that this won't translate into a satisfying listening experience in the home, in the car, or on the pod? But in fact my records are nothing like my live appearances: they are carefully-crafted studio artworks. But devilishly hard to sell....

Backstage at McCabe's I introduced to all and sundry my new character, Harold Nossiter. Many were amused for a while, but when he started taking me over, like a ventriloquist's doll can do, they backed away.

Gigs, gigs, gigs—this year has been full of them and I'm happy for that. If you stop and ponder then awful thoughts of mortality come creeping in. This month, September, I've got the regular Borsht Belt Babies variety shows every Friday, and this weekend it's the annual Orange County Ukulele Festival (for which I'm hosting a concert of "virtuosos" as well as the usual local Hawaiians whom we have to be very reverential to since they consider the ukulele to be their native instrument and regard us mainlanders as like cowboys in redskin country; also I have to bear in mind that when the teen Hawaiian girls demonstrate the hula—undulating their bodies with special emphasis on the waggle of the bottom and thrust of the breasts—we are watching a religious exercise and not a bump and grind show by underage angels).

I continue to enjoy playing Cantalini's by the sea. The management at Cantalini's is so kind to us: free dinner and wine before we settle into our corner chairs and play acoustically to the diners. Sometimes we stroll to the tables — that is, only if we get a welcoming signal from particular diners. And what diners they are! We can't fathom out how it is that so many beautiful and sexy young women like to eat at Cantalini's. We're in our corner playing away at say "Poor Butterfly" and we are awarded a rear view of a young woman in low-slung tight jeans, so low that the leather thong is visible.

We're ever-ready to oblige with a "Happy Birthday," too. The tip bowl is always out in front of us too. This is real work with a real and instant reward: hard cash. The more obliging we are the more tips we make. I'm reminded of the man in the enormous diving bell suit who used to stand on Brighton Pier and give diving demonstrations. He'd remove his globular metal helmet with the glass front and implore: "Don't forget the diver!" Small coins would be hurled at him, some actually entering the upended helmet he held out.

Now that we're back in the past we might as well stay there.

On the subject of gigs (defined as a short single musical engagement), I can remember the very first one I did for money. It was in a corner pub in South London in late 1959. I played piano and sang, my brother Robin was on drums and a new friend, one Johnny Toogood, tootled his clarinet. I'd just left my Public school (boarding school) and was working at Harrods department store in the gramophone record section. Johnny was in ladies lingerie, I believe. He liked to visit me and make off with a few 45s and the odd LP. He had slicked back hair and a nasal twang of indeterminate class; he claimed to have been to Public School, which may have been true because the one he named was very, very minor indeed. My mother nicknamed him "Not Too Good."

Johnny had connections with the trad jazz scene and was soon getting us gigs. He could wail on the old chestnuts and somewhere in the flurry of notes he'd hit a right one — mostly a conjuring trick, like show biz is. I remember that after the South London pub gig the landlord paid us in coins and we carried the money triumphantly, like champion athletes in ancient Greece, to the pavement where under the street lamp we divided it up. What a thrill that was! First gig money ever! My father and uncle arrived to take us home and I was so pleased to show my father that I was now a professional musician. He thoroughly approved, even going to the extent, later on, of lugging our sound equipment through snow and rain to whatever venue we were playing.

In later years I hooked up with ragtime pianist, Professor Dick Zimmerman. We started gigging in the late 1960s after he'd rescued me from rock & roll, setting me on the road backwards. He was what was termed a "forte pianist," so loud you could hear him from blocks away. This might have contributed to the failure of his marriage since he was in the habit of starting a daily performance of his latest cakewalk or rag study prior to breakfast.

It was a relief to have a piano player because I could now concentrate on performing and doing shtick rather than being stuck behind a keyboard, like a clerk at a desk, as I had been since my coffee house days in Seattle back in 1963 when I arrived in America and got my first gig. But Dick being such a forte performer and one who never stopped for breath—in other words, not an accompanist but a star performer on a mission to spread the ragtime word to not only the world but also to the universe— I had my work cut out finding a way to insinuate my vocals in between the storm of notes that Dick fired out. So I'd weave around his phrases, sneaking in a line whenever I could. It was quite a battle, I can tell you. A friendly one though—like a sporting tournament.

Eventually we got celebrated enough to be invited to perform at the Montreux Jazz Festival in Switzerland, quite an honor. We were to open for Art Blakey and His Jazz Messengers, a modern jazz ensemble and black to boot. They had demanded a Bosendorfer grand piano, the top brand. At the concert— shown live on Swiss TV and to be eventually distributed around the world —- I sang a few ragtime novelties, to the bewilderment of the jazz aficionados, and then announced that Professor Dick would perform a classic rag, something to do with hot vegetables. I left the stage to Dickie who immediately made short work of the Bosendorfer.

As I stood in the wings watching him I became aware of a concerned gentleman nearby muttering in French. I spoke a little French and I asked him what was troubling him. Turns out he was the Bosendorfer technician and he was horrified at what Prof Dick was doing to his precious instrument. The piano was indeed shaking and it seemed as if bits would fly off at any moment.

I was reminded of a similar scene a few days earlier, at the London home of a well-to-do magician friend of Dick's, who is something of a close-up trickster himself. After wining and dining Dick had leapt at the rich man's ornate grand piano, a Chinese antique and clearly a never-played piece of valuable furniture, with scrolls and columns and intricate woodcarvings. It was, in fact, acting as an exhibition stand for a priceless collection of Ming vases.

Well, a few bars into "Pork And Beans,"a particularly lively rag, and several of these vases started dancing and sliding. It took the magician, assisted by his wife and myself, to rescue the objets d'art as they slid towards a likely destruction. Dick was unperturbed and continued to play till exhaustion. He was simply following his bliss.

I didn't inform the Swiss piano technician of my partner's propensity. I pretended not to know him. "Qu'est-ce que c'est?" demanded the man, with arms outstretched. "It's ragtime," I replied. "Quelle horreur!" said the man and would have torn his hair had he had any. The Art Blakey group quickly followed our act. They reaped the results of Dick's performance: the Bosendorfer was so out of tune that the pianist's modernistic and hideously ugly chord substitutes sounded like Liberace on a chocolate diet.

The detuning of the Bosendorfer didn't phase Dickie one bit. He continued to tour Europe and the British Isles destroying pianos. He became known as the Ragtime Attila The Hun. On the last day of our stay in England my mother and I took him and his wife, the lovely Diana The Enchantress, to a picturesque country cottage belonging to a well-bred couple, friends of my mother's. The husband was a powerful judge in the law courts of the city of London, but for relaxation he liked to play cool or smooth modern jazz piano, his hero being Bill Evans.

After a long and quite liquidy lunch, followed by croquet (during which Dick and Diana informed our host and hostess that despite the fact that they found Europe quaint and were crazy about castles they remained convinced that America is the greatest country in the world, thus causing the judge to lose control of his mallet), and concluding with a tea of buttered toast, anchovy sandwiches and two kinds of cake, the judge invited the professor to give him an example of this thing called ragtime. "Fire away," said the judge, settling down in his favourite armchair and pulling out his pipe and baccy pouch. He indicated, with a slow movement of a long bony finger, a lovely old Steinway baby grand piano in the corner of their Tudor cottage drawing room, nestling under low and ancient oak beams.

Dick proceeded to batter it so hard that ivories flew off, some hitting treasured landscape watercolors on the wall. Dick finally was persuaded off the piano stool, with some physical help from the judge, where he fell into a stupor. We hauled him to my mother's car and said our farewells and thank yous. "You're so welcome," said the judge's wife through clenched teeth and with a rictus smile," Are you sure you can't stay any longer? Oh well, what a pity, if you must, you must, good bye, goodbye, goodbye!"

Our car refused to start. The Automobile Association was called but was an awful long time arriving. Up to this point the well-to-do couple had been a paragon of politeness, but now the mask fell and they revealed their loatheing of Americans, especially those who destroy pianos with ragtime. They treated us from then on as if we didn't exist. And so we sat stranded in the car in the driveway. My mother puffed a cigarette. I sat and stared straight ahead. Dick and Diana slept.

The judge and his wife simply got on with their life — changing into tennis gear, seeking out their racquets, backing the Jag out of the garage, and shooting off to their party without so much as a wave. We sat for hours until finally the AA man came and repaired the car. Professor Dick slept through it all. What a blissful life he leads, lucky man! I shall be seeing him next month at the annual Sacramento Ragtime Festival where the pianos are built for duty in Iraq. I shall battle once more to try and squeeze my song lyrics through the barrage of his syncopations.

Speaking of pianos, we have just had delivered to our Monrovia digs the piano with which I grew up in London. It has sat gathering dust at our old house in Altadena during the year we've lived here. We'd left it there because we thought it wouldn't be long before we found a new house or moved back to the old one. We can't afford a new house and we can't move back to the old one because the Iranian bitch who oppresses us, and is the reason for our exile, stays healthy and smug next door.

So the piano was moved. I'm so glad it's with us because it exudes comfort every time I look at this solid piece of burnished oak with rounded sides in the art deco style of the 1930s. It's compact but weighs a ton, as the moving men discovered. The piano is stamped all over with gold-lettered notices, announcing itself as an Eavestaff sold by Maxwell of Woking (where I was born in 1941, a day that unspeakable atrocities were happening in a Polish town), and that Minipiano is a registered trade mark and fully protected with "patents granted and applied for" as well as being a "registered design" with the following numbers to prove the matter. That's all on the right side of the instrument. On the left side is this: "As used by HRH Princess Ingrid of Sweden and TRH Princess Elizabeth and Princess Margaret Rose of York." The lid folds so that when closed the Minipiano looks like a solid oak sideboard. Indeed my mother used it as a piece of practical furniture whenever I wasn't around to play. She kept her telephone there, next to her ashtray and made many a long and merry call to friends or family, with her cigarette burning away and a crystal glass of Dubonnet in her free hand.

She had bought the Minipiano for my father as a wedding present in 1936. She paid for it through the installment plans.

My father was quite a good pianist, properly trained as a boy, with a delicate touch, but he could never master syncopation dearly as he wanted to. He idolized the great British syncopation piano wizard Billy Mayerl and owned his sheet music but struggled in vain. He would watch me pound away in a rock & roll manner and wonder how I achieved such rhythms. And, in turn, I wished I could read as well as he could and wished I had his tender keyboard touch. When he played he made the piano sing and hold notes. I shall never forget his beautiful rendition of "Alice Blue Gown." I have a recording of my brother and me singing "Friends And Neighbours" to his accompaniment, circa 1954.

When I started composing rags at the piano he was very encouraging. He was on my side through all my artistic endeavors even though he himself worked as a businessman. Well, really as a salesman for his younger brother's brick and tile company, motoring around England wearing a trilby hat and with a trunk full of builder's merchant materials. A bit of a comedown for a Public

School man, but then this was the price he'd paid for staying loyal to his father. For when his father's business ventures crashed he sank with them.

At Christmas parties the lid of the piano would be opened and I'd become the pianist for a round of songs. Everyone joined in on "Rhymes," a collection of limericks that quickly grew filthier. I can still see my Uncle John, an ex-RAF officer like my father, push forwards with his cry of "I've got one!" and without heeding the warning of his prim and Fundamentalist Christian wife, launch into:

> *"There was a young fellow called Skinner*
> *Who took a young girl out to dinner.*
> *At a quarter to nine they sat down to dine*
> *At a quarter to ten it was in her—*
> *Coda: The dinner, not Skinner—he was in her before dinner"*

I worked out a lot of my songs at the Eavestaff, including my first hit, "This Sporting Life," and as I worked I could hear the shifting of chairs by the upstairs neighbours, nice people who were registering their unease with this mildest of protests. One day, in the 1970s, we were visited by the great American "serious" composer and ragtime buff, William Bolcom, accompanied by his lady friend, the singer Joan Morris. After my mother had served tea Mr. Bolcom was invited to try out the Eavestaff. He remarked on the bell-like sweetness of tone, before accompanying Miss Morris on the standard, "Can't We Be Friends?" She sang beseechingly at him and he goo-goo-eyed her. A little later, back in America, they got married. But at the time my mother, standing in the doorway, was stunned by this public display of affection. "Are all Americans like this?" she asked me later.

So now the piano is safely lodged in an unused fireplace at our Monrovian apartment. When I want a whiff of the past, an equivalent of Proust's cake, I climb under the piano and sniff. All at once my old home on Putney Heath comes rushing back, an aroma of gin and Dubonnet, cigarettes, cigars, macaroni cheese topped with bacon for my return to England treat, and the ghosts from family parties surrounding my mother as she asks me, "Are you ready for the other half?" and I know she's wanting me to open another beer. A breathing time capsule, a door into the past, a piece of oaken immortality. The Eavestaff existed before I was born and it will continue after I'm dead.

In my last report I wrote of how there are only two letter writers left in my life, Andy and Charles, of London. But today I received a letter from England from the Rev. John Stanton-Watts of Wales. I didn't have to tear it open because someone in the post office had already done that. Headed "The Rescue Mission" this is what the

Rev. wrote:

> *Dear Mr. Whitcomb,*
>
> *PRIVATE AND CONFIDENTIAL*
> *Perhaps you have heard of me and my nationwide campaign in the cause of temperance.*
> *Each year for the past fourteen, I have made a tour of Britain delivering a series of lectures on the evils of drink. On these tours, I have been accompanied by my good friend and assistant, Clyde Lynson. Clyde, a young man of good family and excellent background, is a pathetic example of a life ruined by excessive indulgence in whisky and women.*
> *Clyde would appear with me at the lectures and sit on the platform drunk, staring at the audience through bleary and bloodshot eyes, swearing profusely, picking his nose, belching, breaking wind, and making obscene gestures at the ladies, whilst I would point him out as an example of what overindulgence can do to a person.*
> *Last Spring, unfortunately, Clyde died.*
> *A mutual friend has given me your name and I wonder if you would be able to take Clyde's place on my next tour.*
> *Thank you in anticipation.*
> *Signed: John Stanton-Watts (Rev.)*

I was so pleased to get an old-fashioned letter — no matter what the contents. And so much better than those daily emails I get from African ex-businessmen, deposed chiefs and dictators, offering me a million dollars of their money to store in my bank if I'll let them have my bank details, credit card, etc.

NOVEMBER

What is wrong with Simon? There's lots wrong with the world: disasters crowd my paper everyday and NPR news has correspondents in the heart of Baghdad as well as up-to-date reports from traffic helicopters concerning a sigalert on the 210 at Rosemead ("It's a mess," intones the radiophonic voice and he could be referring equally to our whole wide world, but not to worry: Bono will solve everything, aided by Brad Pitt). But what is wrong with Simon?

Simon is the cat that adopted us twelve years ago, appearing suddenly from over the back wall of our house in Altadena. He's a tuxedo — that is, black and white and nothing special but we have grown to love him. He doesn't care for visitors, hissing and almost barking, punching them in the arm or even the face should they choose to get close to him. He lies around the flat all day in various spots, contemplating, staring, considering. Thinking of what? He always used to run to his bowl at the sound of the tuna tin being opened; he liked to lie on whatever newspaper you happened to have spread out on the kitchen table; when you were resting on the bed he'd jump up and face you, stretching out his paws to play your neck, and pretty soon the purring would start.

There's no purring anymore. Simon doesn't eat, he drinks to excess and he mostly abides on an electric heating pad, staring off into nowhere. Or is it that somewhere? I left this keyboard to lie with him, singing "Si-mon," but he showed no interest. He moved away to stare elsewhere. He's been doing odd things in odd places. Of course, why should the outside world have any interest in this nondescript unfriendly cat? Unlike Rollo The Dog, Simon is no great beauty. There will be no stadium concerts for him, beamed globally. But he's important to our world: he gave comfort in that steady presence, that knowingness. Now he knows something else. I hope I can face the end with the same composure.

A few weeks ago we'd played for a private party celebrating the 70th birthday of the manager's mother, a Scots woman. I worked hard that night, roaming the tables, exhorting guests to sing, eventually rendering "I Belong To Glasgow" so that the whole Scottish family, including the manager, were inspired to join together, kick up their heels and sing boisterously, as loud as the Paul Newman customer in the bar.

There was a piquant moment during the evening: I'd spied an African-American and his family in a far booth and so I picked some bluesy numbers to aim at them for their delight, like fish & chips for an Englishman. We did "Frankie And Johnny" and "Shake Rattle And Roll." The inky table was polite but not ecstatic. There was no visible response, no rolling or shaking or even nodding. Then the father signalled to me and I went over.

"Would you play me a George Formby number?" I was amazed. Caught with my trousers down in prejudice in the true sense of the portmanteau word: pre-judgment.

"Would you play 'Leaning On A Lamp Post', please?" Of course, but how do you know of Formby, the ukulele man? "I grew up in Wolverhampton." And he's happy to have left. We did a spirited version of "Lamp Post" and I felt I was now a better person, that I'd been cleansed.

At Cantalini's I had almost brought with me, as reading matter for when I was with my pesto pasta, a large coffee table size book called, "Bryanston—Reflections." Then I thought better of it. Reading it is not good for me, and forcing the unwieldy volume on others is even worse.

I paid almost $90 for this heavy work and when it arrived I ripped off the wrapping and went immediately to the index to see....Yes, I was in there. I was accepted, entombed as part of my old school history. An all-male red brick boarding school, originally built as the country house of Lord and Lady Portman in the early 1900s and turned into a school in 1928 by an Australian clergyman/schoolmaster who left under a cloud, set deep in the heart of Thomas Hardy countryside at the end of a two mile driveway, removed from all civilization, a setting for sending any respectable young boy on a twisted, inverted road that leads to...

There were two photos of me and an extract from my book *Resident Alien*. One photo showed me in sunglasses pulling a face down by the River Stour in 1958. It proved I had been a boy there because I was wearing the school uniform of open necked grey shirt and grey sweater.

The book extract concerned my tussle with the famous Headmaster TF Coade (a thinker and deeply religious in an obscure way) in the Main Hall when I'd taken offense at his caustic remarks about a still-wet modern art poster I'd set up there. I'd called him a philistine and run from him. Then I'd feigned a breakdown in order to escape being expelled.

The school doctor had reasoned with me that my troubles were minor compared with what was happening that moment in Cyprus. "Imagine Sir Hugh Foot, our Governor, and his terrible predicament — Greeks versus Turks — and us British, as usual, caught in the middle. I'm sure that your problems will shrink to their proper size."

I wish I'd taken his advice through the life that followed. Of course, all this material had been sent by me to the publishers in London. There'd been no commitment to use them.

But now here I was sitting in the pantheon of past boys, no longer the school fatty, the difficult schoolboy who was no good at games, the pest who was sent to Coventry (treated as invisible) as a punishment (for what?) by the members of my dormitory. Here I was as an equal with the other teenage Adonises in the big book with the blue cover, an assembly of breathtaking photos of Bryanston: the solidly constructed redbrick mansion fronted by lush greenery, backed by an intense blue Dorset sky with a few fleecy clouds; a dawn scene of mist at the river showing a steamy field and thick mysterious tree clusters in the background, holding the promise of adolescent excitement and experimentation; and also a sturdy boy with perfect shoulders, operating an electric saw on a log in that thick forest, taking part in what was called "pioneering"; the boy has 1950s short hair clean cut and he's wearing the school uniform of open-neck shirt except his is unbuttoned almost to the waist, the very epitome of the ideal youth of Hitler's Germany, an Aryan delight, fit for consumption, with no connection to the effeminate 1960s callow youths with girly hair and action-shunning dispositions who were to take Bryanston from rutty masculinity into the prosaic world of today.

Who was this boy? I didn't remember him from my time at school. What would he look like now? He'd be in his 60s like me. Probably blessed with grandchildren, balding or bald and with a potbelly. As I read the big blue book, "told through the voices of former pupils" (so says the dust jacket blurb) I realized that these romantic youths caught in that brutally short time of pure beauty had mostly gone on to be responsible, dull citizens.

Take, for example, the contribution to the book by a trio who were friends from their very first days at Bryanston in the Junior House, 1947. All three of them have their names as the authors of the entry. Are they still friends today, huffing and puffing and farting as they play Bridge together at parties in some stockbroker-Tudor Home County mansion?

In the book they recall their first night in the Junior House, new bugs fresh from home, and how Tigger Hoare, the master in charge, had made them less homesick: "Just before lights out Tigger came shuffling into the large ground floor dormitory, sat down on the end of one boy's bed — and read everyone a story."

I remember that same outdoor dormitory, with its stiff new sheets and thin blankets, eight years later — and how the new housemaster, Mr. Brewin, would sit too on the edge of certain boy's beds and read or whisper to them. And I remember one boy, faired haired and girlish, order in a shrill but clear and piping voice: "That's quite enough of that, sir!" Mr. Brewin had never honored my bed but he did encourage my acting. Despite my stammer he made me secretary of the Junior Dramatic Society.

The Three Musketeers of 1947 stayed together and were sent on to the same Senior House and then the same study, an attic of many hideaway bolt holes far up in the school's roof. There they decorated with old rugs and blankets and Chianti bottles, and burned toast on toasters and made instant coffee via dodgy electric kettles, and played jazz records.

"Most of the time, though, we were three very fit and healthy seventeen-year-olds taken up with A levels and tennis, hockey, rugger, rowing, and cross-country runs." The very opposite of me—who used the excuse of flat feet to get off from playing any games, so that all I had to do was to take country walks which I'd climax with a tin of cold baked beans studded with pork sausages. These boys in the blue book were the true Apollos of the games field, specimens I could never hope to emulate.

The boys' entry is accompanied by an idyllic photo showing

them rowing down the middle of the steamy river Stour in high summer on an "unauthorized trip," probably to pick up cider from the nearby village shop. A heart-stopping picture in its freezing of an adolescent adventure in a perfect sylvan setting. A coda from the editor tells the whole sorry subsequent story:

Boy A: "After spells in shipping and horticulture he developed a company specializing in paperback books for schools and libraries. Since retirement he has dealt in antique prints."

Boy B: "Following a school ambition he became a dentist. Since retirement he has become a painter in watercolours."

Boy C: "After a career in advertising he took up furniture-making and design."

Sic transit gloria mundi...

They should have served together in some war in a distant country and died in action.

Toting the book around here in California has done me no good at all. The very word Bryanston is magical to me. I look at it and the feelings flood back. But it's meaningless to people over here. I present it like a bible or holy relic or illuminated manuscript at restaurants where our friends gather and they scan it like a high school college yearbook and resume their topic—the war on Iraq, Bush, the price of gas. Why was my time at Bryanston so memorable, so intense? The masters, remembered fondly and admiringly by the Old Boys writing in the new book, meant little to me. For the most part, they had no effect on me at all except to interfere with my dreams and projects.

I realize now that what I liked about Bryanston, apart from the gorgeous countryside, which I ingested rather than actually saw, was that Bryanston was a self-contained world, a boy's town where I struggled to the top, establishing myself as a poster artist, a comedian, an actor, and finally the founder and leader of the school's first rock & roll band. A very convenient little civilization and I've been struggling to recreate it ever since.

I've had letters from my two faithful correspondents, Chas and Andy. Chas points out that my account in last month's Letter of his father's bomber pilot experience in WW2 was inaccurate: his best friend Wigg wasn't in the same plane — he died in another crash. All of Chas's fathers' crew were killed except him.

"My father returned to the crash site after the war and found a piece of foulard scarf worn by one of them."

Chas has just returned from Italy where he visited a museum of torture in Sienna: "Full of old implements with odd descriptions of them, such as why torturers avoided the vital parts of men because of a certain sympathy, but they enjoyed disembowelling women because they feared them and found them mysterious."

Andy's letter was of sterner stuff — a wigging about my writing style or lack of it. He criticizes my recently published book reviews as "clumsily staged projections of yourself" and "striving for effect." But he does praise as "interesting" my current review of two books by George and Diana Melly:

"A courageous if uncertain review of the Mellys who, of course, are sacred cows and beyond criticism in literary London. You lambast them but forgive him at the end for being nice to you."

What he prefers are these posted "Letters":

"There is a wonderful spontaneity in your web journals. Your report from Japan was masterful." But then he spoils it all by going on to advise me to be more careful, to "think about what you want to say when you walk the dog. Compose your piece in your mind. Mull it on the drive to your P.O.Box in Altadena. Mull it further on your swim. Structure it clearly in your mind. Then, when you're ready, splurge forth." This is contradictory, but I believe that when he wrote this letter Andy was on his second or third Scotch in his cottage in the country. How shall I respond? I shall soldier on blindly, as I've always done, fearing nobody even as I'm offended by them, staying free and willful, chattering on down the trail that has no end.

Now we must see to Simon and whether he can be saved.

PS: The letter from the Reverend John Stanton Watts, quoted in last month's Letter, turned out to be a fraud. A joke played on me by somebody who claims to have known me at school.

DECEMBER

Regina and I have formed a husband & wife medical team: administering a life-giving liquid to Simon The Cat via a plastic bag hanging from the top of the kitchen door frame. Regina holds and soothes the crying or complaining cat while I make sure that the liquid is dripping steadily from the bag. It's all over in a few minutes and the procedure — "subcutaneous," to get technical — is an excuse for a moment of togetherness, just as other families get their togetherness at the dinner table or round the television.

The treatment has returned Simon to his old life habits: if Rollo grows excited about, say, a squirrel he has spotted in a tree Simon will respond to his barks by chasing him till he has trapped him and can administer a series of boxing punches. Rollo eventually escapes to hide from his tormentor either under my work table or inside his metal crate.

Thus our life is returning to normal — except for the fact that Simon has been diagnosed with chronic kidney failure, incurable.

With this home treatment he may have up to four years more of life. Our kitchen has become a miniature hospital but I've no complaints because it makes us a team and gives a little purpose to my life, pulling me away temporarily from antique songs and long-dead crooners and equally-dead singing cowboys.

The treatment doesn't have to be given every day so we were able to take our trip to the annual Sacramento Ragtime Festival after we'd injected enough fluid into Simon to last a few days. Our neighbour — a kind one for a change — had agreed to look in on Simon while we were away. Rollo was pleased and shaking with anticipation because he saw us lining up his bowls and food together with the rest of our stuff and he knew that he'd be accompanying us on the trip. He grew very animated when I left AOL and the spooky-cheerful voice uttered, "Goodbye!" He knew that this meant end of work and start of play. Indeed, he grew so animated that Simon had to deliver a few more punches. But soon he'd be away from oppression and en route for Somewhereland. Where? That's what makes a dog's life exciting. You never know what'll happen next, where life will take you. But one thing you're certain of: you'll get your water and your biscuits.

This was taking place in the late afternoon of Wednesday, November 16. Now all we had to do was wait for our friends, the Seilers, a husband and wife medical team (always useful to travel with) to arrive in their "motor home"—what we used to call a "caravan" when I was growing-up in England. But today's caravans are literally homes on the run. And the Seilers' home is gargantuan: our tree-lined and coffin-quiet street darkened and trembled as the monster rolled up, a never-ending metal building on wheels.

There at the helm was Dr. Irv, happy as a sand boy, puffing away on a ciggie, while Dawn, his lovely wife and our nurse, dealt with lingering domestic details relating to their other home (a nailed-down one in Arcadia conveniently situated near the freeway for easy access when instant getaways are called for), on her ever-present, often-jingling cell phone. I must say it has one of the more appealing ringtones, a classical fragment I can't place, but happily not Wagnerian.

After we'd loaded the mansion with ukes, CDs, DVDs, costumes, dog food, almonds, etc., we were able to flow onto the rush hour of the evening freeway and were soon tooling along at great speed with the doctor still happy as the Beach Boys played while he consumed a bag of powdered jelly doughnuts, enjoying them to the last speck of powder, tipping up the bag in order to ensure safe passage for the sugar, and a sure passage this sugar certainly received, but sometimes missing his mouth in order to drop softly like snow flakes onto his shirt, trouser and captain's throne, as all the time he roared us past small fry sedans and pathetic Japanese gas-saving hybrids.

At first I had dared to sit up front with Rollo peering out at the little cars we were creaming past, making me feel at one with the eighteen wheeler juggernaut trucks, high up above the freeway peons. But as the Doc drove faster and the Beach Boys grew louder and the powder flew about in a snowstorm, I grew a little frightened. We seemed to be at sea or in the air and I feared the sudden smash of metal on metal. Of course, I was assured we'd be quite safe in our behemoth, but still, I didn't fancy crushing another car like a beetle. So I retired to the domestic part of the racing home and pretended to be in a real living room.

We were soon making ourselves at home in the lounge, dining room, bathroom, bedroom and so on. The Home is decorated entirely in the USC colors — mats, pennants, towels — because the doctor is a rabid USC football fan. Recently he and Dawn drove the Home thousands of miles, to Indiana, in order to watch a game between USC and Notre Dame. Of course, they don't merely watch — they take part with hollering and hooting and showing off their colors. This is all Greek to me but the Doc has explained that these games are a very significant part of his life, but I only nod and respect. I don't understand. In return he says he doesn't understand cricket, far too complicated.

Somewhere behind the riot of college colors I located a virgin bottle of Gentleman Jack and soon I was comfy in a chair at a table with Jack nestling next to a cold bottle of Newcastle Brown, and my fat book on Senator Joseph McCarthy & His World. This was living! So absorbing was this book that I was only dragged away by the sound and then the sight of a mini-dance taking place within the Home: Regina and Dawn were swing dancing together to my record "You Turn Me On" which had now taken the place of the Beach Boys.

We arrived at the Harris Ranch — a splendid oasis in the middle of the #5 freeway, that straight dull road that cuts across the level fields of the Central Valley and continues, so I'm told, into Canada — at the decent hour of 9 PM — in time for a full Harris beef supper in their restaurant. I was amazed to see even larger Homes in the parking lot, homes with sides that expand out into extra rooms, wings with bay windows. Inside one I could see a giant TV playing scenes of black men in baggy clothes, pointing their fingers accusingly with one hand while wielding radio mikes in the other. A hip-hop program, no doubt.

The great thing about the Harris Ranch is that our steaks, when part of a live cow, are kept north of us, in the real ranch, so that the stench of their biggies and wee-wee doesn't reach us. However, we get it full strength the next day when we pass the forlorn and braying beasts as they stand around on dirty hillocks contemplating their fate. I always feel a bit guilty for a few moments. But this time the moment was doused quickly by a glass of chardonnay from a small Berringer bottle and some more Joe McCarthy.

Too many Berringers en route to Sacramento had the effect of making me despondent and by the time we arrived at our Red Lion Inn, the festival venue, I was feeling the way I used to when returning to boarding school in the 1950s: I dreaded encountering any ragtimers I knew. And in the hotel lobby the very first person I saw was a wall-eyed cretin of a banjo player who has been bugging me since I first arrived in California in the summer of 1963. I smiled and moved on fast with a wave of my hand.

The Doc was fortunate in finding an excellent space in the vast concrete plains of the parking lot at the rear of the hotel. Our new temporary real estate was bordered by two freeways and right at our doorstep was a patch of elderly ferns, shrubs and boulders making the location look like a little garden. We pulled up plastic chairs and so the Home took on a sort of permanence. As the Doc and his wife live within a few feet of the 210 freeway in Arcadia they felt perfectly at home in this setting. The Doc says the steady freeway hum reminds him of the sound of the ocean when, in more affluent days, he owned a cliff top house in Laguna —- but that was in another world when he was with his first wife.

We were intending to catch a little of the pre-festival ragtime bash taking place in one of the hotel conference rooms. But as I approached the door I was accosted by the banjo player. He wanted to know whether I'd written "that great poem" that is track #2 on my CD, *Titanic*. No, you fool, that was written by Thomas Hardy. Is he coming to the festival, too? Does he play ragtime? I gave up and went to bed.

There's not a lot to say about the festival music: if you've heard one ragtime number you've heard the lot, and what you see is the back of the pianist and some of them have pretty wide bottoms I can tell you. In my case I face forward and get animated as much as possible, singing lively stuff and comic songs. Making show. I've learned from bitter experience that if I try to insert a sad ballad — the sentimental songs that really move me — people will come up afterwards and wonder whether I'm ailing, and do I have a virus, etc. At this festival I had the benefit of piano accompaniment by my longtime rag partner Prof Dick Zimmerman, or Zimmerperson as he's calling himself in these sensitive times.

This is the same gentleman I described in detail a couple of letters back: he's the Attila The Hun of pianists, the one who broke so many piano strings all across Europe in one Grand Tour. Dickie was looking a little the worse for wear: matching luggage under his eyes and a slight stoop. But then we're not as young as we used to be. I know that my face is rapidly resembling a crinkled old parchment that should rightly be stored in the Huntington Library archives together with the Dead Sea Scrolls and the Nuremberg Laws.

I crashed into a few mikes while on stage with Dickie and I forgot the words of many of my songs — we hadn't performed these old chestnuts for two years. But it didn't really matter: afterwards a couple came up to congratulate me on my stage presence: "We never care what you sing, it doesn't matter because we just love you as yourself in all your cantankerousness and curmudgeonly manners."

In between performances, at various venues in rooms around the Red Lion complex, I dropped by the Home to see how the Doc was doing. Through the window I saw him stretched out on the sofa with his arm over his eyes and with Rollo beneath in a similar position at his side. The pair resembled one of those stone tombs topped with a sculpture of knights in armor and their hunting dogs beside them that you can see in Westminster Abbey. It was a touching picture spoiled only by the raucous soundtrack — a satellite broadcast of some football game.

I noticed for the first time that the Home has a large sign painted on it saying, grandly and frighteningly: TIOGA." More peaceably there's a homespun sign on the rear bumper saying "FolloW Us To ThE RoSe BoWl."

On Saturday evening we took part in the Grand March at the Ragtime Ball in the Yosemite Room. Grand Marches are child's play — all you do is march around. I can't remember the name of the lady I escorted. Where was Regina? There were so many marchers that the line exited the Yosemite and went on a trek throughout the hotel, invading other venues where serious minded classic ragtimers were rudely interrupted by us troopers. At this distance we could no longer hear the band so we took to singing bawdy barrack room ballads and then the Teddy Bears' Picnic.

It was odd, we all said — like carting coals to Newcastle — that the festival should have imported at enormous expense a band from Hungary to play for our ragtime ball. Surely there are local bands that can play this music? Yes, of course there are — and my Bungalow Boys are just one such band. However the Hungarians proved lively and personable lads, even though they made it clear that their style of preference is progressive jazz of the 1950s — an even more dated music, if you ask me. But, as I said, they were nice fellows and had come a long way.

They really won my heart at the end of the ball, around midnight when the floor was almost empty. Rollo suddenly put in an appearance on the dance floor where, unused to polished parquet, he slid all over the shop, splayed out on all fours one second and rolling over on his back the next. Well, in the true spirit of jazz improvisation, the Hungarians promptly went into an improvised rag exactly matching Rollo's mad movements. This was a highpoint of the festival for me, bringing the event into the present world, showing the purpose of ragtime and jazz.

The other highlights were glimpses of the solitary. Around midnight I heard the wheeze of an accordion and, captivated, found it to be coming from a room inhabited by no audience, no one except an accordionist armed with a very ancient and lovely machine of pearl and chrome and a winking glitter. Hunched over his music the lone accordionist was working so hard to properly render a Scott Joplin rag. The frail old sound was haunting and touching. I talked to the fellow: he hadn't been hired by the festival at all, no, he'd simply blown in from New Jersey and was playing for whomsoever. He was playing for eternity. I congratulated him but he didn't seem to care. After a pause we went into a talk about how hard it is these days to get your bellows mended.

Early next day, passing an open door, I caught a xylophonist practicing in an empty room, getting ready for his lecture on the rags of George Hamilton Green. You all know who George was. The player was so pleased to meet a sympathetic soul. I told him that the instruments I prefer are all sort of illegitimate: xylophones, ukes, accordions, and pianos that are out of tune in the best sense. I never like instruments too much in tune because then they're too pure, too ethereal, too goody-goody, too unreal. I like fallible human sounds.

On the return journey in the Home we listened to the Doc's choice, via satellite radio: a string of old time radio shows: a dramatization of John Ford's *Stagecoach* with the director himself as narrator, sounding remarkably sober, and also a very early adventure starring the Lone Ranger. These kept the Doc happy at the wheel. After all he'd be back pulling teeth early the next day.

I realize that my life these days is spent whizzing from safe place to safe place — the little islands of decent culture (vintage music, balls, festivals) — and trying to avoid today's society. But in reading the paper and listening to NPR I can't avoid the iconography of the mediocre and over-exposed. I mean, how much more can be written and dredged up on the Beatles, Springsteen, Dylan, Sir Elton, Robert Crumb, and all the other wretched poseurs and fakes that seem to have their origin in that most horrid and iconoclastic decade, the 1960s? My heroes are from the years before the Fall, a short but glorious period from around 1890 till 1965. My heroes include Art Gillham, Whispering Jack Smith, Ruth Etting, Bill Haley, Elvis, Charlie Parker, Thelonious Monk, and Roy Orbison. I never tire of them, just as others, it seems, never tire of the Beatles et al.

So — one of our safe places where we can meet and see like-minded people is at the Grande Victorian Balls organized by The Social Daunce Irregulars Of Los Angeles. Who would believe that our city, that black spot of all that is trendy and transient and meretricious, is the nestling ground of all that was worth preserving of our past? We are the curators, the archivists — and we're not chair-bound academics in dusty archives. We are up and jigging about.

The latest ball was held in a big Masonic hall in Pasadena and it was filled to capacity. Regina and I have been attending for many years and know the regulars, some of whom come in from as far as San Diego and the High Desert. But due to recent coverage in *Westways* magazine there were lots of new faces at this ball. And not a few of them were unaware of social graces and etiquette. When people dress up in formal costume I find that their manners improve.

A lot of the newcomers were not dressed in period and thus were lacking in good manners — in other words they behaved as people do today. For example: there were men slouching bemused in jeans; there was one fellow dressed in a wine waiter outfit. I spotted a young man in sort of 1940s swing clothes, including a cockily-tilted fedora. You simply do not wear hats on the dance floor. I pointed him out to our tough major domo and he at once strode over, with his mace swinging, and ordered the wretched boy off the floor. All this in the middle of a Sicilian Circle. I felt a little bad about being a snitch but standards must be enforced in our little world within a world.

Then there were couples waltzing in the wrong direction around the floor thus causing collisions. Jewelry flew, corsages were squashed. During the Virginia Reel a man stopped the proceedings because he insisted on taking a call on his cell phone (which jangled an Elton John tune snippet). He was reprimanded in no uncertain terms by one of the regulars, costumed as Mr. Pickwick. I, incidentally, was wearing the uniform of a Royal Marines full Colonel. I always check up with my brother-in-law, the General, about whether or not I should be impersonating a British officer. "Where are you wearing the uniform this time?" asked the General. When he learned it was at an America event he tartly replied: "I've told you before—and I'll tell you again: it doesn't bloody matter!"

But, standing back and viewing the dance from above in the gallery I was impressed and touched by this perfect picture of Americana at work: lines of couples of all hues and races — many were Asian — trying to be a part of an old culture, one that believed in decorum and decency, good manners and kindness — and rules of conduct. There they all were chasing down the line to the strains of "Dixie."

Next day I revisited the battleground. Every so often I have to return to our old house in Altadena and it's then I realize what a squalid wild westy town it is. It may be fine for bohemians but at my age I'll take middle class boring peace. I lingered for a few seconds in the road, too close to the beastly next-door neighbours. Just a few seconds — but Kaleem happened at that moment to be wandering around her front lawn. Upon seeing me she turned round, bent down and stuck out her fat rump at me. I turned the other cheek.

And returned to the pleasantness of Monrovia. Regina and I, accompanied by two Social Daunce Irregulars left over from the night before, strolled to a Mediterranean café round the corner on Foothill, the old Route 66. Following some excellent hummus and olives and kebabs we repaired to the historic Aztec Hotel in readiness for their Sunday night singsong concerts.

The Aztec is a landmark, pictured in every book about Route 66. It opened in the 1920s and always had a dance floor and nightclub. In the 1930s stars like Clark Gable would motor out for an evening's fun. By the 1950s the fun was limited to sex — the Aztec had become a brothel. And the hotel was now notorious for violent crime. The other day I was telling a friend about the place and he commented: "Yes ... when I was in jail I shared a cell with a guy who'd murdered his wife there in room 102."

But today the Aztec is another safe haven. Restored to its former glory it now has blues and rock bands pumping out in the main Brass Elephant bar, making enough money to allow us to enjoy quieter stuff in the nearby Mayan room. We sat at tables around a dance floor, beneath a mural of "Kinich Ahau—The Sun God." There was a goodly crowd the night we were there. I thought that these folk were here to enjoy listening to good old songs — as audience. But I was wrong: every table held singers, waiting to be called up by keyboard king Jim. They had signed up on a list at Jim's side, some of them as early as 5pm. It was now 7.30. Jim commanded a mighty console of keyboards; at his disposal were effects such as a full string section, a steel guitar and even a whistler.

I've always enjoyed watching non-pros perform — because what they sing reflects their dreams and desires. They're not there for commercial considerations. We heard many a Sinatra follower. The singer not the songwriter is celebrated here. A little squiff of an old man crooned as he clutched the radio mike about "You and the night fill me with desire" and you knew that desire was all he had left. A rail-thin woman from England sang "Hold me, thrill me" and another song about being embraced. She looked china-doll fragile to me. Rather undiplomatically a squat old chap took advantage of the radio mike to work the room, selecting Regina as his victim for "My Funny Valentine": "Is your figure less than Greek? Is your mouth a little weak?" The idea! I bristled.

Later it was, at last, Regina's turn and she sang like an angel: "You'll Never Know" and "Under The Bamboo Tree." She ought to come back again, said Jim from his keyboard kingdom. We took our leave as a woman accompanied by an oxygen tank was starting to sing, "Don't Get Around Much Anymore." Reality had entered even the Mayan Room.

    Happy Holidays. I will be leaving for London on December 27 — that is, if the IRS and the federal tax court will allow my "trial" to be postponed till February. They are having difficulty understanding what it is I do exactly and thus accepting my expenses for such items as Bungalow Boy costs and stagewear. I claim to be an author, composer, performer — a regular renaissance man — but they have never heard of me in today's world of culture. I'm not Sir Elton, as one of their agents so succinctly put it. "But you'd like to be, wouldn't you?"

Intermission and Photo Gallery

Here I am on my father's back, looking at my sister Suzanne (second row from the top, fourth from the left) at a Christmas party at the RAF mess in Scarborough, England, in World War Two, 1942.

Me and my younger brother Robin sitting at the feet of our parents at the seaside in Torquay, Devon, England, one glorious summer, circa 1950.

At Bryanston, a boarding school in Dorset, with my first guitar, bought for me by my father in London's Tin Pan Alley after tense negotiations with a tough salesman who, understandably, was reluctant to accept my old accordion as part payment. The Skiffle craze was at its height and I wanted in on it. Dressed in the school uniform as well as a cowboy plaid shirt, I am strumming a G chord left-handedly. I am 15 and the year is 1957.

Ian Whitcomb performing at Bryanston School, Dorset, with his first electrified guitar + school rock 'n' roll band — 1958

Finally—an electrified guitar! Performing "High Class Baby," a Cliff Richard hit, with my rock 'n'roll group—Bryanston's first—for admiring schoolmates and intrigued masters in the Big Schoolroom, summer 1958. My boarding school swansong. Gaining Weight.

A third year undergraduate in Modern History & Political Thought at Trinity College Dublin, Ireland, 1964. Posing with attitude in Front Square, fresh from a summer in America playing a coffee house; showing off my All-American clothes; thrilled to have just been signed to Jerden Records, Seattle.

A Dublin beat club, late 1964: rocking and sweating, in another macho American shirt, as lead singer of Bluesville MFG, Ireland's first real rock group, just months before we scored Ireland's first American hit with "This Sporting Life" on Tower Records, a Capitol subsidiary.

An elfin gamin, I sit still briefly for a record label publicity photo session inside the Capitol Tower as "You Turn Me On," with Bluesville, rushes up the pop charts and into the Top Ten in the summer of 1965.

Label promo man George Sherlock persuades this teen idol to dress natty as a typical English gent. So it's herringbone suit and deerstalker hat—the antithesis of the Rolling Stones and a fatal career move in late 1965 as teen rebellion rumbles and hippies are on the horizon.

My first songbook, published by the venerable Tin Pan Alley publisher Edward B. Marks. All my own work, plus Dublin gig pix and a brief bio. In the text I predict that American Ragtime coupled with British Music Hall is "the sound of the future." My ambition is "the destruction of nationality and the achievement of world citizenship." Fat chance on either.

Backstage at a 1965 summer spectacular with the Rolling Stones in a Seattle arena. Standing next to me is my manager/publisher/producer Jerry Dennon, the local record czar who originally signed me to Jerden Records.

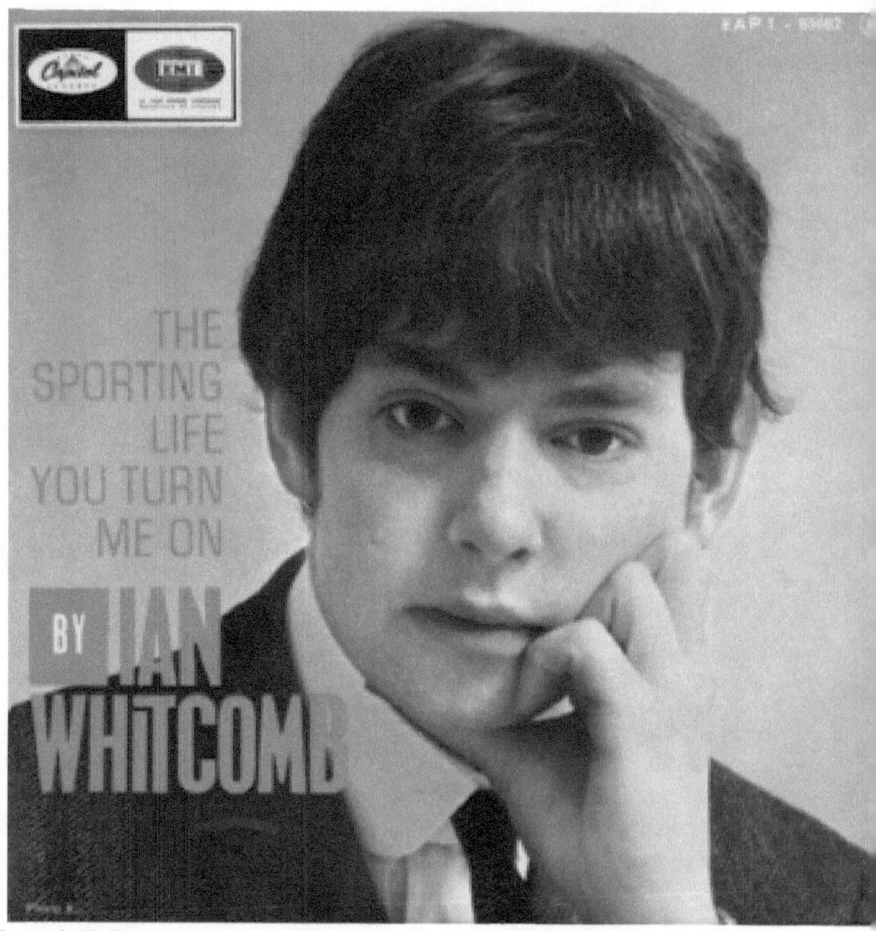

A French E.P. I was big in France for a while and, sharing a bill with the Rolling Stones, I played the famed Olympia Music Hall in Paris, where Piaf had recently performed.

Playing cowboy in the San Fernando Valley in 1968 with actor Christian Roberts, a close friend from England. The horses were owned by veteran animal trainer Ralph McCutcheon. Christian was preparing for a western movie; I was fading as a teen idol.

A newspaper photo, circa 1980, with me posing on the back patio as the proud owner of my very first house, a 1947 one in Altadena, a rather wild town near Pasadena. The house only became a home when Regina entered my life a few years later.

In the living room, by the player piano, harnessed in my musette accordion. Since buying it in 1982 the eerie sound has flooded almost all my recordings.

Writing my daily journal—I have kept one since 1972 and it's the source of these Lotusland Letters—during a break at a Jazz festival near L.A. international airport in 1988.

Leading my 1920s dance band at a public function in a shopping mall in Pasadena in the early 1990s

With wife Regina at a Victorian Grand Ball during Vintage Dance Week in Cincinnati, Ohio in the early 1990s.

In the back patio, demonstrating my favorite ukulele, Ukie—a Martin bought new in 1968—prior to a ukulele festival at the City Of Industry in the late 1990s

The Altadena house, over the years made into a perfect home by Regina, but now unhappily up for sale in these realtor-produced pictures. We had been forced into exile in nearby Monrovia due to a neighbour war that began in 2002 and climaxed in 2004.

2007 and the exiled Whitcombs are back home again! Regina at peace with Rollo during a photo session at the Pasadena Museum of History where I was artist-in-residence and Regina was an advisor for an exhibition on the history of women's handbags.

Rollo and his master en route to the Coffee Gallery, a favorite Altadena resting place and entertainment center, 2008.

Smartly dressed in a 1940s vintage suit with trademark keyboard scarf. But the ukulele isn't Ukie. Who is it?

2006

JANUARY

I'm writing the Letter several days before Christmas and New Year because when you read this I'll be in England. And I hope that I'll be doing all the things I plan to do — dinners with old friends from Trinity College days; staying at my sister's house in Royal Berkshire and my brother's in Wimbledon; being interviewed at BBC Broadcasting House for a flurry of local radio stations; giving a concert on the Isle Of Wight for a DVD production; attending a lunch thrown by *The Oldie* magazine at Simpson's-In-The-Strand; returning on the 13th of January. But, will all of this come to pass? If I've learned one thing in life it's that nothing is as you expect it to be. You're at the mercy of chance and luck. At any moment calamity may occur. Or good fortune from a phone call. Life, like art and music, is a complete and utter mystery to me.

On top of all this I really have no idea what's worth recording and what's mere trivia. The judges, the archivists and social historians maybe haven't yet been born. But here are some of the incidents I felt were worth writing up in my journal lately.

At our local Starbuck's, a short walk down the street — and how Rollo loves the attention when we get there, and how I've enjoyed the ambience lately since they've abandoned Bob Dylan for more seasonal stuff such as Maurice Chevalier and Gene Autry — I offered the young lady server a dime so that she wouldn't have to fish out all the change for my $2.10 regular misto with foam. "That's AWESOME," she said. Such a misuse of that poor word I have never encountered before.

At Russell's, a retro coffee shop where I have sausage and eggs (with large dollops of Dijon mustard) every Monday at 10am, I saw the manager, a Filipino, reprimand a Mexican waiter for speaking in Spanish when placing an order with the cooks. "Only English here!" he ordered quite sharply. And he repeated it to the puzzled waiter. I was relieved because recently I had trouble getting a glass of water from a bus boy there. He kept bringing me more coffee or just smiling and leaving me.

At a Christmas party last night in a historic house in Altadena, with a log fire burning merrily and a cauldron of mulled wine simmering, I was introduced by our host to a woman with an English accent. "You're English!" I said, in order to make conversation. "I am certainly not!" she said, but in a very upper crust English accent. "I'm African!" She looked milk white to me. "But....." "I grew up in Kenya." It turns out her father was a farmer there in the 1950s. "Did you enjoy your time there?" "Not particularly — you see, my father was murdered by the Mau Mau." At that moment I was hailed by an American and I knew I was on safer ground.

My saviour greeted me: "You're the one who was driven from his home by Iranians!" He went on to say that he and his wife have just inherited a large old house in San Gabriel, a township near our Monrovia. What are his neighbours like? Peaceable? "You betcha. They come from a very old culture, you see." His neighbours are all Chinese with more arriving every day. San Gabriel, like nearby Alhambra and the rest of this valley, is rapidly becoming orientalized. "But I'll tell you," said the man, "It's better than where we used to live in Pasadena — the shooting went on all night — black gang bangers killing Latino gang bangers and vice versa."

Yes, it's peaceful and quiet but there won't be much cultural interchange. However, the Asian restaurants are great, if you like duck. My new party friend told me he'd been over to introduce himself to his neighbours. Not one could speak a word of English, but there was much bowing and smiling. My party friend's house is historic, a Craftsman from the turn of the century. His Chinese neighbours have old houses too, but they are hard at work tearing them down and putting up shining McMansions to show how well they're doing in their new land.

At the annual Workman & Temple Family Homestead, held in the City of Industry — near this valley I've been talking about — me and the Bungalow Boys (not forgetting Regina), were recently entertaining from the stage for the annual Christmas celebration. A couple got up to dance on the lawn in front of us: "How is it?" I asked. "Tough," said the man. He was wearing a really snazzy 1950s sports jacket, the kind that is hard to find these days. I have a couple but I really envied his, with its speckles and its little white crosses sprinkled all over.

"I like your jacket," I remarked into the mike at the end of our foxtrot. And bless my soul if he didn't take it off, come up to the stage and hand it up to me. Nobody has ever done this for me before in my life. I've heard the expression "I'll give you the shirt off my back" but I've never seen the cliché in operation. He wouldn't take any money for it; he wouldn't take anything — not even my CDs and DVDs.

The label reads, "Designed by Gregory's of Los Angeles for Vincent Taylor." There's even a date deeper inside the jacket: 12/11/57 — and it was December 11 that very day. 1957 — the year that Pat Boone hit with "Love Letters In The Sand" and I had my first kiss to the record as it played in a flat bottom boat — a punt — on a lake in Suffolk, England. The girl with me was Debbie Briggs — no kiss since has given me that same singular sensation.

The point is: what is relevant, meaningful, fascinating, even interesting, about any of the above? Will future historians be intoxicated by my period details? Will they get a better sense of 2005 from these revelations? Or is Bush's Iraq more memorable?

And now — a memoir. This is sparked by a recent book signing that Regina and I attended at the Gene Autry Museum nearby. *Hollywood Hoofbeats—Trails Blazed Across The Silver Screen*, a beautifully produced coffee table-size book about horses in movies, particularly westerns. The author, Petrine Day Mitchum (Robert Mitchum's daughter), was interested to hear that I had known Ralph McCutcheon, a noted trainer of horses for cowboy pictures. There are lots of references to old Ralph in her books: how he'd been a forest ranger from Colorado before buying his ranch in Panorama City in the San Fernando Valley in the early 1950s. How he was known for voice commands and hand signals rather than whips and pistol shots. How he trained a black horse that became *Black Beauty* in the 1946 version and *Fury* in the TV series, as well as playing Elizabeth Taylor's abused horse in *Giant*.

Ralph's big white King Cotton was the real star of the Cantinflas' vehicle *Pepe*, when he swam lengths in a pool, went up and down stairs, and did a convincing limp. The horse was awarded a PATSY by the American Humane Association.

Before the likes of McCutcheon and a new breed of horse providers there were many unnecessary deaths of horses during filming. There were directors who didn't give a damn about cruelty to animals so long as they got their shot. B. Reeves "Breezy" Eason, for example, was notorious for his inhumane treatment of animal actors. On *The Charge Of The Light Brigade* in 1936 more than 25 horses were killed due to the use of the Running W trip wires and other devices. Errol Flynn, the star of the movie, was furious and went public. But the killing continued: there's an infamous shot of stuntman Cliff Lyons, during the making of *Jesse*

James (1939), steering a wagon, led by two horses, in a spectacular dive off a 75-foot cliff into churning white water. Lyons got over $2000 for the stunt knowing full well that both horses would be killed.

Later, when the Humane Association really got into the act, under the authority of the Hays Office, the stunts were done by Falling Horses, the kind that McCutcheon trained. However, with the abolition of the Hays Office and the consequent flood of permissiveness in the 60s and 70s, directors went back to their old ways with a vengeance: particularly loathesome were Sam Peckinpah (*The Wild Bunch*) and Michael Cimino (*Heaven's Gate*). These days bloodthirstiness involving animals can be avoided by the use of computer effects.

And now to my memoir of good times with Ralph McCutcheon.

In the summer of 1968 I was over in Hollywood on one of my fading rock star trips, armed with a work permit. I'd been making these trips since my banner hit year of 1965, but the hits were long past and I was struggling to keep in the business. This time I was in the company of my best friend Christian Roberts, whom I'd known since he'd been head boy of my brother's boarding school in 1960. Christian loved westerns as much as me and he liked to sing old songs with me in a sort of close harmony. His father was a rich man and had a large estate in Surrey where there were stables and lots of good riding. Chris and I would take a couple of horses out and play cowboy games all day over the Surrey countryside near the busy motorway, pretending we were in the wild west. I remember crawling through the wet grass near the motorway one afternoon, dressed as a redskin when a motorcyclist stopped to address me: "Aren't you a little old to be playing cowboys and Indians?"

As D. H. Lawrence once said, fed up with the England of puritanical petty-mindedness, of total lack of romantic feeling and of childlike exaggeration: "Curse the blasted, jelly-boned swines, the slimy, the belly-wriggling invertebrates, the miserable sodding rotters, the flaming sods, the sniveling, dribbling, dithering palsied pulse-less lot that make up England today.... God, how I hate them! God curse them, funkers. God blast them, wishwash. Exterminate them, slime."

I couldn't match Lawrence. All I could do was to blush in my loincloth and warpaint. Nevertheless I continued to play out horse dramas with Chris — sometimes we were Civil War officers on opposing sides, sometimes we were the Mystery Riders (from the Mascot Pictures serial *Riding With Kit Carson*). Our fist fights and wrestling matches on the heath were quite realistic. We even made an 8mm film called *West Of Staines* with a very involved plot and lots of tracking shots. But this was England and it was raining and our noses were always running.

Here in the Hollywood of the late 60s with everyone beautiful and telling us we were beautiful too, and young girls with long flowing hair and beatific smiles coming to the Canyon and a general message floating in the scented air that life was now offering anything in the realm of the possible, even that the impossible was possible, and that we were in heaven — here bliss it was to be young.

Chris, in fact, was here to meet up with Columbia Pictures executives and get some western riding training. My best friend, since being Head Boy, had graduated from the Royal Academy Of Dramatic Art and immediately was talent-spotted and plunged into movies.

James Clavell, writer and now film director, had cast him as the bad boy, Denham, in *To Sir, With Love,* where he has a boxing match with Sidney Poitier and comes clean in the end so that Lulu can sing her hit song. The movie was a worldwide hit and so my friend became a hot stud for a while, eclipsing me. I was a bit jealous, I'll admit. And now he had landed a big co-starring role in a western called *The Desperados,* playing an outlaw alongside Jack Palance and Neville Brand. God, I was now green with envy! More than anything in the world I'd like to have been a cowboy in westerns. Nothing could be further removed from the dreariness and soddenness of English life than the West.

And Chris had been invited to travel through the looking glass, down the rabbit hole, through the wardrobe, and into the secret garden, the magic kingdom!

Despite my inner turmoil Chris and I remained friends. We traveled across from Heathrow together and on arrival at LAX were greeted by my latest manager, a beaming fellow with crossover hairstyle and bursting memories of his short-lived partnership with Brian Epstein. He had driven to the airport in a long black Cadillac which he announced he'd rented for me, as befitted my status as a teen idol, still potent.

Thanks to Chris's connection with James Clavell — he was now involved with his daughter — we had a nice residence all ready for us: a cottage hideaway up in Laurel Canyon where the beautiful people were thriving, near Frank Zappa's house and the Nitty Gritty Dirt Band. Somewhere nearby was Steve Martin, a neophyte banjo picker with a line in comedy, so they said.

The road was called Lookout Mountain Drive and the cottage had all the modern conveniences. The next day, at breakfast, Chris and I met up with my manager in a coffee shop to discuss my future — not very promising: my hit days were over, I was no heavy metaller, significant singer-songwriter, nor drug proselytizer. Downcast, I then accompanied Chris to Columbia Pictures in Gower Gulch, where he was treated famously. A female production assistant ruined my day by whispering to me: "Aren't you thrilled — doesn't it make you proud — to be associated with such a good-looking guy?"

A Columbia executive called Ralph McCutcheon at his ranch to arrange for Chris to take lessons in western riding — oh, and could his buddy tag along, too?

We arrived in dusty flat Panorama City that afternoon in my Cadillac. The ranch was set amid 1940s one-story homes complete with nice white picket fences. An all-white old-fashioned Anglo-Saxon neighbourhood full of gals and guys and "howdy" in the morning. Today Panorama City is concreted and mini-malled and lived in almost exclusively by Latino and other ethnic groups, but that's the way the cards are falling all over the western world.

Ralph, a grizzled old boy in his 70s wearing a Stetson and a metal bolo tie, greeted us and showed us around his spread with its barns and rows of wagons and stagecoaches and anything necessary for a western. But they weren't making any westerns in his neck of the woods anymore, so Ralph was happy to see us as he had lots of time on his hands. He lived in a long and low and pretty house covered in vines and flowers — that looked like it was an old set from a Hopalong movie, the place where the schoolmistress lives.

And indeed inside we met Ralph's wife Mary Kornman who, I later learned, had been in the early Our Gang silent shorts and had gone on to play sweethearts in B westerns with John Wayne and co. Now Ralph spent most of his day in the tack room yarning. He'd worked with John Ford and Breezy Eason, the horse killer, and he respected them all. He was friendly with Ken Maynard, the western star veteran who now lived and cursed and drank too hard in a trailer in the nastier part of the Valley. He would visit and comfort poor old Ken. Ralph was a tough old varmint, but when he took his hat off and revealed his bald and gleaming head, and when he loosened his dentures and broke out the bottle, he became a kindly grandpa.

He was especially kind, from day one, to us dude westerners from England. He really didn't have to give us any lessons because his trained movie horses did all the work. He introduced us to the famous Fury, now into his twenties. Ralph called him Beaut to his face; he had taught the horse a dozen words so that, from beside the camera on location shoots, he could explain the stunts the script was calling on the animal actor to perform. Beaut responded also to the tone of Ralph's voice. Clearly they loved each other as master and servant. And it's Beaut who remains immortal on the screen, while Ralph has to rely on the likes of me and other writers.

Beaut was out to pasture, enjoying retirement. Ralph led us over to Page, a calm and collected brown horse, a favorite of Charlton Heston and Gregory Peck. After I'd ridden Page I could understand why. You simply drove Page as you would a car: a gentle tap and he was off, a pull left and he went left, etc. You could ride him hell for leather up to the barbed wire fence and he'd stop immediately within an inch of the wire. And he did it all without a protest, without a snort, without recriminations. He was casual like John Wayne. He even loped like John Wayne.

Ralph had a wonderful dog, too, called Rote whom he'd taught to drive the station wagon. At a soft command from Ralph this dog could turn into a fearsome creature, all snarls and bared fangs. We dudes backed away. Ralph was a man not to be trifled with, but he did everything with ease and a kind authority, like so many Americans of his background and era. He was a real Colorado Ranger; he'd served in World War one. He was a man of few words, but well-chosen and to be marked and respected.

So Chris and I started visiting the McCutcheon spread regularly and soon we were accepted as ranch boys. On certain days he'd order a stable hand to load up one of his movie trucks with horses and tackle and ornate western silver saddles and then off we'd go to a stretch of flat country just off the freeway in the region of the Hansen Dam. There we could canter and gallop and play cowboys. The kid ranch hand preferred to hang out at a nearby coffee shop where he could ogle the local female talent, pronouncing with a whoop when he saw a curvy one: "Ahmm in loooove!" It was all very macho American.

One evening Chris and I went whole hog and took a couple of local gals, picked for us by the ranch boy, to the Drive-In. I can't remember what the movie was because I was making progress in the back seat until she told me to stop because her glasses were getting all steamed up. Chris and his gal watched the movie mostly. I felt I'd scored a major victory over my best friend.

After too short a time Chris had to leave in order to start his movie. A western made in Spain, I ask you! A goddamn runaway production. What a crime they didn't shoot in Lone Pine, not so far away, where Hoppy and Gene and Roy had ridden! Ralph could have supplied the animals and wagons. Anyway, I said farewell to my pal as he flew off to play cowboys and get paid for it.

Meanwhile I returned to pursuing ragtime songs and wondering what would become of me. At the end of that fateful year, 1968 — assassinations and war and general mayhem — I returned to the bosom of my family on Putney Heath, living with my mother in the flat where I'd grown up. When I tried to return to Hollywood the following year I was denied a work permit by the INS. I panicked. Stolen from me was that sunny glorious promised land, the boy's town of Southern California. Now I would have to face the cold and wet and matter-of-factness of my homeland.

But, as sometimes happens when I have my back to the wall, I found something profitable to do: I wrote a proposal for a book about the history of pop music from ragtime to rock and I was signed by Penguin Books' top editor, Oliver Caldecott, to a contract and a nice advance. The result, after three hard years, was *After The Ball*.

And during the research for the book I found myself once more, courtesy of the INS, out west and near Ralph McCutcheon's spread. He welcomed me and we became firm friends. He let me ride Page whenever I wished. We chatted lots in the tack room and took a little taste, a sip or so.

I had started contributing articles to the *Los Angeles Times* by this time. In fact the first one had appeared in 1968, just before I'd left for London. Written in a fit of pique by a washed-up and bitter ex-teen idol, my article, splashed on the front page of the entertainment section, attacked what I saw as the growing pretentiousness of pop music, all the pseudo poetics of, say, Procol Harum's "Homburg."

Now this attack was personal and uncalled for since the record had been produced by Denny Cordell, a fellow schoolmate of Christian's and my brother Robin — and also a close friend of mine. I'd introduced Denny to the Blues when he was still a naughty schoolboy. In return Denny had gone on to produce early recordings of mine, backing me with such musicians as Jimmy Page, John Paul Jones, and Mitch Mitchell — all this before their supergroup days. He'd got me jobs with Brian Epstein, even arranged a late evening interview with Epstein. So why had I turned on my friend? Search me — I've done this all my life.

The local L.A. media turned on me roundly and rightly. I was condemned on the air by deejays, the underground FM ones, a new and fearsome breed, being particularly vitriolic. I was rapidly becoming a ragtime reactionary.

But the *Times* liked my feisty confrontational approach and proposed more of such stuff. So on this new trip I wangled an LA Times pass to the Charles Manson trial, at that moment taking place downtown. I can still see that tiny courtroom and the judge saying that if Mr. Manson was willing to behave himself today he could be let in to the courtroom. But that if Mr. Manson chose to create the spectacle of disruption he'd achieved yesterday then he'd have to be returned to his cell. Call him in!

I'll never forget Manson as he shuffled in, handcuffed and in chains. He stopped and slowly panned our faces, giving us the benefit of his Evil Eye. He seemed to be looking hardest at me as if to say, "I'll remember you. And I do remember you — from the past!" Then I too remembered: in 1964 I'd been a guest on McNeill Island, a state penitentiary, up in Seattle during the time I'd been appearing at a coffee house there and had been befriended by the McNeill Island prison chaplain. Anytime you want to come visit and give a talk about England — feel free, he'd said cheerily.

I love to visit prisons and feel I'm not the guilty one so I snapped up his offer. I gave my talk and afterwards asked for questions. And it was then that the fellow who was now Charles Manson, monster murderer, had got up and asked me what the drug trade was like in Britain and was it worth getting involved in. Guards quickly removed him and I took a question about Winston Churchill.

Back to the courtroom: Manson eventually switched off his evil eye and turned his attention to the judge. He started berating him about society and its evils and about the stars and galaxies and the threat of the industrial military complex. The judge warned him three times before removal became necessary.

Thus I was at liberty and it wasn't nearly lunchtime. Outside the courthouse, holding signs protesting their leader's innocence, were female members of the Family. They too fixed me with angry glares. Then I remembered, from my reading about the case, that B Westerns had played a part. Yes, the Spahn Ranch! That was where the Family had holed up and planned dirty deeds. Remnants of them were reportedly still there. I wonder...

I rang Ralph and asked whether he knew Spahn. Yep, that old galoot. Sure. Would Ralph like to ride there with me and say hello to his old pal? Sure. So Ralph and I climbed up into the mountains behind Chatsworth, with the station wagon chugging and Rote, the dog, crying with anticipation of possible protection of his master from owlhoots or varmints, on our way to the Spahn movie ranch, location of a score of Z-grade westerns. The last ones had starred Lash La Rue and were, so I'd been told, soft-core porn flix. Ralph said he wouldn't know about that, Spahn being a good old boy.

On the ranch at the top of the hill in the blazing October sun we were greeted by poor old ailing Spahn. His current home was a trailer. A few feet away from him swayed and shimmered a motley group of hippies, smoking and viewing us with sullen suspiciousness. The Family. But Ralph and Spahn ignored this nouveau trash and set to yarning about the old days, about Charles Starrett, and Smiley Burnette, and gals they'd known and liquor they'd sampled. And all the while the Family glared. What a strange collision of the old B West with the horrid new world of drugs, sex, murder, and rock & roll. No wonder I've been diving into the past ever since.

A little later Ralph and Mary moved to Burbank. On my trips to Hollywood I'd always call up Ralph and arrange to see him. He still had a few horses, still had Page. But in late 1973, when I was working for KCET, a local PBS station, I learned that Mary had died of cancer in June. Ralph wanted to see me, though. We drove out to the William S. Hart ranch and museum. Of course, Ralph had known old Hart. I asked Ralph if I could hire Page for a little western romp in Griffith Park that KCET were going to let me star in. Yep. And he'd toss in a couple of wranglers too, one of whom was a past master at throwing dust just before the camera rolled. These men would be hot from a John Wayne movie. I had lugged across with me from England an early videotape camera and reel-to-reel recorder and so I managed to get that shoot on tape — the dust, the hoofbeats, and me in full cowboy garb riding Page, Wonder horse of the West. My dream had at last come true. I was in a western!

Two years later, Ralph, who had been always tied to Mary in deep love, died. They are buried together back in his hometown of Greeley, Colorado. I'm so glad that his achievements are now safe within that big book, *Hollywood Hoofbeats*. And that my memories of a great animal trainer are in this Letter.

FEBRUARY

In the last Letter, written just before I left for England, I wondered whether all the things I intended to do, the friends and family I wanted to be with, would come to pass. Or that fate would step in the way and spoil my expectations.

But everything turned out fine. Before I go into details let me tell you that just after returning I had a dream in which I was but moments away from being executed in the electric chair. I had no idea what crime I'd committed but I did know that very shortly my time would be up. And that instead of going to heaven I would be simply obliterated. Sent into oblivion. Pffft! Just like that.

The result is that I am now trying to appreciate the little things in life — like the shrub outside the front window shaking in the wind, like the clean, almost 3D, mountains on the horizon. It's very clear at present in Monrovia due to the Santa Anas rushing through the canyons. Last night we came home to a blacked out avenue and for the short duration I enjoyed seeing stars above the blackness and quiet, and reading in bed by candlelight. I felt closer to nature. And then on came the lights and I was back in the slough of civilization and probably happy for that.

Funnily enough, I was at the time reading *Revolutionary Road* by Richard Yates, a 1961 novel of despair set in a bedroom community suburb of western Connecticut. The stifle of a too comfortable existence, of life without wildness, rang a chord within me. Here are the Wheelers, husband and wife, discussing their plan to escape to Europe and a new and exciting life: Frank sits on the coffee table — itself an "original and wonderful thing to do" — and says: "It's like coming out of a Cellophane bag. It's like having been encased in some kind of Cellophane for years without knowing it, and suddenly breaking out. It's a little like the way I felt going up the line the first time, in the war.... I just felt this terrific sense of life. I felt full of blood. Everything looked realer than real; the snow in the fields, the road, the trees, the terrific blue sky all marked up with vapor trails—everything..... I remember we went through this shelled-out town, all broken walls and rubble, and I thought it was beautiful.. I kept thinking: this is really true. This is the truth."

Just earlier the Wheelers had been grousing about those "loathesome little signs people put up in their front yards."

"The 'The' signs, you mean," says his wife, April. "With the people's name in the plural? Like 'The Donaldsons' ?"

"Right! Never 'Donaldson' or 'John J. Donaldson'...You picture the whole cozy little bunch sitting around snug as bunnies in their pajamas toasting marshmallows...My God, when you think how close we came to settling into that kind of an existence."

Yet even today you can see those loathesome little signs, especially in Palm Springs, that most unnatural of places, and what is worse is that now there is a possessive in the sign: "The Donaldson's." Not just a family staked out in what was once wild country, but a family who tell you they own this desert, that it's not God's but "The Donaldson's." After I'd read out the offending passage about signs to Regina she told me that while clearing out her late and dear father's immobile mobile home in Palm Springs she'd found, hidden by the growth of a desert shrub, a sign: "The Enzer's." And I'm not sure that her father was even married when the sign went up.

So I was ready for the adventure of England.

My brother Robin met me at Heathrow. Less than an hour in the parking lot cost seven pounds. I paid at the machine but my ticket wouldn't open the gate. Cars were piling up behind us. "Welcome to Britain," said Robin. The weather was gloomy too. It stayed that way all through the trip. Of course, I'd come over partly to get away from non-stop mindless sun so I should have been happy. And so I was for a few days but after two weeks it began to lose its charm. Robin said this weather brings him down. Yes, but would he like my relentless sun? "Every day, every day," he said. Around Christmas time each year, he continued, the obituary pages of the newspapers are crammed with more people than ever, popping off at relatively early ages, too, like in their 50s and early 60s. The weather.

Back at Robin's house in Wimbledon, "The Molehouse," he cooked the traditional macaroni cheese topped with bacon and soused in Worcestershire sauce, a specialty of our mother's and always served to me on my first night back in the old country. We ate on our laps as we watched a Channel Four extravaganza called "100 Best War Films ".

Following that was a dramatization of the Prince Charles and Camilla affair, including shots of His Highness's bottom thrusting into what would become his second wife. Together the two lovers, aided by Lord Mountbatten, arranged to set up Diana as a Queen of Convenience. Charles was shown to be quite a cocksman: aside from Camilla he bonked various other ladies, mostly encountered in disco clubs. One told His Highness that her friends called her "Yum Yum." He replied: "You're very well put together, Yum Yum." And there followed yet another sex bout. Of course, as the producers stated, the show was pure fiction. "Welcome to Britain," again said Robin.

Following that—my jet lag was causing me to stay rigidly awake—I watched a documentary on pornography. At the far end of the San Fernando Valley, pointed out the British commentator, sits an extreme porno company featuring very, very old women having sex with hunchbacks and cripples and that sort of thing. A few samples were offered. A thriving market, said the Thames Valley-flat voice of the commentator. Meanwhile, Robin worked at his computer on his next project, a book on people who live in odd houses.

Next morning early, I put on my London Fog raincoat and California fedora, and was ready for the cold slog to the Indian-run newsagent called Mike's a few streets away. I was pretending to be British. At the shop I bought the *Daily Mail,* a lively and intelligent tabloid. This I read back at Robin's as I ate taramasalata (fish roe) spread on Ryvita, a rare delicacy in America, but obtainable at every Indian-run corner mini-market in Britain.

An item in the paper caught my eye: in the North of England a mother of two had been shot dead in her home by a neighbour. For years they had been feuding over, respectively, her cats and his pigeons. She claimed he'd poisoned several of her cats with anti-freeze, and in retaliation she'd burned down his pigeon shed. Said a neighbour: "The row had been going on for quite a while although there had never been any big incidents, just shouting. Sue was always so pleasant and the man with the pigeons seemed to be just a typical family man." I cut out the story for Regina. It justifies our decision to move from the threatening Altadena neighbours to the peaceful, if culturally arid, land of Monrovia.

Next I entrained on the Tube for Earl's Court and the flat of one of the three best friends I've got left in London. On the ride I didn't hear one word of English. But everyone was very pleasant, except when addressing their omnipresent cell phones, like actors trying to project to the very back of the theatre.

Chas lives in one room on the third floor of a corner building that overlooks a busy crossroads in Earl's Court. The room is decorated by bookshelves. The overflow books take up most of his couch. He sleeps above the bookshelves and he reaches the bed by a series of imbedded rungs. Lately he has been ill with a mysterious virus. A bevy of ladies come up, separately, to provide him with meals. Often there is smoked salmon and champagne and the celebration can last into the night and beyond. Today he was coughing but this didn't stop him smoking. The room reeked deliciously of tobacco, reminding me of my old prep school master's study back in the early 1950s: the tin shed with the naval photos from World War One, the bound copies of *Jane's Fighting Ships*, which TDM edited, and the wooden cabinet full of Sophie Tucker 78s and the like, the records TDM allowed me to play, and how safe I was because I was pudgy and not the blonde Nordic type boy he favored for reasons other than musical.

One of Chas' ladies called twice during the first few minutes of my being there. Her voice came through on his answerphone speaker: *Darrleeng!* Chas is a lucky man: not only does he have his bevy of ladies, from many nationalities, but he also has a beautiful wife of many years as well as three gorgeous daughters.

On the walk to a late lunch Chas insisted on stopping off at a tobacconist. To my astonishment he bought not a mere packet of cigarettes but an entire carton, at almost fifty pounds sterling. He's the only person I know who, rather than giving up smoking as middle age and ill health take their toll, actually began smoking in his forties, after never having shown the slightest interest in cigarettes as a young man at Trinity College Dublin when we were all puffing and sucking. He's a real original.

We celebrated at a nearby and empty Italian restaurant — spaghetti Bolognese and an entire bottle of red wine, served by a Polish waitress. After this there was no time for any art galleries or museums. On my last visit, if you recall, I had written a scurrilous note in the visitor's book of a famous gallery and then later Chas had led me to the British Museum to view a pornographic act between two animatedly consenting Ancient Greek males, one old and one rather young, painted on a vase and purchased by the museum for millions of pounds of taxpayers' money. There had been questions in Parliament about this purchase.

However, towards the end of my present trip Chas did manage to lead me into the British Museum for a special exhibition of paintings by Samuel Palmer, a 19th century artist associated with William Blake, the poet/painter who saw trees filled with angels and God pressing his forehead against his nursery window—heady stuff straight from the heart. I've always been taken by Palmer's glowingly golden twilights in an idyllic English country setting. "The Lonely Tower" is full of mystery under a sickle moon—I've got a postcard of it propped up in my basement desk at the Huntington Library— and I noticed that the picture I was looking at in the British Museum had been lent by that very same Huntington.

And then I was shocked to see a modern day photograph of the original Tower. Why, I know it! It's located in Surrey and you can see it from the car as you whizz down the A3 roadway. A very mundane building. That's Palmer for you—he mystified the mundane. Next time I whizz by I'll see the Tower afresh through Palmer's eyes. Chas pointed out a quote of Palmer's painted across the wall of one room. Something like this: "The present is for idiots, the past is for poets."

Next he took me to the National Portrait Gallery in Trafalgar Square for the special on artist self-portraits. Salvator Rosa glared down at me truculently. I didn't care for his attitude. At the bottom of the canvas the artist had posted a Latin tag: "Aut tace, aut loquere, silentio meliora." Chas translated, rather pointedly: "Either keep silent or say things that are better than silence." I was pretty quiet for the next few hours.

The BIG EVENT of my trip this time was to attend my sister Suzanne's New Year's Eve party, down in her country cottage which she shares with her husband, the General. And the party certainly came up to scratch. Each year a different member of my sister's social circle throws the event. The last one I attended was held at the house of the prettiest woman in the county (according to my sister's reckoning) and Chas and I arrived ahead of my sister and the General.

I realize I've told this story before, but I failed to report certain things concerning that previous party so here they are.......

We had entered through the wrong door to find ourselves in a crowded Tudor-beamed drawing room, smack dab in the middle of the canapé and drinks segment of the party, a melee of upper class people in frocks and dinner jackets, all braying away and obviously old, old friends and thoroughly like-minded. When they saw Chas and me they gave us the cold shoulder, a quick up and down appraisal and then back to the braying. It must have been the effect of Chas' wild white hair, what's left of it, or else his gleaming brow and piercing eyes. It can't possibly have been me.

Anyway, we retreated. Back outside in the wind and rain we saw that the cavalry had arrived to help us. My sister and the General swept us in via the proper front door and we followed in their wake. Re-entering that same canapé room in the protective custody of my family we were aware of a big change: faces lit up, hands were outstretched, and happy cries and halloos were offered. What a welcome! Oh, and these two other men? They're with you? Well, they must be alright. Yes, do tell me, have you come far? From America? And what, pray, can keep you there? Tell me all about yourself!

In fact, after that the evening became so hospitable that I got a bit nervous. During dinner the strapping woman next to me kept rubbing her thigh against mine and I had to keep excusing myself because her husband, another senior officer of some kind, looked like a man one wouldn't want to tangle with.

Then there were the inevitable party games, including one which involved remembering objects set out on a silver salver before the salver was removed. You only had a minute and all I could remember was a used condom. There were worse things than that but I couldn't remember them.

Finally midnight chimed and we sang Auld Lang Syne and the traditional rocket was set up. "Who's going to do the honors?" announced a veteran of the Household Guards. Chas offered with a flick of his silver lighter. But he wasn't very good at it and finally another General, a veteran of the Gulf War, took over and successfully launched the missile into the Berkshire countryside and possibly somebody else's garden. "Hope we do better than that in the coming Iraq show," commented another senior officer. So this must have been around 2003, I suppose.

Anyway, we had a less strenuous time at my sister's current affair. My brother came down, plus Chas and Andy Wickham. Black tie was de rigueur but Robin got away with a blue velvet jacket and frilly shirt that had a disco flavor about it. I wore a 1939 fin-lapelled dinner jacket that, so the label inside told me, had once been the property of the Right Reverend Percival, Prebend of Bath or some such place. I'd found it in the back of a closet in my bedroom at Robin's house. It had a dead man's muskiness about it but I was filled with an antique correctness and thus ready to take on any amount of high-ranking British officers.

My sister and brother-in-law catered the whole evening—no help at all, no waiters or valet parkers like over here. What a splendid and efficient job they did! And without any fuss. At the start we had the canapés in the drawing room— plates of smoked salmon on toast came around as we drank champagne. In the past I have never mastered the art of circulating, of not being stuck in small talk when eavesdropping on another more interesting conversation that's happening within inches of your bore. I never know how to get away without offense. And, of course, one's chat partner is probably equally bored and trying to get away too.

But tonight I found an excellent way out. Trapped with a man in Seaforth Highlander trews and a limitless knowledge of wines which he'll tell you about at the drop of a hat, I spotted a stooped woman approaching us, staggering under the weight of a plate piled high with smoked salmon. So I came to her aid by grabbing the plate from her: "Here, let me help!" She surrendered and was left to talk to my ex-partner while I was free to buzz around with the heaped plate and thus sample bits of the party talk, like channel surfing with the TV remote.

However, I met my Waterloo: a woman, clearly trying to escape a bore, offered to relieve me of my job. I wasn't having any of that and we had a tug-of-war. I won and so was able to work my way back to Chas and Andy who appeared to be engaged in an intense discussion. It turned out to concern the Indian Mutiny of 1857 and how Al Quaida emerged out of the struggle. All the world's troubles seem to have their origins in the British Empire. But what rugged Imperial heroes thrust themselves into that arena! What brave men of action! A little unscrupulous perhaps but better than the wimpy present day of smart bombs and press conferences.

After dinner we had the party games. But these never really took off and so I was asked to get on the piano and liven things up till midnight. When I sang, "They're Parking Camels Where The Taxis Used To Be" my sister laughed so hard she had to rush off to the lavatory. Later I led a session of limericks to the tune, "Rhymes," and it was surprising to see so many respectable men of industry and warfare, as well as regular churchgoers, step up to offer a dirty verse. My sister had to pay another lavatory visit as a result of my contribution:

There was a young choir girl from Chichester
Made all of the saints in their niches stir.
And each morning at Matins
Her breasts in pink satin
Made the Bishop of Chichester's britches stir.

Soon I was back in London and continuing to visit my friends. This after all was what I had come over to do. No sightseeing, no theatre, no cooing at the countryside. I grew up here. Forget it. No, I was here to spend as much time as I could with my friends and family, storing up the experience so that camel-like I could last another year under the unthinking sun of Los Angeles County. I had meals with my other best friends, Jeremy Lewis and his dear wife Petra—both of whom go back to my Trinity College Dublin days—where Jeremy demonstrated how close I am to his family circle by farting long and loud whenever he felt like it. He's a Man of Letters and his latest commission is to write a book about the Greene family, and not necessarily all about the famous Graham.

Of course, Chas came along to the Lewis dinner since we're all old TCD friends, but he wasn't invited to the next dinner, at the house of Virginia Ironside, the nationally-read Agony Aunt columnist, because he gate-crashed one of her parties once where he stood around staring at her friends rather too blatantly. I later tried to stick up for Chas by telling Virginia that Chas came from a family of old British Empire hands, stretching back to the founding of the East India Company. Why his grandfather had been the Surgeon General of All-India! "If we're playing that game," said Virginia in her most precise voice. "My grandfather was the Viceroy!"

We were joined at Virginia's table — she served a game pie of hare and pheasant, complete with bits of gunshot — by a garrulous but entertaining young man who works for the Society For the Preservation Of Rural England. I was amazed: he talked more than me. He told us breathlessly that he'd just returned from a "very, very, very, very rural part of Wales"— so rural that he'd failed to get a signal on his "mobile" (cell phone over in the USA).

Most mornings I'd make my way up to central London by Tube and then spend the day seeing friends, sometimes the same ones I'd seen the day before. Chas was emerging from a small shop in Earl's Court when I met up with him again. He was stuffing a cigarette packet into his old raincoat. I was wearing an old raincoat too so we both looked like dirty old men.

The Italian restaurant was closed so we had to make do with "Balan's" on the corner. Through the front window we could see tough young men with brute-short haircuts holding hands at table and kissing waiters. Chas ordered the "Fully Monty" which is a fry-up of eggs, bacon, sausage, tomato, baked beans and fried bread—the most English dish you can get.

I thought I saw the customer opposite staring at me. Those days are long over, aren't they? He left and another man sat down there. I thought he too was staring at me. But then Chas pointed out that behind us was a big tilted mirror affording a panoramic view of the entire restaurant. The men were simply looking around, or at themselves, adjusting their dress or hair.

Embarrassed by my narcissistic mistake I grew irritated when my glass of water seemed to be taking too long to arrive. Chas came to my aid by suddenly raising his voice in a military manner to a passing waiter.

"Don't you shout at me," said the man, big and macho. "You sound like my father and I didn't like him. That's the reason I left Cyprus." "My mother is buried there," said Chas. Soon they were chatting cheerily. "We're all very excited about 'Brokeback,'" said the waiter as we left.

That evening Chas delivered me at the front steps of the East India Club in St. James' Square. Not by car, of course, but by foot. I like London because it's all walkable and all seemingly of one piece, a city of stone leading to anyplace you require, by way of stone pavement, stone road, stone alley. Stone that has been through wars going further back than when the Americans started rebelling. On the way you may meet any amount of friends and they may tempt you into a pub in an alley, older than old, entered at a tilted weathered door where inside is discovered a lively group of drinkers and smokers, even at three-thirty in the afternoon.

My appointment was with Andy Wickham and the East India Club is fussy about who comes in, so Chas quickly disappeared. He can certainly apply for membership, especially with his fine family history of service for the Empire in India. Also, as an ex-Public Schoolboy, he's equally eligible: due to economic strictures the East India has had to amalgamate with the Public Schools Club. You see no more Empire builders there but instead plenty of spotty-faced young Public School leavers, often escorted by red-faced older men — possibly their old headmasters or priests.

Andy, dressed in a bespoke dark suit (which he's told me was tailored by Huntsman at a cost of four thousand pounds), eyed my shoes with disapproval. Perfectly sensible hiking boots "engineered by Rockport" to Gore-Tex specifications. He enjoys being disapproving of me. Eventually he led me into the bar, informing me loudly, as he always does, that no women are allowed. He ordered his special Scotch, a favorite of Prince Charles. I ordered the same.

He pointed out with disgust a gaggle of young men, recent members, laughing raucously in a corner and fiddling with their mobiles. One had a great bush of coarse hair tied up at the back so that it wasn't so much a ponytail as a bulbous growth.

At dinner he questioned our waiter about conditions in the man's homeland of Nepal. "Can the King hold back the Communists?" The waiter answered in a qualified affirmative as he filled our glasses from the red wine decanter. Afterwards there was a bit of a scene in the hall at the umbrella stand when Andy discovered that a member had run off with his one hundred and fifteen pound sterling umbrella made from Malaccan rattan palm and stamped with his initials in gold. "What kind of a club is this?" he demanded of the dark men at the desk.

The club manager was summoned and even though Andy and he had attended the same school at the same time no acknowledgement of connection was made — but at least details of the umbrella disappearance were duly noted. "I don't know what the world's coming to," muttered Andy ambiguously as he hailed a taxi.

The next day, Wednesday January 4, was another BIG EVENT, a journey into unknown territory, artistically. Jane Quinn, a tireless promoter of my talents, a well-mannered agent for artists with special needs, has been trying for years to get me a gig in my homeland. Here at last was a possibility: a chance to play at an adults-only holiday hotel near the cliffs on the Isle of Wight.

Together with her sister-in law, another Jane, we motored down to Portsmouth and took the ferry to the island. On the way, Jane filled me in on the nature of the gig. A certain Rodney Hearth, an entrepreneur from the North of England but with a TV cable channel in Spain and a plan to start a family-oriented channel for Europe, would be hosting us at his house and then escorting me down the road to do a solo cabaret at the Bembridge Coast Hotel in front of 400 unsuspecting seniors and all to be filmed with four cameras for Rodney's Heaven Sent Productions "in association with Mediterranean International Television."

I was apprehensive: I haven't done a solo performance since my days playing coffee houses in the Seattle of the early 1960s. I'm used to having a backing band. For various reasons an English band could not be rounded up. Still, I saw this as a challenge to my entertaining skills. I would try to keep the attention of the Brit seniors with only my wit and the Flukie uke I'd carried across with me from Monrovia.

The Isle was shrouded in mists and a mighty wind was blowing when we arrived and drove to "Eastpoint," seat of the Hearths. The house was at the very end of the island, facing France bravely. The wind was whipping up the waves into a dancing white froth. But the house looked thick and sturdy, good for withstanding rough weather. Our host emerged from behind glass double doors. "Oh dear, oh dear! Close your eyes, please! This is unheard of! We are the Sun Spot Centre of the British Isles, I tell you. Come in for a cup of tea!" He had a very strong North Country accent, sounding like a low comedian in a cheap 1930s music hall film. I mean that as a compliment.

We were ushered into a large and well-heated drawing room with a widescreen view of the English Channel and the angry waves. Rodney's delightful wife of many years, Norma, produced a pot of tea and lots of biscuits. No sooner had I started my chatter — forgetting about what Velasquez had said about silence — when Rodney clapped his hands and announced: "Norma! Put away the tea pot and let's get out the cameras for a filmed interview suitable for my show 'Hearth At Home'!" Within a few minutes the Hearth drawing room had been transformed into a TV studio with arc lights and mikes and the husband and wife team manning the cameras.

In the interview I confessed to my worry that my fellow countrymen wouldn't take kindly to an upper class gent with a plummy accent. Rodney assured me I'd go down a treat. Stick to wholesome family stuff, keep to the well-known old chestnuts, ladle on the charm. Not like the decadent stuff you get on the Mainland. Does Rodney ever visit London then? Brrh! No fear! The rot starts at Portsmouth.

Who would I be performing for? 400 people of my age or thereabouts, nice folk who are partaking of a weekend away from the grandchildren and in-laws and the wicked world in general. Their days and nights are organized into certain activities at certain times. This afternoon, for example, they will have seen a vintage TV sitcom on the big screen at 5pm, then it's do-as-you-please till Bingo tonight — immediately followed — ta-ra! — by Ian Whitcomb, brought to you direct from America, immediately followed by Johnny Casson, the famous stand-up comic. Mr. Casson has said in no uncertain terms that Mr. Whitcomb must be off the stage by ten pm because Mr. Casson is coming on then whether Mr. Whitcomb has vacated the stage or not.

So I was being wedged in. I wasn't on the scheduled program. The 400 would be in for a surprise. "Not to worry," said Rodney brightening just as the clouds outside the cinemascope front window were growing black with bile. "Come along now — and let's have a feed."

Rodney is a warm-hearted man from Manchester and he made me feel relaxed. Wife Norma had prepared a virtual feast. There was no mucking about with different courses, no nouvelle cuisine artsy plate decoration with Jackson Pollock swirls surrounding an itsy bitsy piece of filet mignon. Our meal was served up on full plates and all at once, steaming food piled up high as a mountain, like the heaped supper rewards in the last panel of a *Beano* or *Dandy* comic: roast chicken, roast potatoes, Brussels sprouts. Rodney showed his individualism by squeezing American mustard onto his chicken from an industrial plastic container. I think I said Grace in Latin.

I needn't have worried about my reception at The Bembridge. All went well: I was announced by a busty young woman as a star all the way from America —-and out of the shadows I stepped with only a Fluke ukulele as my musical aid. And onto the dance floor with the bold red stage curtain behind me. Into the Valley of Death to face the 400! There they sat, in hushed anticipation, at little tables, to the front and to the sides. Waiting for a nice evening's entertainment. No performance art, no references to Bush or Blair.

I gave them what they wanted, a shower of comfort food, prefacing my 45 minute show with the statement that while the 400 might be thinking I sound like an upper class git and not American at all, "bear with me" (I'd learned this from local telephone operators and railway station announcers)—"And you might have a good time all round."

Early on in the act I discovered that my audience was keen to participate, so I led a singalong to "You Made Me Love You" and "After The Ball." They were ready to join in "Wurzel Fudge, The Village Idiot," quickly mastering the "Ha Ha Hee Hee" chorus and twigging to the punch line—a clean one, to the relief of Rodney and his camera crew. There wasn't a song, known or unknown, that they didn't immediately sing along to. Even my very latest songs, hot from my new CD, they sang with gusto as if they'd been singing them all their lives.

I exited to genuine applause. Johnny Casson, the famous comic, waiting in the wings to go on, was pleased that I'd timed my act to perfection. "Good work, lad," he muttered. I asked whether, like the old-time comedians I used to enjoy in the 1950s, he ended his act with a sentimental song. "No, lad," he replied, "That's a copout." Well, thank you very much indeed.

Out he stepped. "Evening all. What d'you think of these celebrities today who name their kids after the place of conception, eh? I mean, David Beckham — he's calling his son Brooklyn, and then don't forget Paris Hilton. In my day if we'd done that my son would be 'Back Alley' and my daughter 'Billiard Table'." Amazingly Rodney didn't flinch and his cameras rolled on.

There was one last BIG EVENT the following week, three days before my departure: the January Literary Lunch, at Simpson's-in-the-Strand, thrown by *The Oldie*, a magazine to which I occasionally contribute, thanks to Jeremy Lewis, the commissioning editor. I was thrilled and nervous because I would be introduced to the daunting editor and founder Richard Ingrams, an important cultural figure of the early 1960s, a co-founder of the satirical weekly, *Private Eye*, a man of limited patience with dunderheads.

The featured guest speakers were Clive James, TV pundit and *New Yorker* poet and frighteningly clever wit; John Pearson, a one-time *Sunday Times* staffer; and Alexander Waugh, grandson of the very, very famous Evelyn Waugh. All three would be introduced by Ingrams at the end of the lunch and then be permitted to plug their latest books for ten minutes.

Jeremy told me that when authors go on too long Ingrams is known to start banging a glass or harrumph loudly. None of the lunchers are getting any younger and so there have been incidents involving old age: Larry Adler, celebrated harmonica virtuoso, had a heart attack in the middle of one lunch and was carried out by the well-known comedy writer Barry Cryer. But he returned just after the pudding course, assisted by Cryer, and waving a triumphant hand to show he had been spared by the Reaper just a little longer. He has now totally succumbed.

Fortunately there were to be no such dramas today. But I was nervous and had forgotten my Valium. I wore my best stagewear, the same costume I'd worn at the Isle of Wight gig—a 1950s vintage American gangster suit of brown speckles and a matching vintage tie, completed by my trademark piano keyboard scarf. No one paid me any attention. They're like that in Britain. I could thus melt into the background. I was among a literary caste certain of themselves and of what they knew. Many of the lunchers, not even subscribers to

The Oldie, travel up from the fastnesses of the countryside in order to listen to authors speaking briefly and to eat soft and simple prep school food. Mashed potatoes and pork sausages and the like. Maybe a little mincemeat.

Of course, Simpson's is world-renowned for its gleaming metal carveries, pushed by fully armed waiters ready to give you the cut of your choice. *The Oldie* lunch, however, is not in the main dining room but down many stairs, in "The Bishop's Room." This is where I found myself alone in a room full of talkative people. I made myself active by ordering a pre-lunch drink. One glass of house white wine, please. What? Eight pounds! How could I ever live again back in England?

Jeremy now turned up to help me. He introduced me to his guest, Alexander Waugh (grandson of Evelyn), and I didn't have to contribute anything much because I quickly discovered that Waugh likes to talk and doesn't care for interruption, even though Jeremy was throwing him tidbits about me, like headlines from a tabloid — my articles for the magazine concerning Plaster Casters who make molds of erect rock star penises, about my uncle who wrote "Lady of Spain." Waugh now turned to consider me. He said he'd never heard of "Lady Of Spain."

This meant I couldn't follow up with a song title of my uncle's that always gets a laugh: "I've Never Wronged An Onion So Why Should It Make Me Cry." It had certainly done well for me on the Isle of Wight. How I missed that cheery 400 and their comforting laughter and applause!

Jeremy now pulled me away in order to have me meet Richard Ingrams. He knew who I was and was gracious but I could see his eye ranging the room and his body was sideways to me. Soon he was off into the melee; Jeremy explained that as a good host Ingrams has many people to greet.

A man in an apron announced that lunch was ready to be served and we filed in. Jeremy had kindly placed me next to him at the top table, near to Ingrams and the guest speakers. It was as if we were all back at school and I was sitting with the masters while the pupils are at long tables in front of us, set at a right angle. The food was super — I've always loved school food: cauliflower soup, and then some kind of boiled fish, followed by spotted dick for pudding.

The event had started at 12 noon but we didn't get to the speeches till around 2.30pm. By this time some of the older patrons, possibly affected by the rich school food, were beginning to doze off. I saw one, two, and then three in a row go into a pleasant slump. At another table an elderly woman in tweeds and a fishing hat was sitting backwards stiffly with her mouth wide open as if in rigor mortis. This spectacle of general somnolence continued, like a sudden pandemic, during the author speeches.

It acted as a happy diversion during the second speaker since, after a decent start, the going got rough. Thrown off his garrulous stride by the breakdown of the microphone, he went downhill racing, talking fast and incoherently until apprehended by a rather tart-voiced woman at the back of the room: "My dear man, I'm sure what you're saying is absolutely fascinating—indeed I have come as far as Somerset to hear you— but we can't understand a word so PROJECT, for God's sake, PROJECT!"

This must have sent the speaker into a spiral because he went into a mumble stream, forgetting names and dates or else tediously correcting them — "It was in 1962...No, 1965..No, April, 1963..."— and this went on and on. During the ramble— when you could hear a pin drop because everyone was embarrassed into silence — Jeremy entertained me at the top table by pointing out the increasing ranks of sleepers. The other tables, keen for entertainment— some had been reduced to examining the trademarks and lettering on the underside of their saucers and cruets, etc— now followed Jeremy's moving finger so as to be fully informed, to be in on the act.

Eventually Ingrams slipped the lost speaker a note saying "You're time is up." Clive James, a slick professional speaker, took over, cutting his address down to a short selection of anti-Bush jokes.

Afterwards I was flattered to be asked by Jeremy to join him in a stroll with Richard Ingrams. I had no idea where the great man was going but I didn't care. He listened to me amiably as I talked of new ideas for *Oldie* articles; he approved of two of them. Jeremy, pleased that I was hitting it off so well with his boss, gleefully danced between us as we negotiated our way from the Strand and eventually deep into Soho via a sea of foreign-tongued pedestrians.

I was describing my enthusiasm for English B pictures of the 1950s in which every detective wore a trilby and trench coat and drove a Wolseley when Ingrams announced a train station and how he ought to be there if he was to return to his house. And he disappeared into the rich soup of London.

Have I gone and over-done it again? Had I talked too much? "No, no, old man! He likes you. I can tell." assured Jeremy.

So now I have to write up those ideas for *Oldie* articles. The first will be about my experiences at auditions in Hollywood — the humiliations such as the casting calls for British butlers: how the casting director's office gets filled with dozens of Brits in full butler costume, how they come falling off the bus dressed up to the nines in tails and gloves and boiled dickies; how, if it's a call for Scrooges, they arrive in Victorian nightgowns with heads wrapped round with bandages from jaw to pate. Yes, I will write and get those ghastly cattle calls for Brits off my chest, now that I'm home in Monrovia where all is white and calm as the young mothers, singing and swaying in transports of silent joy, push their brand new babies past our window and where the only sound is the tock of this computer.

MARCH

These Letters have become accounts of the past month or memoirs of the 1960s, which is all very well but I believe the original purpose of the Letter was to tell what we're about to do — concerts and such. So for this month, since I haven't got much to say about last month, I'll try to write about the future. Not too much — my friend Chas in London has warned me about excessive verbiage. You must retain certain mysteriousness, he says. Our mutual friend, the late poet Alan Ross, liked poems to be a bit incomprehensible — he'd even edit out a few words of works he published so as to achieve that effect, much to the fury of the poets he'd hacked at. He used to scratch out chunks of my articles for his *London Magazine* arbitrarily and then tell me they were much the better for it. So I suppose in his eyes I became a sort of poet, too.

Well, I'll try to not tell all, but it's a hard job.

First of all, it's March the First as I write and I'm off the wagon. I vowed to abstain while I was in England in January. The decision was made during my sister's New Year's Eve party: a bibulous friend of hers, a man in military kilt who is also a wine connoisseur and who shows it in his face, told me that in February he'd be off the alcohol for that month, an exercise he does every year at this time. Probably quite a good thing in his case as he looked as if coronary time was nigh. But I admired his decision and I vowed to do the same. Having e-mailed Regina that I was becoming teetotal for February I then had to stick to my vow. She was very pleased, having suggested I do this several times over the years. I'm not a drunk, not dependent; I simply wanted to test my will power, and lose some weight, and see how I felt as a dry.

But I felt staid and miserable in the evening when all around me were nursing their glasses of glee. And the world looked and sounded awfully drab. I seemed to be another being, a gaunt and distant visitor, viewing a strange society from a lofty height. Reality was so banal, so unmagical and unspiritual. I counted the days till I could hold a glass of red wine again, get out of jail. I only lost about 6 pounds, too. However, one or two friends did admit, after I pressed them, that stone sober I'm not so explosive, not so contrary. I kept quiet more often, didn't erupt in "Jesus Christ"s.

I think, however, that I prefer the colorful world of wine despite the possibility that its haze masks the real thing. I think I'd rather live in a fantasy. Tonight Regina and I will celebrate at home with a bottle of champagne. And then I'll watch a Buck Jones western....

To March and the future. I'm sure that tomorrow I'll start the day in the same way: take Rollo out down the road, making sure I have a supply of plastic bags so I can collect up his biggies. Monrovians are very alert to dogs' messes on their streets. Altadena was a funkier place, so well-decorated with discarded malt liquor bottles and fried chicken cartons that I never felt I needed to pick up the dog messes. It seemed perfectly natural, indeed downright folksy, to let the biggies join the cartons and bottles.

Rollo ritually pees on the same trees and barks at the same dogs. He's very conservative that way. Sometimes we'll walk as far as Starbucks where I'll order a grande misto (large coffee with steamed milk) and possibly a turkey baguette, trying to ignore the ghastly mewing singer songwriters and the grunting, moaning soul singers pouring from the sound system, as advertised on the CDs that Starbucks offers. We have a very special Starbucks in the shopping center mall: where there's a gang of regulars — Vietnam veterans in their wheel chairs, intent young Asians peering rather too seriously into their laptops, local cops with guns and equipment sticking out. They all love Rollo and because I'm tethered to him this means that I'm dragged into society and this is a good thing for a malcontent.

"What is he?" and I answer the same every time and they reply that, on the contrary, they know what he is and they proceed to tell me. This is the standard procedure, like a church service, or a B western, a ritual that comforts me more and more as I creep into senior citizenship. Which reminds me: a few weeks ago I signed on for Social Security. To do this I had to enter the world of reality and as I was on the wagon the experience was even starker in black & white than my film noirs.

I went to the local sign-on place and was dismayed at the masses already assembled there. The room was full of them so every chair was taken; there was a gaggle of East Indians surrounding an official who was informing them in their own language; there was a guard with a gun, there was no literature in English — every other language, but nothing in English. I flushed red and felt lost. But after an hour or so of reading the L.A. Times, even the sports section, I was rescued and was soon in a cubicle in a big inner room, with not a flower or family photo in sight, sitting opposite a desolate official who took down my particulars, sighing as he did so, and looking puzzled because he didn't know who I was and felt he ought to because he watches television like anybody else does and I'd described myself as an entertainer, hadn't I.

He resembled the IRS paralegal wretch who had given us a third degree interrogation last December, downtown in an equally dispiriting setting in which he'd said, "Bud, I watch a lot of movies and such and I never heard of you." But this Social Security worker, although he had the required dandruff sitting on his dog mess colored jacket, the greasy hair and the dead eyes, was nicer. I could detect no chip. After demanding details about my mother, my birthplace, World War Two, etc, he signed me on and told me to look for the first check next month and to take it easy in my impending old age. Next stop Medicare. Watch out, he warned me, it's a jungle out there. He was nice enough not to ask what exactly I'm retiring from. That would have posed a problem since I've never had a regular job.

To return to my narrative: I did take Rollo down the road and in the evening I did take my first taste of alcohol in 28 days. Regina opened a bottle of California champagne and I drank from a fluted glass. What a shock! It tasted bitter, acrid, horrid. Perhaps, praise the Lord, I have become a total abstainer.

Next evening I tried again to return to the pleasures of the vine. We dined Mexican prior to a Janet Klein & Her Parlour Boys show at the Steve Allen Theatre in Hollywood. I ordered the house wine, which came in a tiny bottle marked Sutter Home. Another foul-tasting drink. Or was it due to the cheapness? Incidentally, the subsequent show went well. Janet was launching her new CD, *Oh!* on which I sing, "Butterflies In The Rain," a song co-authored by my uncle Stanley, and on which I perform a French waltz on accordion, ascribed to one Pierre LeFevre, whose work sounds an awful lot like mine. The Steve Allen is but a part of the Centre For Inquiry. A lot of doubters come here and discuss and reason about the unreasonable and the impossible. There's no mystery in life for them, more's the pity. An upper floor holds the Atheists Club. I wonder if they have a bar.

This Sunday I travel up with other Parlour Boys to Yosemite where we appear at a Speakeasy Salon in the Ahwanee Hotel, part of the annual old-time celebrations. A few years back, you may remember, Regina, Rollo, and I were guests of honor there. We were given a suite and we dined at the same table where Queen Elizabeth had dined. I lectured on the 1920s Jazz age and Regina taught the dances of the era. Then we danced and sang and the band played. Never before had the park rangers allowed such entertainment in the Ahwanee. We were, in fact, blazing a trail for the acceptance of period entertainment at the Ahwanee. But politics stepped in and the Northern California Art Deco people soon took over the gig and so it was curtains for us. Now I'm there just as a Parlour Boy and as such have to come in the servant's entrance and sleep in a cabin out in the woods. Part of my long march backwards.

On my return from Yosemite I will look forward to the regular gatherings at our venerable Salon, starting at 6.30pm.

At Conrad's I will order a red wine and wait for the salonists to arrive. Who they will be is always a surprise. The evening is open to everyone. We are a truly democratic group and thus have to suffer bores as well as boors for our principles. But those who are not of similar mind and mouth usually get the message and don't return. We have lost all our political members. The liberals and conservatives used to clash, the Bush baiters easily sending the Republicans into full retreat, fuming. It's funny how the right wing generally doesn't care for debate. However, the lefties with their holy cant are just as tiresome. So now we are reduced to a stingless group that discusses old films, old songs, old anything.

Jim Dawson is our court jester and he specializes in puns and tales of farters. At the drop of a hat he will tell you that his new book, *Son Of Fart* will be published imminently. He will tell you that his first fart book, *Who Cut The Cheese?* is currently at 35200 in the Amazon book sales chart. Then he'll dig into his Greek salad because, as he says, "It's hard to fuck up a salad." One week he tried the special "seniors" offering of Salisbury steak a la mode and sent our waiter back to the kitchen with a message to congratulate the chef on the quality of his gristle.

No, we're certainly not there for the food — a few of our members have been poisoned by what looked like plague-ridden fried chicken. The location is useful because our corner booth can be expanded by the addition of tables. Our waiter Javier is always at the ready to build the additions as salonists make their grand entrance through the side door of the bar area. Always smiling, always ready with our orders, Javier can be excused if, during the course of our four-hour meetings, he disappears into some inner sanctum in the bowels of the kitchen. But he always returns with a happier face, as if concealing some wondrous secret. He must be a successful waiter because recently he bought a house next to the street where our old house is in Altadena. And bigger than ours.

Next week Regina and I will be having our second session with the IRS. But this, we hope, will not be like the third degree interrogation of last time. We don't have to go downtown to the federal building and face a seedy and bitter paralegal. We will be in pleasanter El Monte sitting opposite an actual agent and one, we hope and pray, known to our accountant, perhaps even on golfing terms. If we can't settle this tax matter then we might a as well give up being entertainers. The IRS refuses to recognize our expenses: stage wear, recording costs, hotels on the road, pens, paper, wigs. Their position is that since we don't work for a corporation and check in to a time machine we don't work at all. Being self-employed sets off an urgent alarm with the IRS. Being in the lower rungs of show biz sets off an even louder one.

If we are stuck with a hefty tax bill then we'll have to take a chunk from the money that Regina recently made off the sale of family land: acres of desert out near Pearblossom left to her by her parents, have been bought by Koreans who intend building yet another church of the desert. The desert is the right place since that's where the three troublesome religions started their ranting.

I must close now and return to my practicing of songs to be performed at our tour of Japan in April. I start with a solo concert in Tokyo and then join Janet and Her Parlour Boys for a tour that will take us down as far as Hiroshima. My memories of that city are of a sleep-deprived night. Our guitarist Tom, after promising that he never snores, proceeded to do so in a stentorian manner the minute his head hit the pillow in the tiny cube unit we shared. Driven wild by the racket I took to the streets where thousands of spirits swirled, roaming for hours, cursing my fate, joining the ghosts of that Atomic 1945.

APRIL

This letter will be short and, I hope, to the point. Only a few minutes ago we signed off on our tax audits for 2001 and 2002. A relief, even though we have to pay a certain sum, but it's nothing like the amount that the IRS has been demanding for over a year. We didn't have to go to court.

I seized a chance to give the rude and disrespectful paralegal — that dandruff flaky shrimp who'd dared to tell me that I should wish I was as successful as Sir Elton John — a piece of my mind: he'd had the cheek to call me in person yesterday when I was at my desk dreaming of old songs and such.

How dare you call me at home, I said. Before he could tell me it was about the tax settlement — all arranged by that really charming IRS agent women, the one who has a model woody wagon with surf board on top on her desk, the one who stood up and shook my hand at the end of our session with her, who told me it had been an honour to meet me and who wished us well with the neighbour problem — I told him that he'd caused us a lot of pain in his third degree interrogation just before Christmas; that I didn't want to talk to him except through our appointed representative; that I didn't trust him or his fellow lawyers. And: is this call being taped?

It all started to escalate so Regina, smilingly, took over. The wretch did admit that he was sorry if he'd given us a hard time. What we've learned from this is that, as a self-employed entertainer, I have to carefully note every expense even to the extent of writing down on the credit card slip what business was done at this or that restaurant, gas station, clothes or record store. For the first time in years we have filed our tax returns prior to April 15.

What else has been going on? My latest article for the British monthly magazine *The Oldie* (this isn't a publication about incontinence pads and wheelchairs, but one of the most distinguished reads in Britain) made the front cover: "How To Be A Hollywood Butler." Now I have to complete research for another commissioned *Oldie* article: on that grand fellow Bob Mitchell, the 93 year old who founded the Mitchell Boy Choir in the 1930s and whose choristers have been featured in over 100 movies including *Angels With Dirty Faces, The Bishop's Wife* and some Roy Rogers and Hopalong Cassidy westerns.

When I visit Bob at his shining Filipino-run assisted living house in Hollywood he's always ready: sitting on the bed in a dark suit and bright tie, immaculate. His voice is strong and deep and he's more together in his life than I'll ever be. Calls are broadcast on his speakerphone as I sit there: "Explain the difference between a symphony orchestra and a philharmonic," demands one rude street voice, an ex-chorister. Bob does so pithily. Another pleads for bail money to get out of jail. Bob has time for them all.

Then we set off for a church organ recital. One was at the world's largest organ in the First Presbyterian Church in an old part of Los Angeles I rarely stray into. Bob knows every hymn in every denomination. He's truly ecumenical: he plays pop songs like "My Sin" for the Christian Scientists who don't believe in hymns; for years he was resident organist at a synagogue that has since rewarded him with a nice pension. He looks good in a skullcap; he speaks fluent Yiddish.

He likes to take my arm as we step outside and into a vehicle. When we get to the church he leaps out and drags me along behind him such is his speed, with his dark suited long tall body leaning steeply forwards, cleaving the air. Death, imminent or otherwise, is not to be seen. The Reaper has skedaddled to the next county, shrieking. In between the church concerts Bob answers my questions about his story. In the 1930s he was holding down two jobs: as music director of the St. Brendan's Church in LA and as the organist and pianist at a local radio station. Eventually he married the two music styles, persuading the station to let the boys perform religious stuff on the air. A sharp woman who was program director spotted a good thing, a potential vaudeville act. She went to see the Corwin Brothers (real name Cohen) to sell them the St. Brendan's Boy Choir. "Lady, what you got we don't need," said the Corwins. But she had a powerful voice and she biffed on: the boys can sing "Eli, Eli" followed by "Home On The Range" — in swingtime. "Now, you're talking!" said the brothers.

And they booked the boys at their Orpheum — on the same bill as Sally Rand, the fan dancer. Miss Rand agreed to add a few more fans and cut the act short. Not long afterwards the boys were billed simply as "Mitchell BoyChoir." That's how I remember them in *The Jolson Story* credits and I supposed there was an actor in the film called Mitch Boychoir and who was probably a Red Indian. But I couldn't spot him among all the different boys. There were two choirs, one Catholic and one Jewish, both supplied by Bob.

I shall be sorry when my research is over and I have to sit down and condense all this gold milk into 1200 words. It's always fair weather adventures with Bob.

Last week we three — Regina, Rollo, and me — went up to San Luis Obispo for a House Concert. I've heard about these affairs before but have never been invited to star. This concert was at the lovely hillside home of Stanley and Carol Stern. Actually they live in Los Osos, near by. Osos means Bears and there used to be fierce Grizzlies lurking in the undergrowth waiting for breakfast back in the days when Indians were the sole inhabitants. The bears ruled, eating indiscriminately, so the Indians were relieved when the Spaniards marched in and shot the bears. Today instead of bears and redskins there are neat rows of satisfied retired folks from L.A. who pity us poor people still swinking for wages down in that clown town big city. God's country is Los Osos and we were informed of this in no uncertain terms. Why travel anywhere else in the world? It's all here: sea, sand, mountains, and utter peace, far from today's babbling diversity. Real life is read about with a shaking of the head via the local paper, *The Fresno Bee*.

There was a curtain-raiser to our house concert: we performed at the startlingly pink Madonna Inn, at the rude hour of 8.30 am: a men's fellowship organization called RAMS, which stands for Retired Active Men, and active they certainly were, chomping on their Danishes and Bear Claws, clad in high-hitched slacks and jump suits, one or two in World War Two pilot outfits, hopping up to give short addresses.

One elderly but sprightly gent gave a five minute talk on the artistic work of Alex Madonna, how he'd used the money he'd made building freeways in order to design every inch of the Inn, adding a room here and one there, developing in an artistic freewheeling way. The result is that the kitchen is so distant from the dining rooms that your chicken-fried or Salisbury steak may well be filched by some starving tourist en route to its far-flung destination.

Also, the gift shop is not, as it should be, the first thing you see when you enter the Inn. Instead it's hidden away on the second floor. At that point in the address our speaker was interrupted by a stern voice from the rear of the meeting room: "My wife found the gift shop right away, buddy!"

Thus I understood what sort of a crowd I would be performing for: stouthearted men, so I gave them "Nobody Loves A Fairy When She's Forty," throwing in the word "Brokeback' for good measure. It's amazing what a great roar of laughter that word "Brokeback" elicits. It's the same effect the F-word used to have before devaluation.

The next evening was our big event: the house concert. We were sold-out and there was a waiting list. I was very flattered. Usually they feature po-faced ragtime pianists who don't talk between numbers, simply rub their hands and adjust the stool. Tonight they had me— an entertainer who talks as much as he sings.

The Sterns managed to squeeze forty people into their drawing room, which already included a grand piano, an electronic keyboard and a library of eclectic books and CDs. There were people right behind me capable of touching my raiment. They were all round me and so close I could smell the sweetness of their breath. Gentle souls in a peaceful environment where no rap is heard.

Regina sang like an angel and stopped me from saying anything that might be misconstrued. And I made a breakthrough that night: I had the nerve to perform several of my keyboard instrumentals as freestanding pieces. "Beautiful," pronounced a bearded man lying in the fireplace a few inches from me. I had begged my fingers to play properly even as I performed — and they had obeyed. I must keep that begging prayer as part of the act. "You don't need a band to accompany you," pronounced our host afterwards. No, I don't. My confidence has returned.

Right after the concert, flush with money (reportable to the IRS, of course), we raced back to Monrovia, a four-hour drive, but with Regina at the wheel it was an easy one, despite attacking rain. A few hours sleep and up I was again, in time to receive Andy Wickham.

He'd called from London three days before to say that he'd been devastated to read in his newspaper that Buck Owens had died suddenly. Andy has always been a true country music aficionado and expert as only a foreigner can be. So affected was he that there and then he'd decided to take the first flight across to L.A. and drive to the Owens "viewing" and funeral service in Bakersfield. The best available flight was First Class and $8,000 but he would be there and hoped I'd accompany him.

In the 1970s Andy had founded the country music division of WB Records; I had been lucky enough to travel with him to Nashville on an expeditionary trip and watch him set up the new department, in company with the WB boss, Mo Ostin. Eventually we made a few C&W singles with Andy as producer and me as songwriter: the first, "Hands," a massage Parlour song, was one of the more commercial of our releases. Another was an epic about a Kansas girl who finds love with a doomed nobleman in his Austrian mountain lodge. This was not a success and Lenny Waronker, head of the A&R side of WB, commented succinctly: "You guys!" Now we wonder how we got away with any of it. After all, pop music is a very serious business and certainly not for overgrown schoolboys. But it was terrific to hobnob with the finest pickers of Nashville, men who'd backed the likes of Patsy Cline.

A year or so earlier, in 1972, Andy had invited me to be his guest at a convention for country music deejays in Bakersfield. The mayor would be on hand to declare this the official West Coast Country Music Week and read out a nicely calligraphed proclamation full of "Whereas this and Whereas that." Buck Owens and Merle Haggard, local heroes would be there to perform — Owens, the businessman/performer and Haggard, the professional bad boy, the envy of Johnny Cash because, unlike Cash, he'd actually spent time in the hoosegow.

This was at a time when Bakersfield, a city noted for nothing but white trash, was bravely trying to establish itself as a rival to Nashville. The Bakersfield Sound, as exemplified by Buck Owens and His Buckaroos was a Telecaster-driven hard electric sound in stark contrast to the choirs and violins of Nashville. A bright future was forecast.

Andy, prior to our departure from Los Angeles, had ordered me to button my lip and not show off. I obeyed and had the time of my life. We checked in to the (now defunct) Bakersfield Inn, sitting right next to that hallmark archway across the main drag that spelled out Bakersfield loudly and proudly. That evening we attended the deejays banquet and show. I had come armed with an early reel-to-reel video recorder and camera, an Akai, and I recorded much of the show. I've since had the reels transferred to VHS and thence to DVD. And I'll continue to transfer as system supersedes system.

Getting back to last week: when Andy arrived in Monrovia for our sad pilgrimage to the funeral of Buck Owens I showed him a snippet of the old videtape. Dressed now in his dark blazer and white shirt, he was amazed and shocked at how long his hair was in 1972 and that he was wearing T-shirt and jeans.

For this closure journey of April 1, 2006, I had packed suits and ties, sober and tasteful. This would probably be our last trip to Bakersfield. We had come full circle from the promise of the Bakersfield challenge to today when there are hardly any classic country stars alive and the rest are poorly or feeble.

Arriving at 5:30pm we were just in time to join the general public for the viewing of Owens, lying in an open casket. Six thousand had already paid their respects. The casket was sitting in front of the stage inside his multi-million dollar entertainment emporium, The Crystal Palace. Only a week ago Owens had consumed a chicken-fried steak, his favourite, in this very room and then, although feeling poorly and ready to depart, had been persuaded by a couple from Oregon, and had gone on stage to sing. Afterwards, alone, he drove back to his ranch, went to bed and experienced the Big Sleep.

As we processed towards the casket we had time to admire the display cabinets of Owens memorabilia: his sequined and embroidered western costumes; the massive bull-horned car he snatched from Elvis. In one cabinet was a blow-up of the cover of an LP, *Buck 'Em,* that Andy had commissioned back in the late 1970s when he'd signed Owens to the WB label.

I was touched by the sobs of a black woman ahead of us. And standing by the rail that separated us from the casket was a tall man in a cowboy hat consoling a grizzled older man who looked like he'd worked the fields in his day. When at last we reached the centre I was shaken at the sight of Owens' dead face. I have seen very few dead people in my life. Open caskets are not the thing in England. Our star looked waxen and Old Testament Prophet-like. His nose was disconcertingly long and droopy; his mouth was set with sides pulled down censoriously. He looked judgmental. I felt certain the real man had left town some time ago. Above on a big screen a sequence of Owens photos showing him in his prime — a full-faced Texan with a thatch of hay hair, a lusty All-American with a taste for a fine assortment of women. We paid our respects and went in search of stiff drinks.

Next day, the Sunday, we had tickets to attend the funeral services in a big Baptist church about a mile away, down a road lined with oil derricks and open fields. The church was large and modern, holding over a thousand worshippers. With our tickets we were able to sit right down in front, just behind the family. Andy's signing up of Owens in the late 1970s had gotten us these good seats. We were an hour ahead of the service but time went pleasantly by as we were entertained by a string of Owens's honky-tonking hits. It was a little odd to hear those characteristic electric guitars ring round the walls of the church. Our favourite Buck number is "Made In Japan." I think I'll learn it for my imminent trip to that country, when I tour with Janet Klein and the Parlour Boys.

The service was tastefully done; the pastor's speeches excellent. He almost converted me to his branch of faith. He made us laugh and cry. He told of the spirit being separated from the body at the time of death — yes, he said,"Death"and didn't employ euphemisms like "passing"— using as a metaphor the image of a Coke can being emptied of its contents.

Once again we were confronted with the waxen and now accusatory face of Buck Owens in that same casket, still in the same suit and red shirt, with the cowboy hat on his breast. The funeral people must have been doing some hard traveling. Would they be returning Buck to the Crystal Palace for the reception? The thought was not pleasant because Buck's face, gleaming more than yesterday, was a little off-putting, especially as we had recently enjoyed a Grand Slam breakfast at a Denny's.

Sturdy four-square hymns were sung; there was even some a capella on "Blessed Assurance." Dwight Yoakam did "In The Garden" very well indeed, introducing it by begging forgiveness for wearing his trademark cowboy hat, explaining that Buck always encouraged him to keep it on since it covered his baldness. It's amazing what a well-shaped, well-placed hat will do. Yoakam, hatted, looked like a pretty kid.

Another singer, a bass voice specialist called Trace Adkins, prefaced his version of "Wayfaring Stranger" by telling us that Buck had advised him to keep hitting that low note because:" It's all you got going for you."

Finally a fat woman came on to sing "Amazing Grace," but before the backing track could roll she told us how Buck had redeemed her from a bad life in the late 1960s when she'd been a hippie who "ate acid and jumped into public fountains." Buck had got her on *Hee Haw* as a regular and today she is an ordained minister.

There were no obvious Hollywood slickster record biz representatives there. Owens' legacy isn't hip or chic; he wasn't an outlaw performer like Merle Haggard, Johnny Cash or Willie Nelson. He pursued the American Dream — capitalism — and he grabbed it and made it real: he owned radio and TV stations, as well as his own song copyrights. But I fear that his lusty honky tonking music is becoming a period piece, a time capsule containing the Okies who settled this sere and arid area during the Great Depression, the Anglos who are now a minority in California, scorned and un-celebrated.

I felt very much a part of the past and few steps nearer to the gray face in the casket. We didn't stay for the reception at the Crystal Palace. We headed back to Vroman's book shop in Pasadena where I bought Andy my favorite novel *Revolutionary Road* by Richard Yates, another dead figure from the past.

Now I must prepare for the upcoming Japan tour as the rain pelts down outside this Monrovian apartment window. I start the tour with a solo concert in Tokyo. A fortnight ago I was concerned lest I could hold a concert audience with only my voice, uke, and piano. But now thanks to the recent house concert experience I have the confidence to be the one-man band I once was.

However, will the Japanese understand a word I say? So much of my act depends on language and accent and style. But I will dazzle them with style and the spirit of the west, of old Anglos and steady harmonies and strong hearts. I fueled myself last night with my first chicken-fried steak. It was delicious, a real surprise and a real comfort. I had placed the godlike food of Buck Owens inside of me. In Japan I will smile and display my body language. I will sing "Made In Japan." Or maybe not.

MAY

IN THE LAND OF KAMPAI

I ended last month's letter with words of anticipation about the upcoming Japan Tour. Now, as I write, this is history and so I will write it up, using my daily journal as a crib. Of course, the material from the journal will be carefully selected: I will not expose some of my darker remarks. You'll have to go to the Huntington Library manuscripts department to read these —- and good luck gaining entrance.

Regina left first for Japan — but she wasn't on a music biz tour, she was going as a Buddhist taking part in a pilgrimage ("Tozan") to the Nichiren Shoshu Temple for the inauguration of the new High Priest. We never saw each other in Japan. I dropped her off at LAX on Wednesday, April 12, where she was immediately enfolded into the large group of fellow pilgrims; I knew she was in safe hands. No chanting on plane, read instructions. Softly does it in hotel, for fear of disturbing others. There'll be plenty of time for chanting once you get to the Temple. She had an inspirational time, refreshing and peace-giving.

I'd lost a day when I arrived in Japan. I wasn't quite sure which one. Nor was I ever sure what day of the week it was. No matter — it was all a whirl of activity, of being shepherded around and bowed to and treated well. A land of smiles. On the United flight I skimmed through a textbook history of Japan & Its Culture (4th edition). I didn't really believe that they're descended from the Sun Goddess, whoever she is when she's at home. I noted from the book that they are racially Mongolian, with the characteristic "fold in the eyelid, yellow tinge in pigmentation, black hair, flat face, high cheekbone, and limbs proportionately short in relation to trunk."

I studied one of my fellow passengers, a native, as she walked back from the lavatory; my study revealed that she wasn't a girl but a beautiful boy, like a perfect toy. He gave me a funny look so I rummaged in my bag for the other history book I'd brought with me. A rather unfortunate title, *Race War!* and an even more unfortunate cover: within a Rising Sun is a caricature from WW2 of a Japanese soldier whipping a stooping European POW. The thesis of this academic tome (by a black professor) is how British racism and colonialism were exploited by the Japanese thus making it easier for their conquest of Hong Kong and Singapore. The gimmick was to claim to be the noble liberators of the world's oppressed peoples of color. While reading this incendiary book I covered the cover with a copy of *Newsweek*.

Mind you, until the invasion, the British did have a wonderful time sex-frolicking out East: Christopher Isherwood, slumming in 1939 Hong Kong, shivered with delight as he lay naked in a local bathhouse being erotically soaped and massaged by a Chinese youth. It was, he wrote, "like a sex fantasy." A British officer recalled how, "in lieu of women of my own class, I took to men, boys, animals, melons, and finally, masturbation." Exotic places, as always, were receptacles for pent-up sex urges.

Tiring of the history books I turned my attention to the string of hopeless movies. *Harry Potter & The Goblet Of Fire* seemed — at least on the airplane screen where all movies are reduced to their substance because any style is lost in a fog war of trolleys and lavatory-bound passengers — to consist of nothing but adolescent Harry in tedious contests with monsters where he always wins by wielding his magical wand — a cop-out if I ever saw one. His pal Ron has turned into a gawky shapeless lump with one expression — a pull-down of the sides of his mouth. There's a constant look of surprise or shock on the faces of the Potter kid heroes.

Anyway, it was all over in 11 hours. The trouble is that arrival in Japan wasn't new to me, was no adventure. I'd been here before on the first tour, a year and a half ago. This time, though, I was alone, in the vanguard of the Janet Klein & Her Parlour Boys tour. Our promoters, Toms Cabin had arranged for me to do a solo concert in Tokyo on Sunday, a day before the arrival of the Parlour Boys.

At Narita airport I was met by none other than the main man himself: Hiroshi Asada, who named Tom's Cabin, in 1975, after his son Tom, without considering that there's an old book called *Uncle Tom's Cabin*, forgetting the blackface minstrel shows trailing Stowe's well-meant anti-slavery propaganda novel.

Hiroshi drove us at breakneck speed in his Honda Odyssey to my hotel in Tokyo. En route he told me in his excellent English of his love of American country music and of the self-same 1950s pop that I grew up on — Johnnie Ray and Frankie Laine and Guy Mitchell. Hiroshi and I are almost the same age. But like most Japanese he is lean and hungry-looking. His car radio was tuned to American Armed Forces Radio, the only station in these parts he could tolerate.

My hotel, a chain called "Met," set next to a subway station, was designed for hard-traveling businessmen. You took an elevator to the fifth floor. Below me lay a view of the railway line; across from me, even late on a Saturday night, were people working — a class of earnest students under the strict direction of a tall European teacher in a mortar board... Rest, take a shower, and I'll pick you up for dinner, instructed Hiroshi, after he'd deposited my bags, as well as an enormous accordion, as big as a refrigerator. He'd hired me this monster especially for the tour. Called Excelsior, it was lined with buttons with names I had no understanding of. But then, I'm not really an accordionist. I just play one.

The bathrooms are always the same: cleverly molded modules containing wrapped toothbrushes, toothpaste, razor. The lavatory seats are armed with buttons that will sluice your bowels out gently with soapsudded jets. There are other options too but I wasn't brave enough to try them.

For dinner Hiroshi chose a small place in a warren of restaurants, upstairs in a tall building. All buildings, it seems, are tall and new in Tokyo, and everything seems to take place on an upper floor or beneath the ground. We were joined by the leader of the band that was to accompany me at tomorrow's solo concert: Juta and his wife Me. Juta's band is called The Rat Orchestra and I chose them because I'd seen them during our previous tour — playing an impeccably accurate version of a Boswell Sisters record of the early 1930s. You could close your eyes and you were listening to the Boswells, but with a fascinating oriental twist.

Our restaurant wasn't too traditional — you didn't have to remove your shoes — but it did have the long low tables and the equally low benches, forcing me to sort of squat boy scout-style, except that I can't really do that for long so I was reduced to sprawling sideways. Uncomfortable as it was there was no stopping my laying into the hot sake. Dish after dish appeared and I gobbled up the little portions, hoping to be eventually sated. But no, never. Juta's lady kept refilling my sake cup. I toasted us all several times with the only word I had learned from Regina's lengthy printout of Japanese etiquette — a list of do's and don't, plus a few useful words: "Kampai," which means "Cheers" in America or "Bottoms up!" in England.

We kampai'd for hours, getting through two big jugs of sake. I congratulated my hosts on their choice of restaurant, adding that I'd never had such tasty Japanese cuisine. Gently Juta informed me that this was in fact a Korean barbecue joint.

I tottered into my bedroom sake-ed out, and in no mood for more evidence of Japanese taunting of British upper class twits who'd been remaindered in Hong Kong in WW2. I threw my books to the floor and instead watched the BBC World News — horror stories from around the world told to me by po-faced English presenters in that awful, flat Thames Estuary accent that these days rules the airwaves. How I miss those steady, level and decent voices of the old BBC, voices that saw us through all the horrors of WW2!

Sunday was my solo concert day. Church bells were chiming as

I rose. Somewhere, many miles away, Regina would be chanting. I descended to the ground floor, armed with a hotel coupon offering a free breakfast at Beck's Coffee Shop, and also a view of the subway entrance, thus affording the sight of earnest locals hurrying to catch trains, and all this set to a soundtrack of curious bell-like music, sweet and ethereal, like heaven is supposed to sound.

My coupon entitled me to a tray containing a dollop of scrambled egg topped with a thin strip of raw bacon, a squeeze of tomato ketchup, a lettuce leaf, plus a toasted ham and cheese sandwich on white bread. And coffee. Ambrosial! A spiritual experience for me, right here in this coffee shop as the bells chimed and the neatly dressed passengers hurried by, and then Vic Damone came on to sing "Tenderly." This was my church. These were my people. I was a god.

As I swallowed the milky scrambled egg I perused *The Japan Times* (established in 1897): "Princess Aiko took part in children's games, clapping and plucking 'yo-yo' balloons from a water tank. She took home three such balloons." A full-page article by the Syrian ambassador addressed "my esteemed Japanese readers" and called them to take note of the fact that Syria is where "the first musical note ever composed was discovered." The Cameroonian ambassador called for investment in his country now that it had become a "pillar of reform."

My first appointment of the day was at the HMV store in Tokyo — an appearance with Janet Klein, followed by a signing and "shake hands" session. Janet and her husband Robert had arrived in Japan days before me and had been holidaying at the coast in an old-fashioned town, sleeping native on the floor and attending a kabuki play.

Executives from both our record labels were waiting for us backstage at HMV. My company, Vivid Sound, has released a compilation CD called "Lone Pine Blues," covered in cartoon graphics of me as a funny old man in spats and top hat. This is supposed to convey the sort of funny old music that I record. Do my Japanese fans know that "Happy," one of the CD's songs, ends with Regina wishing that her lover were deep in the ground because then the wretched cheat will be happy for ever after?

Janet and I shared the stage for 30 minutes; I accompanied her on my ukulele (Ukie had agreed to the trip after much persuasion) as she sang "Hello Bluebird." Then I did "Shake, Rattle & Roll," and the audience of young people clapped along, always smiling. Unnerving — all these undeserved smiles. I come from a land of the glum and the cynical — England.

Afterwards we descended to the floor and signed CDs and shook hands and bowed.

My solo concert took place that evening in a suburb of Tokyo called Shimokitzawa at a club called La Cana. A neighbourhood of narrow streets and no cars, one that in the days before the war would no doubt have been a fantasy of gay lanterns, swishing kimonos, and a general mysteriousness. The club was downstairs and so tiny there was no backstage area, no green room or dressing room. No wonder the signs said "Sold Out!" Instead of chairs there were benches. My backing band, The Rat Orchestra, was excellent: they had learned every note and phrase and nuance of my records — and I was rather shaken: I've never played these exactly like the recordings. We had fashioned the arrangements there and then in the studio. My Bungalow Boys had never performed my songs exactly like the records — the ones that they had played on. I got lost a couple of times. I was amazed, staggered, impressed, humbled.

Instead of singing "Hello, hello, hello!" I substituted "Kampai" and the audience joined in. On every number they clapped along. The Rat leader, Juta, acted as interpreter — for my act is as much speech as music — and after my speech and the deathly silence Juta would translate and then there'd be the reward of peals of refreshing laughter. I called for more "Kampai" and my call was answered by glass after glass of Jim Beam. I toasted Tokyo, Japan, the World, the Universe. For a hundred minutes I kept them happy and they made me ecstatic.

I ended with my own song "Goodnight": *And when the darkness turns to endless night I'll live for ever after through your laughter and smiles.* Never have those words seemed so true and so moving.

Afterwards there was more shake-hands and record signing. Many of the fans had copies of my vinyl albums, even obscure ones like *On The Pier*, only issued in England. Hiroshi hosted me and the Rat Orchestra to a late night dinner at a traditional restaurant where I had to remove my shoes. This was an effort, thanks to Jim Beam. We had dish after dish of unknown substances (to me), and beer after beer. I toasted Japan and its superb culture and in particular this marvelous cuisine. "May I point out," said the Rat Orchestra leader, very politely, "That this is a Chinese restaurant." I'd done it again! I was feeling woozy and barely made it to my room. This time I watched CNN.

Next day, Monday, I again availed myself of the complimentary Beck's breakfast. As I ate and sipped I watched the army of commuters marching to their trains. Suits, ties, dresses. Not one baseball-cap-on-backwards. What a civilized country! I had time to kill so I sat and watched and pondered till Kazumi, the girl who works for Tom's Cabin, arrived to entertain me until Hiroshi could drive me to my next hotel — in nearby Yokohama, where I would rendezvous with Janet and the rest of the Parlour Boys.

Kazumi is a charming girl, always in jeans and a parka, very gamin, like a newsboy. She walked me around noisy Tokyo, guiding me so that I never barged into members of the teeming masses. Nothing but tall new buildings looming and spouting J-pop (Japanese popular music) accompanied by video pictures flashing down from big screens attached to the buildings. Pretty pictures of pretty people of indeterminate sex, like dolls or children, always smiley-smile. Could we ever have fought such a charming smiley race? I never saw an old person. Indeed I was the only oldie around.

Kazumi would like to come to California and study sociology, she told me, as she negotiated our way. We lunched in a noodle bar, where Kazumi, upon my prompting, told me that she had written her college thesis on *The Jazz Singer* (the Jolson version), and the problems of minstrelsy. I dropped the subject. She has seen *The Third Man*; her passion is Jean-Pierre Leaud, the star of many Truffaut movies.

We browsed Tower Records — much better than any of the American versions — where I saw all my records well-displayed. Kazumi found a Japanese book on British Invasion groups in which I got a mention. She translated: apparently I am known as a singer of homosexual songs, or something. She was very sorry. Let us see more sites.

We traveled by subway to Hiroshi's Tom's Cabin office, a smart building somewhere in outer Tokyo. Is there even one old building left in Tokyo? Were all the old ones destroyed in the war? Or is this newness a result of the local adoration of the very, very latest?

Hiroshi was busy with business so I waited in a reception area where I amused myself by selecting CDs from his vast library. His taste is my taste — I listened to Connie Francis and Milton Brown & His Brownies. Eventually Hiroshi emerged from an inner sanctum and we raced to his Honda van and then whooshed down the freeway to Yokohama. I couldn't tell where Tokyo ended and Yokohama began. I did spot a patch of green and even a little bit of river at one point.

Hiroshi dropped me at the hotel, The Business Sun, in a rather seedy and even seamy part of Yokohama. He had to return forthwith for urgent business. We will meet again at 3.15 tomorrow. It was now 5pm. So now here I was alone and with only one word of Japanese: "Kampai." The hotel was horrid: very cramped, a place for midgets. But — oh joy! — there were Janet and Robert's bags neatly lined up in the reception area. They would arrive soon, I felt sure, and rescue me. Two elderly spinster headmistress types manned the reception desk. They could speak no word of English. There was nowhere to hang my clothes in my room. The view from the window was of a wall a few feet away.

So I took a walk, making sure I traveled close to the walls and only went round the block, for fear of getting lost. I walked this block many times. I kept returning, after each round, to see if Janet and Robert had picked up their bags. But no — there sat the bags, complacently orphaned.

I set off one last time. So many eateries and bars, so many strip joints, so little English. Eventually I chose a place that had the word "Cocktails" in the window. It was called "Fu Fu" and the server boys were very attentive, too much so perhaps — androgynous anime boys. I ordered a vodka martini. They understood. Soon I felt high as a kite. The boys metamorphosed into girls. I wrote a waltz song in my head:

"Have a martini! Put two olives in.
Don't be a meany — fill it up to the brim.
Whether it's vodka or whether it's gin
Have a martini and let life begin!"

Emboldened I left and went in search of sensible grub, possibly something American for a change. The local food had a tendency to leave me unsatisfied. I saw a basement dive with a sign: "Grass Roots." Ah! I descended and found myself in a room decorated with low-hanging silver-painted twigs, sheets of corrugated iron and rickety rocking chairs. A sort of bayou atmosphere. When the waiter arrived — another cartoon boy — I pointed at a photo in the menu. It looked like fish and when it arrived it smelled like fish. And so it was — and I ate it up while listening to grunted blues and hot jazz on the sound system. It would have been nice to hear some old Japanese music in Japan. Do we have McArthur and Perry to blame? Or is it in the nature of the people to reject their vintage culture?

I returned to the Business Sun hotel, avoiding the women of the night, ducking my head as I entered my room, putting on the robe, negotiating my way past my bags, finding the tiny bed, taking a Valium, going to sleep.

On Tuesday, in the morning, I was sitting writing up my journal in the reception area, next to a tall receptacle for cigarette butts, and a sign saying "No Smoking In Bed," when out of the elevator stepped Janet and Robert, looking fresh as daisies and altogether All-American. Rescued at last!

For the rest of the trip they protected me — Robert making sure I drank glasses of water to offset the sake, Janet sewing up my vintage suits when they ripped.

The Parlour Boys flew in late that afternoon and we did our first show at Thumbs Up, a club atop a high-rise in Yokohama, another bayou reeker. A success. Every show in the ensuing tour was a success. What can I say? At every show I played a piano, usually a beautiful Yamaha grand. With every performance the band grew tighter and more polished. Too polished? We must never lose our contrariness, ornery-ness, cantankerousness. Our individuality. The Boys, this time, consisted of: Dave Jones (bass), Tom Marion (guitar), and Dan Weinstein (trombone, violin, and euphonium). We got along famously. What can I say? Oh, we were so polite to each other — having had our explosions back in the USA at rehearsals.

Next day we climbed into our respective vans and set off for the next leg of the grand tour. I rode always with Janet and Robert since they had been dubbed the King and Queen. I was the Archbishop of Canterbury. The rest of the Boys rode ahead of us in a smoke-belching van driven ferociously by Hiroshi. Kazumi, our driver, uttering tiny pathetic cries of "Oh!" followed in the Honda. She was having a hard job keeping up with Hiroshi. The countryside soon palled — mountains with scrubby little trees and tunnels forged through. And so on and so forth. I had witnessed and noted all this on our first trip.

Kazumi kept in touch with the racing Hiroshi via her cell phone: "Moshi! moshi!" and "Hi hi hi." We amused ourselves observing odd signs in a kind of distressed English: a restaurant offering "Slow Food" (as opposed to Fast?), a café called Coffee Steak, a strip joint called Guilty Club, a Cow's Café, a hotel advertising "Bridal Suites plus Chapel," a clothes store called Juvenile Delinquent.

Whenever we turned into a gas station the service folk, male and female and uniformed to the nines, would dash out to frantically signal us in and fill us up and clean our windows; all at a brisk pace, almost with a synchronicity seen in Olympic Games swim teams. Meanwhile we would saunter off to the food vendors. I wasn't brave, usually settling for a white bread sandwich. Janet and Robert were adventurous, tasting such delights as bulls' testicles fried in batter and fish eyes in jelly.

In Hiroshima we appeared at the same smart club we'd played in last time. I took Hiroshima in my stride. No visit to the Peace Museum this time. I'd done my penance. The club Quattro is at the top of a glittering and curvy building. As always, excellent sound and lighting, excellent piano — nothing like this in California. The opening band, "Fresh Lemons," sported ukuleles, an accordion, and a comely woman banging melodiously on a set of Trinidadian steel drums. They began with a tip-top version of "Brazil" and soared upwards from there. I was in a transport of delight. Why aren't there bands like this back in the USA? In Japan they have embraced the latest in technology while simultaneously conserving the old songs with love and respect.

After the show, while we were signing CDs and doing the shake-hands, a woman approached me and said, "You are beautiful." What did she mean? My soul or my presence? Or was it the only phrase she knew in English, possibly inspired by the country song by Ray Stevens, "Everything Is Beautiful — in its own way." Still puzzled, I joined our group at a late night restaurant called Okonomigaki: a long counter with stools where the chefs quickly whip up delightful fare of unknown origin at a steel cooking plate right in front of you. Careful not to put your elbows on that plate, as I did.

The grand finale was a haystack of bamboo shoots mixed with fried eggs and I know not what. As we left, at some unearthly hour, a businessman came up and knelt at my feet and took my hand to kiss it. Another person to tell me I'm beautiful? No — he'd mistaken me for an American — Hiroshi explained. The fellow was simply thanking me, as an American, for having given Japan the NFL and Super Bowl.

Our next gig was in the city of Matsuyama. I'm told it was an island though I never really was aware of coast or sea. Korea was hovering nearby. The venue was at The Monk Club, named after Thelonius Monk, the famous black jazz pianist/composer (known in England as "The Loneliest Plunk"). Our hosts greeted us with gift bags of rosemary and guidebooks to the town. They were two dentists with a taste for obscure and naughty songs.

The club turned out to be like someone's living room but instead of library shelves of books they were filled with LPs. This was a record club, very popular in these parts. You go in and order your drink and select an album. Or was this the next club we played? It's all a little hazy now — the gigs are merging into one.

The band got better and better as we progressed up and down Japan, sometimes driving for eight hours at a stretch. Kazumi tried to tell me about her favorite kinds of music and singers but what I understood to be "Beans and Roast Beef" turned out, more prosaically, to be "Bing Crosby." Janet quietly took out her sewing kit and mended a rip in my 1949 gangster suit; Robert enquired as to whether the prunes they'd lent me were having the desired effect.

I do particularly remember the afterglow of our penultimate concert: this was in Osaka at another Club Quattro. A group of fans led us up to the top floor of a swank building and into a world of old-fashioned Japan. Shoes had to be removed; the narrow floors of the corridors were of glass and flowing beneath this glass was a stream full of flashing fishes, gurgling with delight. There were many rooms in peaceful brown tones, of exquisite proportions, rigid angles, slotted wood — no nails used in the making of this palace.

Although none of our fans could speak much English we all got along famously by using body language. One of the women was attired in traditional kimono and sash and even those high stilted wooden shoes, making her shuffle as she walked. I broke out Ukie, who was impatient to join in the revels, and we sang "Kampai." Then, in an adventurous mood, I taught our hosts some WW2 songs — we sang "Hitler Has Only Got One Ball," the men forming an ad hoc rhythm section by banging their chopsticks on the glasses and plates, the women standing up on the bench to join Janet in a line dance. This was definitely a novel cultural event.

Our final concert took place back in Tokyo at yet another Club Quattro. We had come full circle and were now in the centre of What's Happening. The place was packed. I sang "Chattanoogie Shoe Shine Boy," in the style of Jerry Lee Lewis, with the opening act, my old Rat Orchestra pals. The Parlour Boys were joined by our one-time drummer George, wearing a washboard like a bullet-roof vest. He moved to a remote part of Japan a few years ago and loves it, even though he speaks not a word of the language; he's engaged to a sweet local girl who, likewise, speaks not a word of English. "But we have no problem in the bedroom," winked George. He hates the food, never watches TV, and stays mostly at his drum studio or at home where he reads imported American novels. "But I'm so glad to be out of the L.A. rat race, know what I mean?"

At the afterglow party Janet sang and danced on the table tops hotly pursued by a pert little local girl who had earlier introduced herself in this way: "I copy you." And so she has, but in Japanese. It is all too cute but Janet puts up with it, encourages it, even giving the girl the names of 1920s female singers who should be studied: Ruth Etting, Annette Hanshaw, etc.

And so our second tour ended — on a note of triumph: we had had larger audiences than the first time. Hopefully we will return again soon. It seems that the further I stray from my homeland the more I am appreciated. So be it. I have no nostalgia for England — especially as my September tour of my homeland has been cancelled, with the bookers stating they had no interest in me, no knowledge of me. To hell with England! I feel like DH Lawrence.

Besides, my England is rapidly disappearing. My England consisted of people and so many are dying off. The recent death of my Uncle John marks the end of the old generation. Now I am the old generation. Death and decay in all around I see.

Regina was there to meet me at LAX. She had sad news: Ann, the wife of my best friend Chas Sprawson, had been killed in a car accident while I was away. She had flown with a group of her Bridge-playing friends from Gloucestershire to spend a holiday in Crete admiring the flowers that bloom there at Easter. On Good Friday night, in foul weather, she was a passenger in a car on a narrow mountain road when round the corner came another car and there was a collision.

Ann was my age. I remember her from back in my first year at Trinity College, Dublin, 1962. She was the loveliest girl on campus, everyone agreed. I can see her now, walking across Front Square in her shy hunched way, corn hair covering her face. She was very popular with the TCD jazz band, of which I was a member. We were all surprised when Chas, a sports blood and classicist, won her hand. After their marriage they set up a beautiful house in Minchinhampton, deep in the Cotswolds. Ann's decorating taste was impeccable. They had three lovely daughters, all artistic. I visited them many times and went on many picnics and sang many songs with them in loamy rich fields in that distant past in the intoxicating countryside of the England I once loved.

The last time I saw Ann was in January — I hadn't been with her for years — and I joined her and their eldest daughter and Chas for tea in an old-fashioned tearoom in Piccadilly. We laughed as we used to laugh, deeply and replenishingly. Ann was part of the England I miss.

A few days after my return, Regina and I threw our first Springtime Dance at the historic Aztec Hotel in Monrovia, where once Clark Gable and Jean Harlow cavorted and where in later years men used to come to murder their wives. We had a grand turnout; the dance floor of the Mayan Room was filled to capacity; there was some bumping. Our dancers came in a wide variety of costume, from white tie and tails, through royal Ruritanian court dress to hape haole Hawaiian.

The Bungalow Boys surpassed themselves in their strict adherence to dance rhythms: fox trots, waltzes, tangos, even a schottische. This is the only band around these parts that actually plays for dancers — rather than for themselves, in endless jazz solos and riffing in the thump-thump of 4/4 time — and that's why the dancers came from as far as Santa Barbara and San Diego. We even had our own Secret Service agent, Fred.

As a special guest George Probert sat in, literally, blasting away at his soprano sax, stuck in his mouth at a rakish angle like a cigar. Can that man blow! (Now I'm getting rather jazzy). He has recorded not only with the Firehouse Five but also with Bob Scobey and Kid Ory, exemplars of the real jazz — decent Dixieland roots music.

A noble effort by Regina in setting up this affair, and we hope to repeat it. But not for at least another year. Now we must return to the task of finding a safe house in a safe area, hopefully right here in Monrovia. Rollo and Simon are glad we are back. They sit at our feet in peace and comfort, traveling to faraway places only in dreams....

JUNE

These letters seem to generally turn out to be records of the previous month and sometimes memoirs from long ago rather than plugs for future performances. This month I'm going to return to over 40 years ago and write a reminiscence of my student days at Trinity College, Dublin. The reason is that I may be contributing to a book of memoirs by past Trinity students of my generation and so I'll use this Letter as a first draft. Sometimes my rushed first drafts are better — more heartfelt and free from literary affectations — than my published articles.

Actually, I've just finished a rewrite of a new article for *The Oldie*. This one is about 93 year old Bob Mitchell, the organizer of the famous Boy Choir. I wrote about him in a Letter a couple of months ago. I treasure my times with Bob — it's always an adventure. Our last one was at Vitello's restaurant in Studio City where he was accompanying would-be singers in the Green Room on Opera Night. Poor old Bob had to put up with the most awful nonsense — singers conducting him and telling him off when he offered them vocal tips, and soaring off into unknown spaces and then having to land these stray notes— which they only did due to Bob's providing them with a parachute of piano notes to guide them down to a soft landing on a safe chord. What a kind man! On our way back to his digs he reminded me of Vitello's connection with Robert Blake: "He must have been a gentleman — he gave her a Last Supper before, allegedly, polishing her off."

Nothing much happened in May anyway. Regina and I went through the same old motions of looking at Open Houses and coming up empty-handed. The ones in our price range are always too small. It seems that you pay extra for space not style. We just went round a charming 1913 bungalow up the road from us in Monrovia — but, yet again, too cozy. We like Monrovia because it's a well-run city inhabited by like-minded people. In contrast Altadena was like living in the Wild West — lovely old houses and lots of history but gangs and graffiti and the constant thud of hip-hop from roaring cars as throngs of slouching or swaggering baggy pantsers with caps on backwards milled about weighed down by attitude. Diversity? No — more like being smothered to death by the mud of debased cultures.

We did perform at the Shakespeare Club in Pasadena near Suicide Bridge. There was no sign of Shakespeare but lots of good fellowship and a full bar. A ladies club that raises lots of money for the less privileged.

I also appeared on a panel on stage at the Alex Theatre in Glendale for Q & A prior to a screening of "A Hard Day's Night." Gordon Waller — of Peter & Gordon — joined me. We had toured together on a Dick Clark Caravan of Stars in the summer of 1965 at the height of a pop fame. At the Alex show I was amazed to find myself full of praise for the Beatles — as songwriters at the end of the grand tradition of Tin Pan Alley — and for stating this I received a round of applause.

The movie was better than I remembered. I realize now that the whole image of the Beatles as kooky personalities was created by Richard Lester, the film's director. The Beatles were never able to escape that image. In that regard, they were a careful concoction, like the Monkees.

I first saw the film in the Seattle of 1964 when I was on vacation from Trinity College and appearing in a local coffee house as an entertainer from London — "Via Liverpool." I had painted the sign on the coffee house wall myself. The year before I'd been peddling cute British music hall songs in this same student establishment; now, thanks to Beatlemania, I could sing rock & roll without being laughed at as a bowler hat twerp, or derided by the folkies as having sold out to capitalism.

As I watched the film, in the company of my local girl friend — possibly the one who gave me the catchphrase "You turn me on" — I told myself that I too could be a rock & roll star and, by God, next year I would return to America as a conqueror. And I did.

Which brings me to Trinity days — and how I got to be there.

I was supposed to leave my Public School, which meant private and boarding, at the end of the winter term, 1958. I had made a kind of mark at Bryanston, but not through the normal channels — not sport, not serious music, not serious writing, not through academic success. I had made my mark by being funny in school plays, by starting the school's first rock & roll band, by causing scenes with senior masters, by calling the Head Boy a "bugger," and the Headmaster, T.F. Coade, a "philistine" when he dared to disparage my still-wet "action" painting, which, exhibited in the Main Hall, had stained his sports jacket with red paint while he was examining my artwork in closer detail.

A much respected and beloved English Literature master, Wilfred Cowley, had been with the Head at the time of this incident and, when I had defied orders to stay put for the Head to deliver a few words to me and raced off down the Main Corridor, the beloved master had shouted, "I'll get him!" Later I surrendered and asked to see the school psychiatrist, pretending I was having a breakdown. The beloved master and I had never seen eye to eye: although my stories, printed in the School Magazine, had been popular with the boys, he had pronounced them "tedious and laboured." I had declared war on the Staff.

In other words, I had been thoroughly bolshie.

And through this childish behavior I had become something of a hero, to the junior boys. "Can I be both a respectable member of the school, even be a prefect — and also be like Whitcomb?" asked one junior of his housemaster. Looking again at my end of term report for 1958 through senior eyes I sympathize with the attitude of Bryanston's masters. I think their assessments were correct. Judge for yourself:

Maths: He batters at the subject with argumentative fury, impatient with himself, with me, and with the world, when the mystery does not at once unfold.

History: Superbly ingenious, an extraordinary haphazard mind. Nobody can teach him anything if he doesn't choose to be taught.

English: An extraordinary fellow of apparently boundless frivolity. His written style is too conversational. Must improve his reading matter.

Art: Keen on this subject but must begin to realize that there is more to art than speed boats, aeroplanes, guns, soldiers, and sudden death. Once he gets these action subjects out of his system we can then get down to more serious endeavours.

Music: Could be taught to play quite well if he were prepared to practice — but as he says he has no intention of doing this, the decision to stop piano lessons is a wise one.

Housemaster's Report: Has enough intelligence to grow up to be a useful citizen but won't grow up if he can help it. Loses control of himself at least once a day and ceases to be a rational creature. Must learn self-control and resist the temptation to be an exhibitionist.

But at the end of what should have been my final term I achieved a great success in a revue written by us boys. I played King Lear and a camp scoutmaster and was cheered to the rafters of the gym. My father, in the area on his job as a building materials salesman, had stopped by and sneaked a seat at the back. I was so happy that he'd seen the exhibitionist side channeled to good effect. And that Christmas, back at home in our family flat on Putney Heath, I grew nostalgic for Bryanston and wanted to return to the scene of my recent glory. I begged my father to write to the H.M and ask whether I could return for one year and properly redeem myself. Surprisingly, Mr. Coade replied that I would be welcomed back so long as the "volcano was thoroughly extinguished," and that, if so, he had a good part for me in his upcoming summer production of

T.S. Eliot's *Murder In The Cathedral*: I could play a Tempter.

Was I excited! A reprieve, a return to paradise, a turning back of the clock! Childhood extended! To remain a boy when I should have been becoming a man and joining the work force! An escape, a dream come true! A boy who had left the school and then returned for another year was unheard of in the history of Bryanston. Most boys couldn't wait to get out of the hothouse and into the real world.

The summer of 1959 was a glorious one for me. The intoxicatingly lush countryside of Dorset made me reel in romanticism. I was able at times to lie in the long grass with my firm friends and assess the scene as if I were a camera, or a god far above. I couldn't bear for this dreamy time to end. When I said goodbye — together with Mr. Coade who was also leaving after almost thirty years of service to youth — I was already in a sorry state. This continued back at home in the autumn of 1959.

Without the timetabled days of Bryanston, without the structured world, the organization in which every hour was accounted for in advance, where bells told you where next to go, without all this support I was completely at sea. What to do with this new and free time? Where were my friends? Why weren't they at home when I rang? How could I spend my time? Never mind — there were films to be made, songs to be written, books, too. I had so many things I needed to create that I went into a cold sweat and wound up doing nothing except brooding and wishing I were back in the safety of school.

Note: I just Googled T. F. Coade and found only a paltry two pages, mostly concerning his book, "The Burning Bow." Compare this with the 70,000 or so entries, nice and nasty, on me, his contrary pupil. I'm not proud of this. I'm amazed that a headmaster with so much influence on so many boys is a mere mention on the Internet. As for the other masters who played such a great part — indeed, who terrified or infuriated me — in my life at Bryanston, I can find hardly a mention. If you want to see what an idyllic setting Bryanston sits in, try Googling the school. Why you might even send your children there — that is, if you have $50,000 a year to spare on education. Anyway, it's now all sensible and modern, and co-educational, so all the mystery, horror and romanticism of emotional deprivation and frustrated passion, is gone with the wind.

My parents, always bending to my every desire, tried to find a way for me to enter show business. I had told them I wanted to be a film director and at once. Among their closest friends was a couple, John and Janie Bryan, whom they had known since before the war. Janie had worked as a film editor in the 1930s with David Lean;

John had been an art director, his sets having won him an Oscar. He had designed *Oliver Twist* and *Great Expectations* for David Lean; he'd gone on to be a producer (*The Purple Plain*, *The Million Pound Note*, *The Spanish Gardener*); he'd let me visit his sets and lunch at the studio with Peter Finch; he was grooming me to become a film technician in the last great days of the British studios. I called him "Uncle."

And when I left school, he promised, he'd get me a job on a production. *Tunes Of Glory*, a picture to be directed by his old associate from the Lean days, Ronald Neame, was to start shooting at Shepperton Studios in February, 1960. Hang on and he'd find me a position.

Meanwhile, I had to fill in a few months. Harrods department store accepted me as a sales assistant in their record department. But as usual, I had complaints: the thick carpets affected my flat feet, I didn't get along with my fellow workers, I despised the pop pap I had to sell. And at Christmas time, instead of joining my fellow staffers at their party in an inner office, I volunteered to man the counter. While they were living it up on sherry and crisps I gave away the inventory as gifts to startled customers. Presley, Adam Faith, Nat King Cole? Take it with my compliments — and a merry Christmas to you!

At Shepperton studios I was the lowest of the low — a Fifth Assistant Director. Translation: tea boy and dogsbody. I failed to properly Roneo (duplicate) tomorrow's scenes, failed to properly collate them, spilled hot tea on the director and producer at an important office meeting, discussed the art of Pudovkin and Eisenstein in a loud voice on the set as Alec Guinness and John Mills were preparing a scene — implying that *Tunes Of Glory* was commercial piffle compared with these Russian masters of the cinematic art.

As a result, the First Assistant Director, Colin Brewer, whose job it was to order "Quiet on the set!" in a loud voice prior to the suited and gentlemanly director Neame's hushed announcement of "Action," added this to his order: "Quiet on the set! And shut up, Ian!" I lent my Grundig tape recorder to Alec Guinness so that he could rehearse his Scottish accent. He was grateful in a hushed but impersonal way. I used to watch him quietly prepare his next scene in a corner of the set. John Mills was the opposite — simply sailing into his scenes. We were all allowed to watch the daily rushes and we agreed that Mills was chewing up the scenery. How wrong we were! His performance is a classic.

The stunt men used to shock me by opening up dirty magazines in my face or else goosing me. According to them, most of the male actors in the film were "poofs." I shared a taxi home with Dennis Price but he never touched me. Instead we talked about school and he told me he'd been a "dry bob" at Radley — meaning he hadn't been in the river rowing team. That was as close as I got to the creators. I learned nothing. The female production office assistant, Miss Whitty, referred to me as "The boy" with a sneer.

As soon as *Tunes* wrapped up John Bryan got me a job in the editing room at Pinewood for his new picture, a comedy called *There Was a Crooked Man*, starring the very popular Norman Wisdom. Here again I failed utterly. I had no interest in hanging up the "trims" — the strips of film of each angle taken; I wanted action not this dull routine of gluing bits of film together for rough cuts. They gave me menial jobs outside of film gluing such as finding out what a taxi fare from Shepherd's Bush to Piccadilly would have cost in 1945. This I failed to accomplish. The editor, Peter Hunt, always immaculate in suit and white gloves, gave up on me. "Typical Bryanston arrogance," he declared. I think he went on to direct a Bond film. You can check on all these people online through the Movie Data Base.

In the canteen I generally sat alone, but once the first assistant editor condescended to engage me in conversation. I told him how currently I was enthralled with the work of boogie-woogie pianist Albert Ammons. "That stuff is mere musical masturbation," he sniffed and turned away to talk to someone else. I remember his name to this day, Desmond Lowden, and that he limped badly. Eventually, I was told to report to "Uncle" John Bryan in his office. "We're very disappointed in you," he said.

But he was kind enough to find my one last job in the British Cinema — as an assistant editor in a documentary company called Athos Films in Soho Square, in the heart of London's West End. This turned out to be a little more creative: I worked on a BBC film about Leni Riefenstahl and was thus able to study her films carefully and realize how wickedly beautiful she was. One day the chief editor took a break and left me to edit a sequence. I waited breathlessly outside the screening room as the cut was projected later. Howls of anger. "Ian! Get your cards and coppers and leave!" ordered a red-faced Bert Eggleton, one of the bosses. I had glued strips of film upside down, right way round, upside down. The result was an art film that was not appreciated. Clearly the technical side of the film industry was not for me.

In fact, all this time I had been taking evening classes in order to sit for an A Level exam in history which would qualify me for entry into Trinity College, Dublin. What I had realized early on in my film career was that I missed school; I wanted my adolescence to be extended, perhaps forever. University seemed to be the answer. Anything to postpone adulthood.

At Bryanston I had been warned off any ambitions I might have had about going to a proper university: Oxford or Cambridge. My tutor, Mr. Dingle (I'll never forget the names of these wretches, as you can see), waved my ambitions away: "Don't even consider it. We're aiming our big guns at Oxford and Cambridge."

Why Trinity? Well, it was easier to be admitted. All I had to have was a History A Level diploma. My other two A Levels, achieved at Bryanston, were in Art and English. Quite useless. My uncle had an oil industry colleague in Dublin, Albert Le Brocquy, who had been at Trinity in the days of the great uprising of 1916. A lunch was arranged; I was charmed by the old man. That was that. So in the evenings I studied with a private tutor in a house near Harrods: a Mr. Davies who packed his pipe with great care, fiddling with it like an artist as we read aloud from our European history books "Nice style," he'd comment every now and then as we read G.M. Trevelyan. After a few classes and much reading I took the exam in a big hall near London Airport. Afterwards, as a reward, my mother treated me to a real novelty: a full Chinese lunch in Putney. Plenty of crispy noodles and sweet fried pork, every bit as tasty as fish and chips.

The examiners awarded me an A Level with "Distinction." My Bryanston A Levels had taken two years of study. This homemade one took a few months. Which shows how most of my time at school had been spent in my own music making and mucking about with my gang. And this, of course, is what I wanted to continue at Trinity under the guise of scholarship. I had chosen just the right place, as I was to discover in the autumn of 1961 when I arrived in Dublin as a Junior Freshman in Modern History & Political Thought.

And on this note, this cliffhanger, I will leave my memoir till next month. I meant to take us right inside TCD and end up with my rock success. But something tells me I've covered this in past Letters. So next month I'll write about my first year at TCD.

From "The Trinity Handbook" (circa 1960):
Living in rooms in college is a unique and complex experience. The walls, once adorned, become the mirror of the student resident's personality. How depressing they can appear on a murky, joyless morning, but how splendid and intimate at night. For only when evening falls can rooms really come into their own. Round college fires, over supper, world problems, politics, religion and sex, in that order, are discussed far into the night, while Beethoven or Brubeck tries to make himself heard. Perhaps the only feature common to every resident's day is Commons, where between well-rounded sentences there is an ordered camaraderie which will remain in the memory when the rest of College life is forgotten.

JULY

July 10 is Proust's birthdate and Jelly Roll Morton's deathdate. It's also my birthday and I happen to enjoy the work of both these varmints. Maybe we have something in common: one was a gossip and the other a braggart, but the joy is in the work.

This birthday makes me 65 so I am a genuine old codger in the flesh, not just in attitude. I've been a malcontent, even a curmudgeon, for many years. Now I have the lines and wrinkles that befit grouchiness. You'll not see much of this in the website photo gallery. Oh no! Up there, I keep posting older pictures so as to keep the Dorian Gray image going.

But the upside of old age is that I now get Social Security money and Medicare benefits as well as a senior rate at the Athletic Club. This lowering of our expenses will help offset the speeding ticket I was handed last week at the tail end of our otherwise therapeutic mini-holiday here in California.

Yes, it was unfair, as they always are: for most of the trip Regina had been driving like a skilled demon, allowing me to sit back and listen to lovely old music via the CD player, and also to repeatedly play cassettes of the loads of Irving Berlin obscurities that Dick Hyman keeps sending me to learn for the upcoming Oregon Festival of American Music in Eugene, Oregon, this August, to which you're all coming, I know. "You Cannot Make Your Shimmy Shake On Tea," "If I Had My Way I'd Live Among The Gypsies," etc — great stuff that can swiftly whisk you away from mundane matters like Baghdad.

But on the last leg I had taken the wheel and was beetling along happily in a daze of Billy Cotton & His Band music. I'd played "Big Head" several times, noting it might be a good addition to my repertoire at Janet Klein's shows. Everybody could shout out "Big Head!" at the appropriate moments. Audience participation always works well — witness, "We All Went Up The Mountain" where I get people to crouch beneath their seats at the start of the climb and then stand up and stretch and wave when we reach the top. After that we start the descent and return to the original crouching position, making sure we've stopped to help any stranded mountaineers or auctioneers we might have encountered on the way down.

This number never fails and always fills me with a feeling of power such as Hitler or Mussolini must have experienced when on the rant at a public meeting. Of course, my form of exhibitionism is quite footling and does no harm.

So there I was tootling and beetling and in another and much better world — Doreen Stephens, Cotton's female vocalist, was singing "They're Changing Guards At Buckingham Palace"— when after rounding a slight bend I suddenly saw a parked highway patrol car. I glanced at the speedometer — something I hadn't been doing while Cotton commanded my attention — and saw I was over the 80 mph mark. I slowed down — too late! On came the lights and the game was up.

He was a calm and polite young officer, but like them all, unbending and unreasonable. Rollo only barked half-heartedly, a good sign. Must be a nice man at heart. Rollo senses bad people immediately…………..

A few days ago I was walking him down our street and we approached a shuffling Arab or middle eastern man or someone who isn't like-minded—I've passed this fellow lots of times: constantly shuffling down our street smiling about something. Rollo normally does a friendly lunge at folks but this time he sensed something nasty about this street gypsy so he accompanied the lunge with a stern bark. The man jumped and then stood back and accused Rollo of biting him. How could he have bitten you—there's no tear in your clothing. "He bite me!"

And the fellow pulled his trousers down right there on our street. He had a disgusting flaccid grey skin, the color of condemned brisket; I could see blotches here and there. Selecting one particularly darkly diseased blotch, he announced that that was the result of the bite. "And if it make blood I call in the police and they call animal control and—abra cadabra!—No more dog!" I apologized profusely, I begged, I almost kneeled to this lump of lies and unreasonableness. "Thassallright!" he mumbled and off he shuffled into the clammy haze of the San Gabriel Valley……………

So Rollo sniffs out the bad people. And this officer was not bad, just automaton-like. He told me his radar gun had clocked me at 81mph. Did he know that the British invented radar? He's giving me a ticket. But, officer, I was driving in the slow lane and I was doing that because we've been tailgated by hoggish SUVs this entire trip. If I went within the speed limit I'd have been rear-ended many times. What should I do? "Sir, I am aware that the other cars are speeding but you are the one I'm ticketing. It's just bad luck. Now you be careful and have a safe trip. The Santa Maria courts are kind, sir. You will possibly be able to pay by mail." But I haven't had a ticket in years, I'm about to be 65, I have to get my license renewed next year.

"You have a safe trip, sir." Regina's hand was firmly on mine. Always a good diplomatic brake. She had last used this when that IRS paralegal was sneering about how I'd like to be Elton John, wouldn't I, because Sir Elton was a success.

We proceeded on our way in an orderly fashion. I never want to hear "Changing The Guard At Buckingham Palace" again. At Calabasas we pulled into a palatial shopping centre full of white columns and shades of ancient Greece, a spot recommended by Regina. You need a tall and calming cup of Starbucks' misto, she said.

Well, we were sitting outside at a table, refreshing ourselves, with Rollo ever so well behaved, when a thin-haired senior decided to stop by. And when I say stop I mean stop. He wouldn't go away. He peppered me with questions: "Do I detect an accent? Yes I do! Are you a cockney, a limey, a bloke, or a chap?" Not waiting or even wishing an answer—the man was spouting—he carried on: he knew a lot of Britishers, some of them geniuses. Take Peter Noone – he'd met him—why, he lives not far away and he's a bona fide genius, not only does he sing and dance but he wrote all those hit sings like "I'm Henery The Eighth," yes, he wrote 'em.

Regina had had her foot firmly on mine all the way through this harangue. But I couldn't contain myself anymore. I stood up and announced:

"'I'm Henery The Eighth I Am' was written by Fred Murray and R.P. Weston and published in 1911 by Francis Day & Hunter. It became a hit through the untiring performances of Harry Champion. So there!"

"Hey, are you in the music business! You know what? Next you'll be telling me that you used to be a rock star!"

We upped and left at this point. I mean, if he'd condescended like this to a black or Latino he could have been brought before a court. But it's the lot of the British to be the latest whipped minority.

I got a little amelioration from the message center on our return: three people had heard me mentioned by Rush Limbaugh on his radio show. Three people thus revealing their conservative bent. What had he said? He was talking about how the Democrats were getting all in a lather about some matter: "Yep, they're running round breathing 'huh, huh, huh' like Ian Whitcomb on his record." Not forgotten after all! A household name—in certain households, but I bet they're spotlessly clean.

And now for the second part of my reminiscence of student days at Trinity College Dublin, 1961................

I couldn't bear to travel alone so I enlisted my childhood friend Speedy McKeachie to accompany me to this foreign country. I'd known Speedy since I was nine or ten; he lived with his parents in the same block of flats as our family: Wildcroft Manor, mock-Tudor 1930s on the edge of Wimbledon Common. Speedy was American—his father was a bigwig at the London branch of an American advertising agency. Together with my younger brother Robin we used to play Cowboy & Indian games out on the common in the early evening, inspired by what we'd just seen on BBC television on Children's Hour—Hopalong Cassidy and other riders of the range. We also had a game called North & South Armies in which I always volunteered to play the Confederates, possibly because I liked being the loser, the underdog. Robin, being the youngest, used to have to put up with being the eternal Indian. Men in dirty mackintoshes lurked in nearby bushes but they never bothered me. I was fat but happy. They bothered my brother but that's a hushed-up episode involving the police and my memory is hazy or suppressed.

I think we were still playing these games up into our late teens. I continued to play them in my mind even into the 1960s. I kept telling myself I was a late teenager who hadn't properly experienced what I'd read a teenager should experience, that I should start behaving like one before it's too late, should be rocking and rolling and being generally bolshie, and shouting out "Bird!" whenever a girl came into view.

But by October 1961, when I was supposed to report to Trinity as a Junior Freshman in Modern History & Political Thought, I had just reached the age of 20 so I could no longer pretend to be a teenager nor play cowboy games in the bushes. Why was I studying History when all my interests were in music? Or, to be more precise, "music of a kind" (as my tutor at Bryanston School had put it, he being classically inclined). Looking back, I regret that I didn't enroll in Trinity's fine music department and be forced to learn to read and write music just as well as I could read and write English (Although, oddly enough, I'm still not clear as to what an adjective or adverb is, even though I suppose I use them all the time).

Speedy McKeachie traveled with me on the Aer Lingus plane from London Airport to Dublin. This was my first commercial flight but I can't remember being excited about it. I must have been absorbed in feelings of dread about what was in store for me in this alien country. Must have been wondering what on earth had possessed me to leave my country of origin and venture into this strange land about which I knew little.

There were no Irish connections in our family. In fact, my grandfather, whom I much admired, was a Cromwellian—which means that he regarded the Irish as barbaric and only fit to be conquered. England had been half-heartedly attempting to conquer the Irish for donkey's years. As with the Scots, we gave up ever believing we'd subdue such savages into meekness, into Little Englanders or passive natives. My grandfather told me that, like the blacks, the Irish were essentially lazy, needing merely a jug of ale and a loaf of bread for satisfaction.

On arrival in Dublin Speedy and I made our way to my assigned digs. On first look Dublin appeared to be a dirty city, not at all fair like in the song. The digs were in a grim terrace of Georgian brick buildings in one of the city's many squares. Of course, the whole city had been built and designed by the English—grand and solid and imposing—but the rulers and aristocrats were no longer there and instead the place seemed like some deserted Roman Empire outpost in which the barbarians had taken root, spreading their stringy tentacles everywhere, climbing grimy and sweaty over noble architecture with their sacks of potatoes and meat patties, artworks that had been fashioned by reasonable people in a vanished age of high civilization.

What right had I to have such thoughts when in my luggage I carried a Dansette record player and a collection of LPs featuring Hank Snow, Muddy Waters and George Formby? What did I know about the grand old culture?

Pembroke Square was my address and we walked up the stone steps and rang the brass bell. A pinched-faced woman answered it: Mrs. Eagar, my future landlady, welcomed me in school-marm fashion, with much sniffing and looking me up and down in judgment. She showed me where I'd be sharing an upstairs room with a fellow undergraduate, an Englishman from Cambridgeshire, one Beverly Lovelace. He had already reported in and was hanging up his gaudy school blazer with its ghastly gold stick-out badge. He was a stringy tall chap with a long nose from which hung a dewdrop, trapped like an icicle but in imminent danger of falling.

I avoided this disgusting sight to take in the miserable room with its stinking oil heater, leaning wardrobe, rough wooden table with washbasins, and enormous and ancient commode. I could see that my roommate had been taking advantage of this commode: there was a steaming turd resting in it, the size of a pocket battleship.

Avoiding this exhibit, I turned my attention to the walls: framed pictures of fierce-looking Irishmen (patriots who'd lost their lives terrorizing my countrymen, very often blown to bits by their own bombs—as I learned later in my studies in both classroom and bar). Dominating the walls was a large reproduction of the Manifesto for Irish Independence, published by rebels in 1916. Mrs. Eagar rattled off the first part of this pompous document, but after a while even she wilted from the purple rhetoric and announced perkily and in a lilt worthy of Molly Malone: "I'll tell ye more later but now I must be away a-making of yer tea. Ye'll be getting black pudding and soda bread, of course."

Speedy informed her that we had other plans. I shook hands with my future roommate, Beverly (What an appallingly common name!) who was standing dumbfounded, scratching his crotch (behind the fabric of which was an enormous and sexually-dormant weapon, as I was to learn as the year went by—why is that that ugly men have such enormous dongs?). I made a mental note to wash my hands as soon as I could—- for fear that earlier dewdrops from his nose might still be still lingering on his hand.

Speedy and I took a taxi into Dublin to have a decca at Trinity itself and to get a meal.

Trinity was impressive alright, what with the statues of Burke and Co and the square where Oscar Wilde had had rooms and the Front Gate porters dressed like huntsmen and all saluting you and calling you "Sir." But the surrounding streets looked like a set from a Sweeney Todd, The Demon Barber of Fleet Street, the Tod Slaughter version, not the dreadful Sondheim musical.

Everyone seemed downtrodden or else clerkly, there were so many priests in black and nuns like swans, buses careened round the corners on two wheels, with conductors crossing themselves in religious fervor. Beggars were all over the place. Drunks would be striding along one second and then suddenly stop, look at their watch, and fall like stiff planks straight onto the pavement, with a cry of "Next!"

There was an imposing statue of Lord Nelson in the middle of the main street. This made me feel at home for a moment. Every other business seemed to be a cinema—advertising films that had first played in England years ago: Humphrey Bogart and Mickey Rooney and The Marx Brothers. Each picture palace had a long queue lining the wall, huddled up from the constant drizzle. As we passed The Royal Regal I couldn't help but notice a commissionaire dressed like a Russian general walking up and down the line telling the plot of the film taking place inside. "And now Mr. Bogart is pulling out a gun with a nasty sneer to his face—wait and I'll run inside and take a peek and come right back to tell you the rest."

Speedy and I found, between the cinemas, a restaurant: The Green Rooster, really no more than a coffee shop or snack bar. But outside it was a riot of flashing neon and seemed American in a blowsy way. We must have been hovering in uncertainty because suddenly a massive man with a beefy face emerged out of the shadows. He looked over six feet and was clad in a blue military overcoat that overflowed onto the pavement. This coat was stuck with medals and ribbons and silver hanging ropes; clamped down on his head was an oversized peaked cap wrapped round with gold filigree. Saluting us he boomed: "Come in my fine gentlemen and welcome to our hostelry! Your pleasure is our desire." "What have you got?" asked the always direct and practical Speedy. "Your lordship, you just name it! We got fish, burgers, black and white pudding, peas all mushed how you likes 'em, and everything comes with chips!" We went in.

The following day Speedy left for London and I faced my first breakfast at Mrs. Eagar's. This was a general fry-up and was the first of what was to be the norm: fried bread, egg, tomato, black pudding (a sausage containing dubious animal insides). That was the main course: we were started off with an hors d'oeuvre of porridge

— you could stick a fork in it and the fork wouldn't budge if you threw a salt cellar at it, but I didn't because I was still in a state of culture shock.

After a few digs into the porridge I came up with a clipping from a local newspaper, tasting as good as the gruel. Opening it up later I found it was an obituary of an IRA commander who had killed a lot of British officers during The Troubles during the early 1920s. Perhaps Mrs. Eagar was operating a propaganda campaign as a sort of initiation.

With stomach gurgling and complaining I set off for my first lectures. Beverly Lovelace had disappeared. I never found out what course he was taking. We hardly ever saw each other. I got on one of the buses I'd seen careening around corners the night before — and discovered what made them nearly topple over: when passing a religious building at a corner the conductor and driver would be obliged to cross themselves, the driver somehow making his vehicle bend in supplication. An unnerving experience but one that I grew used to in the ensuing years.

After several enquiries as to where junior freshmen in Modern History were supposed to assemble, I located the venue: the Museum Building in one of the squares that made up Trinity. The university had been founded in Good Queen Bess's days and was a Protestant bastion in a Catholic Republic. It resembled a broken down Oxbridge college, but I was happy to be any kind of undergraduate, happy to be an overgrown boy delaying the day I should have to enter the jungle of real work.

In the huge marble hall of the Museum Building I was shocked to see the motley collection of what would be my fellow students: pasty-faced and plug-ugly Northern Irish in their old school blazers and chattering in that impenetrable and querulous accent; also a gaggle of blacks in smart business suits, carrying umbrellas and cackling high-pitched.

I didn't dare approach any of them to ask whether this was the right place for our meeting. But then I spied a tall blonde Viking-looking chap in big glasses and wearing a reassuring World War Two flying jacket — who I felt must be English and therefore must be worth talking to, one who would understand me. I approached him — or did he approach me?

Anyway, we guessed from first sight we were kindred spirits. And we were. We talked about Ian Fleming and James Bond, my saviour's deep and resonant voice beating out the babble of Ulster accents and African bleating. I had found a fellow soul in this alien environment. We immediately became friends — and indeed Jeremy Lewis has been a best friend ever since. He described that first encounter in his memoir, *Playing For Time:*

I am a "stout, disreputable figure with prehensile fingers, a very loud brown and white tweed jacket and a rolling, nautical gait." I don't remember that jacket but it sounds promising. I suppose I do have long fingers — I like to think of them as artistic, a sensitive — and others have noted the way I sway when I walk. This walk was no doubt due to flat feet and fatness. I was very aware of being overweight and a possible figure of fun. On top of this I had a stammer. But none of these handicaps stopped my rushing, impatient energy.

In the lecture hall, I sat on the same bench as Jeremy and was introduced to his roommate, David Shaw, a swarthy, almost Semitic fellow, but who had a decent English accent and a fine umbrella. We waited awhile until all of a sudden in strode our Head of History, Professor Moody. An imposing figure what with his big head and gown floating behind him, keeping company with his flowing white hair. We were all in our gowns too — I had hastily donned mine as I entered the hall, for to be without one was to be "academically nude."

We waited for the great man to speak: "Students!" he bellowed, with only the faintest Irish accent. "I pose a simple question. What is history?" There was a pause and we knew better than to answer this rhetorical question.

"What is history?"

A rather common Thames Valley voice piped up: "I could have a go...." I was horrified to see it was a callow youth of the Beverly Lovelace type and he was sitting right there on our bench.

Professor Moody rightly chose to ignore the interruption: "I'll tell you what history is! HISTORY IS THE PAST!"

Then he rambled on while we mulled this over. Finally he stopped. "There will be an examination at the end of your first year. You must make the midway mark in order to continue your studies.. Any questions? No. Fine, fine..."

Our embarrassing bench mate spoke again. "But sir—what if you get 49%? Will you be kind enough to let us continue?"

Moody glared at him for a long moment and then marched out with a dramatic sweep of his gown. Jeremy, me, and David repaired to a bar for some ale and pork pies. I invented a delicious lunch consisting of a soft cheese called Galtee mashed into a brown sauce called T.D.— the local equivalent of H.P. sauce, a British mixture named after our own Houses Of Parliament.

Pub lunches were to be our ritual for the rest of our student days. We breezed or snoozed through lectures. We uttered catch phrases like "Leges Henrici" and "sake and soke" and "Skinner V. The East India Company" as if they were magical incantations; we knew there had been a famous Battle of The Cabbage Patch and that priests had a medieval habit of creeping from field to field and bog to bog; we were asked to write an essay answering the question

"Were The Early Irish Tribal In Nature?" Eventually some of our lectures moved into the bars.

I was to spend most of my early days in the company of Jeremy and David, sometimes following their ways and views, sometimes resisting (for example, when they decided to wear Churchillian boiler sits and false beards in public). But as time went by and I lost weight and found my feet in college society and in Dublin clubs, I spent more time with the local jazz players and blues fiends, eventually founding my own rock band, Bluesville, and making a name in college and in Dublin as a beat merchant. And even a name as a sexy youth. A chest expander and a diet had effected this. By the end of my time at TCD I had made a record that had flown to Number 8 in the American hit chart. And I had received a note from one of my fans, which Jeremy and David affixed to the wall of our college room: "Dear Ian, I would like to have intercoarse (sic) at your earliest convenience. Yours, Moira."

AUGUST

It's Saturday morning and I dreamed last night that our neighbours had stuck a green metal gate — complete with lock and chain — in the middle of our tall wooden fence in the old house in Altadena. Were they intending to sally through and visit us with bowls of raspberries and cream, heaped with sugar from a bag of Tate & Lyle?

Or were they intending to stake out and size up their newly appropriated land? And how would our student renters deal with this? I informed Regina, in the dream, and she smiled a "told-you-so" smile: give them an inch and they'll take a mile. I had never stood up to them back when we lived there, she reminded me. Over two years ago, two years.....

But Regina was impressed by my show of action the other night when we were returning from a gig at the Hammer Museum in Westwood. The Ventura freeway (I never go by numbers, I like to humanize the freeways) was at a standstill — some dreadful multi-car, multi-body parts accident ahead; the waltz of a million police lights in dancing colors. We remained in line obediently.

However, to the right, in the emergency vehicle lane, were cheats trying to queue barge by zooming down the lane and then edging in ahead. And compliant fools were letting them get away with it. Regina kept within inches of the law-abiding car ahead. Just as we thought, a car in the emergency lane started edging in to make us stop and let them take their cheating place.

I wasn't having it — but I made a survey of the occupants. Latinos, yes — but no males so no danger of being shot when I let fly my invective. My employment of four letter words surprised both Regina and myself. Leaving aside the street lingo, what I told them was that we weren't letting them in — indeed we didn't care if they crashed into us because we have a beat-up old Honda whereas their vehicle looked like its hubcaps and low suspension and hood ornaments had been given tender loving care on many a weekend: thus they wouldn't be inclined to blemish it in a collision.

I embellished my address with a few more four-letter words spoken at high volume in order to round off the argument. The Latino girl driver was amazed. Then she uttered a seemingly extraordinary statement:

"Do I know you? No, I don't know you!"

On reflection I suppose that she said this because my short stubby words are regularly used by her circle and thus she was surprised to find them used by a stranger.

Regina was very impressed by my boldness. We celebrated back "home" with brut champagne.

For my 65th birthday Regina gave me a weapon to deal with anti-social situations: a gizmo that attaches to my key ring — so I can whip it out and click at an offending TV set, whooshing it into blackness and silence. You know, those annoying TVs in bars blaring out sports and news and reality shows and all at the same time.

Well, we were in a really friendly local Mexican restaurant the other night and we'd had a really well served dinner. I boasted to the company about my gizmo and they didn't believe me. So, as we were leaving, I fired it fast at the TV set in the bar. Larry King was up there in his suspenders talking serious matters —- suddenly he was disappeared. Did I run for cover fast! I hid behind an SUV in the parking lot. I felt so guilty.

What I really need is a gizmo for turning off cell phones. Apparently you can buy them, but they're illegal. Another way we waste our nights and days is watching YouTube. Someone introduced me to this and now I tune in far too much. People post videos of themselves or, more to our point, of old entertainers. I've watched George Formby, Fats Domino and Bill Haley. Of course, I popped my name in and up came my 1965 *Shindig* appearance in which I sang "You Turn Me On." So far 155 people have watched this clip and two have posted comments: "The strangest hit of the 60s and he's really camping up..... Read Ian's biography and find out he's not so weird."

Regina has gone north to Stanford to be part of a Waltz Week, with a little Swing thrown in, under the direction of our old friend Richard Powers, the social dance maven. So I am "batching" it — and trying to do all my daily duties: I managed to inject Simon The

Cat with his life-supporting fluid yesterday in the part of the kitchen that has now the look of a hospital. In the night, in bed, I let him clamber on top of me so he can start that steady purr of contentment; but when I turn, telling him I've had enough and must sleep, he gets ratty and hisses and hits and bites me. Sometimes he attacks Rollo for no reason with swinging (de-clawed) paws but Rollo takes it all in his stride. In the end the night is calm and the three of us go into our respective dreams.

The woman in the old boarding house opposite our bedroom is peculiar. She leaves her kitchen door open permanently and I can also see clear into her bedroom. No shame. From either party. I watched her last night pairing off with another woman, both in identical black outfits. After sizing each other up like wrestlers they left the room and I hoped I'd next see them in the open door kitchen. But, alas, no. What were they about to get up to? The woman, in her thirties I'd guess, keeps changing her hair color. She's not pretty but she does have a sturdy body.

She spends a lot of time sitting outside her kitchen door on a wooden landing, smoking, or else talking loudly into a mobile phone. God, she's loud. A few weeks ago she set out festive tables and chairs, with towers of paper cups, and buckets full of plastic cutlery and party favors. But nobody came to the party, except a black woman and her baby. The party set-up is still there, looking rather forlorn. Dusty leaves are gradually blanketing the site of what should have been a terrific evening. And this abandoned festive site has been joined recently by three Tiki metal torches that flame through the night, causing Regina to worry about our safety in case a fire breaks out. This morning, as I rose alone, scattering animals from the bed, I was relieved to see that the Tiki torches were extinguished.

This is my morning ritual:

I go to the bathroom where I sit and read. Fittingly, the permanent book there is volume two of our friend Jim Dawson's gathering of facts on farts. I peruse the opening chapter, a refresher course on the constituents in a fart: three-fifths is odorless gas, the unpleasantness is created by trace amounts of ammonia, hydrogen sulfide and skatole. I'm none the wiser but better informed. I turn to some easier material — the joke section: what does a gay man call a fart? Answer: a mating call.

I reflect that this joke is a variation of one collected in J.Legman's famous book, *Rationale Of The Dirty Joke*, in the section dealing with flatulence and sex: a Frenchman is making slow but skilful love to a girl, starting at her forehead and working down methodically item by item. He has reached the area beneath her neck when, in her excitement, she lets fly a corker of a fart. "Be patient, mon ami!" commands the artist-lover. "I will get to you presently." Legman annotates this story with the fact that it was collected in

Brooklyn on February 2, 1942.

After the bathroom exercise I repair to the kitchen where I down a Lovastatin (keeps the cholesterol down) and Propecia (does double duty as a prostate pacifier and claims to keep your hair on) with orange juice drunk straight from the carton – when Regina's away or not looking. Then it's walk time for Rollo who stretches his legs in anticipation. His leash is equipped on the lines of an Everest attempt: attached is a bag containing treats, a muzzle, and a fabric bag that will hold water; there's also a round plastic affair that dispenses plastic bags for collecting his biggies. Monrovia is such a squeaky clean city: picking up dogs' mess is a must — you never know when you're being watched. On the walk I let Rollo lead — there's no other way, he simply tugs me along, allowing passersby to make their age-old and tiresome joke about the dog taking the master for a walk.

Next it's off to the Pasadena Athletic Club, nine miles down the road. On the commuter-clogged drive I play a cassette containing song demos for my upcoming concerts at the Oregon Festival of American Music. I have over a dozen Irving Berlin numbers, well known and obscure, to learn. The demos were made by that renowned pianist Dick Hyman, singing in a voice similar to Mr. Berlin's. I told Dick this but he didn't take it as a compliment. I must say that though I'm happy to learn "You Cannot Make Your Shimmy Shake On Tea" I find it hard to digest the later super-patriot stuff that Berlin turned out after he started hob-nobbing with Presidents and Generals. I mean would you, in today's climate, like to go on stage and give voice to: "This is a great country, a great country....Hats off to America, the land of the free and the brave!....If this is flag waving, can you think of a better one to wave?" This from the man who in 1910 was writing double-entendres relating to the size of black genitalia, as in "Alexander And His Clarinet," another song I have to learn, and am happy to learn.

Be that as it may, after skillful negotiating with SUVs that tailgate, I arrive at the Athletic Club for my morning exercise, culminating in a swim. The rumor has been confirmed that the greedy millionaire family that runs the club has sold it to equally greedy Iranians who intend to pull the institution down and build condos. Pasadena is awash in condos as it is. Has the family who owns the venerable Athletic Club no sense of social responsibility? They already have oodles of money and don't need anymore. Couldn't they stipulate in the sale of the club (that they are no longer interested in running) that the buyer must continue it as a health club? After all, the place thrives and makes money. And what a great social gathering center! : there's Tony The Hat who wanders around the men's locker room naked and ranting of Shakespeare and the bad men he, Tony, bumped off in the old days; there's personal trainer Lenny who talks ten-a-penny as he takes you through your exercises, telling of his latest radio show, the one where he gets in touch with the dead and tells the listener that, yes, his late mother is enjoying heaven but at the moment she has a nasty cold; and there are police chiefs and lawyers and successful market players to give you free advice even as you avert your eyes from their football bellies and dropping dongs.

This morning, as I was leaving the shower area after a refreshing shave (isn't shaving a wonderful experience, almost a religious one? You feel, as you wipe away the excess foam and water, that you have washed away your sins — and speaking of sensual/religious experiences, Regina hired the daughter of friends of ours to come to the apartment and give one of her professional massages: I was so relaxed as she kneaded away at every proper part of me, even those near normally erogenous zones, that I was transported into a reverie, helped by the music I had chosen — Isham Jones and Annette Hanshaw in her version of "My Sin" — in which I was on some distant desert island shore in the midst of swaying dancers, beauties of both sexes, wreathed in smiles of rapture and all-knowingness, and when our masseuse gently woke me I was sorry to leave this satisfying and relaxing vacation — and all effected on a magic carpet massage mattress in the confines of our Monrovia apartment. So why travel? Get a good massage!..........)

Where was I? Oh, yes — leaving the shower area at the athletic club... Well, a little bald man in his senior years, but probably not much senior to me, gently stopped me to ask whether it was in the rules for a member to take a towel with him or her to the pool. "You see, I'm a new boy here." I told him it was not necessary, and I felt very sorry for him — because he'd been the subject of a con or scam. The greedy family that has sold the club is, it seems, still selling membership to unsuspecting clients. I like feeling sorry for people so I didn't tell him about the scam.

The next leg of my regular morning routine is the one I relish: breakfast spread over an hour. The place I enjoy most is Russell's, a faux old-time eatery in Old Towne Pasadena. They know me so well now that immediately I sit down at the counter they confirm that my order will be a "lite" breakfast — one egg basted with two plump pork sausages, sourdough toast, and a bowl of fruit instead of hashed browns. The fruit bowl is brought prior to the main meal which, of course, is so un-American — so tiny — that it comes on a child's plate. The Dijon mustard is not forgotten — it is plonked upside down on the counter in front of me. So now I'm ready. The coffee, in a sensible thick white mug, awaits too and there's classical musak in the background — Elgar to be exact — playing as the waiters run around doing their business.

Now comes the time to open the folded *Los Angeles Times*. I never take a peek preview. Yes, it's the same old mayhem in full colour: ruined buildings in the Middle East. "Militants Warn of 'Open War'." My eyes glaze as once again I read of Sunnis and Shiites. Which is which? Who are the good people? I think Sunnis are not actually very sunny but Shiites may be shits. But as I fork sausage onto egg onto toast and dip it in Dijon all's right with the world (because I'm not stuck in the middle of it) for a few minutes.

And I can look forward to another evening's gig with Janet Klein & Her Parlour Boys. Of course, none of us are boys anymore but the title has a certain ring to it. We will be performing in a historic downtown building once again. Last month it was the 1911 Palace Theatre where Jolson trod and whipped up a frenzy as he sang "You Made Me Love You! — I didn't wanna do it!" Then there was the wedding atop the Oviatt building, an Art Deco treasure, in the penthouse plaza where Mr. Oviatt, a men's haberdasher par excellence, used to entertain young ladies by moonlight in the 1920s.

Tonight it's the Bradbury Building, built in 1893 and fitted with elevators even then. The day whisks past and soon, after feeding the pets, I'm inside the thick brick building admiring the landings with their black ironwork. This was built, we're told, as a visionary indoor city. Life would be an urban indoor dream. What I like about downtown is the solidity of the stone buildings, how they interlink and intersect almost organically, how you could get lost in the alleys and corridors and mysterious passages of this man-made universe that spreads itself in brick and mortar both overground and underground. Most excitingly underground.

I'm reminded of the subterranean cavern world described in *The Princess And The Goblin* by George Macdonald, a book I had as a child and still have now even here in our Monrovia apartment of the moment.

The gig is a birthday party for a young couple. She's Australian and he's Chinese by way of Singapore. Armed with an education that includes Cambridge and Edinburgh he's emerged as a financial wizard with the first name of Wesley. Now they live well and in style in the grand Los Feliz district near Griffith Park, where Regina and I would love to live if we only had the money. The Parlour Boys play on the second floor landing while Janet is placed a floor below us, all on her own. And on the ground floor is the party itself. All I can see are the tops of their heads and the shrimp and oysters and liquor they're digging into. We do our stuff and it's appreciated. There's an Australian fellow there, a family member who's flown over for the occasion, a senior like self, who is intrigued by my ukulele. "I know a few chords myself" he confides in me. "Nothing to write home about."

He asks me if I'll oblige with a George Formby number. Thoughtlessly I launch into "I'm the Husband Of The Wife Of Mr.

Wu," a part of the Mr. Wu saga. As I'm singing and strumming and the Aussie is smiling I see that our birthday king, Wesley, is smiling too but it is a rictus smile, a smile that is the apogee of Far Eastern inscrutability. Of course! This is one of those Incorrect songs.

I was incorrect the other night at Cantalini's restaurant when entertaining a pair of appreciative lesbian ladies. They were giving me the thumbs up and the winks and smiles — until I sang, unthinkingly, a local favorite, "I Wonder Where My Little Hula Girl Has Gone" with the line about finding her in a bar and sticking her back in her little grass shack. The sunny demeanor of the lesbians changed rapidly. "Where have you been hiding?" thundered the more macho of the two. "Get real!"

After the gig at the Bradbury Building the janitor, also a historian, takes us on a tour of the subterranean world. Deep down there's a 1920s speakeasy. These days it's just a big stone basement room stacked with ruined cornices and columns. The only intact decoration is an ornate ceiling of hammered metal.

But in the 1920s it was ablaze with drinkers and dancers and even murderers. The historian points to the back where there's a walled-up entrance. Used to be a tunnel, one of several fanning out from the Bradbury. These tunnels led to such places as the Hall of Justice, the City Hall, and other seats of power. After sentencing bootleggers the judges would saunter down the tunnel and enter the big room for a refreshing beer or cocktail of their choice. I wonder whose band played here. Those were the days....

Now to the days I promised, at the end of my last Letter, to try to continue dredging up my first years at Trinity College, Dublin, Eire. Last month I only got as far as the first day's lecture. I wrote to my TCD friend, Jeremy Lewis, to ask how he manages to time travel He replied that he finds that "if one concentrates hard enough and gets into a semi-trance then the memories come bubbling up from the semi-conscious, and one thing leads to another."

I wish I could descend into that dark realm as easily as Jeremy. What a great land to re-enter with the knowledge that you're comfy-cozy safe, able to say hello to friends who've said goodbye forever!

Let's attempt the descent.......

That first Trinity term was quite short. It started in October and was ended well before Christmas. I don't remember much of what was said at our lectures but I do remember that Dr. Lydon, who took us for general European history, had a very red face, fit to burst. But it was a smiley face and he recommended the class to go and see *El Cid* if we wanted to get a good idea of what life was like in Old Spain. We liked that approach to education. He later suggested we all meet in a nearby bar for a lecture on medieval Ireland.

On the other hand Miss Otway-Ruthven was formidable as a battleship, sweeping into the frigid lecture hall with gown attempting to catch up with her. At once she'd proceed, in a Scottish upper class drawl, to read out the roll call. It began "Amangala, Baggs, Bennett, Best, Blackley....." Why do I remember the Bs and then there's a gap until "Lammert"? Memory is pitted with lacunae.

There were several Africans in our class and Miss Otway-Ruthven seemed to take pleasure in mispronouncing their names despite their (mild) protestations. For example, Mr. Amangala's name came out sounding like his family were washing machine mangle men, or maybe that they mangled words, whereas he had told her and us, with utmost patience, that his name should be pronounced with the emphasis on the latter part, as in a gala or fete.

Because he was black I made a beeline for Mr. Amangala, who was always rigged out in dark business suit and tie, and not at all the syncopation-riddled savage. I was jazz and blues mad at this time and convinced that blacks were born with the big beat pulsing inside them. I must learn their secret. I was dying to be black. I believed some of Mr. Amangala's rhythmic essence might radiate out and seep into my body if I could lure him into my room and switch him on with some hot jazz.

Eventually he agreed to come to my digs, where I served him a rich iced cake and tea. Then I played him Louis Armstrong and Kid Ory and such. He enjoyed the cake and tea but seemed embarrassed by the jazz. With a bow he bid me a polite goodnight, adding that he would see me at the constitutional history lecture tomorrow.

Later I learned he was a keen admirer of Gilbert & Sullivan, a pair I loatheed and had been trying to escape from for years. Still we remained at a polite distance in our years at college. When I came to pop chart fame in my last year and was playing at the Trinity Ball with my band Bluesville, I remember spotting him standing at the back of the cheering, raving crowd. He was mouthing something to me but I couldn't make it out. Somebody informed me that he was saying, "I've got it!" meaning he'd at last got the Big Beat.

I later read in the Old Boy's magazine that he'd been killed leading his regiment in a battle between his country of Nigeria and some other one close by.

My mind was on jazz and hardly ever on European history or political thought. I couldn't bear to bury myself in the books. I needed to be in the fray. Very soon in my first weeks I had joined the Trinity Jazz Club. They met in rooms high up and there in an overcoat I made myself known by sitting at the piano and pounding out a Jimmy Yancey boogie blues. The jazzers were impressed. I had found a niche since there appeared to be nobody else into boogie pounding. I knew how to crush several notes down together, thus producing an ugly clash but one that triggered a response from the club members: "Yeagh, yeagh, man!" and the like.

That was my entry card into the jazz life and soon I was a member of the TCD Jazz Band. We played wherever we were welcome: in pubs and tennis clubs, and even on mountainsides in the rain. We appeared in the annual Carnival of Nations, held at St. Anthony's Hall down on the quays near the River Liffey. Representing Ireland, on a bill that included acts ranging from Sweden to South Africa, we were unfortunately caught short when our name was suddenly announced by the jovial host, a divinity student.

For just as we were waiting our cue there had been a disagreement within the band. The trombonist had asked the clarinetist what key the first blues was in. "Zed Sharp!" shouted the inebriated clarinetist. The trombonist, a burly fellow from a distant British colony, responded by swinging his instrument at the head of the supposed funnyman. As the curtain rose on this celebration of how music can break barriers and spread peace, the audience was presented with two jazzers bashing each other, for at this stage of the fight the clarinetist was retaliating with swipes of his licorice stick. The act was glimpsed for only a few seconds before the curtain was rung down. The compere improvised with a few choice limericks and then brought on the Icelandic Saga-tellers.

In the Christmas holidays I took a job in Putney at the local brewery. I was officially a brewer's drayman, which meant mucking in with the workers on the beer lorries, helping them load and unload the beer. This was my first close contact with the working classes and I was terrified of speaking, lest my accent annoy them. Luckily they had a hard job understanding me at all. Mostly I stuttered. They referred to me as squire or your lordship. I learned that life for them was about getting away with as much thievery as they could. Screw the management was their ideology. We drank a lot of beer and put it down to "ullage" (bottles broken in transit).

In the Summer break, a long one, I celebrated my 21st birthday, but not, surprisingly, with my parents, with my family. Instead I chose to join some fleeting friends — having a rugby football connection — at their rented holiday house in the South of France at Juan Les Pins. I remember that the sand was hot and dirty, that you rented your postage stamp of beach and just lay there soaking in a sun that never much appeared in England—throughout my childhood our summer holidays were always wet and any plans we made for that day invariably ruined by downpours, which I didn't mind because it gave me another chance to pore over my American comic books, all-action, 68 big pages, don't take less, bannered on the cover, cheaply printed in the North of England I noticed, which took away from the beefy detectives and cowboys inside, bred on

Texas cattle which showed in their muscles and defined chests, while I steadily grew porkier and my parents worried and consulted doctors.

The Mediterranean was waveless and sticky. I was embarrassed to be seen porcine in my swimsuit. Everyone, female or male, seemed to be in tiny bikinis. Bikini was the sexiest word I'd ever heard and I avoided thinking about it. I took to wandering off with my sketchbook. I took against my hosts because they seemed content among themselves with private jokes, excluding me. They did throw a little 21st birthday party for me at a local restaurant and I cheered up a little.

Next day I caught the train home. In the carriage I was befriended by two French boys on their way to sightsee in London. I wished I was as slim and as handsome as they. I wished I was a teenage French boy.

Back home at 18, Wildcroft Manor, Putney Heath, my father welcomed me. Where was my mother? Away with my grandfather or my sister's family, perhaps. My father cooked me supper all by himself. It was a stew and very good too. He was fond of his cooking and took great pride in his carving skills on Sundays when we had roast beef. But he always gave himself the worst piece, the gristle. My mother would tease him about this, saying that he enjoyed being a "martyr."

My father was a quiet man and I always felt restrained in his presence but I had the greatest respect for him. And I loved him without ever telling him so. Nor did he ever tell me that he loved me. Love was never mentioned in our flat, even though we actually all adored each other, would die for each other. I never saw my father in a temper but I was told by my sister that he did have one.

I remember that when I caused a family scene only about a year before — we were in a restaurant being hosted by my grandfather and in the small talk I dared to contradict my grandfather over whether President Kennedy's father was once one of the richest men in America, which I claimed he was and my grandfather scoffed and I told him off brusquely and there was a horrible silence —- my father quietly got up and left the room as the rest of the family expressed their shock and dismay.

But, as I say, my older sister says she experienced his temper. One evening in the 1950s she'd been calling him "Big Ears" — she was good at that sort of thing — and he responded by throwing the telephone at her. I think it missed.

My father always let my mother do the talking, do the bubbling, be the merry one. He was content with his golf, billiards and boxing on the TV. My mother and I scolded him for liking such a violent sport. Now I feel ashamed of scolding him. He once tried to explain the facts of life to me as he stood in the bathroom shaving. I noticed, squeamishly, that he had little red pimples on his body. At the end of his caged explanation of the facts of life I ran to my mother and said: "Daddy is being disgusting, disgusting!" And that was the last time that the matter of sex ever came up — except that when I was about to leave for my first term at Bryanston, a boarding school, he told me: "Never let another boy touch you, ever." I never did — nor did they ever want to.

He always encouraged my musical endeavors, slogging up to London's West End to haggle with slick musical instrument salesmen when I'd decided to trade in my accordion for a guitar. How awful for him, a gentle well educated man, to have to deal with such brutes! I have an image of him trudging through the snow lugging sound equipment for one of my early pub gigs. He put up with my rock & roll, never complaining. But when I played him a Joplinesque rag I'd composed, "Luscious Slices," he pronounced it very good and asked me the secret of syncopation. He could never syncopate, he said, though he'd very much like to.

At the start of my second year at TCD I moved from Mrs. Eagar's to the Montrose Guest House in the grander neighbourhood of Ballsbridge. Here I shared a single bedroom with my pals Jeremy Lewis and David Shaw. I decided to keep a diary. It tells of all my little trials and troubles, of living at rather too close quarters and yet of getting by.

Jeremy reminded me recently that I was prone to diving into moods. I also dived back into my prep school past, pretending to be a school master, reading *The Wind In The Willows*, watching with disgust as Jeremy awkwardly tried to woo a female classmate of ours during a visit to their digs and at teatime at that.

For myself I tried to banish lust. "Maybe lust can be channeled," I wrote in my diary. "For me, life is what other people see of you on the surface. Never let them delve deep inside."

By November I was in a turmoil about the deadline for delivery of an essay. I'd managed to scrape through our first year's exams, while my roommates had done much better, but then, you see, they had actually read the set books. I used to get Jeremy to give me a précis on long walks around Dublin. A very kind friend he was. I did a silly thing with the impending essay — I wrote it in my mind before I had read the set texts. Eventually, by flashlight under the blankets in our room, as the others slept, I read the main textbook and next evening I dashed off a passionate essay attacking Karl Marx for being juvenile. Jeremy said it was excellent. So now, until the end of term, I could rest in peace, and finish *The Wind In The Willows*.

The last diary entry is for November 25, 1962:

A horrible, lethargic Sunday. Such days are hard enough to

take in England, pleasant land, but here, in alien country, they're unmitigated hell. Why is Sunday so depressing?
 Lay in bed till 2 pm. So did Jeremy and David.
 In the afternoon we went for a walk in Phoenix Park. Very foggy, very cold, very hostile. Everyone seemed against us. Objects suddenly loomed up in front of us. Everything dripped. The dripping sounded like psalm-reading. Nearby two rough-looking natives were bashing at each other with hockey sticks — the local sport: Hurling. Barbarous. Names like Ryan and McGee had been chalked on the frieze at the base of the Duke of Wellington's monument. I felt very sorry. For my family and the past.
 Then I lost J&D. Deliberately. I lost them and I walked off deeper and deeper into the thick fog until it enveloped me completely. I felt good at last. I felt I had come home to where I belonged. I looked forward to Christmas at home in England, at Wildcroft Manor.

Here the diary stops. A few days later, at the beginning of December, I returned for supper at our boarding house and was handed a telegram by one of our landlady's uniformed maids. It told me to call home at once. When I at last reached Putney 7978 I heard the voice of my aunt Nancy.
 "Are you sitting down?........Take a deep breath......Daddy died last night."
 A pause.
 "I'll say it again, dear. Daddy died last night."
 "Yes, I see...."
 My mother now came on the phone: I was to bring with me my dark suit and I was to come back as soon as possible.
 "I see..."
 My roommates escorted me to the ferryboat and that night I made the rough crossing to Holyhead, reading a history textbook about Sir Walter Raleigh, and then took the train to London. Much of what followed is a blur. But there are moments.
 I learned that my father had come home from the office and told my mother, back from golf and having early cocktails with my aunt, that if they didn't mind he wouldn't join them right now as he felt a little on the tired side.
 He went to the twin-bedded room and lay down and never woke up.
 We all behaved most sensibly in the days following his death. There was very little crying. My brother Robin was at boarding school and, for some reason, was not allowed to attend the funeral. My father was buried in Old Woking cemetery near his parents. I had been born in Woking in 1941. At the church service, as the coffin was being borne down the aisle, I saw my mother staring

fixedly at it as it passed, her eyes following it, her neck stretched out, until it reached its place. She seemed like an actress in a silent film melodrama. I've never forgotten that stare, very unnerving. She never cried. At the graveside, just as the coffin was reaching its final resting place my favorite Uncle tossed in my father's old felt hat.

I now found the word "Daddy" to be so painful that I have never used it again in reference to him. I have never really been reconciled to the fact of my father's death. Nor has my brother. Nor, really, my sister. I wish I'd known him better. If only we'd had that long talk on that long walk. I see him in my dreams but, of course, he never speaks.

SEPTEMBER

These days I use my daily journal as the source of material for these Letters. This is the journal I have kept since 1972.

People snoop into my current journals at their peril. A pre-Regina girl friend once trespassed there and was rewarded with heavy volts of shock. "You don't like me!" she shrieked. "You shouldn't read other people's diaries," I retorted. Which is the real me — the one that walks and talks or the one who writes?

Damned if I know. Regina never peeks, despite the big black volume laying in plain sight on my desk.

I open it now and see that this one was started on July 31, the day I left for the Oregon Festival of American Music. Today I wrote the entry for August 27, just under a month later: I have filled 121 pages with my scrawl. This scrawl is notoriously hard to decipher — a good safeguard. However, a learned and well-read friend of mine told me that he has, at times, managed to crack the code.

But — 121 pages! Let's see whether there's anything that's fit for the public eye......................

I'll try to make this Letter short, to the point, and for the public record............................

The topic of this year's Festival was "Irving Berlin's America" — right up my alley. Dick Hyman had rewarded me with a crowded schedule of concerts to keep me busy. I must have things to do in order to stave off Black Dog moods. In our current life we have two close friends under sentence of death from cancer, and also, since reaching 65 on July 10, I am keenly aware of being on a sled on the downward slope. Therefore I must use my time wisely, a time that rushes on headlong at a furious speed. When I was a child time hung heavy like a constipated cloud. When on earth will that hour be up? I would ask in despair as the Latin class stuck on the clock that never moved. When will the referee blow that whistle and stop this endless football match?

As in past glorious years I was billeted at the Marriott Residence Inn, Eugene, close to a wide and fast flowing river with an accompanying pathway always crowded with determined joggers and bicyclists hell-bent on life-extending violent exercise. Actually, they're a bloody nuisance: whenever I went out on my early morning walk along this path I'd keep hearing from behind the cried order, "On your left!" and suddenly a jogger or cyclist would whoosh past and always while I'd been contemplating the rushing, heedless water.

Dick Hyman and our resident orchestra conductor James Paul were also billeted at the Inn. So was the virtuoso peripatetic jazz reedman Ken Peplowski. I always savored breakfast because then I could sit with them, pretending to eat but in fact hanging on their every wise musical word (when they weren't Bush-bashing), and waiting for the right moment to ask them some technical question about the use of upper intervals in harmony or about the prevalence of chromaticism in Irving Berlin. They were always very patient with me. "You're very talented, Ian — in your own peculiar way." In other words: stick to it, don't stray from your particular Alley.

Dick drove me in to central Eugene and on the way I could continue to pepper the Master with musical questions. He rewarded me with the observation that "A Couple Of Swells" (from *Easter Parade*) is really written in march form. I was pondering this as I entered the Shedd Institute, a complex of rooms in a big building that was once a church and religious college. The organizers of the American Music Festival have had every room de-sanctified thoroughly, and scrubbed clean as well. I completed the cleansing process a few years back when I performed a vigorous version of "Whole Lotta Shakin' Goin' On" on a platform close to where once hung Our Lord.

As it turned out "A Couple Of Swells" was the first number I was scheduled to rehearse. Not with Dick but with the director of the musical, *Annie Get Your Gun*, which was to be the highlight of the festival. My partner was veteran song-and dance man Bill Hulings, thoroughly trained and experienced in Broadway moves and delivery. What I hadn't expected was that director Richard Jessup had choreographed every line of the song for Bill and me. We would be a team.

And I was in a panic. You see, I never work in teams. I'm not a team player in any sense of the word. I'm the leader, I'm anti-social. I'm a one-man show. Which means I'm free to forget lyrics on stage and keep going by making them up. I can make up my own moves as I'm going along, too. I improvise. I'm like a vaudeville jazzman.

But this wouldn't do. If I didn't learn the steps, learn to

synchronize with my partner, I would screw up the act — and we were scheduled to perform the number at the opening night gala show in a couple of days. I can't learn it, I can't learn it, I protested. I'll muck you up. No you won't, said the gentle stage director. Bill mastered the moves right away. I gabbled and gabbled excuses — please forgive me — look, I know what I'll do: I'll pretend to be your shadow as in "Me And My Shadow" and I'll imitate your move a split second after you've done it: or, I'll pretend to be an idiot and deliberately be out of synch with you and that would be a funny act……..

And on and on, ad nauseam.

The actor and the director looked at me blankly. And I went all hot and cold, flashing back to schooldays in the 1950s when I'd first started using this charade of excuses —- as to why I couldn't learn maths their way, or algebra, or music. Music! That's why I'd never learned to play music the right way. Had only learnt to play it my way. Aha! Like Irving Berlin!

I was back on form, back in the rut.

Eventually I managed an approximation of the choreography, promising that all would be right on the night. At noon I was whisked off to a Rotary Club lunch, where, after the solemn invocation and singing of the national anthem (not yet "God Bless America," still that impossible English drinking song), I gave the members "I'll See You In C-U-B-A" followed by "My Sweetie," ranging the room with Ukie. Straight after that it was rehearsal time for the Gala: I was to perform "Mandy," with Ukie, accompanied by a 28 person mixed choir and an orchestra. I was happy to hear a teenage member of the choir pronounce: "Ukuleles Rock!"

Thursday was the day of the great Gala Concert in the 2,500 seat Hult Theatre. This is where they would also be presenting a version of *Annie Get Your Gun* — I say "version," because this is the recent Bernadette Peters one, cleansed of anything that might offend Native Americans. Thus that grand comedy song, "I'm An Indian Too" has been banished. What would Mr. Berlin feel about this political correctness? After all, in his early days he churned out ethnic comedy songs. They were typed by the trade as "coon," "wop," "yid," etc. Possibly Mr. Berlin would have agreed with today's sensitivities and would have offered to write some new PC material.

Before our afternoon dress rehearsal I had a task in my guise as lecturer: talking about Tin Pan Alley to a group of vigorous Elder Hostellers, just arrived and settling in. They'd finished breakfast in one of the rooms in the labyrinth that constitutes the Shedd Institute. I've been coming here for five years and I still get lost in this maze of rooms. The Elders are not to be trifled with, they take life seriously and aren't afraid of voicing opinions and complaints: today the eggs were too spicy and there's much too much cheese on the omelettetes, if you could call them that, they told me.

I braced for my lecturing, but all went swimmingly. After all, I'm an Elder, too. One fellow asked me for a definition of Tin Pan Alley. I launched into it, getting smiles and laughs. At the end my questioner thanked me, telling me that his one question had clocked a 15-minute answer but that he was happy with it.

All went well at the dress rehearsal, too — the director and Bill patiently went through the dance steps with me. I tried to synch in. A classical woman vocalist called Maria did "Always" in the style of Handel. Afterwards I caught the end of a lecture on Mr. Berlin by Robert Kimball, the keeper of the flame. He has published the complete lyrics and he had a twenty-year telephone relationship with the great man. H tossed us a tidbit: Mr. Berlin went to see *A Clockwork Orange* and liked it; he also liked some Beatle songs. He was up with the times. And he knew that by the end of the 1960s his own time was up: "It was as if I owned a store and people no longer wanted to buy what I had to sell," he told Kimball. So he shut up shop.

I walked back from the lecture in the company of Ray Charles, the white Ray Charles, the man who headed fine vocal groups in the 1950s. Ray told me that when Berlin's last musical, *Mr. President* was in try-outs he was invited up, with other recording musicians, to the songwriter's hotel suite to talk about the possibility of their recording some of the show numbers. Ray was known for his special arrangements. After the meeting Berlin took him by the arm, and escorted him to the door. "You know," he confided in that husky whisper voice, "I write some pretty good special material." Still Berlin the merchant— ready with whatever the customer requires. "You want the pants altered? No problem!"

And what of the Festival Opening Gala Concert? I love the thrill of an opening, of waiting in the wings, ready to stride confidently onto the stage and look out into that sea of darkness knowing that there throb hundreds of hearts waiting to be amused. And I can give it to them! So much easier than ordinary one-to-one relationships!

Some guest, a local bank manager or other, standing in the wings next to Dick Hyman, asked him whether he ever gets "butterflies in the stomach" on these occasions. Calm as a cucumber Dick replied, "I am, shall we say, in a state of extreme readiness." And onto the stage he strode.

I was the first vocal act to perform. "Mandy" went smoothly, easing into "I Love A Piano," which I sang to Dick as he tickled the ivories. Maria Jette, the diva, brought down the house with her Handel-inspired Berlin renditions. And then came "A Couple Of Swells."

Bill had rehearsed me over and over in the dressing room. But once on stage, as in the past, I forgot everything and just lapsed into a series of comic steps and stumbles, with much grinning out into that sea of darkness. But we were a hit. Everyone said so at the reception afterwards. A fan of my 1960s rock records, a stout and rubicund party, declared himself "amazed" and insisted on buying me a drink, which was nice because those drinks are expensive.

The rest of the two-week festival was a blur of excitement that was all over too soon. I enjoyed every minute, so long as I could be in the centre of the action. I had meant to take a trip outside of Eugene and see some countryside, see the sea, the mountains, the desert. I have meant to do this ever since I first came to Eugene in 1998. But it has never come to pass. The fever of the music and musicians holds me. I want to discuss chords and how to speed-read music, I want to learn more about modulation and the Devil's Interval.

At night, after the shows, back in my room at the Inn, with a Sierra Nevada in hand, I would press on the TV instead of opening heavy books that are good for you. A channel of record held me in thrall: CSPAN — I joined a camera for an hour as it tried to follow President Bush around some military establishment which he was visiting.

Switch-smiling and shaking hands with alacrity, gleaming with sweat, Bush was spreading confidence to some sort of military personnel group, all of whom were wearing Boy Scout hats. The smiles contrasted with the grim thuggishness of the men behind him — Secret Service types who look like they shaved and bathed exactly on the hour, stuck with ear-plugs they fiddled with, and firing scowls at anyone who dared speak to the President or ask for his autograph or just smile at him.

A strange spectacle of smiles and scowls. A far cry from Berlin. Or was it? Our songwriter just loved hanging out with Presidents, more's the pity. I believe it ruined his writing. I believe he could have contributed some sassy rock & roll songs, akin in spirit to his ragtime ones, if he'd only stopped flag-waving and sucking-up to the powerful.

By the end of our grand finale concert, in which I sang not only "You Cannot Make Your Shimmy Shake On Tea" but also, "God Bless America" (I finally have mastered the words), we were all Berlined-out. We'd had quite enough of him. We'd heard him cannibalize himself — a stretch of "Cheek To Cheek" was earlier tried out in "Smile And Show Your Dimple" and then "Mandy." Oh, and "Dimple's" chorus melody is almost the same as "Easter Parade." We were tired of his tricksy syncopations of the "Puttin' On The Ritz" variety — a bit stilted — and we were tired of his chromaticism — see "White Christmas."

But now, a few weeks later, I am reconciled to the best of Berlin.

The problem with extensive Berlin exposure is the problem with all composers and, indeed, all artists. We only have a small bag of tricks. We are really only exposing ourselves and we are therefore limited, handcuffed, as humans in this world. Sometimes, at our best, we break on through to heaven or wherever it all comes from, and then we are angelic and at one with — whomsoever.

From Eugene I flew to Providence, Rhode Island — to take part in the annual Newport Vintage Dance Week. Luckily I had an absorbing new book to read on the daylong journey: *The Looming Tower — Al-Qaeda And The Road To 9/11* by Lawrence Wright. The lesson is not to mess with other people's cultures, to stay clear of Islamists — they're still smarting from the Crusades, they still live mentally in the Middle Ages.

Thus they hate western cultures. Mr. Qutb, the Egyptian writer and founder of the modern Islamist movement, was swept on a road of revenge by his experiences in America in the late 1940s when he was a student. In particular he was shocked and excited by brazen American Woman "who knows full well the beauties of her body, her face, her exciting eyes, her bulging breasts, her full buttocks and her smooth legs."

The culmination of shock came at a Sunday evening dance in a church hall in Greeley, CO, where "the room convulsed with the feverish music from the gramophone. Dancing naked legs filled the hall, arms draped around the waists, chests met chests, lips met lips, and the atmosphere was full of love."

Love! That's what extremists can't abide. The minister gazed approvingly and dimmed the lights in order to play a record of "Baby, It's Cold Outside," a 1949 Academy Award winning song by Frank Loesser. So Frank, you chain-smoking fiend — we have you to blame! Because after this dance scene Mr. Qutb sunk into an "estrangement" of soul and body and withdrew from all his classes at Colorado State College. Back in Egypt, in his writings, he advocated the killing of all infidels. The activist torch was taken on later by Osama bin Laden who, after a childhood infatuation with *Bonanza* and *Fury* suddenly, in his teens, renounced and denounced the West. He hated music, calling it "The Devil's Flute." Even when Arabic tunes were played he stuck his fingers in his ears and writhed in agony, the poor fool.

With a head full of hatred I landed in leafy lush Rhode Island and was soon safe in a dormitory room not far from a bed containing a sleeping Regina. Dance Week was taking place at Portsmouth Abbey Preparatory School, a quiet establishment — self-contained, surrounded by grass and long green swards leading to the bay, sprinkled with silent gliding monks going to and fro from the monastery to the abbey. Who could see this as Western decadence?

Well, I suppose we vintage dancers are reactionaries — reacting to the awfulness of the 21st century by indulging in Victorian Dance and its associated etiquette of decency, of good manners, of considering others, of unselfishness, of community.

We had a week of dance classes — the waltz, the quadrille, the tango — and at night we took over robber baron mansions for our balls. There we were seen in all our sartorial splendor — the women in ball gowns with hoopskirts and laces, the men in white tie and tails. All was graciousness. The racket of our present times was held momentarily at bay. During the week I gave a lecture and a concert. I wrote a schottische called "Dance Of The Voles." It was a happy time of good fellowship all round, a social time as much as a dancing time — but tinged with sadness: our leader and dance director and our close friend, Patri Pugliese, had announced to the assembled dancers in our very first night that he is a condemned man: he has been stricken with liver cancer, there is no hope, he has only a month or so to live. "And then that's it," he said. He is not one who believes in an after-life. He faces the facts. With his imminent departure in mind we were determined to give Patri a good, active time.

For me this culminated in a spontaneous dance we did in the auditorium of the prep school on our last afternoon. What happened was that after my lecture on Irving Berlin I put on a recording of a tango, "Dreams Of Old L.A.," one that I'd written at the very first vintage dance week that Regina and I had attended.

Then I went into my own peculiar and eccentric improvised dance steps — and suddenly I found that Patri and members of his family were shadowing me. In fact they were in synch with me. It was a remarkable and uplifting experience. It was an answer to the clod-footed mess I'd made on stage at the Oregon Festival. Here at last I was free from the strictures of choreography, free to express myself.

And here was Patri and his family following and then becoming part of a whole. We were as one happy whole. Even Osama would have succumbed. He had to. Luckily a friend was snapping some of the dance on his video camera. You can see the last few moments of this extravaganza on YouTube.

OCTOBER

I only have two regular correspondents these days — I mean who write me letters in longhand with fountain pens, who then fold the sheets, placing them in an envelope, who lick and seal by hand-smoothing, who then step outside, possibly in pelting rain, perhaps negotiating their way through jostling crowds containing not a few turbaned gentlemen and women who have taken the veil, to post their hand-made art in a solid red letter box.

My correspondents — in London, of course — are my two old friends from the 1960s: Charles Sprawson and Andy Wickham.

Charles uses the Airletter form, emblazoned with the red crown of the Royal Mail. This confines him to a mere page and a half of unlined paper, but every word is priceless.

In the latest letter he describes a luncheon at my sister's country cottage, where she lives with her husband the General. Charles was accompanied by a lovely, literate, well-spoken, well-connected, Bridge-playing lady called Margaret, his constant companion. "There were three Generals present. The top one, Guthrie, who's always on the phone to Blair, boasted that the Welsh Guards' (he's the head of them) recent intake of officers were all from State Schools." Charles, of course, is from a decent public school like any gentleman — in fact, he refuses to read a newspaper obituary if the deceased isn't a Public School man.

"When I said I thought it was a pity, the General looked puzzled and before an argument developed we were luckily called into lunch by your sister — 'Soup's up!' — where Guthrie sat next to Margaret — and of course they got along very well because she knows how to deal with men."

In contrast, Andy writes on traditionally small writing paper — never "note paper" for that is only for the bourgeoisie — of thick bond with his address embossed on the top right-hand corner. His pen, possibly a Parker or Waterman or even a Mont Blanc, has a thick nib and he always uses a light blue ink. Some months his letters go on for over a dozen pages, carefully constructed in the mandarin style and with never a crossed-out word (well, sometimes he makes a mistake but instead of crossing out he whites out with brush and bottle). His letters are often so amusing that I read them out to Regina as we sit in our front porch of an evening, with glasses of wine and a view of the young mothers passing by with their baby carriages.

But in Andy's latest letter, prior to his arrival on our doorstep next week, he takes me to task for being too wordy in my Letter: "It would seem that our epistolary arrangement — which I greatly enjoy — is that in exchange for my desperate efforts I get a hurried note and a Letter From Lotusland. This latter is invariably entertaining, though the last seemed a trifle brief — ruthless editing, no doubt, having expunged many crucial details. What colour socks, for example, were you wearing on your first day at Trinity College, Dublin? I think we should be told. Blog on!"

Sucks to you, Andy! I'm my own unedited Proust, I'm a Wikipedian. I write because I am and I put in as many details as I can remember. And anyway, Andy, one evening while we were strolling in the West End of London you listed every item of clothing you were wearing from your Huntsman suit, your Turnbull & Asser shirt, your Old Cheltonian tie, down to your special underwear and — your socks.

So now I intend to write up a Day In The Life. Precisely, last Tuesday, September 26. Who else keeps such a detailed record? An unexamined life is not worth living, said someone. I may not properly examine but at least I record. And what I write makes a change from reading about Shiites, Sunnis, detainees, Al Qaeda, Al Jolson, militias, the Golden Mosque, insurgents, deadly standoffs in schools, obesity in Mississippi, and soap opera lonelygirls on YouTube.......
YouTube is addictive.....and potentially dangerous. The other day I dived into an almost-porn site — it was skimpy bathing suits — but no sooner had I got there when the computer froze and I was, in a manner of speaking, caught with my pants down and in a cataleptic state at that. Would Regina return from shopping and discover this awful picture? I hadn't a clue about shutting down the machine — nothing short of throwing it out the window.
I called a computer nerd pal and he talked me down. The machine shut off with a drowning bell like a ship sinking beneath the waves. Since then I delve circumspectly: ploughing through the 75,000 entries under my name. Nothing very exciting — offers of old CDs and books of mine.
But I had surges of nostalgia when I ran across an offer on Amazon of a DVD compilation of *The Old Grey Whistle Test*. This was a long-running "serious" show of "serious" rock music presented in a tiny studio at the BBC. This was Rock without the Roll. This was America, Alice Cooper, Rory Gallagher, Tom Paxton, and I-don't-know. I was fired after a few months.
I was hired as the first presenter of the series, back in 1971 when I was living at home in London with my mother and writing the final chapters of my book, *After The Ball* for Penguin. I had given a lively lecture on Pop in The Movies at the National Film Theatre and the lady who'd hired me then recommended me to Michael Appleton (or "Apples" as his colleagues called him — but I never did; I couldn't stand the man what with his long and shampooed and well-blown hair down to his shoulders, his leather jacket, his passion for "serious" rock and the upper-class drawl that revealed his betrayal of his decent upbringing).
Before I could reveal my true colours I was offered the job of on-camera announcer for the new show. I couldn't resist the chance to perform, to show off, whatever the cause. I was the Lord Haw Haw or Tokyo Rose of the 1970s. Anything for the limelight, a com-

plete tart.

For months we prepared for the first night, live on the air, all over the British Isles and much of Europe. We had excited conferences in the office at White City in BBC Television Centre. I cycled to and from work. I studied other hosts and interviewers; I was determined to master the art. On the day of our first show Appleton gave me a box of cue cards and had me write down questions I should ask my first guest, Tom Paxton, the balding serious singer of serious folk songs.

Then, just prior to our live broadcast, Appleton rehearsed me, having me read out the introductions using the autocue set in top of the camera. As you all know, I am a stutterer and stammerer, but usually I'm fine when performing, when the words are written out for me in advance; then I can control the flow, I haven't got to feel my way in expressing an emotion, I'm fluent because I am not creating any ideas, merely reciting.

However, in rehearsal, for some reason, I stuttered on the very title of the show — "The Old Grey W-w-wwhistle Test."

"Whoops! Hang about!" said Appleton over the intercom from the control booth. "We have a problem." Hadn't he known all along that occasionally I stumble on a word? From this "wwwhistle" moment on I was persona non grata, I didn't exist, I was ignored. Around me bustled and buzzed technicians rearranging the program. I sat transfixed, feeling like a cripple, an embarrassment. "Sorry, mate," mumbled a soundman, but he was apologizing because he'd bumped me with a mike, not because he took pity on my state.

Appleton had a top-level conference and decided that he himself would do the announcing of the groups by crouching beside a camera. But what to do about the Tom Paxton interview? The singer was already in make-up. He'd let me tackle that. He'd take a chance.

The old folk singer was very pleasant and I managed to avoid tricky words — like ones that begin with W or L. The opening show went off OK. Everyone congratulated each other at the little wine and cheese party afterwards. My stutter was not mentioned. It was all very polite, very English.

But immediately the search was on for another announcer. I recommended everyone I could think of, all my actor friends. I was allowed to stay on as an interviewer. In this capacity I managed to have good TV talks with the father of the Everly Brothers, Memphis Slim, the blues pianist, and Bob Hite, a member of Canned Heat, who, in response to my asinine cue-carded question (approved by Appleton): "What exactly is or are the blues?" answered cockily: "The blues is Al Bowlly."

Of course, I knew what the blues is and who Al Bowlly was — bloody hell, I'd spent years researching all this for my forthcoming books! But I had to shine it on and be polite to this smug bugger when all the while I was cursing myself for not having stayed on the other side, as an artist, not having to humiliate myself by pretending to be a TV interviewer.

But some of my suggestions were accepted. I arranged to have Gene Vincent, a real rock & roll original, the creator of "Be Bop A Lula," on the program. I had read that John Lennon considered "Be Bop A Lula" to be the very quintessence of rock & roll. So did I. The only trouble was that Gene Vincent suddenly went and died. Instead I arranged for the veteran TV rock show producer Jack Good, creator of *Shindig* and *Oh, Boy!* to take part in a tribute. Jack agreed but rather spoiled the decorum of the occasion by stating bluntly that he didn't think much of Vincent as a singer; that, if the truth be known, the arch-rocker would have looked like a Casper Milquetoast had Jack not encouraged him to accentuate his gammy leg, ordering him to drag it around the stage, and to limp, clad in the black leather outfit and metal pendant that Jack had costumed him to make him resemble the Richard The Third of rock & roll.

"No, old boy!" chuckled Jack, live on camera. "Vincent was my creation!"

Appleton went bananas in the control room. "This won't do," he fumed at me later. My time was nearly up as a BBC man. The manager of some art rock group complained about my ignorance of the current scene. "You're supposed to be a journalist," he admonished me."You should be reading up about what's happening."

I needed to get back into the fray as an artist. I needed to be free to singer-songwrite about "The Notable Yacht Club Of Staines," as I used to in the 1960s; songs that were my equivalent of the Old Testament imagery of Bob Dylan.

Before leaving this account of my time on *The Old Grey Whistle Test* — a silly title if there ever was! — one curious thing is worth telling: Andrew Lloyd Webber came in to talk about Joseph and his Dream Coat: we were all fascinated by his array of accents, how he'd switch quite suddenly in the middle of an interview from cockney to upper class, to north country, to Scottish or whatever. He seemed very insecure. We ran the videotape over several times to watch this amazing quick-change act.

I must also record that when I'd return home after a broadcast, to our family flat on Putney Heath where my mother lived as a widow, to the little bedroom which used to be my sister's but was now mine, I used to invariably find a note from my mother telling me how good I had been on that particular show, how well I had handled myself, how peculiar some of these Americans appeared to be, and how proud she was of me. At the side of the note would be a chocolate biscuit and a tumbler of scotch, for my health.

After I left the "Test" it went from strength to strength, for year after year, becoming a classic. Everybody who was anybody in rock appeared on it. Appleton even allowed me to do a quick number, in the middle 1970s, when I had a short run as a Warner Bros Records artist. My run was entirely due to an inmate being allowed to run the asylum for a while: Derek Taylor, an old friend from my Hollywood days, was Big Man at WB for a swift glorious moment and he set about doling out contracts to those he considered original and daft. So he released my strange country narrative song, "A Friend Of A Friend Of Mine."

On the show I performed it with only my ukulele as accompaniment. Just as I was about to go on camera I felt a tug at my sleeve. I turned and saw an unprepossessing fellow with a brutally short haircut and clad in a dog's mess-colored tweed jacket. "Hello, Ian. You remember me? Eric?" No. "Eric... Eric Clapton."

Oh, of course — back in the late 1960s in California when you were touring with Cream and we were with the same management and did some appearances together — can you believe it — and afterwards we'd sit around and smoke and sing old songs together such as "Your Baby Has Gone Down The Plughole," which we'd both recorded in our own manner...

"Yes," says Eric. "And you know what? You were a character back then — and you are still a character!" He had heard a test pressing of my country narrative song, concerning a tale of hippies descending on a friendly host and how they take over his house and ruin his life until the host calls up his clan and they come from factory field and farm and mash the hippies into fine ground round.

Now, where was I? We were about to go on a "Day In The Life Of" tour, like James Joyce in *Ulysses*, except more coherent, less artsy.

I can't face telling you about every minute of that day — although my daily journal for Tuesday, September 26 does so.

So...I put my sports bag in the Honda and set off for the Pasadena Athletic Club, a doomed cathedral — it's been sold to Iranians and is in escrow. This escrow will be ended next summer and then we'll all have to find another safe place in which to stretch, lift weights, swim, go to the lavatory, fart, shower and shoot the breeze. I certainly shan't miss the old fools of the locker room, with their long wizened trailing dingle-dangles, banging on about the ball game they watched on TV last night. Watch, watch, watch — that's all they seem to do.

No, I mustn't complain because without them I'd have no audience.

In the car, en route to Pasadena, stuck in the morning commute on Route 66, I put on a CD rather than listen to the drip drip drip of unctuousness from the local NPR station. Sig alerts, and unchanging weather conditions, fires, and news for parents of fifth graders.

Wanting to keep up with the present world I recently bought the new Bob Dylan album, *Modern Times*. I'd read that it's Number One in the nation. A man of my age with a Number One album, beating out the hip-hoppers and rappers and Justin Timberlake! What's the old fellow up to? Well, I had to pull over and recover after I played track #7.

"Beyond The Horizon" is a note for note, chord for chord rip-off of the 1935 classic, "Red Sails In The Sunset,"a hit song written by Will Grosz and Jimmy Kennedy. The latter I got to know quite well when I was researching *After The Ball*. A sweet man from Dublin, who also wrote the words to "Isle Of Capri" and "The Teddy Bears Picnic." I was horrified at this Dylan steal. I examined the CD notes: "All Songs Written by Bob Dylan."

Mind you, anybody who knows "Red Sails In The Sunset" will recognize the contours, but the trouble is that Dylan, having never had more than a handful of notes at his command is, at 65, reduced to a croak of about two discernible notes. So I suppose he'll get away with it again — he's notorious for stealing his tunes from old folk songs but then those old folk songs were public domain to start with. But this was different. This is a copyrighted song. My old friend Jimmy wrote the words with love and care — he told me of being inspired by seeing a fishing boat at twilight in Dublin Bay — and he has relatives alive who need to be clothed and fed.

Dylan should have been decent and honest enough to acknowledge his source. Soon as I could I contacted some music publishing colleagues and they gave me the email address of Shapiro-Bernstein, the veteran New York publisher and holder of the Sunset copyright. Later I got an e-mail note thanking me for my "insight." Not a peep back from them since. I also left word with the *L.A.Times* and other papers. No response. Then I happened to mention my discovery to a couple of Dylanologists.

I discovered why I was hitting a brick wall.

Bob Dylan is such a cultural icon that he's as sacrosanct as Mohammed. To dare to attack him, to call him a tune thief, is to commit sacrilege and to risk being targeted. The attitude of the Dylanologists is that if their God, the consummate artist, chooses to use some meretricious Tin Pan Alley hack song as the bedding for his art then so be it. It is written! And the publishers of the "Sunset" song should feel honored that their trash has been picked up, picked over, and absorbed into the mighty work of a genius.

I have given up on this mission to expose the Master as a robber. Instead I have taken a hint from him and written a train song which uses an old blues form as the music bed: "The Reckoning Train." I scribbled it out in a Hollywood restaurant with a vodka martini at my side as I waited for a late friend. I'm sure that's how the Master works. You let yourself go and scribble.. Then you set your verses to whatever is at hand. In this case I chose the blues form that is in "Mystery Train" and "Down In The Bottom" and, it so happens, in another song on this new Dylan album, "Rollin' and Tumblin." My effort has images of brindle cows and staring foxes and a sense of impending doom with a day of judgment a-comin'. Note how I clip my G's in the Dylan manner. Authenticity, street cred.

I fumed about Dylan The Thief as I swam at the Club; I was only simmering by the time I was sitting at the counter of the Pie 'n' Burger contemplating with relish the place of buttery basted eggs and the thick crisp bacon. Within moments I was happily munching and crunching as I read of sectarian killings in Baghdad and President Bush's boast that he's not illiterate, that he has read "Three Shakespeares so far this year."

Next stop was the Huntington Library, where I keep a desk under the stairs in a dark basement with no windows. A very secret burrow and I love its seclusion. Books are my only company plus the occasional ghost of an aged scholar abandoned in this netherworld many years ago and still unremembered.

On entering the Library I was surrounded by fetching young women who now run the special events department, women I'd never seen before. We finalized the concert I'm to give on Sunday for the General Public in Friend's Hall. The theme is Railroads and I will sing "The Wreck Of The Old 97" as well as the "Reckoning Train."

We also discussed a Titanic-themed cabaret evening for next year, should I still be alive. An evening of food and wine in a setting decorated like a dining room aboard the doomed ship. Wine, women, song — and a fee. How much money have I made out of this tragedy? I shudder to think.

After this I drove up to my P.O. Box in Altadena, making sure I went past our old house, hoping that there would be ambulances outside carting away the Evil One, or, even better, a For Sale sign. No such luck. We'd been informed by a neighbour that the Iranian was well on her way to greener pastures. But when Regina dropped by our property the other day she could distinctly hear loud cackling and snorting from the Evil One's backyard: the bitch was addressing her cell phone. She has friends? They must be fellow terrorists. And I must remember never to trust the word of a neighbour who is a Jehovah's Witness.

At the P.O. Box were cheques: for my songs that have been in movies now playing on TVs in the Far East. And even further afield. Good — we can have a decent dinner tonight and maybe a movie if there's anything worth watching. At home I got online at once to see if any more of my videos are up on YouTube. Yes, there's a few from the 1960s and also our classic feature short of 1992, made on location in Lone Pine, *Inspector To The Rescue*. Take a look. My pride in being available for screening 24 hours a day is spoiled by the fact that everyone else I know is for viewing up there, too — even performers I consider to be rank amateurs. The price for online democracy.

Then I went to my email. There was a letter from a Mr. Lee, Plastic Surgeon, in Malaysia. He is impressed by my songs in the movie, *Last Call* which he saw last night on the Hallmark Channel in his comfortable unit in Kuala Lumpar. Is it possible, kind sir, to get a CD of this exquisite music? Of course.

Then I saw a notice bannered across the top of his letter: "This material has been scanned for national security reasons." Well, I never. Modern times have reached *ianwhitcomb1*.

There were more work offers that afternoon, a radio play for me to co-star in, opposite Jo Ann Worley and Norman Lloyd; a gig for Ukie, Me & Regina at Universal Studios for the Assembled Set Dressers Of America; my article on Bob Mitchell of the Mitchell Boychoir is at last to appear in the November issue of *The Oldie"*in England.

And I managed to finish an instrumental I'd started writing last Sunday at Cantalini's when I felt like playing a Parisian two-beat number because the night before, at old Bob Board's Bijou Kinema at his cabin up in the Hollywood Hills he'd screened a documentary on Edith Piaf and she'd kept singing one of those yearning stretched repetitive French melodies like "The Poor People Of Paris," and so I made one up. Next day I stripped and polished — and decided that instead of being a Piaf sound-alike it would be a train number for the upcoming Huntington concert. The train number had to have a title: my mother used to read to my brother and me from a storybook and I wish I knew the title because I'd dearly love to re-read that story and regain lost times. But I do remember that the story involved one Ginger Winer, a cat, and how he took his pals Mr. Rah Bitt and Mr. Squeer-Rell for a train trip to the seaside where they inspected cockleshells, dipped in the briny with their trousers rolled up to the knees, and ended the day with candy floss and kish and fips on the pier.

So naturally I titled my instrumental, "Ginger Winer's Holiday Train" and it will have its premiere this Sunday at the Train Event.

No excuse then to be gloomy and wonder whether I'll ever work again. But no excuse to be happy and self-satisfied either: news from San Diego, where Regina's sister lives with her husband and son, is not good. Lanny's cancer has spread and spreads and now it's pressing and pushing and shoving into his throat. The poor fellow — confined to a hospital bed in his home hospice situation with a nurse and a doctor and much prayer.

He'd like to exit this world with a gentle tap from morphine the way my mother went. If only death could be a matter of going gently off to sleep like in the richly coloured stained glass picture of the Great War soldier in the church window of my prep school church. As the parson droned and the boys fidgeted and coughed, I looked at this serene boy private lying stately at the side of the battlefield. The legend underneath him stated "He went to sleep on the Somme, 1916."

My father told my mother he was going to take a nap but he never woke up — that must have been a painless departure. Oh no, corrected Regina, as we drove on this Tuesday evening to our night's entertainment. Oh no, she said, you don't know your father died peacefully. He may have been writhing in great pain, you don't know, no one goes easily. Regina knows about the facts of real life. She's canny. I've been avoiding Mr. Death all my life but even in my high bright sturdy Looming Tower he'll eventually find me and no amount of protestation from Ukie will stop him.

We were on our way into Old Pasadena for some free food: "Enjoy The Taste of Old Pasadena 2006" said our invitation from the friendly folk at Keller-Williams Realtors. From 5:30, when the grazing was advertised to begin, till 8:30 we wandered Bloom-like from restaurant to restaurant sampling the local cuisine.

Mostly we were confined in our sampling to the pavement where employees doled out tiny portions on paper plates while inside, sitting at nice tables groaning with full plates of delicious food, were real paying customers.

We were eating Happy Hour food. Still we got a taste of the bustling new, trendy, youthful, Old Pasadena and its global fare. Why travel? It's all here without the hassle: Italian focaccia bread, chocolate flown in from Belgium every Tuesday by Leonidas The Chocolatier; home-brewed ale at Gordon Biersch; curry from Hurry Curry; chicken wings and hot panted big-breasted girl waitresses at Hooters; paella at Barcelona, California sushi at Famima! — The Premium Experience, a Japanese Seven Eleven.

By 8pm the pavements were filled with hungry people wearing the same coloured wristbands as us. We were caught in a swill-sea of the General Public. But suddenly we were rescued.

I was hailed: "Meester Weetcoomb!" A waiter outside a new Mexican restaurant was hailing and smiling. Of course, it was Jesse, our helpful generous waiter from years back when my Monday night Salon used to meet at Mijares, a Mex joint nearby, the spot where Paul McCartney can be found because there he's unrecognized especially when Monday night football is playing on the banks of TVs hanging from the walls.

Jesse had left Mijares under a cloud, accused of being in cahoots with the barman in order to serve us margaritas at a budget price. I remember the night of his departure. I entered at the usual time for our Salon. The owner — a wall-eyed creep who never recognized my illustrious rocker past and loved telling me that Paul McCartney, whom he called "Paul," had been there only a night ago — confronted me: "Jesse is no longer your waiter" Why? "He's in the parking lot being arrested by the police for fraud and you were working with him I think." How dare you talk to me like that! So we moved to Conrad's Coffee Shop and Family Restaurant where there may be long-dead sandwiches, cobwebbed french fries and even old customers resting under the booth seats, but at least they treat us right

Jesse welcomed us into his new place of work, pointing out the massive pillars and huge paintings depicting the glories of Aztec or Mayan life or whatever it was — a noble and god-like ancient culture that seems a far cry from the chips and salsa and fat bottoms of today. I remember a more recent past — when this Mexican restaurant was a Ruby's Diner, where Elvis and Danny & The Juniors could be heard in rotation.

The management emerged all rubbing their hands with glee, offering us 15% discount coupons. And pamphlets describing a history of La Huasteca Restaurant. It dates from 2004 and offers "a true sample of the Mexican cuisine that has been served throughout the last century in the cities, towns and countryside pueblos of Old Mexico. Our coordinator will assist you in choosing your perfect menu."

Is there any live music? Not yet but maybe. I then told the assembled company about how my fellow Parlour Boy, Tom Marion had caused a sensation at Conrad's a short time ago. How he'd naturally brought his guitar and, after a beer or two, had started playing a lively march melody.

Suddenly from out of the kitchen and from doors and holes I'd never seen before, from under the table, from the men's room, from out of the woodwork so to speak — came Mexicans dancing and singing and throwing up their hands in glee. To our delight and amazement they entertained us in this colourful folk manner till the march finished.

Then, as suddenly as they'd appeared, as in a dream, they scuttled. It was as if all of imported Mexico, legal and illegal, had been called to the front by a clarion call of national importance. The INS would have had a field day. Later, after normality returned, I asked Tom what magic music he had been playing. He said it was a famous revolutionary tune from the days of Pancho Villa and that the lyrics were an incendiary attack on gringos of all shapes and sizes.

My story fell on stony ground. Management and even Jesse stared. So we shuffled off to our next free venue, which, happily, was a Wine Cellar where a would-be actor and voice-over star, was pouring three kinds of wines for our inspection and judgment. And that ended the night of tasting. Oh, except for our stopping off at the Dog Park — a recent gift from the City of Pasadena — where we let the long-suffering Rollo have lots of leg lifts. The poor devil had been waiting in the Honda all this time while we were out sampling. He was able in the darkness to find a bitch and do some humping. To his chagrin there was also a big black male dog who fancied our hetero hound and who kept trying to make it into a threesome. Rollo growled him off. But the dog persisted. What an eternal triangle! So eventually we hauled Rollo off and retired to our Monrovia camp-apartment where I went to bed in a Trinity College Old Boy's tie. I want my correspondent Andy to know that. I went to bed in a tie and the overall color was green. Meanwhile, as I blog on, the New Crusades continue.

NOVEMBER

While Regina was in San Diego acting like an angel during the last days of our poor brother-in-law as he lost his struggle with a creeping cancer that eventually shut him down, I was in charge of holding the fort here in Monrovia.

"Holding the fort" comes ready-made, off-the-peg. No, the real "fort" is our old home in Altadena where lies the woman who trades in claiming to have terminal cancer but in fact is lying in order to get sympathy and attention from gullible Jehovah's Witness neighbours. My brother-in-law, Lanny—a splendid man with great talent as an inventor and blessed with a sweet disposition—has to die before his time while the venomous Iranian steams ahead, spewing contumely. If only God would reveal himself and explain his grand plan. But, lacking the presence of the Great Inventor, we soldier on, victims, perhaps, of a monstrous practical joke—sentience—played by a heartless Nature.

Life in our Monrovia apartment was peaceful, but we missed the missus. Clothes that need washing pile up; I can't find the can opener; I'll never get used to the idea of jabbing a needle into Simon in order to fill him with life-giving fluid. The kitchen table area looks like a hospital operating room. I talk to the pets, Rollo The Dog and Simon The Cat. They follow me from room to room. They sleep on me and near me when I'm in bed. If Simon gets a go at the dental floss after I've finished with it then Rollo jumps up and comes over so that he can have a go at it too.

I have an alternate world in my dreams. I've kept a Dream Book since March of 1972, recording the memorable ones. Most nights—not worth noting — it's the same comfortable London of the late 1940s: grimy and dark, stuck with tall black looming buildings, and smelling of hot coal and oil. I change trains constantly, ending my journey either at my mother's flat in time for a drink before supper, or going to a rickety shack by the seaside, surrounded by sand, where the waves beat a steady rhythm on the pebbles.

While Regina was away I took the seaside train — with interruptions from Ginger Winer and his animal pals who were whooping it up in First Class, singing songs of carrots and milk—and found, upon arrival, an invitation to a gathering from new neigbours across the sand.

The clapboard house turned out to be the summer residence of relatives of Irving Berlin. Was I thrilled! This dream world is terrific because, not only is everybody who was dead now alive, but I have met choice ones at gatherings. To name a few: "Whispering" Jack Smith—in a corner at a cocktail party—Adolf Hitler—at a church fete where he revealed that he is a keen ukulele player.

The Berlin family retreat was a modest place. I noticed scratches on cupboards and ottomans. A son who resembled a younger Irving introduced me to the Master. He looked very chipper, in a tweed jacket and Ascot. Everybody had lots of tight curly black hair and was sleek and sallow, but generally welcoming.

There were no less than three pianos in the drawing room and the Master wanted to talk and play music. It was hard to hear him because he spoke in a whisper and the rain was pelting down, beating out a contradictory rhythm to that of the eternal waves.

With a grin he opened a Regina music box and out came a tinkling "Swedish Rhapsody." I was surprised at his choice because he didn't write this tune. Next moment he'd secreted himself behind a Chinese screen. We could hear him banging on a keyboard. A relative signaled to me to climb on top of a steamer trunk. We were afforded a view of the Master at work. I was interested to see he wasn't playing in his favourite key of F#—he was in the People's Key of C.

He introduced a new song, playing a queer little scramble of a flourish, as if cleaning the keys with an invisible feather duster. Then he performed the sort of primeval Tin Pan Alley waltz ballad that I've always adored. I forced myself to wake up and jump out of bed. I dashed to the electronic keyboard, switched it on and clamped on the headphones. I had to get the words and music down before dawn and consciousness would whisk them away.

Here are the words. For the music, you'll have to wait till I've recorded it. Or maybe you can drop in some Sunday night to Cantalini's and we'll play it for you...

LOVE NEVER MAKES A MISTAKE

Verse:

Sages say this, sages say that.
They think that they've worked it all out.
Should have done this—
Went and did that—
Now you're hooked and you're cooked like a trout.

I say it all had to happen.
I know what life's all about.

Chorus:

Love never makes a mistake, dear.
Love never gets it all wrong.
You said the moment you met me
Life came as sweet as a song.
Even tho' friends had their doubts and
Said you'd be trouble and strife.
Love never makes a mistake so
We'll be together for life!

Andy Wickham arrived in Los Angeles at the beginning of October. He had traveled first class by plane in order to spend a week in Costa Mesa attending a Russian production of Wagner's Ring Cycle, accompanied by relevant lectures by world-class experts. He denies being a Ringhead, but I think this comes pretty close. I never associated Wagner with the nearness of surfers (Huntington Beach, where the art was first demonstrated by George Freeth)—and yet, on second thought, Wagner's superfan Hitler would certainly have approved of the Aryan looks and ripple stomachs of the wave fraternity.

Andy was in the company of his longtime mentor and walking lecturer, Dr. Randolph Fischer, a Wagnerian who has racked up a dozen Ring Cycles and has around 50 CD versions of the opera and is game for more. Dr. Fischer, whom I got to know through Andy in early 1970s Hollywood, now makes his home in the High Desert, surrounded by imminent fires, permanent rocks and sand, and lots of marines. The latter he teaches instant history and literature to at a nearby base. He lives alone in a small apartment in Joshua Tree where he keeps in touch with the real world via BBC broadcasts and quality magazines.

They had invited me to join them for a day—during a break in the action— at Andy's hotel, the towering new hotel Westin, sitting pretty amidst other gleaming towers in that spanking new city where once roamed sheep and such. Local developer Henry Segerstrum's name is cut, painted and plastered everywhere. A vast concert hall was recently erected in his name.

Randy and Andy greeted me from their couch in the main lobby of the Westin. Randy sprang forward to grasp my hand: "Cherished friend!" They told me breathlessly that I'd just missed the Maestro himself, conductor Valery Gergiev, a dynamic man. Randy had bowed to him, as is his wont, and wished him a "Bravo, Maestro!" followed by a bow.

I was treated to a stream of very un-American men and women passing us in the lobby, all dressed in black, very lean and tall, and mostly puffing away at ciggies. Members of the Kirov, from St. Petersburg. We repaired, across a stone bridge with no river underneath, to a shopping mall and a branch of "Baja Fresh." Andy loves this place, a discovery for him, he'd had breakfast and lunch here every day of the opera. Can't get enough of the salsa and the Mexican beer.

And what had the performances been like? Up to snuff? They told me that as there'd been a contretemps between the director and other Kirov powers prior to departure for the tour, the Cycle was without direction and thus it was every man for himself. The result was that cues were missed and there'd be cries of direction in basso Russian from the wings and other places during a performance. But, as Andy pointed out, at least this was *The Ring* in its original setting and not forced into the modern world. He told me of a production set in a McDonald's where Rhine Maidens sang between tables set with burgers and fries...At this point his attention was caught by an overhanging TV screen: CNN was reporting on the recent murder of a female Russian investigative journalist. Andy told us whodunit: an order from President Putin, a dictator Andy admires.

Randy kept looking at his watch—he had to leave us soon for appointments in L.A. for this was a day when the operas were rested. Not even a lecture—I'd like to have been at these. Andy said there were lots of expatriate English lecturers hired, all good. But the best was a Simon Williams from the University of Santa Barbara. Very suave and pukka. Andy hadn't yet found out what school he'd been to.

In lieu of high culture experiences Andy and I decided to walk through two malls—one up market and the next very low market—to an Edwards cinema complex. We caught an afternoon showing of *The Departed*, which was certainly high drama but not high culture. On the way back we got lost but in our wanderings we ran across a Victoria's Secret. Andy got me to accompany him inside so that he could buy a pair of ladies' knickers that happened to be in the colours of his old school. For one of his lady friends, of course.

And instead of Shostakovich in the evening we went to a Japanese restaurant and had sushi. Andy had a laughing fit up at the counter as the chef made a display of expertly slicing halibut and shark. The fit was caused by his remembering that once, in the presence of Dr. Fischer, our teacher, I'd had confusion about whether Bach was Renaissance or Baroque. Embarrassed and apoplectic, I spluttered: "I know nothing!" Andy immediately pulled out his leather-bound pocket notebook and jotted down my foolish statement. "Priceless! Priceless!" he chortled.

After Andy left for London and the pleasantness of his Chelsea flat overlooking the Thames and his country cottage near a stream and after Regina left for the impending tragedy in San Diego, I submerged myself in the world of YouTube. Not the crassness of boys fighting and cats playing the guitar, not even the over 20 songs that I can be seen singing. No, none of such stuff: instead I entered a visual jukebox where at the click of a mouse I could watch many of my favourite singers of the past. I became a tubie—a video junkie following my bliss from artist to artist...........I was hooked.

First you have to type in the name for the search. I typed in what I considered to be an obscure one.

I was rewarded with Chas McDevitt & His Skiffle Group in a scene from *The Tommy Steele Story,* made in 1957. I hadn't seen Chas and the lads since that year of release. Four guitars thrashing away, backed by an upright bass and an intense washboard. Fronting is Nancy Whiskey, of Glasgow, singing soprano to the obbligato whistling of Chas. They're in outdoor clothes: tight jeans and open-neck shirts. All very healthy.

Such a sunny scene is very much in contrast to the gloomy story of a boy with a future at the end of a rope. The 1904 song by Elizabeth Cotton, "Freight Train," landed Chas & Co. not only in the British Top Ten but was also big in America—long before the Beatles.

I have seen this clip several times and love the earnest breeziness of the players and the sweet natural smile of Nancy when she looks into the camera ever so shyly every so often. Melts me.

After Chas I clicked on Lonnie Donegan, Alma Cogan, and Johnnie Ray –very neurotic as he sings "Cry" in 1953 with a big band backing, running off the stage at the end like a scared rabbit. A haunted boy.

Guy Mitchell is more manly: square-jawed and solid, performing "Singing The Blues" in a 1980 rendition on stage accompanied by The Four Lads. The record hit in the mid fifties but it's a truly extraordinary rendition because the arrangement is fairly true to the original— right down to the insidiously catchy whistling riff here played energetically by four flautists.

Needing more educational material (and curious to see if my friends and colleagues are up on YouTube) I typed up Dick Hyman. He's seen demonstrating some keyboard devices used by Art Tatum.

The camera is overhead so you can see exactly what notes and fingering made up the Tatum virtuoso tricks. Dick slows down the lick and examines it, like a spoilsport showing you a magician's tricks. Now that I know how the flash licks are done I'm not so in awe of Mr. Tatum. All music is just maths. The trick is to make it sound human. I wonder how long this free treasure trove will remain before the corporate copyright owners swipe it off the screen.

My best discovery was finding extracts from Carlos Gardel movies. I've always been fond of this Argentinian hero. I respond emotionally to the macho anguish of his tango singing even though I can't understand a word.

Gardel, who was actually born in France, looks like the archetypal Latin lover-gentleman on the screen: tight-fitting dark pin stripe suit, striped tie and rakish fedora. And, of course, plastered lambent hair. Much oil has been used. When he sings the classic "Mi Buenos Aires Querido" to the captain at the rail of an ocean liner Gardel has his hand on the captain's shoulder at the start but by the end, at the big finish, the hand, with fingers now splayed, is pressing hard on the breast area of the man's uniform. Nothing queer—just a man among men. A well-mannered, correct man who was never familiar and whose ardour was clean and never sexual. The tango tune is reminiscent of Victor Herbert's earlier ballad, "Ah Sweet Mystery Of Life," but never mind—it takes on a new guise in Gardel's strong and meaty hands. This isn't a Bob Dylan steal. Notice how much he has in common with Al Jolson.

The video had been viewed 3000 times—so it read when I last visited. Underneath there's space for comments. All in Spanish—except: "Awesome! Awesome!"

I am returning to England in November—to visit family and friends. Regina found me a really cheap round trip ticket without my asking. She will be staying behind to take care of the apartment and pets.

Regina has just e-mailed me from San Diego: she writes that the first thing her sister said after the death of her husband Lanny was: "Who will pour?" This is what my mother asked at the time of my father's death in December, 1962. It was right between tea and cocktail time.

DECEMBER

I've just returned from two weeks in London and I should be jet-lagged and disorientated but I'm not. I'm happy to be back in Monrovia. I promised Regina that this time round I wouldn't go moaning about how terrific England is and how I'd rather live there; about how London is set in stone, has been there for centuries and how you can walk its twenty thousand streets on solid slabs of stone, stone that is substantial and won't accept any nonsense, no babble about receiving the rapture, or fundamental religions. No, no — if London hears anything like that it replies: "Pull the other one — it's got bells on!"

Here are some of the highlights of the trip.

The purpose was to see my brother and sister and my two best friends over there, Jeremy Lewis and Chas Sprawson. Regina had arranged all this. She had grabbed a cheap ticket on British Airways that she'd spotted online. She'd had to grab it that second otherwise it would be gone in a trice. She knew I'd been pining to see my family and friends again. Very thoughtful. And for the trip she'd bought me a mini-traveling kit containing a tiny toothpaste tube, tiny deodorant stick, even tinier laxative pills (with special directions about not taking too many).

I've never understood why, in all of my forty odd years of flying across the Atlantic, the flight from L.A. to London is never full, but coming back it's always choc-a-bloc. Is this because, in actuality, the world wants to go to Los Angeles and not so much to London? The general opinion is that L.A. is LaLaland, Clowntown, Tinseltown, a hellhole, and that London is a centre of civilization—theatres, galleries, museums, etc. Of course, I believe in L.A. which is why I live here.

Anyway, the British Airways plane was pretty empty so I had a row all to myself. Was this an early boycott of the airline due to the female employee who had been ordered to remove the tiny cross around her neck because it was Christian? Heathrow was buzzing with airport workers in turbans, skullcaps and Arabic veils when I arrived. A multi-cultural festival………..

Back to my flight: this is my chance to concentrate on decent literature, not yet Proust, but an English writer I've always enjoyed, provided I have the time and the peace. As we jetted over plains, frozen lakes, tundra and then ocean, I dug into Patrick Hamilton's *Twenty Thousand Streets Under The Sky,* a trilogy of stories set in 1930s London. Soon, with help from free bottles of red wine, I was snug in a setting of smoky, beery pubs, tarts, clattery corner house cafes, and carpeted cinemas offering instant romance…….

Bob and Ella, who work as waiter and barmaid in a London pub, are having a night off, at the pictures:

"*He asked for two two-and-fours, and Ella could take it or leave it. She being at the time under the eyes of a tall, vigilant, and rather inquisitive attendant in uniform, took it. Whereat the attendant, satisfied of their honesty, pulled back the door, and the waiter and barmaid went through into an atmosphere of dim, shaded lights and heavy carpets. Here they were met by two voluptuous but doll-like young creatures wearing pert brown dresses and enormous bows in their hair, and the whole thing was decidedly Eastern. With profound and charming veneration one of these seductresses put forth a nail-glinting and powdered hand, gathered Bob's tickets, and with a pleasant manner at once ushered himself and Ella down the centre gangway....*

At last they were settled. In a few moments they were a part of the audience. That is to say their faces had abandoned every trace of the sensibility and character they had borne outside, and had taken on instead the blank, calm, inhuman stare of the picturegoer—an expression which would observe the wrecking of ships, the burning of cities, the fall of empires, the projection of pies, and the flooding of countries with an unchanging and grave equanimity."

My sanctuary was interrupted by the voice of our captain, a voice rather too urbane, and oozing an unctuous calm, the kind he'd use, no doubt, had a terrorist been at that moment pressing a sharpened thumbtack into his back: "Hello, people — sorry to bother your slumber but we'll be landing shortly. Sorry about the weather — drizzly and a trifle soggy all around, but Trafalgar Square's still there, Helen Mirren's on the throne, and *Strictly Come Dancing* will be on the telly as per usual. So nothing changes in the Land Of Beckham. Needless to say, it was our pleasure serving you today, understand."

My brother Robin was there to meet me as I exited with the two battered Samsonite suitcases I originally bought for the Australian ragtime tour in 1984. Robin recently retired from Dulwich College prep school where he'd been a popular sports teacher for decades. Before that, as some of you know, he played drums with Sonny & Cher and is immortalized as the tambourine player on "I Got You Babe." He's four years younger than me. In his sporty new Volvo, with optimistic sunroof, he drove me through the gray drizzle and hurried drivers to his terrace home, The Molehouse in Wimbledon.

Robin has recently acquired a new dog. Well, not a new dog exactly—she's five years old and called Coco. He didn't name her; he was offered her by farm folk in Wales who had too many dogs. She doesn't care to be left alone, as I witnessed when he opened the door of The Molehouse. Phew! A smell of biggies—and then the sight of brown lumps spread equally over the white carpet that Robin had had cleaned in preparation for my arrival.

Quickly he cleaned up the mess and soon the house was exuding that school-nostalgic aroma of muscular disinfectant. I felt sorry for Coco—she so dotes on Robin and only wants to be at his side or behind him at all times. Unlike Rollo who likes to be in front of the action. She's so quiet and looks like she suffered in the past. But it's a problem for Robin—he can't leave her for even the shortest time without her barking and crying for him. Then the old bag next door—this is a terrace house so that Robin shares a wall with his neighbours—gets angry and turns up a talk radio station full blast. And I can't tell you how grating is the continuous sound of the new British accent: cockney without melody. In contrast, American talk show hosts are pure honey.

So I see a tragedy in the making. Robin's movements are now restricted, for he's determined to keep Coco. He says his life revolves around Coco, the Roehampton Country Cub, and his super new TV set—a flat widescreen Panasonic that stretches across the far corner of his living room. He demonstrated its powers with a quick viewing of a BBC travelogue broadcast in High Definition.

We were swooped down the north coast of Scotland peeping into the tiniest cracks in mountains, examining the varieties of grains of seashore sand, and when the host's face — celebrity talk-head David Dimbleby — popped up I could count every facial pockmark had I wanted to. It seemed our helicoptered camera might at any moment collide with another film crew documenting fissures and wave textures from the south of Scotland upward. Very impressed, but I begged for rest.

I went upstairs and nodded off in my usual room, rising later in time for a delicious version of my mother's traditional macaroni cheese dish, washed down with lots of Retsina. In fact, I drank the whole bottle. I was on holiday, you see.

The meal was accompanied by a viewing of a popular celebrity chef show—one of those "Reality" shows that dominate British TV – starring Gordon Ramsay. Each week he takes over a restaurant on the brink of bankruptcy and shows and tells them how to extract. His every other word is "fuck" and this gets tiresome but he makes his points and saves the place—in this case, the stubborn owner of a pretentious restaurant on the Coast Del Sol in Spain who was offering 70 dishes ranging from curry to spaghetti and chips. His signature dish was a disgusting mixture of prawns with chocolate chilli sauce. "Fuck this shit!" says Gordon and goes to work with a push and a shove. Boggled by this and addled by wine I toddled up to bed.

An edited version of my daily journal:

WEDNESDAY, NOVEMBER 15

Breakfasted off taramasalata (a salty fish roe paste unobtainable over here) and Ryvita crispbread—all thoughtfully bought for me in advance of my trip by Robin—as I read the tabloid "Daily Mail" and the broadsheet "Daily Telegraph." Pretty much the same stories in both but differently presented. Much livelier than the po-faced, taking-itself-too-seriously "Los Angeles Times." Bought the papers—from an array of daily national papers—at the little shop at the end of the road, where sits a little Indian woman and has done for years but she never recognizes me. All the little shops are run by Indians. Or else it's Pakistanis. No love lost between the two nations. Hindus v. Muslims. The story of modern Europe. Is Britain yet a part of Europe? On my return to "The Molehouse" I saw a fully veiled Muslim woman being helped out of a Mercedes by a fellow practitioner in what looked like a fez.

Intended to accompany Robin on his afternoon trip to see a rich man who owns an odd mod house on a gated estate in Weybridge, where reside such stars as Sir Cliff Richard and Sir Sean Connery. Knights from humble places. Earlier I'd rung another new Knight, but this one from the same class that knights used to come from: Sir Tim Rice. Known Tim for decades but lost touch. Got through his assistants in a trice. Very friendly. We talked of YouTube and how he'd just watched Dell Shannon and Ral Donner. Told him about my presence on the Tube. He promised to watch. What's he up to? "Oh, nothing—just hanging in, you know." Hanging in! He has "Evita" in a revival in the West End and "Blondel" coming on next week. Not to mention all the Disney songs with Sir Elton. Started sweating—must be jet lag. Promised to keep in touch.

Robin's research is for a book project on people who live in odd houses, "Home Sweet Home." As I said, I wanted to be with him. But he looked in on me in my bedroom and saw I was flat on my back covered in "The Daily Telegraph" and snoring. So he left. Woke around cocktail time—6pm. Robin preparing an elaborate dinner he'd got from a Gordon Ramsay cookbook, or was it from Jamie Oliver, another celeb chef? Beef bourguignon. Watched him making it while he told me how he'd had a contretemps on the road on way back from the rich man's estate. A "Four By Four" (GB term for SUV) had tailgated and flashed lights. Robin stayed at the correct safe speed. Infuriated Four by Four overtook, but as he did Robin gave him the two-finger sign. Four by Four screeches to halt in heavy traffic. Driver, a beefy brute, gets out, marches over and screams Gordon Ramsay words at Robin. Ends with a kick to the Volvo. Coco sleeps peacefully.

After dinner I watched one of Robin's thousand cable channels: a live broadcast from the House of Commons. Amazed to see only four MPs listening to speech by the honorable member from Banbury. And, of those four MPs, three were chatting while the other was asleep with mouth wide open.

THURSDAY, NOVEMBER 16

At Jeremy's suggestion I phone veteran comedy scriptwriter

Barry Cryer to fix up a meeting with me, him and J at a Soho pub. No idea how Cryer knows about me but he treated me like a celebrity. He gets hired for "Oldie" magazine literary lunches if a big name drops out at last minute. Always good for a joke. Told me how Spike Milligan, at an "Oldie" lunch, had been approached by a sycophantic reader who stuck out his hand and said, "I want to shake the hand of a truly great British gentleman." "Fuck off," replied the famous Goon, "I'm Irish."

Up to Earl's Court by Tube. Sat opposite a scarfed Muslim woman but buried myself in my "Daily Mail," making sure she could see a headline concerned about plans to build the biggest mosque in the world near London Airport. Is this what Olympic Games visitors ought to be seeing as they fly in?— screamed the paper.

Chas Sprawson lives in a one-room flat once owned by an employee of John Cleese. Chas has left the man's double-barreled name on the nameplate outside. Up the dark and gloomy staircase. Chas in better health than last time. Blue workshirt undone almost to navel. Still smoking up a storm.

We lunched al fresco at a pavement café run by Egyptians. Patrick Hamilton was run down and badly hurt not far from here in the 1930s. We ate croque monsieurs in the wind and rain as traffic crashed past us. Next we walked up West to a posh art gallery where Chas was to pick up an expensive Victorian seascape in oil. This he will take next Monday by plane to Dublin where he will deposit it with his wealthy client, a tax exile. The gallery owner is very upper class and turns out to be the nephew of Celia Johnson, co-star of "Brief Encounter."

After that, with Chas in charge of a brown-paper parceled-up painting worth thousands of pounds, we popped into Harrods to see if the record department, where I once worked in late 1959, was still operating. It isn't, but there are lots of plasma TVs and video games. But I did see the extraordinarily vulgar bronze statues of Princess Diana and Dodie Fayed (son of the owner of Harrods and man who is still being denied British citizenship). The display bashes you in the eye as you enter the store:

Diana and Dodie are hand in hand, tugged through the air by a dove. "Innocent Victims" proclaims a large lapidary notice. There's a book to sign. People were lining up to write their thoughts. I signed: "Tunefully, Osama Dun Rovin." Not very clever, but it's a gesture.

Had a bit of trouble getting on a Tube at rush hour. Jampacked. Had to wait through three trains before we could squeeze in. Chas deposited his precious painting on the toes of a tall lout. Luckily the man was wearing heavy army boots and didn't notice. Back at the Chas flat I fell asleep, jet-lagged again, while "The Way

To The Stars," a great World War Two RAF film starring John Mills, played on the video.

Around 7pm we walked through hard rain to Margaret Vyner's flat in Onslow Square. A lovely lady, she is Chas' boon companion these days. Was the great beauty of Oxford in the early 1950s, and knows High Society intimately but never boasts. Always has a tray of drinks, complete with soda syphon, at the ready, and a pile of new hardbacks on her dining room table. Just returned from a weekend in Kelvedon. I know Kelvedon as a rather dull town in Essex full of common people. What was she doing there? Why, staying at Kelvedon Hall with Lord Kelvedon, of course. All matter of fact, no side stuff.

On to the Chelsea Art Club for dinner with Margaret's younger sister and husband, an investment broker in the City. Never met them before. Club full of the usual unemployed posing as artists. Man in next urinal to me— the club booker of the jazz bands who annoyingly compete with one's conversation in the bar, muttered, "Must hire Humphrey Lyttleton to blow his horn before he croaks." Food is always good — sensibly English. Except I ordered broiled tuna — and promptly got attacked by the investment broker, Ivan. "Why are you having tuna when you can get that in the Land Of George Doubleya Bush?"

Tried to engage him in pleasantries but was met with nastiness. He simply hates America, a common position over here among moneyed people of the old school. Tried to convince me that there's no city in L.A., merely sprawl. I tried to explain that Los Angeles is a county and that within that county are cities like Pasadena and even, er..., Monrovia. He'd have none of it — no, no — he knew, he's been there — and only San Francisco is a city.

As we got up to leave at the end of the evening Ivan, turning sideways slightly to address me, said: "Goodbye. I don't even know your name and have no idea what you do. But even if you told me I wouldn't remember because I have no interest whatsoever."

Chas and Margaret hadn't noticed any of this internecine strife. They said they'd seen me smiling constantly and assumed that Ivan and I were busy "bonding."

NOVEMBER 19, SUNDAY

In contrast to last night's indoor activities we had a day at the seaside. Robin drove Coco and me to Brighton. An unnaturally bright and sunny day—so everybody else seemed to have the same idea: approach to Brighton choked with cars. Brighton! Where variety stars like Max Miller retired; Laurence Olivier had a house here too. And the two piers! The Palace and The West, full of chocolate bar machines (empty due to the war), and Real American Doughnuts. Which pier was it where, in 1950, I came across the *fun box containing a golliwog who mimed to Al Jolson's "Swanee" if you put in a penny? The Jolson experience was seminal, telling me that America was my country, the place of song and promise and freedom and Dixie.*

But there's only one pier left and it calls itself a generic "Brighton Pier." The other one was destroyed a few years ago. How? All that's left are some rusty metal poles, a sort of skeleton sitting in the slate-grey water. Robin suggested a trad fish'n'chip lunch on the Promenade. We sat down at a table outside once such emporium. Coco quietly settled herself with the slightest wheeze.

An unpleasant-looking man nearby, sprawled in a deck chair, remarked: "We don't ALL like dogs, you know." Robin: "Sounds like your problem." The man reacted badly. We ordered our fish'n'chips. Two children came up and petted Coco. "Some people, you see, DO like dogs," said Robin. The man came over, snarling: "Say any more like that I'll have to ask you to leave." He was the proprietor. I bent down over my lunch, huddled into my raincoat, and pulled down my fedora. I was not anxious to get involved in the action even if I did resemble a Scotland Yard detective from a 1950s B picture. A couple approached and admired Coco, stroking him. Robin started to speak. "I warned you," said the man. I strolled up to him and enquired about whether I was eating plaice or cod. "Cod," he said. "And very nice indeed," I continued. "I'd like to congratulate you on the quality of your fish, not to mention the firmness of your chips." He looked blankly at me. Then: "Thank you, squire....You know, I really do like dogs. It's just that he didn't ask me – the proprietor's – permission...." Then Robin congratulated him on the cod's texture. All was well. I have learned from life in Los Angeles to avoid confrontation at all costs. That's why we relocated to Monrovia.

After lunch we moved on to Seaford, where we'd both been at boarding school in the 1950s. Took a bracing walk on the cliffs of Seaford Head, with the wind buffeting and my nose running and my fedora in danger of flying away and across to France. The cliffs of the Seven Sisters were ahead of us. I pictured RAF officers on leave in the summer of 1939 lying with their girls on the cliff top grass after a lazy picnic. Only a jealous nation could have wanted to fly warplanes over to destroy such an idyll. On the horizon was a panoramic spread of black cloud with a sheet of rain spitting straight down to the sea. Looked like a cinematic special effect. CGI? Robin pronounced the scene to be Spielbergian.

Anxious to see what has become of Newlands, our old prep school, we dropped in. The newspapers had written of the school being sold on the sly by the greedy family of our old headmaster, H. M. Chittenden, a reluctant expert in the administration of the cane. We were relieved to find the place still operating. Lines of school buses marked "Newlands Ltd," sitting smartly in the driveway. We were peeping through the front room window — into the hall where our parents used to wait for us to rush out and greet them, even kiss them, so happy were we to be taken out from this hell at rare visiting weekends, relieved to see that mummy and daddy were still alive, that we hadn't been removed from them and home for ever—when suddenly an SUV roared up. And out stepped a thickset man with a boxer's face. "Hello, I'm the headmaster. Call me Buster!"

He recognized Robin as a fellow sports master. They'd been at conferences together. Buster invited us in, keen to show us the improvements being made to the school. Yes, they'd been saved by parents who'd forked up a cool 4 million to keep the place going. School's never been in better nick. Yeagh, yeagh, yeagh! Look at the cafeteria and the new music school with the computer keyboards!

But I pointed out the spot where I'd slugged a bully called Bayliss after Robin had told me that the boy had beaten him up. And I also showed Buster the urinal where a boy called Buston had peed on me in the summer of 1954 and how I'd been to see the headmaster. The old HM: "And what exactly occurred?" "Sir—Buston was excused all over me!" You see, in order to be allowed to go to the lavatory during class you had to raise your hand and ask, "Sir, may I be excused?"

The new HM: "We've come a long way since those days. A long way."

Then, growing excited, he went on to tell us of the success of their music and arts department, of how they now have a theatrical agency within the school itself, supplying boys and girls—they've been co-educational for decades — for movies and musicals. Buster's very own daughter was recently a finalist in the TV reality show about finding a Maria for Lord Webber's new version of "The Sound Of Music." Bryony's her name, you must have seen her.

I still wanted to regain my past. Can we see the boards where the names of Old Boys are painted? Still there, thank heavens. Still the names of the scholars, the swots, in gold, and then the names with crosses against them to show that they'd died in battle in world wars one and two. The Big Schoolroom has been broken up into smaller classrooms. I couldn't find the spot where there used to be a calendar slab. Everyday TDM, the vice-headmaster, would ceremoniously peel off yesterday and reveal today's date—with a different limerick. There's one I've never forgotten. Found myself reciting it to Buster:

"There was a young fellow from Sydenham
Who lost his best pants with a quid in 'em

He found 'em again
Down in Petticoat Lane
But there wasn't a quid but a yid in 'em"

"As I said—we've come a long way," said Buster and we thanked him for the tour, congratulating him, in the same way we did with the fish'n'chip shop proprietor, on all the improvements, all the modernization. "Times move—and we move with them!" said Buster.

MONDAY, NOVEMBER 20

To "Hatchard's," the nobby bookshop in Piccadilly, not far from the sushi bar where the Russian ex-spy may have been poisoned. The tabloids are describing the poison as like a mini-atom bomb. Andy Wickham had told me to meet him there at 2pm. Persuaded me, within seconds, to buy a book, "Murder In Samarkand," by the sacked British ambassador to Uzbekistan, the country to which Bush's men send suspected terrorists that they aren't allowed to torture in America. The Uzbeks are fond of boiling Islamists alive.

Andy was in high spirits, squirrelly really. Said that my "genius" is only experienced in person when I get "curdled" by things going wrong. From Hatchard's we tubed to the Guildhall in the City where we saw an exhibition of paintings by William Frith, famous for "Derby Day." Andy was shaken at being let in for only a pound. We're seniors—or Old Age Pensioners, as they call us over here. Andy didn't think much of the Friths. What impressed him, in a gloomy way, was afterwards, as we worked our way back to the tube: the sight of row upon row, floor upon floor, of today's office workers seen through glass as they sat in steel towers gazing into computers. Neo-Dickensian workhouse. We saw a girl smile as she gazed. This is happening all over the world right now, said Andy. Even the smile?

Next we hit the National Gallery where we saw some Cezannes. More to Andy's liking. Shattering, he said. He showed little interest in what I've been up to. Seriously, he suddenly said, as we entered a taxi—he'd become fed up with the tube and all the scrum of hoi polloi—seriously, he said from the cushions of the taxi, you should write a Juke Box musical about being an upper class boy who found himself in rock & roll. Unique. I said I'd ponder this.

We had cocktails at one of his clubs, The East India. Then on to the Polish Quarter Club in Queen's Gate. Rather a mausoleum: high rooms and elegance, lots of oils of celebrated past Poles on the walls, but nobody around except waiters and receptionists. All real Poles, though. Tried to make conversation with the barman about how my RAF father in WW2 had arranged for the Polish air force— stationed in Scarborough where we were—to march past my baby carriage and, at a command, turn and salute me. The barman looked blank. Andy scolded me. "Everyone knows about their air force being here in the war. That's tourist stuff." Since he was picking up the bill I said nothing. Later we got into a discussion about perfect records. He says that Elvis' "Suspicion" is perfection. I countered with "Mess Of Blues." Nonsense, he said. There's no melody. I ate humble pie. But he did walk with me to the tube.

TUESDAY, NOVEMBER 21
Bought a suit at Baron's of Piccadilly—a double-breasted with bold grey pinstripes, my idea of a 1940s gangster suit, but maybe it's a little more like a London banker. "Suits you to a T," sir, said the assistant. I must have shopped here a dozen times over the years but the staff never remember me. I asked whether it's true that the Baron name is connected with Sacha Baron Cohen, better known as "Borat." The assistants went quiet. Yes, yes, his uncle owns the shop, but we don't talk about the boy. A disgrace to the family. Can I interest you in some ties for your suit?

Wandered around the West End to kill time till I could report to Virginia Ironside's house in Shepherd's Bush for dinner. Trudge, trudge, trudge, through wind and rain, dodging people all the time. Such negotiation! Never collided though. None of the record stores have any of my CDs. Nor have I a book in any bookshop. I am back to being a member of the public. The words of one of the masters at Bryanston came back: "Don't you sometimes consider, Whitcomb, that some of us have to constitute the audience?"

Jeremy and wife Petra were the other dinner guests. Virginia is currently enjoying a late success—her novel in the form of a diary called "No, I Don't Want To Join A Book Club" has been published by a major imprint and has so far been translated into 14 languages, including Croatian. She showed me the Dutch version. Julie Walters is slated to star in the TV version. She'll be over to the USA early next year for a six-city promotion tour. "So now I know what it must have been like for you when you hit the top of the charts with 'Nervous'." It was actually "You Turn Me On" but I didn't argue. I congratulated her on this autumnal success. And Jeremy has two books in the works. And Robin has his house book project. Still, I take comfort in the fact that Chas hasn't published anything since his lone book, "Haunts Of The Black Masseur" in the late 1980s, about the time when I had my last real book-book out.

We had the typical Virginia exotic GB dinner: last time it was grouse and I found the shotgun pellets a bit too much; this time it was pigeon—a brown lump that I couldn't or wouldn't penetrate. Instead I made a meal out of the carrots and squash. Later Jeremy & Petra told me the secret is to cut into the carcass to get to the meat. But I pictured Trafalgar Square and those pigeons and their white biggies. Jeremy has a nice meeting planned for tomorrow: I'm to meet up with Barry Cryer, the jokester.

WEDNESDAY, NOVEMBER 22.
Up the shuddering 1930s lift in the narrow building in Newman Street, just north of Soho, Fitzrovian territory. "The Oldie" magazine is on the top floor all in one room. You step out of the lift, you have been alone since you entered the building, nothing stirs, except pre-war ghosts. Then—you open the "Oldie" door and you're slap bang in a hive of activity. The staff sit at their desks in a small room as if in school. At the end by the window is the headmaster, Richard Ingrams, another famous name. In the early 1960s he founded "Private Eye," the satirical weekly that is still a power in Britain. He's very quiet but has an air that encourages veneration. He laughs at my stories. He authorized me to go ahead and write an article about a night at Cantalini's restaurant. I hope I can achieve this without libelling anybody. Jeremy is the commissioning editor. Oh, yes—there he is in his tweed jacket. He'd like me to meet Barry Cryer. I swing round, almost hitting an editor at her computer.

And there is the great scriptwriter. I've already checked him out on the Internet movie database. What a lot of credits! Wrote for The Two Ronnies, for Morecambe & Wise, Frankie Howerd, Tommy Cooper. Golden Age of British Comedy. He's all over me—so thrilled to meet me. But how does he know of me? "I just do!" he says in a sort of North Country accent. Lots of salt and pepper hair, wearing jeans, early 70s.

Jeremy, Barry and I retire to a friendly pub in an alley off Newman Street. I like this pub: you go through a hole in the wall and there you are. They serve hot meat pies and well-poured Guinness. That's what we all order. For the next two hours, as the bar gets fuller and fuller and hotter and hotter, despite thunderstorms outside, Jeremy and I are audience as Barry delivers a stream of jokes.

When a pause comes Jeremy encourages me to tell some of mine, the ones that used to make him laugh on long car trips during our Dublin days. I try to tell one or two but Barry knows the punch lines, or else I mess them up by forgetting important details. I'm nervous. He takes over. "Look," he says, "If you don't find a joke funny you don't have to laugh—club rules, club rules."

He knows the origins of jokes, explains that no one makes up a joke from scratch; jokes are based on real life incidents.

Oh, I see, I say. Like in the 1950s when King Farouk was being driven down a long and straight road in the Egyptian desert with no other traffic except a British army lorry coming in the other direction and first seen dozens of miles away and it runs straight into the royal car; and then at the official enquiry, when the sergeant driver is asked by the president of the court to describe what happened, the sergeant says:

"I was proceeding along the said road when I found my lorry in collision with a motorcar. I alighted, walked over to the vehicle in question and opened the door. Inside I observed two wogs......"

The president of the court interrupted.

"Sergeant, you are referring to His Royal Majesty, King Farouk, King of Egypt. You will please re-phrase your statement"

" Yes, sir! Well, sir, I opened the door of the vehicle and saw the King of Egypt — and another wog."

Barry, observing club rules, nodded and carried on with another joke, prompted no doubt by my attempt.

"A Jewish gent is telling a friend: 'I was in court the other day as a witness — but I ended up in jail'. 'How was that?' 'Well I was called to the witness stand and told to put my hand on the bible. 'What is your name?' asks the judge, 'Maurice Abrahams', I reply. 'Are you Jewish?' 'What the fuck d'you think I am!'

We all laughed, notwithstanding club rules, and then I quickly ordered another round.

FRIDAY, NOVEMBER 24

Met up with Suzanne, at Old Woking graveyard. Robin had driven me and my suitcases down there. I would be removing to Suzanne's country cottage for the rest of this trip. We met in the graveyard to tidy up our parents' tombstone. A peaceful plot. Whenever I visit the weather is grim and the trees look thin and desolate. What an awful time that was back in the winter of 1962 when our father suddenly died quite unexpectedly. He was only 58. I don't think we've ever really got over it, especially Robin. He was at boarding school and, for reasons we've never understood, wasn't allowed to attend the funeral. I always remember Uncle John tossing in our father's favourite old felt hat just as the gravediggers were about to start covering the coffin with earth.

I will end the diary extracts here. For when I came to stay with my sister and brother-in-law, the General, my time was one of utmost peace and tranquility. The days drifted by in pure delight. I slept well, ate well, was thoroughly taken care of. Breaded plaice filets with roast parsnips, pork pie and lettuce, roast lamb, and mostly eaten in the sunroom while lightning stalked about, as we watched a string of reality TV shows, starting with BBC's *Strictly Come Dancing*—which is on every night of the week—followed by *The X Factor*, a vocal talent contest, and triumvirated by *Get Me Out Of*

Here—I'm a Celebrity! By this time we had all taken a few dozing time-out spells. Then we rounded off a pleasant evening's entertainment—I hope that the after-life is like this—by watching the News. I was surprised that whenever a member of the government appears they speak in such a strong Scotch burr that I can't figure out what they're talking about. England has been taken over by the Scotch. But by this time I'd had a goodly quantity of red wine and was ready for bed.

I had bought a massive biography of comic magician Tommy Cooper, the bruin in the fez who laughed when his tricks went wrong, and I was getting buried into it before nodding off in the comfy bed............

On the plane coming home—a gruelling eleven hour journey — Cooper's life kept me occupied: a vanished world of 1950s British showbiz and Cooper himself, lucky man, was able to retreat even further into childhood. Couldn't change a fuse and didn't have to, obsessed with new conjuring tricks, loved coming home to his wife's roast beef, or pork with crackling, died on stage in the middle of his act, in front of two million TV viewers. The last sound he heard was laughter. Lucky, lucky man.

Here's one of his routines, between tricks:

I said to the waiter, 'This chicken I've got here's cold.' He said, 'It should be. It's been dead two weeks.' I said, 'Not only that, he's got one leg shorter than the other.' He said, 'What do you want to do? Eat it or dance with it?' I said 'Forget the chicken. Give me a lobster.' So he brought a lobster. I looked at it. I said, 'Just a minute. It's only got one claw.' He said, 'It's been in a fight.' I said, 'Give me the winner.'

Regina and Rollo met me at LAX. She didn't feel the above routine was right for me. She suggested I was over-tired. She kindly suggested we have dinner at Cantalini's. After all, it's nearby, in Playa Del Rey. We didn't discuss how we're going to deal with our renters leaving and the task of finding suitable new ones and if that doesn't work out will we return, tails between our legs, defeated, to our Altadena house hoping the nightmare with the neighbours doesn't return......

Everyone at Cantalini's welcomed me back, said they'd missed me. I'd missed them too. This is my world, where my trio can rise from our corner and work the room with song and dance. This is where we form a line to perform "Me And My Shadow," where Rusty tap dances on her plank, and Ann, the tall lady with the black beehive, commands more Elvis songs and I always oblige. Where the tip jar fills and the wine is ever ready.

375

2007

JANUARY

As I write this we are not yet into the New Year. I'll be letting in 2007 at Cantalini's. Our little band will be sitting in the corner and playing, no doubt, "Auld Lang Syne" when midnight strikes. The money — and good money it is — will be the first I make in the New Year and I hope this will continue through the year because God knows we need it at present.

Our Caltech students left the Altadena house at the end of November and now it sits cold and empty of dwellers. Workers are in there from time to time, ripping away the carpets so as to restore the hardwood floors; installing a new basin and better plumbing in the bathroom. Meanwhile, the poor old maple tree in the back garden is slowly being taken down by experts — it was dying and had become a stronghold for bad-tempered bees. Soon there will be a view of the San Gabriel Mountains and more of our big and unsightly fence, the Berlin wall we had erected at the height of our Troubles four years ago.

But who will live in this restored and repaired house? Will we find decent reliable renters? Or will we put it up for sale? Or will we return there? I feel that to return there would be foolish, even dangerous. The house I knew and loved was one of long ago, a memory house of when I was young and carefree. Much as I'd like to live in the past even I realize that it can't be done except through books and movies and songs. Regina is practical, she is of this world, and she understands that we have to find a safe hiding place as the years whiz by. There's not enough room in old books or a piece of sheet music. You can't climb into a photograph.

So it looks like we'll stay here in Monrovia in the 1907 craftsman with the fine porch and the parade of nice people strolling by, and the cinemas and restaurants and Starbucks within walking distance — stay here and consider selling the Altadeda house and thus getting rid of that poisoned air.

The New Year is for Resolutions. One of my main ones is to spend less time writing these Letters and more time at my Huntington Library desk, under the stairs in the basement, trying to develop some themes that may become stories that may become a book that somebody might publish. That, at least, is my intention. Of course, there will also be, above ground, gigs and lectures to deliver and e-mails to read and write.

One thing I am determined to cut down on is my YouTubing. This has become a drug: watching Johnnie Ray sing "Cry" leads me to Guy Mitchell and to Hank Williams, and then, of course, I can't resist popping into my library of videos to see how many new hits we have and whether anyone has posted a comment. This MUST stop!

So this Letter will be a short one. I hope. December's was so long — it took me about two weeks to write. If this continued then I should be spending all month writing the Letter. And the next one would be a description of writing the Letter.

Our main event in December was a trip up North for the annual Christmas party thrown by the massive and rambunctious Ukulele Club of Santa Cruz, followed by a day touring the secret world of Pixar Animation studios.

As per tradition we stopped off en route up North at Gorman, that rather desolate gas'n 'food 'n 'antiques town in the mountains between L.A. and the San Joaquin Valley. At the "Antiques" store — which actually has nothing much older than a few decades ago, meaning too many posters of John Wayne in *True Grit*, and Michael Jackson pin-cushions — Regina located a pair of high-heel shoes with taps on them. Now who would want to tap in high heels? She says she has some job for these items.

While she burrowed away I enjoyed some local folklore: an old white varmint, unshaven naturally and in from his mountain condo, was engaging the overflowing white hillbilly woman store minder:

She: "What you doin' in these parts?'
He: "I come up to har-ass you"
She: "You did?
He: "Yep, I really did. See, I wake up this morning and I says to meself, 'What am I gonna do today?'"
She: "And what exactly did you decide?"
He: "I decided to come up here and har-ass you!"
She: "Well, let's get down to it!"

Rollo missed this exchange since he was guarding the car — a brand new rented one, made by Ford, a white vehicle of the kind you never see anywhere except in rental company lots. It had a CD player that could deal with homemade CDs and this meant that at last I could spin the Bob Dylan radio shows that George DiCaprio presented me with a few weeks ago. None of my other machines can deal with Dylan. And as I'm obsessed with the man this was an opportunity to give him a chance.

Well, Dylan turns out to be a very attractive disc-jockey, much more deep folksy than that charlatan smoothie G. Keillor, a savvy-smart New York egghead whose real name is Gary and who rubs leather-patched tweed jacket elbows with slick all-knowing *New Yorker* writers. Dylan may be a faker but I find his fakery entertaining and unpretentious. I was amazed that he devoted a whole hour show to dogs. He loves dogs, opining that anybody who doesn't like dogs doesn't have a heart. And he played, with a straight face, Patti Page's "How Much Is That Doggie In the Window." I was glad too that he saluted "Old Shep." Nothing tongue-in-cheek about his presentation. He's the new Will Rogers, with the difference that while Will wrote all of his own material the Dylan show is trailed with a credit list of writers and researchers almost as long as your current movies.

Dylan tells jokes, too:
Dog#1: "I'm goin' crazy!"
Dog#2: "Then go see a psychiatrist"
Dog#1: "I cain't — I'm not allowed up on the couch." Very good stuff— so to hell with the intellectual critics who see Dylan as an obscurantist poet to be deconstructed and dumped on the head with a Nobel.

With canine quips still ringing in our ears we pulled in, around dusk, to our favorite Interstate #5 hotel, The Harris Ranch, where the smell of cow biggies lies ahead to the north, thus not spoiling our anticipated tri-tip beef dinner. We swam in the heated ranch pool, Olympic-size and, thankfully, free of urinating children and thus glistening with limpid water, as opposed to yellow ochre. While Rollo chased the feral cats, permanent residents, I took note of the sheriff's prisoner bus parked in the Harris lot where normally RVs and motor homes nestle and bulge and retract. Were the prisoners enjoying tri-tips too?

We suffered one of those lockjawed *Five Easy Pieces* waitresses at our ranch house restaurant booth. She started her act by slinging our water glasses down hard on the table, as she demanded, "Beverages?" Why not simply, "Would you like a drink?" But I have adopted a new demeanor: pure passivity. I will tolerate any bad behavior, except that of an armed person threatening me, Regina, or Rollo. So I sat and quietly examined the pictures hanging in our booth: an 1880s print of an English countryside scene, "The Huntsman's Pet" juxtaposed with a B&W photo of "California's

First Cotton Oil Mill," muck and toil and hard gumption and American know-how — much more down to earth?

I was tiring of looking at these and both of us were thirsting for beverages. "Where is our Guinness?" I asked the waitress as she flew by like a witch. After all, twenty minutes had gone by. She looked astonished: "I have to get them, ya know!" I turned my attention to two grizzled cowboy types, older gents in an animated conversation at the booth opposite. Regina suggested that they had lived in *Brokeback Mountain* many many years ago.

In the ranch store I admired the marbled beef sides, but not the cool jazz sax version of "Silent Night." Why do jazzers so dislike a decent melody? Why do they arrogantly assume that they can instantly make up better ones? On an impulse I bought a book called, *Secrets of Closing The Sale* by a beaming senior called Zig Zigler. Key Advice: "Project warmth and integrity." I've always felt that America is based on salesmanship.

Next day at breakfast I watched a solitary man methodically pour ketchup over his bacon, eggs and cottage fries, blanketing the entire display like in a slasher movie murder scene. Regina gently explained that there are people like this — she has witnessed them smothering an expensive steak with ketchup, even doing this to a decorated lobster tail all the way from Maine.

Onward! We arrived in Santa Cruz — a proud city of libertines and eccentrics who will tell you at the drop of a hat that theirs is the authentic Surf City, notwithstanding Jan & Dean — as the afternoon darkened and the massed ukesters were heading towards the Italian restaurant for their annual shindig. They must have been in a hurry because when we arrived all dollied up in finest clothes and bang on time, much of the buffet had already been punished to death. We made do with some pasta and salsa chips. Of course, I didn't complain because I'm in my new mood and also because you have to love ukesters who are also surfers, benevolently wreathed in smiles and wearing Hawaiian shirts fresh from the cleaners.

We were seated next to Tiki King, possibly a bank manager by day, who kindly offered me a Jack Daniels and which I thoughtlessly accepted. I have promised Regina I would abstain from Jack because every time I drink it the result is a steady snoring in the night. And then I had another: the reason being that my opening act, good people in normal life, were dressed as undertakers and, as a change, performing jolly Christmas songs in minor keys. "Silent Night" sounded like a fatalistic dirge from a concentration camp concert.

Now this was all well and amusing but it went on too long. Timing is everything in entertainment. By the time Regina and I were introduced the festivities were drawing to a close. And I needed yet another Jack. But the years have taught me how to hold a crowd and not to hold them too long: I got them to join me in a chorus of

"Why Does Everybody Call Me Big Head?" — they enjoyed calling me Big Head — and we managed to get them to crouch down and then stand up and stretch high, while swaying in the Woodstock manner, for the reliable warhorse, "We All Went Up The Mountain." The evening was saved.

But during the night Jack Daniels strutted his stuff: I must have been snoring like mad, making a racket like the prune-faced cow in the Bill Bailey song: next morning I awoke to find myself alone in bed, guarded only by Rollo. Poor Regina had retreated to a sofa in a far room of our host's house.

And this was the day when we were to be the honored guests at Pixar Animation.

On the drive up to Emeryville, seat of Pixar, Regina gave me a chant card and together we did morning gongyo: *Nam Myoho Renge Kyo*, etc. Soon we were settled and back to normality.

Emeryville, far from being the sylvan village I'd imagined, is a rather grim attachment to Oakland and we all know how Oakland can be when the malt liquor's flowing and the trigger fingers are itching.

Stuck in the middle of a landscape of industrial crate buildings is a secure site and inside is a long solid and forbidding structure where dreams are made by the magic of electricity. We received our passes, identifying ourselves as "Strangers From The Outside!" I was armed with my Martin uke and my George Formby banjo-uke, plus a music stand and reams of sheet music.

We passed through formidable glass doors set in the exact middle of the studio building — a very symmetrical affair indeed, more like an institution than a fun factory — and suddenly there we were in a vast and booming atrium bustling with people moving methodically hither and thither, full of purpose, with headphones and laptops, all dressed for the beach. I could have been father to any of them.

Indeed, I was treated paternally. Our host, Lee arrived at Reception in a Hawaiian shirt and a full schedule. So pleased were they all that I had come to play for them. The animators, directors and what-have-you would be assembling around 1:30 pm. He himself would have to leave after a little while since he had meetings. A feature he'll be directing? Top secret. However, his uke was waiting and he was ready for instruction or, at the very least, a jam.

All the while he was talking I had ideas rushing around inside of me concerning the possibility of perhaps writing songs for the studio. I suppressed a shiver. And a stutter. No, of course, I wouldn't be invited or commissioned. Randy Newman writes their songs, down somewhere in Beverly Hills. No, no, I was there purely as an entertainer. Don't go and spoil it with a sales pitch...

Consulting his watch Lee announced that in a few minutes we were expected in the theater for a special screening. We made a royal progress down the atrium towards the theater. Floors with glass fronts towered above us on either side. Were there watchers? Was I over-dressed in suit and tie and keyboard scarf and fedora? "No — you look great!" Regina was a paragon of calmness compared to me. So Lee turned to her.

He explained that Pixar is carefully planned as a self-contained culture, a society where everybody mingles freely like an ancient Greek democracy. There are no cliques, no separation of suits and artists. You could bump into a creative person at any second, even as you were ordering a lunch wrap at the cafeteria, and there could ensue a discussion about a story point or a budgeting concern.

All deserving of high praise — but why was I constantly reminded of Cal Tech or some science lab?

In the theater we were treated to a program of shorts and finishing with a look at their current feature in progress: *Ratatouille*, about a Parisian rat with a taste for haute cuisine. I noticed that Lee sat very still and serious throughout the screening.

The lights went up and I commented that their rat character is the spirit of Bugs Bunny. I also mentioned that Regina works in child care and that her charges love to watch *Toy Story* and *Monsters, Inc.* over and over again. Lee, seated a row in front of us, was quick to explain that Pixar makes movies for all age groups and demographics. Further — in fact, they make movies for themselves first.

Afterwards we were taken upstairs for a tour. Computers hummed everywhere. We saw a room housing banks of monstrous ones making an even bolder sound. What if there's a power failure? They have their own generating plant. They could hold out here for ages. A totally self-contained world, a powerhouse producing entertainment product for worldwide consumption, all demographics, all religions, atheists and vegetarians.

We dropped in on an animator, Mark, hard at work on a rat scene. From a keyboard identical to the one I'm typing on now he summoned up a 3D rat and turned it around 360 degrees and then, from a sidebar on his screen, displayed the options available for facial expression and limb gesture. Another key produced a film noir lighting effect suitable for the scene he was working on. In answer to my question Lee assured me that there are pencils and paper to be found in the studio, and that they are used when necessary.

After lunch at the splendid cafeteria where high executives and plain old janitors mixed and mingled and ordered healthy dishes, Lee led us up to a conference room. There I spread out song sheets. "Shall we start?" said Lee. And so pretty soon I had a passel of animators and directors strumming their ukes as they bent over copies of such songs as "The Uke Is On The March" and "Ukulele Heaven." I even led them in "My Dog Has Fleas." So engrossed was Lee that he missed the start of his meeting and an assistant (who in the old days would have been called a "secretary") entered to beseech him to leave the fun and attend to business.

As we were saying goodbye my dam burst and I blurted out a plea for perhaps a chance to contribute a Pixar song. After all I am a bit of a pixie, if not actually pixilated. Too late did I realize that Pixel is the operative word.

"When the right project comes up," said Lee as he beat his retreat. "You can be sure we will be considering you."

And then we were out of the rabbit hole and into the harsh world of Oakland. And then we were back in our solid Monrovian craftsman house and facing the testing time of Christmas. And now, having conquered, we're making resolutions and hoping for that break that brings money so that our family — Rollo and Simon — can live in our own sealed and peaceful world, far from alarm, far from Baghdad, in a land of unadulterated harmony.

Postscript:

Late again in posting this Letter. New Year's Eve has come and gone in an 8 hour flash: the Cantalini's experience beginning with the vodka martini in the tiny cramped Harbor Bar among the lined lady lushes, the delicious pre-gig salmon dinner at the table near the lavatory, the seated four piece acoustic combo of Fred, Tom, Dave and me playing sweet old melodies from our corner for the first seating, the evening progressing into 50s rock when the Elvis lady demanded songs by her star, the paper top hats and tiaras perched on the heads of the later diners, and the party favors and noisemakers, the hubbub increasing, Rusty tapping up a storm on her portable dance board floor as we play her fiercely-directed "Ain't She Sweet," Nick with his arm round my shoulder as we swayed in characteristic Flanagan & Allen style to "Underneath The Arches," then the count down to 2007 and the free champagne and "Auld Lang Syne" and the hugs and wishes, then our final number, "Happy Trails," slightly spoiled by the old Scot who insisted on following our finale with his "Hello Dolly" complete with Satchmo imitation, and finally a sepulchral quiet descending as the huge bills appeared and the parties divvied up, or didn't, leaving someone with a large credit card slip to sign.

And, back in Monrovia, Regina has kissed the pets at midnight and long been asleep, crossing a peaceful bridge from 2006 to 2007.

I walk the dog this morning as the new year races along with nothing to show for it, and see the sad severed Christmas trees piled like so many bushy corpses along our road and I worry what the future brings. Will there be enough work or shall I just pretend I'm a retired... but a retired *what?* And the self-explaining begins all over again.

FEBRUARY

The Merry-Go-Round of Show Biz picked me up and threw me down four times over the last month or so. How I long to be on that ride, in the swim, on the radar — a member of World Entertainment once more! "We can't all be superstars," e-mailed my old friend Roy from London. No, but just a spot of limelight keeps my heart warm and stable.

What happened was this: a music-for-movies company called for a "quote" on "You Turn Me On." When do you need this quote? Like, yesterday — the movie's released next week. What's the context? A restaurant scene in a new film, *Factory Girl*, about Edie Sedgwick and Andy Warhol. Not my period, although I lived through it: Warhol's *Interview* magazine ran an interview with me back in 1973 and I was introduced to the man himself at his Factory in New York.

"Say hello to Ian Whitcomb," said the introducer, head of promotion at United Artists Records, my company at the time.

(*Under The Ragtime Moon* had just been released in the USA, minus the cover illustration of happy picaninnies dancing on the old plantation to Uncle Remus' banjo, because the black head of R&B deemed it offensive).

I shook Warhol's hand in the normal British firm manner. He grimaced and withdrew his hand quickly with an "Ohhh!"

And that's the story of Andy and me. Frankly I think he's as big a charlatan as Bob Dylan — and you'll only read this opinion here since no other media will accept what I say. My protestations about Dylan The Song Thief have been ignored or rejected so far by *The L.A. Weekly*, *The L.A. Times*, and, to my great dismay, by *The Oldie,* the English monthly that has always accepted everything I send them. I sent in my accusation about Dylan for a regular column they feature entitled "RANT." But the editor, in that sweet civilized local way, said it "doesn't quite work."

Fearing I might be short-changed by the film people — and fearing my female movie music representative — I called up Julie and told her of the request. She'd get right onto it. She knew the company, she knew the scene. I sat back and pictured a cool $25,000, like I got when "You Turn Me On" was used in *Encino Man* back in the 1980s. And that was only for the publishing because Hollywood Pictures chose one Crystal Waters to re-cut my masterpiece. In this case, *Factory Girl* would be licensing the whole thing—master recording as well as publishing.

I waited. Suitable new tenants for our Altadena house came and went. A new bathroom continued to be built. Rooms were re-painted. Ghosts roamed the empty house at dead of night, talking of things I'd done and left undone. Bills piled up. Never mind — the movie money would take care of all that.

Next week Julie emailed with Good News. A fax with a formal contract for a minute's use of my record had come through. $15,000 for the licensing. Yippee! I went online to find out facts about *Factory Girl*..........

Produced by the hefty Weinstein Company and starring a hottie called Sienna Miller, and in trouble due to a threatened lawsuit by Bob Dylan — God, how he dogs my life! — due to his understanding that he's being portrayed in the film as a lover who abandoned Edie Sedgwick and thus encouraged her to suicide. Lou Reed, a man who's never produced a note of beauty, has denounced the movie as "vicious." The premiere has been cancelled. But the Weinsteins are tough cookies and I felt sure they'd beat back the enemy.

Christmas was dealt with. We went to a few parties, at one of which a caustic friend — English of course — on learning from me about my impending movie money, stated with relish that he and his partner, being Academy members, had already received their "for your consideration" DVD copy of *Factory Girl* and that they'd watched it and that there is not a whiff of my song anywhere.

Julie, always so receptive to my pleading calls, assured me that all was well: they're stripping the film of the old music and putting in new numbers. Mine's among them. Is this because the Lou Reeds and Dylans have told respectable artists not to allow their work into such a disreputable film? No, no.........

Then a short and rotten review appeared in the *L. A. Times*. A tiny ad said it would open just before the New Year at only one theatre — and, just my luck, it *would* have to be a wretched multiplex in a hideous shopping complex on the Westside. Traveling to the Westside these days is an epic trek due to traffic indigestion.

But I was determined to see *Factory Girl*. Regina agreed to join me on the journey. Will Ryan, who haunts our dreams, agreed to meet us at this Westside Pavilion complex.

And so, on Tuesday, Jan 2, we convened at a fast food mall in this dreadful Pavilion where clangor banged around and the world and her children dug into stir-fry, burgers and curly fries. Will was recognizable in this melee in his broad-brimmed Jungle Jim hat. We retired to a "theatre" no bigger than a mogul's screening room. The "film" was delayed because they were having trouble with the DVD projector. It has come to that. No more clatter and jerk and scratch and blur and stars in the right hand corner at the end of the reel. No more filmy romance. A video!

We sat and we watched and we waited. Unmitigated rubbish. No "You Turn Me On." Plenty of "Psychotic Reaction" and "Shakin' All Over," but no "You Turn Me On."

We waited right till the very end of the credits when the clutter of trade signs come on and we're assured that no animal has been mistreated. No "You Turn Me On." Our New Year had been shattered. The vision of $15000 retreated like Richard The Third's ghosts in the old movie. We went to the Food Mall. I hadn't the will power to stir the tea bag in the paper cup. I just watched the brown cloud emerge to wander around the bottom. A world I wanted to leap into.

Julie was surprised. She'd still got the song request. She'd simply sign it and send it in. You never know. Yes, you never know — I held out hope that the song might be in a later digital print when there's a wider release. After all, this short Westside run was merely to qualify for the Academy Awards, right? I always live in hope.

Hope stood up to be counted on the Saturday night when Regina and I were part of a real Show Biz table at a West Hollywood supper club called Gardenia. Never mind that we were gypped out of over $100 for a miserable meal with Sutter Creek wine at $12 a glass, served by disgruntled insurgents. Never mind that the woman cabaret star slowed every once-peppy 1920s song — such as "How Could Red Riding Hood Have Been So Very Good And Still Keep The Wolf From The Door?" a number I perform at breakneck vaudeville speed with Janet Klein and Her Parlour Boys — to a cataleptic crawl, pointing up the words with slow motion hand and finger gestures as if dealing out Brecht or Sondheim, those joyless creatures. Never mind: Leonard Maltin, one of our company and a Man Who's In The Know, announced that the Weinstein Company has sent out frantic notices stating that Academy members should pay no attention to the DVD of *Factory Girl* since the movie is being re-edited completely. Did this mean new music? Maybe. The movie opens the Santa Barbara Film Festival at the end of the month. Should we drive up there to check it out? We could take Rollo to the dog beach, see our friends, and have marzipan at Mrs. Andersen's Scandinavian restaurant on Main Street.

In the diary entry for Monday, Jan 15, I wrote a headline: "THE SONG IS IN!" I had returned from morning exercise at the doomed Pasadena Athletic Club. Regina was in the midst of her chanting — Nam Myoho Renge Kyo — as I turned on the computer to look at my e-mails. And there it was, a message from Julie@music-forthemasses.net on the subject of "Good News":

"The Weinstein Co. requested your W9 so they could process your payment for *Factory Girl*. I've asked for an e.t.a. and will let you know when it should arrive." Yippee and again yippee! I dared to go in front of Regina as she chanted and give her the thumbs up and execute a little leap. Rollo and Simon appeared in order to find out what was up. I told them all: our debts would be paid — and we could wipe out the image of Regina, Will and me sitting sadly and silent, staring one to the other in that tacky tiny Westside shack masquerading as a cinema.

So often — I wrote in my diary—things turn out OK in my life as long as I have patience. Of course, I added, the chanting helped. Just like decades ago, when I was first courting Regina, and we were looking for a parking spot in Santa Monica and nothing seemed available until she chanted and, lo and behold, a space suddenly opened up. And so we had a week of merriment.

Until I again returned in the morning from the Athletic Club. This time I found Regina feverishly vacuuming. I went up to her and asked if everything was alright. She shook her head. She asked me to hold her. As I did she said, "Bad News — Julie just called to say that the song has been dropped." But it was a dead certainty. But...

Later Julie sent me the paper trail:

From Angela Leus/Manager, Motion Picture Music, The Weinstein Company: "FYI, unfortunately 'You Turn Me On/Ian Whitcomb ended up coming out of the film last minute...Purely a creative issue, not financial."

Julie: "Angela, would you double check this before I have to let down the artist? In my 15 yrs. of doing this I've never seen something not make it at this juncture...and I'm really dreading having to deliver such news."

Angela: "Yes, during the holidays when we initially sent the license request, it was still in the picture — but the filmmakers went back in and were changing things around until the very last second, unfortunately. I'm sorry."

Up until then I had been reacting with pleasure to the news pictures of Helen Mirren being feted at functions. There she was all smiles, with her equally smiley husband, Taylor Hackford. Friends of ours, you know, though we haven't heard from them in ages. And there's Jeremy Irons with whom I worked on *Last Call* and who enquired as to the name of my tailor. And Bill Condon, director of *Dream Girls* — he had me sing "Teddy Bears Picnic" with the Universal Studios orchestra for a film he directed years ago. Yes, I know them and they know me. At least they will now that I'm back on the Merry-Go-Round.

But after I'd been flung off I loatheed their bloody faces. I turned to the sports pages at breakfast rather than have to read about their success, their lives in the clouds, sprawled on the pantheon. And here I was, back again in the shadows, embracing the mud, a civilian once more. An accordionist and ukulele player. One of Janet Klein's

Parlour Boys. Humility is fine but not all the time.

But look at it this way: before the first Weinstein offer for my song I was in a fairly blissful state and I didn't have that extra $15000. I knew nothing about it. Of course, I was in a completely blissful state before July 10, 1941. And so I will be in a certain amount of years time.

Meanwhile, other news from the month of January:

I made the long journey out to the cavernous Anaheim Convention Center for the annual bash of the Music Merchants of America (NAMM). I hate the damned affair — nothing but salesmen and cacophony. Show-offs trying out trumpets, drums, electric guitars, announcing their nothingness to the world like an over-amplified version of cell phone abusers in public places. And they always have to show how fast they can play, like a kid boasting of how big his dong is. Nothing to do with quality, nothing to do with precious, carefully considered musical notes.

But I was only there for one purpose: to meet with two music publishers in order to find out whether my work would see light of day. A man called Link (an appropriate name since he's about as emotional as a sausage) smilingly interrupted me as I started my speech about how well my songbook would sell, to tell me that at this point the company would have to pass on my project. This year they'd be focusing on books branded with household names — such as Norah Jones, Diana Krall. Never heard of them, I said to myself. "I quite understand," I said to Link.

On to the Mel Bay stand where, after finally catching the eye of boss Bill, I was able to grab a few seconds with him. Is the *Ian Whitcomb Songbook* on schedule? You know, I added, we have "You Turn Me On" in that book and the song is featured in an upcoming big movie called *Factory Girl*. Bill's eyes lighted up. Go and see his female assistant — she takes care of all that. When I got to her and repeated the *Factory Girl* story she smilingly gave me an affirmative. The songbook will be, therefore, bumped up and be published in June. Victory! Now I could leave this hellish racket.

In the last few days I have been spending hours at our old house in Altadena — battleground of the neighbour war, location of my book, *Resident Alien* — as Regina's assistant. We are getting it presentable for showing to prospective renters. In the back garden I carried out orders to collect the terra cotta pots and stack them behind the shed. Memories flooded back: this shed is really a playhouse and we bought it years ago as a retreat for me. The plan was that I would bask there in the late afternoon with a good book and a glass of wine. But I only got to do it once. And the room gradually became a repository for broken chairs and redundant videos. Spiders found a good home there, spinning intricate webs that stretched from the metal globe of a pre-1947 civilization (when a British red covered almost everywhere) across to the wall where was pinned a color copy of the Victorian painting of the sailor boy lying by his mother's grave, "Home From The Sea."

As I worked around the rest of the garden I was reminded of dreams and schemes I'd had which, once realized, turned out not to have been such a good idea. The gazebo, for instance — a plastic outdoor palace with intimations of the Delhi Durbar, where I would recline on white chairs as I played my ukulele and invented songs. But the only event I remember is my niece, newly arrived from an England she'd left forever, sprawled on the chaise longue with a wine and a cigarette and laughing loud at the thought of having left the restrictions of England for a fresh start in Australia.

And I used to have three ponds, all of which I lovingly created. I cherished the microcosms where lilies and water grasses provided a life for the koi I introduced. I would drift off to sleep happy that the fishes were frolicking in a habitat that I had god-like made for them. But the fish died. The frog disappeared, too. They remained on my conscience for some time and then, like everything else in life, they evaporated from my mind.

And there's the red brick floor in the outside area beyond the back porch, enclosed on one side by a wall of the house, and on the other the Berlin-style wall/fence that keeps the hostile neighbours from us (except in nightmares in which they scale the fence and chase a gardening Regina and then set fire to our cacti), and by the stately sweet cedar-smelling room that Mr. Brown built all by himself. This enclosed area was, in the chimera of my imagination, to be a place of calm, a place in which to meditate. It was inspired by an Italian piazza I'd seen as a set on the stage of the Pasadena Playhouse. All my life I've been trying to clamber onto a stage and live in an ideal set peopled by deathless actors in a play that ends with everything tied up peacefully together and everybody singing a good old song. A play that, after a suitable interval for refreshments, starts all over again. And the cycle continues for ever and ever, amen.

A few days ago I completed a new comic song, originally thought up in Japan. And last Saturday night, at The Fret House in Old Covina, I introduced the number, encouraging everyone to join in the chorus. And did they ever! Heartwarming, as satisfying as the cocktail that is the subject of the song. So here are the lyrics. Maybe this is the song we will sing in the everlasting afterlife. We must be patient, I tell myself.

HAVE A MARTINI !

Verse:
This world just gets grimmer and grimmer
We seem to be deep in a dive
And chances are slimmer and slimmer
That our kind of song will survive
But I have an answer to this
So follow my highway to bliss!

Chorus:
Have a martini!
Put two olives in
Don't be a meany
Fill it up to the brim
Whether it's vodka
Or whether it's gin
Have a martini
And let life begin!

Patter:
I can eas'ly prove that I can hold my liquor
No quotation ever proves to be a sticker
"Peter piper picked a pickled peppercorn" — how's that?
"Sister susie's sewing shirts for soldiers" and then
"Mary had a little lamb" — you see, I told ya
I can shay mosht almost anythink — oh drat!
There's only one proper way out
So fill up your glasses and shout:

Chorus:
Have a martini!
Put two olives in
Don't be a meany
Fill it up to the brim
Whether it's vodka
Or whether it's gin
Have a martini
And let life begin!

Words & Music By Ian Whitcomb. Copyright: Ian Whitcomb Songs.

MARCH

Is this called "Breaking News" or "A Story We're Following"?

We are moving back to our house in Altadena, our home. The reason is because the woman neighbour who plagued our lives is dead of brain cancer. "Ding Dong—the Witch is Dead!" said one of our friends, meaning well.

Regina sent a card with a sincere personal sentiment. I offered my condolences to the husband — and we meant it. I'm sorry for him, and for their adopted son. I'm happy for their dogs who will now, I hope, get the attention they deserve. No longer will they shiver all day in the wind and the rain. And I'm happy that, on hearing the news and being assured that this news was correct, Regina felt better about making plans for our return; garden improvements such as removal of the cacti; improving the kitchen. This is going to be the house as it should have been. Already, over the last few months — in preparation for the next renters — workmen re-built the bathroom, even to the extent of a shower door.

Now, a shower door is not something you just pick up at Home Depot. Oh no, it has to be made to measure by skilled craftsmen. We had a neighbour, a nice chap and long dead, called Shower Door Dave. His sole job, his calling, was selling these things and he lived well, with a swimming pool. I know because he once popped his glistening head over the back garden wall to ask me to please stop trimming our maple tree because this trimming had caused loss of crucial shade and he and his wife liked the shade when they were lazing in the nude on a hot summer day by the side of their pool. Come and have a look. Dave had made a tidy sum from shower door sales.

Just prior to the above Good News, oddly enough, Regina had been having nightmares about working in our garden when suddenly the bad neighbour's husband clambers over the wall and starts setting fire to everything. And I had dreamed that he'd scaled his wrought iron fence, the one next to our driveway, in order to tear off vital parts of my parked Honda. Curious, because the man has been on speaking terms with me over the last two months, even to the extent of inviting me to inspect where he'd had his intrusive bougainvillea cut back in response to our pleas, even as his wife lay in her deathbed deep in the Iranian barracks they'd remodeled their house into. How I wish their house had been left as the charming 1940s Californian cottage it was when I moved into Altadena in the Spring of 1979! How I wish I could turn the clock back to then and be young again and with an impending radio show and a house full of crazy tenants! What am I talking about? This was all BR —

before Regina came along and by her very aura sent my recalcitrant renters fleeing like thieves in the night. No, no — but I'm so pleased to be returning in order to start life anew in the old homestead.

The house has been a regular character in my dreams. In one of the better recent ones I noticed a rectangular hole cut into a wall in the drawing room. Peering through I saw a full-scale theatrical 35mm projector and Regina busying about with a reel of film. "I treated myself to all this," she explained. And what is in the reel? *The Way We Were*, with Redford and Streisand. She proceeded to screen it. I turned round to discover that the room had become a theatre auditorium, and Standing Room Only at that. So I stood in front of the screen and asked the audience whether they'd support weekly showings of the best in B Westerns and selected musicals to our liking. A roar of approval.

So what do I mean by this being an unresolved story? Well, we still can't believe that a death can bring life to us. And is she really dead? I keep seeing, as in a horror film, a wraith-like head in Arab scarf suddenly rising over our fence and keening and cackling and claiming to be fit as a fiddle and ready for fatwa.

However, when I visit the house, which is every day, I notice, in my mind's eye, how cheerful the garden has become in the light of the news, how inviting the old wooden bench and the pond where once was a thriving cosmos of koi and frog, how gleaming the refinished hardwood floors and crying for tea dances, how the dining room is calling for dinners with our friends where toasts will continue into the night, how we will once again host Orphans Christmas where musical friends, with mandolins, ukuleles and saws, will form ad hoc bands and there will be laughter and fox-trotting and perhaps even a Grand March. And then we'll retire to the new screening room where we'll watch Whispering Jack Smith and Ukulele Ike, as we all sprawl on the mammoth bed, bigger than a Kalifornia King.

The other Breaking News concerns the subject of last month's Letter: the movie *Factory Girl* and the flitting in and out of "You Turn Me On":

A friend and follower e-mailed me to say that he wasn't sure whether congratulations were in order but—-

"Last night on the David Letterman Show the band played 'You Turn Me On'. It was like this: they showed a clip from 'Factory Girl' which featured the song as background music. Then at the end of the segment Paul Shaffer and the band went into a raucous rendition of your song. Unfortunately, there was then a commercial. When we were back, the band was still working the song and Letterman even sang along a little. Just 'la la la', no real lyrics. Hope you get a royalty — it made my evening, Seeya, Jim."

Well, you could knock me down with a feather. I had thought it was closure on this awful matter, this yo-yo. I'd been trying to forget — hastily turning the newspaper page when faced with an ad for the dreadful movie, hoping the thing would vanish without trace.

Quickly I rang Julie, my representative. Galvanized, she asked me to please try to get evidence, a DVD, a VHS. Luckily our friend Dr. Irv Seiler, not a night owl, has a Tivo machine on which he records all the late show chattering for viewing next day at his dental practice, in between root canal sessions and the like. He invited me into his bedroom where, with the new wife present, we checked out the recording.

Yes, yes, yes! "You Turn Me On" is clearly heard underneath the prattle of Sienna Miller and others in a scene where they're swapping clothes or something. You can clearly hear me sing, "Come on and do the Jerk with me."

So: is the song back in the movie? Or, more likely, had somebody at The Weinstein Company goofed and sent the TV show a clip from the version of the film when my song was included?

No matter. Julie assured me that this is certainly a case of unauthorized use of my music in order to promote a movie. Like a trailer. The Weinsteins must pay up. I recently saw a photo of Harvey Weinstein waving Oscar like it was a hand grenade and did he look like a tough customer! Wouldn't like to tangle with him or his bodyguards.

Julie said we must go in fully armed. She's hired a hotshot attorney from a company with a string of names, down on Wilshire Boulevard. The female attorney, with an impressive double-barreled name, has already fired off a terse but polite e-mail to the Weinstein music woman. "Please let me know how you would handle. Thank you for your help in resolving this. Best regards......" The money demanded is enough to pay off the debt on our house remodeling.

To be continued.

PS: if we should lose and end up with nothing, who's footing the legal tab? I hate to think about it.

Meanwhile, everywhere I look I see the face of Helen Mirren, escorted by her smiling husband Taylor Hackford, or acknowledging a congratulatory hand from Leonardo DiCaprio — and I should be full of fulsome good feelings for their success and flattered that we know them and their families. But instead I get a sour mash stomach, knowing that, with such success, and owned by the world, I shall never hear from them again, until their star is sinking.

And then I start evaluating my own career and seeing myself as sinking even as my stomach growls and groans. I dread that someday I'll be strumming in a café corner and in will come these stars for a birthday and management will nod me to go play "Happy

Birthday" and one of the stars will peer at me through shades and say, "Don't I know you from somewhere?" and management will signal me back to my corner.

God, I'm glad we're moving back to the Pasadena area, nearer to civilization. I mean Show Business. Monrovia is all very well but it's a dormitory with a main street like a movie set. When, almost three years ago, I told a casting agent friend that we were moving to Monrovia he replied:" So you're trying to get closer to Broadway!"

I have a business on the side, making money off a ship that sank in 1912. A little back-story: a few years ago, after my CD, *Titanic — Music As Played On The Fateful Voyage*, had run its commercial course I had a call from my friend, Harold Bronson, founder of Rhino Records and about to retire, having sold the company to the mighty Time-Warner.

Harold asked whether I'd like a few leftover copies of the Grammy-award winner now that it was deleted from the catalogue. Yes, I could take maybe 50. How about 24,000, asked Harold in his quiet manner. Phew! I'd love to have them all but there isn't room in our garage. What will be the fate of these CDs otherwise? They will be pulped by Time-Warner and marked down as a tax write-off at a dollar a disc. Oh no, I can't have that, I said.

So I made a few calls in order to find a home for the Titanic.

The California State Library offered to take a few thousand, as did The Huntington Library, The Alex Film Society, the L.A. Historical Association, and the family of Leonardo DiCaprio. There was also my uke-playing friend, Will Ryan, the man who haunts my dreams: he kindly took in a lot of boxes to be stored in the bowels of his rustic retreat deep in a Hollywood canyon.

How he coped, at his modest house, with the arrival of the records I have never asked. In my own case, an 18 wheeler truck rolled down our Altadena street pulling down power lines and ripping off the limbs of trees. Our garage bulged after the offloading. And I wondered how the Time-Warner powers reacted when they got the trucking bills and realized there would be no tax write-off.

So, over the years, the CD has been given away and away to good people. Sometimes I had to force them to accept the gift. I took to slinging them out on any occasion to whomsoever. There were just too many. One friend told me that he and his wife were growing tired of having the boxes stored under their bed, especially as the bed was starting to sag. And the boxes were hard.

Then, a year ago, some friends were visiting a Titanic exhibition in San Francisco and heard the strains of my record. They mentioned to the man at the souvenir stand that they knew the producer and how nice it was to hear his music. You know him?

Why, we've been trying to stock this CD forever! We're told it's been deleted. Can you get copies then?

On learning this, I contacted the salesman and he described a burgeoning business called *RMS Titanic* with exhibits rolling round the country and always a demand for souvenirs to sell in the shop. He ordered a few boxes from me. We set up a business. Then I ran out of product. I diplomatically asked my friends and a few of the institutions whether they'd let me take back any boxes they still had and perhaps didn't want. Please. They responded with kindness, never enquiring what I needed the CDs for — and I've been supplying the Titanic salesman ever since. I've even met him and he wears an RMS Titanic sweatshirt and criss-crosses America in an SUV full of Titanic spin-offs including my record. He'd stopped off at our Monrovia garage to pick up the latest thousand copies I'd managed to round up.

This could be your legacy for life, said the salesman, as he loaded in the last boxes. I must lay my hands on more, for the sake of Regina, Rollo, Simon and future dinners at our Monday night Salon. Aha — there's Will Ryan.

Yes, he said, somewhere in the hinterland of his house he was certain there lay a cache of Titanics. Could I then come round and help him dig?

Will is a collector of pop culture of the best kind: comic books, encyclopedias of the B western, a history of Republic Pictures, the complete Krazy Kat, the framed original painting of the Monogram Pictures title logo. His stuff has taken over his rustic house, spilling into every room so that you can't tell where the bedroom ends and the living room begins.

Somewhere there lies a kitchen but it has long been concealed by mountains of books, records, piles of papers. Somewhere submerged is a grand piano that used to belong to Mel Blanc.

It is truly a wondrous landscape of collectibles. But where does Will sleep and where does he eat? Last Saturday we started exploring and eventually struck gold in a recess of his house: eleven boxes, the last of Titanic, and not too badly mildewed. They were under a consignment of 8-track cartridges of The Best of Roy Rogers.

I promised Will several free dinners as a reward. Fortunately he's a vegetarian and never touches alcohol.

Down the winding road leading back to Hollywood proper from the fastness of his rustic bungalow, I looked out for the house I rented back in the idyllic summer of 1966: 2001 Nichols Canyon. The last house on the right, just before a dell and up against a steep canyon wall. Today the house hides behind a fence but I managed to get a fleeting glimpse as I drove by, enough to trigger memories..................

I'd gone in with fellow Englishman David Mallet, an ex-Public schoolboy who'd come to Hollywood as an assistant to *Shindig* producer Jack Good. We'd met on the set of the TV show when I was at my hottest in the summer of 1965.

David, although only twenty, was extremely self-assured, brimming over with vim and vigor. Not surprising: his father was a knight and had been a British Ambassador; the family had a country house in Kent. David had no fear of anybody and backed this up with a breezy way of talking, sailing through any kind of resistance. Rapidly he became my friend and then my record producer. I think we shared a girl friend at one time. Of course, I only discovered this later, after he confessed. He said my brother had had her too.

I left America at the end of the summer at the height of my pop success in order to return to Dublin and sit for my history degree at Trinity College. When I returned in 1966 my perch in stardom was rickety. I lay sweating in the murphy bed in the tacky Hollywood apartment block on Cherokee remembering my swell hotel bed in Seattle the year before when I'd lain there around midnight, wine glass in hand, gazing at the cover of my first album—me and the model standing sexy beside an AC/Cobra parked on Mulholland Drive. Top of the World! But no more....

Still, I kept busy recording for Tower Records under the guidance of David. We made some singles, and then an album of Tin Pan Alley and Ragtime songs — the start of my continuing march backwards: *Ian Whitcomb's Mod, Mod Music Hall*.

Around early summer David suggested we share a rental house on Nichols Canyon, just off Hollywood Boulevard. He'd been recommended the place by Derek Taylor who'd recently vacated for a larger spread. Derek, celebrated as the Beatles publicist and Brian Epstein's right-hand man (he'd ghosted Epstein's memoir, *A Cellarful of Noise*), had moved to L.A. and was a much in demand publicist. He represented the Beach Boys, the Byrds, and me. We got along famously. He liked to have me sit beside his pool at night and read aloud extracts from the Epstein book. He said I sounded just like Eppy, and how he and his wife Joan laughed with glee as they supped off wine and spirits.

The house was long and white and low. It had a family feel, but David and I were two peripatetic bachelors. We never cooked and never had proper parties. Dust and insects settled into the house, making a home. Girls would come and go, sometimes when we were away. I was always on tour it seems.

I know I had a piano there and, after a tour that had taken me to Denver where I'd spent hours watching Ragtime Bob Darch until he fell off the barroom piano stool, I returned with a clutch of sheet music Bob had given me. In Nichols Canyon I spent happy hours picking out such songs as "Sadie Salome — Go Home!" David was off working with a group of teenagers he'd run across and dubbed "Somebody's Chyldren." They backed Mae West on the album David produced: *Way Out West*, released by Tower that year and containing "Turn On" and "N-N-Nervous!"

I was living at the house when Doug Weston, boss of The Troubadour, rolled up with his personal assistant and secretary in order to check me out before booking me to open there in September. This was quite a decision because hitherto this world-famous Mecca of acoustic folk acts had never permitted an electric rocker on the stage. I performed with David's teenage band but in the second part of the show I sat alone at the piano and played "Sadie Salome" and "A Lemon In The Garden Of Love." The *L.A. Times* man gave me a pleasant review. "Quite good," he wrote.

It became de rigueur to take part in my show: Derek Taylor came many times, banging the table and singing "We'll Meet Again"; stoned hippies made it a point to get involved in "Where Did Robinson Crusoe Go With Friday On Saturday Night?"— their fevered brains conjuring up weird doings on the island, akin to what the Teddy Bears were up to in the wood at their picnic

One night, after the show, Doug Weston introduced me to some members of my audience: Christopher Isherwood, Don Bachardy, and David Hockney. I was stunned. I'd been an Isherwood fan since schooldays. "Very nice," he said and Hockney smilingly agreed. Bachardy, an artist and Isherwood's longtime companion, told me I had a "very interesting and unusual face" and might I sit for him. Wow, yes! I flashed on boys who'd yelled "fatty" at school, and my sister who liked to call me "King Farouk." But all that was back in the squelchy, torpid Fifties.

So Don came up to the house and sketched me in the bedroom as I gazed out of the window into the darkling canyon, dreaming. The ink drawings made me look like a sort of Rupert Brooke, an ideal English schoolboy, what I never was at school, and I asked Don if this was what I really seem to be. "I only draw what I see," he replied, sounding like Isherwood. You can see these early pictures on the home page of this website.

Chad & Jeremy came to catch me at The Troubadour. They offered me a slot on their upcoming tour — providing I cooled down my act by not lying on the floor and not licking the mike, that sort of thing. I agreed. By this time I was featuring my ukulele at shows, and on the tour I sang "Robinson Crusoe," since my single was in the West Coast top twenty and might even break into the national charts. It only made #101 — "Bubbling Under," as *Billboard* called it. I also included "Winchester Cathedral" in my act because everyone assumed the vocalist on the hit was me. If you remember, this was the summer when old-timey or vaudeville sounds were hitting the charts: Sopwith Camel, The Lovin' Spoonful, and of course, The New Vaudeville Band. I felt there was a chance for me to show off my newly discovered Tin Pan Alley songs. The trend turned out to be no more than that, and soon we were back in heaviness and, of course, psychedelia was lurking round the corner, waiting for the Summer of Love, and all the concomitant hatred.

At the end of October I returned from the tour to find an empty house. Then the phone rang. It was David telling me to leave at once as the house was haunted. He said he'd been asleep in his bedroom a few nights ago when he was woken by an icy blast and, sitting up, saw a hideous old man rising from the floor and leering at him with extreme malevolence. Terrified, and still in his pajamas, he raced off in his Jaguar to some friend and had been in sanctuary there ever since.

I stayed on at the house, braver than the ambassador's son, but I did check up on David's strange story. The couple he was staying with — parents of the lead singer in the teenage band — assured me that David had turned up white as a sheet around one in the morning and had begged to be let in.

I told Isherwood about the ghost and he was interested. "Very spooky" he said, and asked to come up and see for himself. He stood in David's bedroom and, rolling up and down on the tips of his toes, he jerked his thumbs in his cowboy belt and pronounced, once more: "Very spooky!" His guess was that David had seen the ghost of some early 19th century redskin who'd been booted out of the canyon by invading whites. I later learned that Isherwood had more than a passing interest in spooks and specters: he was in the habit of haunting people he didn't care for but was too much of a gentleman to tell them so at parties and such. He too would rise from the floor at the end of the bed, shooting a rictus grin.

As a result of Isherwood's suggestion that a dead Indian was spoiling my rental I organized an exorcism. Some robed guru — and there were plenty of them around that year — officiated, bringing along with him a retinue of open-toed shoe women banging gongs and clashing finger cymbals, handing round fat cigarettes for toking. The circus went on for hours but the dead redskin rightly decided not to put in an appearance. He had better things to do, bigger fish to fry in richer canyons, no doubt.

As Christmas approached I felt lonely and homesick so I packed up and gave the landlord back his key. David came on the same plane, having decided to return to England as he had a yen to become a TV producer. Which is exactly what he did and still does — he now shoots Rod Stewart and Elton John but never talks to them.

I spent Christmas at home with my family in London, but came the New Year and I was back in Hollywood, trying once again. A year of exhuming old songs for recording. When would I ever realize that I was marching to a different drum?

Tower Records, for a while, before their patience ran out, went along with my whims, releasing *Yellow Underground*, an album containing not only "Sadie Salome" but also a twenty minute spoken word track, "Memoirs of An Old Soldier," based on a 1920s book by a warrior of the British Empire. At a preview listening session in the Tower offices Mike Curb, then producing savvy kid pop and later to do those soundtrack albums for *Wild In The Streets* and *The Wild Angels,* burst into laughter, breaking the angry silence of the assembled executives.

I was entering a battle against the forces of progressive rock, of Jimi Hendrix and Cream, and heavy metal and worse — a battle I was to lose and to keep on losing until I reached Outer Monrovia. But, like McArthur, I shall return...

APRIL

I'm in a state of confusion. This is probably due to our move back to Altadena, following the demise of the woman next door. So much stuff to shift — it's like the nightmare of those endless marching broomsticks in the Mickey Mouse cartoon. No sooner have I lifted countless CDs from the apartment shelves and forced them into cardboard boxes than I turn back and see that there are still countless more to be removed.

It's the same with the books. And there are books everywhere, even under the bed, as there were in the old house. In the new and reconfigured house there will no longer be corridors made narrow and nearly impassable by bulging bookshelves. In the old days only one person could squeeze by and it was in such a situation that one morning years ago, before Regina, I encountered a stranger, a black woman, making her way past me and failing the negotiation. "Who are you?" I demanded and she replied, "Who are *you*?" This wasn't the first time these words were spoken in the house I owned. Many were the strangers who claimed residence there.

But day by day I convey books, CDs, cassettes, DVDs, in my Honda to Altadena and park them in the sparkling, empty, pristine house, with the newly refinished hardwood floors and the new bathroom with the shower door and the new rugs and new carpet. A house waiting to be aesthetically and sensibly decorated by Regina. She has a free hand — I've told her so.

She entered a beastly bachelor boarding house in the late 1980s when she joined me. My presence shouted from every wall, every closet. My record covers in frames, my CDs towering near the rows of books I'd written. Now she can start on an empty stage and fashion the house into the home she has in her mind's eye. It's as if the clock has been rolled back and a new play begun.

Speaking of plays, I am mindful of what Shakespeare said about life being like an actor strutting and fretting his hour upon the stage, spitting out lots of sound and fury, all signifying nothing. Today I was listening to an NPR interview with a smooth-voiced Oxford science writer, the kind of self-confident, self-satisfied, super-rational English bastard who terrifies me.

A passionate atheist, he was telling us that we're all descended from a piece of pre-historic bacteria, rather than being the children of the kindly man upstairs with the white beard and brandy snifter. I suppose that makes me a relative of Mrs. Flu and Mr. AIDS. But what about our moral sense, asked the interviewer. Doesn't our code of ethics, our conscience, separate us from mere germs? No, said the snotty-nosed academic with the silver tongue: being nice and kind to other people is only a carry over from the days when, as cavemen, we had to get on with each other so as to keep the tribe preserved. And so on. It made me wonder whether all this moving we're doing, this attempt to restart our lives in Altadena is worth it — for just a few years of calm before the oblivion to come..........

I hope my CD masters don't deteriorate. The LPs will last longer, so the experts say. And the paper my writing is on will last for centuries, if the illuminated manuscripts in the Huntington Library are anything to go by. Legacy...it's the only way to go.

An update on the Breaking News item from last month: our attorney with the double-barrel name from the company with a string of names, situated on the better end of Wilshire Boulevard, informs my agent Julie— by e-mail naturally— that the matter with the Weinstein Company has been resolved. They have agreed to pay the full amount we demanded for the unauthorized use of "You Turn Me On" in the clip from *Factory Girl* as shown on the David Letterman TV show.

All a mistake, they say. It will never happen again. (What a pity! I could have done with the extra money.) Your song isn't in the final release, they say, and this was an earlier version, a mishap—-and perhaps you'd be so kind as to give us a break by taking a few thousand dollars less?

Our attorney suggested that this might be a good move because the Weinsteins use a lot of songs in their movies and if we gave them a break then they'd beam kindly on us when we propose a song of mine in the future.

This brings to mind the morals and ethics business mentioned above and how being kind helps keep the tribe intact and furthers existence. Self-serving, really. But in this case I didn't feel like being kind, nor did my agent Julie. It was *us* and not *them* who discovered the mistake, thanks to my vigilant late night viewing fan. The

Weinsteins would have let it go, hoping we had missed the illicit clip. They aren't in the business of being nice guys—you only have to see the hulking threatening gangster figure of Harvey to understand—and so we're asking for the full amount and not expecting any future work from their company.

Well, that wraps the matter up and so a check should be on the way. But it hasn't arrived yet and isn't even reported to be in the proverbial mail.

STOP PRESS! I just got an e-mail from Julie stating that the Weinsteins will have a check rushed round to our Monrovia apartment via special messenger sometime next week.

We will continue to follow this story for you.

I'm looking forward, as a devotee of *schadenfreude*, to the upcoming Phil Spector Show on TV, live from a Pasadena courtroom. What will be his chosen couture of the day, what his headdress? Will he wear the tumbleweed wig he had been favoring? Of course, we live so close by I could attend in person, but those courts still echo with the nastiness of our encounters there with the woman next door. I still remember her snarling at me when I identified her to the judge as being of an Arabic complexion: "I am Aryan, Aryan!—Get your geography right!" But the judge agreed that the woman did indeed look dusky. It's funny—I still can't believe she's left this world, I keep expecting her to rise from over the back fence and spew vitriol and other words of four letters.

Anyway, I had a skirmish with Phil Spector about a decade ago. Not a nice man. In fact, pretty unpleasant. But like lots of people I'd been captivated by his Little Symphonies For The Kids, those loamy mushes of pubescent longings he'd reduced to a 45rpm disc. I even recorded my version of "Be My Baby" (which you can watch me perform on YouTube). I used to see him hanging out at the bar in Martoni's, the Hollywood watering hole of the record biz in the 1960s. His session men played on my records. In later years my Bungalow Boy fiddle player, Bobby Bruce, was death-threatened by Spector and his waving pistol. All Bobby was doing was laughing at the immensity of a particular Wall Of Sound. Bobby, a WW2 marine, had survived Iwo Jima, but the Spector incident had him shaking. He could hardly drive home.

Here's how my skirmish came to be:

Through a Spector acolyte I'd been invited up to the mogul's lair as a guest at one of his soirees. He was then living in a splendid 1920s Spanish-style mansion in Pasadena. My inviter advised me to keep mum and listen to the wise words of the Master, to be like all the other arse-licking guests assembling in a semi-circle around the enormous fireplace, big as a reasonable person's house.

I recognized the motley crew as the sycophants you see at rock revival shows and doo-wop festivals. Amazingly, Rodney Bingenheimer wasn't present. Yes, there they were, these lily-livered drips who'd run after their idol with a roll of lavatory paper should they be so commanded. And here was I— in their company, of their company. I was guilty as hell. I was an arse-licker in training.

Standing in the enormous fireplace, wearing shoulder-length fright wig, blue shades, frilly regency shirt, raucous scotch tweed jacket and 4-inch Cuban heels, and warming his bottom from an electric log fire on this sweltering September day, our host offered us midget curling sandwiches followed by a rambling and tedious lecture on pop history. The sycophants followed him in awed silence as he took us on a royal tour of the halls. Stopping at an exhibition stand cradling John Lennon's guitar, our host pulled from his tweed pocket a guitar pick and waved it in a circle as if he was a shaman or witch doctor about to perform a miracle

"Can you believe this?" he crowed. "I have here a Nick Lucas guitar pick." Silence and awe. "Yeagh—a lot of people don't know who he was. But I do." Silence and awe. "Yeagh—he was a crooner of the flapper age but not—I repeat NOT— a guitarist. It's a fraudulent pick!" Shock and awe. Murmuring. I had to pipe up.

"Excuse me—but Nick Lucas was one of the greatest pioneer guitarists in pop history." A tremendous wave of shock and no awe.

Silence.

" I repeat....," said Spector. And he did.

And I continued to do battle: "Nick Lucas wrote the first real guitar instruction book. Many future stars of the Grand Ol' Opry learned from his book. He was very influential and a good person. I am proud to have known him." You could hear a sliver of midget sandwich drop.

Spector pretended he hadn't heard a thing. But he must have pressed a secret button or something because when Dr. Demento excused himself to go home as he had a long drive, our host smiled Cheshire cat style and waved the back flap of his tweed jacket. "Good luck," he said.

We soon discovered we were prisoners in the mansion. Every door had been locked. And they stayed locked for a couple of hours with everybody pretending all was well. I pretended to be invisible. Spector helped me.

Eventually we were allowed to file out. Nobody spoke much, least of all to me. Needless to say I never got invited back. One of those present that night, and one who remains a good and loyal friend of mine, tells me that lately, even as the trial hovers, the man has been throwing dinner parties at an expensive Pasadena steak house. Those disciples lucky enough to be invited are not only free to order the entrée of their choice but are also issued a round metal badge reading, "TEAM SPECTOR." The trial starts this month and I shall be watching.

I continue to play in Janet Klein's band as an aging Parlour Boy. Last month we performed at the Ahwanee hotel up in Yosemite and on the way there, in the Parlour Boy van, I wrote my first Rap song. The inspiration was a pipe lying in the cup holder in the front seat. A pipe of peace, one that seemed to be giving consolation and generally spreading good fellowship around the van. I'm not a smoker but I enjoy the aroma. Reminds me of the 1960s, of lubricious go-go girls and the promise of fun in the dark in Griffith Park or on a late night couch in Hollywood.

And as I watched and smelled the peace pipe I was inspired to write a companion song to my recent effort, "Have A Martini," a number that has people joining in wherever we sing it. So I started a chant and the Boys joined in and when I ran out of material they came to my rescue with technical lingo dating from the heady 1970s.

As we entered Yosemite and drove through majestic forests and saw the magnificent and god-proving steep cliff walls and the waterfalls gushing with no fear of tomorrow, I completed my rap song in the notebook I like to carry. We performed it that evening to startled members of the Art Deco Society who had just been listening to Janet Klein trilling jolly songs of the Jazz Age.

A week later, drunk with creativity, Dave and Dan and I made an acapella recording of "Smoke That Pipe!" at a genuine rap studio in a charming stucco house in South Central Los Angeles. The only people driving-by had been us. A more peaceful part of the world you couldn't imagine. And the peach cobblers are to die for. Our recording seemed to disturb the engineers. "You guys are crazy!" they concluded.

You decide for yourself. The lyrics follow. Help yourself.

Incidentally, we hope to make a video of us — known on the CD label as "Sir Ian & His Royal Tokers"— performing the song live and with special finger pointing and our own gang gestures. This will be posted on YouTube where the world is at liberty to watch.

Unfortunately the world doesn't seem to be watching my videos. At least not much of the world. I mean, I was thrilled to see the viewing numbers for some of my stuff, but others lie stuck in the mere hundreds. And I was truly humbled when, prompted by my niece in Australia, I visited a video on YouTube produced and directed by her three pre-teen children. The story, animated via stop-motion, consists of a battle on their living room floor between two Lego-like creatures or machines. I was amazed and impressed — indeed, I was in shock and awe — at the number of visitors to their little epic: numbers creeping into the thousands.

How could this be when such epics as me on the Johnny Carson

Show singing "Baby Your Mother" have only garnered a few hundred hits?

Regina, ever wise to the ways of the modern world, educated me: the Australian kids have cleverly marketed their video as "Bionical," a buzzword for a cool new toy — thus attracting loads of viewers. What word should I use for my offerings? What word can encompass my world?

SMOKE THAT PIPE!

Vamp:
 BONG, BONG, BONG, HIT! — BONG BONG!

Chorus:
SMOKE THAT PIPE—
SMOKE THAT PIPE—
GET A LITTLE HEAD RUSH WHEN YOU
SMOKE THAT PIPE!
MY GOOD TIMES
YOU CAN'T SWIPE
GET A LITTLE HEAD RUSH WHEN YOU
SMOKE THAT PIPE!

Verse:
WHEN YOU HEADIN' DOWN THE HIGHWAY
 IN A BRAND NEW VAN
AND YOU LOOKIN' OUT HARD TO AVOID THE MAN
AND YOU FEELIN' KINDA GOOD
LIKE YOU REALLY OUGHTA SHOULD
YOU WOULD FEEL MUCH BETTER
IF YOU ONLY WOULD…

Chorus…………..

Verse:
WHEN YOU BUSTIN' OUT THE CHRONIC
AND THE GOOD SKUNK BUD
IT'LL ACT JUST LIKE A TONIC—
KNOCK YOU IN THE MUD.
IT'S A REAL OLD PRESCRIPTION
FOR THE DEEP DOWN BLUES
YEAGH— THIS MEDICINE IS BITCHIN'
AND IT'S BETTER THAN BOOZE!
Chorus…

Vamp: BONG! HIT! — BONG! BONG!

Verse:
ACAPULCO GOLD—COLUMBIAN GOLD—PANAMA RED—
MAUI—WOWEE!
HUMBOLT COUNTY AND LEBANESE OIL
AFGHANISTAN HASH
ALL WRAPPED IN FOIL

Vamp:
BONGS, etc………

Verse:
NOW THIS MAY BE A MYSTERY TO SOME OF YOU FOLKS
SO WE'LL GIVE A LITTLE HISTORY OF ALL THESE TOKES
AND THEN WHILE WE FIX YOU UP A FEW MORE SPLIFFS
LISTEN AS WE LINE YOU UP A FEW MORE RIFFS!……..

ZIGZAG PAPERS, REEFERS AND TEA
GANJA AND ROACHES TO SET YOU FREE.
BOMBERS AND PINNERS
DOOBIES AND SHIT
LET'S GET WASTED!
TAKE ANOTHER HIT!

Chorus:
SMOKE THAT PIPE!
SMOKE THAT PIPE!
GET A LITTLE HEAD RUSH WHEN YOU SMOKE THAT PIPE—
MY GOOD TIMES
YOU CAN'T SWIPE
GET A LITTLE HEAD RUSH WHEN YOU SMOKE THAT PIPE!

MAY

I'm writing this Letter more than a week before the start of May because this Apple cube computer is to be carefully removed by the skilled hands of an ex-Apple executive (and friend of ours) tomorrow. He will then convey it to our sparkling re-furbished house/home in Altadena where he will carefully and skillfully set it up in the room that is to be Regina's office. We will tell him how clever he is and he will nod vigorously in agreement.

It's all part of the continuing Move that started over a month ago when we got the good news that all might now be quiet on the old front line where once foul language was hurled at us from over the fence together with chicken bones intended to choke Rollo The Dog.

So far the widower neighbour has been co-operative, but you never know. At least he has removed the metal plate sign that warned, "Beware! Electric Fence!" that hung from his spear-tipped iron-bar fence. And even better: he moved the wrought-iron mailbox he'd erected on *our* property. This had been a source of contention for several years: he refused to move the thing and we were at our wit's end as to what to do — a sheriff, one of many called to our house, suggested that we hack it down with an axe. His partner, asked his opinion about what we should do in the long run, opined: "Move, buddy, move. Because the situation where we can really take action is when you become statistics and we arrange for you to be carried away to the morgue." We took his advice. In retrospect our situation reminds me of the recent Virginia Tech massacre: in our case two people teetering over the verge of madness, giving signs of incipient violence, but who could not be incarcerated until they'd slain someone. A good reason for a pre-emptive Saddam-like strike.

Can I predict the future? Will we still be here on May 1 when this Letter is posted? These days life is rolling along too well: Regina is smiling again; we have — in the Altadena house — a new driveway of gray paving stone like the approach to a French chateau; a gleaming new bathroom; and a library rising slowly from a once desolate part of the back garden. Oh, and the cheque from the Weinstein Company cleared the bank — another amazing event, considering that the thuggish brothers have had a string of big screen flops. And my song, "Have A Martini!" gathers followers like a hot Early Christian prophet wherever I sing it: appearing with Janet Klein & Her Parlour Boys last weekend at an ex-brothel in downtown Los Angeles called Bordello, I had hardly opened my mouth to sing when an entire table rose to its feet and, as one man, sang "Have a Martini!" — getting the words right. Afterwards they told me that they'd learned it from an earlier performance of mine and that they'd just come from an office party where they'd given a rendition. I can't stop this monster — it's as all-conquering as "You Turn Me On." We are mixing and re-mixing the recording almost daily, polishing the little gem so that it will shine brightly for all time, adding counterpoint as if it were a piece of Bach.

I used to believe I have a good memory, especially for my past. But a recent e-mail has shaken that belief: a retiree in Great Falls, Montana, writes to remind me of an unpleasant situation in Seattle, 1965. He was a DJ on radio station KTW and he says that I was a weekly visitor, coming in to play the piano and talk to the jocks. "In the many hours you spent at the piano, we probably knew more about you than most DJs of that era EVER could. We recorded a few of your efforts, but I'll never know what happened to those tapes, which is very sad."

One day, he writes, I brought in my girl friend and a jock called Bill took a fancy to her and later got in touch with her, which led to canoodling. Says the writer: "I was not HAPPY, and I don't know how you found out, but you were very irate with both of us... One evening you stopped in to see me and you asked, 'You knew about this, didn't you?' I replied, 'Yes, I did, and I didn't want to get involved'. Please believe me, Ian, that I did NOT condone it, but you said, 'A friend would have TOLD me what was going on'."

This was all news to me. Eager as I was to snuggle up safe in the past again, none of the story rang any bells at all. No train took me down the beloved time tunnel. The Montana man sent me photos of himself and of Bill sitting at the mike in KTW. Still nothing jogged my memory. The letter went on to recount how Bill Bray (aka Sam Kelly) drifted to other stations, always fooling around with someone's wife or girlfriend, always in trouble, and eventually disappearing completely. The writer hired a private detective to find Bill. No record of his death, even though there was a rumor he'd been killed in a car crash in Nevada. Then his ex-wife contacted the writer, wanting to know all about him. Then she disappeared too.

I was mystified too. Was this a case of mistaken identity? Was he remembering some other one-trick pony rocker from England? No, the man must be for real because he mentions Jerry Dennon, my recording manager. But try as I could, almost to the point of dunking little Proust cakes, I could remember nothing of this station, these jocks, or even the girl friend. Not that I didn't have one — I had a few, one of whom delivered, from a late night couch in the middle of a petting session, the phrase "You turn me on," thus setting me on the road to a fortune. I can't even remember her name, though.

Nor can I remember the dark-haired Italianate girl who lured me to her apartment in the summer of 1964, on the night of my birthday, where, around dawn, I took the plunge and entered the world of lubriciousness . God, how guilty I felt after the swift sensation had subsided! I took my leave of her as quickly as possible. I confessed to the Catholic friends at whose house I was staying, and asked whether they could recommend a suitable priest. I was terrified lest she would get pregnant.

And the capper of my misery was that Jerry Dennon had at this very time offered me a contract with Jerden Records. I could return to Trinity College for the winter term as an incipient rock star! I remember sitting in his office and signing papers and feeling gloomy when I should have been jubilant. I remember all this but I can't remember KTW and my correspondent. At the end of his letter he asked for forgiveness. I gave it.

Quickly he replied, "I sincerely appreciate your forgiveness, ending a 42-year feud! I am really glad you did not burn out and have been able to continue in music. I cannot picture you driving a bus, as I eventually ended up doing for a living."

There's a photo decorating this Letter, as it did last month and you probably wonder what it's all about. Unlike the pix of the DJs, this is one that brings back a certain recognition: a Christmas party in the Royal Air Force Mess in Scarborough, Yorkshire, taken in the depths of World War Two, in 1942. I recognize my father, in uniform, on the right, bending slightly to let the child on his shoulders get a better look at his sister. I am the child and my sister Suzanne is sitting in the centre of the children. She is the attractive girl, looking a little serious. But then so many of the children look serious, like they're not having much fun, while the adults are putting on the smiles. Santa Claus (or Father Christmas, as we call him over there) is wearing a rather tatty outfit.

"Don't you know there's a war on!" I can hear the ghosts of the time admonish. Everybody endured privations — my mother told me that whenever she saw a queue she automatically joined it without regard to what was being sold. On reaching the head of one such line, and with me in her arms, she found that oranges, a rare fruit, were on offer. Finding no money in her purse she resorted to digging out the shilling coin she had lodged in my belly button when I was a baby in order to keep the button from popping out.

At the very top of the photo I see the bottom of a bass drum and some band stands. So there must have been music at the party. I wonder what the band played. Was it "The Lambeth Walk" and "The Teddy Bears' Picnic"? I like to think so, for ever since I have been musically trying to get back to that time by having my dance band play period arrangements of these songs. They say that the music one hears as a child is the music that remains the most potent, so dear to your heart.

I was born on July 10, 1941 in Woking, Surrey. We moved up north to Scarborough shortly after that, joining my father who was Wing Commander of the Initial Training Wing or ITW, which is why I'm Ian Timothy Whitcomb. My father had nobly volunteered to join the RAF immediately after Britain declared war on Germany in 1939. His younger brother stayed safe in the building industry. In civilian life my father had been at his own father's side, assisting him through various entrepreneurial enterprises. These included, excitingly, car manufacturing (the Bean), motion picture making (British Screen Classics) and finally television (The Baird System). My grandfather, Hubert Whitcomb, was in the right businesses but seems to have backed the wrong horses — all of these companies eventually failed and by the time I was born he was bankrupt. No more castle on the Scottish island, no more chauffeur-driven Rolls Royce. He died just after I was born. I'd love to have known him because he sounds like a goer and a doer, an entirely self-made man (his father had been the village carpenter) and even though he failed I admire his attempt to get something done, to make a mark.

I wish I could set myself back in those wartime years in Scarborough but the brain yields nothing beyond the isolated memories I've had forever, memories having nothing to do with the screams and groans and death-jerking going on across the English Channel, memories of a feeling of being tucked away far from alarm, in a cocoon where no-one can find you even though they're calling out for you and you can hear the laughter and jokes as they troop off to tea without you and how they'll miss you...

Snapshots:

Confined to a pram (baby carriage) in a hut on a golf course overlooking Scarborough Bay where at any moment enemy bombers might drop a load... a delicious feeling of wanting to drop one myself in the pram but resisting... Daddy somewhere below on the links playing a round in a rest period from his RAF duties... the appetizing smell of petrol mingled with leather which must have been coming from his car... The Polish Air Force marching past my pram, parked outside our flat by the sea front, and obeying the "Eyes right!" order, climaxed by their commander saluting me... The underground café by the sea, safe from bombs, where you could get that rare delicacy of fried bacon, fried eggs, and fried bread, while a model railway train, high above, ran continuously round the room... Running breathlessly through the dusk towards the beckoning sounds of a fun-fair, filled with anticipation of the thrills to be had from the roundabout and the bumper cars and the ghost train tunnel where in the blackness slimy string will brush across your cheeks as you clatter past and ghouls will suddenly spring up... Knowing that the family suspected that I had been responsible for a little fire in our flat due to my fascination for matches, knowing this and getting a chill-thrill... Digging in the sand of the bay for treasures to be dumped in the Mickey Mouse bucket and seeing the flat grey mud colored water and the barbed wire on either side of me and the concrete gun emplacements... and then that exciting time when Daddy pointed out the fleet of funny-looking lorries with bottoms like boats that were racing towards the waves and, amazingly, riding in and actually floating, becoming real boats... American vehicles, he explained, called DUKWs... And Americans loomed again when we left Scarborough in 1945 at the end of the war and traveled by train to London — my mother, my sister and my new baby brother Robin — to meet up with my father, newly de-mobbed, and how at the station an American soldier, beautifully attired in a silk uniform that fitted him to a T, helped my mother out of the train asking, "Ain't yer folks here to meet ya?" and me being enraptured... and moving to Suffolk by the sea to live in a house by a lake stuck with islands called Pirate's Lair and Peggoty's House, to spend days rowing around The Meare discovering things like a floating metal cylinder upon which I scrambled and then straddled and paddled until men in uniform took my toy away because it was an unexploded bomb; and yes my grandfather, the one who lived here in Thorpeness in the big house and who had kept his money made in oil, and doled out some of it to his daughter, my mother, with the understanding that it was for her and not my father for, as his reasoning ran, if my mother had chosen to marry a man who couldn't make a pot of money then why should he be supported by his in-laws; yes Uncle Jack, as he liked to be called to show he was young at heart and a good sport with a bellyful of dirty jokes, owned five farms because that's what his doctor told him to buy before the war in order to recover from the breakdown caused by one of his disgruntled employees bursting into his office to threaten him with a waved revolver, yes and then Uncle Jack would offer me a Guinness mixed with champagne and chortle when my mother refused the offer and so he drank it instead and told once again the story of how KaKa, his wife whom we never saw much but we knew she was somewhere in the house because we'd hear a kind of mad laughter now and then, had been returning from a local hotel lunch in a taxi bumping along the Aldeburgh-Thorpeness road right by the grim grey sea when suddenly a Nazi plane strafed the cab with a solid rat-tat-tat and how she'd held tight to her hat and swore she'd never order the fish at that hotel ever again; yes and how we'd been given a half-breed sheep dog called Panda and I'd spend hours with him roaming the countryside looking for the village called Nutwood where Rupert Bear lived, yes and how I loved Panda in such a way that I threw him into the lake just to see how he'd cope with the situation but when I saw him struggling and crying out, a hitherto unknown emotion surged up in me — pity, wonderful pity! — and I jumped in and pulled him out; yes and one day, as I was riding my tricycle, a boy I hardly knew stopped me by the village shop to tell me casually that he knew something I didn't know, "And what's that?" and he shot back, "Get me a choc-ice and I'll tell you," but he told me all the same and the news was that the war had ended which didn't mean a lot to me but we did get my mother to treat us to ice cream, the only brand around at that time, El Dorado, made from margarine and with a fishy aftertaste but what did we know — had we any idea that though the war had officially ended in 1945 it would carry on regardless for us until the mid-1950s? What I did know was that there was colour in this drabness and it was provided by Americans from the nearby air base who would suddenly burst into our world with the glorious roar of a massive automobile with front like a great mouth full of radiant teeth and the disgorging of godlike creatures, beautifully proportioned, in creamy clothes with children equally godlike in blue jeans and cowboy shirts and how I wanted to be transported to the magical place from where they came...

When you read this we will be, once more, back in Altadena in the old house, but with a stage clean of the old stuff, a stage being stocked by Regina for a new production, a transformation, a chance to make a fresh start. I will miss much about Monrovia: the peachy clean families strolling by; Rollo watching with ears pricked as I drive past the front window; Rollo, let out by Regina, rushing out, wriggling with glee, to greet me when I pull into the parking lot; our fellow renters and their cheerful noises such as the can-can tune banged out by the little girl next door, and the roar of the young Cal Tech professor who lives behind us as he rushes off to yet another distant state for interviews for a tenure in bio-physics; being able to walk to Starbucks and being handed the *misto* before I can say the word; walking to the Aztec, that relic of a 1920s roadhouse, to have a martini at sunset in the courtyard near the tiny pond with the bridge and the mural of an exotic temple by placid river, and looking up at the palm trees fronting the mountains and for a moment actually being at peace.

Monrovia is a clean machine with Disneyland homes and I shan't miss having to stoop to pick up Rollo's biggies in a plastic bag. Back home in funky Altadena, free as the frontier, I will once again let the biggies drop to gradually return to nature. Ashes to ashes and dust to dust. Biggies to be absorbed back from whence it came. As will happen to us all.

JUNE

After three and a half years in exile here I am back at our house in Altadena and typing the Letter. I say type because I've been told by my literary friends that what I do on these website pages is not writing but typing. Even worse, some refer to it disdainfully as mere blogging. A *Los Angeles Times* writer reminds us that "blogging is a form of speech, not of writing." Another adds that: "The act of writing for print, with its implications of permanence, concentrates the mind most wonderfully. It imposes on writer and reader a sense of responsibility that mere yammering does not. It is the difference between cocktail-party chat and logically reasoned discourse that sits still on a page, inviting serious engagement."

Well and thoughtfully put, but how were these passages written? On a computer I'll be bound. And so what is the difference in thought process between writing for the blog and writing for print?

I can only speak for myself: when I type these Letters I use my recent journals as memory aids but after that I let the juices flow, trying not to be flowery, to polish, to write for posterity — and by so doing mask my true feelings. The result may not be slick and pretty but, as an English friend and critic has told me, at least it's honest and passionate and rocky-racy, and not forced, labored and self-conscious.

And now down to business. This, as usual, will be an account of the past month and not of June. The First of May saw us back in the house but surrounded by boxes. Regina is taking her time to design the new set for our real-life stage and I hope the play will be less fraught than before. On a mundane level, I had never realized how small the rooms are in this house. But the warren has an appeal for me going back to childhood. I like to hide away as if in caves and tunnels where alarm can't find you.

Unfortunately trouble was found straight away within the house: the workmen who were supposed to have put in a new bathroom floor, a new kitchen floor, to have restored the hardwood floors, etc, had not done their work properly. The new bathroom basin leaked, the tiles were cracked or crooked, the floor creaked as never before; the hardwood floors had strange circles and lines, and in the kitchen the lino peeled off as if in a sneer.

Understandably Regina was shaken. So the workmen will have to return to right their wrongs, but what a waste of time and money! We'd never have remained in Monrovia, paying hefty rent, had we known that the work was to be this sloppy.

Meanwhile I have been making myself scarce — taking Rollo down the old roads, happy to see he remembers his favorite leg-lift bushes and trees, and the yards holding dogs that dislike him. He was upset that one of his archenemies, a really raucous creature, is no longer with us. Rollo had prepared for the encounter with bounds and leaps. And on our walks along the road with no sidewalk I was happy to be greeted by neighbours with smiles and claps and welcome homes. Many, as is their wont, stopped their cars to chat from behind the wheel, a dangerous local habit.

For a fortnight it was a honeymoon. But this ended a few days ago. Returning from our local organic health food store where we had enjoyed a vegan "yummy yam" dinner followed by an informative documentary on how America is going the way of ancient Rome and will fall soon, we were happy to see that our bad neighbour's vine, always hideous and always reaching out to strangle Regina's roses, had finally bitten the dust. The wretched vine tangle was lying in their driveway — and now we had a clear view down the road and now the roses could see the light and breath the air and enjoy life.

Next day, from over the now naked iron fence (with spear tips) I congratulated the husband, widower of the woman. He was not as happy as us. In fact he was furious, accusing us of cutting the wires that had been holding up the dying mess, that this is a vendetta but he wasn't going to let this get him down, oh no, he was going to sell the house. How relieved I was! "Yes, I'm going to sell the house — to a black family with ten kids!" If he hoped that would bother us he was wrong. Most of our neighbours are black and a more charming, peaceable bunch of folks would be hard to find. Still, his wrath rattled me. Was he planning a new assault? No, he'd said he wouldn't let the vine collapse bring him down too. As I write this a gang of Latino workers, masked and armed with wires, are trying to re-attach the hideous vines. We will miss the view and the light but at least we won't see so much of his glowering face and stooping body. What a misery guts!

On Sunday, May 6, my old friend Curtis Harrington, film director and bon viveur, died. Another friend told me pretty quickly by phone. Curtis had died alone in his art nouveau-style bedroom in the Hollywood Hills. No pain, no nothing. Proper doctors had been offering to take care of his dickey heart but Curtis, a firm believer in the power of homeopathy, paid them no heed. So he died. Still, he had reached a ripe old age — over 80, so they say, though Curtis liked to lop off a few years every now and then.

My telephone friend instructed me to call the *Los Angles Times* obituary writer because I was one of four people recommended to deliver some suitable quotes. I did this and was told there was no more space but thanks all the same.

So I called my friend back and asked whether there was anything else I could do. Yes there is, he said, you can assemble some excerpts from your radio shows, the ones where Curtis was your guest; now listen, we don't want to hear your voice, we only want his; we'll play the excerpts over a montage of photographs of Curtis which will precede the main memorial video presentation at the service in the Academy Of Motion Pictures theatre, a week after the funeral at Forever Hollywood.

Usually, in other cultures, there's an interval of several months between the funeral and the memorial. You mourn at the funeral and then you wait a bit before throwing a celebration of the life. That could mean a few laughs and perhaps some warts and all thrown into the festivities. I mentioned this shortness between funeral and memorial to an old Hollywood hand. He replied: "You gotta act fast out here — let a few months go by and the guy's forgotten. Remember: change is all!"

Time, therefore, was of the essence. I worked fast but it was tricky. The only available radio shows with Curtis were on audiocassettes and these were buried somewhere in the mess of boxes newly dumped and piled in and around our house. After midnight, in the darkness of our bedroom, I cast my mind back to our recent move, picturing where those cassettes could be. Eventually the image of the location appeared and early next morning I tugged out the box from the mountain in the garage and found the trove.

All day I played the shows, enjoying the repartee and joshing of Curtis and me back in those great days of ether freedom when I hosted a two hour show on KPCC in Pasadena from ten in the evening till midnight. We'd totter in to the studio, primed with good food and drink, brimming with bonhomie and wit, freed of all inhibitions. A Gallagher & Shean, a Smith & Dale, Abbott & Costello, Flanagan & Allen. What a team! I found great stuff in which, egged on by me, Curtis reminisced on the awfulness of French lavatories in the 1950s, on a misunderstanding concerning the word "douche," and also delivered a brief history of the brassiere — among other topics. It was funny and sad. It was riddled with his extraordinary laugh, his golden hallmark. I wanted to pick up the phone and call to remind him of those japes and larks of the air.

I noted the excerpts and then I drove out, with the precious cassettes, beyond Hollywood to my friend Jim Bedoian's house where we spent five hours transferring the bits onto a master CD. Jim quickly designed a cover and contents and then I rushed over to my friend, the event producer, back in Hollywood. "Bless you," he said. Such friends I have!

However, life is full of surprises and I got a rude one. They didn't want my voice, they didn't want the double act, they just wanted Curtis alone. I had "disobeyed orders": the CD was useless. I blustered; I apologized. Regina and I attended the funeral as circumspectly as we could.

There was a good turnout at Forever Hollywood, where resting in niches are the likes of Rudolph Valentino, Peter Finch and, more recently, Lana Clarkson, victim (allegedly) of Phil Spector and one of his many guns. The chapel was full to capacity. A cellist played mournfully, the same cellist who'd been playing when Curtis had his last margarita at Lucy's El Adobe, near Paramount, the night before he died. We acknowledged friends and stayed respectful. Then there was a commotion: I recognized another old friend, a sort-of friend, the avant-garde filmmaker and scurrilous author Kenneth (*Hollywood Babylon*) Anger, getting ejected from the chapel. Bald as an egg and orange of hue, he was loudly stating "You're throwing me out! This will be on the front page of the Times tomorrow!"

Turns out he'd arrived with a camera crew and was doing an on-camera commentary even as the lens thrust into the open casket where Curtis lay in state, beautifully dressed in a white jacket, but helpless to prevent this travesty. Curtis and Kenneth had become estranged over the years. In fact, Curtis couldn't stand Kenneth. For myself, I'd had decent relations with the man—first encountering him as a voice screaming with excitement at the screen in the National Film Theatre, London....

Clara Bow, the Jazz Age vamp, was horse-whipping Gilbert Roland, her handsome leading man and both were thoroughly enjoying themselves but nothing like as much as Kenneth. He was about to die. He was howling. We were introduced later. We got to know each other to the extent that he arranged to let Regina and me adopt the late Rudy Vallee's dog, Inspector. At the time, Kenneth was living in the middle of Latino gangbanger country and he'd already seen one of his dogs shot to death.

We picked up Inspector and his belongings: a scrapbook of pictures showing him destroying Rudy Vallee's memorabilia, one of his former master's famous megaphones, and a packet of hot dogs.

Lately I've been out of contact with Kenneth which is annoying because I wanted to talk to him about his unauthorized use of my recordings in his latest movie, *Mouse Heaven*. The Disney people weren't too pleased with his unauthorized use of Mickey Mouse either.

Returning to the scene:

As mourners we had been invited "to take a last look"at Curtis. And so, camera-free, we did. Yes, it was him alright but strangely larger than life. His painted face seemed fuller and flatter and there was drool coming from the side of his mouth. I didn't linger long. No sooner were we back in our rear seats than Kenneth Anger returned, sans camera and crew, striding to the front row and plonking himself down.

The oration was delivered by the old actor Jack Larsen, cub photographer on the *Superman* series back in the 1950s. His speech was dignified and measured. Within seconds he was interrupted by Anger: "Speak up!" And challenged: "It was never a coven that we were involved in!" and "I financed Curtis' trip to Italy." There followed a descent into heckling punctuated by use of the "fuck" word.

Finally Anger took over from the gentlemanly Larsen. He announced that everyone was wrong: Curtis was in fact 86 years and died of prostate cancer, the disease that he, Anger, is going to die of. He even gave us the exact date when he'd die: Halloween, 2008. "I will be laid to rest right here and there will be a service — but unlike this one *mine* will be by *reservation only*." Much laughter. The mourners had become audience and were enjoying the show. But I could feel Curtis writhing in his casket. His enemy was having the last laugh.

Less than a week later came the more celebratory memorial service at the Linwood Dunn theatre, operated by the Academy. Another decent turnout — to hear "Remarks By Curtis' Friends" and to watch a documentary-in-progress about his work. No sign of Kenneth Anger — he had been deliberately misled into believing the memorial would be held the following week. I rather missed him.

There were sonorous quotations from Shakespeare again: at the funeral it had been all about how everyone, even boys and girls, eventually ends up as dust; tonight it was Hamlet's dithering on whether there's life after death or not, but that finally, "Readiness Is All."

I missed Curtis' laugh, which had been preserved on my radio excerpts CD. But I was happy that at least they chose one of the songs I'd added to the excerpts: "Limehouse Blues," Curtis' favourite song.

The speakers were mostly articulate. Dennis Hopper was silent emotion, exuding a vibe-like eloquence. A master of the dramatic pause. He had competition from Norman Lloyd, a master of the pause that gets attention. As I didn't get invited to tell my memories of my good friend I'll leave you with a few.

Curtis first came to me as a laugh slicing through a summer twilight in 1971. We were watching some early talkie musical in a house in the hills above Mulholland Drive; his sharp laugh signalled that a presence worth attending to was imminent. We became instant friends, sharing a preference for the past and a loatheing of the present. Curtis was more extreme than me — he had no time for rock & roll or for anything that smacked of sentimentality. So he shuddered at "I'll Be Seeing You" and the like, those comforting heart-tug ballads that I enjoy wallowing within.

He showed a keen interest in what other artists were up to. He was never mean about the success of his friends, unlike me. When I told him I'd got a song in a movie he was genuinely pleased, even excited.

Around the time I first met him I was polishing off a Mae West album I'd been producing for MGM records. Miss West was to put her voice on "Great Balls Of Fire" at a local studio and I managed to smuggle Curtis into the control room where he hid in a closet, unseen by our star. He never forgot the experience but I can't remember anything untoward happening that evening. Mr. Novak, her bodyguard, kept his hand away from his gun. Miss West did the job, with my conducting her every phrase due to her problem with bar counting. She was a natural and liked to spread out over and above the prison-like bars.

In return Curtis was my guide into film appreciation. He took me to my first viewing of *It's A Wonderful Life* at the Vagabond, an art film theatre. He knew this would be a revelation, a cultural discovery, and it was. In contrast he took me to a porn theatre on Hollywood Boulevard to see *The Devil In Miss Jones*, pointing out the artistic camera angles surrounding Miss Jones' breasts and the way the lighting caressed the rear of her male partner.

I was eventually invited to the famous parties held in his Mediterranean house with the art nouveau interior. He had promised to let me in providing I stopped confusing art nouveau with art deco. I promised I'd do my best. I admired the Marlene Dietrich shoe displayed in a glass case and the stone cupids. I gazed at the still green water of the swimming pool, recently installed thanks to Curtis' stock market skill: he'd been to a preview of *Star Wars* and had rightly reckoned that shares in 20th Century Fox would skyrocket so he invested and — voila! – a pool of Roman proportions and with appropriate statuary.

Then it was into the melee and there I met Roman Polanski and Shelley Winters and more. I was introduced to Samuel Fuller, a master of screen violence. "You think my movies are violent — why you British made the most violent film ever: *Brief Encounter!*" Obviously I was puzzled. "That affair between Trevor Howard and Celia Johnson. Behind the twee tea and crumpet sweetness is a seething violence. British repression in a capped volcano! The mind is more powerful than the sword or bullet or knife. Get me?"

Curtis acted as host and chef on these occasions, disappearing into a tumultuous mess of a kitchen to whip up a simple but delicious pasta or fruit compote. Once I was asked to bring to the party a crate of cheap red wine. Upon delivering it Curtis had me join him backstage to steam off the labels and replace them with vintage classic labels from famous French vineyards.

And there were the angled lights over the gilt framed prints of Pre-Raphaelite masterpieces such as one could buy at London Underground kiosks. I had some but mine weren't set like Curtis'. He showed me how important appearance was.

Once he condescended to visit me for an al fresco dinner in my Altadena house. This was before Regina entered my life and cleaned it up. My life and my house were a bit of a mess. There were curtains made from Waikiki Beach scene prints and such was their vulgarity that Curtis was forced to cover his eyes and twist his body away while passing these offenses. At that stage I had boarders occupying almost every room and they were not of the highest social calibre, though they were young. One of the youngest had prepared a boil-in-the-bag spaghetti dinner but the sauce was one of Heinz 57 varieties, the tomato one. Curtis had taken the precaution of bringing his own sauce, mixed by his own hand from secret recipes handed down from olde world chefs. As he took his leave he said, "Next time we shall meet at a place of my choice."

At our private dinners at local restaurants — where there must be lots of customers squashing us on either side for without whirling people of the right sort Curtis was not amused — he would talk easily of the past, about his great affection for James Whale, director of *Frankenstein*. Suddenly Curtis was in tears, remembering the critical and commercial neglect suffered by the director. But swiftly his sadness evaporated when an eavesdropping waiter, hearing the word "movie," sat down and joined us. Upon learning that the boy was really an actor in need of discovery Curtis offered to see what he could do.

We talked of our mutual acquaintance Christopher Isherwood and how the latter, who could be a nasty drunk, had punched Curtis in the face at the end of a party just as Curtis was offering his hand to say goodbye and thanks. Isherwood was in a rage because he'd earlier spotted Curtis in conversation with Isherwood's boy companion Don Bachardy. Curtis sued and won a few dollars. Later Isherwood had a habit of entering Curtis' dreams and more: he would rise up at the end of Curtis' bed and shoot out a grimace of dripping menace. And Curtis was by this time well awake.

I was flattered to be in his circle for it was well known that he couldn't stand being near "low class" people. That is why, when he was ailing in his last weeks of life, he refused an offer to move to the Motion Picture Home in Calabasas. "Crawling with low class minds," he explained. His stroke had been serious enough to force him into a hospital despite his distrust of western medicine.

He was finally persuaded to enter after being reliably informed that at the Cedars Sinai hospital he would run into gangs of stars, including longtime regular Elizabeth Taylor. Why, there might even be all-star wheelchair races down the corridors. The day I visited him the stars were clearly having their day off and I could see that Curtis was in no-man's land in a world of practical ethnics, skilled at placing patients on bedpans. A man of his sensibilities and sensitivity didn't care for this at all but he faced the modern world bravely.

We formed an unbeatable team on my KPCC radio show in the

1990s. He eagerly agreed to be a guest whatever the theme of the night. Usually we drifted away from that theme so that a show about crooners became a series of vignettes on life in Paris in the 50s, of pissoirs and douches, of his landlady who'd been Proust's housekeeper. From there we'd discuss how neither of us had ever got through all of Proust but that Curtis had been at a dinner where Werner Hertzog, noted film director, had boasted that he had read every word of the massive Warren Report in one week without a proper break and that it is a monumental and important read, as important as the Bible. Oliver Stone, one of the guests, had just made *JFK*, a film rebutting the Warren Report, and he took Herzog's declaration to be a put-down of his movie. Proust would have enjoyed the social tension.

And so the program went drifting by from subject to subject without rhyme or reason into the night and up until the midnight hour. Radio that would be impossible in today's dreary compartmentalized world.

Fortunately I have those radio shows preserved on cassette. Curtis' personality is caught and is a part of his art, complementing his movies.

Where do individuals — all of us — go after the body is reduced to dust? Do they float about somewhere, barging into each other and having exchanges? Does Hitler share jokes with Ukulele Ike? Do we meet God's father at the 19th hole?

I can't bear to think that we return to a core, a mighty Oneness Thing. Or worse — that we become a tree or a frog or an ant. That's why I'm so glad I have those cassettes.

PS: a week ago I attended the Phil Spector trial at the invitation of Jim Dawson, a longtime supporter of the eccentric producer and a proud wearer of a "Team Spector" button.

Because I arrived earlier than Jim I sat where the sheriff told me to: on the left, on the prosecution side. In that position, behind the sexy Asian woman prosecutor, in a tight pant suit that did justice to a pert little bottom, I agreed with every word hurled against Spector. Clearly the man must be guilty.

But then in walked Jim and beckoned me to come sit with him on the defense side, right behind the latest Mrs. Spector, a comely young lady. Sotto voce, Jim introduced us: she offered me a cough lozenge, we chatted, and pretty soon I found her to be delightful. So delightful that soon I was rooting for her side. Clearly there were grounds for "reasonable doubt" in this case. I grew to loathe the Asian lawyer. I accepted a "Team Spector" button.

My position solidified when, at the lunch break announcement, the man himself, clad in a knee-length Edwardian-style jacket and wearing, for a change, a conservative wig, shuffled over to be with his wife. She introduced us and his face, hitherto either glowing or addled, transformed itself into wreaths of smiles. He must have forgotten the incident when he'd locked me in his mansion. What he remembered was "You Turn Me On" and how he laughed!—the laugh ringing out in this unsmiling courtroom, a place that might some day embrace his doom. We talked of Sonny Bono, of Mike Stoller, of my admiration for his recording of "I Saw Mommy Kissing Santa Claus."

I was telling him how our jackets had similar pinstripes when Mrs. S announced: "Now we must be popping home to Alhambra for a bite. So nice to meet you!" And then Phil Spector leaned forward and gave me a terrific bear hug for what seemed like an eternity. I was now his man. The truth, for the moment, must be admitted.

JULY

After 75 years as a haven of health and good fellowship the Pasadena Athletic Club has closed down as of the end of June. I am sad and furious. Sad because I shall miss the members, despite never getting introduced to many of the regulars. I shall miss their ritual greeting to each other: "There he is!" followed by joshing and banter and talk of how well a team played yesterday on television. I shall miss the trainer whose sports car vanity plate states "Medium" and who, for a fee, can summon up one's dead and then tell you that their golf handicap is awesome and getting more so. This trainer hardly ever supervises his clients. No, he lolls nearby on an exercise machine, doing needlework on his Blackberry or else making cell phone calls. Sometimes he'll take a break to talk about the fabulous tournedos he had at a new restaurant. He's not in good shape, but always has lots of clients, mostly rich men who, in turn, tell their trainer about how the new Mercedes handles on a sharp turn as compared with the Alfa.

I shall miss the well-shaped mother in tights who orders everybody to see *Jersey Boys*; and the glistening and super-packed upper bodies and posteriors of the few as they to-and fro on great overwrought-iron machines; I shall even miss the naked old men in the locker room with their enormous elongated dongs which seem to get longer as they grow older, sad engines out to pasture, long past their pleasure days.

On the last day of operation I took my usual morning lap swim in the sensibly long and wide pool. Thank God that my oppressor abandoned ship some time ago! There used to be an Arab woman, a hideous creature in a bathing cap who floundered about like a beached whale in her attempt at a crawl and refused to let me share a lane when the other lanes were taken. Club rules dictated that this was common courtesy. But she wouldn't make room and brushed me as we passed so at the next opportunity I performed a mighty sweep of the arm, as if executing an Olympian crawl thus creating a wave that smacked water all over her pasty face.

On this last morning I had a lane all to myself. Most of the pool was laneless — devoted to the Water Aerobics class of many years. Today, as a brave farewell, the class was fit to bursting, with the ladies (and the lone gent) wearing party hats — a choice of stars & stripes chef hats or else wire affairs that attached to their heads and wobbled about like antennae worn by space aliens. To martial music from a boom box, and under the leadership of their buxom trainer woman, the class marched swishingly up and down the pool in pairs, chattering merrily all the while.

Then it dawned on me this was what the athletic club was all about. Not physical jerks but community: a meeting place safe from the dangers of today, a social circle for people to talk and talk, not necessarily of anything in particular, nothing earth-shaking, but just plain old talk. Fellowship. And that's what being alive is for. That's why we have our Monday night salon at Conrad's, the family coffee shop with the cardboard food and the kitchen I wouldn't dare to examine closely. We go for the company. So when my friend Paul from San Francisco, the art historian and bon viveur, condescended to attend the Salon and then had the nerve to send back his jug of house red wine, referring to it as a "carafe," and demanding a better vintage, we said goodbye and good riddance to him. It's not the wine, it's the folks!

Yes, I shall miss the Pasadena Athletic Club. And I'm furious that the family who owned it sold out for a mess of pottage to the tune of $30 million. Have they no civic sense, no feeling for the community? And they sold out to Iranians who have announced that they will tear the building down, destroying the trees in the process (how ethnics hate greenery!) in order to erect thousands of condos, a hotel and retail stores. As if we need any more in Pasadena! The city is infested with them and the traffic gets more and more clogged. This destruction of culture has been green-lighted by a city council led by a mayor whose wife is a dedicated preservationist, always saving craftsman bungalows and the like. Saving them for the very rich, no doubt, moving them to the right neighbourhoods, so that they can be enjoyed in peace while we are left in a wasteland studded with condos built with Arab money.

It all makes me want to retreat into the past. So I will...

I had a dream last night that it was my birthday and nobody came to the party — not my father, my mother, not my favorite uncle.

Mind you, they're all dead, but that's no excuse in a dream. That's what dreams are made for. I saw Rollo The Dog uncharacteristically take a bite out of Simon The Cat but Regina said it didn't matter and anyway by that time the scene had changed to a windy golf course and there I found my beloved dead family, out rummaging in the gorse for a lost ball. My grandfather was in attendance too, in golfing tweeds, and full of really good jokes. It was like old times.

Perhaps I was in the past due to my recent reading about Edith Piaf in the late 1940s, and in particular how her boxer lover, Marcel Cerdan ("Le Bombardier Marocain") had died in a plane crash over the Azores en route for New York and his woman. The date was October 27, 1949, when I was a month into my first term at boarding school and the hell and the bewilderment and the feeling of being abandoned flooded back and yet I want to be there again. At Newlands, Seaford, Sussex-By-The-Sea, The World, The Universe. Far, far from home.

At home, in the family flat on Putney Heath, London, S.W. 15, I had heard, just before being taken away, a beautiful song called "Take Me To Your Heart," the English version of Piaf's "La Vie En Rose." I had been transported, a journey I sorely need at this point in my life.

Life up till then had been lovely. The war had been spent in my pram until, in 1945, we caught a train from Scarborough to London — where another train was on fire — and from there we puffed to the Suffolk coast, to a fairy tale village called Thorpeness, with a lake and a castle and a House In The Clouds. Here dwelt my grandfather in a big house by a windmill with a golf course on his doorstep and toy soldiers for me to play with and somewhere in the recesses was my grandmother but she didn't appear much because she was "unwell." Bottles secreted into her bedroom drawers told a story I was only later, much later, to learn. "Uncle Jack" (he hated to be known as a granddad) was my mother's father and he was oil rich with five farms nearby that I've told you about in a previous Letter — the farms he was told to buy by his doctor in order to take his mind off his depression.

At The Mill House my grandfather dispensed jokes and glasses of Guinness mixed with champagne. We watched him drink with his friends after golf, encouraging the local vicar to drink up and have the other half. The vicar, I later found out, was on my grandfather's pay roll and after he'd say farewell and hope to see us all in church and had shut the mighty Tudor front door of the Mill House my grandfather would announce ritually: "That's the one hundred and sixty fifth free drink he's had off me." Or whatever number the poor little chap had reached. Everybody laughed like hell and trooped into lunch.

We lived a few minutes walk away down the lane in a house by the lake. I spent my days on my tricycle, with our sheepdog Panda running alongside, in search of adventure.

One day we tried to find Nutwood, home of Rupert Bear. We failed. Another day I tried to drown Panda in the lake but experienced pity — what a delicious feeling! — and pulled him out.

On other days I was entertained with sweets from a twinkly old man who seemed to live alone without a wife or anybody. He was very free with the sweets and called me Tommy Tomkins and wrote a poem about me. Sometimes I sat on his knee as he bounced us to a song — "We're off to Brighton! We're off to Brighton!"

Next thing we were off to London, eventually to the flat on Putney Heath, near Wimbledon where the tennis takes place. Life was still lovely, especially when my father walked me to my first school, just down Putney Hill, a big stony house called Glengyle. We wore blazers and caps and sang beautiful hymns, as beautiful as the Piaf song — ones about Jesus hanging on a green hill faraway and there was something tingly and exciting about his hanging there and suffering all for us. I wanted to be up there with him. I loved hearing about his death, about his selflessness.

On my way home from school I liked to stop at a smelly refreshment stand, like a gypsy caravan. For a penny I could buy a doorstep slice of bread slathered with a sort of butter that tasted fishy. There was also ice cream to be purchased but this was made from margarine. The war had been declared over but it was still on to a certain extent.

I sang and I sang, leading my gang in a crocodile down the hill from Glengyle to Jack's Snack Bar where we had a school lunch treat — fried eggs, fried bread, fried everything. My mother, out shopping, had sneaked a glimpse of me at work entertaining gaily. She was so happy, because at home I'd been showing a tendency to stutter and stammer. The summer of 1949 came and it was lovely, too. I'm sure all hell was loose in the rest of the world but I knew nothing about that. We had sports day down by the Thames and again I sang as the boys competed. My brother Robin was now attending Glengyle and he was proving to be good at games. At home, though, he had a tendency to disappear and once he was gone for so long my parents called the police. "He must be dead by now," I told my mother. But they found him near the Wimbledon Lawn Tennis Club, sucking his thumb, happy as a sand boy. He got an ice cream as a relief reward — made of real cream. I wanted one, too.

Then one afternoon, in pouring rain, my parents took me up to London proper in a black taxi with tip-up seats. I sat in the tip-up. As we neared the West End the buildings got darker and darker until they were black. Only the cinemas blazed. We ended up in a black and dark hotel in a tearoom. My parents had me sit down to meet two rather swotty boys of my age, both in glasses and both very plain. They were Jones and Lefroy and they would be New Boys like me at Newlands School in September. But this was July and that meant there was ages and ages till September. My eighth birthday was coming up on July 10. Maybe I'd get that Daisy Red Ryder air gun with the pump action. Still, September would arrive one way or the other and I didn't like the idea of boarding school and I didn't much care for these two with the drips running out of their noses and their lack of interest in pop songs and comic books. We kept our own counsel as the parents chatted. I grabbed the chocolate éclair.

September came though and I now realized I was never going back to Glengyle. It was goodbye to hymns and friends and fishy bread and that sports day by the river. I stared out of my bedroom window, out beyond the bars and into nothingness. My mother tried to stave off my tears. She said she didn't want to send me away, nor did my father. It was just that if you came from our background then you had to send your children away so that they would get the right, the correct start in life. It was all for my good.

Nothing stops time and doom. On the day of leaving I was escorted by my parents to Victoria Station. The news theatre above the platform tried its best with Bugs Bunny and news from Russia and pictures of the King and Queen and men who twisted each other's noses and poked eyes. But it was all over in 75 minutes. "This is where we came in," said my father. Next I was taken up to meet the engine driver, wreathed in steam, a blackface hefty brute with a twinkle in his eyes as he shoveled on the coal and let me touch the hot iron levers. But now was the hour of doom: time to say goodbye; my mother had to turn away even as my father shook my hand and said, "Good luck, old boy." A master with a pipe he waved like a conductor took over. I was gently pushed into the uniformed throng. I avoided every boy on that journey to Dread Town. And now my memories go blank except that I remember finally getting into an iron bedstead in a big room at the top of that big red house and feeling the stinging cold of starched sheets and trying to make the world go away. I had seen the last of my parents, my family. That I knew. And the only comfort was that as the days and weeks went by and as I fell into the rhythm of Newlands life and formed my own gang and band and started drawing pictures of cowboys and GIs and sudden death, so the faces I had loved in another life faded.

Let's move back to the present:
I have sent in my two articles about Richard Rodgers for inclusion in the program book for the Oregon Festival Of American Music which, once again, I'll be performing at in August. Now I have to learn a whole bunch of Rodgers & Hart songs for various

concerts. These are tricky ones to remember – Hart's lyrics are too, too clever. I'm really a Walter Donaldson man. And many of the songs I've never heard of.

It's peaceful on the frontline here now that we have no belligerent Arab woman — although I still have wide-awake nightmares that she'll suddenly rise like a fearful Phoenix and say, "Fuck you, Whitcombs!" like she used to. However, the surviving one, the stooping diminutive husband, has been pleasant enough in his way. He left for a vacation in Oregon and let us have the keys to his front gate so we can use his pool if we wish. This I did the other night and it was odd to see our house from the ex-enemy's vantage point. I was in the very area where, four years or so ago, he and his wife boasted loudly—intending for us to hear and fear— of installing a machine gun on their garage roof so that they would then have a suitable nest for picking us off.

I swam around the pool in the nude and admired the moon and the trees and listened to the birds and regretted that we'd ever got into this mess. It was as if I'd died but was now permitted by some kindly God to restart— like Scrooge, only nicer.

Back to our side of the fence: the pond in the converted hot tub —where once, in the days before Regina arrived to clean up the ship, sex orgies took place when I had a house full of lodgers who, when I was away in England, would have fun— is now running smoothly with water gushing from the faux mill and tiny goldfish milling about with useful mosquito-eating fish. The denizens of the pond scurry away under rocks and stones when raccoons descend in the night to try to consume them

On Wednesday June 13 Regina and I were given awards at a trendy local restaurant, together with local rich people, as "Contemporary History Makers" by the Pasadena Museum Of History (where I'm currently "Artist In Residence").

While the other awardees had forked out several thousand dollars for their tables we were actually making money: I had been employed to provide music with my Bungalow Boys. At dinner Regina and I sat next to an interesting man, full of beans: he used to be a top cancer specialist but now he's discovered a more lucrative career as a director of a company that makes armor plating for Humvees in Baghdad. "I tell you," he said," there's a lot of loot in this war! You should get into it with your ukulele!"

The month of June also saw the release of a movie called *Fido*, a Canadian zombie comedy starring Billy Connolly and containing two of my songs. Regina and I battled frightful traffic to get from Pasadena to Santa Monica in order to catch the noon screening at the Nuart, the only theater in L.A playing this picture. But it was worth the slog: a charming zombie film set in the 1950s and shot in rich

Technicolor. And my song "When You're There" comes on at an important plot moment — when the wife is falling in love with her pet zombie, Fido. We see their soppy faces and we hear nothing but Regina's dulcet voice as she sings my song. Very pleasing and we clutched each other with glee. Unfortunately the film is yet another of those money losers I seem to get involved with. No doubt it will eventually be classed as a "cult classic" but a fat lot of good that is to me financially.

I was hired to play atmosphere French accordion at the premiere of Pixar's *Ratatouille* at the Kodak Theater in Hollywood, a real, old-fashioned event. Of course, as I've written in a previous Letter, we had been given the red carpet treatment last year by the powers-that-be up in Pixar's studio in Emeryville. But here I was — an employee at the event. However, with the use of a Disney contact, we managed to wangle a ticket for Regina to the screening and reception. I stayed at my post with the other employee, waiting upstairs in the ballroom together with the magicians and men in stilts and girls in shorts and army of waiters till our commander, clad in earphones and mikes, told us to get into action as soon as the guests poured in to grab the Wolfgang Puck delicacies once the credits started running.

After my job I sneaked off stage to join Regina at her table and sneak a little ratatouille. I sat there amazed as Regina got to her feet to shimmy with a seven-foot male clown on stilts.

I've also been correcting the proofs of my latest Mel Bay offering, *The Ian Whitcomb Songbook* which will finally published this month of July almost in time for my 66th birthday. This book has been over three years in the making. It was finished as we moved from Altadena to Monrovia back in those dark days of 2004.

Finally it will see light of day just as we see light of day in a new life. Regina is happier than I've seen her in many a year. I hope you are all happy, too. For at last I am able to pull my head out of our old battleground and have a look at the world around and see how happy one can be. How long will it all last?

AUGUST

This HAS to be a short one. (I'm inspired to use caps by Ms. Rowling). This WILL be SHORT. It's what I tell Regina every time I sit down at the Apple to tap in the Letter with the middle finger of my left hand.

This time I must be brief because I have to get back to trying to learn the mass of songs that are on my plate for the Oregon Festival Of American Music which starts at the beginning of August.

Having to master 26 songs is my own fault. Each year I beg the festival boss, Jim Ralph, to have more time on stage. Now this was fine when we were featuring the Fabulous Fifties and I could do "Hound Dog" without thinking, plus other simple songs I had known since my teen years; it was fine when we had two weeks of Irving Berlin last year. Berlin is right down my Alley. Indeed, many of the numbers I chose myself.

But this year the focus is on the lofty and hallowed Richard Rodgers and to my embarrassment I find I know hardly any of his work — "work" as opposed to the easy on-the-ear accessibility of Tin Pan Alley. I admire, respect, and am in awe of Mr. Rodgers but I don't find his work fits my stage persona. He seems a little stern and didactic; he stated from the start that he intended to rise above the inanities of mere pop song; he was a "musical dramatist" not a tunesmith. Boy, he must have been annoyed when "Blue Moon," his sole pop song became the best seller of all his oeuvre! Thanks to Elvis and the Doo-Woppers. But even "Blue Moon" isn't in my repertoire. Now I'm having to learn the thing in all its moon-june glory.

Still, being a pop it's not hard to remember. Now, some of the others are really tough, and obscure, too. Have you ever heard, for example, "It's A Lovely Day for A Murder,"or "There's Always Room For One More"? And the verses to some of the Rodgers & Hart songs — songs that have become such evergreen standards that you can watch slimy neo-crooners on YouTube swishing and swaying and mike-clutching to them — are so smart they're tricksy, perplexing. Why, I had to call up my clever writer friend Chas Sprawson in his London flat, on an evening when he was watching an important Test Match (cricket between England and India) and get him to explain this line from the verse of "Have You Met Miss Jones?": "We mustn't wait — the nearest moment that we marry is too late." I'm not sure I understand even after Chas' explanation. But I admire Larry Hart's being able to get out of his emotional skin and put himself in the character of a married man. After all, as we know from the latest biographies of Hart, he was a permanent bachelor, prone to indulging in sleazy and lubricious nocturnal activities with sailors and what-not, set up by his procurer friend, the pernicious queer dentist "Doc" Bender. Hart would often report for work with the anal-retentive Rodgers at the composer's spic'n'span home, sporting a black eye and a few bruises, the results of the previous night's rough trade encounters.

As the festival boss retorted when I moaned about the 26 songs I have to learn: "Every year you ask for more material — so here you are! Enjoy!" I shall certainly enjoy being accompanied once again by Dick Hyman on piano and, for the first time, Bucky Pizzarelli on guitar. Bucky played on Vaughn Monroe's hit version of "Riders In

The Sky" back in the late 1940s. I bought the 78 in Putney High Street at that time. He also played on all those great Guy Mitchell hits like "Singing The Blues" and "Knee Deep In The Blues," as part of the Ray Conniff rhythm section. I bought those 78s fresh in the High Street too. In a recent phone call, Bucky confided that the Conniff secret formula was three guitars and a ukulele. The uke gave it a jolly bouncy edge.

So, for the past month, I've been shutting myself in the Music Room, a free-standing building behind our main house, and studying the songs at the keyboard, pretending I'm a past-master at reading music. All the while around me improvements are being made in our compound, so many changes that old friends and boarders who stayed here in the old days wouldn't recognize the place. Apart from the French chateau cobblestone driveway and the London Club library building, which I'm sure I've told you about, we now have a new garage door with cute little windows, resembling a chocolate box Tudor cottage. Resting now on the cobblestones is a Honda Element we bought last week— a box on wheels serving as a van, nicely safe and high.

And yesterday we almost became the owners of a 'laundry center' by Kenmore. (I'm not exactly sure why we need a new washer and dryer, but there you are — I never question Madame). The Sears men came in a big truck to deliver and install the tall machine but looked at each other in amazement when, upon plugging it in and turning the knobs, the Kenmore, "top of the line," proceeded to do the reverse of what the knobs said. The machine washed instead of drying and vice versa. A bold Sears man opened the dryer to be greeted by a fierce stream of water slapping him in the face. Odd noises then came from all parts of the machine — bells and whistles and grunts. The Sears men, after looking perplexed, broke out into laughter. Regina joined them. I just stared. I couldn't see the joke.

For the record: the month of July....................
The following is from my daily journal. Much of what I jot down is of no interest. Eg: "Sunday, July 1: it gets hotter and hotter. I feel bloated. Too much ice cream last night."

A month of gigs: The Bungalow Boys played our annual July 4th party in Brentwood at the house of the retired shrink, Dr. Zeitlin. We have done this party for over a decade. Nobody gets any younger. The number of guests declines each year. A dance floor is laid out in the back yard but fewer and fewer can get up and dance. One dear woman, victim of a stroke, was led by her husband around the floor in a firm clutch. They managed a few slow foxtrots, an inspiring sight to see.

We stick to the music of the 20s and 30s. Is our sound going to atrophy and eventually die — either on its own or via murder by Rod Stewart? I was glad to see a couple of children at the party. They left after the food was offered. We love the July 4 food, especially the plump hot dogs and the potato salad liberally mixed with bacon bits. I was happy to find that even in affluent Brentwood there are neighbour problems — a dog barked from over the wall continuously throughout the evening, eventually smothered when the Santa Monica fireworks display began and we struck up "I'm A Yankee Doodle Dandy."

Friday, July 6. My concert at the charming Backstage cabaret in the Coffee Gallery. Almost every day I buy my coffee at the Coffee Gallery on Lake Ave in Altadena, where the local sages sit for hours at the big round table solving the world's problems for free. Every now and then I transform from a customer into a star, striding through the Gallery, past my fans and into the Backstage. We had a Sold Out house, but that's not hard here because the place is only allowed to hold 48. More than that and the Fire Marshall appears with his gang of muscular men.

While singing "Home Is Where Your Heart Is," an old Bud Flanagan number, I almost choked up, thinking of our return to Altadena. Why was I getting all emotional to a simple commercial pop song? Is this sentimentality?

Regina sang beautifully and tunefully, while tending in her arms one of her babysit charges, Clarissa. The latter, shy at first, later got so badly bitten by the stage bug that she demanded to join us on a regular basis fot the rest of the show. Happily, our friend, Richard Payatt, a self-styled authority figure and an adept at the martial arts, gently removed her.

Afterwards we retired with a few friends, members of the London Club, to the Library. Led by Richard we christened the building with toasts and cigars. I want the cigar smell to imbed itself, mingle with the cedar, and then exude civilization. On the shelves P.G. Wodehouse rubs shoulders with Dante and James M. Cain.

On the following Monday we — Regina, Rollo and I — set off on a trip to Santa Barbara, after leaving the termite men tenting the house. A clever idea of Regina's — to combine termite extermination with my birthday. As before, though, it was really Rollo's holiday: we headed for Dog Beach, officially known as "Arroyo Burro" and, before that, in simpler times, as "Hendry's." This haven is just off the freeway north of Santa Barbara and there Rollo can scamper about legally and try to mount other dogs. Regina and I took a plunge in the sea. Most refreshing but I'm always fearful that I'll bump up against the bloated white body of a dead female. After the dog walk we enjoyed, as usual, a Martini at the Brown Pelican, a restaurant right on the beach. I tell myself this is better, or as good as, any seaside in England.

Next we drove to Main Street and Mrs. Andersen's, a Scandinavian restaurant that sells delicious marzipan pastries, and healthy herring. Mrs. A., buxom and Earth Motherly, is always on hand to embrace us. Regina used to be scared of her but not any more. Our local friend Richard Payatt joined us. Among his many accomplishments he is also the founder of The London Club and an expert on toasts and British military uniforms. He's also a wine expert and so he earnestly instructed the waitress on the correct way to open good wine, explaining as he tore and screwed that he manages no less than four restaurants. What he didn't say is that they are known under the collective title of Taco Bell.

His 8-year-old son Marshall was with us. Marshall is brainy and articulate. He tends to deliver speeches, on a host of topics, from the top of the restaurant stairs. After dinner, back at the Payatt house, Richard was preparing to read more of *The Iliad* to Marshall. I offered to relieve Richard. I like reading to children and rather pride myself on my style. But Marshall declined my offer: "No offense and all that."

Next day, July 10, was my 66th birthday. We celebrated by taking Rollo to Dog Beach, after a morning spent watching World War Two flying pictures on the motel room's TV. We don't subscribe to cable and so watching Turner Classic Movies is a real treat. In the evening we went to the Payatt house where we watched my chosen movie, *Champagne Charlie*. Everyone joined in the choruses.

At the weekend I had two gigs out at the Workman & Temple Family Homestead in the City Of Industry. That dreaded title! It's always hard to persuade friends to come and see us there for the first time. "Industry" makes them shudder. But in fact our music is made in a sylvan setting beside a fully stocked pond or else inside the walls of the 1920s Spanish adobe compound. This year the event was titled " Ticket To The Twenties."

On Saturday I was part of Janet Klein's band as a Parlour Boy. For the first time we Boys all got along well together, even praising each other's playing. What a change! Several members of the London Club were present, dressed in period costumes and spreading tasty picnics on the grass in front of the bandstand. One member, an expansive fellow called Jerry, a retired banker and dedicated Sherlock Holmesian, sat spread in a deck chair with what looked like a refreshing ice drink in his hand. Beautiful cut glass. I accepted his offer of a sip. It turned out to be a gin and tonic, even though prohibition was being tightly enforced. Very refreshing — I had another and another sip. After that the gig swam by and there was even more bonhomie within the Parlour Boys, stopping short of actual embraces.

Next day it was the turn of my Dance Band, a group that like *Brigadoon* only appears at certain times. This is an annual event and I just love standing in front of a ten-piece band to conduct and call off the tempos. The musicians are all true blue pros who can read at sight anything that's put in front of them. One time our lead reedman played a squashed fly — and what an exotic chord resulted from the blend! The Dance Band has been playing the Homestead summer event since 1988. I shan't forget the first time: afterwards, at a Pasadena Mexican restaurant, in the middle of my second margarita, I posed this question to Regina: "What would you say if I asked you to marry me?" "Ian ... I'm not going to address a hypothetical question like *that*. When you want to propose you can do so.," she wisely replied. We were married the very next year.

Had a reply to the last letter I wrote to Andy Wickham. He says he enjoyed the latest Lotusland Letter, especially "your evocative description of the news cinema on Victoria Station and the feeling of foreboding when your father said:' This is where we came in'. I like the sound of your father, though returning to school is a well-worn subject."

However, Andy concludes his letter by reminding me that dwelling in the past is a bad thing. He quotes this exchange between Ratty and Mole in the finale of "The Killing of Mr. Toad":
"What's that sound, Ratty?"
"It's the wind in the reeds"
"What's it saying, Ratty?"
"Forget, forget...."
Curtain.

Apart from personal mail, the other thing I like getting in the mail is *Reminisce* ("The Magazine That Brings Back More Good Times") — of course, Andy would hate it. The readers, all Americans of the old school, write each article. They're always about poor people and so I have restrained myself from contributing: my family did rather too well in the Depression. Emotional suffering is another matter.

I'll end with a sample letter from the magazine's "Stirring Up Memories" department. The letter must have impressed the editors since it's appeared twice in successive issues. Or maybe this is due to the age of the staff...

"In the '30s, my grandpa Carl Wackernah owned Carl's Delicatessen, located in Jacksonville, Florida. On top of one of the counters were three big crocks. One was filled with pickled pig's feet, another, pickled eggs and the third pickled ROOSTER COMBS! I never had the courage to try one, but still I wonder how they tasted."

Oh dear! I broke my promise — this Letter is not very short. But

I typed as fast as I could and without much thought.......

SEPTEMBER

Improvements at our house continue to be made daily, under the direction of Regina. At this point we have: a new driveway, garage door, insulation, kitchen floor, bathroom with shower doors, three piece sofa set, and, at the rear of the back yard where once was desolation, a spanking new library building.

So what can I moan about? The weather. I can't stand this perpetual sun. I need seasons. I need rain to pelt down so that I have good reason to stay indoors and read or write. Sun is for holidays and I can't make every day a holiday because I'm not retired even though I'm of the age.

The best of August was spent working. Well, the kind of "work" I enjoy. I was rehearsing or performing almost every day at the Oregon Festival of American Music in Eugene and though I was worried I'd have to go on stage and perform a song I hardly knew — all was well in the end. When I was under-rehearsed I resorted to comic business. Two solid weeks of Richard Rodgers; 25 new songs for me to perform. But I returned home satisfied. I'd become a cool ballad singer at the final concert; jaded jazz accompanists had applauded me. No more having to be funny all the time.

Culled from my journal:

Sunday, July 29 — a happier airport take-off for Eugene. For the past four years I've left an unprotected wife to face possible attacks from savages. This time there's only peace and quiet. Goodbye for a while to Mexicans and Blacks. Eugene is white as a sheet. Everyone running around in shorts with thighs flexing. This year they've stuck me in a different hotel, The Valley River Inn, further from the festival action, set in a sea of parking lots surrounding a vast shopping mall with, in the distance, a Macy's and a Regal cinema and — aah, how reassuring! — a Starbucks: I shall be able to buy "The New York Times." None of the performers have yet arrived. The Willamette river flows peacefully by, slow and inexorable. No problems. Very reassuring.

After checking in and unpacking, I walk down the bike path — there are bike paths everywhere — beside the river to find the Marriott Residence Inn where I always used to stay in past years. Where Dick Hyman, my father figure mentor, stays and where every morning I would time it to be at the free breakfast simultaneously with Dick and his wife Julia; there we could discuss the war, or Bush, or the curious harmonies of Richard Rodgers.

How many years in succession have I been playing this festival? Since 2002 when I came for the Gershwin Transformations and sang "Fascinating Rhythm" with Ukie, in the style of Cliff Edwards. The Ralphs, the couple who started the festival back in the early 1990s are cultural saints. Each year they spend their own money presenting classic American song and dance with lectures and movies plus a full-scale musical or two and all in the space of ten days. A feast of Gershwin, Porter, Berlin, Rodgers — as well as other less stellar names. There's nothing like it anywhere else in America. Or the World for that matter. I am in heaven.

And now I'm hiking down the bike path, heeding the speeding bicyclists racing up my rear with shouted warning, "On your left!" Finally I arrive at the restaurant — Mc Something or Rather's — beside the river where so often in the past I've dined deliciously alone on ahi tuna on a roll, washed down with local India pale ale by Hammerhead and a whiskey by J Daniels, and all with a book in front of me.

Tonight it's a biography of Lorenz Hart. However, the table next to me is getting my attention: alarmingly rigid elderly couple hosted by their dumpy son. There's stilted table talk. The mother bangs on about some trivial thing while the husband gazes disinterestedly into the middle distance as he picks his teeth. They are all drinking Cokes. There's murder in the air. The son fidgets and then, in the middle of a long pause, talks of his church-going today. He attended twice. The mother smiles. The father continues to stare off somewhere. Is it towards the men's room? Would he like to be tapping a message with his feet inside a stall? Already I'm beginning to yearn for Mexicans and Blacks and all the bustling color of L.A.

Monday onwards—it's now a blur of rehearsals, concerts, lectures, of mingling with fellow singers and musicians. An artist among artists. A pro. Just my meat. Wish I did this all year round. Scurrying around with plenty to do, thus avoiding that awful sitting in repose, taking stock of life and concluding that it's all sound and fury, strutting and fretting, and in the end the endless angry silence.

Rehearsals for the opening night gala concert, "Where Or When." My two songs, "The Girl Friend" and "Honey Bun" are rushed through in one go. Maybe this is a backhanded compliment as I'm such a reliable old pro. The operatic diva gets the lion's share of attention. She's now a regular on "A Prairie Home Companion." Our new musical director, Ken Peplowski, keeps assuring me: "I'm so glad you're here!" This is nice, until I hear him telling others the same thing.

Incidentally, Ken, an Anglophile with a taste for George

Formby and the Goons, tells me that he once met Spike Milligan and the great comedian told him that the name, Peplowski, sounded like a custard pie hitting a wall and then slithering slowly down to earth.

Wednesday: opening night gala. In the morning I delivered my first lecture/talk/presentation to the Elder Hostellers. This is a merry group of feisty oldsters (actually not much older than myself) who every year pay for a week's room and board at the festival in order to get to see everything: concerts, musicals, talks. They're very smart and you have to be on your toes. My first talk was about how Richard Rodgers, despite having an aversion to swing and jazz and not liking his songs to be garbled by jazzers and crooners, was to live to hear his songs become rock fodder: Elvis cut "Blue Moon" and then the doo wop Marcels went to Number One with it.

As an example of how singers could show no mercy — sticking in the word "now" every so often — I played Buddy Greco's slaughtering of "Lady Is A Tramp." I was amazed at how well it went down with the hostellers. They ate it up. Their leader informed me that Greco really swung — unlike the version I'd just played: Sophie Tucker, speak-singing with clear enunciation, which would have been thoroughly approved of by Rodgers & Hart. Added the spokesman: "I have perfect pitch — and I'm telling you: this woman can't sing!" I stood speechless. But: these people are the bread and butter of the festival and they must be obeyed.

At the afternoon rehearsal in the big concert hall I was thrilled to meet Bucky Pizzarelli, the octogenarian guitarist who started with Vaughn Monroe, strumming on "Riders In The Sky," a 78 I bought in 1949. I mentioned him in last month's Letter. Bucky confirmed that indeed it was he who provides the lively solo on Connie Francis' "Lipstick On Your Collar" and he's proud of it, too. So refreshing to hear this from a jazzer. He became fascinated by my ukulele. Kept smiling at it as if it was a pet animal. Where could he buy one, he asked. Tomorrow we'll have breakfast.

The concert came off fine. I didn't do much. Didn't even take a curtain call. But I was at high energy on my numbers, although I'm not sold on the lyrics of either. But these are stage songs and probably work better in context. Rodgers always was at pains to describe himself as a musical dramatist, not a mere one-off songwriter.

Afterwards we all came back in the van, diva and musical director and jazz sidemen, plus the elderly Max Wilk, noted musical theatre author. I had a nasty feeling he'd crossed me some years back. "Yes," he confirmed. "You met me in London and asked for advice on a book you were writing about Irving Berlin." Oh, yes, and what happened? "I told you to fuck off," he said with a laugh. You can't help liking old Max. His favorite expression is "Oh, pull-eeze!"

After being dropped off we hung around the hotel entrance telling jokes. Bucky told about a man whose wife fell gravely ill at a restaurant after eating the halibut. After six hours in emergency the surgeon comes out and says: "She'll live — but it'll be tough on you: she needs 24 hour-a-day attention; you'll have to have her fed and bathed and taken to the toilet; she'll never speak again — let's face it: she's a vegetable." The husband looks devastated. Then the surgeon slaps him on the back and says, "Just kidding — she died!"

I couldn't compete on this level. Nor with the string of one-liners that the jazzmen reeled off as if they'd done this for years. When the dirty limericks started I took a backseat. The opera diva, Maria, came out with some of the filthiest. One was about a woman from Azores with sores. Ken followed up with a leper story involving a barman dipping his chips in the man's arm. I guess this is the way performers relax after a taxing concert where the demand is to stretch their techniques to the max. I have no technique so I don't have a store of salty stories. I just play myself, only bigger.

Thursday: nothing planned so I rented a bike and became an Oregonian, speeding along the bike path by the river, joining the clan of healthy ones in abbreivated shorts, glimpsing the kids floating down the river on rafts and inner tubes, envying the two boys who ran to the bank shouting, "Wanna swim, or wanna fish? Or wanna do both!" Went back to my room to practice a song I'm having awful trouble with: "A Lovely Day For A Murder" from the musical "Higher and Higher." Really odd number of bars, doesn't follow the Alley norm, has lots of repeated notes, and is klezmeric. Dick Hyman, with us on piano for only the first week, told me he'd help me. Must have seen how red-faced embarrassed I became at rehearsal when I couldn't read the rhythm patterns. I cursed myself. Very self-conscious about this musical illiteracy. I seem to have reams of sheet music in my room but it's all Greek to me until I play a CD of a song on the boom box they've lent me. Only then do the dots on the page make sense and match. Music remains a mystery.

I'm discovering characteristics in Rodgers' melodies. He adores scales, climbing up and down them from "Manhattan" through "My Heart Stood Still" to the apogee of them all," Do Re Mi." I have to sing that at an upcoming concert.

Friday: joined the jolly Bucky on the terrace of the hotel dining *room, as the river calmly flowed by and bikers zoomed along the bank opposite. Bucky has a Roman nose and a New Jersey gruff accent that makes him sound like a mobster. Ken assured me that New Jersey folk affect this so that they can get respect and attention from waiters. He's really a pussycat. Told me he never had formal instruction but learnt guitar from listening to his uncles. All his family were weekend musicians and were brilliant. Could have toured the country with the top bands but they didn't want to leave the home turf, couldn't miss the home cooked pasta and the evenings on the front porch.*

Bucky talked of his tour of Israel. He was over there on a jazz gig but he had time off to hire a guide to drive him around. A college professor who couldn't stop lecturing. So many walls, was Bucky's summing up of Israel.

Max Wilk, another octogenarian, joined us on the terrace. He's been hired to give talks to the oldsters. He actually knew Rodgers & Hart. He saw Hart ordering crates of wine and spirits for his benders with Doc Bender, the sinister dentist who also procured for Hart. Max shocked his Hosteller audience yesterday by reciting doggerel by Hart about Bender buggering about with a waggling chorus line of bottoms-out and bending chorus boys. "Lucky Bender! — He's on the Enda!" This didn't go down well with the festival authorities.

At the afternoon concert, "On Your Toes," held in the Shedd building, once a church, I stumbled during "Murder." Mortifying because I'd got it right twice running during the morning rehearsal. But we all made mistakes this afternoon, even master pianist Dick Hyman. And none of the audience realized this. As long as they don't realize something's wrong they'll go along with you. Never embarrass them by showing off your mistake. Concert hall pianists observe this rule. If they forget the Beethoven passage they simply make it up. Keep going, keep smiling — that's the secret. Purvey confidence and it'll spread to the audience like a disease.

In the evening I sat in the balcony of the vast concert hall over at the Hult centre and saw the full-scale production of "South Pacific." Three bloody hours long. Now I see how "Honey Bun" fits — as a parody of a cheap burlesque number. "Some Enchanted Evening" works as a beautiful opening catch phrase. I realize it's the same opening phrase as in "With A Song In My Heart." And then, later, back in my room, as I was playing a 1915 arrangement by Frank Saddler of a Jerome Kern song, "Till The Clouds Roll By," I heard imbedded there, in between the phrases, those same opening 5 catchy notes in a clinging bunch. Only connect.

Next week, the final one: I savour every moment here. Soon it will all be over and I'll be back trying to kill the days. Bucky left on

Sunday morning at 4 am. I spied him from my window. Woke just in time. His next stop is Nairn, Scotland, for some jazz party or gathering. A remarkable man. It's the gigging that keeps him alive and kicking. Last night, at McGrath's, the fish joint across the parking lot, he told me about the first jazz party he'd been to, back in the 1950s. That's when a rich fellow started throwing parties where he'd pay big bucks to lure in the big jazz stars, the legends. In the 50s there wasn't so much call for these stars due to the coming of rock & roll. So this Colorado millionaire could indulge his love by hiring his favorites.

At this, the first jazz party, he'd roped in Teddy Wilson and Joe Venuti among the stars to amuse him in his house. A house so high in the mountains that both Count Basie and Duke Ellington had collapsed due to the thinness of the air and could be seen lying together on a couch, stretched out like noble knights on Westminster Abbey tombs.

Teddy Wilson had never met Venuti and he told him how much he'd loved his recording of "You Took Advantage of Me" and how he'd give anything to hear it. Venuti fished out his violin and started playing the request. Wilson, who'd been enjoying the host's scotch, spread out on a couch to revel. Soon he was so deeply asleep that Venuti packed up his fiddle and went to bed. Next morning the famous fiddler rose around noon in time for caviar and lox. Afterwards, retiring to the lounge for a cigar, he found the famous pianist still recumbent and now snoring up a storm. So Venuti pulled out his fiddle and finished off the Rodgers & Hart song. Wilson awoke, like a fairy tale princess, and delivered a beatific smile: "Man, that was positively dreamy!"

Max Wilk has discovered that he can get his beloved New York Times at the Starbucks. I escort him down there, negotiating cars and bikes en route. Max inhabits another wonderful world where I hope to join him in a few years time. I notice that both he and Dick Hyman are at sea without their blessed New York Times. At one lunch Hyman spread open the paper in front of us all and proceeded to read all about Baghdad and Bush even as we told hilarious stories.

On the return journey from Starbucks, and with his Times rolled up under his arm, Max told me a story about Sophie Tucker. The way our conversations go is that I'll suddenly state a song title and this will trigger Max into singing it. Such as "Who Paid the Rent for Mrs Rip Van Winkle." We can construct whole conversations using only song titles. Then, feeling bad about this guilt-ridden pleasure, he'll declaim: "What crap these songs are!" — compared to such giants as Rodgers & Hart. But he sings the songs with gusto and I join in. This is an interesting phenomenon:

I've done the same with jazz virtuoso Derek Smith, another performer at the festival who is relieving the departing Dick Hyman. Derek, an Englishman who came to America in the 50s because America was where the True Jazz lay, disdains anything that's not pure jazz. Yet once at dinner, a few festivals ago, after we'd had a few drinks, I started singing WW2 songs like "When They Sound The Last All Clear," a Vera Lynn number, and a very rousing rendition of "Run Rabbit Run" as sung by Flanagan & Allen. Derek joined in with passion, as if hypnotized. Next day he gave me a rare glare and waved a dismissive hand at me, as if I'd caught him in a compromising position. Derek has an extraordinary laugh. He'd laugh if you told him there's a hurricane approaching with a tornado hard on its heels. The only time he doesn't laugh is when you tell him a joke. Or do what I did: resurrecting rubbish songs. Actually, they're great songs, memory finders, releasing the souls in those starved of pure emotion.

So there was old Max as I steered him through the parking lot sea back to our hotel. I was singing "Some of These Days" to ease the trek. This led him into a stream of consciousness about Sophie Tucker. He told me she used to hire men to service her over the years. One such lover was working away at the lady, building the act with ardent sayings until, just before the hoped for climax, he asked sweatingly: "What am I doing for you baby, what am I doing?" From her silk pillows, as she relaxed underneath the energetic hired man, Miss Tucker replied: "What are you doing? You're taking my fucking money."

Saturday: the last day. The last show. The flowers that were fresh in a vase when I arrived have wilted and are turning brittle. I've been relieved to have gotten through concerts where I've only rehearsed a song once and then had to fake it on stage that afternoon. I did that Saturday with a Rodgers & Hammerstein song called "All I Owe Ioway."

In that case I didn't even know the tune even though I had the music in front of me. But I made a success of it by doing a comic turn: wrapping the endless ream of scotch-taped pages round my body like a shroud and exiting with a little funeral dance. But you can only get away with only so much faking. I had reached the limit.

For the finale concert, "Something Wonderful," music director Ken asked me to sing two ballads absolutely straight: "I know you can ham it up and be funny— but I'd like to see you sing a ballad." I was determined to be straight. I recalled the scene in "The Singing Fool" where Al Jolson is a singing waiter and tells the cabaret pianist Bert Fiske that he's going to sing a ballad. "You're screwy — you can't sing a ballad." "Many a screwy guy has sung a ballad," says Jolson and goes into a melodramatic reading of "It All Depends On You." Terrific.

The two songs selected by Ken are "It's Easy To Remember" and "Have You Met Miss Jones?" Now it seems like everybody and his wife knows these songs — except me. I guess I've always avoided such classy stuff because definitive versions have been recorded by Crosby and Clooney and the like. I've always gone for novelty, for neglected songs that I can make my own. I've been determined to make the numbers my own, to try to find out what they're about and interpret them as such. "Miss Jones" in particular seemed like a little novel told in a minute or so, encased in 32 bars. Encountered casually at a social gathering Miss Jones stops the singer in his tracks, causing him to lose his breath and then, in the next line, he owns the earth and sky. Suddenly he's meeting Miss Jones every day — and this will happen till he dies.

On the big stage this evening I walked on slowly, dressed in my British pinstripe suit. The audience was expecting something funny. There were anticipatory laughs. But I stood serious and recited the verse, ending with the warning, "We mustn't wait — the nearest moment that we marry is too late." Seize the moment — for otherwise it might be gone forever. After the recitation and the ensuing frightening silence I went into the song and I sang. I actually sang. I hit notes. Mr Rodgers' notes.

Afterwards even the jazz sidemen applauded me. I had become a smooth, cool interpreter of ballads by big name theatre writers. Had joined the club. I was closer to Michael Feinstein and the rarified, perfumed aroma of New York cabaret and hooded eyes and rapidly discarded gestures. No more telling frantically of where Robinson Crusoe went on a Saturday night or of asking what to get a Nudist for its Birthday. No more Hungry Women......

Afterwards I sat up late in the bar of the Valley River Inn with the sidemen, all great in-demand jazzers, and drank and yarned. Thanks for hanging out with us, said an ace guitarist from New Jersey. You're one of the guys, a fellow musician. I went to bed on a cloud.

The following week, when back in Altadena and trying to resume the old life, James Ralph, creator of the festival, kindly e-mailed a review from the local paper, *The Register Guard*, written by one Tom Manoff. An afterward informed us that he's also classical music critic for National Public Radio's *All Things Considered*. Here is what he said of my foray into balladry:

"This was the challenge throughout the festival: how do you go up against the famous performances of Rodgers' music, heard live especially, or endlessly in film and on recordings? That was the unspoken subtext for the singers. The best answer was to bring something new and personal to the music, but to bring it with class. Whitcomb always does. He may have lost a few high notes at this point in his career, but he still spins magic from these songs."

Phew! I hardly ever get reviewed. And here I was being judged as if I really was a singer and not a personality, a diseur. I don't think I've ever possessed those high notes — but this was praise indeed. However, when I told Janet Klein — she of Janet Klein & Her Parlour Boys of which I'm one — she e-mailed a plaintive query: "I hope you're nor going to desert us for the jizzy-jazz world. I hope you'll still sing ' The Window Cleaner' and 'I'm Happy When I'm Hiking'."

OCTOBER

A few days ago I was driving my elderly Honda Accord on the freeway when some thoughts, flitting like birds across my sky, jammed together as one and I shuddered with a realization that my life was absurd:

A: I'd just finished playing Pontius Pilate to my friend, Will Ryan's Judas Iscariot, in a Crucifixion radio play for worldwide broadcast (including Bechuanaland). The heroine is a little girl called Britney who finds herself dropped into this lurid episode where, confronted with the idea of crosses and nails, she comments: "Ewww!" None of the actors were practicing Christians; Jesus was played by a practicing Jew; we all made jokes in between takes; outside, in Burbank's harsh streets, security fences and spotlights warned graffiti artists to stay away. Will and I tried to get the Colorado-based producers interested in having us do a future production in which we are dueling uke players.

B: I was coaxing the very ill Accord to please get me home without a seizure because I wanted to catch a PBS documentary on California in World War Two. The paper had praised the authenticity of the film—Zoot Suit riots, internment camps, and Japanese submarines sinking American ships off the West Coast—and I was anxious to see it: four of my songs had been licensed by the producers. Once more, like Zelig, I had inserted myself into history. There had been a musical revision.

And someone somewhere nagged that I was a fraud.

I was reminded of a bit in a noir novel I'm currently reading — Eric Knight's *You Play The Black And The Red Comes Up* — where a Hollywood star tells the hero that the local climate sends everyone mad:

"You see those mountains just like I do. Well, they're not there. We only think they're there. And they're not. It's just a movie set. If you go round the other side of that mountain, you'll see nothing but two-by-fours that hold up the canvas...And you see this restaurant?

Well, it isn't here. It's a process shot. All Hollywood is a process shot. It's a background just projected on to ground glass. And the only reason nobody knows that is because we're all mad."

With all this in mind I started up Lake Avenue towards the mountains and home. The car protested, flaring up into an angry roar, refusing to get into the right gear. At any moment it might give up the ghost. And then I realized the fragility of life, of how much I'd sealed myself off from hardship and the street outside and the weather while cruising in the past with Al Bowlly and Whispering Jack Smith as I creamed past people worlds away holding placards telling of their hunger.

As I stuttered up Lake I saw two burnt out souls waiting for the bus that never arrives, their faces dark brown and their eyes hollow, seeking beyond the expected bus into some distant land of promise.

At last the Honda shuddered to a halt in the sanctuary of our driveway. What would I do without my car? Why, I'd walk, ride the bus, and spend more time reading and writing! I'd get by! I'd be a real honest-to-goodness worker. And then I took comfort in realizing that I am already a worker—once a week at Cantalini's, where I work the tables with accordion, ukulele, and vocals, carefully — skillfully — avoiding the waiters as they career about with loaded plates of pasta and such. Yes, when I'm at the restaurant I'm just one of the workers, part of a team. Earning money by the sweat of my brow.

I felt good as I entered the house, ready for a cocktail.

Last Sunday we had a full house at Cantalini's Salerno Beach Italian Restaurant, to give the full name. The original owner, a full-blooded Italian, was showing his gratitude to America for landing on that beach and liberating his country. I remember this man as a rather intimidating presence. He paid a return visit a few years after Lisa, the present owner, took over and made it better. Waving a cigar and banging the table for more wine, he was seated as King at the end of a long table, beneath the trademark jungle of Chianti bottles and exotic plants and junk that hung perilously from the ceiling. I remember him commanding us to play Italian favorites to which he sang in a beefy Mario Lanza style. His friends applauded as if on cue. Then he addressed a fellow diner at his elbow with a shouted aria and the man responded with an equally loud blast of opera. They continued to shout at each other musically, like fighter planes in high battle. Then I sang a sentimental American ballad and the old owner laughed uproariously, waving me away with his cigar. I remember that the jungle above seemed to have descended during the night's festivities.

The bottles and stuff have since been removed and now there is a clear view to the wooden ceiling. An industrial look. A clean and tidy and law-abiding look. I miss the bottles, but they were becoming dangerous as they lowered themselves. One night a Chianti bottle, unannounced, plunged to the floor, narrowly missing the Elvis Lady. This was a good thing for the lady but not at all good for the restaurant since the subsequent banishment of the bottle jungle meant disqualification from the updated version of a best-selling book on bizarre Los Angeles.

Anyway — back to last Sunday. We had a full house and a noisy one at that. I had to really push those accordion bellows to be heard. I felt sorry for the poor old wheezy Hohner, a veteran of the early 1930s. Leaks may develop. Dave Jones, on bass, says he couldn't hear me even when I bellowed in my loudest voice. Customers must have been having too good a time.

Still the Elvis Lady, a stately CPA with tall bouffant and an Elvis obsesssion, caught my eye with her smile and I launched into our 1950s rock & roll medley: "Blue Suede Shoes," "Shake Rattle And Roll" and then a slowdown for a ballad such as "One Night." While I was belting out the latter I saw Regina walk by outside. She had been dining here with friends, a rare event. Well, we were approaching our first break and I wanted to tell her to fetch Rollo from the Element and then bring him to the door to be admired. Such is the nature of our show that I can break into any number with whatever's on my mind. So I chose the approach to the bridge of "One Night" to rush to a window and rap while informing Regina of my wish. She nodded and I was just in time to sing the line: "I ain't never did no wrong!" a double negative that always goes down a treat.

This trick of interpolating new material into a song is one I've found very effective. I use it to make political statements or op-ed commentaries. For example, a few days ago The Bungalow Boys were playing for a fancy event in Pasadena and the mayor delivered a feel-good speech from our stage. I followed up with "Home In Pasadena" but made sure that during the second verse I delivered an ad hoc speech about how the city should cease permitting seemingly unrestricted development — condos and hotels and the like. The mayor was startled, I could tell by the shake from his shoulders.

Dave can really slap out that boogie shuffle bass so that we don't need drums. (So skilled is he at the slapping that I can forgive his occasional taking and making cell phone calls even as we are playing). Fred is a past master at rockabilly guitar licks. I thrash at the Fluke ukulele. Together we create a unique sound, if you like that sort of thing. The Elvis Lady was satisfied and placed her usual $20 into the bowl that sits on the stool in front of our musician's corner.

Tonight we were graced by the presence of Nick Santa Maria, the musical comedy actor, who had motored in especially from Las Vegas where he has been performing in an endless run of "The Producers." He obliged us with "You're Nobody Till Somebody

Loves You" with all the expected Vegas histrionics and then we did our party piece, "Underneath The Arches" as made famous by the great British team of Flanagan & Allen.

We stand in the aisle between the kitchen and the tables and after the first chorus we process slowly— Nick (as Allen) with his hand on my shoulder in a friendly way— down the aisle towards the restaurant entrance, taking care not to bump into waiters going about their business—as we too are going about ours. Remember, this is work for me, even though I enjoy it, I wallow in it, I couldn't do without it.

On this occasion I took the act further than ever before—leading Nick out the front and into the street. The band followed and soon we were true buskers, singing to the stars and cars and to the occasional startled biker or young person hurrying to a rap show or an older one hurrying to get home in time to catch the first part of Ken Burns' very own War.

Tom Marion had joined us on this night, playing electric mandolin, but he didn't care to join us in the street. I don't know why. Perhaps he was in a regal mood what with his crisp white shirt and bow tie, unusual for him. He'd been polite to Regina earlier, thanking her for her thoughtful gift of an old but serviceable pair or ladies' stiletto high-heeled shoes. They will be a grand addition to his collection. The Elvis Lady has noted Tom ogling a particularly bright pair that she sometimes wears.

Tom usually plays with his Italian trio on alternate Sundays to me. I envy his treasury of tunes from all over the world: some nights, so I'm told, he'll pull out a Mexican revolutionary march and as he plays he'll lead the band into the kitchen where dancing and frolics soon follow due to the power of these marches. People come out of the woodwork to celebrate with jigging and hand clapping and shouts of "caramba!"— only to disappear as fast and mysteriously as they arrived. In this way Tom is a magician. In other ways he's a nuisance—purloining cubes of Parmesan and invariably getting caught in flagrante delicto, resulting in a tongue-lashing from headmistress Lisa.

I have aimed a few songs into the kitchen hatch but have been met only by wan smiles. However, I really believe that the staff, on the whole, accept me as a fellow worker.

I love Cantalini's. I love the rituals. The ritual of arriving by five and going straight into the dinky Harbor Bar for my vodka martini with two olives. The overhead TV displays violent motor sports. The hard faced drinkers on the stools stare at the screen or talk tough, as tough as the women. I love conveying the triangular shaped glass, full to the brim, from the bar to the restaurant without spilling a drop. I love the Caesar salad with the real anchovies followed by the nice piece of salmon with capers. I even love the broccoli. I love the way

Clive or Brian, the managers, reel off smoothly but with enthusiasm the specials of the day. Artists in their way.

All too soon it's 6.30 and time to strap on the Hohner, round up the Boys, and start to play: instrumentals at the start until we see that the diners are ready for vocals. They're really very kind—they clap after almost every number, even as they chew and swallow.

Here are notes on some of songs I enjoy singing from our corner—but I stand when I sing them:

"You Ought To See Sally On Sunday": Harry Woods wrote this in the early 1930s. I like the detail of Sally walking out in her "dainty Sunday clothes— with her hat on one side." And how "you might pass her by on a Monday when her long weary workday is thro'." The melody rollicks along, fox-trotting.

"Maybe — She'll Write Me/Phone Me." A 1922 perky foxtrot by Turk, Snyder, & Ahlert — seasoned pros — this has an extraordinary chorus suggesting that the departed love might be in Hong Kong or else working in a grocery store "laying eggs in windows," or further, she might be in Frisco using Crisco for her face massage. Whichever, the singer doesn't care "as long as she comes back home."

"I Double Dare You," a 1937 swinger by Terry Shand and Jimmy Eaton, has one of those built-in drives that makes it race along merrily. I have chosen to alter a few lines: "I double dare you to take off your blouse/I double dare you to not get aroused." No customer has ever been startled by these new words. Perhaps they weren't paying sharp attention. Perhaps they recognized our music as comfort food.

We usually end the night — at 9.30pm — with "A Thousand Goodnights"or "Happy Trails" but I rather like "When You Come To The End of The Day," a 1929 waltz by Frank Westphal, a bandleader who was also Sophie Tucker's husband for a while.

After that, it's ice cream for Dave and resistance to crème caramel for me. The tips are divided up and then off we go in Dave's pickup truck. I'm ready for his take on world events, how mayhem is just around the corner and how he knows how to prevent it.

NOVEMBER

Breakfast with reading matter is an event I enjoy — as much as the first Martini at Cantalini's or reading a book in the bath. I love to eat tasty food as I read about others' catastrophes or else digest ideas on the current state of civilization. Over Krab salad, lentils, capers and coffee I did read about Kennedy & Swanson but I also, foolishly, read other stuff and it infuriated me: an article in the "Opinion" section on "The dissonance of the 20th Century" echoing "in the works of its classical composers." I should have known this would be glossy tosh as it was written by a glib *New Yorker* writer called Alex Ross. That wretched magazine, to which I subscribe because it's virtually free, (they're begging for subscribers because they're threatened, thank God, by this Internet and us bloggers), I find insufferably smug.

We are told, in that typical authoritarian way of the quality press, that the "horrors of World War One made it practically impossible for most young composers to indulge in lush Romantic textures." And that the resulting reaction, from atonality to minimalism caused a revolution so great that "neither classical nor popular music was quite the same afterward." He cites the Velvet Underground as being receivers of Schoenberg's "angst-ridden utterances."

What has any of this to do with my musical universe? Nothing whatsoever. Just ignorant waffle from yet another officer of the Kulture Kops. Isham Jones, Irving Berlin, even Cole Porter — were delivering utterly romantic and lush music through the 20th century. I'm still doing this too. Our music floats above the vulgar convulsions of everyday "reality." Me and my friends operate in an alternate universe that the mainstream media knows nothing of.

Turning with disgust from this article I was soon oppressed by more tiresome cant about cultural icons we're ordered to revere. I'm sick to death of facing articles on Springsteen, Dylan, and Bono. At least I don't have to listen to the fraudsters. There's a review of a 560-page biography of Gram Parsons, a spoiled rich 60s kid whose only claim to fame is that his body was kidnapped for burning in the desert. And then we're promised, next week, reviews of two more books on the Beatles. Is there no end to this? All that John and Paul did, to merry melodies, was reiterate truisms such as money can't buy you love, followed up, after lashings of dope, with visions of a semolina pilchard climbing up the Eiffel Tower.

I'd rather hear Gus Kahn, in a beautiful and touching late 1920s song, ask me what I do at the end of the day:
Do you ever watch the setting sun?
And dream of things that you might have done?
Do you turn from your work with a smile?
Do you feel that it's all worth the while?

This is what was playing in the Element after breakfast as I drove Rollo The Dog up to the foothills for a walk and a look at the magnificent panorama of Los Angeles below us, a simmering promise of what might be.

I looked forward to stepping into a specially salted bath prepared for me by Regina. There I would open a new biography of the great stand-up comic character Mrs. Shufflewick (as portrayed by Rex

Jameson) — a seemingly prissy auntie in a hat stuck full of grapes and old brush, with a two hundred quid fur round her tiny shoulders paid for by "two hundred fellows with a quid each." The shabby genteel lady had been a star in the dying days of British variety in the 1950s. I had been lucky enough to catch her show in the 1970s in some gay pub. She was sitting sedately in an armchair, scotch at the ready, and telling us how she'd been to see her doctor who asked her whether she'd had a checkup lately. "No — but I did have a couple of Hungarians." In the bath I wanted to learn more about the lady and her other self, Rex. I'd got as far as the childhood at the seaside, living with foster parents...

"Auntie Mabel was a wonderful person. She had a thing about cats. But I was terrified of Uncle George. He used to kick all the cats out of the back door and then she'd let them in round the front. She used to have a lady friend and they would go out together to the pub on Sunday mornings....Auntie used to put a bottle of bleach and a bottle of cider down by the side of the stove. So when she and her friend came back from the pub after closing time they'd have a little drop to keep them going. One day her friend picked up the bleach instead of the cider. She was dead in about ten minutes."

Rex Jameson, I'm happy to report, had no time for serious theatre or literature or anything like that. He liked nothing better than sitting in a darkened Odeon puffing on a Woodbine as he watched one of the "Doctor"or "Carry On" films (although he also yearned for the vanished pre-war sophistication of Adolph Menjou et al), prior to a night's consumption of stouts and Scotches later at the pub. And on till closing time or when he got thrown out....

On the evening of November 7, and every subsequent Wednesday from 10 pm till midnight I shall be spreading the Word — similar in tone to the above but seasoned with our kind of music — via Internet Radio at the studio of LuxuriaMusic.com, located in the quaint neighbourhood of Frogtown. This is a tiny enclave bounded by several freeways and the concreted LA River. The studio is in a wooden 1914 apartment building redolent of film noir settings; next door is a pickle factory and opposite is Dolly Madison's bakery, not far from the Home of The Twinkie.

I like the idea a lot.

I like the idea of the potential of being picked up anywhere in the world, so long as the listener is at their computer. Pretty soon, I'm told, you'll be able to listen to Internet Radio just like ordinary radio. That is: all around the house and in the car. Meanwhile I'll be trying to recapture the mix that was my old show: records, historic background, chat and gossip about my week, guests from everywhere, dogs and Jack Daniels.

When I started in radio back in the early 1980s I had no plan and no ambition. My first radio slot, on KROQ in Pasadena, was offered to me. I wasn't begging. It was an evolution. You see, I'd been a guest on this maverick free-form, alternative rock station due to the pleadings of the talent booker at the nearby Ice House. In those days that venerable nightclub was on its last legs as a music showcase. Stand-up comics were howling in the wings. In the Sixties it had been cutting edge, with acts like Steve Martin. I'd first appeared there shortly after a stint in 1966 at Doug Weston's Troubadour in West Hollywood where I'd trail-blazed as the first rock act to be permitted to perform on a hitherto folk-only stage.

Now, after well over a decade, I was back with my old sidekick pianist "Ragtime" Dick Zimmerman and the booker wanted some publicity so he'd contacted KROQ. A deejay called "The Insane" Daryll Wayne agreed to interview me, as an Oldie from the British Invasion. We got along so well he had me back for subsequent chats and then, when I took one of my trips back home to England, he had me phone in the latest pop news gleaned from the London music papers. Wherever I was on a Saturday at 6pm British time I'd go to a public phone booth and call in the news. I remember calling in one balmy summer evening from the Suffolk seaside village where we'd once lived from 1945 to 1947. Boaters were splashing on the lake, tennis players were crying points to each other on grassy courts, upper class British youth was at its loveliest and I was brimming with anticipation for the dance and barbecue to be held later that evening at the country club. In clashing contrast here I was, stuck in a stuffy ironclad phone booth calling in news of gob-spitting punks and slick New Age popsters. My heart wasn't in it but I liked the radio exposure.

Upon returning to Altadena — I'd only been a short while in the house I still live in — "The Insane" soberly asked whether I'd be interested in taking a regular slot on KROQ. You betcha!

Yes, but on Saturday mornings from 6am to 10am. Yes, yes. So that was how my radio career began. Rising almost at dawn, filling a shopping bag with LPs, taking the dog Beefy with me in the Honda, stopping at the AM/PM for bitter coffee served by friendly Armenians, climbing the steps into the shaky box building on Los Robles, just beyond Colorado, stepping over the vomit-colored shag rug, entering the cramped control room.

Since I can hardly place a tone arm on a turntable without causing scratches, the management had arranged for me to have an "engineer" — a callow youth with a liking for Oingo Boingo. Still he did serve to keep me up on what was current even as I made him spin Al Jolson, Jerry Lee Lewis and Vera Lynn. There'd been a pre-show meeting at a local sandwich bar with the brand new music director, Rick Carroll. A rather weasely and antsy character, he turned out to be the architect of the KROQ format, one that eventually spread over America, making the station the powerhouse it is today, so I'm told.

So I'm told. For I was, as usual, floating in a cloud of my own, ready to grasp any opportunity to sell my spin on life. Carroll hadn't much time for eating. Instead he spread out on the table a large sheet with a circle. This was the "pie" sliced up into segments for each hour. I was to play this record here and that there. The artists' names meant nothing to me. What about my own choices? I would be given a few minutes at the end of each hour. Not enough — but I didn't tell him that. I simply went about my own business when on the air, guessing he'd not be listening.

For a while I was format free. I played old rock & roll and rockabilly and Al Bowlly and so on. A brutish fellow I partly knew (from jungly excursions into R&B clubs in Compton and Gardena and so forth) was invited up to man the phones and deal with listeners who dared to question my taste in music. He'd tell them to fuck off or come up and meet him outside in the parking lot. Meanwhile my dog Beefy was laying turds on the vomit carpet but not so anyone would ever notice. The turds merged with the overall funk that was KROQ.

Eventually Carroll latched in to what I was up to and freedom was curtailed. It started early one shift when he called in to know why the fuck I was playing this French geek. "You mean Jacques Brel?" Stick to the pie, he ordered. "We hired you for your Brit accent, not for your taste." I took his point. The four hours became onerous and I began to wonder why I was on the air. I'd leave the engineer to play Roq of The Eighties crap for most of the hour while I walked the dog round Pasadena. Then I'd return in time to play some more Brel. Sometimes when the phones were quiet I felt like I was simply in a crabby room playing records to myself. What was the point of all this? But gradually I acquired a following and then there were other perks: girls who thought I sounded cute and let's make a blind date. Some turned out winners. I mean — they followed through. I can still feel that pleasant tingle ache even after all these years. How exciting it was to take off after the show on an adventure in the unknown, climbing over the mountains into La Habra for a tryst with, say, Leslie, who'd purred to me on the phone: "Your greenhouse or mine?" She just adored boys called Ian. Yes, she did — and she left me to marry a British Navy short order cook called Ian, moving from beautiful La Habra to a cul-de-sac terrace house in Southampton on the smelly greasy grey south coast of England.

I hardly ever fraternized with the other KROQ jocks. They were too into the music, or into drugs. I tried to keep them out of my life until one morning, around 8 am, when a certain female jock had the effrontery to lay a line of cocaine out in front of me as I sat at the mike delivering a public service announcement about the dangers of overindulging. This was the limit! I blew the wretched stuff off the desk and smacked her with a Bill Haley LP.

It's amazing to me that I lasted four years at KROQ. Towards the end there were several attempts to usurp my chair. I'd find a new jock perched there and I'd bodily remove him. But in the end I came to realize that this wasn't my scene — at least not at this station. And they'd found another Brit, a lower class oik with a Thames estuary twang — Richard Blade he called himself. Said he went to school near Oxford. But not in Oxford, not at a real college. He reminded me of a Butlin's Holiday Camp redcoat. So I resigned. At least, I think I did. What actually happened is buried in my journal of that time and I haven't the energy to wade though those volumes.

Broadcasting had given me a taste for commentary, for recounting my adventures, for stirring it up. The music was simply a breather between the chatter. I've carried on in the same vein at KCRW and KPCC. Let me give you an example of stirring it up:

The night before one of my Saturday morning stints, I'd been dining locally and royally with my friend Joe Wambaugh, the celebrated cop book author. One of the guests was the police chief of Montebello, a city situated somewhere, and — boy! — was he having a good time! The booze was flowing freely and at one point the chief clambered onto the table to demonstrate a goose step while shouting Nazi marching songs. Very amusing indeed, if you like that sort of thing.

Next morning on the air, still woozy from the night before and treating the mike like it was an old and trusted friend, I blabbered about the event, naming names and all that. I guess I thought that nobody was paying any attention at this unholy hour. But I was forgetting my burgeoning gang of fans.

The teenage son of the mayor of Montebello was listening keenly. He was a loyal fan. He loved the story and told his father. Now the father was up for reelection and his rival for office was this very police chief. As my old housemaster used to say to me: there were severe repercussions. Joe Wambaugh hired me a lawyer and together we embarked for this distant city to meet all the concerned parties and set matters straight. At the local Taco Bell I explained to the gathering that the chief had merely been giving an ethno-musicological demonstration of centuries old European folk songs and dances. No more, no less.

Luckily no one had taped the show so my story could not be challenged. The mayor's boy was duly chastised and made a special study of European culture. The chief was so happy with me that he offered a ride-along in Montebello in the police car of my choice at any time of day or night. He strongly recommended night because that's where the action was. I took him up on his offer and had the time of my life with his officers as we chased robbers and non-robbers or else crept up on copulating couples in parked and steamy cars. We'd wait until climax was nigh and then pounce with flashlight and "Boo!" All good material for a writer is the way I looked at it.

After a short interval there came an invitation from a KCRW "programmer" (NPR stations, hoity-toity, don't descend to Deejays or jocks), a fellow Englishman who'd sometimes called me on the air to congratulate my spinning, say, a George Formby. Would I like to do an early afternoon show at the little Santa Monica college station? How much? Nothing. A mere college station! Was it worth it? Could I tape the shows? Santa Monica's a long way from Altadena. No.

Well, I agreed because I can't resist the lure of the mike, a mouthpiece into the wider world, a way to get my propaganda across, to change minds, and soothe harried hearts. Let's face it: power! We shall see whether I can spread my word across the world in this new venture at LuxuriaMusic.com. Stay tuned…

DECEMBER

Two Incidents In The Life Of A Disappointed Man:

Incident #1:

I had stopped at the post office and found, to my delight, that the editors at *The Oldie* magazine had sent me two copies of their Christmas annual because they'd included an article of mine. The one I wrote about Cynthia Plaster Caster and her moulds of engorged rock star dongs and how she'd always wanted to plate and plaster me but somehow I'd eluded her since 1965.

The annual, in the tradition of British annuals, was hardbound in very stiff board and resembled those children's comic annuals I used to get for Christmas in the 1950s and treasure. I mean, *The Beano Book* and *Knockout*, and even the rather straight-laced and educational *Eagle* (featuring Dan Dare, Pilot Of The Future).

So I was thrilled to be in an annual and to know that this analog object would outlast CDs and DVDs, would maybe last forever — if kept at the right temperature down in the bowels of The Huntington Library archives. Clutching it in one hand while the other held Rollo The Dog on the leash, I headed hard up the pavement to the tables outside our local health food café, "Oh Happy Day." I intended to celebrate by gloating over the book while I drank an organic ginger beer.

The café is run by a sweet altruistic man in an Afro-Cuban pillbox cap perched on a kindly face that's always pasty on account,

I believe, of rabid vegetarianism. The man welcomes in the world, particularly members of the Third, Fourth and even Fifth worlds, to his place. And if they haven't got a cent he donates bowls of bean soup, or boiled cabbage, etc. The result is that there are some dubious characters haunting the place, including our local beggar. Now, we used to give loose change to this black beggar but we've stopped since we caught him on a cell phone and then saw him zoom off in a newish sedan. Catching a plane to Vegas, no doubt.

Anyhow. I tethered Rollo to the table and entered "Oh Happy Day" for my refreshment. While inside I heard him barking which is something he does in a friendly way. I looked out and saw his tail wagging. Of course. Taking my time, I paid for the drink and sauntered out to enjoy it while perusing *The Oldie Annual*.

Well, I was met by a tableau. Living statues, really — except for the dog. He can't control the tail wagging, you see. A middle aged black couple was frozen to the pavement, standing stock-still and staring at Rollo, who was wagging and barking with glee. He was also free as a bird, off the leash. I suppose, due to my excitement over the annual, I'd not hitched him up properly.

So I gathered him by the collar and led him back to the table where I hitched him up properly. I nodded politely to the couple and settled down to the ginger beer and the hardback. But life was not going to be allowed to flow peacefully. The tableau sprang to life, like Pygmalion's sculpture of the maiden except that I wasn't in love with this one.

The woman said, "You control that dog — he's dangerous!" "But madam he didn't bite you." "Not yet, he didn't. But he scared me a heap." "He's a lovely dog and he loves the world."

Now the man re-animated. "All you have to do is apologize, that's all." And I was about to apologize when suddenly a woolly head shot up from the depths of a sports car parked opposite me. A Jaguar if I'm not mistaken. No time to consider. "I'm a witness, a witness!" bellowed the head as if experiencing a rapture on the road to full-blown BornAgainLand.

"I witness that dog making to assault these brothers here!" Like Jesus turning the other cheek, I turned back to my annual and my drink. Next thing he'd leapt from the car with the skill of an Olympic athlete and he was approaching me. I saw bulging biceps and tattoos. But, such was his fear of Rollo, that he made a wide berth on his way into the health café. He didn't look like one with a taste for wheat grass and baked yams. As he sloped by, shaking like a leaf on a tree, he fired a parting shot: "Now you listen up and you listen up hard! If yo dog bite then I'll tell you what I do — I stab you not once but two times! Yes, I stab you twice!" This was becoming quite a drama and so I closed *The Oldie*. Wisely I decided to keep my own counsel. Luckily the middle-aged black couple took up the slack:

"Come now," said the man, who I now noticed was wearing a tasteful tweed sports jacket. "Come now," he admonished the militant young black. "We don't need that kind of talk. Easy up, easy up."

The irate black entered the café. The couple moved on. I sat and pondered. Yes, it might be wise if I moved on too. The drama was ended. No-one had been bitten. But in a nugget I had witnessed a sociological situation of these times. Next week I read in the *Los Angeles Times* about a poll showing that middle class blacks feel they have more in common with middle class whites than with their young black high-rapping, high-fiving brethren. They are choosing to disassociate themselves from their underclass, even when its members drive Jaguars.

Incident #2:

We'd had a satisfying dinner at Big Mama's Rib Shack on Lake Avenue, not far from my house. We were: Will, his lady doctor friend Nancy, and me. Regina was visiting her sister in San Diego otherwise this incident would never have happened. Dr. Nancy, god bless her, needed a bottle of something stimulating before we all repaired to my house to watch a Gene Autry movie on the new 50-inch screen.

I pointed out a liquor store down the street and off dashed Nancy at an impressive sprint. Will and I followed in the Element, parking it in the lot. We came out of the store with a decent white wine and proceeded to the car. The lot seemed rather crowded now: blacks were ambling in and out of the store, giving the sort of wide berth to a group near the store wall that the Jaguar blackman had given to me and Rollo in Incident #1.

I took a closer look: a half dozen teenagers were engaged in spray-painting the plain white wall. I couldn't believe my eyes. I was watching articles in the newspaper coming to life. I was actually witnessing a "Tagging Crew" committing graffiti crime. I was flabbergasted and furious. Caught in the act! All the frustration I've accumulated over the years against Third Worlders who smear their taste over walls, freeway signs, parked vans, rocks in the park, burst out of me in one Lear-like howl. Will and Nancy retreated to the Element and hid behind its van-like bulk. Then I approached the gang and said, "What do you think you're doing! Desecration, that's what it is! Stop it at once!" That sort of thing. One of the boys turned round and weighed me up. He laughed and shouted to his friends: "Take a look at this old guy!" They did, and they all laughed too.

I didn't care for their lack of fear, of respect. I resorted to name-calling: filthy Mexican swine, that sort of thing. They continued to laugh. Then one of them — who I noticed was wearing a dark blue blazer and an ascot — came close up and announced: " You're too old to be wearing a cowboy shirt and a cowboy belt buckle. Grow up!" The gang agreed. Now I saw that they were all wearing blue blazers and ascots. College boys? They calmly climbed into a Mercedes. I couldn't stop my stream of abuse. I went up to the car with the abuse at full tilt. As my face closed in on the back window I was hit by a gob of spit. Red spit with lumps in it. The car started to move away, but not before I'd flung my rolled copy of the *L.A Weekly* into the back seat. "Thanks! We haven't picked up this week's edition yet," said one of the boys. And off they went. And there was I, standing stupidly with red stuff on my cowboy shirt. Looked like blood.

But it wasn't blood. It was red licorice. And it didn't fool the big black butch policewoman who responded to our call. She handed me a tissue. Then she leaned casually against her vehicle and lectured me: "You should know better, a grown man like you, than to go after taggers. They may be armed. Let us do our job and you do yours — by going home because it's past your bedtime." Dr Nancy handed the policewoman the license number of the Mercedes. She's clever, is Nancy. The policewoman tucked it away as if it was a used gum wrapper.

We enjoyed the Gene Autry and not another word was said about the incident. The police called just when Gene was singing, "You're The One Rose That's Left In My Heart." They said they'd traced the Mercedes to a house in San Marino. That's a pricey neighbourhood. Would I be available for an identification parade? No I would not be available. I'd had enough of this farce of my own creation. I returned to the better world on the TV screen...................

My new Internet radio show on LuxuriaMusic.com was launched at 10pm on Wednesday, November 7. It was very much the format of the old KPCC show: the opening theme music, "Good Evening" followed by a lively set led by The Ferko String Band's "Hello," then a tribute to Ted Lewis, and a set of saloon songs. What's different is that listeners can join the chat room via their keyboards and chatter to their heart's content. I'm happy to report that most of the chat concerned the show. My *Sunday Times* journalist friend, Bill Kay, filled me in with details about Ted Lewis' real name and hometown; Regina kept the chatterers in line by telling them to pay attention to the music when she found that they were going astray into unrelated topics.

Another gimmick is the mini-TV camera that can be pointed at me if I wish. I did wish and I liked what I saw: the primitive nature of the camera wasn't able to capture the deep lines on my face so that I resembled myself as a young man. A time machine effect. You have to be on guard, though, against nose-picking or facial tics.

Two of the chat room regulars also have these cameras and I was able to see them at work as they typed in. But the question is: What is the point of the video extra? I don't know — except that it can be done. And it shows that we can all be potential video stars — should the world choose to watch. In my case, on this premiere show, only a tint portion chose: there's a chilling numbers board on our studio screen informing us of the exact amount of listeners at any one time. I never reached the 90s on opening night. Chuck, the program director (and also my engineer) told me that the highest number reached by Luxuria at any time is around 5am when office workers in England log in to hear the steady stream of lounge and exotica fed to them from a sort of juke box. What they don't want as they work is someone like me talking away. However, I'm still determined to make the world clamour to my door for a listen — and a look.

It has been a time for old friends: Andy Wickham arrived from London and we took our annual trip to the High Desert to see our mentor from the early 1970s, Dr. Randolph Fischer. Back then the doctor led us into the world of classical music and German history. These days he teaches liberal arts to kid marines at the local base.

Andy drove us in his rented car and I was content to listen to his words of wisdom as he weaved the freeway: global warming is a fraud, Putin is a great leader, Proust must be read in toto and never listened to on CDs as I do, Phil Spector killed the woman but should get off because he's a genius and geniuses are above the law, and I've been getting wrong the story of how we once were introduced to Tennessee Williams by Christopher Isherwood. Yes, it was at Musso & Frank's, and yes, Isherwood was in the middle of a story in which he was the centre of attention — a Berlin story, no doubt — and, yes, he was no longer the evening's star when Mr. Williams suddenly made a stage entrance from the rear of the restaurant, supported by two beach boys. But, Andy said, the great playwright did not announce himself — as I've told it — with the words, "Chris — you old bugger!" No, what he actually said was, "Aha! And what have we here?" meaning that he suspected Andy and I of being pickup tricks.

On the drive back to Pasadena — after a good time with Dr. Fischer during which the history of the Austro-Hungarian Empire had been narrated in detail by the doctor until Andy managed to change the subject to his recent trip to Ethiopia and how there's no McDonald's there — Andy turned to me and said: "Seriously, why don't you have those facial lines removed — you look like W.H. Auden." Now the great poet, in late life, had a face resembling a crossword puzzle grill. I told Andy that I like my lines — they show everybody what I've been through.

I even laughed at that one. I could have retaliated by telling my best friend his face is puffy and saggy, but I didn't because he knows it is.

A few days later it was auld lang syne again when Regina and I went to dinner at the Los Feliz home of my old school friend, James Scott. We were study mates at Bryanston in the late 1950s. James went on to be an Academy Award director and a painter. He has a place in France — 60 acres including a forest or two. While Regina chatted with his wife Yolanda, I intoned names from our schooldays as they popped into my head. For example, "Gestetner." James remembered that the school authorities had unwisely put Gestetner in the same dormitory as Mohammed Talal, the unbalanced younger brother of the Crown Prince of Jordan. Soon the Arab was chasing the Jew down school corridors, firing his pistol at the fleeing boy. I'd forgotten that incident.

Yesterday, on the Sunday that I play at Cantalini's, I went for a noon sitting with Don Bachardy. Don has been drawing and painting me since 1966 when he and Chris came to my show at The Troubadour in West Hollywood. "You have an interesting face," he told me — but he's said that to a lot of people. He paints every day and so has a constant need for models.

I find it therapeutic to sit in the studio chair and gaze out over Santa Monica Bay, letting my thoughts wander onto the meaning of life (e.g.: Be kind to your friends and never let the sun go down on your anger) as Don peers at me and paints his bold strokes.

"I think I'm going to stop now," he said, as he usually says, after 75 minutes. I knew it was 75 because that's the length of the Bach CD that I'd chosen to play in the background. I was very glad to hear the last of it, as the schematic running up and down scales had been driving away my thoughts on life and lost loves, had been driving me crazy.

At one point, as the afternoon shadows lengthened to produce a plein air film noir effect, my long-dead father appeared at the top of the distant mountain ridge to tell me that he needed to have a serious talk with me. So, as I said, Don called a halt at a good moment.

He let me have a look. A decent resemblance. And brutally honest: the crossword grid of facial lines was there. "I'm happy with myself as I am," I told Don. He agreed with this idea. And he also agreed that even though he'd read every word of Proust he saw nothing wrong with enjoying him on a CD, even as read by a hammy thespian. On that note we parted.

The painting will be filed away together with all the other subjects, including Andy Wickham and Regina. Ashes to ashes and dust to dust, but we live on in Don's cabinets. There we lie in state, immortalized, in company with Charles Laughton, Vivien Leigh, Sir Lawrence Olivier, Igor Stravinsky, Fred Astaire, Sir Elton John, and on and on ad nauseam but Christmas is coming.

So ... Happy Christmas!

2008

JANUARY

I hope these Letters aren't like those newsletters we get every Christmas from people we hardly know where they pour out, in that fake handwriting font, facts about their family's aneurysms, angiograms, new grandchildren, lovely vacations full of lovely people and places, and the stent that Rita had inserted into a heart artery recently.

I hope. But I soldier on...............

Notes from December of last year: continuing from where I left off last month — at a painting session.

Sunday, Dec 2: A sitting for artist Don Bachardy in his (lovely) house on a cliff top in Santa Monica. Don has been depicting me, off and on, since late 1966. We were introduced that year at The Troubadour nightclub where I was pioneering myself from teen rock idol into vaudevillian. Doug Weston, the owner, was breaking new ground by inviting a Rocker into his folk club and he'd invited a catholic audience to witness the event. He introduced me to David Hockney, Christopher Isherwood and Don Bachardy. I was startled to be in such cultural company.

The ink drawings Don did, as I sat stony-faced for hours in a sunny dusty room at the Hollywood canyon house I was renting, rendered me up as the ideal English boarding school boy, a Rupert Brookesian face wreathed in curls and sporting provocative, though innocent, rosebud lips. Could this really be me? I mean, I'd always wanted to look like this but... "I only draw what I see," said Don in that high, clipped voice he'd learned from Isherwood.

Since then Don has been drawing only what he sees. And so, over the years, his Dorian Gray (me), like a very slow dissolve in a monster movie transformation scene, has accumulated lines in the face, wattles and sags in the neck and bags under the eyes. These are the stages of character building and people tell you how distinguished you look.

Don has lived alone since Christopher died but inside the house are shelves of duplicate Isherwood books, the framed school photo of a naughty schoolboy longing to escape to sensual happiness in some exciting strange land, and latter day paintings of the famous author as aged lion. No smiles anywhere. There aren't any smiles in Don's works because you have to sit for hours. How do the nude male models, hanging next to Christopher, in Don's studio, keep their equipment from atrophying? As I took my seat near the window I noticed one lad with huge ripe red balls but I said not a word.

I had taken pains to wear conservative attire befitting my age: the dark pinstripe banker's suit I'd bought in Piccadilly during my last English trip, matched with a Trinity College Dublin striped tie. In the old days I'd shown off in muscle shirts, abbreviated shorts, tight jeans and even nothing at all. "Those days, alas, are gone/And the light that erstwhile shone/Was the light of a falling star!" sang the song in my brain while I stared, as instructed, into Don's eyes as he painted mine, and then, much later and after being given permission and while Bach was on the CD player, I gazed out the window and into the canyon and further — into the back roads of an unplanned and unconsidered life.

Tuesday, December 4: Holiday time is jollity time and it's approaching. The papers say that, contrary to popular belief, this is not the season for suicides, according to a new survey. But old friends, younger than me, are dying around me. I got an e-mail from Earl Angevine telling me of his brother Roy's death. He used the word death rather than the "passed away" euphemism. Even worse is the one about how the dead person isn't dead at all but has just popped into another room. Or maybe popped out to get a loaf of bread and a packet of cheroots?

Anyway, Roy's death whisked me back to the summer of 1963 when, on my first trip to America, I'd stopped off in Seattle to see my cousin Anna (now dead, too) and had landed a job in a student-run coffee house at 92 Yesler in Pioneer Square. Earl, piano, and Roy, bass, were the house Dixieland band at the club, keeping folkies and radicals at bay. We had a shared interest in ragtime and an aversion to flaxen-haired girls wailing about being ten thousand miles from home as they strummed guitars bought by their gray flannel suited fathers. Little did we know that the dentist drill whir-'n'-whine of Dylan was just around the corner — the finger getting ready to point and accuse Mr. Jones and his ilk.

Next year I was brought back to the coffee house and the Angevine boys invited me to stay at their parent's waterfront house. They were a decent God-fearing Catholic family with solid maple sideboard topped with a row of black derby ragtime hats and lacy tablecloth on the solid maple dining room table. At meals we'd start with grace and then tuck into an assortment of dishes including wobbling jelly nestling in a bed of lettuce and macaroni cheese and, later, hot apple pie a la mode. There was a solid oak player piano in that room and I used to bang out "Your Baby Has Gone Down The Plug Hole" as Mrs. A. pronounced she'd be hornswoggled. I shared a room with the boys and, knowing that they knew priests and the like, I confessed one night to having destroyed my virginity with a local dark-eyed girl on my birthday. I can't recall Roy and Earl's reaction. I do know I considered converting to their faith or at least consulting a Father but by that time the holidays were over and I needed to fly back to Trinity College and rejoin my history class.

Wednesday, December 19: a Christmas party! The first one.

Joe Wambaugh (the famous ex-cop thriller novelist) and his longtime wife Dee have been trying to arrange a get-together with us since this time last year. But my "busy schedule" prevented it. Busy schedule? What the hell was I doing that was so important? Strumming and pushing and pulling and belting away in a corner at Cantalini's I suppose; gigging as a Janet Klein Parlour Boy. Nothing compared with what Joe's been up to: publishing *Hollywood Station*, a best-seller, and following it up with a sequel; dealing with Hollywood concerning a TV series based on the books. Joe's in the real world of hardheaded show biz and the monetary rewards.

I've known Joe and Dee since 1979 when I was assigned to interview him for a British entertainment organization. I bought a tape recorder especially for the assignment. I was expecting Joe to be a tough customer. But he turned out to be a pussycat — with tiger traits if called for. He was then living on a large San Marino estate (near Pasadena), and preparing the movie of his hit book, *The Onion Field*. We fast became friends. I was invited to his parties where I was called upon to sing "The Laughing Policeman." He had me play a death row convict (no lines) in the film. He thought it would be a laugh. The director had to stop filming in order to show me how to properly push a broom. In the bit where a convict slits his wrists I got splattered with fake blood. Or am I remembering this wrong? Check the movie. Everything's available these days.

The original little reunion had swollen into a quite large Christmas party: a guest list of 60, including the pundit celebrity Ben Stein and a soap opera creator together with his longtime companion. "But you're still the main star," reassured Dee. Of course, I would be singing "The Laughing Policeman" at some stage.

Dee is a demon at designing mansions in the desert. Her latest is a natural affair at the foot of the mountains at the top end of the

Thunderbird Estates in Rancho Mirage, on the ritzier side of Palm Springs. It's cozy but also spacious enough for big parties or receptions. The frowning guard had checked our names at the gate and now we were safe and sound from Muslim, black, Red Indian or Mexican bandit. Wire-fenced off from us, but sometimes glimpsed romantically as they roamed the rocks behind the estate were longhorned sheep, even further might be lions, and hundreds of miles away, right at the end of the mountain range, might well be illegals hiding out till it was safe to sneak down for garden work or even a Jack In A Box job.

We had our own freestanding guesthouse, with TV (Ben Stein was glimpsed as a talking head on CNN, as we entered the suite) and a white bathrobe in the bathroom closet. Rollo The Dog was immediately made welcome for this is a household in which dogs are equal to humans. He joined a pack of six others and there was much friendly bottom-sniffing. Joe, having heard about "Have A Martini!" offered me one from the long bar set up in the pool area. The piano player arrived and without any ado got down to cocktail standards. Guests were arriving even before the advertised hour of 6pm. The desert is an early community. I met many old acquaintances including the erstwhile lead guitarist of "The Applejacks," a group from the English Midlands who made the charts in 1964 with "Tell Me When" but failed to make it as successful British Invaders. The guitarist is now a building contractor and Dee is one of his clients. In fact, he had built this house. We talked of the 60s and his hometown of Solihull. "Brrh!" he shivered. "Glad I'm not over there any more. The moment I landed in America I knew it were place for me."

Another old acquaintance was Howard Lincoln, onetime host at Monahan's Pub in Pasadena back in the early 1980s. Joe had taken me to this cheerful hostelry, with its warrens of little booths with curtains you could close for privacy. Later I had entertained many a first time girl friend in a booth and there had been delightful foreplay following a pint or two. Monahan's is long gone and the site is now an up market space with no carpets so that the racket of customers clatter-bouncing around from naked floor to naked wall means no-one can understand anyone else, which doesn't matter these days since no-one is saying anything of any import. Typically, in full view of customers Mexican cooks toss mountain goat cheese and imported walnuts into salads with unpronounceable foreign names. In the old days the specialty of the house was Irish rarebit — toasted cheese soaked in Guinness.

Howard had been a bit of a lad in those days. Fond of liquid refreshments and other matter. At tonight's party I learned from him that his collar was on backwards due to his having had an epiphany one day in the mid 1980s. He was on Colorado Boulevard minding his own business when he suddenly saw Jesus Christ walking across the street at Lake Avenue. Our Lord was crossing normally — the electric sign had given him permission — and he was in company with the usual lunch crowd.

But Howard knew this was a sign for him, Howard, to forsake his wasteful ways and answer the call. I had questions: Was Jesus carrying a shopping bag? Had he perhaps been buying LPs at Canterbury Records? After all, the store is very near and Canterbury is an apt name. "Let him continue," advised Joe.

Well, Howard decided to go the whole hog as a Christian: he became a Catholic and worked his way through seminary. Now he's a full-blown Father and his ten-minute homilies at his church are a big hit, as big an attraction as the octogenarian showgirls at the Palm Springs Follies. He's like a rock star, said Joe, switching on the killer smile that displays his milk-white full set of immaculate teeth.

Saturday, December 22: Regina's brother, Earl, had arranged for the family to attend "The Glory Of Christmas," a splashy event at the world-famous Crystal Cathedral, lair of the Rev. Robert Schuller, not too far from Disneyland. You can sit in the parking lot and enjoy the service if you wish, but I don't believe the speakers were switched on today so Rollo had to keep his own company in the rear of the Honda Element.

The Cathedral is made of iron and glass and inside it's like a great aerodrome hangar or a rock arena. Above us hung thousands of stage lights and speakers ready to rival the stars and moon and thunder even further above us. The extravaganza was advertised to begin at 4:30pm. But lo! There was silence.

This silence went on for some time until the children started getting restless. Then a Roman soldier, swinging his kilt, strode up the vaudeville-style gangplank running down the middle of the cathedral and, on a rock near Bethlehem, shouted out harshly, that they were "experiencing audio problems" but to "hang in there because God is on our side."

I turned to converse with a pasty-faced old fellow on my right. Had he been here before? Where was he from? He ignored me, buried deep in his glossy program. I pressed on with more questions. No response. Was he deaf or an Anglophobe or was he undergoing a rapture? Finally, I resorted to my program, too. If you can't beat 'em, join 'em.

I read, in a note by the extravaganza's director, how Mary and Joseph had been sent on a voyage of personal discovery outside the parameters of their usual "comfort zone." From here I turned to the music and was fascinated to see songwriter credits ranging from Johnny Carl and Buddy Green to such teams as Wesley/Mendelssohn and Watts/Handel. Musical accompaniment was credited to the London Symphony and the Seattle Symphony. This church has money. But where were the players?

It became clear when at last the power came on. "Thank the Lord," announced a big voice from the cathedral heavens, a voice as deep as God himself might sound. Then the voice — I guess it was Dr. Schuller — began the narration of the Nativity, being careful to be abreast with the latest biblical scholarship, informing us that Jesus was "probably" born in Bethlehem "Possibly on Christmas day."

Soon the action began. Down the aisles came Romans mounted on real horses, and from the side came townspeople leading goats and sheep, and then Wise Men on camels, and finally, in full costume, a man with a pooper scooper. No sooner had we taken in all this local color when angels descended on us from both sides at high speed smiling like Pasadena Rose Parade queens — eight of them, I counted — and one stopping to hover over us so near that I could peer up her robes. No revelation. Later Regina assured me our angel was clad in blue panties.

And all the while great music swelled and poured from the speakers as characters sang, a sort of Christian karaoke. I could have done without the debased black gospel melismatics offered by a white Mary. Such excess: Eight notes where one will do nicely. Let me tell you — you can't beat simple "Silent Night" for pure melody. And the symphony boys did a great job, putting the Lloyd Webber and Ray Charles simulators to shame. "Oh Come All Ye Faithful" rounded off the show and roused me into almost having an epiphany. But then I realized this was just the work of fellow musicians, of mere mortals, and, following this, that God is within us, not out there.

Well, God was there in one sense: I saw a pale unelectric shy moon sitting like a debutante way up above the far side of the Crystal Cathedral. For me that good old moon stole the show.

And yet, and yet....

This extravaganza for the Glory of God turned out to be for me a display of the Wonder of Man: a show of stirring music in a soaring cathedral made by loving, devoted craftsmen. I felt the same ineffable emotion that I was to feel a few minutes before midnight on Jan 31st, 2007, when the merrymaking, funny-hatted diners at Cantalini's, my particular heaven on earth, I sang "Have A Martini" as One Man — without ever having heard it before and with no prompting from me. That's the Great Mystery and we must let it be until All is eventually revealed in Good Time.

After the cathedral show we trooped out and into the quotidian and increasingly clamorous world of now. We dined at Outback, the faux Aussie chain, where the rock and beer flowed. I had a Jack Daniels and a Sierra Nevada and after that I noted how beautiful is Regina's family, how pretty and noble some of us can look. Is this a sign of god? If so, where do ugly people fit in?

People. The holidays have shown me how important people are in my life. They're a better study than literature, painting, sculpture, etc. Maybe those annual letters full of lovely people are telling the truth after all.

People came to our Orphan's Christmas Day Party, the first in several years, the first one since our return to Altadena. Regina invented the Orphan's Party many years ago for those who had no place to go, nothing to celebrate on Christmas Day: they're Jewish, Buddhist, Hindu, Pagan, or have no family to be with.

So these people filled our house and exorcised the horrid sadness that had floated there. The horror was gone, no longer even appearing in Regina's nightmares — the evil woman clambering over the back fence with face aflame — and now here we were welcoming people and telling them to help themselves to food and drink and would they like a tour of the improved and expanding estate? Notice the new driveway, the garage door, the two new cars, the Library with the *Beano Book* and *Eagle Annual* and *Girl* on display. Here's Robert Armstrong, all the way from Northern California, with his slide guitar and musical saw and soon we'll be playing and singing and dancing. There's loads of honey-baked ham and roast turkey and cranberry sauce and pecan pie. There's even *Monsters Inc.* for the children. And there's a week of parties and gatherings to follow. Even as I write I'm thinking about tonight's gig at Cantalini's when I'll be sitting in the usual corner with Dave and Fred and Tom playing for the people, listening to the noisemakers, watching the legs rub against each other and hands clasp under the table as the rich blood of life flows on.

FEBRUARY

As I grow older, far from entering a golden age that the old songs promised, I find myself instead stuck in a junkyard lined with tin where little things spin me into a whirlwind of tizzy fits.

Take yesterday, for instance. Regina has been housebound with a nasty mysterious virus and I have been acting as nurse. She expressed a craving for watermelon juice so off I went in the Element to the gargantuan new Whole Foods emporium in Pasadena in order to satisfy this craving.

"Watermelon NOT plain melon," I said to myself as I opened the grocer van door and leaned in to retrieve some of the many CDs scattered on seats and floor. "Must put the Prousts in a safe place," I was saying as the door slammed into me. It does that all the time; it has a mind of its own. "Jesus Christ!" I said to the door.

On the journey I played back a CD of Wednesday's Internet radio show to find out how many times I'd "ummed" or "errrred" or said "because" or "anyway," or clicked my palate. I was depressed to learn that I'd committed these air crimes several times. Then: "Bong! Bong! Bong!" continuously until I gave in and clunked the seatbelt on.

In the underground parking structure I parked cleanly and shut the door. "Clunk!" The seatbelt again: I'd slammed the door into the seatbelt, getting my revenge for its having slammed into me earlier. Serves you right for hanging out of the cab and not staying put in your proper place! I shoved it back and shut the door — "Klang!" What a tinny vehicle!

No strife at Whole Foods, none at all. Staffed with helpful youngsters eager to lead you to whatever takes your fancy — be it pilchards from the Scottish Isles or capers from the Czech Republic. Antonio guided me swiftly down long corridors of exotic foods — letting me stop en route to sample a soft smelly mountain goat cheese stuffed with walnuts, or else to scoop up a handful of those delicious Chinese glazed crackers — until, presto, we came to a halt at Naked Juices. And there was a plastic container of melon juice. As I said, and as the world says, No Problem.

The problems began in the cinema I decided to drop into on the way home. The Paseo theatres have stadium seating so that there's no-one in the row in front to get in the way. Besides, ladies don't wear big flower hats anymore. But the seats are close stacked like before and just as I'd settled into a fairly empty row I felt a thump behind me. Then another. I could feel creatures breathing down my back and what was worse I could hear the crunch of popcorn and the crackle of wrapping being torn.

The Pacific Theatres disembodied voice now asked us to please refrain from talking during the movie as it spoils the enjoyment of others. *Let There Be Blood* commenced — a long stretch of no talking — refreshingly like a silent film — as the histrionic Daniel Day-Lewis mined for riches. Perhaps frightened by the comparative silence the creatures behind me started their own dialog. Or perhaps they felt more at home talking to the screen, as they would while tele-watching a football game or a hospital drama.

At any rate, I put up with it for a while because I was fearful of overreacting and saying something I might regret — as I have done in the past. Years ago, at the Chinese Theatre in Hollywood, my friend Andy Wickham, seated on my left, told me to make the people on my right stop talking. We were watching *Mean Streets* and were getting pretty engrossed in the incipient violence. I'm always obliging my friend Andy. He issues orders, I carry them out.

So I told the invisible man on my left to stop talking. A pause.

And then he hissed, as he pressed a hard object into my side: "Meester, you say another word and you get stabbed! OK?" I had dared to order a Mexican gangster around. For the rest of the film I sat silent and rigid, the incipient violence beside me far outweighing the mayhem on the screen.

At the Paseo, I tried hard to be quiescent. But on and on went the talking behind me, even as Day-Lewis found mineral wealth and broke his leg and keened in his best Shakespearian manner. Finally I turned round and said: "Please stop talking."

I couldn't help seeing what the couple looked like. Revoltingly fat, one glutinous lump, like a monstrous jellyfish from outer space, connected by a giant tub of popcorn down the sides of which flowed liquid butter.

At my words, astonished eyes peered at me through the folds of their faces. They were stunned into silence. I returned to my viewing.

Now Day-Lewis was rejoicing in discovering black goo at the bottom of a well. More promising than popcorn butter. Maybe we'd be rewarded with a gushing oil derrick to keep the fat couple quiet with awe. But no! The dialog started up again and I had to once more turn around and address them. This time they kept quiet and remained so as indeed oil gushed and characters were placed in jeopardy.

Suddenly — a scuffling noise from the end of my row. I turned. A man had got up and was making his way towards my couple. I heard him say, "Fucking well stop kicking the back of my fucking seat!" Did I detect a Liverpool accent? "I'm only giving you one fucking warning."

Peace reigned for the rest of the film, allowing us to enjoy Day-Lewis' descent into homicidal madness, climaxing with his beating out the brains of a fellow performer in the bowling alley of the Doheny Mansion.

Not entirely satisfied I made my way to the car. You know those underground parking lots. I felt like Stanley in an urban jungle. And there are so many bloody Elements. Finally I located the van and started the adventure of finding an exit. Failing to do so but discovering I was in the vicinity of Gelson's, the upscale market, I parked in their own special lot. I knew that at Gelson's I could get my parking ticket validated again and I reckoned that that would add free time to the Paseo validation I already had. Are you following me?

As I was in Gelson's I thought I might pick up some nutritious greens for the poorly Regina from their salad bar. I immediately noticed a thickset and runty Asian woman stolidly and slowly making her way down the bar filling a plastic container with everything on offer. There was something in her manner that really got my goat. As if there was nobody else in the world but her, as if she was the Queen making an inspection of Gelson's. That stubborn Asian stance.

I had no intention of waiting in line with her, proceeding at her majesty's pace. So I hopped ahead and pondered whether it would be sweet corn and/or garbanzo beans. I could feel her creeping towards me and, if I chose to, I could have made my corn/garbanzo decision faster. But I chose not to. This woman was exuding arrogance and I wouldn't stand for it. I summoned up Kipling and The Road To Mandalay and all those brave Empire builders who'd fought and sweated and hacked in hideous hot climes to bring the sweet reason and nobility of an English Public Schoolboy to the baying teeming masses of the Orient where life was cheap and brutish and short.

She was furious at me for standing my ground, like the brave squares of soldiers at Waterloo. She glared. I stood at attention, container in hand, still considering various vegetable options and possibilities. She glared again and made a big business of moving past me from behind. Now it was her turn to impede my progress down the line. A Mexican standoff ensued. I stared, she stared.

Finally I spoke: "Don't give me that look, madam!" Like the cinema couple she expressed astonishment, not the usual oriental inscrutability. "You are a very rude person," I added and then stalked off with my container only half-filled. Nevertheless, I was feeling satisfied.

Until I found the parking lot exit booth. The ticket collector, a pleasant enough Middle Easterner, politely informed me that I owed $8, the full amount. "But not only did I validate once — at the cinema — but twice — at Gelson's." "Ah, but you see, sir, by doing that you invalidated your ticket." I felt like screaming. "Hold on, sir. I will wipe out the digits and we will commence again. Please to give me $4." I felt like protesting that the fee was only $2 last week but I quickly handed over the cash. In my rear view mirror, at the wheel of a Lexus, was the Asian salad bar woman. At least, I think it was her. But you never can tell.

At the end of the last Letter I was eagerly anticipating New Year's Eve at Cantalini's, the highpoint of my year as chief minstrel in the Elysium of my life. As usual we had the specially augmented corner orchestra: Me, Dave on bass, and two string players — Fred and Tom (between them they play guitar, Dobro, steel, mandolin and banjo). What a joyous sound! And me calling the tunes.

Only trouble is: Fred — Mr. Relaxayvoo — doesn't exactly feel at ease with the mercurial, unpredictable Tom. Put it down to the latter's Sicilian ancestry. He's a secret consumer of Southern Comfort. I've never seen his source but I've suffered from the effects — he gets argumentative, taking offense at the tiniest thing.

He also has a habit of filching chunks of Parmesan cheese from the box sitting on the serving hatch just above him. Tom always seats himself next to the hatch. He's been caught filching several times and has been reprimanded by Lisa, the ample owner. "You're a naughty and disgusting little boy."

Tom and Fred are so different by temperament but stunning when they lock into a song and trade or compete musically. They're like a runaway racing train sparking magic for the delight of the diners. Tonight they were in paper hats and armed with noisemakers, courtesy of Lisa. There were three sittings and we played for five hours with very brief breaks. Just as we were snuggling into our breaks Lisa would come up clapping her hands and chivvying with: "We're losing the energy! Get back to work as soon as possible!"

Because of the frisson from Fred I sat Tom as far away as possible. He ended up bang underneath the serving hatch. In retrospect I should have arranged it differently. Anyway, they were a long way apart. Dave stood between Tom and me. We played like a tight unit for an hour and the diners appreciated our music, clapping after each number even as their nice dinners lay spread in front of them. But then trouble started.

Strapped into my accordion I was leading a German medley comprising "Oh, Mein Papa," "The Faithful Hussar" and "The Happy Wanderer." We were into the last tune and had just got through the part where you sing "Val der ree, val der rah — my knapsack on my back!" when Dave stage-whispered to me: "You gotta move me someplace else — Tom's driving me crazy!" Be more explicit, please. "He's ordering me to go into double time in the val der ree part — I told him it's your gig, you're the boss, but he keeps going on about it — you gotta move me!"

I asked him to please hang on and not explode because this is New Year's Eve and we're supposed to be providing mirth and merriment and general bonhomie. Please. He complied with my request.

At the break I acted as Headmaster and told the bad boy to stop pestering Dave. "But I always double the tempo in the val der ree part!" he protested. Yes, and I noted the silly smile and I smelled the Southern Comfort. At least he wasn't being argumentative. We saw the evening through till 2008 and "Auld Lang Syne" without further trouble.

On Jan 11 we attended the famous movie maven Leonard Maltin's delayed Boxing Day party. This is a gimmick affair where guests bring along Christmas presents they loathe and despise in order to trade off with other guests. Such is the affluence of some of the guests that we sometimes come home a little richer in material objects: some ornate candles, a few tonic wines, and, this year, a complete French maid outfit. Not to name-drop — but Buck Henry helped me fit into the outfit — I was told I looked like Proust's Baron De Charlus in drag — and then I made a sudden appearance in the middle of the show biz throng gathered in the library where I got laughs, even from Stan Freberg.

Mike Stoller of Leiber & Stoller was seen to crack a very tiny smile. He's not a smiler. Too busy thinking about the bottom line, perhaps: of lost royalties, and starting lawsuits against perceived stealers of his songs like "Hound Dog." It was odd to discover him in the library, and then to spend time in the drawing room at the other end of the sprawling ranch house with fellow songwriter Richard Sherman of the Sherman Brothers. You all know what they wrote, of course. Those cheery Disney songs as well as "It's A Small World" and Califragi..expe..ali..etc. Life as a jolly holiday.

Well, there was, typically, chattering about the latest movies and somebody brought up *Sweeney Todd*. A television producer, creator of strings of cop shows in the 1970s, pronounced "Todd" as superb. Dick Sherman thought otherwise. "Sondheim can't write a decent tune," he said. I've never seen the normally affable Dick so spirited.

"The trouble with you," said the TV series veteran, "Is that you see life through rose-colored glasses. All that supercalifragi stuff and midgets parading down Disneyland, proud of their stunted growth."

"Yes, but he can't write melody," continued Dick. "It's all so angular."

"Face it — life is shit and Sondheim tells it like it is."

"Yes, but..."

"Dick! I've known you since you were a kid in short pants. And I know that you've had dark patches — even hell."

"Yes, but..."

"What about that first wife of yours? You should have lobotomized her. Why don't your songs reflect that, eh? Instead of Poppins and Califragi and all that shit?"

Rather than responding to these fighting words with a righteous defensive ardor Dick Sherman slumped in a chair and reflected.

"Yes, you may well be right. Just imagine: a life spent writing about the sunny side of the street and the joys of being sixteen!"

A mighty icon of children all over the world was sinking into the safety of plush cushions! I consoled the great songwriter by leaning down and whispering to him of my love for "You're Sixteen"— the Johnny Burnette original, not the Ringo Starr travesty.

"It was written as a schottische," said Dick softly. "And when you sing it please be true to the lyrics."

Dick, you see, doesn't care for my changing the line to "You're Sixteen, you're ILLEGAL and you're mine" when I do it at parties.

I couldn't take sides on the Sondheim-as-melodist issue since I hadn't seen the film. When I did see it, a few days later, I agreed with both sides. Life appeared to be shit and so did the songs.

On January 20 I returned to Cantalini's for a gig commandeered by the unpredictable but sometimes brilliant Tom Marion. This would be an Italian music night and my job is to sit quietly and follow Tom's leadership on mandolin as he takes us through tarantellas and waltzes and polkas and such. Tempos depend on his mood of the moment.

The first hour was placid and we got applause — which was better than last Sunday when it had been my gig: nobody except the Elvis Lady paid us any attention. All they did was eat and make conversation. I mean, I ask you! The worst offender was a long table of lesbians right in front of us — gabbling away without a break. I couldn't get their attention even when I leaned over the table with Ukie in hand and one eye closed to sing "Shake, Rattle and Roll" with special emphasis on the second verse: "I'm like a one-eyed cat peeping in a SEAFOOD store." No reaction whatsoever. What can a man do?

Well, tonight was fine for a while. Applause, smiles, and tips placed in the little basket on the footstool in front of us. Yes, all was fine until Lisa sent over one of her women to tell Tom he was in the doghouse for filching another lump of Parmesan. Oh no, not again!

As it happens he hadn't been stealing. What he'd done was to reach up for his shot glass of Southern Comfort, which happened to be on the same ledge as the cheese container. So he was innocent except that, from his past record, he appeared to be guilty.

With all the fury of a wronged man he slammed down his mandolin and stormed up to Lisa who was, as usual, enthroned and tackling a whole pizza at the far end of the restaurant. We stayed at our post in the corner, watching for battle signs. We saw raised arms and much gesticulation. Tom returned dark with anger. The rest of the night was hell as he rushed us through overcharged tarantellas as if we were leading a Dark Ages death dance. There was no break between numbers, they just tumbled on regardless; we had a hard job catching up with this demonic figure. We were breathless by the end. Cheese and Southern Comfort had poisoned the air, putting us off any chocolate cake we might fancy.

Finally: my weekly radio show broadcast via the Internet at luxuriamusic.com continues to get smoother. I doubt if it'll ever get slick, will ever sound like real radio. But my irascibility is e-vaporating. I don't lash out so often at any handy group, person or race. However, Bob Dylan got it in the neck as so he should for song stealing.

Last week I read extracts from George Orwell's *The Road To*

Wigan Pier and played Jack Hodges, *The Raspberry King,* with his famous song filled with what sounds like a duck farting. At my invitation my new good and trusted friend Bill Kay, money columnist for the *Sunday Times* sat in with us.

This is what he wrote in his blog: "In a shabby house on the other side of the tracks, a 66-year-old man hunches over a briefcase and mutters haltingly about his past life. He speaks in the cultured accent of a minor public school, of the sort the BBC prized 40 years ago. Stumbling occasionally, he corrects himself without apology or embarrassment, as if trying to fix his memories in his own mind and only incidentally for the benefit of his audience. He has maybe 100 people silently attending his mantra, devotees of an obscure cult which claims no religious or ethnic status."

Maybe so, but what reaches the world is another world, a magical one, that is mine and mine alone. The ether absorbs it and there it floats forever, seeking a fellow spirit who will say, "Welcome home!"

MARCH

The absent-minded Professor is a legendary figure and I passed him by as an uninteresting fiction.

Now I'm becoming such a character, except that I'm not a professor: my degree was second rank in the second class in Modern History at Trinity College Dublin, 1965, and I never bothered to pick up the scroll.

At this point I suppose it's at the humorous stage. A couple of examples: onstage with Janet Klein & Her Parlour Boys, a few weeks ago at The Coffee Gallery in Altadena, I was strapping myself into the accordion and having enormous difficulty. The machine kept banging my head over and over no matter how I tried to lift it. Pain was increasing and the audience growing restive, concerned, puzzled. Then Janet gently inquired: "Why are you trying to lift it over your head? Surely it straps on your shoulders?" She was right and I was so grateful. The show went on.

But if I had succeeded in getting the Hohner over my head where would it have ended up? A question not to be considered.

Then there was the home screening of the Academy Award nominee, *Away from Her*. The opening played and I was pleased to see Julie Christie again after all these years, remembering how we'd met in the darkened bar of The Plough And Sail at the San Ysidro Ranch in Montecito, near Santa Barbara in the summer of 1973 — you see, I remember all these details of the past but keep forgetting how to deal with the simplest matters of today's living — and how she sat there alone in dark glasses and how she'd liked my old songs and invited me to visit her at the Malibu cottage where she was the guest of a prominent member of the Guinness brewing family, some duke or other, and when I took her up on her offer I found her calmly employed in needlework but she did let me give her a brotherly kiss on the cheek.......

In the movie, some runty Canadian actor was driving a car away from the aging but still handsome Christie — earlier, she'd put the cutlery in the fridge and they'd both looked at each other knowingly — and I was getting the feeling that this was going to be a noble and sensitive tragedy of mental deterioration because there was noble music on the soundtrack. But this soaring opera diva — all very well in the kitchen and car scenes— was now interfering with the dialog in the hospital. No sound mix Oscars for this movie! Or was my hearing losing its ability to separate sounds?

As I do with most difficulties or mysteries, I called to Regina. She came in from the kitchen, where she'd been washing up, and assessed the situation.

"You've got the radio on," she deduced. She pressed a button and returned to her work.

KUSC, the local classical station had been playing the Ring Cycle, and thus competing with the movie. This was made possible by the stack of black machines that constitute our home entertainment system. Had it not been for Regina's deduction I would have watched a very different *Away From Her*. Might have been better, actually. Still, it's all very worrying.......

MACHINE GUN IN THE NIGHT

When Wednesday arrives I'm always pleased because that's "Putting The Radio Show Together Day." The main theme for the two hours is predicated by whatever my current research is. For the next few months this theme will have to do with music between the Great Crash and the end of World War Two: *Hard Times* is the title of this year's Oregon Festival Of American Music.

As usual, thank God, I've been hired to take part, and on top of my chores as lecturer to the seniors (The Elder Hostellers as they're called) and ukulele minstrel to the kiddies, I'm to produce and perform in a concert titled "Brother Can You Spare A Dime?" This entails my digging up protest songs and dust bowl ballads, naturally, as well as a little Gene Autry to sugar the pill; possibly I can slip in a George Formby song such as "In A Little Wigan Garden" since that depicts the horrors of slum life in Northern England in the 1930s, around the time when George Orwell went up there to examine how the other half lived and discovered how dreadful and disgusting it was, from his viewpoint as an Old Etonian (He'd had his West End tailor run up a tramp outfit for his slumming trip).

So my day is spent reading up on, say, folk music and left wing politics and then selecting appropriate recordings. Of course when the moment comes to broadcast I usually shy away from descending straight into agit-prop union songs and complaints about capitalism. Instead I start off with a slew of lively music — Billy Cotton with "The Night The Floor Fell In" or "Big Head,"selections from *Me And My Girl*, the "Lambeth Walk" musical.

And, of course, I talk an awful lot because the records arouse detours into odd corners — as happened when I played 1913's "Flower Garden Ball" which led me into a recent article in the London papers about a brouhaha at the BBC over a usually harmless radio show for gardeners during which a flower known as "Black Man's Willy" was discussed and there were, as my old housemaster used to say, "severe repercussions" involving the BBC's Complaint Unit. An abject apology was issued.

However, on Internet radio you can say whatever you like — and so I do. Last week Chuck, who runs the station and engineers for me, put on the CD I'd selected:"At The Vicarage Party," a dirty limerick song requested by our friendly dentist.

Out came a disturbing and infuriating rap number. Now: the CD label read *Comedy Songs* but the pressing plant had mistakenly pressed another company's music. Rap! I had Chuck instantly remove this trash — but then, rashly, I launched into a diatribe about this awful sound and from there I proceeded to make a sweeping condemnation of black culture, seeing as how this was Black History Month — about how they've regressed from the genteel plaints of life on the old plantation to boasts about "hoes" and guns and having it off in alleys or wherever. How far has this culture fallen! And we are supposed to respect the music of this oppressed race?!...

At this point I noticed the crestfallen expression on Chuck's face and I desisted. He said — as "The Naughty Lady Of Shady Lane" played — that it's unfair to lash out at an entire race just because the pressing plant made a mistake.

Until a week or so ago the studio at LuxuriaMusic.com was a shambles. My friend William Kay described it nicely in his blog: "Push open the unlocked door and you walk up a short set of stairs to what must once have been a living room. A sofa reminds you of its former role, but it is now otherwise littered with detritus: broken chairs, piles of cardboard boxes overflowing with records and books, a discarded restaurant sign...Beyond the main room is another smaller one — the studio. Just enough room for a console and a desk with a couple of computer screens, and a few chairs round the side. A torso displays a luxuriamusic T shirt, standing next to a plastic blowup dog."

Well-expressed Bill, but you didn't mention the smells from a too-near lavatory and the clump of shoes from the floor above as a would-be screenwriter paces for inspiration and the ukulele strums of the handsome professional woman who lives across the hallway.

Nor did you write of the helicopter clatter and police sirens that follow the roar of cars passing too close to our world of dance bands and minstrelsy and slide guitars in the moonlight.

Recently, though, the station has been cleaned-up and re-arranged. Now, as you enter the "living room," you might be in a Raymond Chandler noir detective's office. There's a long and venerable desk and on it an art deco lamp and an upright metal file holder neatly stuffed with paperwork. All the detritus has gone. I pulled out a piece of paperwork. It was an ad for an underwear sale. This was a movie set — and all the better for that.

Chuck explained that the makeover was done to impress a potential financial backer who recently visited the station. For his grand tour there was a live and beautiful female stenographer stationed at the desk, appropriately painting her fingernails red as he entered. Looks like he's going to shell out some money. Does that mean I'll be paid?.........

Chuck asked me to hand over my first CD for the show......

At 10pm, in the newly squeaky-clean studio, as the chat room wound down (under the eagle eye of headmistress Regina who makes sure that the keyboard chatterers, both national and international, stay tuned to what musical drift I'm sailing on, and who, from her office back at home, tells me when my hair is awry or when I'm bending my head too low so that the web cam can reveal a thinning spot on my scalp) and my "Goodnight" song was spinning happily — there came a startling report:

"Rat-tat-tat-tat-tat" — something like that only boomier and doomier. Nothing like the "Rooty-toot-toot" in the Frankie & Johnny lyric of the song I'd been playing earlier. Funny how a gory murder in a Gilded Age St Louis slum can be smoothed out through the folk process into a merry and catchy number.

The shots were so steady we knew they'd come from an automatic weapon. And they sounded like the shooter was just outside the window. I stood up. "Don't get near the window," said Chuck calmly but firmly. Of course, I had to go and have a look outside. After all I was wearing my down jacket with the LA County Sheriff (Volunteer) arm badges on. The street was dim, dark, and empty. The industrial buildings housing Wonder Bread, Dolly Madison Cakes and Twinkies stood quiet and intact. The moon wobbled in a puddle.

"You're asking to be shot — wearing that jacket," said Chuck when I returned. We sat and waited. Soon we heard the siren wails and the chopper clatter. "Don't worry," said Chuck. "They only kill each other. But being a looky-loo in that absurd jacket could put you in the line of fire."

Two days later a headline in the *Los Angeles Times* read, "Two Killed In Gang Shootout." Turns out that Luxuria is slap bang in the middle of turf claimed by a venerable Mexican-American gang called "The Avenues." The police actually know where their HQ is — down the road on Drew Street. (Then why don't they go there and round them up?) Linked to the Mexican Mafia prison gang, these thugs have been shooting and killing since at least the 1950s. They kill children and blacks; sometimes they'll warn you by drawing outlines of human bodies on your driveway. Not on our driveway of course. But I must stop wearing that silly jacket.

CONFESSIONS OF A DECEIVER

A certain party is claiming the copyright on "The White Star March" which I wrote under a pseudonym as a bookend for my 1997 CD *Titanic — Music As Heard On The Fateful Voyage*. The party's arrangement, claiming to be from an 1880s vintage number and thus in the public domain, is to be performed by the BBC Concert Orchestra at a concert in London this month.

I could stand it no longer. I decided to come clean and confessed to the BBC. Far from throwing up their hands at this deception they say this makes for a very interesting story and would I like to guest on one of their stations.

I've been deceiving for decades. Here is my confession:

To the best of my knowledge I began using pen names in 1966 when I wrote an old-timey song called "Poor Little Bird." As the songwriters I used the names of two villages in Dorset, England, near Bryanston, the school I had attended in the 1950s.

The song, credited to Sturminster Newton & Melbury Bubb, appeared on my second LP for Tower Records, *Ian Whitcomb's Mod, Mod Music Hall*, together with a waltz I'd written for a college show back in 1964 in my undergraduate days at Trinity College, Dublin: "August, 1914."

For the LP I used the name "Colonel Alexander Weston Jarvis" based on a real soldier, Colonel Weston Jarvis, C.M.G., M.V.O, whose memoirs, *Jottings From An Active Life*, published by Heath Cranton Ltd, London, 1928, had amused me for years. In fact, on my next LP I recited extracts from this book on a lengthy track that caused consternation among the Tower executives who had been looking forward to another "You Turn Me On" smash.

"Poor Little Bird" would have remained my little joke had not a certain Ernie Carson, Dixieland cornetist and bandleader, decided to include his version in a 1980 LP, *At The Hooker's Ball*. There was no credit to me on either disc or sleeve. Instead the notes read: 'Poor Little Bird' is one of those ditties of mysterious origin that Bill Rutan (the banjoist and vocalist) seems to come up with. The sentimental aura of the tune gets quite a working over from Rutan's characteristically saloon style vocal and Carson's sardonic solo comment."

I've never demanded a cent from this steal, happy to be a folk artist lost in the mists of time. Besides, Dixieland discs don't sell enough copies to warrant a lawsuit threat.

By the way, there are a couple of folk songs on the Tower LP that I added fake names to and then claimed new arrangement of a PD song: "The Awful Tale Of Maggie May" says "Arranged by Prof. Siegfried Gildenblatten," while "Your Baby Has Gone Down The Plug-Hole"seems to have been written by two notable socialists, Sidney Webb and H. Hyndman, and one communist, F. Engels. No one has ever commented to me about this.

On my next LP, *Yellow Underground*, I included my ragtime two-step, "Sandcastle — A Day By The Sea" (1967). Here was where I introduced F. Arthur Nouveau, known to his friends as Art. A nice-looking sheet music edition was published by The Maple Leaf Club of Los Angeles. On the back was printed the story of the rag's inspiration:

"My wife and I had journeyed to Scarborough for a sea-side jaunt. Young Albert, our son, built sandcastles and I watched a bank clerk remove his collar and carefully peel a hard-boiled egg, then add a little salt and slowly munch his bread and butter. Suddenly he dropped the egg in the sand and his spectacles steamed up. But I was distracted from this pathetic scene by cries and a lot of pointing to the sky. I looked up and saw a huge black cloud strongly resembling the shape of Germany."

If you want a free copy of this music then say so. We have too many littering up our house.

In 1973 my British publisher, Essex Music, put out a collection of my songs and instrumentals. Most were under pseudonyms but all were heavily copyrighted. New names included Buck Murphy ("Wigwam Wigwalk"), described as a Tin Pan Alley ragtime songwriter who was so long-lived he was able to offer "Blue Danube Rock'n'Roll." In stark contrast was Jack Engels ("That Twentieth Century Rag"), an activist in the union movement, who tried and failed to organize Tin Pan Alley writers. Later he became the darling of the Greenwich Village folk song set for whom he wrote "There's No Place Lusher Than The Steppes Of Old Russia" before beating a retreat, hotly pursued by anti-communists.

I also introduced Oliver De Cologne as the writer of a risqué and fruity song, "I Want To Ask You A Personal Question, Aubrey Dear," also known as, "Can I Borrow Bobby, Tonight?" In *After*

The Ball I'd written that the song had been sent to me by a liberation group, The Jolly Boys Of America, with the suggestion that I record it as a follow-up to "You Turn Me On."

I mail it to my record company and get back a cable from Gene Klopmaster, vice-president who informs me that "songs of a homosexual nature" are "the kiss of death' in this industry, adding that he knows the business because he has "walked with Sinatra."

Incidentally, Oliver De Cologne — also known as O. De Cologne — is still working for Ian Whitcomb Songs. He recently wrote a new kind of drinking song in the waltz-time of the old beer celebrations: "Have A Martini!" has been recorded as a duet by me and Janet Klein and will be on her forthcoming CD, together with a new offering by her French writer Pierre LeFevre, another Ian Whitcomb Songs staff composer, entitled "Au Bal Musette."

One of the Sturminster Newton & Melbury Bubb songs in the Essex folio was "Hip Hooray For Neville Chamberlain." Next thing I know is that it's featured in the opening medley of a hit London musical, *Happy As a Sandbag*, a celebration of "All the Fun Of The Forties," especially during World War Two. There was an LP on Decca Records. I never wised them up since, as I said, we were copyrighted up to the hilt.

And so my trickery went on. I haven't even mentioned the invented passages in my books — the 1897 poem about the boy hanging from the tree ascribed to limp-wristed, incense-burning Piers Brighton, quoted in *Lotusland* and *Rock Odyssey* and now appearing in a new book about Jim Morrison. Or how Vanity Fair darling Nick Tosches, in *Where Dead Voices Gather*, mistakenly thought that my made-up 1917 news quote from "Alcide Yellow Nunez"— about how the blues is natural "like the flow of a stream, the lope of a buzzard, the rock and the roll of well-oiled wheel on steady rails" — was from a real newspaper and that he could swipe it from my book, *The Beckoning Fairground* and pretend he'd researched the original source.

We caught him nicely; the arrogance of his publisher, Little Brown — treating me like a neophyte biting at the heels of such a noted writer as Tosches — didn't frighten my lawyer from accusing them of plagiarism. They paid up and removed the stolen quotes.

Now we reach "The White Star March" and why it came to be.

In 1997, after researching the actual music that might have been played aboard the *Titanic* in 1912, I felt we needed a sparkling and peppy march, played as if we were at the ship's launching, to open the themed disc, as well as a dismal and melancholy slow rag, played as if underwater, to end with. So the two pieces would act as bookends.

(At the Huntington Library I had turned up a lot of graphic material including an instrumental from 1887, "The White Star

Polka-March" by J.T.Gardner. I took a look and found it to be pretty pedestrian. However, the cover was splendid, so we used that.)

I composed the two pastiches — the other I titled "Raggin' The Waves" — at my mother's Eavestaff Mini-Piano right here in our living room, within Regina's earshot. "White Star" was then taken down by David Pinto, in whose Pasadena studio I produced the album, and played into his computer using a sampled electric organ. Next he added a piano; we completed the track with Bobby Bruce's violin.

After the record was released and did well, even getting a Grammy (for packaging) and a nomination (for my notes), Dick Hyman, music advisor for the Oregon Festival Of American Music had a band arrangement made for their 1998 concert celebrating music of the Titanic era. The arranger had, however, tinkered with the tunes and I pointed this out to Dick Hyman who then spent hours re-writing the march so that it sounded close to our recording. I was thrilled to hear a big band play my little march. I tried so hard not to let the cat out of the bag.

In 1999 Dick reprised the "White Star March" at a concert held at the famous 92nd Street YMCA in New York. This time he had Rick Benjamin, leader of The Paragon Ragtime Orchestra, arrange it to be played by his ensemble. Again there were changes to my melody, especially at the end. But this time it was too late for corrections.

In 2001 I was pleased and surprised to find my march as part of a program of "Theatre and Dance Music of the Ragtime Era" on a CD called *More Candy*. The music was played by The Paragon; the arrangement the same as the Y one commissioned by Dick Hyman; but my march was now called "The White Star Line March."

I let the matter lie in peace.

And now we reach February of this year.

Here's an e-mail I received: *"The BBC Concert Orchestra would like to perform an arrangement of the White Star March. Do you have a score of the arrangement you did for your Titanic CD that you would be willing to hire?"*

In my haste and excitement — to be performed by a concert orchestra! — I couldn't find the Oregon arrangement of "White Star" so I left word with the Paragon people asking whether they still had their arrangement. They did. I recommended theirs to the BBC. They liked it — strings and things.

And then I found the Oregon arrangement — full of brass and saxes. Too unwieldy for the concert orchestra. The BBC would rent the Paragon arrangement. Fine.

Assuming this concert would be another tribute to Titanic I kept mum about my deception. But how I wanted to join Beethoven and

Brahms up on their pantheon! As one who has been performed by a concert orchestra! But I kept mum, as I say.

Even so, I was intrigued as to why Rick Benjamin's arrangement differed from my tune at the end of the final strain. I felt my original last four bars were pretty good — very Ian, my kind of music hall, jolly and jaunty.

I e-mailed Mr. Benjamin asking whether he'd used the Hyman version, or the music published (and copyrighted) in my Titanic Songbook, or whether he'd taken it from my CD.

This was his reply:

"My arrangement is based on the original 1880s J.T. Gardner piano solo sheet I dug out of the Library Of Congress in the early 1990s. Around 1993 the Paragon Ragtime Orchestra and I were invited to do a concert of 'Music of the Transatlantic Lines' for the New York Historical Society. . and thus had to arrange it for the occasion. After that concert, it sat in the files until 1999, when I had it engraved, copyrighted, and performed with you and Dick Hyman at the 'Y'."

"I don't have your Mel Bay songbook or your record, so I don't know how similar or different my arrangement is from yours. I suspect it's very different. My arrangement is quite a 'free' one: I didn't cleave exactly to Gardner's original 1887 melodies or form. I changed a few harmonies, revised the bass progressions (some were faulty — that is, retrograde), and invented counterpoint for the woodwinds and cello. So I called the result 'White Star Line'."

I was astounded, shocked and disgusted. Here was an outright blatant lie. The Paragon Ragtime Orchestra's recording is exactly the same as my march. Except for the mucking about at the end.

I must say, the thought did strike me that maybe I had been channeling the long-dead J.T. Gardner when I'd banged out the tune and set the harmonies on my little piano over a decade ago.

I was going to let sleeping dogs lie (these off-the-peg clichés are really useful aren't they?) until I learned from the BBC that the concert has nothing to do with Titanic at all. It will be a program of "wacky music" chosen by the host, Danny Baker, a popular broadcaster and contributor to the *Times*. Then the penny dropped: I remembered: Danny Baker has been playing my march over the years — I knew because I've been receiving nice publishing and writer royalties from BMI via PRS.

And further: the BBC tell me that Danny is a fan of mine, has lots of my records and would I like to come on his show when I'm over in London next month?

That did it. I told the BBC that not only was I the actual composer of "The White Star March" but that I had copyrighted it and that this should be revealed at the performance. They were delighted to hear my revelation/confession. They said it makes for an interesting story and even more reason to go on Mr. Baker's radio show.

But what to do about Mr. Benjamin? Nothing.

I too had been mendacious in my way. And — to use a mess of clichés thereby creating a crazy picture — with my chickens coming home to roost I have been hoisted by my own petard, and so, having made my bed I will now have to lie in it.

The moral is: "Oh, what a tangled web we weave when first we practice to deceive," as the old poet once said.

Or, as my old scoutmaster would say," You're always playing the fool so it serves you bloody well right, Whitcomb!"

* *

Minutes of The Salon, held at Conrad's Family Restaurant & Cocktail Bar, Pasadena, Monday, February 25.

Co-founder Ian Whitcomb arrived with his wife Regina at the stroke of 6pm, grumbling about how the meeting time has gradually grown earlier and earlier, how he and fellow founder Jim Dawson used to meet at 8pm, in liquid preparation for Ian's 10pm radio show at local NPR station KPCC, back in 1994 or so.

Ian complained that nowadays if you don't get to Conrad's by 6pm you'll be stuck at the end of the table and not necessarily with people of your choice (or of their choice, for that matter), adding that anyway it doesn't matter if he doesn't arrive at all since the Salon seems to get along quite nicely without him as has happened on those few occasions when he's been away in England....

Regina told him to stop. In they proceeded, leaving Rollo The Dog inside the Element to bark, sleep, and guard to his heart's content.

As usual Ian was quite wrong: the Whitcombs were the first to arrive. Javier, the matinee idol Mexican waiter who has put up with the Salonists for years with a smile and a habit of disappearing (for a quick visit to his homeland?) after a couple of hours of attending to the gathering's needs (such as setting up separate checks, remembering that Ian has beets with his salad, and adding extra tables and chairs as more members join the group), immediately set in front of Ian a carafe of the restaurant's best Burgundy, much to the chagrin of Regina who, rightly, is concerned with such after effects as snoring.

We must interject here to point out that when we write "best Burgundy" we are being kind. There is only one Burgundy offered at Conrad's and it is surreptitiously poured from a huge Costco-style jug from behind the bar by Carlos, a noisy man who had never been too keen on our party until a few weeks ago when Ian slipped him a pretty tip — since when he's transformed himself into the epitome of the beaming Mine Host. However, last week he wasn't so jolly and thus Ian will have to consider tipping him again, rather as one recharges a battery.

In defense of Carlos we must add that he did us a service one night many years ago when one of our newer members, a rather pretentious academic commuting between Frisco and San Marino, sent back his carafe of Chardonnay with an order to see the wine list and wine waiter. Carlos eventually appeared, arms akimbo, and laughed heartily, like a bandito, at our member's request.

At 6:05 Bill and Lynne arrived, characteristically full of beans, and conversation proper began. Ian put a downer on the evening by telling about a newspaper article he'd just read in *The Daily Telegraph* of London concerning a long-closed children's home on the island of Jersey where police are discovering the bodies of murdered and abused children dating back decades.

At this point Regina called a halt and a new topic was quickly introduced: the Six Degrees of Separation. Since Ian knows nothing about this subject he attended to his salad and anticipated how fresh the "Fresh Trout" would actually be and whether it's a good idea to decorate it with a thick slice of onion, as is his habit.

Next, through the side door, like actors making a first appearance in a play, came Barbara and Bobb. They were carrying glossy brochures courtesy of the Los Angeles Italian Festival at the Chinese Theater in Hollywood. This had been a free film festival, sponsored by the Italian embassy, and so Barbara and Bobb took in as many films as they could stomach.

Meanwhile Edgar, the librarian, had slipped into a seat and was sipping his first beer, quiet as a dormouse. And full of benevolent smiles.

Jim, co-founder and a retired pornographer who has made a name for himself as the author of two books on the history of farting, was not so quiet. When the subject of the Academy Awards show came up he railed against the slick and glib song products of those self-satisfied Beverly Hills songwriters — the tinselly rubbish in Disney's *Enchanted* — and how glad he was that the tiny and cheaply-made movie *Once,* from Dublin, got the award as Best Song. Ian agreed — not that he cared for the lumbering number, but because he was touched by the pathos and modesty of the Czech girl with the long nose and long skirt who played grand piano as she partnered songwriter Glen Hansard.

As more members arrived, including Altadena town councilor Steve and his nurse wife Jeanette, your minutes stenographer had trouble keeping up with the many topics that were buzzing around him. A characteristic LA noise had descended on the evening, even there in folksy Conrad's. Your scribe did manage to hear Andy Schwartz, our legal counsel, excitedly tell of how he'd made a successful bid on a vintage photograph of a grisly car crash and how "terrific" it was. "I'm telling you!" he added. He illustrated his excitement with little claps and yelps.

Rollo put in an appearance, led by Regina, and members were relieved that management wasn't around to order him out. Perhaps they too were making a visit to Mexico. Rollo had time to work the table and take compliments as well as a little nourishment — a bit of bread roll here and some bacon there.

By 9pm proceedings were at their merriest and loudest. Javier had disappeared. Regina now signaled to Ian that it was time to go. Luckily, because he was sitting at a regular place and not on his usual throne-booth, there was no need for him to make an exit from under the table, as is the case when attendance is so great and he is hemmed in at the rear of the main booth. However, Ian wants it put on record that he has in the past enjoyed descending into this netherworld for there he has encountered interesting folk and relics of the past, part of Conrad's rich history and heritage.

The meeting closed around 9.30. Your writer is guessing the actual time because he and Regina left a still well-attended meeting in order to be home in time for *Law & Order*.

APRIL

Here is the report on my recent English trip:

People ask, "How was England?" and I say it was fine except for too many foreign accents. Were they Polish or Russian or both? I say that there was always a ceiling of slate grey, that I spent too much time on public transport but that, like troops in the trenches or certain concentration camp prisoners, I grew fond of my suffering, and now, back in the land of still wide open spaces and worlds within one's car, of isolation in a county containing multi-millions, I miss being constantly in motion in bus or tube or moving staircase, wearing my Philip Marlowe raincoat and fedora, scanning the outrage screams rushing up at me from inky newspapers — tons of them — and listening to the babble of tongues around me as they tell intimate details of their lives into mobile phones — all Greek to me, of course. And I miss the closed circuit TV cameras recording everybody everywhere, and I miss the disembodied female voice in the soothing classless accent announcing that the next stop is Parson's Green and that this train ends at Mornington Crescent, and I miss the interruption of her balm by a live and raspy cockney voice regretting to inform us that many trains on many lines are delayed indefinitely due to points failure, sabotage, bodies on the line, etc.

I don't miss having to carry handy tissues to deal with a constantly dripping nose caused by the weather and such.

Regina and Rollo saw me off at LAX. Travelling steerage class on the ticket bought months ago very cheaply from British Airways. As usual the flight over to London is undersold. Most of the passengers appear to be Poles. Australians are identified by shorts, T-shirts and flip-flops, even though it's been announced that the weather in London is cold and wet, with a big storm approaching.

Aisle seat with an empty one next to me; a polite half-caste girl at the window doing Japanese puzzles. But she keeps getting up to go to the lavatory and on the third time, just when I'm tucked in for the duration, stuck with a tray of dinner remains, cruising on Jack Daniels with beer chaser and nursing a red wine in plastic cup, she upsets my equilibrium. Burgundy splashes down my shirt, seeps into my T-shirt, and settles on my corduroys. "So sorry, darling — can I offer you my sparkling water?"

"Brokeback Mountain," "The Bourne Ultimatum" and "The Assassination of Jesse James" see me through the rest of the flight. You poke your finger at the screen if you're fed up with the movie. Poof! — and millions of dollars of work and vanity is made to vanish. Very satisfying.

Staying at my brother Robin's house near Wimbledon: "The Molehouse," very comfortable in my old room, the one with two beds where his sons used to sleep when they were up from their Devon home, away from their mother. But these days I'm the only visitor since the sons decided to start a new life in Australia. The youngest is doing manual work for an Aborigine.

Have there been any phone calls or e-mails from the BBC? I'm expecting an invite to guest on the Danny Baker Show prior to the show at the Hackney Empire, hosted by Mr. Baker, at which the BBC Concert Orchestra will play my "White Star March." No, says Robin. Then, seeing my face fall. "At least — not yet."

Robin has set out the food and drink he knows I like: taramasalata and Retsina, a Greek wine that some say tastes like diesel oil. Then he sets about preparing the macaroni cheese and bacon dish that our mother always used to greet me with on the first night of my trips home from America.

He's become something of a cook in the years he's lived alone, and as he cooks I watch his favourite show, chef Gordon Ramsey cursing out an LA restaurateur so toughly that the man is reduced to tears. The "fucks" fly from Chef Gordon like bullets from a Spitfire. Speaking plainly is his trademark.

Robin goes up to bed, followed by his faithful dog Coco, at 10pm because he has to rise early for a newish job — supervising the rugger at Colet's, the prep school for St Paul's. A year or so ago he had retired from sports teaching at Dulwich College Prep but such is his talent he's been called back and is happy to be in harness again.

Thursday: in the morning I'm on my own and planning my first trip up to London proper. My first rendezvous is with Chas Sprawson. The journey is one I shall take many times on this two week trip: leave the Molehouse in raincoat and hat under threatening sky and walk to the bus stop at Raines Park station.

Conveniently there are now electric message screens at the sheltered stops with information on how many minutes till the next bus: 8,7,6,5,4,3,2,1 — "Bus Due!" All the passengers have passes; I'm the only one paying cash — two little gold-coloured pound coins for a ride of about a mile or so. If I lived here I'd qualify for a free pass as an oldster, a pass that would let me travel anywhere in London. A day ticket on the Underground will cost me almost 6 pounds. Money is going to disappear fast, I can see. Lucky that I'm able to use pounds sterling from my British account, money that's built up from the royalties from my uncle's song lyrics like "Lady Of Spain" and "Let's All Sing Like The Birdies Sing."

You see, Auntie Irene left her husband's royalties to my mother who, in turn, left it to my brother, my sister and me. Nice that I like these songs and have recorded a couple. He wrote several that George Formby and Gracie Fields used too. Nice that I like their work also.

On the tube I sit among the cell phoners and start to read the library of newspapers I just bought. There are about ten offered daily, all roaring away in their fashion. "The Daily Mail," an intelligent tabloid, disappoints me in the latest report from the children's home in Jersey where skeletons and graves were being discovered a week or so ago and a juicy story was starting to unfold.

Now I read that the skeletons are probably animal bones and the graves are props leftover from a TV cop series shot on the island decades ago. What a swiz!

At Earl's Court, en route to Chas, I line up at a hole-in-the wall cash dispenser. There's always people around these places, always a line, with a machine happily spewing. How well-off must people be over here! Almost before I've fingered my pin number the machine, like an over-hot teenager climaxing, shoots out a wad of notes with a satisfied grunt.

Chas lives a lovely life: he can dump his garbage in a solid public bin, built in the reign of Queen Victoria, that sits right outside his front door on that ever noisome corner in the Earl's Court Road.

Well, it's not exactly his front door because the building houses hordes and Chas knows none of them intimately. Sometimes though, inadvertently, he hears their intimate moments: a couple screwing and screaming and moaning as the bed rhythmically squeaks above or below or beside his one room. Chas enjoys such noise, and the sleuthing out of its source.

One of his treasures is a cassette tape I made in the early 1970s of a couple at work above me in the Studio City apartment building I was temporarily living in. The action of the copulating pair had woken me up so often that I decided to create taped evidence and confront them. But I never did because, quite by accident, I met a voluptuous British Airways stewardess at a party and in the small talk discovered she lived above me and, in spite of a screwy schedule, was fond of entertaining. "Let's face it — I'm a fun person!"

I kept the tape until I could find a decent home for it. Chas loves the rhythms of the pair and likes to imagine what techniques they're employing. It always seemed to me as if they kept coming apart, with one of the partners falling out of the bed and then climbing back in to start the process all over again, hoping to reach a triumphant finale.

To gain entry to his building you have to press a buzzer under a strange double-barrelled name I can never remember. It's the name of the previous occupier, a man who left over a decade ago. Some say he was the gay secretary of John Cleese and that he's since died of a social disease. I do know for certain that Cleese now lives comfortably in Santa Barbara. Chas refuses to remove the nameplate.

I'm in with a click so I know he's at home. In the hallway gloom I try to see whether there's any mail for Chas laid out in the left hand ledge. I'm doing my best for him. In the past I'd send letters and packages containing my new CDs or recordings of my radio show but they'd never reach him — because of this ledge arrangement. Naturally people would steal anything promising especially if it came from America. So now I address my mail to Chas' leading lady who lives up the road in a posher and safer area.

I climb the dark stairs. As I reach his floor a memory returns: of the time I was making this climb and suddenly, from the vicinity of Chas' landing, descended a woman clad and muffled up in layers of clothing, like an ultra-orthodox Muslim. She rushed past me, then changed her mind and rushed back up and past the landing she'd emerged from, heading for some higher region, perhaps beyond the roof. This spectre, Chas later explained, turned out to be one of his string of ladies of a certain age. This one is Polish but has lived here many years, solidly married and with children.

Chas chuckles as I enter his flat. He's supposed to be writing a book for publication next month about the man who swam the Amazon from source to sea. You should be working at it, I say. He chuckles again and tells me he hasn't written a word yet.

When he does he'll be writing as usual in longhand, then taking it to another flat for an elderly woman, wreathed in tobacco smoke, to type out. He's old-fashioned that way. I should also tell you he's had a technician de-activate the seatbelts in his gas-belching Mercedes. He loathees seatbelts and safety devices of any sort. When we first met at Trinity in the 1960s he was the only one in our group who didn't smoke. As the years went by and we all gave up smoking on health grounds so Chas took up the practice. Now he's up to about twenty a day and buys his ciggies in cartons. I see him as the last of the fearless adventurers. I see him on Everest or in Antarctica at the dawn of the last century.

Through wind and rain we push on to "Daquise," the Polish restaurant in South Kensington, for lunch with Thompson, an old TCD man, recently retired from prep school mastering. Even as a young undergraduate Thompson wore a walrus moustache and a spare tire round both neck and waist. Now they look natural for his age, but the deep black three-piece suit seems rather funereal. He's already downing strong Polish beer and getting ready to tuck in to an atypical lunch of two over-fried eggs atop mashed potatoes. He rises with a clatter to greet us in a voice that clearly has refereed many a boisterous soccer game.

We talk of Public Schools and of which were genuine and which copycat. "Marlborough was upstart in aping Eton — the real thing — by calling their headmaster 'The Master'." Several diners, some pretty and slim girls, turn to stare. "Am I too loud?"

While Thompson is in the lavatory, and I'm digging into traditional Polish potato pancakes, Chas explains that because Paul looks so like a caricature of the traditional cane-swishing (and possibly pederastic schoolmaster) he has difficulty keeping his job over the years.

After lunch Chas and I slog on to Knightsbridge where we drop in on a fruity-voiced art dealer called Peter who has aristocratic connections and thus can get his hands on fine old paintings from distressed landed gentry in need of hard cash.

Peter's gallery specializes in Churchilliana and, as well as portraits, there are lots of busts of the great bulldog. Chas doesn't at present have a market for Churchill. But he is interested in the small Turner landscape over there on the floor.

"Two hundred thousand?" he mumbles.

"Much more than that," says Peter. He refuses to disclose

exactly how much. This is the first time I've ever heard an actual figure mentioned in Chas' art dealings and I've followed him avidly over the years. It's most exciting.

We continue on up to the West End where, after a cursory round of the Cranach exhibition at the Royal Academy — too much German Renaissance gore for me, blood streaming from the nose and mouth of Christ and John The Baptist's head on a platter in a sauce of blood and pipes — we take a stroll down the streets where the commercial galleries are and where I can enjoy watching Chas at work, an art that conceals art. I'd much rather be taken behind the scenes than be a mere gawking praise-uttering spectator, a member of the bloody public.

Chas spots a hunting scene in one gallery and quickly enters. His customary dirty raincoat and open neck shirt contrasts with the salesman's dark suit and spotted bow tie.

Chas is greeted warmly. He says he has a client in Jersey who collects such hunting scenes. The couple, though, would like one where the horses are jumping the hedgerow from right to left. "And there's maybe a kill going on in the mid-distance?" adds the salesman. "Sorry — can't oblige you there." He leads us to a tiny oil in a big gold frame "This is a good one — look at the texture — you can almost feel the velvet of the coats." Chas says he'll call back for it on Monday.

The galleries trust him, letting him take the paintings in his car over to the islands via the car ferry. The Channel Islands are a haven for tax evaders. After preliminaries — drinks, or lunch, possibly a few laps in the heated pool — Chas closes the sale: a check is discreetly slipped to him and there you are. Smooth as that.

Except that last time the client commented, "One of these days I'd love you to sell me a painting I actually like." On hearing this our salesman, back at today's gallery, cocks his thumb at Chas, winks at me and says, " Now I call that quite a real compliment!"

I tell the man we've just been to the Cranach exhibition. Is he going? "Not likely! Like taking a busman's holiday. Selling the stuff is quite enough for yours truly. At weekends I want to get away from the smell of oil and varnish."

In the evening we revisit "Daquise" — this time with the most top-drawer of Chas' ladies. I have the potato pancakes again.

I make my weary but happy way back to my brother's house via tube, bus and walk. The evening paper has a story about the craze for teenage binge drinking and there are photos of tight-skirted girls throwing up in the street; a local mullah nick-named "Osama Bin London" has been jailed "indefinitely" for training future terrorists near Finsbury Park station, as well as organizing paintball sessions for young Muslims and for boasting that the 52 deaths caused by the 2005 bombings were "not even breakfast for me."

The BBC is promising 17 hours of non-stop sport on TV this weekend.

No calls, as yet, from the BBC, requesting me to be on The Danny Baker Show.

Friday: I go up again and see Chas. This time we lunch at his club, The Chelsea Arts, teeming with professional bohemians and people of no fixed abode. We sit outside in the garden in a tent erected especially for smokers. It feels like the Delhi Durbar of either 1903 or 1911. I tell Chas that Robin and I may be visiting our old prep school in Seaford this coming Sunday. "Then you have to get me that painting of Balfour." Which painting?

Turns out he remembers that decades ago I took him on a tour of our old school and in one of the dormitories there was an oil of British Prime Minister Lord Balfour. He'd wanted to sneak it off the wall then but I'd protested: I had fond memories of when I slept in that dormitory under the painting; of how TDM, vice headmaster, would make us sit on the edge of his bath and talk to us of this and that and let us find his soap; of how HM, the head, would, as a special treat, drum out a military tattoo beat with his fingers on the wall. No, I won't agree to steal Lord Balfour.

Today, in the tent, and with him treating me to a Cumberland sausage lunch, he's trying again. He has clients in Ireland who collect pictures of Prime Ministers and will pay well. They've only 26 to go till they're complete. Look, he says, you can easily whip it off the wall, nobody will notice, they have no appreciation of art...

I'm inclined to agree: the headmaster that Robin and I met last time we were at Newlands was called Buster and wanted to talk of rap and getting his students into West End shows and movies and such. I tell Chas that if we see the head we'll broach the subject and see if he wants to sell.

After lunch we went up west and took in a few more galleries, saw some salesmen, but no prospects. In a second hand bookshop in Charing Cross Road I had a hard job wrenching Chas away from a book about mass murderer Giles De Rey, an associate of Joan Of Arc, who was eventually caught and then executed by having his innards removed, followed by his nails and then was finished off by a red hot poker stuck up his bottom. The final burning proved to be rather an anti-climax.

Chas doesn't buy the book. I guess he'd gutted it by the time I was able to remove him. Frankly we were killing time till we could report in to a tiny theatre in Jermyn Street where my friend Steve Ross, doyen of the New York cabaret scene, is presenting his latest show. Steve started the revival of the white tie and tails entertainer at the grand piano cooing clever songs from the golden age — Gershwin, Porter, Berlin. Very smooth, sophisticated, civilized.

Strangely, Steve seems to like my breezy vaudeville approach. We've stayed in touch for years. He was very good to my mother, taking tea with her whenever he was in town.

At 6pm we go to the box office to get our tickets to "The Great American Songbook In London." The woman behind the glass is also the owner and a no-nonsense cockney. I had noticed a framed photo, near the box office cage, of Judy Campbell, the actress who introduced "A Nightingale Sang In Berkeley Square" in a London revue of the late 1930s.

I mention this, as an icebreaker, to the tough woman. "You're standing on her carpet," she says, like a drill sergeant. I ask about seats for tonight. Sold out!

Steve Ross suddenly materializes from the gloom below. He looks very different in mufti — no bow tie or white tuxedo. He's in jeans and a parka.

"Who said you could go down there?" says the tough woman. "Thinks he owns the place, he does! Acts like the Queen Of Sheba — but we love him, don't we dears?"

Steve gives us the All-American bear hug. Chas is taken off-guard. "I'm performing one of your numbers tonight, Ian — 'You've Got To Show It To Mother', the one you wrote under another name — but don't be upset that neither name is credited in the programme. They made a mistake and put Noel Coward's name instead — so you're in good company." The bossy lady is shaking her head; he tells her that surely we can sit at the cabaret table, the prop that's right on the stage.

So that's what we do, even though we're both in raincoats and tieless.

The theatre is dinky, only holding about 60 patrons and all of them bundled up against wind and rain. There's much coughing and sneezing, but then that's par for the course in England whatever the time of year.

The boss lady offers us all champagne in a plastic container. Chas and I, on stage at our little prop table and sharing the spotlight with Steve, do our best at pretending to be pre-war sophisticates. Pity we can't smoke.

We have a good view of Steve's neck and silvery hair. I'm glad he's not facing us because Chas might deliver one of his death ray stares — like the one he gave Frank Sinatra at almost point blank range when, like now, we were placed too close: at the apron of the Albert Hall stage. Sinatra was playing Mr. Rat Pack, snapping his fingers and totally in control when he swung round and was hit by Chas' deadly stare. For a second or two the Cool One was unnerved and lost a beat of "Lady is A Tramp."

My song is in a medley devoted to Sir Noel Coward. Afterwards Steve announces that it's not often that he's able to introduce the composer of a song but....and he makes me take a bow. Nobody has the faintest idea who the hell I am. But I'm flattered to be in the show.

Later, in the tube, it strikes me that he generally never ever identifies the writer of this song as me — he's been including it in his show for years — for good reason: it would spoil the atmosphere. After all, he's trying to resurrect an age of sophistication, of smart set stuff by Porter and Coward. If the Whitcomb name is stuck in then the spell is broken. Who wants to hear about some upper class git from the Beatle era?

This is another example of the "White Star March" syndrome I've saddled myself with — my use of pen names to fool people into believing they're hearing gems from the golden age means that I usually can't then get up and reveal I'm the real author. So I was in a roundabout way, grateful to Steve Ross.

Sunday: Still no word from the BBC. The papers are warning of a monster storm approaching slated to last several days. Trees will be uprooted, roofs whipped off, and people will die. Don't go to work, advise the headlines. That's no problem because, according to these same papers, a third of the population are on disability pay and benefits. Not working and getting government money for it can get you around $60,000 a year.

The day is clear and calm. Robin, me and Coco The Dog, travel down to the Sussex coast. Brighton is full of aggressive bikers so we move on to Seaford. Here we take the ritual walk up on the cliffs at Seaford Head, and then down to the row of cottages that play an important role in "Atonement," one of the latest batch of British Heritage pictures.

I try to soak in the beauty of the Cuckmere Valley. The view will have to last for a year or more.

Still no storm. In fact, it's crisp and sunny. We drop in on Newlands. Outside the front door a man in a track suit is washing his car. Similarly dressed but not the same man we encountered on our last trip. That was Buster. This man, Bill, is better spoken and tells us he's the new Head. Buster left under a cloud we learn.

The new Head keeps staring at the Los Angeles County Sheriff's badge on my jacket. I try another icebreaker: I tell him that I came as a New Boy to Newlands in the winter of 1949.

He reels backwards. "That's like medieval times, man!" he says. I tell him about TDM and of sitting on the side of his bath as he talked to us. "Definitely medieval," says the new Head with a frown. "The guy would be in prison in a flash if he was operating today." But I have fond memories of TDM. He introduced me to Sophie Tucker records.

I bring up the Lord Balfour painting and its location in my old dorm. Bill laughs and says that there are no more boarders here and the dorms have been closed down for ages. The painting could be anywhere or nowhere. All a long time ago, like back in the Dark Ages.

I tell him it could be valuable and that I have a possible buyer. He perks up. He's interested. E-mail me, he says. We'll make a search and report. TDM — yes, I heard about that guy! Quite a character.

Back in London I phone Chas and give him the news. But you know I haven't got a computer, he says, nor am I going to get one.

Tuesday: The trumpeted storm hit London yesterday. I saw no uprooted trees or dead people — but that's the British press for you. They get a lot of lawsuits but none from God.

No word from the Danny Baker Show. He said, in print, that he has many of my records.

Anyway, today was a big event: The Annual Oldie Of The Year Awards Luncheon at Simpson's-in-the Strand. Oldie magazine editor Richard Ingrams (he founded "Private Eye," the satirical weekly started in the early 1960s) has kindly invited me. I was pleased to see that the article on my Internet radio show — how Farting Jack e-mailed his response from England during a broadcast — is in the "Ex Pat" column of the April issue. They were distributing it to the VIPS at the luncheon. (Note that it wasn't a common "lunch" but a proper "luncheon").

I arrived early, just before noon, all dressed up in my 1940s vintage American gangster suit, but nobody made any comments. There was already a gaggle of press photographers at the entrance. When I was in the cocktail room I saw why: Sir Peter O'Toole, Sir David Hockney and other Sirs. Seems to me that almost every other person here is a knight. I was introduced to a pixilated and frail Sir Peter as "Ian Whitcomb." He rather condescendingly replied, "Well, hello Ian Whitcomb," adding a look of bewilderment.

I went on to tell him how, on his first night in L.A. in 1963, he was arrested with Lenny Bruce after cops found pot in their car. The arresting officer let him off after the actor pleaded about having a big picture set in Arabia about to be released and that it might make him a star. This officer was none other than Joseph Wambaugh. O'Toole looked blank and turned to greet somebody who might make sense.

Next I met Sir David Hockney who's very deaf these days. After translation of my story, courtesy of his boyfriend, Hockney appeared to remember the time he and Christopher Isherwood and Don Bachady came to see my show at the Troubadour in

Hollywood in 1966. Today he smiled and rewarded me with a metal button stating "End Bossiness Sooner," part of the painter's campaign against the new and draconian anti-smoking laws.

Lunch was announced in stentorian tones by a major domo and this was followed by an even louder stream of expletives from an older man nearby clad in heavy country tweeds. Suffering from dementia or Asberger's Syndrome, no doubt. In true British style he was politely ignored.

I was seated near Diane Cilento, once married to Sean Connery. Next to me was the great comedy scriptwriter Barry Cryer and we exchanged a few jokes. He likes to say to me: "We were there, Whitcomb, weren't we? That's what I tell the young people of today: we were bloody well there!" Opposite me was the rabidly left wing film director Ken Loach and I was terrified. But he turned out to be a delight — gentle, soft spoken and agreeable. We agreed that all the Oscar winning films are tosh.

The menu was printed on thick board. Sensible prep school food: steak and kidney pudding followed by treacle sponge and custard. My friend Jeremy Lewis, ex-TCD and now an editor at "The Oldie," rushed up to ask me the name of the song that mentions "Mornington Crescent." Who wants to know? John Julius Norwich. The name rings a faint bell. Lead me to him.

The 2nd Viscount Norwich listened intently as I sang "The Night I Appeared As Macbeth" with the line — in the context of a theater audience's reaction to our singer — "They made me a present of Mornington Crescent/They threw it a brick at a time."

Norwich was grateful, so was his wife. Emboldened I went on to tell him that I once sat on the bed of an old woman called Lady Diana Manners and sang "Burlington Bertie From Bow" to her because it contains the line, "I've just had a banana with Lady Diana" and she'd never heard it before, even though she'd been young and famous when it was popular in 1913.

"I know the song," said Norwich quietly but firmly. Then I went on to tell him that this woman had danced with Prince Yusupov at a London Ball just before World War One. Yes, she'd danced with the man who was later to assassinate Rasputin—yet, as I sat on her bed, she asked what ever had become of that nice young Russian.

"I knew the prince quite well," said Norwich.

As I made my way back to my table Jeremy informed me that the "old woman," Lady Diana Manners, was the mother of John Julius. I was shattered. Yes, and his father was Duff Cooper, one of Churchill's wartime ministers.

Luckily, I have no stories about Duff Cooper. I think Norwich was the quintessence of restraint. He could have just told me to bugger off.

For the record: among the awards, presented by BBC disc

jockey Sir Terry Wogan, was one for Sir David Hockney ("Gasper Of The Year").

Also for the record: on the Tube going home a black youth got up to offer me his seat, the one with the sign above stating, "Priority Seat — For those who may have difficulty standing." I was flabbergasted. This was a first. Do I look that old? I refused his offer sharply but later felt bad about it.

Thursday: to Manchester, up North, to give two lectures for the University of Salford's Popular Music Dept. I got this gig through a chap I'd never met till today: Dave Sanjek, who used to work in BMI's archives in New York. Knew his late father Russell, a fine gentleman and one of the original staff at BMI when it started in 1940. Very helpful at the time I was researching "After The Ball," my first book, in 1970.

Not worried about what I'm going to say since I've given these ad hoc talks many times to schools back in L.A. In fact, I love talking, especially when no one can interrupt — turn me on and I can't stop flowing. Dave has only recently been appointed professor of pop. Said farewell to America for the time being. Promises me a fee and expenses. I'm to explain to the kids the importance of Tin Pan Alley. The faculty has had difficulty trying to get the kids interested in such an antique era. No problem — that's my fiefdom. I've got a briefcase weighed down with my books, songbooks, CDs, DVDs, and copies of my latest radio shows. Always trying to plant a legacy since I'll never have any children of my own.

Robin drops me at Wimbledon station bang during rush hour. A horrid experience. The train loads at every stop until I'm squashed against vile bodies—unwanted flesh, breasts and the like. If there's an erection we're in trouble; a fart knows no father; I can't open my paper; nobody offers me the senior citizen seat. It's every man for himself. I miss L.A. with its freedom of the car, endless freeways, and music of my choice. A self-contained, sealed-off world.

At Euston station I am helped to a self-service ticket machine by a kindly Muslim. There an equally kindly Pakistani operates the machine for me. I seek advice on restaurants. A black security guard advises me that there's nothing but junk food on the station — Burger King, McDonald's, Starbuck's. I locate "Delice De France," a one-off, where another blackman, wreathed in smiles and about to burst into calypso, prepares me a "croque monsieur." He tells me, with a wink: "Better known as cheese on toast."

A long wait at Euston: the PA announces that the Manchester trains have been cancelled due to "vandalism at the points" near Stoke-on-Trent. Two hours later I'm aboard a sleek streamlined train operated by "Virgin," Sir Richard Branson's company.

In the "Daily Mail" I read that Sir Tim Rice will be organizing the weekend's entertainment at Lord Lloyd-Webber's 60th birthday party on an island near Africa. The 60 guests will be flown there from a private airfield somewhere in England. Among the guests will be Sir Michael Caine. The affair is costing the birthday king 5 million pounds. Throwing birthday parties for themselves has become fashionable among the super-rich, says "The Daily Mail."

I'd heard about this party from Sir Tim Rice himself, an old friend dating back to the 1970s. "Everyone seems to be a knight over here," I'd complained to him in my phone call. "And you'd have been one too if you hadn't exiled yourself in America" was his comeback.

En route I'm determined to absorb and remember the passing countryside, remembering George Orwell, dressed as a workingman as he travelled up North in the 1930s to see for himself the sufferings of the downtrodden. I make notes: fields, cows, a well-stacked woman walking her poodle beside a stodgy canal, plastic bags pinned to bramble bushes. "The Daily Mail" has a campaign going against these plastic bags. The culprit is Tesco, they say. On the outskirts of Burton-on-Trent is a warehouse: "Jones & Shufflebottom — Better Known As 'Shuffs'." Aha! Northern humour even as I see a Starbuck's . But as we pull in to Manchester Piccadilly I see a train spotter, in raincoat and flat hat, and I relax.

Dave Sanjek, long-haired, tall, and studious, is full of information. I don't have to add anything. He loves Manchester already. We race through the city to lunch at "Istanbul"; from the taxi I'm impressed by the solid, stately brick buildings built in Victorian times when Manchester was an economic dynamo and Britain ruled the world. Proud substantial edifices built on the sweat of labor. Statues of Free Traders. The massive Quaker Meeting Hall. Dave attends regularly. He points out the pub where Marx and Engels used to drink while they worked up "Das Kapital" and other schemes to destroy capitalism and bring on the communist millennium.

Salford University is weather-beaten and well-used. Doors have lost their paint. I like that. Not much to say about my lectures. I do my act in an amphitheatre; a faculty member puts on my CDs of ragtime and Alley ballads, I play a bit of Jerry Lee Lewis piano. Afterwards the faculty says I've done a good job making the quaint subject of Tin Pan Alley entertaining to the kids. Many have guitars slung on their backs. They certainly aren't rich and spoiled in the USC manner.

I'd been pleased to find out, at question time, that they have little respect for Bob Dylan or Bruce Springsteen. They're keen on blues and jazz and roots music. Rolling Stones and Beatles are beyond the pale to them. My Tin Pan Alley was prehistory but I'd *made them laugh and that's a start.*

Afterwards Dave takes me to dinner at a 19th century chophouse. He reels off names of those he respects in the West Coast. Most of them have connections with luxuriamusic.com. Amazing. I feel less isolated being stuck out on the western frontier. I ask whether there's a chance I might find a regular gig lecturing on Tin Pan Alley here at Salford. We'll see, says Dave.

We had such a good time at the chophouse I almost missed the last train. This one meandered and for a while I thought we were heading for Scotland. Perish the thought! At midnight I was making my way to the Tube for Wimbledon. "No chance, mate," said a security man. "There's a passenger under the train at Mornington Crescent." I wasn't back safe at The Molehouse till the early hours.

Friday: I'm getting to be a regular commuter and feeling I'm fooling Londoners into believing me to be one of them and not just an expat. Up to the West End again—to buy Regina's presents: rose chocolates and flourless almond cake at Fortnum & Mason – where I managed to avoid being served by the older man in the frock coat with the unbearable deep dent in his forehead; a coffee table book called "Emperors, Kings & Queens – The History Of Connections, Marriages and Feuds Between the Royal Families of Great Britain and Europe" – quite a mouthful and quite a weight. But at a "useful bargain price," said the black suited assistant. So, with the savings, I treated myself to a facsimile map of the British Empire in 1906.

Walking across Leicester Square on my way to the Tube I reckoned that not a word of English was heard. However the foreigners appeared pleasant if brisk. Everyone is terribly busy, judging by the intensity of the cell phone concentration.

Saturday: entrained at Waterloo for my sister Suzanne's cottage deep in the Royal Berkshire countryside, where she lives with her husband The General. A relief.

Getting there was a problem because I had trouble operating the mobile phone lent to me by Robin. I was supposed to call to report departure from Waterloo – only I couldn't work the machine. The more buttons I pressed the more options flashed on the screen, including "Erase." Soon all my precious contact numbers, entered by my thoughtful brother, were vanishing as in a magic trick. I panicked. The destruction stopped as if in response to the panic. One number remained intact like a beacon: Robin's. I got through and he said he'd call Suzanne and tell her I was on my way. The businessman next to me seemed displeased but said not a word. When he alighted at Woking he cast me a black glower.

Only when I stood up to get out at Basingstoke did I realize how

I had caused his displeasure. Above was a sign stating that this compartment is "The Quiet Zone" and that under no circumstances should mobile phones be used. I wish I could have told the businessman that I agreed with him, that I'm on his side in the fight against incivility in the misuse of modern technology.

At the cottage I was safe for the remaining days of my trip. Sealed off from the racket and rush of today. My sister whipped up meal after scrumptious meal from the simplest ingredients — sausage with cauliflower cheese, nothing American — and we ate from trays on our knees as we sat in the conservatory watching the rains come in and "The Seventh Veil" and "Brief Encounter" plus a stream of cooking shows, including one in which the chefs of Britain compete at coming up with new ways to serve old favourites — pig's trotters, jugged hare, steak and kidney pudding — so you'd never recognize them, you'd think you were eating nouvelle.

Chas came down to the cottage one day with his best lady and I watched as the foursome played Bridge. In between rubbers I entertained at the piano. After tea and champagne Chas and his lady left and we three sat down to a toad-in-hole supper. The BBC news reported that Sir Paul McCartney will get off lightly in his divorce proceedings — a mere 25 million pounds for Lady Mucca.

Sir Macca's female lawyer was seen arriving in court immaculately coiffured like Margaret Thatcher but leaving looking like Hilary Clinton. A furious Lady Mucca had soaked her with a well-aimed carafe of water.

Every paper was full of the story when I left next day. I was able to see every paper because, for some reason, the British Airways woman who took my ticket at the gate up-graded me to business class. I had a seat that reclined into a bed, champagne prior to departure, smoked salmon for lunch and no one near. I got so settled into luxury that when some paupers from steerage dared to invade our section for a view of the rich I summoned an attendant and had them removed. A velvet rope was duly erected.

Regina met me at LAX with Rollo in tow. At Cantalini's she brought me down gently, decompressing me back to our reality.

The BBC never summoned me to be Danny Baker's radio guest. But thanks to the Internet I have managed to hear a re-run of the broadcast of the concert he hosted at the Hackney Empire during which the BBC Concert Orchestra performed my march. Mr. Baker announced it, describing me as a "genius" and going on to say that the tune about to be played is a "core theme" of his shows. He was just saying that I'd composed the march when he corrected himself. No, I'd "collected" it or something. And the orchestra played "The White Star LINE March." My tune — but with a new title given to it by Mr. Rick Benjamin. So he has won after all and I must sink back into the depths of anonymity, the mysterious begetter of folk music.

Strange for someone who is so garrulous.

MAY

The last Letter was so long in the making (and long in the reading, too). In April nothing happened to compare with the London adventures. And I can't foresee what May will bring me.

So I'm going to stream through a day in my life — Tuesday, April 22, which is today — and see what I come up with, trying to be as truthful as possible but also trying to be funny or at least amusing. Trying not to be a blogosphere bore................

Of course, being constantly borne back into the past, having been hurled off the boat that carries those shiny, smiley positive thinkers into the current leading to the sunrise of a bright affirmative future, I have to begin with last night at Conrad's.

Lynne gave me a clipping, a review of Simon Gray's latest volume of diaries. Gray is a 70-year-old English playwright and a curmudgeon; I suppose that Lynne considers me to be like Gray in manner and, in a B-picture way, I suppose I am. He keeps looking back across the years at the mistakes he's made; the memory of a party is better than the actual party itself; writing down a worry is a "completely unworrying experience... Yes, I had fun writing down my worry."

I couldn't agree more.

Here's an unpleasant in-flight experience that, by being recorded in all its horrid detail, has been exorcised and made golden, like a bloody battle in a gilded frame.

Gray is sitting next to a woman with a bad cold: "She is now blowing her nose on little shreds of Kleenex about twice a minute, long, thick, wet blows, then she screws up the Kleenex and places it in a paper cup, already bulging, in the back of the seat in front of her. There is an already full paper cup beside the one she has now nearly filled. She is frankly a very disgusting person to find yourself sitting next to on a flight."

I suspect that when he gets home he'll smoke his cares away, coughing and gasping so much "anyone who wanted to murder me would simply have to say three funny things in a row."

I had to read this clipping back home, just before nodding off, because I couldn't miss any of the Salon activity. From the corner booth I surveyed our assembled tables stretching off into the middle of the cocktail bar. Everyone was engaged in chat and there was no way to tune into all of it, although a few hours later I made a royal progress down the line, lightly squeezing the shoulders of Salonists, cupping my ear to catch a gem, a bon mot.

Up at our end, in the booth, Lynne, from Yorkshire, had been complaining about the lack of liquid disinfectants in America and later telling of the "huge left wing bits" inside her. This was in response to my having just said that Woody Guthrie described himself as apolitical — "Left wing, right wing, chicken wing — I just wanna sing songs anywhere, anyplace." I'd brought Woody up, you see, because I'm researching him for my lecture at the upcoming Oregon Festival Of Music. You can bring any subject up at our meetings, but you may be ignored or spoken over, like hobnail boots on fresh grass. Will had made a list of diminutives for "Elizabeth": Bette, Eliza, Lizzy, Lisa, Liza, Betty, and — don't forget, said Lynne — Lillibet, which was The Queen's nickname as a child..............

Yes, it's not profound stuff but at least they kept off Bush and Obama.

When they're all talking at once I have to conduct them with a pointed finger and a hush sign..........

Glenn is taking Lynne and Bill to the theatre organ concert at the Nethercutt Museum this Saturday night. I told them they'd have a good time — though not necessarily because of the quality of music — if Gordon, the swishy MC, has invited one of his fruity friends to perform. When Regina and I were last there, courtesy of Glenn, we watched the swaying back of an imported Australian organist called Reg as he pumped away at the grand machine. As per the dress code he was wearing a dinner jacket — to start with. But as soon as he'd finished the selection of show tunes, climaxing with "I Feel Pretty," he spun around and stripped off the formal black to reveal a skintight blue muscle shirt moving to six-pack abs. Then he stuck out his tongue as an affectionate greeting to a young African-American sitting in the front row. The young man, similarly attired, got up and raised his hands like a boxer celebrating a knockout.

"Reg won't be performing Saturday," said Glenn quietly but firmly. And that was that. I ordered a bread pudding. And another Burgundy.

And now to this morning.

6.35 am: What were my dreams last night? Regina is saying something to me in her own dream and it's lyrical and light, a far cry from the nightmares she used to have when the woman next door shouted maledictions over the fence. I offer a suitable reply. Beside the bed sits the Dream Book I've kept since March, 1972. The last entry was two years ago, back when we were in exile in Monrovia:

"I accompany Irving Berlin as he sings a fast version of 'God Bless America'. I play a wrong chord & he gives me a black look. Afterwards I rush to keep up with him as he races down an endless corridor. When I reach him I offer, as we race, a profuse apology, telling him how much I love his songs and how sorry I am about that wrong chord. He says, 'I don't know the right ones myself! But you, of all people, should!'

Get up.

Rollo has to have his pills, as do I. On his walk I always let him decide which way we're going and on which bush or garbage can he's going to lift his leg. Sometimes passers-by offer comments like "What kind of dog is that?" and then they proceed to tell us exactly what he is; or else it's, "Are you walking him or is he walking you? Ha, Ha!"and "Where's the saddle?" "Do he bite?" I really hate. The only comment I like is, "He's beautiful." Pity he can't appreciate the "beautiful." Well, maybe not: it did me no good, except for a thrilling tingle, when I got that tossed at me back in the late 1960s/early 70s.

A smart car pulls up at the curb of a neighbour's house. A black man in a high bobble hat gets out and starts rummaging through the cans for recyclable bottles for cashing in. This is illegal but he doesn't care; he has a certain swagger as he works the street. Rollo barks at him. He glares. An elderly black man with a walking stick approaches. He has Uncle Remus white hair. "Yo, bro!" he greets the looter with. I mind my own business, as is proper. Illegal it may be to loot garbage cans but then, the other day, we put out an old rocking chair for the taking and it disappeared in a trice. I visualize the old man in that chair as he rocks contentedly in a steady rhythm while the bobble hatter struts and strums a banjo. The scene makes for serenity, clearing away the clouds. Time to drive to Cal Tech for my swim.

The Honda Element is a tin box on wheels, practical for instruments and dog. They say you can wash it out by simply pointing a hose inside and going full flush. I don't think I'll try that — too much of my office is in there, like CDs I'm researching with, and books, and my Huntington (Reader In Rare Books) ID, and the drawing block with no drawings in it as yet. One of these days I'll do some plein air sketching. One of these days.

So much to do as the seconds rush by to become years. Life was slower in the early 1950s when we sat in the prep school classroom counting the drops as they slid down the pane. We sang, "Nothing to do! Nothing to make, nothing to take!" Now I'm in a rush to get to the pool in order to complete my laps before closing time at 9 am. Don't want to listen to any more radio bleating about the doomed Middle East so I turn on the CD that Glenn gave me last night, his latest radio show, the one that's heard in Catalina and certain parts of New Zealand.

A "tribute" to Bessie Smith has her praising her man's "thing" and how he uses it, Eagle-Rocking her with one steady roll, turning her over for some Balling the Jack. Afterwards Glenn, in steady measured tones tells us that Bessie Smith wrote, "I'm Wild About That Thing" in collaboration with H.Weberman. "I couldn't find out what the 'H' stood for." Unusual because Glenn always gives us a wealth of facts. Like, for instance, that the "Thing" song was recorded on April 7, 1927 for the Columbia label. He knows the matrix number too.

Nice to spend time in this sealed world of shellac and dates and numbers, where no harm can come to you, except for a crack or a breakage; where Smith's fatal car crash and Pine Top's death (caught in barroom crossfire as he ordered the girl with the red dress to get up and boogie to his piano playing) is reduced to the cleanliness of encased history.

Back on the radio, pundits are wondering whether the old war hero will trounce the semi-black and the female and end up as Chief. So I try another CD, one I found as a freebee in the *Independent* when I was last in London. Newspapers are doing this in a desperate attempt to keep readers. Every day classic movies are offered on DVD; on CD we got classic 20th Century poets. It just fell out of the pages, great works landing with hardly a noise.

An excruciating Thames Estuary-accented bluestocking female academic introduces the likes of T.S. Eliot and Siegfried Sassoon reading their most famous poems. She apologizes for their "rather quaint way of speaking," meaning they have educated accents and pronounce clearly and beautifully while she is nastily nasal and toneless. Philip Larkin she approves of since he's from the North and isn't posh and spent his life buried in a library in god-forsaken Hull.

Now in the Element, as I progress slowly in rush hour traffic down Lake Avenue towards the Cal Tech pool, following Bessie Smith and her thinly-veiled phallic appreciation, amid mad Mexicans interlacing on bicycles and hard-faced black business women steering even as they address the phone in their ear, Larkin recites "The Whitsun Weddings."

He speaks in such a conversational manner that he sounds not a bit like my idea of a great poet but more as if he's telling me over coffee or a beer about a railway journey to London. Sounds like this: "That Whitsun I was late getting away — not till about one-twenty on the sunlit Saturday did my three-quarters-empty train pull out, all windows down, all cushions hot, all sense of being in a hurry gone..." Yes, yes, and how about another pint, now? Don't worry; I'll get it — just hold the thought...

Sailing along fine but now he gets poetic. I mean — I don't understand: the flow of the story has become stuck in a brackish pond: wedding girls on the cool platform, hitherto amusingly "grinning and pomaded" in "parodies of fashion" are now "posed irresolutely, watching us go, as if out on the end of an event waving goodbye to something that survived it." *Out on the end of an event?* But I let the words wash me on, as teachers have told me to do with poetry, and soon I'm back in the hot train passing poplars casting long shadows and an Odeon and someone running up to bowl, as we hurry towards London, "shuffling gouts of steam."

Nice, oh very nice — and I'm whisked deliciously back to the early 1960s and a hot summer day of my own with wincing sweet memories of loves that never came to be. And as we arrive, and I'm deep in a dream even here in the horrid blatant present, Larkin casts darkness once again: he talks of this "frail traveling coincidence" (what coincidence?).

"And as the tightened brakes took hold, there swelled a sense of falling, like an arrow-shower sent out of sight, somewhere becoming rain." Yes, it's seductive over the speakers in the morning rush hour, and it waves away today but I don't quite understand. Still, I take comfort in something old H.D. Thoreau said, "Every man will be a poet if he can." Well, I tried once. I tried to deceive Alan Ross, the poet-editor of *London Magazine* into accepting a song lyric of mine as a real poem. You don't fool me, he laughed. He was a friend and had published my prose articles. But he was guarding the secret of poetry closely and he wouldn't explain.

Is it about how you lay out the lines? In the above poem I haven't laid them out as Larkin did. He broke up his seeming conversation so that on the page his voice looks like a poem. But in the car he sounded very chummy indeed and might offer me a Silk Cut or a pink gin.

This is the song I tried to foist off on the editor: I've tried to make it look poetic:

> *It's ball time for you but it's wall time for me*
> *Why do I get in a sweat?*
> *Under this fat there's a soft furry cat*
> *Craving for you to set free.....*

> *The waltz that you promised to dance with me—*
> *I've been waiting all evening in vain.*
> *You've danced with my friends even strangers too*
> *While I watched through the cold window pane.*
> *You know I would treat you so tenderly*
> *We would fly round the room then we'd soar.*
> *But you seem to surmise a rather odd look in my eyes*

And I'm back on the sidelines once more.

The Cal Tech men's locker room, in grey and off-white, is hangar-like and empty. Paint is peeling and flutters down like confetti at a Hilary gathering. Time has passed it by and I like that. In period lettering on one wall are past Track & Field records by long-dead athletes — A.E. Housman would love to peruse and imagine; a warning notice that was already up, in equally dated lettering, in the mid 1980s when I first got into the Cal Tech pool, is still there on the other wall: "Lockers Are Being Broken Into By A Thief." Well over twenty years later and the thief is still at it.

Back then Chas Sprawson had wangled us passes into the pool by posing as a visiting mathematics professor with me as his assistant. Neither of us can add up very well, let alone subtract. Later I discovered that Huntington Library Readers are eligible, so there'd been no need to go through the deception in the Cal Tech office that had had me trembling like I used to at prep school when, say, I'd been accused of "deliberately and malignantly" turning on taps in the changing room and leaving the scene. "One of the worst examples of sabotage I've seen in a long career," said the headmaster prior to his caning me on the thigh.

I shave at a chipped basin in the washroom area. The carefully-written want ad on the partition separating basins from urinal stalls is still there, I'm glad to see: "Call (818) 555-2230 — muscular men only!" The usual trousers-down-at-the-ankles person is occupying the end cubicle. Never a sound from him, no fart, no heaving, no ecstasy, no nothing. And he's still there when I leave. Day after day this is the situation and it never gets resolved.

There's nothing to write about the lap swimming. Because such swimming is boring. But the sky is bright and blue and the mountains sit the same as ever. "They're very old, those mountains," said my real estate man when I bought the house hard by the San Gabriels in 1979. "Very old indeed — and that's why they crumble and move every now and then." I like to look at sky and mountains while I'm doing the beastly boring laps. Today I have a little bother getting a lane. Common courtesy suggests that a swimmer should welcome a lane-sharer. For several laps I try to get the man's attention but he is heads-down oblivious, a very serious swimmer. Finally I get into the lane and he's forced to acknowledge my presence. He stares at me incomprehensibly from behind his goggles. He is Asian. "Do you mind if we split the lane?" I say. "You go leave pool at once!" What? An elderly man in the next lane intercedes. "He is new to this country — just proceed in the normal way" And I do and there is no trouble.

At last the task is over and I can get ready for breakfast, lovely breakfast — to the accompaniment of drastic newspaper stories.

Nothing like enjoying an omelette as you read about disasters in foreign lands.

Meanwhile: "Turn Water Off To Conserve Water When Using Soap" is another sign I puzzle over in the shower room. Have done for years. And also: "Please Dry Off In Drying Room," Today I find this Drying Room. The sign is in Art Deco.

I push open the door. Inside is nothing but old dynamos and giant magnets and test tubes attached to rubber hoses, like Dr Frankenstein's lab. I thought that Cal Techies were into space exploration and finding a substitute for gasoline. Get on with it!

Back under the shower I'm forced to listen to guttural utterances from the other shower room. A brute, a Turk built like a brick shithouse, is there every morning at this time, hawking up phlegm, a fearful racket. Is it to annoy me or is it due to a condition inherited by the Turk from his land of origin? I steal his towel.

On the way out I pass the guard desk. Carlos is sitting cross-legged, chair pushed back against the wall, like Henry Fonda in *My Darling Clementine*, only he's not Fonda. I know what he's going to say — and he says it: "Warming up out there, eh? We're so lucky!" In the dog days of August he has, "Hot enough for you?" I like him for his predictability, I like him because I feel safe knowing that seasons will change and so will Presidents but Carlos will stick to the script.

Carlos! Another Carlos commandeers the bar at Conrad's, site of the Salon. This Carlos is subversive, not a supporter of our group. And I've tipped him nice bills to win him but lately he's reverted to his old ways. Maybe the money ran out, like in a parking meter. Anyway, last night we arrived to find our corner booth, the HQ from where I reign, occupied by a couple, deep in fried food. No way could waiters start to build our table line from the booth to the end of the room. Members had to make do with separate tables for two, as if in secluded island outposts. Carlos, it turned out, had given the HQ away to a mere couple before our own waiter, Javier, was aware of the mischief. We fumed on our islands until the fried food couple, taking their time as they shared jokes with Carlos, vacated.

Breakfast. Today is an egg day and I will have it at the Coffee Gallery, our local social centre for Altadenans. Food and drink are only a part of the scene here: paintings for sale hang over us, toys and books are on the shelves, the laptop mobile office workers are already heads down and looking in. As I move in to order my usual omelette (the way Chef Jeff likes to make it) I see and hear a scruffy man in loser's clothes telling the world via his cell phone that he is buzzing with business: "I got productions ready to go, go, go-go! You name 'em, I got 'em. And you know what? If you green light the movie I'll make you head of production with your very own office!"

I take a spot near the Round Table by the door. Like my Salon this has a Chief and he is Steve, a town councilor. Every morning he presides for hours, sketching housing developments or else reading the paper, cocking an ear and every so often joining the heavy table talk. We all know there are problems in our world today but here, at this round table, all are solved daily. If only the Establishment would venture here and listen in. But you'd never guess from their clothing and cars that these are mighty minds. And mighty angry as well.

However, Fly, the South Seas islands barista up at the counter, doesn't appreciate the brainstormers. He mutters, "Just my luck the stereo's bust when I need it most for burying the bullshit!"

Meanwhile, a black woman in dreadlocks and a dark pinstriped business suit has the floor at the Table: the subject, as ever these days, is Obama. "See, he's all positive energy — he understands people out there are vampires and will pull you down but he's here talking stuff that ain't been talked for years and he goes with the signs of the times and we all can feel the change, I mean FEEL the change." "It's palpable," adds Steve. "Whatever" says the woman and, having made her speech, leaves the Coffee Gallery.

As I eat the omelettete I read in the *Los Angeles Times* about car crashes and gang slayings and Tibetans clashing with Chinese and each bite gives satisfaction. Here's a full page ad for a new movie, "Iron Man," showing a metal male with a perfectly proportioned body; and here, opposite is a photo of kids splashing in the sea at Dockweiler State Beach watched by their parents. All are fat as Xmas pigs and, thankfully, fully-clothed. It strikes me that if you were invading America all you'd have to do would be to push Americans in a line from coast to coast and there'd be a domino effect. All fall down and go phlaaatt.

From mid-morning till mid-afternoon there's not much to relate. I'm coasting, acting automatic — making the bed, putting away dishes, getting out of Regina's hair, writing my journal in the freestanding office in the back garden. Ah, the journal! There's where the unvarnished truth lies — or as close as I'll ever get — soon to be buried in the Huntington Library Archives. And if any future scholar ever opens them there'll be a hard job breaking the code of my scrawl. Even I can't decipher it. So what is the point of the journal I've kept since 1972? Let's not get into Samuel Beckett territory.

Around 4pm, as the bloody sun starts beating down again, I start assembling records for tonight's show at *luxuriamusic.com* in Frogtown. I meant to survey protest songs of the 1930s, songs for political action, of coal miner strikes and textile worker strikes and of standing steady with the union and of Woody Guthrie in stiff pungent underwear and his patron trying to push him into a hot bath, and then we're diving into a left-wing New York night club to hear

Billie Holiday sing "Strange Fruit," written nearby by a white Jewish schoolmaster of reddish persuasion, describing a burnt black body hanging from a Dixie tree. And all the while the ghost of Lenin is cackling, "Such self-loathing liberals will hand us the microphone with which we will proceed to bludgeon them."

But I find a way to procrastinate on the dreaded protest survey. In the garage I stumble on a hitherto hidden cache of vintage 45 rpm singles, favourites of mine that I'd bought with my own money in the 1960s, piles of them, dusty or sticky, but longing to be spun once again.

I find "Having A Party" sung by Ronnie Mitchell on the obscure Blue Cat label, 1964. A white promo copy — I'd got it in Seattle that year, on the brink of my pop stardom, when Jerry Dennon, my recording manager let me have a few minutes inside his record distributorship warehouse. It was understood that I could loot at will — for a few minutes.

In the garage, from other piles, I select Lloyd Price, Fats Domino, The Stokes, Fats Waller, Bob Lind, Buck Owens, George Morgan, Vicki Carr, Billy Cotton, Tommy Steele......... I'd have enough stuff to hold back the whole gang of whining, complaining Stalinist folkies!

The list is made, the big legal briefcase filled, and off I go in the Element heading for Ripple Road in Frogtown, a strange place bounded by two freeways and the L.A River, home of Wonder Bread and Dolly Madison Cakes, and a pickle factory. Hardly a soul lives there, save for the occupants of the 1914 wooden apartment building (trucked in from elsewhere) where LuxuriaMusic.com operates from. At night a noir life commences when local Mexican gang-bangers shoot each other up — but you've heard much of this before, in earlier Letters. I told you about the night that, seconds after my broadcast, a machine gun rat-tat-tatted just outside the building.

The less said about dinner at Astroburger, up the road off Fletcher, the better. Often I have a party with me — Will and his guitar, Mary and her noisemaker, and others. Tonight I was alone, with my Woody Guthrie biography, a work tool. The intractable Argentinean waiter with the dyed black matador hair (who I tried to win months ago by speaking of tango and Carlos Gardel) refused to accept that I was dining alone and kept trying to get me to move to a bigger table. So I ate my gyro and fried zucchini in an unsettled state, taking in with every bite more of the revolting behavior of cultural hero Woody Guthrie: how he ripped up Burl Ives's sheets, while guesting at the folk singer's apartment, by sleeping in his sharp-toed cowboy boots; how he attempted three times to steal silver and gold objects at a society woman's party but was foiled each time.

From 8pm to 10pm, as usual, I broadcast from the littered room in the Frogtown apartment. Chuck rides the controls as, perched in a flexible plastic chair, I hand him 45s from the other side. "Having A Party" is every bit as good as I remember it and I'd forgotten there's a ukulele driving the band along. Ukes have been the catsup on so many old hits from Guy Mitchell's "Singing The Blues" and Johnnie Ray's "Just Walking In The Rain" to Connie Francis' "Everybody's Somebody's Fool."

The chat room traffic is heavy but hardly any of it is relevant to my show, probably because Regina isn't there to monitor and control. She left earlier for San Diego and a vintage dance festival. I drink as many cups as water as I can stomach in the hope that this would curb the clicking I hear when speaking. I haven't got false teeth so what's causing this awful noise?

But then what does it matter? Chuck has tallied up the current listenership: it wavers at 88. There's a sudden dip when I talk about words like "Negress " and "Jewess' and say it's a pity they're no longer allowed.

In the second hour I'm shattered by a series of pistol shots quite near, just after I've played Bob Lind's "San Francisco Woman" which mentions seeds and stems and maintaining and drinking wine from paper cups and washing without use of machines and the sound whirls me back to glorious summer days in the mid 1960s with my hippie girl friends like Dale Vann (last heard of as an inmate of a mental asylum) and Jackie Hyde (who left me to marry Arlo Guthrie). The smell of the sycamores reminding me of thrills to come...........

Pistol shots! Are the gangbangers gaining entry; are they coming up the stairs to get satisfaction for all the slurs I make on them and other ethnics? Is this the End Game?

No. It's only Chuck having fun with his sound effects. But the damage has been done; my nerves are writhing like a speared snake. Only a double shot of Jack Daniels can cure me and I shall down my medicine at home while watching, as pleasurable penance "Wasn't That A Mighty Day? — The Story of African American Gospel"

And so, cleansed and reeling, to bed.

JUNE

I should have marked the words of that old Music Hall song, "As A Friend":
As a friend I would advise thee,
As a friend.
Stand on me for I've been through it.
What you're going to do — don't do it!
As a friend.

You see, my rather stern letter to Rick Benjamin, leader and owner of the "Celebrated Paragon Ragtime Orchestra," accusing him of trying to filch my 'White Star March' by copyrighting his version (claiming he'd dug up the public domain original from deepest archives at the Library of Congress) was ill-advised.

In fact, nobody had advised me to be accusatory except my own hasty heart. Raw emotion had got the better of me. I'd boiled over at the prospect of losing the little tune I'd made up at home here on the family piano. I'd forgotten that I was practicing deception. The world of Titanic had become my playground of invention.

Back came a six-page reply from Mr. Benjamin throbbing with righteous indignation: "To say that the contents were a shock would be a severe understatement." I had, he wrote, been "deliberately representing 'The White Star March' as a genuine, authentic, historic, musical artifact of a real 19th century composer named J.T. Gardner." If he'd known the tune was mine he'd never have agreed to arrange it: "My professional work involves — exclusively — the preservation and performance of authentic 19th and early 20th Century music. I do not *under any circumstances* play music by contemporary composers...the thought of that alone is now appalling."

Finally he enumerates facts he must have from me — and at once: "I need to know *exactly* what you have told the BBC regarding the attribution of this piece," and he goes on about "needing to know" all details about the performance, including number of tickets sold, name of venue, names of other performers... etc..."

I went red in the face. I was back in school again, on the headmaster's carpet. Then I noticed that a copy had been sent to his legal counsel. Panicked, I called Mr. Benjamin's East Coast number. Over and over, hour after hour. A patient clear-spoken lady assistant took the calls. Gradually, as morning turned into afternoon we got to know each other.

Around teatime she informed me that Mr. Benjamin was actually in the building. She would let him know. A long pause. Finally he came on the line. I was amazed: his voice was that of a whelp — piping, pip-squeaked.

Nevertheless, I groveled. Excuses poured out: extenuating circumstances, misunderstanding, that sort of thing. I couldn't stop talking. Would he accept my humble apology? Nay, my repentance! For I had sinned...

Perhaps he would, he said — given time.

The tables had turned on me. From being the wronged composer I had become a deceiver, a musical James Frey.

What you're going to do — don't do it, as a friend.

The correspondence — e-mails printed out on an Epson — now sits secure in manila files in a metal cabinet. In some distant time we will read it and smile and shake our heads at such silly strife. What a vale of unnecessary energy and tears we inhabit!

We don't write many personal letters these days. Haven't heard from Chas in a while — the last letter was sent in '07 in the usual Air Letter. These folding one-sheets limit him a lot but he still manages to cram in the details:
"Blue Moon," he writes, "I first heard in the Lesbian film *Desert Hearts*; the second time was while cleaning out the school lavatories in May, '61; Fellini used it in *8 1/2* when Anouk Aimee walks down a street in Rome. When are you coming to Italy? You'd love it, all the swimming and the lunches and dinners with Etonians in the hills around — we could laugh at them all, though I'm sure you'd like them."

That's why I haven't heard from Chas since I returned from London in March — the old devil's been swanning around Tuscany, among all the history and good taste and singsong Italians and wine and pasta. Long lunches followed by long sleeps. Living it up with his aristocratic pals.

And he says I'd love it all — but I wouldn't because, as Regina tells me, I can't just relax, sit down and enjoy a holiday. I have to be involved in a project, learning a song, performing, or whining about how I'm not getting enough performing gigs. Of course, Regina would adore Italy and the Italian men. But she says resignedly that her dream will never come true as long as I'm alive.

By now Chas must be back in his flat in Earl's Court above the roaring streets with the constant traffic and guttural Poles and petrol and tobacco fumes. Outside he'll be hurrying through the rain to the cigarette shop wearing his filthy raincoat. But inside! He bloody well better be heads down into the book he has to have ready for the publishers by the summer — the one about the man who swam the Amazon from source to sea; the man he never saw swimming it but who, according to this last letter, he flew out to interview in his homeland, a newish country called Slovenia. There they swam together in the Adriatic and then in a "thermal pool where he does 12,00 lengths every day." The interviews, writes Chas, weren't a great success because the Slovenian's English "wasn't too good" so "I'll have to use my imagination for once."

Yesterday I was thrilled to receive one of Andy Wickham's many-paged letters, the third this year, I believe.

On notepaper bearing the insignia of "The East India Devonshire Sports & Public Schools Club" (three clubs amalgamated into one for economic reasons) he began with a quote from Cal Worthington, the celebrated TV car sales evangelist: "It's a GIANT mart/From the dealer with a heart!"Commented Andy: "The poetry still resonates."

Next we were told of his week watching cricket up North in "Gracie Fields country where mosques and Asians now rule — lots of curries but no more clogs." Last night, by chance, I'd watched a clean print of Our Gracie's first feature, *Sally In Our Alley* where she plays a goodhearted but tough girl in a close-knit community of flat-hatted, mufflered and shawled true Northerners. No curries yet but plenty of hotpot, tripe and chips.

From there he went on to thank me for my telephoned birthday greetings message to him. I'd added, stupidly, a peevish note on how our mutual friend Van Dyke Parks, now my neighbour in Pasadena, had seemed, in a reply to my e-mail to him, to be mysteriously reluctant to receive visitors. Andy's reply was that, in his considered opinion, Van Dyke may find me "overbearing and indiscreet and simply doesn't want to see you (Come in Sky Saxon with 'You're Pushing Too Hard')."

But now Andy must wind up his letter because he has to collect his Jaguar from the garage in Kensington. While he was cricketing up North the car was stripped of all its insignia including the little cats on the radiator grill and the boot. This is modern Britain, a working democracy. However, Andy assures me, "Michael Quinn — Old Cheltonian, grandson of Sir William Lyons who created the marque — has promised to restore it by 3pm and it is now 2.30pm."

He concludes by instructing me to keep my pecker up and to remember what Bobby Day said about the "Rockin' Robin":

He outbopped the buzzard and the oriole.

He adds: "And you can, too. It's never too late"

The rest of my correspondence is of the e-mail kind and thus not as carefully constructed. I have been having exchanges with Cary Ginell, an expert on country music, during which I have made the mistake of casting aspersions on those sacrosanct figures of folk music, Pete Seeger and Woody Guthrie. I called the former a head-up, chin-jutting sanctimonious killjoy and communist dupe; the latter, I wrote, was in it for the free food and pussy. Besides, he never took a bath.

Ginell retorted that he's always been a firm follower of these two, that they were noble fighters in a just cause, unlike those "Tin Pan Alley writers who were just looking for a hook to make money."

Thus I can see trouble ahead when I hand in the article I've just finished for the Oregon Festival Of American Music's concert programme. Why is it that if you compose from a high and mighty perch you will be respected even though your songs are tuneless rubbish? But if you're no more than a journeyman entertainer you can be passed by as if you were me and the boys strumming out beautiful but socially insignificant melodies from a corner of Cantalini's Italian Restaurant in Playa Del Rey. I must try to be high-minded and pretentious.

Much as I enjoy the anticipation of good news when the steady, congratulatory AOL voice announces, "You've got mail!" I also half-know that much of it will be nothing but annoying: streams of badly-written jokes by people who can't tell jokes, offers of millions of dollars from recently-deposed African big-wigs, Viagra ads, and the body measurements of young women for my consideration.

JULY

I had an operation in June. It's been instant gratification telling people that I've had an operation. They get a concerned look and I let a few beats go by before telling them that the operation was for a hernia, an old man's problem generally. In my case I had my first hernia operation when I was 29. The bulge in the groin grew so big and my trousers were so fashionably tight (in those early disco days) that for a while I became the toast of London's gay society.

But I never get as far as that story because after hearing the hernia word people's interest fades away fast. It would be nice to contract an illness that gets longer attention.

However, the hospital stay was most enjoyable. Dr. Pettigrew, the tall blond British-born surgeon, had seen my bulge the day before and booked me in at the Huntington Hospital pronto. What a neat and tidy place it is! The reception area is like a hotel. Fountains plash in a friendly way. No stench of boiled cabbage. Maybe I'm remembering England. I know more about English hospitals where I used to visit my mother. Usually she was in a private ward because she'd got insurance. None of that National Health for us. But one time, in an emergency, she had to be dumped in a public ward. Within minutes she was robbed of her purse and jewelry. Sign language had to be used because mastery of basic English was wobbly in that particular ward.

I was in a state because I had forgotten to bring any legal I.D. "Don't be silly," said Regina when I called her in a panic on the cell phone, "Who on earth would fake their way onto an operating table?" I didn't say anything since I, for one, would fake it in order to get some future sympathy.

A hell of a lot of forms to fill out. No wonder I had been told to report in at 8am for a noon appointment. Why did they want to know whether I wear false eyelashes? What about pantyhose? And then: "Is anyone using your money or your house illegally? Are you in a relationship that creates fear? Any spiritual practices to be observed during hospitalization?"

I complained to the black female receiving clerk. "I don't make the rules," she said. Then she warmed: "I agree they axe lots of strange questions." Two Nigerian women, very jolly, wheeled me upstairs to a holding room where I was placed on a gurney. "I like your questions," said one. "Nobody ever asks us anything." The room was very cold. Outside, in Pasadena, they were having a heat wave. "The cold is to kill the germs," said the other Nigerian. "Who's that strange man on the front of your book?" I shouldn't have brought the Russ Columbo biography — the cover photo makes him look like a raging queen and I don't believe he was.

I changed the subject to the current state of Zimbabwe. Yes, said the nurses in unison, they were better off when there were whites running the farms. Next came a Nicaraguan nurse and her partner from Peru. They had trouble locating a vein for my IV. Why had I chosen today for the operation when I'm behind on my crooner article (hence the Russ Columbo book) for the Oregon Festival Of American Music and tomorrow there's the Luxuria radio show and the day after that I'm playing with Janet Klein & Her Parlour Boys at the Steve Allen Theatre?

An old crone started screaming and moaning, moaning and screaming from a nearby room. "Don't you worry about that," said the Peruvian, patting my chest. "She's just coming out of anesthetic." Do they always come out? "Not always," she said gaily.

Arriving just in time came Dr Pettigrew, in full white costume complete with pillbox hat. "How are we today then? Not so dusty?" He showed me a booklet with illustrations of the upcoming procedure. He explained how a TV camera with pincers attached would be inserted into my stomach and how he'd then proceed to do all the surgery from the far end of the theatre by viewing my inside on a TV monitor and manipulating knobs (or something like that — I was getting squeamish and thus wasn't listening carefully). "And," he said, "It's all in high def. telly with awesome color!" Then he started trying to show me how my stomach worked but I interrupted. There's the problem of fainting, I explained. I also get sympathy pains whenever women chat about giving birth. "No problem" he said, "Showtime at high noon!" and went off to check the cameras in the theatre. What about sound, I thought. Do they have a 24-track board?

Russ Columbo had been thoroughly read and re-read by the time the nurses came to convey me to the operating theatre. Corridor ceilings rushed past me and I was reminded of the 10pm hospital drama shows that Regina likes to watch. Minus the blood. On the stage, lying helpless and trusting, wondering whether I'd soon be meeting, on the Other Side, friends who've said goodbye, I heard the voice of a nurse and, opening my eyes, saw a bonny apple-cheeked woman gazing at me. "Yes, it is Ian Whitcomb and what a thrill for us! I remember you from way back. You were a turn-on then and — you know what? — you still look great!"

I was trying to thank her when I felt a slight jab. The anesthetist was starting his work and so, basking in fandom, I slipped away into nothingness..................

A few seconds later I was finding it hard to breath and feeling nauseous. And I was blind, in a world of screams, farts and belches. "Is anybody there?" I asked. Dr Pettigrew materialized to tell me that during the "op" he'd disentangled three hernias in the course of just under two hours. "But I remember nothing!" I said. "That's it! No pain, no nothing!" he replied.

The next moment I was back in the freezing holding room. I saw burning Humvees, keening Arab women prostrating themselves on dead sons, African natives leaping and chanting, a smiling and bewildered George W. Bush. Eventually the nurses agreed to turn it off. Regina had left her Buddhist meeting and was on her way. I was happy I could impress her in a wheelchair when she pulled up in the Element. The last thing I remember was the start of *Lars and The Real Girl* glimpsed from the sofa in our drawing room. It seemed rather a surreal movie.

Next day I felt awful. Regina persuaded me to cancel all gigs. That afternoon I went to take what I hoped would be a pleasant nap, inspired by a book about early crooners (to which I had contributed an introduction). But the nap became a nightmare. Leading a monstrous regiment of angry crooners, waving microphones at me as they advanced, was a business-suited gent with a toothbrush moustache and hair like a lavatory brush. "I am Mr. Lambdin Kay," he was shouting. "And never forget the Mister!"

Now I had written of Mr. Lambdin Kay in the crooner book introduction. He was station manager of WSB Atlanta, the first big radio station of Dixie. He gave Art Gillham, a pioneer crooner who'd performed on the station, his soubriquet as "The Whispering Pianist." Earlier he'd allowed Fiddlin' John Carson on the air, thus paving the way for Fiddlin' John to become a pioneer of country music. And all this from a dapper gent in a dinner suit and with a fearsome moustache. But now, in my nightmare, Mr. Lambdin Kay was angry at me about something.

When I had recovered I started work on two articles for the Oregon Festival Of American Music. And I made sure that Mr. Lambdin Kay was mentioned several times in both pieces even though he was really a minor player. He no longer haunts me. And although I'm much better I think I've contracted another ailment. A pain in the throat whenever I sing loudly of Dixie or even of Shake, Rattle and Roll. But I'm happy to have another complaint to keep me going.

On Friday, the thirteenth, while Regina was enjoying a holiday in Lake Tahoe at a resort spa, I foolishly offered the use of our house to a band from San Francisco. It was like this:

Janet Klein, whose Parlour Boys I join at concerts and shows, had told me she'd be guesting with this band at the Coffee Gallery Backstage, our local entertainment centre. Jack Maverick, a noted bohemian guitarist and a friend I'd not seen in ages, was advertised as being in this band, The Dixie Darlings. I thought I'd put in an appearance; probably be invited up to sing or at least announced as being in the audience. I often drop in to the Backstage to patronize the place. Of a morning I'm to be found having coffee in the front room and possibly enjoying an omelettete specially prepared by chef Jeff who sleeps on a couch on the premises or sometimes in the back alley.

The morning of the San Francisco band offer I'd been eavesdropping on a particularly vociferous bearded man in a ponytail who was telling his companion in no uncertain manner how he'd be a star if only those who organize house concerts didn't always hire established stars of folk music. He dropped some names but I'd never heard of any of them. This evil system doesn't give him a chance. "You see," he told his friend (who didn't seem to mind never getting a word in), "You see, if we establish a beachhead in the house concert scene then that will lead to us performing at bigger venues — like this place. Who knows? — one day we may indeed play McCabe's Guitar Shop in Santa Monica!" "You mean both of us? But I'm merely a computer repair man." "I was employing the country music use of 'We', the royal 'We'," said the man, annoyed by his friend's ignorance of show biz.

I resisted joining in to tell them how I'd played not only the Coffee Gallery but also McCabe's and even the Hollywood Bowl — in my time. But I kept mum, returning to news of Afghanistan, even though I was bursting.

Returning to the Dixie Darlings:

I rang Janet to say I'd be dropping in on the show. She said that it was all rather a mess because she'd told the band they could rest up in her Alhambra house after their long trip by car from San Francisco without realizing she'd be out on the dreaded West Side at work on printing business and would never be home in time... So I said they could rest up at our house in Altadena, a block or so from the Coffee Gallery. Janet was most grateful. Yes, I'd like to see Jack again. And he adores Rollo.

Around 4pm I had a call from one of the Dixie boys. Somebody called "Frazzled Out Frank." Yes, they'd arrived at the Gallery and were ready to avail themselves of my hospitality. Come on round, I said. I felt sure they'd know who I was because Jack would have told them.

As they piled out of a dusty battered old Toyota I looked in vain for Jack. The leader, a swarthy fellow with swept-back black shiny hair, told me Jack wasn't on this gig. Bobbing about in the background was a lean and hungry-looking man in a beret (always an indication of trouble) puffing on a cheroot. "Hey guys — let's crash — and fast!" There was another man, much older — almost as old as me — who didn't say anything but looked like someone you wouldn't want to trifle with in a cowboy bar. He had a mass of thick grey hair in a battle line low on his brow, like Irishmen and alcoholics have. Another bad sign. There were other band members bouncing about but I never counted them.

They made a mad dash for the house. Instrument cases were dumped on the carpet. Bodies found their way onto the couch and chairs. We had only just had the house cleaned at great expense by a very anal housekeeper — I was glad Regina was out-of-town — and I made a speech about keeping the house clean, to no response. The beret man ran to the piano and started banging out a Jelly Roll Morton number as if his life depended on it. My poor little mini-piano, a wedding present from my mother to my father, couldn't bear it — resisting every blow, refusing to respond. "Wow – what a weird piano," said the beret. I told him it's not supposed to be played so hard and loud. "Weird, man," he replied. I then showed him how the piano responds best to peaceful chime-like sounds. He wasn't impressed.

Next I did a silly thing. I took them on a tour of the house, showing off my office and the record albums on the wall and the press photos of me as a rocker in the 60s and my CDs all in a row. Surely they would now recognize me! Not the response I was expecting: they merely appraised and discussed each room as a potential changing room, green room, place to crash in or smoke in.

Which is what they did, while I retreated to the lavatory to plan and to ponder. Clearly they had no knowledge of my musical pedigree. I was put in mind of the time, back in the late 1960s, in London at my mother's flat when I was alone and suddenly there came a ring on our front door bell. When I opened the door I was confronted by a band of costumed hippies fresh from San Francisco. The leader, a youth with no eyebrows, announced himself as a "friend of a friend of a friend" and said they'd like to crash. My mother was away on a golfing holiday (like Regina was away in Lake Tahoe) so I was at sea. Foolishly I allowed them in. They soon made themselves at home with their hash and guitar music (uglier and angrier than the Doors). I locked myself in my bedroom and waited till dawn. They clattered about the kitchen making breakfast. An hour later they'd gone and I could come out of hiding. (I wrote a song about this frightening episode which was recorded in Nashville by Corky Mayberry and released by Warner Bros Records in the

1970s.)

Friday The Thirteenth was similar. After a couple of hours of crashing, the Dixie Darlings left. In parting the hirsute cowboy man said, over his shoulder, "See, we didn't make no mess!"

I sat there stunned — a bit miffed, even annoyed. Even so, I went to their show that evening. It was all over amplified, a noisy welter of hopped-up electric vo-do-de-o-do. The beret man raced from keyboard to sax and back again. Freneticism was in the air. I sat against the back wall, incognito. Janet Klein, as their guest, flitted about and waved her arms, doing her stuff to the best of her ability — but was overwhelmed by the Dixie Darlings's rock approach to 1920s goodtime songs.

Afterwards I made myself scarce and ambled a weary way home. Presently I was apprehended by Joan, a neighbour, who introduced me to her partner, a well-dressed Asian man. She said he was an art photographer. They'd been at the show. They were indifferent to the act. I didn't tell them the humiliation I'd suffered earlier.

Then something nice happened. The photographer confessed he was a super-fan of mine, had many of my records, even a DVD or two. In return I enquired about his origins. Turns out his parents were Japanese-Americans and were interned in World War Two at the infamous camp near Lone Pine where the Roy Rogers and Gene Autry pictures had been shot. I told him how Rollo and I had once been lost in a snowstorm up there and were heading for the camp when we were rescued by a National Geographic photographer in an SUV. We were making connections, me and the Japanese-American photographer. Joan looked bemused.

Eventually I reached home. There I straightened up the living room, throwing away the roaches, patting the poor piano goodnight. Then I told Rollo that all was well once more.

AUGUST

Recently I entertained hopes that Rollo The Dog might become the latter-day Rin Tin Tin. It started like this: Rollo and I attended the finale of the annual Wiggle Waggle Walk in the park near Pasadena's Rose Bowl: a fairground of dog vendors. We browsed the food and trainer stands. Rollo accepted treats and sampled behavior pointers from sturdy female trainers. When food was offered he'd be so very obedient. When back with me he became boss once more.

A stand called "Hollywood Woof Woof & Meow" attracted me. Evangelical girls offered to sign the dog up for movie roles. Alert to "agents" who offer stardom and then demand that we pay them rather than vice versa, the real show biz way, I asked whether this was the case. No, no, they assured me, keeping the smiles going all the time.

A few weeks later we got a call from "Woof Woof": We're really interested in your dog. In fact, we're excited! Could you bring him down to our studios this Sunday for an audition?

Not this weekend — I have a gig. I'm in show business too, you know.

> Pause.
> Next weekend?
> Fine.
> Oh, and make sure you bring all members of the household.
> You mean Simon The Cat?
> No, no — just any other significant others like partners, wives.
> Fine.

However, two days before our appointment with destiny Rollo took a fall. Well, we believe it was a fall — possibly on that damned slippery decorative hardwood floor in the dining room. What happened was we returned from Regina's lasic eye surgery to find Rollo limping about and very low in spirit. Day by day he grew worse. My journal tells the story:

"He no longer races to the door when I come home; no longer runs round madly in circles; just lies around all day, doesn't want to eat, won't get up, shivers on the bed at night, sometimes convulses; I feel helpless; all I can do is to offer him the comfort of my body as he lies next to me on the bed we lifted him onto... The good old days are gone"

He'd get better, then relapse. On the appointed Sunday he seemed fine in the morning. Maybe the old days were returning. Maybe my mother would reappear looking fresh as a daisy and in her twenties and sunnily stating she never died.

At any rate, Rollo, wearing his best blue harness and with a red bow tied round his neck, was lifted into the car at noon. Ready for his stab at stardom. At least, that's what I thought. He himself seemed in a daze, perhaps in another world. Regina was cagey. This could be a scam, she suggested. Notice they insist on both of us being there. That's in case you sign something silly and come home and I spot the catch. In California you have three days to cancel a contract, you know.

I didn't know — but since I have long ceased to have chances to grab the brass ring, have indeed missed the bus, I wanted at least to get the reflected glory of a new Rin Tin Tin. Besides, we both believe Rollo to be King of Kings.

We pulled into the lot of Studio City's Empire studios, and immediately saw signs directing us to "The Yellow Brick Road to Animal Glory (& Management Company)." Some were askew, propped up against office walls. We followed paw signs leading us down long nondescript corridors hung with movie posters for ghastly movies we'd managed to avoid. Rounding one final corner we were greeted by Tom Cruise's face beaming beatifically.

At last there we were at the Woof Woof Control center. A woman dressed in a black pantsuit hove over to greet us: "So glad you're here!" Smiles a dentist would have envied. "And what an awesome dog!" Rollo was sunken and dragging at the leash. With a flopping sound he crashed to the floor to rest. I began to feel guilty about bringing him to this dreary space that resembled a hospital waiting room. And where were the other auditioning dogs? Regina took over: "Our dog is not at his best. You should see him when he's well." The woman looked me up and down and nodded. "No, I mean the dog," said Regina. "He's terrific!" said the woman looking down at the comatose Rollo.

Meanwhile I was observing an Arabic man in a terrifyingly dark business suit who was moving fast from computer to computer inside a glass walled office. Our holding space seemed surrounded by these glass-walled offices all of which were occupied by dark suited swarthies accompanied by agile females, young and razor attractive. The setting was eerily similar to that of an auto sales dealership. Somewhere no doubt was lurking the Deal Closure Room. Regina was right. She's always right.

Now the Arabic man rushed out and crossed our path, carefully avoiding any contact with an animal. However, he hadn't seen the collapsed Rollo and thus brushed against him, getting hairs on his trouser leg. Violently, like a terrorist dealing with the blood of a child, he swiped at the hairs as he made his way into an office opposite.

"Please sit down and make yourself comfortable for you will presently be viewing a video of some importance," announced our woman. On the big flat screen a man sat stroking his dog as he explained that when the call comes you must hit the ground running. "The Woof Woof folk informed me there's an epic shooting in Alaska and I'd better be there fast. So I hopped the first plane and we were on the set next day at dawn to audition. That's how on the ball are Woof Woof and Meow." He didn't tell us whether his dog got the part. Or who paid the airfare.

There was no time to ask because our woman now told us that any moment the trainer would appear for "evaluation." And appear he did, as if on cue, like an actor in a farce full of the carefully-timed opening and closing of doors.

Justin The Trainer, a willowy young man in fatigues, rattled off his credits with eyes closed, as if bored or perhaps embarrassed. He sounded like an airline attendant delivering safety instructions. "Any questions?"

Next he tried to put Rollo through his paces. But Rollo had to be helped from the safe spot on the floor.

"He's not been well," said Regina.

Justin kept a straight face and proceeded to set down a small box and then, positioning himself behind the box, with a treat held out in one hand as if offering tribute to God, he tried to lure the ailing animal up onto the perch.

"Step up, step up!"

We both joined in, hoping to make him rise from the dead like Lazarus. Power of the spirit and all that.

But Rollo would have none of this malarkey. He agreed to slowly rise; he even approached the box, but then, sensibly, he negotiated his way round the box in order to accept the proffered treat.

"Sit" said Justin. Rollo refused. "It's quite painful for him," said Regina.

Justin marched smartly to the other side of the room.

"Come" he ordered. Rollo stayed where he was, for there was no treat in sight.

"You should see him when he's well" said Regina.

"Come" said Justin.

"Look, let me show you one of his tricks," said Regina.

The trainer, sighing, stood back and folded his arms.

Regina persuaded Rollo to come over to her and give her a wet kiss with his tongue.

"See," she said.

The pantsuit woman reappeared.

Justin will make his assessment in a few minutes. "In the meantime please join me in my office where I'd like you to fill in a few questions on our questionnaire."

The image of the auto dealership.

One of the questions was: "What is your goal for your animal?" I wrote, "I want him to be adored world wide."

She smiled at this when she read it. Then she went further and cackled. Quickly she pulled herself together. She was in command, behind her desk. There seemed to be nothing personal on this desk. No framed photos of loved ones; or stuffed animals.

She produced a contract and slid it across the desk

"Can we take this home with us for study?" asked Regina.

"I'm afraid you cannot."

A rather long pause.

Then:

"Ah, here's Justin with the assessment!"

The trainer sheepishly sidled in, slipped a sheet to her, and sidled out.

The woman studied it for a few seconds. Then she stood up. She seemed taller than before.

"Congratulations! Justin has accepted your animal for a course of intensive training! Let's see..." She pulled down reading glasses from where they had been perching (together with dark glasses) on top of her mass of wet-look black hair. "Let's see...he scored highly in the 'Food Motivation' category and in 'Intelligence'."

I thought of the treat and the box avoidance.

She slid the contract closer across the desk. It was in danger of falling. The phrase, "pushing the envelope" came to mind.

I took a quick look at the document: months of training and further assessment culminating in graduation and readiness for motion picture auditions..........

Total: $6,500. Easy payments can be arranged.

Finally I took over.

"I think there's a little misunderstanding here"

"A misunderstanding? How is that?" She was acknowledging me for the first time. Actually, she was peering at me.

Loudly and clearly I announced, "I am in show business, you know. I am a member of both unions — SAG and AFTRA. I have a theatrical and commercials agent. I have a manager."

"I'm very happy for you but..."

"So *you* pay us. We don't pay you."

Oddly enough, within the next few days Rollo got much better and was soon back to his old self. Now, once again, he barks, he jumps up on the bed, he farts, he rolls on his back like a puppy.

I like to believe that the restoration started when I asserted myself as leader of our pack to the woman in the pantsuit.

A SLIGHT PAUSE

I don't quite know why but a great sadness has clumped down on me, a soggy cloak imposed from above. This sadness cloak is making me stoop.

I think it set in yesterday when, swimming in the Cal Tech pool, I got to thinking about Saturday's show at The Coffee Gallery Backstage and how well it went, not so much because of what I sang or how I sang it — we performed warhorses like "Eleven Thirty

Saturday Night" and "Everywhere You Go" — but because the audience took part, laughing at everything I said even when it wasn't particularly funny. Even laughing among themselves. Was something left undone?

But there was a reverent hush — at least I think it was reverent — when I sang "The Yellow Bird" about how I wished for my long-dead father to return and how he visited our garden that very night, letting me explain and saying he understood, so that when he left in the morning I felt cleansed.

Yes, people kept quiet and afterwards they applauded. Of course, it was then back to the comedy concerning high jinks on "Hi Tiddley Hi Ti Island" where the girls wear their skirts a trifle short and some are simply wrapped in thought.

"You should stick to the comic stuff because you're the king of music hall," advised Bob, the booker, later. But I don't agree. I let it get personal.

It was a good and natural show. Everyone got pleasure. They sang lustily on "Have A Martini!" encouraged by Janet Klein on one side of me and Regina on the other. There was almost a friendly rivalry going on, you might say.

Nevertheless — the gloom started as I swam and thought about why I had turned down an offer by a professional video cameraman to film the concert with a three-camera set-up at no expense. My treat for your birthday, he wrote in an e-mail.

Yet I said no. Why? I still don't know. And as I slide faster and faster towards 70 I find I understand less and less. Not that I understood much in the first place.

So the result is that a memorable evening has gone forever, never captured as an entertainment artifact. Only a memory. With a little editing what happened in that back room could have been fashioned into a splendid affair in riotous color and sonorous sound with clever angles and wipes and dissolves and decorative titling. The finished product could then have been duplicated endlessly onto shiny discs, one of which would be salted away in the depths of the Huntington Library, safe for posterity, for future researchers seeking to discover what made the early 21st century tick. The disc would join the archive holding my journals, letters, laundry lists, pressed flowers, etc.— all the clutter of febrile gathering over the years, all the litter that I hope may someday be piled up into a mighty tower of culture, of social history, of something as fascinating as Early Feminist Movements On The Far West Frontier.

Of course, maybe nobody will ever venture so deep into the archives, way past the Isherwood, Amis and Bukowski collections. And if they did discover my trove would they bother to crack the code of my journals? For only I can decipher them at a normal speed. Perhaps they're scrawled and scribbled because of the secrets and admissions, spite, hate and jealousy.

I went back to the Library yesterday. I needed some peace and quiet. Too much running around, multi-tasking and getting nothing completed; too much regret that an anticipated-with-glee event like the Monday night salon at Conrad's seems to be over as soon as it's begun.
Speeding towards the grave, ever faster....
Perhaps in the cool and silence of my basement at the Huntington I might stop time for a while... And after only a few minutes of silent prayer at my desk under the staircase I felt someone beckoning me to follow.
He led me through a suite of tall and stately rooms, ones I'd never been into before, ones I don't believe the authorities know exist. On either side the walls held still pictures of glimpses of a past paradise, hardly reflected upon at the time, now painted from different angles so that I was seeing everything anew.
Of twilight drinks at Wildcroft Manor hosted by my mother from her wingtip tobacco-stained, gin-rich chair; of her inviting guests to "have the other half," to help yourself to nuts and crisps and Kit Kat because "The Wildcroft Arms is always open," as the evening light painted the flowerbeds outside the lounge window into edible colors and a summer thunderstorm waited its cue to pounce in a neighbourly way. Of Uncle John elbowing his way through the dining room crowd at my mother's 60th birthday so that he could join me at the piano and contribute a dirty limerick (about a pansy who hailed from Khartoum taking a lesbian up to his room) to the tune of "Rhymes," even as his new wife warned, "Don't you dare, John!" Of my father, after giving us a tennis lesson, leading my brother and me down sandy paths towards the Thorpeness Country Club and supper before the Saturday dance and him telling us what to expect from life and warning of pitfalls and me gazing elsewhere with a look that said we shan't pass this way ever again together so fix it with the Brownie of your inward eye. Of my mother sitting on the staircase at Christmas softly crying for reasons none of us understood and our father not home yet from the office and the time of their golf appointment long past. Of DUKWs blazing with big stars trundling down the beach and plunging into the sea at Scarborough beach; of the smell of tired, stained and satisfying leather and of petrol I'd have liked to drink, in the garage as I sat there watching far below my father playing golf on the cliff top green while war planes flew over us growling in triumph; of my mother singing softly to me, in a voice of liquid gold, as sirens keened outside the flat window, and of feeling coddled in utter tranquility, a tranquility mingled with expectation — that something wonderful could happen soon and that I might have a part in it.

Then the stranger led me into a long dank room where there were no pictures, where there was nothing but a kindly pink light. Turn around, he seemed to say. Start again from another angle bearing in mind that your task is to stop talking for a few seconds in order to consider the meaning of love. Of love. Others you encountered the first time around gave you lashings of love and left no bill. Even so, try to pay them back.

And now we have a slight pause. After that you may proceed through the door. Don't forget to lead the singing as you march back.

The End

www.ingramcontent.com/pod-product-compliance
Lightning Source LLC
Chambersburg PA
CBHW021953160426
43197CB00007B/122